25 Events That Shaped Asian American History

Advisory Board

25 Events That Shaped Asian American History

An Encyclopedia of the American Mosaic

Lan Dong, Editor

GREENWOOD™

An Imprint of ABC-CLIO, LLC
Santa Barbara, California • Denver, Colorado

Library of Congress Cataloging-in-Publication Data

Names: Dong, Lan, 1974- editor.
Title: 25 events that shaped Asian American history : an encyclopedia
    of the American mosaic / Lan Dong, editor.
Other titles: Twenty five events that shaped Asian American history
Description: First edition. | Santa Barbara, CA : Greenwood, an imprint of
    ABC-CLIO, LLC, 2019. | Includes bibliographical references and index. |
    Identifiers: LCCN 2018046439 (print) | LCCN 2018047012 (ebook) |
    ISBN 9781440860898 (ebook) | ISBN 9781440860881 (hard copy : alk. paper)
Subjects: LCSH: Asian Americans—History—Encyclopedias.
Classification: LCC E184.A75 (ebook) | LCC E184.A75 A125 2019 (print) |
    DDC 973/.0495—dc23
LC record available at https://lccn.loc.gov/2018046439

ISBN: 978-1-4408-6088-1 (print)
      978-1-4408-6089-8 (ebook)

23 22 21 20 19   1 2 3 4 5

This book is also available as an eBook.

Greenwood
An Imprint of ABC-CLIO, LLC

ABC-CLIO, LLC
147 Castilian Drive
Santa Barbara, California 93117
www.abc-clio.com

This book is printed on acid-free paper ∞

Manufactured in the United States of America

Contents

Preface

Asian Americans have made significant contributions to American history, society, and culture since the nineteenth century, when they started arriving in the United States in considerable numbers. Asian American history has become an important component of high school social studies curricula that recommend the inclusion and expansion of culturally diverse historical viewpoints. It has also become a common topic at colleges and universities, both in general education classes that aim at broadening students' knowledge about the complex history of the United States and raising their awareness of varied perspectives, and in upper-division courses that study specific topics in American history, race relations, and multiculturalism, among others. The essays included in *25 Events That Shaped Asian American History* will be valuable to high school students (especially seniors and students in honors and Advanced Placement classes), undergraduate college students (especially those taking classes related to race and ethnicity, multiculturalism, Asian American studies, and American history), and general readers seeking carefully selected information on Asian American history. The book will be a useful addition to school and public libraries, academic libraries at colleges and universities, and research libraries.

This project, as part of a series of reference works on the American mosaic, presents twenty-five key historical events in the Asian American experience through well-developed, accessible essays, detailed chronologies, biographies, sidebars, primary documents, and images that provide narrative and visual information on high-interest topics. It is unique in its scope and structure. While most reference books on Asian American history broadly cover and usually organize events in chronological order, this book seeks to offer greater depth of study, contextualize specific actions and procedures, and highlight connections between historical events and present-day concerns. To this end, each essay not only is anchored by a key event but also ties together a variety of other national and international events to showcase the historical trajectory of Asian American experience in this country and demonstrate its complexity and long-lasting impact. The key events are vetted in consultation with leading scholars in Asian American studies to ensure a balance between coverage and depth. The overlapping among some of the essays not only demonstrate the far-reaching and important influences of key events but also provide multiple perspectives of the same historical past.

Readers will notice the following features of the essays: chronologies that cover significant events, movements, court cases, and other information related to the title events; narratives that detail the key events, their importance and impact, and other related events in Asian American history; biographies of notable figures who have played significant roles in shaping Asian American history; sidebars that highlight political, religious and community organizations and leaders, controversies, landmark legislations, and other historical phenomena; document excerpts that present primary sources closely tied to the topics of the essays and are paired with introductions to help the reader contextualize the documents and connect them with the key events; and a list of sources for further reading.

The essays are organized into five sections. Part 1: Early Immigration and Development focuses on major events in the nineteenth century. Part 2: Citizenship and Community Building addresses contested court cases, federal and state legislations, international treaties, and other topics around the turn of the century and the early twentieth century. Part 3: Conflicts and Politics weaves together the complex history of Asian Americans and national and international encounters in the first half of the twentieth century. Part 4: Activism and the Post-1965 Era introduces to the reader Asian Americans' engagement with political and social actions, as well as the changing trends in immigration in the mid-to-late twentieth century. Last but not least, Part 5: Heritage and Legacy examines connections between historical and contemporary events and the Asian American experience from the late twentieth century to the new millennium. Within each section, the essays are presented in the chronological order of the title events. This structure allows the reader to identify the key events easily and at the same time connect the essays thematically, thus making the book user-friendly to lay readers who may not have a wealth of prior knowledge of Asian American history, as well as to experts whose specialty is Asian American history.

This book collects the research and writing of professionals from the United States, Canada, and Japan, including leading and emerging scholars in Anthropology, Asian American Studies, Education, English, Ethnic Studies, Gender and Sexuality Studies, History, Legal Studies, Sociology, and other fields. Their expertise in and dedication to these academic disciplines and interdisciplinary fields ensure the coverage and depth of the essays, ranging from early immigration in the nineteenth century to the Trump Travel Ban in 2017. Together their essays address a variety of topics in Asian American history, from the California gold rush to the Japanese American internment, from the Delano Grape Strike and Boycott to the Vietnam

War and refugee migration from Southeast Asia, and from the Los Angeles riots to 9/11 and Islamophobia. The contributors' varied training and background help present a balanced representation of key events that are not only crucial in Asian American history but also significant in American history at large.

The "Bibliography of Recommended Resources" at the end of the book lists selected resources helpful for students, educators, scholars, and general readers who are interested in further studying Asian American history.

Acknowledgments

This project would not have been possible without the support of Kim Kennedy-White, Jane Glenn, and Barbara Patterson, who assisted me every step of the way. Over the past three years, ABC-CLIO's editorial and marketing teams worked tirelessly to keep the project on schedule. Their dedication made everything proceed smoothly. I am indebted to the members of the advisory board for this book: Dr. Jonathan H. X. Lee (San Francisco State University), Dr. Franklin Ng (California State University, Fresno), Dr. Cathy Schlund-Vials (University of Connecticut), and Dr. Judy Tzu-Chun Wu (University of California, Irvine). They have been generous with their time and expertise. Their guidance helped shape this project. Numerous scholars in Asian American studies have inspired and continue to inspire me; my colleagues at the University of Illinois Springfield have provided intellectual camaraderie and friendship at various points along the way. My deepest gratitude goes to all the contributors from the United States, Canada, and Japan who are experts in Anthropology, Asian American Studies, Education, English, Ethnic Studies, Gender and Sexuality Studies, History, Legal Studies, Sociology, and other fields. Their expertise in various disciplines and interdisciplinary fields ensure the coverage and depth of the key events in Asian American history included in this book. It has been a humbling experience working with and learning from all of them. I extend special thanks to my editorial assistants, Veronica Hartman and Nicole Overcash, who patiently offered assistance during the lengthy process of copyediting, fact checking, and proofreading. All errors and faults are my responsibility. Last but not least, I thank my family and friends for always being there for me.

Marie-Therese C. Sulit would like to thank Marcus Daitch, working under the supervision of Derek Sanderson, for their assistance in researching the essay, "9/11 and Islamophobia, 2001–2018."

Introduction

"Asian" refers to a person whose origins are in the Far East, Southeast Asia, or the Indian subcontinent. According to the 2010 census, the Asian American population grew faster than any other race group in the United States between 2000 and 2010. Historically, K–12 education does not provide students and general readers with detailed knowledge of Asian Americans' long history in the United States and its lasting impact on American life. Misconceptions and racial stereotypes of Asian American individuals and communities still prevail today. This book offers the reader a comprehensive understanding of the key events in Asian American history and the ways in which they have helped shape American society.

As David K. Yoo and Eiichiro Azuma have pointed out, the study of Asian American history emerged in the 1960s and 1970s as part of the efforts to document and analyze subjects who often are missing or marginalized in mainstream historical narratives. The 1980s and early 1990s began to see synthesized Asian American history in publications, followed by the establishment of Asian American and ethnic studies programs at colleges and universities, making it possible for students to specialize in Asian American history. The field of Asian American history took transnational and cultural turns in the mid-1990s, emphasizing an interpretive and integrative framework. Since the 1990s, Asian American history has become recognized as relevant and beneficial for other academic fields of study (Yoo and Azuma 2016, 1–6).

It is no easy task to write about Asian American history. Competing ideologies are abundant in chronicles of Asian American history, partly because Asian immigration to the United States has been controversial (Chan 2003, ix). Narrowing down the topics to only twenty-five key events without sacrificing coverage presents an extraordinary challenge. After all, Asian Americans have a complex history in this country. Different from most reference works on Asian American history, the essays included in *25 Events that Shaped Asian American History* are not organized by national groups; nor do they always provide coverage commensurate with these groups' population sizes. Instead, the topics are anchors that tie together many other events, reveal Asian immigrants' and Asian Americans' struggles with acceptance and equal opportunity, as well as recognize and celebrate their contributions to American life. The essays are the results of research in the existing literature on the subject and consultation with experts in Asian American studies.

Using accessible language, the essays guide the reader through a rather long time span—from the nineteenth century to the twenty-first century—and, in the process, cultivate historical perspectives of and reflection on Asian American communities. To help the reader contextualize the narratives, the essays include primary documents and excerpts that influenced and reflected cultural perceptions, informed policies and regulations, and helped shape Asian American experience since the nineteenth century. They include, but are not limited to, government documents (such as the 1877 Report of the Joint Special Committee to Investigate Chinese Immigration, President Theodore Roosevelt's "Sixth Annual Message" delivered to the Senate and House of Representatives in 1906, and Senator Daniel K. Inouye's congressional statements regarding Asian/Pacific American Heritage Month), landmark and controversial legislation (for example, the Chinese Exclusion Act of 1882, the California Alien Land Law of 1913, the Immigration and Nationality Act of 1965, and the Refugee Act of 1980), political documents (for instance, Hawaiian Queen Lili'uokalani's letter protesting annexation, Proclamation 4650, and Executive Order 13769, commonly known as the 2017 Trump Travel Ban), and personal essays (such as "My Last Day At Home" by Herbert Yoshiwaka and "Remembering Vincent Chin" by Thomas Perez). These document excerpts are accompanied by the editor's introductions. Together they help contextualize the key events discussed in the essays and help the reader understand the connections between various events and their long-lasting historical and cultural impact. These empirical historical evidences provide a glimpse of what happened then and how it affected the Asian American experience.

The essays included in "Part 1: Early Immigration and Development" use key events—the California gold rush, *People v. Hall*, the Central Pacific Railroad's recruitment of Chinese workers, the Chinese Exclusion Act, and Hawaii becoming a U.S. territory—to provide a historical trajectory of Asian immigration in the early years. Racial segregation and discrimination, particularly in immigration policies, heavily regulated and restricted the number of immigrants from Asia who could enter the country and limited their rights (such as their eligibility for naturalization) from the late nineteenth century to the mid-twentieth century. These early practices not only directly affected Asian immigrants and Asian American communities at the time, but they also laid the political and legal foundation for restricting immigration to the United States and fostered institutionalized racism and xenophobia. Collectively, these five essays reveal to the reader why Asian immigrants began to arrive in considerable numbers in the mid-nineteenth century, how the general public's perceptions of them changed, how historical events a century and a half ago have long-term impact on Asian Americans and American society at large, and in what ways these events are still relevant and significant to today's immigration policies and cultural climate.

Despite political barriers and hostility, Asian immigrants continued to enter the United States, build communities for themselves, and fight for their rights. "Part 2: Citizenship and Community Building" introduces to the reader how Asian American history is closely tied to international relations and community building. The key events that serve as anchors in these essays reflect such a focus—*United States v. Wong Kim Ark*, the Gentlemen's Agreement between the United States and Japan, the opening of Angel Island in San Francisco Bay, the establishment of the first Sikh gurdwara in the United States in Stockton, California, and the Webb-Haney Act (also known as the California Alien Land Law). Many local communities and organizations laid the foundation for collecting archives and documenting history in oral, print, and other media. They have helped preserve valuable materials for the study of Asian American history.

"Part 3: Conflicts and Politics" continues to guide the reader in exploring various kinds of struggles, conflicts, and changes that have had significant impact on Asian Americans and have helped shape the history of the United States. Together, essays on *United States v. Bhagat Singh Thind*, *Gong Lum v. Rice*, Japanese American internment, the Luce-Celler Act, and the Korean War cover a broad range of domestic and international events. Some are well known; others may seem obscure to general readers. They call the reader's attention to the unexplored and underexplored aspects and different perspectives of widely recognized events, such as the Korean War. They also introduce less familiar cases, legislation, and events that are, nonetheless, of significance in Asian American history, for example: the Luce-Celler Act of 1946.

"Part 4: Activism and the Post-1965 Era" focuses on major events, politics, and activism in the 1960s and 1970s and includes essays on Daniel K. Inouye, the first Asian American U.S. senator, the Delano Grape Strike and Boycott, the Vietnam War and refugee migration from Southeast Asia, the Immigration and Nationality Act, and the first Asian American studies program at San Francisco State College. These essays help the reader piece together a trajectory of Asian Americans' social and political involvement, from grassroots movements in the early years to organized demonstrations and protests later on, and from community-based activism to the establishment of academic departments, programs, and associations.

Finally, "Part 5: Heritage and Legacy" explores the challenges Asian Americans have faced since the 1970s. The essays included in this section address *Lau v. Nichols*, Asian/Pacific American Heritage Week, the murder of Vincent Chin, the Los Angeles riots, and 9/11 and Islamophobia. Together they remind the reader to understand Asian American history within the larger context of race relations in the United States, post-9/11 immigration policies, and the 2016 presidential and the 2018 mid-term elections.

The term "Asian American" is contested among scholars and readers. It includes over forty national and regional groups whose experiences in this country vary vastly. It is not the goal of the twenty-five essays in this project to be all-inclusive in terms of representing all aspects of Asian American history. Rather, they reveal the historical trajectory of Asian American experience in this country, examine its long-term impact on American life in general, and call the reader's attention to the connection between the past and the present. Collectively, these essays help the reader gain a nuanced understanding of how Asian Americans have contributed to American history and society, how they have helped develop and transform this country, and how their experience is an integral part of the American mosaic. The essays included in this book are by no means exhaustive overviews. After all, it is impossible for a single volume to cover all aspects of Asian American history. These historically informed and culturally engaging essays hope to prompt the reader's interest in further exploring Asian American experiences, past and present; to foster discussions on the connections among economic development, international relations, and immigration, as well as how these connections affect policies and legislations and vice versa; and to look at history on both the micro and macro levels.

Further Reading

Chan, Sucheng. 1991. *Asian Americans: An Interpretive History*. New York: Twayne.

Chan, Sucheng. 2003. "Introduction: Underexplored Topics, Emerging Frameworks." In *Remapping Asian American History*, edited by Sucheng Chan, ix–xxii. Walnut Creek, CA: Alta Mira Press.

Chan, Sucheng, ed. 2003. *Remapping Asian American History*. Walnut Creek, CA: Alta Mira Press.

Himilce, Novas, Lan Cao, and Rosemary Silva. 2004. *Everything You Need to Know about Asian-American History*. New York: Plume.

Hsu, Madeline Y. 2017. *Asian American History: A Very Short Introduction*. Oxford, UK: Oxford University Press.

Kurashige, Lon and Alice Yang Murray, eds. 2003. *Major Problems in Asian American History: Documents and Essays*. Boston: Houghton Mifflin.

Lee, Jonathan H. X. and Christen T. Sasaki, eds. 2016. *Asian American History: Primary Documents of the Asian American Experience*. San Diego: Cognella Academic Publishing.

Ling, Huping, ed. 2008. *Emerging Voices: Experiences of Underrepresented Asian Americans*. New Brunswick, NJ: Rutgers University Press.

Ling, Huping and Allan Austin, eds. 2010. *Asian American History and Culture: An Encyclopedia*. Armonk, NY: M. E. Sharpe.

Okihiro, Gary Y. 2001. *The Columbia Guide to Asian American History*. New York: Columbia University Press.

Takaki, Ronald T. 1989. *Strangers from a Different Shore: A History of Asian Americans*. Boston: Little, Brown & Company.

Yoo, David K. and Eiichiro Azuma. 2016. "Introduction." In *The Oxford Handbook of Asian American History*, edited by David K. Yoo and Eiichiro Azuma, 1–10. Oxford, UK: Oxford University Press.

Yoo, David K. and Eiichiro Azuma, eds. 2016. *The Oxford Handbook of Asian American History*. Oxford, UK: Oxford University Press.

1
Early Immigration and Development

California Gold Rush, 1848–1855

Ying Ma

Chronology

January 24, 1848	Gold is first found in the Sacramento Valley, marking the beginning of the gold rush era in American history.
August 19, 1848	The *New York Herald* becomes the first major eastern American newspaper to report the gold rush in California.
December 5, 1848	President James Polk confirms the discovery of gold in California.
1848	The first Chinese immigrants arrive in San Francisco.
1849	The number of immigrants from around the world reaches its peak in California as they join other gold seekers, popularly known as Forty-Niners.
December 20, 1849	Peter Hardeman Burnett becomes the first governor of the state of California. He is a proponent of exclusive policies toward foreign miners and later supports the Chinese Exclusion Act of 1882.
April 13, 1850	California passes the Foreign Miners' Tax Act, which imposes a twenty-dollar monthly tax on foreign miners.
September 9, 1850	Two years after becoming an American territory as a result of the Mexican-American War, California becomes the thirty-first state of America as its population rapidly grows.
1851	The Foreign Miners' Tax Act is repealed. The state revenue is impacted after 10,000 Mexican and other Latin American miners leave the mining fields.

1852	The Foreign Miners' License Tax Act is passed, replacing the Foreign Miners' Tax Act and imposing a three-dollar monthly tax on foreign miners.
1852	Gold mining reaches its peak, with $81 million worth of gold extracted.
1852	More than 20,000 Chinese immigrants arrive in San Francisco.
1852	A commutation tax is passed, which requires incoming ships to post a $500 bond for each foreign passenger, unless each pays a five- to fifty-dollar fee to commute the bond.
1853	The Foreign Miners' License Tax is increased to four dollars a month.
1854	The California Supreme Court in *People v. Hall* rules that Chinese individuals have no rights to testify against whites in state courts.
1855	A capitation tax is passed, which requires incoming ships to pay fifty dollars for each foreigner who is ineligible to become a U.S. citizen.
1855	The Foreign Miners' Tax is increased to six dollars a month, with a two-dollar increase every year.
1860	California levies a tax on all Chinese fishermen.
1862	California passes a police tax that requires every Chinese person who is not employed in mining or in rice, sugar, tea, or coffee production to pay a monthly tax of two dollars and fifty cents.
1868	The Burlingame Treaty declares that the United States and China have a favorable relationship with each other and that the citizens of each country can move freely between the two countries.
1868	The Fourteenth Amendment to the U.S. Constitution declares that anyone born in the United States should be granted U.S. citizenship, but it is not extended to the Chinese.
1870	The Civil Rights Act is passed, extending the right of naturalization to African Americans but still denying Asians citizenship. The act rules the Foreign Miners' Tax and other anti-Chinese laws as unconstitutional.
1882	The Chinese Exclusion Act is passed by Congress, prohibiting the immigration of Chinese laborers for ten years. It is the first

federal law to single out an ethnic group to be excluded from immigration.

1892 The Geary Act is passed. It extends the Chinese Exclusion Act by another ten years.

1907 The Gentlemen's Agreement between the United States and Japan scales back Japanese immigration to the United States.

1913 The California Alien Land Law is passed, depriving Asians of the right to own land in California.

1917 The Immigration Act of 1917 bars immigration from the Asiatic Barred Zones.

1924 The Immigration Act is passed by Congress to exclude aliens ineligible for citizenship from immigration, a category that included almost all Asian immigrants.

Narrative

The first large wave of Asian immigration to the United States occurred in the mid-1800s. However, the anti-Asian immigration policy soon after created enormous obstacles preventing Asian immigrants from entering America. The Chinese immigrants' experiences during the California gold rush marked the beginning of the racial formation of Asian Americans. The widespread anti-Asian sentiment, along with other restrictive legislation on Asian Americans, had profound effects on this racial minority, greatly discouraging Asian Americans from participating in American political and civil life.

Asian immigrants came to the United States in sizeable numbers between the 1840s and 1880s. The discovery of gold in California in 1848 triggered an influx of people from all over the world, seeking fortune in this Western land. Foreign laborers from countries such as Mexico, Australia, and China made up a significant portion of the newcomers. The population in California thus increased rapidly, bringing in new business and eventually making California the thirty-first state of America in 1850. The influx of foreigners aroused questions regarding the desirability of the "un-American" races (Paul 1938, 181). Thomas Green, a member of California's first legislature, warned that "the wonderful gold discovery . . . has excited the wildest cupidity, which threatens California with an emigration overwhelming in number and dangerous in character" (1850, 493). This resonated with public hostility toward immigrants, which was often accompanied by racial mobs and race riots. The Mexican miners were targeted first. They were attacked by armed

Four Chinese miners stand near a sluice box in Aubine Ravine, California, ca. 1852. Chinese immigrants came to the United States in sizeable numbers in the mid-nineteenth century, following the discovery of gold in California in 1848. These early immigrants were predominantly young men. (Fotosearch/Getty Images)

white American miners shouting, "California for the Americans," and asked Mexican miners to either pay more taxes or leave the area (Gendzel 2009, 77). A race riot broke out in the Grass Valley, one of the richest gold camps in California, in 1851 due to resentment toward foreign miners. The following year, a petition was raised to ban foreigners from the town (Mann 1972, 497).

Like many others who came to California during this time, the Chinese came for the gold rush. When gold was first found, there were few Chinese in the state. An estimated 50 Chinese immigrants lived in California in 1849, and that number swelled to 4,000 in 1850 (Bancroft 1888, 124). In 1852, about 20,000 Chinese immigrants arrived, marking the first large wave of Chinese immigration to the United States. According to a special state census report in 1852, there were 25,000 Chinese, or more than one-third of the total foreign population, in California (Kanazawa 2005, 781). Early Chinese immigrants were primarily males. Most of them were peasants desperate to leave their home country for opportunities elsewhere to make a living because of the political and economic turmoil in China. China was in a dire situation at the time. Having suffered multiple natural disasters such as famine and flooding, people struggled to support their families or to simply get by. The Chinese government was faced with external invasion by Western powers and internal turmoil such as the Taiping Rebellion. The government's corruption and ineptness had caused starvation, warfare, and death. Trying to find a way out, the early Chinese immigrants left their families behind, hoping to bring back fortune after they worked on the "Gold Mountain." Consequently, they were known as "sojourners" because few of them intended to stay in the United States permanently (Nee and Sanders 1985, 77).

The presence of foreign workers was perceived as competition for jobs by white workers, even though many of the white workers were immigrants or children

Some Push Factors of Chinese Immigration in the Nineteenth Century

In the 1800s, China was in a deep crisis. The population had increased quickly in the late 1700s and early 1800s, and by the 1850s, the population had reached over 430 million. However, the food supply did not keep pace with population growth, and farming land became insufficient for a large population. Multiple natural disasters also caused massive crop failures, leading to starvation and death. Huang He (the Yellow River) changed its course many times in history and was prone to flooding. In 1852, it again shifted its course, moving north. Devastating flooding followed for the rest of the century (Marks 2012, 236). From 1876 to 1879, the great famine hit central China, and about nine million people died.

These difficulties were accompanied by political turmoil. The Chinese government (under the rule of the Qing Dynasty) was losing control over its people and showed ineptness dealing with Western powers. China was defeated in the first Opium War in 1842, followed by treaty after treaty signed with Western countries. These treaties required large amounts of compensation paid to the Western powers. They were subsequently passed on to the people by the government, often through higher taxes. Overburdened by taxes and economic difficulty, the people rose up against Qing rule. The Taiping Rebellion, which started in 1850 in Guangxi, soon swept the country. This uprising lasted fourteen years and was the largest since the Qing Dynasty was established. For several decades, China was far from peaceful. People were starved, killed, or displaced, and the rest were desperate for opportunities to survive, even when it meant going abroad.

Early Chinese immigrants to California were mostly from the Pearl River Delta area, north of Hong Kong. The establishment of Hong Kong as one of the international ports had tremendous impacts on its surrounding areas. The imports through Hong Kong greatly damaged local cottage industries, forcing a mass departure of people looking for opportunities overseas. Meanwhile, Hong Kong provided a portal for people to migrate overseas (McKeown 1999, 313–14). For centuries, people in southeastern China have emigrated to Southeast Asia, such as Indonesia and Malaysia. In the mid-nineteenth century, transportation development made it possible for them to travel even farther. The news of gold in California provided incentive for them to explore the new world.

of immigrants. Their sense of white supremacy made them believe they were entitled to privileges, while others, especially people of color, did not deserve the same rights. Chinese immigrants were targets of such nativism and racism. Most Chinese workers came from impoverished areas in China. Many borrowed money to pay for their passage to America and had to live stingy lives to pay back these loans. They were also considered the hope for their families in China. Most of their earnings were sent back home as remittances (Boswell 1986, 357). Compared to white miners, Chinese miners spent much less on themselves, and this also aroused resentment. Consequently, they were accused of bringing down the living standard.

In the meantime, the capital-intensive mining industry began to replace placer mining. At the beginning of the gold rush, miners used pans and cradles to excavate gold, usually working alone or in small groups. They were called placer miners. Later, hydraulic mining was invented, and quartz mining also made great advances. Both of them were more efficient ways of extracting gold and attracted large-scale capital investments. Mining companies began to become a big player in the gold industry and needed waged laborers to work for them (Kanazawa 2005, 782). The emergence of mining companies worked against the interests of individual placer miners. White miners blamed Chinese immigrants for their willingness to work for lower wages and treated them as scapegoats for their income loss. Attempts to exclude Chinese miners were found in most of the mining counties in the mid-nineteenth century. For example, about sixty Chinese miners were driven away by the white miners in Tuolumne County in 1849 (Chung 2011, 31). The tension between white miners and foreign miners intensified from 1853 to 1854 when the gold prices dropped. White miners responded with race riots. They not only drove Chinese and other foreign miners out of the mining fields but also took away their profitable mining claims (Boswell 1986, 356).

Alongside the prevalent anti-Chinese sentiment, local government passed discriminative legislation. In 1850, a Foreign Miners' Tax Act was enacted, requiring foreign miners to pay twenty dollars each month for a mining license. Consequently, many foreign workers, especially Mexican miners, who were the largest foreign group at that time, were driven away from the mining regions by this extra expense. This act was repealed in the subsequent year. However, a new Foreign Miners' License Tax Act was passed in 1852, when large numbers of Chinese immigrants began to arrive. They became the new targets of the state for collecting tax revenue. The new tax act imposed a three-dollar tax per month on foreign miners. One year later, the tax was raised to four dollars per month. After two years, another change was made to the act, and this time, it specifically targeted Chinese miners. The new legislation attempted to increase the tax by two dollars per month every year for foreigners ineligible to become American citizens. By that time, only

Chinese immigrants fit this description. California Governor John Bigler labeled the Chinese "nonassimilable" and unable to gain citizenship because only "free white persons" could be naturalized by the nationalization law (Torok 1996, 63; Wang 1991, 193). The Foreign Miners' License Tax Act remained in effect until 1870, and it created about one-quarter to one-half of the state's revenue and was almost entirely generated by Chinese workers (Gendzel 2009, 77).

Moreover, there were measures to restrict foreigners coming to California, especially to limit Chinese immigrants. In 1852 and 1853, a commutation tax was enacted, requiring incoming ships to post a $500 bond for each foreign passenger. In practice, the bond was commuted to between five and fifty dollars a head, and the cost was passed on to the passengers. Even though this law did not explicitly state any specific nationality, its main targets were nonetheless the Chinese (Chan 2000, 74). In 1855, another capitation tax was passed. It was titled "An Act to Discourage the Immigration to this State of Persons Who Cannot Become Citizens Thereof," and required incoming ships to pay fifty dollars for each foreigner ineligible to become an American citizen. This legislation evidently targeted Chinese immigrants, since according to the federal naturalization law, they were not eligible for citizenship (Kanazawa 2005, 786–87). These are merely a few examples of the dominant white nativists' desire to drive away foreigners. Ironically, these legislations did not deter the Chinese from coming to the United States. On the contrary, they produced a counter effect. To pay off their debts for coming to America, Chinese had to stay and work for even longer periods of time (Gendzel 2009, 77).

The presence of Chinese immigrants in large numbers on the West Coast also added a new twist to the white and black racial dichotomy (Chan 2000, 67). By 1853, the Chinese had become the largest minority group in California. As the first large Asian immigrant group settled in America, they experienced the first wave of anti-Asian sentiment and discrimination. Behind the anti-Chinese sentiment was a combination of racism and nativism. The Chinese were constantly referred to as "aliens," as they were never considered part of the American people. They were ridiculed because they looked different from the predominantly white population and had different cultural practices. Few of them were Christians or spoke English well. Their clothes, custom, language, and lifestyle all became evidence that they were not Americans, but rather an inferior race.

The stereotypical images of Chinese immigrants at the time were predominantly negative. For example, in one editorial of the journal *Mining and Scientific Press*, Chinese were called "half-civilized beings" (1860, 4). Chinese, Native Americans, and African Americans were put together as people of color (Caldwell 1971, 124). In the popular media, "people of color" always meant inferiority. In the book *The Land of Gold* by Hinton Helper, both Chinese and blacks were characteristically filthy and degraded (Caldwell 1971, 127). Along with other anti-color accounts, whites and people of color were depicted as opposites—whites as moral and superior, and people of color as immoral and inferior.

Moreover, Chinese workers were always compared to black slaves and referred to as "coolies." The coolie system was like indentured labor, in which people repaid their passage dues by providing a certain amount of years of service to the money lender. That was not the case for Chinese immigrants. In fact, most Chinese migrants were helped by their relatives or associations and used the "credit-ticket system," repaying passage loans with money earned later (Wing 2005, 4). However, this Chinese coolie stereotype frequently appeared in the media and strengthened white workers' antipathy toward the Chinese. White miners saw Chinese laborers as slaves and wanted the mines open only to free labor. In a minority report submitted to the state of California in 1852, a law was called for to deal with the unfair competition between the "inferior population of Asian" and "the labor of our own people" (Paul 1938, 187). Some mining counties attempted to expel Chinese miners. For example, in 1852 the miners in Yuba County passed a resolution to prevent the Chinese from holding mining claims and from staying in the area (Chung 2011, 35).

The racial discrimination went beyond the mining fields; Chinese workers were barred from certain jobs commonly associated with higher prestige. In a study on the social structure in Grass Valley and Nevada City, two of the most productive and richest counties in California, author Ralph Mann found that, like African Americans, not only were the Chinese put at the very bottom of the social ladder, but they were also spatially segregated from other groups (1972, 499, 503). From the historical experience of early Chinese immigrants, we can see that the racial line hardened during the early 1850s. The distinction between whites and nonwhites was made clear and protected by discriminative laws. As argued by Sucheng Chan, this racial stratification is exemplified by the split labor market, where the dominant white group takes the more prestigious and higher-paying jobs, while racial minorities take the menial and lower-paying jobs (2000, 78–79).

The infamous *People v. Hall* case of the California Supreme Court is clear evidence that Chinese immigrants faced institutional racism. The Court ruled that Chinese people could not testify against a white man. As a result, George Hall, a white man, was set free because the charge that he murdered a Chinese man was based on three other Chinese men's testimony. In addition, the Court ruled that Chinese immigrants were ineligible to become citizens due to their inferiority. The Court statement labeled them:

> a race of people whom nature has marked as inferior, and who are incapable of progress or intellectual development beyond a certain point, as their history has shown; differing in language, opinions, color and physical conformation; between whom and ourselves nature has placed an

impassable difference, is now presented, and for them is claimed, not only the right to swear away the life of a citizen, but the further privilege of participating with us in administering the affairs of our Government. (*People v. Hall* 1854)

This case set the tone for anti-Chinese judicial rulings, putting the Chinese in a very disadvantaged position. It denied them legal protection, and they became easy targets for violence and abuse. In 1862 alone, eighty-eight Chinese were murdered by whites, but only two of the accused perpetrators were convicted.

Faced with enormous hostility from white workers and injustice from the state legislation, some Chinese immigrants were unable to continue working in the mining fields at all. To survive, they turned to "women's work" that other miners were unwilling to engage in. Because of the heavy concentration of work in the mining industry at the time, the workforce in California was composed mainly of men. The rapid population increase created a need for domestic work. However, domestic work was traditionally relegated to women, and male workers were reluctant to participate in it. Chinese workers who were expelled from the mining fields became cooks, laundrymen, housekeepers, and other types of domestic workers. Chinese men who took these jobs were considered less threatening to white workers' employment. However, by working "female jobs," Chinese men set in motion another long-lasting stereotype. Yen Le Espiritu (1997) has studied the image of Asian men as they were perceived in North America and argues that Asian men were victims of both racism and sexism. In mass media, Asian men were depicted as both hypermasculine and effeminate. On the one hand, they appeared to be a threatening force to white workers in the labor market, taking away jobs and driving down wages and living standards. On the other hand, they were also described as asexual or effeminate in an effort to decrease their sexual attractiveness to white women.

Despite the popular notion that Chinese people were indifferent to the political environment, they fought for their rights from the very beginning. When Governor Bigler denounced Chinese immigrants in 1852, a Chinese merchant named Norman Asing wrote a letter to the newspaper *Daily Alta California*. His letter pointed out the discrimination against Chinese immigrants and argued that California did not have the right to restrict immigration (McClain 1984, 538–39). When Chinese workers were accused of indentured labor, the community leaders of Chinese laborers' associations compiled documentation and showed it to the state legislators to refute the accusation. They also successfully convinced the legislators that Chinese workers were beneficial to the state and should be treated with justice. As a result of their efforts, the legislators eventually increased the mining tax by only one dollar a month, instead of three to four dollars (Chan 2000, 76; McClain 1984, 540–43).

The Credit-Ticket System

The credit-ticket system was a prevalent route to immigration in the mid-to-late nineteenth century. Even though some scholars believe that the credit-ticket system was the same as indentured labor, others argue that there were key differences that set the two systems apart. When Chinese laborers set their destination as California, few of them were able to afford the passage fare, which usually ranged from forty to fifty dollars. While some of them had help from families, relatives, or others to pay for the fare, most of them used the credit-ticket system. Their creditors were often shipping companies, labor recruiters, or future employers.

One of the most prominent creditors for Chinese laborers was "Six Companies," officially known as the Chinese Consolidated Benevolent Association. Six Companies was initially made up of different *huiguans*, which were generally associations based on the birthplace where the Chinese immigrants came from. These *huiguans* not only helped and supported workers traveling overseas, but they were also responsible for these workers' lives in California, providing shelters, tools for mining, and other necessities. Moreover, they facilitated the transportation of corpses back to China because to Chinese people, it is important to be buried in their birthplace. It is true that the "Six Companies" and many other similar associations charged interest when lending money to Chinese workers, as well as monthly fees for memberships. But they also served as an essential shield protecting Chinese workers in this new land. In other words, it was a combination of credit and networking (McKeown 1999, 317).

Another important difference between the credit-ticket system and the indentured servitude is how the debt was paid back. In the indentured servitude system, laborers were bound to a specific employer for a certain number of years. When the Chinese used the credit-ticket system, they were required to pay back the loan plus interest, but they were not usually contracted to a specific employer. So in general, they were "free" laborers.

Many Chinese were outraged by the *People v. Hall* ruling. One Chinese merchant, Lai Chun-Chuen, wrote an open letter to Governor Bigler to protest the Court's decision. The ruling also encountered challenges from the white community. For example, William Speer, an advocate for Chinese workers, published articles in the newspaper *Oriental* strongly opposing the ruling. Protests arose from the white community. In the late 1860s, there was an organized campaign aimed to overturn the Court decision (McClain 1984, 551). However, the anti-Chinese movement overwhelmed the resistance from Chinese immigrants and their white advocates and sympathizers. In fact, the *People v. Hall* decision was extended to civil cases in 1863 and continued to deprive Chinese people of justice for many years (Chung 2011, 37). In the following decades, Chinese people were denied citizenship, stripped of property, barred from marrying other races, and eventually forbidden to come to America at all.

Biographies of Notable Figures

John Bigler (1805–1871)

John Bigler served as the third governor of California from 1852 to 1856. A successful politician, Bigler was strongly against Chinese immigrants. During his terms, multiple discriminative laws against the Chinese were passed.

Bigler was born in 1805 in Pennsylvania. Before moving to California, he worked in the printing industry for many years. Later, he became a newspaper editor and then studied law. When the news of gold in California spread, he decided to practice law on the West Coast. However, he was not able to find a job in law there. He joined the Democratic Party and was elected to the California state assembly in 1849. He became the Speaker for the assembly and began to rise to power. In 1851, he was nominated by the Democratic Party to run for governor and won the race. In 1853, he was nominated again and was re-elected as governor for a second term.

During his terms as California governor, Bigler took a stance against Chinese immigrants. Chinese immigrants began to arrive in the state in 1848, but in very small numbers. It wasn't until 1852 that large numbers of Chinese arrived ashore and anti-Chinese sentiment began to spread. Bigler subsequently used this sentiment to strengthen his political power. In 1852, Bigler sent the legislature a special message, accusing Chinese immigrants of being "coolie" laborers and advocating the restriction of immigration from Asia. In 1852, Bigler reinstated the Foreign Miners' Tax, which was originally introduced in 1850 by Governor Peter Burnett but was repealed in 1851. The 1852 Foreign Miners' Tax targeted Chinese workers exclusively. In the following years, several other anti-Chinese legislation measures were passed, including a commutation tax and a capitation tax. Bigler's popularity reached its peak in 1854 and 1855. He was nominated to run for a third term but was defeated by the nativist Know-Nothing Party nominee, Neely Johnson.

In 1857, Bigler was appointed as U.S. Minister to Chile. After that, his political career declined. He was railroad commissioner for the Central Pacific Railroad in 1867 and then returned to his old career as a newspaper editor for the *State Capital Reporter* until he passed away in 1871 at the age of sixty-six.

Norman Asing (dates unknown)

Norman Asing was born in Sang Yuen, a village in southeastern China. He was a successful merchant in San Francisco and a leader for the Chinese Workers' Association. Around 1820, Asing arrived in New York and later relocated to Charleston, South Carolina. There he converted to Christianity and obtained U.S. citizenship. Like many others, he moved to California in 1849 during the gold rush. He opened a Macao and Woosung restaurant in Chinatown and soon became a spokesman for the Chinese community. He helped establish the Yeong Wo Association, the first Chinese mutual aid society. The association provided assistance to new Chinese immigrants, and Asing became a prominent figure among the Chinese in America. In 1854, he was selected as the "foreign consul" and considered a leader in the Chinese community in San Francisco.

After California Governor John Bigler denounced Chinese immigrants' citizenship and attempted to restrict Chinese immigration, Asing wrote a letter to the *Daily Alta California*, the leading newspaper in San Francisco. In the letter, he defended Chinese workers and rebutted Bigler's accusations toward Chinese immigrants. The editor of the newspaper actually backed Asing and stated that Chinese workers were industrious and beneficial to the state. Asing's letter is an example of how early Chinese immigrants fought back against nativism and racism.

DOCUMENT EXCERPTS

John Sutter's Account of the First Discovery of Gold in California (1854)

On January 24, 1848, a man named James Marshall discovered gold in a stream near the foothills of the Sierra Nevada of California. Stories about the discovery of gold traveled, prompting thousands of prospectors and settlers to relocate to California in search of their fortunes. Among these newcomers were Chinese immigrants. The gold rush was the first event to inspire a significant number of Chinese to immigrate to the United States. After their arrival, anti-Chinese sentiment began to grow in the state. This article is by John Sutter, a merchant whose fort was close to the stream where Marshall discovered gold. It was first published as a letter sheet in San Francisco in 1854, recounting Marshall's extraordinary discovery.

"I was sitting one afternoon," said the Captain, "just after my siesta, engaged, by the bye, in writing a letter to a relation of mine at Lucern, when I was interrupted by Mr. [James] Marshall, a gentleman with whom I had frequent business transactions—bursting hurriedly into the room. From the unusual agitation in his manner I imagined that something serious had occurred, and, as we involuntarily do in this part of the world, I at once glanced to see if my rifle was in its proper place. You should know that the mere appearance of Mr. Marshall at that moment at the Fort, was quite enough to surprise me, as he had but two days before left the place to make some alterations in a mill for sawing pine planks, which he had just run up for me, some miles higher up the Americanos [American River]. When he had recovered himself a little, he told me that, however great my surprise might be at his unexpected reappearance, it would be much greater when I heard the intelligence he had come to bring me. 'Intelligence,' he added, 'which if properly profited by, would put both of us in possession of unheard-of-wealth—millions and millions of dollars, in fact.' I frankly own, [words missing in manuscript] when I heard this that I though[t] something had touched Marhsall's [sic]brain, when suddenly all my misgivings were put at an end to by his flinging on the table a handful of scales of pure virgin gold. I was fairly thunderstruck and asked him to explain what all this meant, when he went on to say, that according to my instructions, he had thrown the mill-wheel out of gear, to let the whole body of water in the dam find a passage through the tail race, which was previously to narrow to allow the water to run of[f] in sufficient quantity, whereby the wheel was prevented from efficiently performing its work. By this alteration the narrow channel was considerably enlarged, and a mass of sand and gravel carried of[f] by the force of the torrent. Early in the morning after this took place, Mr. Marshall was walking along the left Bank of the stream when he perceived something which he at first took for a piece of opal, a dark transparent stone, very common here—glittering on one of the spots laid bare by the suddenly crumbling away of the bank. He paid not attention to this, but while he was giving directions to the workmen, having observed several similar glittering fragments, his curiosity was so far excited, that he stooped down and picked one of them up. 'Do you know,' said Mr. Marshall to me, 'I positively debated within myself two or three times whether I should take the trouble to bend my back to pick up one of the pieces and had decided on not doing so when farther on, another glittering morsel caught my eye—the largest of the pieces now before you. I condescended to pick it up, and to my astonishment found that it was a thin scale of what appears to be pure gold.' He then gathered some twenty or thirty pieces which on examination convinced him that his suppositions were correct. His first impression was, that this gold had been lost or buried there, by some early Indian tribe—perhaps some of those mysterious inhabitations of the west, of whom we have no account, but who dwelt on this continent centuries ago, and built those cities and temples, the ruins of which are scattered about these solidary wilds. On proceeding, however, to examine the neighboring soil, he discovered that it was more or less auriferous. This at once decided him. He mounted his horse, and rode down to me as fast as it could carry him with the news.

"At the conclusion of Mr. Marshall's account, and when I had convinced myself, from the specimens he had bought with him, that it was not exaggerated, I felt as much excited as himself. I eagerly inquired if he had shown the gold to the work-people at the mill and was glad to hear that he had not spoken to a single person about it. We agreed not to mention the circumstances to any one, and arranged to set off early the next day for the mill. On our arrival, just before sundown, we poked the sand about in various places, and before long succeeded in collecting between us more than an ounce of gold, mixed up with a good deal of sand. I stayed at Mr. Marshall's that night, and the next day we proceeded some little distance up the south Fork and found that gold existed along the whole course, not only in the bed of the main stream, where the [water] had subsided but in every little dried-up creek and ravine. Indeed, I think it is more plentiful in these latter places, for I myself, with nothing more than a small knife, picked out from [a] dry gorge, a little way up the mountain, a solid lump of gold which weighted nearly an ounce and a half.

"Notwithstanding our precaution not to be observed, as soon as we came back to the mill we noticed by the excitement of the working people that we had been dogged about, and to complete our disappointment, one of the Indians who had worked at the gold mine in the neighborhood of La Paz cried out in showing us some specimens picked up by himself,—Oro!—Oro—Oro!!!—"

Source: *Capt. Sutter's Account of the First Discovery of the Gold.* Lithograph. San Francisco: Britton & Rey, c. 1854.

See also: Angel Island Opens in San Francisco Bay, 1910; Central Pacific Railroad Recruits Chinese Workers, 1865; The Chinese Exclusion Act, 1882

Further Reading

Bancroft, Hubert Howe. 1888. "Broader Effects of the Gold Discovery, 1848–1849." In *History of California*. Vol. 6, 110–125. San Francisco: The History Company. https://archive.org/details/worksofhuberthow23bancrich

Boswell, Terry. 1986. "A Split Labor Market Analysis of Discrimination against Chinese Immigrants, 1850–1882." *American Sociological Review* 51: 352–371.

Caldwell, Dan. 1971. "The Negroization of the Chinese Stereotype in California." *Southern California Quarterly* 53, no. 2: 123–131.

Chan, Sucheng. 2000. "A People of Exceptional Character: Ethnic Diversity, Nativism, and Racism in the California Gold Rush." *California History* 79, no. 2: 44–85.

Chung, Sue Fawn. 2011. *In Pursuit of Gold: Chinese American Miners and Merchants in the American West.* Urbana: University of Illinois Press.

Espiritu, Yen Le. 1997. *Asian American Women and Men: Labor, Laws, and Love.* Thousand Oaks, CA: Sage.

Gendzel, Glen. 2009. "It Didn't Start with Proposition 187: One Hundred and Fifty Years of Nativist Legislation in California." *Journal of the West* 48, no. 2: 76–85.

Green, Thomas J. 1850. "Report on Mines and Foreign Miners." *California Senate Journal* 1st sess. Appendix S: 493–497.

Kanazawa, Mark. 2005. "Immigration, Exclusion, and Taxation: Anti-Chinese Legislation in Gold Rush California." *The Journal of Economic History* 65, no. 3: 779–805.

Mann, Ralph. 1972. "The Decade after the Gold Rush: Social Structure in Grass Valley and Nevada City, California, 1850–1860." *Pacific Historical Review* 41, no. 4: 484–504.

Marks, Robert B. 2012. *China: Its Environment and History*. 2nd ed. Lanham, MD: Rowman & Littlefield.

McClain, Charles J. 1984. "The Chinese Struggle for Civil Rights in Nineteenth Century America: The First Phase, 1850–1870." *California Law Review* 72, no. 4: 529–568.

McKeown, Adam. 1999. "Conceptualizing Chinese Diasporas, 1842 to 1949." *The Journal of Asian Studies* 58, no. 2: 306–337.

Mining and Scientific Press. 1860. Editorial. 12: 4. San Francisco.

Nee, Victor and Jimy Sanders. 1985. "The Road to Parity: Determinants of the Socioeconomic Achievements of Asian Americans." *Ethnic and Racial Studies* 8, no. 1: 75–93.

Paul, Rodman W. 1938. "The Origin of Chinese Issue in California." *The Mississippi Valley Historical Review* 25, no. 2: 181–196.

People v. Hall, 4 Cal. 399, 1854 WL 765 (Cal.).

Torok, John Hayakawa. 1996. "Reconstruction and Racial Nativism: Chinese Immigrants and the Debates on the Thirteenth, Fourteenth, and Fifteenth Amendments and Civil Rights Laws." *Asian American Law Journal* 3: 55–103.

Wang, L. Ling-chi. 1991. "Roots and Changing Identity of the Chinese in the United States." *Daedalus* 120, no. 2: 181–206.

Wing, Bob. 2005. "Crossing Race and Nationality: The Racial Formation of Asian Americans, 1852–1965." *Monthly Review* 57, no. 7: 1–18.

People v. Hall, 1854

Andrea Kwon

Chronology

1830   Federal census records three Chinese residing in the United States.

1844   The United States and China sign treaty of "peace, amity, and commerce," the first treaty between the two countries.

1848   Gold is discovered in California, prompting various groups of foreign- and U.S.-born prospectors to stream into the state. Chinese immigrants join the gold rush in significant numbers, starting in the early 1850s.

1849 Anti-Chinese riot breaks out in Tuolumne County, California. White miners drive out sixty Chinese workers employed by a British mining company.

1850 California's state legislature enacts the first Foreign Miners' Tax, requiring foreign miners to obtain licenses and levying a twenty-dollar monthly license fee. The tax is repealed the following year but is renewed in 1852 and amended in subsequent years. Chinese immigrants are the primary targets of the renewed tax.

1852 More than 20,000 Chinese immigrants arrive in California.

1852 California enacts a commutation tax aimed at limiting Chinese immigration. Ship owners are required to post a $500 bond for each arriving foreign passenger. The bond can be commuted by payment of five to ten dollars per passenger.

1853 Jury in Nevada County, California, finds George Hall guilty of killing Ling Sing. At trial, three Chinese testify as witnesses to the murder. Hall appeals conviction to the state's Supreme Court.

1854 *People v. Hall.* California Supreme Court rules that Chinese should not be permitted to testify for or against whites in criminal cases. George Hall's guilty verdict is reversed.

1855 California enacts a capitation tax again targeting Chinese immigrants. Entitled "An Act to Discourage the Immigration to this State of Persons Who Cannot Become Citizens thereof," the law levies a fifty-dollar tax for every such person landing in California.

1858 California passes legislation to prevent further immigration of "Chinese or Mongolians" to the state.

1859 *Speer v. See Yup Company.* Invoking the precedent of *People v. Hall,* the California Supreme Court rules that Chinese witnesses are not allowed to testify in any civil suit in which white persons are parties.

1860 Census records approximately 35,000 Chinese in the United States out of a total population of 31.4 million. The vast majority of Chinese immigrants continue to reside in California and are concentrated in mining regions.

1862 California imposes a monthly police tax of two dollars and fifty cents on every Chinese resident over eighteen years of age, with some exceptions. Collectors are allowed to seize and sell the property of those who refuse to pay the tax.

1862 *Lin Sing v. Washburn.* California Supreme Court rules the Chinese Police Tax unconstitutional because it violates the federal government's power over foreign commerce. The case marks the first time a Chinese resident challenges the validity of a state law as violating the U.S. Constitution or federal law.

1863 California codifies the ban on Chinese testimony in both criminal and civil cases.

1865 Central Pacific Railroad Company begins recruiting Chinese workers to build the western portion of the transcontinental railroad. Chinese labor plays a pivotal role in the railroad's completion in 1869.

1865 *People v. Awa*. Criminal case in which California Supreme Court rules that Chinese witnesses are permitted to testify on behalf of a Chinese defendant, since the plaintiff (the People) is not an individual white person.

1865 Arizona Territory, using California as a model, prohibits Chinese from testifying for or against whites in court.

1868 United States and China sign the Burlingame-Seward Treaty, which recognizes the right of free migration and emigration between the two countries.

1869 *People v. Washington*. California Supreme Court affirms lower court's decision that testimony by Chinese witnesses against a U.S.-born "mulatto" is inadmissible.

1870 *People v. Brady*. California Supreme Court holds that the state's ban on Chinese testimony does not violate the Fourteenth Amendment of the U.S. Constitution.

1870 Federal Civil Rights Act extends basic civil rights to "all persons" within the jurisdiction of the United States, including the right to give evidence in court.

1872 California repeals Chinese testimony ban by omission from codification in its Penal Code and Code of Civil Procedure, effective January 1, 1873. The ban is officially repealed in 1955.

1872 *People v. McGuire*. California Supreme Court rules that the decision in *People v. Brady* must be followed until California's new codes take effect in 1873.

1878 *In re Ah Yup*. Federal case in which the U.S. circuit court in California rules Chinese are ineligible for naturalized citizenship because they are not "white persons."

1882 Congress passes the Chinese Exclusion Act, suspending the entry of Chinese laborers for ten years and barring all Chinese from obtaining U.S. citizenship. The act is renewed in 1892 and 1902 and extended in 1904.

Narrative

People v. Hall (4 Cal. 399) was a California Supreme Court case in which people of Chinese descent were denied the right to testify against whites in court. The case came before the state Supreme Court in 1854, after a jury in Nevada County had convicted George W. Hall of murdering a Chinese miner named Ling Sing. Subsequently the Court reversed Hall's conviction, ruling that the trial testimony from three Chinese witnesses was inadmissible because members of the "Mongolian race" should not be allowed to give evidence for or against white persons. Handed down during an era of rising anti-Asian sentiment, the decision in *People v. Hall* hinged on notions of racial inferiority and embodied one of numerous legalized attempts to restrict the rights, and ultimately presence, of Chinese immigrants in nineteenth-century America.

Early Chinese Immigration and Rising Hostility

The events surrounding *People v. Hall* coincided with the beginnings of the first major period of Chinese immigration to the United States. Although smaller groups of Chinese had arrived on the eastern seaboard and in Hawaii (then an independent kingdom) by the early 1800s, it was after the 1848 discovery of gold in California, and especially starting in the early 1850s, that substantial numbers of Chinese immigrants started arriving in America, primarily to join the gold rush. These early migrants were part of a larger emigration from China to different regions around the globe during the nineteenth century. Internal social, political, and economic upheavals in China, as well as disruptions caused by Western intrusions into Asia and the concomitant recruitment of migrant laborers, contributed to the mass movement of Chinese mainly to southeast Asia but also to countries such as the United States, Australia, Cuba, Canada, Peru, and New Zealand. The overwhelming majority of immigrants to the United States were from the Pearl River Delta in southeastern China, an area that had long served as the center for China's foreign trade. By the mid-nineteenth century, the delta had become the main conduit of contact and commerce with the United States, and accordingly where news of the American gold rush likely would have been first received.

The Chinese who crossed the Pacific for the United States were also participants of a wider, international influx of foreigners into California following the revelation of gold in the Sierra Nevada foothills. Itself a newly acquired U.S. territory in 1848, California almost immediately became the destination for thousands of foreign-born migrants, the largest groups initially from Mexico and later from Europe and China, while others originated in Chile, Hawaii, Canada, Australia, and elsewhere. Like most of these newcomers, Chinese immigrants were predominantly young and male and had come to the gold fields in search of wealth and economic opportunities, contrary to popular perceptions of the Chinese as "coolies," or unfree labor. Few would actually strike gold; as their numbers increased, many would encounter mounting hostility and discrimination.

While at first Chinese immigrants met with a degree of welcome, particularly by business interests keen on a potential new labor source, their presence quickly elicited animosity from European Americans, who saw the Chinese not only as economic but also social and cultural threats. In the mining districts, where the Chinese were concentrated, white workers complained of unfair competition based on the false view that Chinese miners were contract laborers. Throughout various districts, they tried to exclude the Chinese from mining; in some cases, Chi-

Chinese immigrants at the San Francisco custom house in 1877. In *People v. Hall*, the California Supreme Court ruled that Chinese immigrants were not permitted to testify for or against whites in criminal cases. This race-based barring of testimony ended in the 1870s, but Chinese immigrants continued to experience unequal treatment in the court system. (Library of Congress)

nese immigrants were physically attacked or expelled from existing settlements. In 1852, for example, a group of white miners swept through Mormon Bar and Horseshoe Bar on California's American River, assaulting and driving out hundreds of Chinese from their encampments (Pfaelzer 2008, 10). Racialized by the majority white society as "uncivilized" and "heathen," the Chinese became frequent targets of harassment, mob riots, expulsions, thefts, and other violent treatment.

Anti-Chinese sentiment soon extended beyond local agitation. Starting in the early 1850s, California's state legislature passed a series of acts aimed expressly at Chinese immigrants and residents. The Foreign Miners' Tax, which required foreigners to obtain licenses and pay a monthly tax if they wished to mine for gold, had been first enacted in 1850 but was revived in 1852 in the wake of a growing Chinese population. Directed primarily at Chinese miners, the tax and later amendments resulted in exploitative collection practices and engendered further violence against the Chinese. In 1852, the legislature also imposed the so-called "commutation tax," intended to curb Chinese migration to California. The tax required ship owners either to post a $500 bond for each foreign passenger on their vessels or to commute the bond with a smaller per capita payment that in practice was usually paid by the immigrants themselves (McClain 1994, 12–13). Over the ensuing years, dozens of other discriminatory laws and ordinances would be passed both on the state and municipal levels, particularly in San Francisco, even as Chinese immigrants became an increasingly crucial labor force in the railroad, agricultural, fishing, and other industries.

Such legislation received the endorsement of public leaders like California's governor John Bigler, who in 1852 announced to the state legislature that "measures must be adopted to check this tide of Asiatic immigration." Referring to the Naturalization Act of 1790, Bigler reminded his audience that according to federal law only the alien who was "'a free white person" could become a citizen of the United States. Continued immigration from China, the governor asserted, would endanger "public tranquility" and the "interests of our people" (Bigler 1852). Bigler's warnings reflected the shared belief among European Americans that California, like the rest of the United States, was providentially destined for the expansion and conquest of white Protestant civilization. By the early 1850s, the ideology of "Manifest Destiny" had already begun to transform California into a racially stratified society, as whites sought to secure their status through the legal and de facto subordination of nonwhites (Almaguer 2009, 32–33). Indeed Bigler's calls for action against the Chinese—not least his contention that they shouldn't testify in courts—would not go unheeded.

Hall's Trial and Appeal

It was in the context of this nascent but virulent anti-Chinese movement that *People v. Hall* was heard by the California Supreme Court in 1854. The previous year, a grand jury in Nevada County, in the heart of Sierra Nevada gold country, had indicted George Hall, John Hall, and Samuel Wiseman for the murder of a Chinese resident named Ling Sing. Killed during an attempted robbery at a Chinese mining camp, Ling Sing had suffered multiple wounds after being shot in the back with a shotgun. The indictment charged George Hall with the shooting, while John Hall and Wiseman were named as accessories (Traynor 2017, 3). During the trial, the prosecution called several witnesses on behalf of the state, including three Chinese witnesses who testified with the assistance of a translator. George Hall was found guilty; the judge sentenced him to be hanged. "I had not the slightest doubt,"

Responding to Governor Bigler

Early on, Chinese immigrants to California actively protested their discriminatory treatment and defended themselves against the misrepresentations perpetuated by mainstream society. In 1852, for instance, in response to Governor John Bigler's anti-Chinese speech to the California state legislature, Norman Asing penned an open letter in which he presented a point-by-point rebuttal to Bigler's claims. "Your opinions through a message to a legislative body have weight, and perhaps none more so with the people," Asing admonished, "for the effects of your late message have been thus far to prejudice the public mind against my people, to enable those who wait for the opportunity to hunt them down" (Yung, Chang, and Lai 2006, 10–12).

Asing found Bigler's arguments both "reprehensible" and illogical. He reminded Bigler of the United States' own history, which he noted was dwarfed by China's centuries-long civilization, and added that "immigration made you what you are—your nation what it is." Rejecting Bigler's assumption that Chinese immigrants had no interest in settling in America or making it their home, Asing assured the governor that "many of us, and many more, will acquire a domicile amongst you" (Yung et al. 2006, 10–12). Bigler's targeting of the Chinese continued throughout his tenure as California governor, just as Chinese immigrants continued to challenge the various forms of discrimination their communities encountered. Confronting derogatory portrayals and stereotypes was an important part of that resistance and a struggle that would remain pertinent to the historical Asian American experience.

William Stewart, the prosecuting district attorney in the trial, later wrote, "that Hall killed the Chinaman" (Stewart 1908, 78).

Hall appealed his conviction to the Supreme Court of California. At the time, three justices sat on the bench: Hugh Murray, Alexander Wells, and Solomon Heydenfeldt. All three were relatively recent arrivals to the frontier state, having been part of the inpouring of migrants into California after 1848, and more specifically the surge of U.S.-born Americans who made the journey westward from various regions. Murray was born in Missouri, Wells in New York City, and Heydenfeldt in South Carolina. None was over the age of forty when *People v. Hall* was adjudicated, with Chief Justice Murray the youngest of the panel at only twenty-nine years. All three justices were members of the Democratic Party. Dominant in early California politics, the state's Democrats were embroiled in the 1850s in an internal struggle between proslavery forces on the one hand, and on the other, Free Soilers who wanted to make California the exclusive preserve of white workers (Smith 2013, 8–9). Later, Murray would join the anti-Catholic, anti-immigrant American Party (or Know-Nothings), a political party that proved short-lived but gained national attention in the mid-1850s.

During George Hall's initial trial, the defense had made no objection to the Chinese witnesses, but Hall's counsel (and soon-to-be California attorney general) John McConnell now argued before the Supreme Court that the evidence provided by the witnesses was invalid. Stewart later recalled that McConnell cited an existing statute forbidding Native American testimony: "Mr. McConnell made a short speech in the opening, saying that Chinese testimony was inadmissible; that the matter came under the statute which provided that the testimony of an Indian should not be taken against a white man." Stewart, who from the outset assumed "of course that the [supreme] court would have to dismiss the case" since no objection had been presented at trial, noted that "in his conclusion Mr. McConnell made a very elaborate argument, attempting to prove that the Chinese and Indians were of the same race." To Stewart's "surprise," the Court agreed (Stewart 1908, 79).

Murray delivered the Court's majority opinion. Justice Heydenfeldt concurred, and Justice Wells dissented without further comment. The court began its opinion by establishing that Hall, "a free white citizen of this State," had been convicted of murder "upon the testimony of Chinese witnesses," and thus the central issue for the justices was "the admissibility of such evidence." To make that determination, the Court turned to Section 14 of California's Crimes and Punishments Act of 1850, which provided, "No Black or Mulatto person, or Indian, shall be permitted to give evidence in favor of, or against, any white person" (1850 Cal. Stat. 229, 230). The "true point at which we are anxious to arrive," the majority opinion stated, was the "legal signification of the words, 'Black, Mulatto, Indian and White person.'" Moreover, the Court set out to inquire whether California's legislature adopted those words as "generic terms" or whether the lawmakers intended a more specific application (People v. Hall).

Focusing on the term "Indian," the Court then proceeded into a set of supposed historical, ethnological, and juridical considerations to show that "the name of Indian, from the time of Columbus to the present day, has been used to designate, not alone the North American Indian, but the whole of the Mongolian race." Columbus may have called the people of San Salvador Island "Indians" by mistake (since he believed he had landed near India), the Court said, but the term nonetheless became widely adopted thereafter to refer to "the aboriginals of the New World, as well as of Asia." According to the Court, during the period when early U.S. legislation—upon which California based its 1850 criminal statute—was formulated, the "universal opinion of [the] day" was that humans were divided into three broad but distinct types, a theory supported by such figures as scientific racism proponent Georges Cuvier. Because "Indian" as a general term encompassing Asians was the commonly accepted understanding of early American legislators, that meaning "then became fixed by law" by the principles of statutory construction (*People v. Hall*, 400, 402).

Likewise, California's state legislature, the opinion continued, intended the language in the 1850 law to be used in a generic way—to propose otherwise "would be an insult to the good sense of the Legislature." That any legislature would prohibit African and Native Americans from testifying but simultaneously turn "loose upon the community" people like the Chinese, "who have nothing in common with us, in language, country or laws," seemed to the Court hardly plausible. California's ban on Indian testimony, in the Court's view, clearly entailed a ban on Chinese testimony as well. Yet the opinion went a step further. Even if Native Americans and Asians were not of the same racial type, "the words 'Black person'" in the statute, the Court argued, "must be taken as contradistinguished from White, and necessarily excludes all races other than the Caucasian." To the Court it was apparent that California's legislators had designed the law to protect white persons from the "corrupting influences of degraded castes," namely the testimony of "everyone who is not of white blood" (*People v. Hall*, 403, 404).

In closing, the opinion shifted to a foreboding tone, warning of the purported consequences should the Chinese be allowed to testify: Not only would they eventually obtain equal citizenship rights, but "we might soon see them at the polls, in the jury box, upon the bench, and in our legislative halls." This was not mere conjecture but "an actual and present danger," the Court declared (*People v. Hall*, 404). Reflective of the blatant racism and the racial fears underlying its arguments, the Court wrote,

> The anomalous spectacle of a distinct people, living in our community . . . whose mendacity is proverbial; a race of people whom nature has marked as inferior, and who are incapable of progress or intellectual development beyond a certain point . . . is now presented, and for them is claimed, not only the right to swear away the life of a citizen, but the further privilege of participating with us in administering the affairs of our Government. (*People v. Hall*, 404–405)

Other points aside, the imperative of "public policy," the Court maintained, would have impelled the justices toward the same conclusion. As the final ruling, Murray held that the testimony given by Chinese witnesses at Hall's trial was inadmissible. Hall's conviction was reversed and the case sent back to the lower court, but without other available evidence for prosecution, Hall was never retried.

Consequences of People v. Hall

People v. Hall had significant ramifications for Chinese immigrants in America and their communities. Denied the right to bear witness, the Chinese became even greater targets of violence and abuse because perpetrators could commit such acts with virtual impunity. An 1862 committee report in the California state legislature showed that whites had killed at least eighty-eight Chinese, eleven of whom were murdered by collectors of the Foreign Miners' Tax. "It is a well-known fact," the committee remarked, "that there has been a wholesale system of wrong and outrage practiced upon the Chinese population of this state, which would disgrace the most barbarous nation upon earth" (Chan 2000, 76). The following year, in line with the ruling in *People v. Hall*, California codified the ban on Chinese testimony by amending its criminal statute to explicitly prohibit "Mongolian" and "Chinese" witnesses from testifying against whites. In 1863 the legislature revised its regulations for civil proceedings to disqualify Chinese witnesses in civil cases as well.

The Chinese objected vociferously to the decision in *People v. Hall* and its implications. Historian Charles McClain has noted that of all the injustices Chinese immigrants faced in the 1850s and 1860s, their exclusion from the witness stand "rankled most deeply"; removing the ban "was consistently the chief item on the agenda of the community leadership" (McClain 1994, 23). In the wake of *People v. Hall*, for instance, Lai Chun-chuen, writing on behalf of the San Francisco Chinese Merchants Exchange, wrote an open letter addressed to the governor, legislature, and people of California in which he criticized the state's practice of barring Chinese witnesses. While Lai's statement revealed its own ethnocentrism, he pointedly refuted some of the misperceptions European American society held about the Chinese and urged that the harassment of Chinese immigrants cease (Lai 1885, 3–6). As would become one of their primary strategies for opposing discriminatory legislation, the Chinese also used the judicial system as they attempted to overturn the testimonial exclusion, albeit with limited success, as in the case of *People v. Awa* (1865).

Not until the early 1870s, almost two decades after *People v. Hall*, would California lift its statutory prohibition of Chinese testimony. In 1870, as part of the federal Civil Rights Act, Congress passed a bill providing certain essential rights—including the right to give evidence—to "all persons" in the United States and not solely to citizens, as had been stipulated in previous civil rights legislation. Enacted as Section 16 of the act, the bill also prohibited any state from singling out particular immigrants for taxation or other charges, declaring null and void state laws that conflicted with this provision. Although the bill did not specifically mention people of Chinese descent, its provisions were undoubtedly designed to apply to the Chinese and owed in no small measure to the persistence of the Chinese

People v. Awa

In 1865, two years after the state of California formally codified its prohibition of Chinese testimony against white persons, *People v. Awa* (27 Cal. 638) went before the California Supreme Court. The case involved a Chinese defendant who had been convicted of manslaughter after evidence given by a Chinese witness, on behalf of the defense, was excluded based on the 1863 statute. On appeal, the Court reversed the conviction and ordered a new trial. Writing for the majority, Justice Lorenzo Sawyer argued that California's statutory restriction on witnesses had to be interpreted in favor of life, liberty, and public justice. According to the Court, since the plaintiff was the State—in other words, the "people as a political organization" and not an individual "white person"—the testimony ban did not apply in this case.

Yet if the majority opinion demonstrated a relatively narrow application of the ban, Chief Justice Silas Sanderson also reaffirmed the legal privilege of whites. He wrote in his concurring opinion that in cases where a Caucasian was the defendant of a criminal action, the Chinese were still disqualified as "incompetent witnesses." Chinese witnesses, in other words, were allowed to testify in criminal cases when the defendant was Chinese, but not when the defendant was white. Only a partial victory, *People v. Awa* nonetheless reflected early strategic efforts by Chinese immigrants to employ American mainstream institutions, perhaps most notably the courts, as they sought to ameliorate the racist policies and legislation enacted against them.

community in fighting for its basic civil rights. In accordance with federal law, California finally removed the testimony ban two years later by omitting it from the state's 1872 penal and civil procedure codes, and officially in 1955.

Even with the formal end to the race-based barring of testimony, however, the Chinese continued to experience unequal treatment as witnesses in court. In California and elsewhere, state and federal courts often regarded testimony by Chinese persons as not credible or requiring heightened scrutiny. This presumption was later applied to other witnesses of Asian descent, a pattern consistent with the conclusion in *People v. Hall* that Asians as a whole were not white. More broadly, the same principle would help fuel an increasingly strident exclusionary movement aimed not only at the Chinese but also in time at other immigrants from Asia whom the dominant society perceived as undesirable and racially inferior. If *People v. Hall* lost legal force after the 1870s, the racialized prejudice that had informed the decision would prove tenacious well into the twentieth century.

DOCUMENT EXCERPTS

People v. Hall *Ruling (1854)*

In 1853, a Caucasian man named George Hall was convicted of murdering Chinese miner Ling Sing. Several Chinese immigrants provided testimonies in the case. Hall appealed the verdict to the California Supreme Court in October 1854. The Court ruled that the Chinese witnesses' testimony was inadmissible under the assertion that Chinese were an "inferior race," calling their intellect into question and describing "an impassible difference" between their race and the Caucasian race. The Court therefore decided that these testimonies were illegitimate sources from which to draw life-changing conclusions. The ensuing discriminatory ruling, included below set Hall free.

The People, Respondent v. George W. Hall, Appellant

Supreme Court of the State of California, 1854

Mr. Ch. J. Murray delivered the opinion of the Court. Mr. J. Heydenfeldt concurred.

The appellant, a free white citizen of this State, was convicted of murder upon the testimony of Chinese witnesses.

The point involved in this case is the admissibility of such evidence.

The 394th section of the Act Concerning Civil Cases provides that no Indian or Negro shall be allowed to testify as a witness in any action or a proceeding in which a white person is a party.

The 14th section of the Act of April 16th, 1850, regulating Criminal Proceedings, provides that "No black or mulatto person, or Indian, shall be allowed to give evidence in favor of, or against a white man."

The true point at which we are anxious to arrive is, the legal signification of the words, "black, mulatto, Indian, and white person," and whether the Legislature adopted them as generic terms, or intended to limit their application to specific types of the human species. . . .

The Act of Congress, in defining that description of aliens may become naturalized citizens, provides that every "free white citizen," etc. . . .

If the term "white," as used in the Constitution, was not understood in its generic sense as including the Caucasian race, and necessarily excluding all others, where was the necessary of providing for the admission of Indians to the privilege of voting, by special legislation?

We are of the opinion that the words "white," "Negro," "mulatto," "Indian," and "black person," wherever they occur in our Constitution and laws, must be taken in their generic sense, and that, even admitting the Indian of this continent is not of the Mongolian type, that the words "black person," in the 14th section, must be taken as contradistinguished from white, and necessary excludes all races other than the Caucasian.

We have carefully considered all the consequences resulting from a different rule of construction, and are satisfied that even in a doubtful case, we would be impelled to this decision on ground of public policy.

The same rule which would admit them to testify, would admit them to all the equal rights of citizenship, and we might soon see them at the polls, in the jury box, upon the bench, and in our legislative halls.

This is not a speculation which exists in the excited and overheated imagination of the patriot and statesman, but it is an actual and present danger.

The anomalous spectacle of a distinct people, living in our community, recognizing no laws of this State, except through necessity, bringing with them their prejudices and national feuds, in which they indulge in open violation of law; whose mendacity is proverbial; a race of people whom nature has marked as inferior, and who are incapable of progress or intellectual development beyond a certain point, as their history has shown; differing in language, opinions, color, and physical conformation; between whom and ourselves nature has placed an impassable difference, is now presented, and for them it claims, not only the right to swear away the life of a citizen, but the further privilege of participating with us in administering the affairs of our Government.

These facts were before the Legislature that framed this Act, and have been known as matters of public history to every subsequent Legislature.

There can be no doubt as to the intention of Legislature, and that if it had ever been anticipated that this class of people were not embraced in the prohibition, then such specific words would have been employed as would have put the matter beyond any possible controversy.

For these reasons, we are of opinion that the testimony was inadmissible.

The judgment is reversed and the cause remanded.

Source: *The People of the State of California v. George W. Hall* or *People v. Hall*, 4 Cal. 399 (1854).

See also: Central Pacific Railroad Recruits Chinese Workers, 1865; The Chinese Exclusion Act, 1882; *United States v. Wong Kim Ark*, 1898

Further Reading

Almaguer, Tomás. 2009. *Racial Fault Lines: The Historical Origins of White Supremacy in California*. Berkeley: University of California Press.

Bigler, John. 1852. "Governor's Special Message," *Daily Alta California*, April 25. https://cdnc.ucr.edu/cgi-bin/cdnc?a=d&d=DAC18520425.2.7

Chan, Sucheng. 2000. "A People of Exceptional Character: Ethnic Diversity, Nativism, and Racism in the California Gold Rush." In *Rooted in Barbarous Soil: People, Culture, and Community in Gold Rush California*, edited by Kevin Starr and Richard J. Orsi, 44–85. Berkeley: University of California Press.

Chin, Gabriel J. 2013. "'A Chinaman's Chance' in Court: Asian Pacific Americans and Racial Rules of Evidence." *UC Irvine Law Review* 3, no. 4 (December): 965–990. https:// scholarship.law.uci.edu/ucilr/vol3/iss4/8

Lai, Chun-chuen. 1855. *Remarks of the Chinese Merchants of San Francisco, upon Governor Bigler's Message, and Some Common Objections; with Some Explanations of the Character of the Chinese Companies, and the Laboring Class in California*. San Francisco: Whitton, Towne & Co.

Lee, Erika. 2015. *The Making of Asian America: A History*. New York: Simon & Schuster.

McClain, Charles J. 1994. *In Search of Equality: The Chinese Struggle against Discrimination in Nineteenth-Century America*. Berkeley: University of California Press.

People v. Hall. 4 Cal. 399, 1854 WL 765.

Pfaelzer, Jean. 2008. *Driven Out: The Forgotten War against Chinese Americans*. Berkeley: University of California Press.

Salyer, Lucy E. 1995. *Laws Harsh as Tigers: Chinese Immigrants and the Shaping of Modern Immigration Law*. Chapel Hill: The University of North Carolina Press.

Smith, Stacey L. 2013. *Freedom's Frontier: California and the Struggle over Unfree Labor, Emancipation, and Reconstruction*. Chapel Hill: The University of North California Press.

Stewart, William M. 1908. *Reminiscences of Senator William M. Stewart of Nevada*. Edited by George Rothwell Brown. New York: The Neale Publishing Company. https://archive .org/details/reminiscencesofs00stewrich

Traynor, Michael. 2017. "The Infamous Case of *People v. Hall* (1854): An Odious Symbol of Its Time." *California Supreme Court Historical Society Newsletter* (Spring/Summer): 1–8.

Yung, Judy, Gordon H. Chang, and Him Mark Lai, eds. and comps. 2006. *Chinese American Voices: From the Gold Rush to the Present*. Berkeley: University of California Press.

Central Pacific Railroad Recruits Chinese Workers, 1865

Tena L. Helton

Chronology

1850–1853 Under pressure from white miners, the California legislature passes laws to limit Chinese participation in gold mining, including the Foreign Miners' License Tax Law, which levies three dollars a month in

1852 and increases another two dollars per year beginning in 1855. Local communities also legally bar Chinese mining claims. This begins a pattern of legislation to exclude Chinese from labor perceived to compete with whites.

1854	The California State Supreme Court rules that the Chinese, among other people of color, cannot testify against white people in criminal trials in state courts.
1854	California Chinese create benevolent societies called the Six Chinese Companies, or just "Six Companies," to help immigrants find work, navigate the prejudices and laws of California, and facilitate connections back home.
1855	The California legislature passes a measure to limit Chinese immigration by requiring fifty dollars for each ship passenger who is ineligible to become a U.S. citizen. This is repealed in 1856, in part because it violates the U.S. Constitution's clause settling the authority to negotiate with foreign powers upon the federal government.
1856	After much lobbying and both sympathetic and racist committee discussions, the Foreign Miners' License Tax is reduced to four dollars a month.
1858	The California legislature passes "An Act to Prevent the Further Immigration of Chinese or Mongolians to This State." This act criminalizes Chinese immigration outright by punishing those who facilitate entry into the state by a misdemeanor and a fine of $400 to $600.
1859	The Chinese government allows its subjects to emigrate permanently to other nations.
1861	The Central Pacific Railroad is incorporated. Leveraging the wave of anti-Chinese sentiment, Amasa Leland Stanford is elected governor of California.
1862	The Pacific Railway Act authorizes the Central Pacific and Union Pacific Railroads to complete the transcontinental railroad.
1863	Central Pacific workers lay the first rail in Sacramento, California.
1864	Central Pacific employment records show that twenty-three Chinese are employed as laborers.
1865	Central Pacific begins recruiting larger numbers of Chinese workers, resulting in an overall Chinese workforce of between 10,000 and 24,000 at its height.

June 1867	Two thousand Chinese laborers strike to demand higher pay and better working conditions. After eight days, they return to work after bosses withhold food.
1867	After five years, the Central Pacific completes the most challenging stretch of work over the Sierra Nevada by completing the Summit Tunnel at Donner Pass.
1868	An expansion of the Treaty of Tianjin of 1858, the Burlingame-Seward Treaty is signed on July 28 and ratified on November 23, 1869. The treaty offers hope of better treatment of Chinese immigrants in California. Its revision as the Angell Treaty of 1880 suspended Chinese immigration, a precursor to the Chinese Exclusion Act of 1882, which deleted free immigration clauses completely.
1869	On May 10, the ceremonial "Golden Spike" is driven in Promontory Summit, Utah Territory. The ceremonial spike and tie are both removed to be returned to California; the Chinese replace it with typical material and drive the real last spike.
	Although some Chinese remain to work on associated railroad lines, most are released from Central Pacific employ and must find jobs in other places.
1870	Chinese begin to move into other parts of the country, including railroad work in the American South. Six hundred Chinese help build railroads in Tennessee and Alabama. Two hundred and fifty Chinese work for the Houston and Texas Central Railroad.

Narrative

Demand for railroad laborers was high in 1865. The Central Pacific, commissioned by Congress's Pacific Railway Act of 1862, needed to speed its eastward progress in building the railroad from Sacramento, California. Competition from the Union Pacific, building westward from Omaha, Nebraska, was growing. However, by 1864, only thirty-one miles of track had been laid by the Central Pacific (Chen 1980, 66). A labor shortage, due in part to the American Civil War and to competing industries such as mining and agriculture, spurred a need to recruit more workers (Kung 1962, 230). Early in 1864, a small crew of twenty-three California Chinese was employed by the Central Pacific Railroad (Chew 2004, 37). In early 1865, the company hired more. Soon, the available Chinese labor was depleted while demand remained high, and the company decided to recruit workers from China itself. Historians estimate that the company employed between 10,000 and 23,000 Chinese

Chinese laborers work on the Central Pacific Railroad during the late 1800s. The laborers usually worked long hours, in harsh conditions, and with lower pay than their white counterparts. (Library of Congress)

workers at the height of employment, which made up about 90 percent of the workforce who prepared the land and laid the track for the westernmost portion of the transcontinental railroad. These Chinese laborers demonstrated an enduring and inspirational contribution to American economic and cultural history.

Working for the Central Pacific

The Central Pacific Railway Company was formed in June 1861 by the "big four" investors: Mark Hopkins Jr. (1813–1878), Collis Potter Huntington (1821–1900), Charles Crocker (1822–1888), and Amasa Leland Stanford (1824–1893). Crocker directed construction; his superintendent, James Harvey Strobridge (1827–1921), had the closest contact with both skilled and unskilled laborers. An initial advertising campaign to hire 5,000 workers yielded no more than 800 white workers. Strobridge found most of these white workers to be "unsteady men, unreliable. Some of them would stay a few days, and some would not go to work at all. Some would stay until pay-day, get a little money, get drunk, and clear out. Finally, we resorted to Chinamen" (U.S. Congress 1877, 723). Strobridge was not initially in favor of hiring the Chinese, believing them too small and weak for hard labor or for drilling and exploding rock, despite having proved themselves by working on other railways (Chen 1980, 67). However, Crocker convinced him to try the Chinese, arguing that they had built the Great Wall and invented gunpowder and so were likely to know how to do the job (Tsai 1986, 15–16).

By 1868, many California Chinese had left mining areas in favor of the railroad construction, and more were needed to fulfill labor demands. Most of the Chinese laborers hailed from impoverished Cantonese areas, primarily Sunwui and Toishan in the Sze Yup area (Steiner 1979, 132). The Dutch merchant Cornelius Koopmanschap and agents from Sisson, Wallace, & Company (Chen 1980, 71) recruited men from these areas near Hong Kong. From Hong Kong, the trip to San Francisco was relatively short: sixty days by ship (Chen 1980, 65). The agents paid for seventy-five dollars of supplies and travel, which the Chinese agreed to pay back in U.S. gold in regular installments over the first seven months they were employed by the railroad (Barth 1964, 118). Direct contracts with the Chinese in China, along with displacement from mining and other recruiting efforts, resulted in dramatically higher numbers of Chinese in the Central Pacific labor force. Strobridge cited a ratio of 10,000 Chinese workers to no more than 2,500 white workers at the height of employment for the Central Pacific (U.S. Congress 1877, 723).

The Chinese laborers were plentiful enough that the crew supervisors had sufficient workers to report daily, even if they were not always the same workers, and contemporary observers noted that the Chinese laborers were efficient and effective, despite being paid less than white workers. The company paid each crew supervisor monthly (twenty-six working days). Supervisors first deducted expenses for a cook and supplies from wages, then paid each laborer. The exact difference in pay between whites and Chinese is unclear, although Strobridge and Crocker both later testified that they generally paid white laborers more than Chinese. White unskilled laborers were paid an average of thirty-five dollars a month plus food and lodging, while the same class of Chinese workers was paid thirty dollars a month but had to pay for their own food and housing, which Strobridge assessed an important factor in the cost of their labor. The pay differential was concerning, but working conditions were the sorest point, leading to an eight-day Chinese worker strike in June 1867. The difference in pay for unskilled and skilled labor between Chinese and white workers ended up saving the company $5 million (Saxton 1971, 63). Most Chinese workers were remarkably frugal and managed to save between thirteen (Chen 1980, 76) and twenty dollars a month (Tsai 1986, 16), a significant amount to send back to their families in China.

Many Chinese laborers chose to live in dugouts in the earth rather than use the cloth tents provided by the company (Chinn, Lai, and Choy 1969, 43–48). Crew supervisors furnished food and a cook, as well as bathing water. The crews ate

Workers Strike

The Central Pacific's focus on completing the work was driven by Union Pacific competition and by profit. More track laid meant more money made, and the more quickly it was laid, the better, but this required a massive labor force. That labor, primarily Chinese, worked almost around the clock six days a week in harsh conditions, enduring unrecorded injuries and deaths in a dangerous workplace. They received two-thirds the pay of white counterparts (Ong 1985, 122).

In June 1867, 2,000 Chinese working in the tunnels of the Sierra Nevada laid down their picks and shovels and did not work for eight days, a peaceful protest. The Chinese demanded an increase in pay to forty dollars a month through a designated spokesman, which is what white laborers were paid at the time. They also demanded daily work hours limited to ten in the open and eight in the tunnels. Chinese laborers worked longer in the tunnels than white men, and they wanted equal requirements for equal pay. They also wanted better treatment by the company foremen, who, according to the *Sacramento Union*, would physically beat or restrain workers who wanted to leave railroad employment. Charles Crocker, however, testified that a system of fines was levied when men did not work or when the company had to employ foremen and horses even when there were not enough laborers for them to supervise (U.S. Congress 1877, 669).

According to Crocker, the Chinese circulated a document among themselves on a Saturday and then stopped working two days later. Crocker's response was to "coerce" them by withholding provisions and then making a speech, refusing to give into their demands but "forgiving" the strike if they returned by the following Monday (U.S. Congress 1877, 669). He believed the strike was a plot by the rival Union Pacific to delay work. Alarmed by the work stoppage, the Central Pacific also wired to the east to inquire about hiring recently freed blacks to replace the Chinese workers (Chinn, Lai, and Choy 1969, 43–48). Without continued support from additional Chinese workers, Crocker's tactics succeeded, and the laborers returned to work. Although it was the only Chinese strike reported on the Central Pacific, it nevertheless set the stage for participation of Asians in other labor movements, and it demonstrated that the Chinese were not simple, docile people to be unfairly exploited.

traditional Chinese fare, a more nutritionally balanced diet than their white counterparts, including some foods imported from Hong Kong and Canton. Other habits kept them healthier as well, including regular bathing and drinking luke-warm tea instead of untreated water stored in empty whiskey barrels.

In the beginning, fifty Chinese in twelve-hour shifts, six days a week, cleared the land of trees, stumps, and rocks, hauled away debris, and laid down rails and crossties for the track. Soon Strobridge came to feel that their ability to do heavy work was equal to whites, and he found them much more reliable, honest, and con-stant than the white unskilled workers. Within six months, the Chinese were fully incorporated into the work of the railroad as laborers, driving horses, tunneling, and blasting, and they "became expert at all kinds of work: grading, drilling, masonry, and demolition" (Chen 1980, 71). Without heavy machinery to aid them, they did this work by hand, often chiseling out rock that was impervious to blasting pow-der. At Summit Tunnel, a shaft was drilled into the mountain, and laborers chipped rock as hard as steel on four faces from the inside out. They progressed an average of only eight inches a day (Lewis 1938, 77). To complete hillside blasting at diffi-cult locations such as Cape Horn, workers were lowered via ropes to drill and deto-nate explosive powder. Although disputed, some historians maintain that the workers used their native knowledge and imported reeds to weave baskets. They then used the baskets to lower themselves over the sides of steep rock faces to set charges and blast away rock (Chang 2003, 59).

The work was dirty, tedious, backbreaking, and dangerous. Workers of all races had to grade the land, dig tunnels through rock, build bridges and trestles, and lay track in deep snow and scorching temperatures through California, Nevada, and part of Utah Territory. The terrain was extreme; weather conditions were often horri-ble. For example, the Sierra Nevada is famed for extreme snowfall, and the winters of 1865–1866 and 1866–1867 were particularly harsh. In 1865, "sixty-foot drifts of snow had to be shoveled away before the graders could even reach the roadbed. Nearly half the work force of 9,000 men were set to clearing snow" (Chen 1980, 70). In such conditions, laborers had to work day and night in three eight-hour shifts to build ten tunnels within a twenty-mile section of the railroad. Newspaper accounts and engineer reports describe workers buried under avalanches or frozen to death. Other accidents also resulted in injuries and deaths. Fortunately, the hygienic hab-its of the Chinese workers reduced the likelihood of death from the spread of dis-ease. Just how many died in the construction of the railroad remains unclear; the company did not keep records of deaths. However, using primary documents and newspaper reports, historians have estimated that anywhere from 50 to 1,200 Chi-nese workers died during the construction of the Central Pacific. Typically, the Chi-nese would temporarily bury the dead and later transport the remains back to their families in China.

The Politics of Chinese Labor

Chinese labor was not popular among much of the white population in California. The fear of migrant labor resulted in political pressure to pass laws to restrict immigration and immigrant rights. In the decade before the Central Pacific began recruitment of the Chinese, the state of California took steps to limit Chinese immigration or to deter Chinese residents from competing with white labor in the mining industry. For example, the California Assembly passed a tax that targeted foreign miners and a "commutation" tax that discouraged immigration, a cost that was passed on to foreign passengers in the price of travel. Another example was "An Act to Protect Free White Labor against Competition with Chinese Coolie Labor, and to Discourage the Immigration of the Chinese into the State of California," also passed by the California legislature. This act instituted a "Police Tax" on all Chinese over eighteen years old who had not paid the Foreign Miners' Tax. It required them to pay two dollars and fifty cents per person, which was collected on the spot from the person or the employer. If not paid, the person or employer forfeited property, which could be seized and sold within an hour. This act was challenged in the California Supreme Court, which found that it and other immigration taxation measures were federal matters to decide. Besides taxation, the Chinese were not allowed to bear witness in criminal or, later, civil trials. Discriminatory laws and practices resulted from the fear that the Chinese were going to take jobs from or undercut the wages of whites and not contribute significantly to the local economy (McClain 1994, 10).

The language barrier and specific economic and cultural behaviors may have contributed to the resentment, along with labor tactics employed by the railroad. Chinese workers were recruited to fill a labor gap but were also used as a tactic against whites who threatened to strike in spring 1865. When whites backed down, the company hired the Chinese anyway (Chang 2003, 55–56). Also, to avoid racial tension, the railroad created "section houses" that segregated the Chinese from other groups, emphasizing the cultural and language differences between groups and exacerbating stereotypes (Carson 2005, 96). The Chinese did not engage in the same off-duty pursuits as whites, who spent much of their downtime drinking and carousing, according to Strobridge. Although the Chinese workers gambled among themselves, they did not squander their pay in the same way as whites, and they often used their Sundays to take care of domestic tasks. In general, observers noted that they were hard-working, orderly, and frugal, a stark contrast to the whites.

The Central Pacific's fulfillment of labor needs likely exacerbated the concern that white labor was being displaced and "degraded." After all, the company could secure Chinese labor more cheaply than white labor. Seven years after the transcontinental railroad was completed in Promontory Summit, Utah Territory, on

May 10, 1869, Crocker and Strobridge were called to testify in Congress's Joint Special Committee to Investigate Chinese Immigration about the company's use of Chinese labor for railroad construction. Many of the committee's questions show bias toward white labor and resentment toward the Central Pacific for utilizing Chinese labor and making significant profit when they perhaps could have employed more white men (and thus had to pay more). Crocker's responses to the committee reveal his attitude toward race and Chinese labor. He maintained that he was "compelled" to use Chinese labor when white labor was neither plentiful nor consistent. He argued that he would have preferred to use white labor; however, he said, the recruitment of Chinese labor encouraged more whites to work for the company than before Chinese recruitment. The result, he said, was that whites had greater opportunity to work beyond menial jobs. Recruiting Chinese labor was thus better for whites who had never seen opportunities beyond repetitive, manual labor (U.S. Congress 1877, 667–668).

This justification is consistent with Strobridge's recollection. Employment of white laborers increased as employment of the Chinese rose, Strobridge said, and "[w]e made foremen of the most intelligent of the white men, teamsters, and hostlers" (U.S. Congress 1877, 723). The bulk of workers, however, were common laborers. A statistical analysis of census data of the Central Pacific and the Union Pacific suggests that "Chinese workers were significantly more likely than natives and Europeans to be classified as laborers and perform the physical work required in railroad construction" and much less likely to be foremen or skilled workers (Carson 2005, 93). Moving up the ranks to a worker with skills that could be transferable to other industries was therefore unlikely, effectively truncating upward mobility for Chinese workers.

Beyond Construction

The consistent and cheap labor provided by the Chinese was instrumental to completing one of the most important American engineering feats of the nineteenth century. Were it not for the Chinese workforce, the railroad could not have been built as quickly as it was. Without the railroad, migrants traveling from the east could not have gotten to California in less than six months. The railroad cut travel time to mere weeks, making the West far more accessible and far more likely to be developed. Ironically, Chinese passengers were racially segregated when traveling the railroad they were instrumental in building.

After the completion of the transcontinental railroad, some Chinese workers were redeployed to work on other regional railroad lines, but most had to find other work. Some returned to mining camps, which by that point were increasingly corporatized. Some became field workers; in fact, without the labor and ingenuity of

Chinese workers, the fertile land of the Sacramento–San Joaquin delta would not have been reclaimed from floods (Bhandari 2011, 8). Some became fishermen, and others worked in canneries in the Pacific Northwest. Some participated in cigar manufacturing. A significant number also provided domestic labor in cities such as San Francisco. Still others returned to China.

Current scholars of Chinese American history, archeology, and culture are attempting to establish a fuller story of the Chinese who labored for the Central Pacific. They are unearthing artifacts from along the tracks, gathering oral histories, and searching for letters sent home. Recognizing the market and the cultural forces at play during the mid-nineteenth century may increase understanding of similar arguments and fears about immigrant groups who come to the United States to improve their families' circumstances and thereby increase the power of the U.S. economy. Perhaps these nineteenth-century stories will mitigate negative modern attitudes and behaviors toward migrant labor.

Biographies of Notable Figures

Amasa Leland Stanford (1824–1893)

Amasa Leland Stanford was one of the "Big Four" investors of the Central Pacific Railway Company, established June 28, 1861. Stanford was the front man for the Central Pacific investors, giving speeches and shaking hands with those who could assist the successful construction of the railroad. He presided over the "Golden Spike" ceremony celebrating the completion of the transcontinental railroad on May 10, 1869. With his partners' encouragement, he became a wartime California governor (1861–1862). Twenty-three years later, he became a U.S. senator (1885–1893) for the state. As a partner of the Central Pacific, Stanford was important in providing the opportunity for Chinese labor. As a politician, he was important as a figure who exacerbated Chinese oppression. His political power and money made him an influential figure in California history.

Stanford was born in New York to a large family with six sons who made its living through manual farming labor and by innkeeping. Showing early aptitude and interest in academic subjects, he and a younger brother were sent to school. Stanford went to Cazenovia Seminary, a Methodist school near Syracuse, New York, where he performed well for the year he attended. He left without graduating in 1845. By 1848 he was admitted to the New York Bar and moved to Wisconsin to practice law. There he became involved with local politics. Upon a return visit to Albany, he married Jane Lathrop and then returned to Wisconsin.

Two years later, in 1852, his home and law library were destroyed in a fire, along with most of the rest of the town of Port Washington, Wisconsin. Stanford decided to move west and enter the grocery business with his brothers, who were already in California with stores of their own. When his first attempt to run a store near a tapped-out mine failed, he and his partner started another in Michigan Bluff, which prospered. When his brothers moved to San Francisco, Stanford took over management of the Sacramento store. During this time, he acquired interest in a mine that the owners had gone bankrupt trying to develop. Stanford received majority share in the mine thanks to their misfortune. Luckily for him, it began producing, and Stanford began accumulating even greater wealth. Over his lifetime, Stanford was a founder, director, or president of other influential businesses as well, including what is now Wells Fargo, Pacific Life, and the Southern Pacific Railroad.

Shortly after hitting it big with the mine, Stanford returned to Albany. However, the pace of living was too sedate for him after the excitement and movement of California. Jane agreed to return to California, where, in 1856, Stanford helped organize the Republican Party in Sacramento. In June 1861, he was elected president of the Central Pacific. In September, he was elected governor of California for a two-year term.

Unfortunately, his success in politics was built in part upon anti-Chinese sentiment. While Stanford employed Chinese workers and praised their industriousness, as governor he also signed into law measures to limit their ability to succeed. One example is California's Anti-Coolie Act of 1862, which enacted a "police tax" of two dollars and fifty cents on every person "of the Mongolian" race who wanted to engage in business. His rhetoric aligned with the racism of the time as well. Not known as a very good extemporaneous speaker, Stanford wrote and delivered his speeches with much forethought. In a message to the California legislature in January 1862, he argued that the Chinese immigrating to California were "dregs" who were harming whites and discouraging "desirable immigration."

Stanford capitalized on his political success in business, although his relationship with his partners on the Central Pacific was not always smooth. His primary nemesis was Collis Huntington, who disdained Stanford's need for the limelight and was particularly concerned with Stanford's conspicuous consumption when it was time to pay back the bonds secured by the federal government for the railroad. Huntington wanted to plead poverty and have the bonds forgiven. Stanford went out and bought his wife a very expensive piece of jewelry, which was reported from coast to coast. Huntington's ousting Stanford from the presidency of the Southern Pacific was also widely seen as retaliation for having won the Senate election over Huntington's friend, Aaron Sargent.

The money that Stanford made from the labor of thousands of Chinese workers on the Central Pacific allowed him to invest in other projects so that he could accumulate greater wealth. And he spent that wealth. His homes were lavish, he traveled luxuriously to Europe, he collected art, he bred racehorses, and he owned an expansive farm. He and Jane also founded Leland Stanford Junior University in 1885 in memory of their son, who died of typhoid fever the year before at fifteen years old. Due to Stanford's own interest in mechanical devices and new technologies, the school was intended to be private and devoted to "useful" education. It opened in 1891. Without Jane's economies after Stanford's death at Palo Alto in 1893, the school that would become Stanford University would not have survived, and without the wealth derived from Chinese labor, both on the railroad and at the school itself, it would not have been established in the first place. Stanford's legacy, then, is built upon the labor of Chinese immigrants.

James Harvey Strobridge (1827–1921)

James Harvey Strobridge was the superintendent of construction for the Central Pacific and reported directly to one of the Big Four investors, Charles Crocker. He stood more than six feet tall and had himself worked in mines in California and on railroads in Vermont, where he had been a foreman. Strobridge was an organized leader but also a rough man known to be quick-tempered and demanding, particularly of Chinese workers.

Strobridge was born on a farm in Vermont but came to California in 1849 to mine gold. He attempted other jobs as well; when Crocker hired him for the Central Pacific, he was a foreman at a mountain mine. While supervising construction for the Central Pacific, Strobridge stayed on the line, setting up living quarters with his wife in a boxcar. He was not a supervisor from afar; he was close to the work, even losing an eye due to an accident from a delayed explosion.

Driven and stubborn, Strobridge was also competitive. According to construction engineer and president of the Santa Fe Railroad W. B. Storey, when a Union Pacific representative found the Central Pacific's progress far behind Union Pacific's, Strobridge reportedly stepped up effort even more, finishing one of the toughest parts of the railway at Summit Tunnel in one year instead of three by putting laborers to work on all four faces of the tunnel. He could have utilized a newly invented compressed air drill that both Stanford and Edwin Bryant Crocker, Charles's brother and legal counsel to the Central Pacific, insisted upon using to speed up the process. But Strobridge flatly refused, costing two million dollars in the process and nearly breaking up the partnership (Lewis 1938, 79, 183).

That competitive streak was also tactical. When Charles Crocker bet that the Central Pacific could beat the Union Pacific in a daily track-laying record, Strobridge seemed to resist, saying the reward was not worth the cost. He waited until the Union Pacific had no opportunity to better the record and then laid 10.25 miles of track in a single day (Galloway 1950, 88).

Strobridge was forthright and at times profane. He spoke rudely to the common laborers, as Crocker recalled. When Crocker asked that Strobridge speak to them more humanely, Strobridge resisted, arguing that workers were "brutes" and could only understand that type of communication. Crocker became convinced of Strobridge's position. Decades later, other acquaintances reported that some of this rudeness was posturing to maintain a tough reputation. Most reports concur that workers were afraid of him.

Whether a posture or reality, Strobridge was serious about the workers who were constructing the railroad, and he was highly attuned to how different classes of labor performed at and away from work. Unapologetically, he testified in Congress in 1876 that he was "very much prejudiced against Chinese labor" (U.S. Congress 1877, 723) when Crocker brought up the initial plan to hire them to build the railroad. However, he said that he altered his opinion as the Chinese workers learned the job and did the work as well as white laborers. Strobridge stated that among workers, Chinese were preferable because they did not cause problems once they were paid and off the clock. He disdained the intemperance of the white men and would even arrange to delay liquor licenses of saloons near the railroad line. When the ceremonial "Golden Spike" was driven to signal the end of construction in 1869, no Chinese were included in the famous photograph marking the occasion, but Strobridge invited a group of Chinese workers to lunch to celebrate their contributions. Nevertheless, he maintained the racial prejudices of the nineteenth century, stating that he would have preferred white workers over Chinese whenever possible.

After completing construction for the Central Pacific, Strobridge became a farmer near Hayward, California. He returned to railroad work periodically, using Chinese laborers and white—mostly Irish—foremen to build railroad lines until 1889, when he retired from railroading permanently. He died in 1921 in Hayward.

DOCUMENT EXCERPTS

Disclaimer

When reading this document, it is important to remember the context. Although some of the language used may be offensive to the modern reader, we have not removed objectionable material from the texts in order that they remain an accurate reflection of the attitudes of their time and place.

Chinese Police Tax Law, April 26, 1862 (Excerpts)

In 1862, California passed a Police Tax Law that required every Chinese person who was not employed in mining or in rice, sugar, tea, or coffee production to pay a monthly tax of two dollars and fifty cents. This law identified Chinese as the "Mongolian race." The title of the act, "An Act to Protect Free White Labor against Competition with Chinese Coolie Labor, and to Discourage the Immigration of the Chinese into the State of California," explicitly states its exclusionist, nativist, and racist intention against Chinese immigrants.

AN ACT TO PROTECT FREE WHITE LABOR AGAINST COMPETITION WITH CHINESE COOLIE LABOR, AND TO DISCOURAGE THE IMMIGRATION OF THE CHINESE INTO THE STATE OF CALIFORNIA

April 26, 1862

The People of the State of California, represented in Senate and Assembly, do enact as follows:

SECTION 1. There is hereby levied on each person, male and female, of the Mongolian race, of the age of eighteen years and upwards, residing in this State, except such as shall, under laws now existing, or which may hereafter be enacted, take out licenses to work in the mines, or to prosecute some kind of business, a monthly capitation tax of two dollars and fifty cents, which tax shall be known as the Chinese Police Tax; provided, That all Mongolians exclusively engaged in the production and manufacture of the following articles shall be exempt from the provisions of this Act, viz: sugar, rice, coffee, tea. . . .

SECTION 4. The Collector shall collect the Chinese police tax, provided for in this Act, from all person refusing to pay such tax, and sell the same at public auction, by giving notice by proclamation one hour previous to such sale; and shall deliver the property, together with a bill of sale thereof, to the person agreeing to pay, and paying, the highest thereof, which delivery and bill of sale shall transfer to such person a good and sufficient title to the property. And after deducing the tax and necessary expenses incurred by reason of such refusal, seizure, and sale of property, the Collector shall return the surplus of the proceeds of the sale, if any, to the person whose property was sold; provided, That should any person, liable to pay the tax imposed in this Act, in any county in this State, escape into any other County, with the intention to evade the payment of such tax, then, and in that event, it shall be lawful for the Collector, when he shall collect Chinese police taxes, as provided for in this section, shall deliver to each of the persons paying such taxes a police tax receipt, with the blanks properly filled; provided, further, That any Mongolian, or Mongolians, may pay the above named tax to the County Treasurer, who is hereby authorized to receipt for the same in the same manner as the Collector. And any Mongolian, so paying said tax to the Treasurer of the County, if paid monthly, shall be entitled to a reduction of twenty percent of said tax. And if paid in advance for the year next ensuing, such Mongolian, or Mongolians, shall be entitled to a reduction of thirty-three and one third percent on said tax. But in all cases where the County Treasurer receipts for said tax yearly in advance, he shall do it by issuing for each month separately; and any Mongolian who shall exhibit a County Treasurer's receipt, as above provided, to the Collector for the month for which said receipt was given.

SECTION 5. Any person charged with the collection of Chinese police taxes, who shall give any receipt other than the one prescribed in this Act, or receive money for such taxes without giving the necessary receipt therefor, or who shall insert more than one name in any receipt, shall be guilty of a felony, and, upon conviction thereof, shall be fined in a sum not exceeding one thousand dollars, and be imprisoned in the State Prison for a period not exceeding one year.

SECTION 6. Any Tax Collector who shall sell, or cause to be sold, any police tax receipt, with the date of the sale left blank, or which shall not be dated and signed, and blanks filled with ink, by the Controller, Auditor, and Tax Collector, and any person who shall make any alteration, or cause the same to be made, in any police tax receipt, shall be deemed guilty of a felony, and, on conviction thereof, shall be fined in a sum not exceeding one thousand dollars, and imprisoned in the State prison for a period not exceeding 2 years; and the police tax receipt so sold, with blank date, or which shall not be signed and dated, and blanks filled with ink, as aforesaid, or which shall have been altered, shall be received in evidence in any Court of competent jurisdiction.

SECTION 7. Any person or company who shall hire persons liable to pay the Chinese police tax shall be held responsible for the payment of the tax due from each person so hired; and no employer shall be released from this liability on the ground that the employee in indebted to him (the employer), and the Collector may proceed against any such employer in the same manner as he might against the original party owing the taxes. The Collector shall have power to require any person or company believed to be indebted to, or to have any money, gold dust, or property of any kind, belonging to any person liable for police taxes, or in which such person is interested, in his or their possession, or under his or their control, to answer, under oath, as to such indebtedness, or the possession of such money, gold dust, or other property. In case a party is indebted, or has possession or control of any moneys, gold dust, or other property, as aforesaid, of such person liable for police taxes, he may collect from such party the amount of such taxes, and may require the delivery of such money, gold dust, or other property, as aforesaid; and in all cases the receipt of the Collector to said party shall be a complete bar to any demand made against said party, or his legal representatives, for the amounts of money, gold dust, or property, embraced therein.

SECTION 8. The Collector shall receive for his service, in collecting police taxes, twenty percent of all moneys which he shall collect from persons owing such taxes.

All of the residue, after deducting the percentage of the Collector, forty percent shall be paid into the County Treasury, for the use of the State, forty percent into the general County Fund, for the use of the County, and the remaining twenty percent into the School Fund, for the benefit of schools within the County; provided, That in counties where the Tax Collector receives a specific salary, he shall not be required to pay the percentage allowed for collecting the police tax into the County Treasury, but shall be allowed to retain the same for his own use and benefit; provided, That where he shall collect the police tax by Deputy, the percentage shall go to the Deputy . . .

SECTION 10. It is hereby made the duty of the various officers charged with the execution of the provisions of this Act, to carry out said provisions by themselves of Deputies; and for the faithful performance of their said duties in the premises, they shall be liable on their official bonds, respectively. The Treasurer of the respective counties shall make their statements and settlements under this Act with the Controller of State, at the same time and in the same manner they make their settlements under the general Revenue Act.

SECTION 11. This Act shall be take effect and be in force from and after the first day of May, next ensuing.

Source: "An Act to Protect Free White Labor Against Competition with Chinese Coolie Labor, and to Discourage the Immigration of the Chinese into the State of California" (April 26, 1862). Legislative Assembly of the Territory of Washington, 1864.

See also: Angel Island Opens in San Francisco Bay, 1910; California Gold Rush, 1848–1855; The Chinese Exclusion Act, 1882

Further Reading

Ambrose, Stephen E. 2000. *Nothing Like It in the World: The Men Who Built the Transcontinental Railroad 1863–1869*. New York: Simon & Schuster.

Bain, David Hayward. 1999. *Empire Express: Building the First Transcontinental Railroad*. New York: Viking Penguin.

Barth, Gunther. 1964. *Bitter Strength: A History of the Chinese in the United States 1850–1870*. Cambridge, MA: Harvard University Press.

Bhandari, Sudhanshu. 2011. "Discrimination and Perseverance amongst the Chinese in California in the Nineteenth and Early-Twentieth Centuries." *China Report* 47: 1–24.

Carson, Scott. 2005. "Chinese Sojourn Labor and the American Transcontinental Railroad." *Journal of Institutional and Theoretical Economics* 161: 80–102.

Chang, Iris. 2003. *The Chinese in America: A Narrative History*. New York: Viking.

Chen, Jack. 1980. *The Chinese of America*. San Francisco: Harper & Row.

Chew, William F. 2004. *Nameless Builders of the Transcontinental Railway: The Chinese Workers of the Central Pacific Railroad*. Victoria, British Columbia: Trafford.

Chinn, Thomas, H. Mark Lai, and Philip P. Choy. 1969. *A History of the Chinese in America: A Syllabus*. San Francisco: Chinese Historical Society of America. http://cprr.org/Museum/Chinese_Syllabus.html

Chiu, Ping. 1967. *Chinese Labor in California, 1850–1880: An Economic Study*. Madison: State Historical Society of Wisconsin.

Galloway, John Debo. 1950. *The Transcontinental Railroad*. New York: Simmons-Boardman. http://penelope.uchicago.edu/Thayer/E/Gazetteer/Places/America/United_States/_Topics/history/_Texts/GALFTR/4*.html

Griswold, Wesley S. 1962. *A Work of Giants: Building the First Transcontinental Railroad*. New York: McGraw-Hill.

Kraus, George. 1969. "Chinese Laborers and the Construction of the Central Pacific." *Utah Historical Quarterly* 37: 40–57.

Kung, Shien-Woo. 1962. *Chinese in American Life: Some Aspects of Their History, Status, Problems, and Contributions*. Seattle: University of Washington Press.

Lewis, Oscar. 1938. *The Big Four: The Story of Huntington, Stanford, Hopkins, and Crocker, and of the Building of the Central Pacific*. New York: Alfred A. Knopf.

McClain, Charles. 1994. *In Search of Equality: The Chinese Struggle against Discrimination in Nineteenth-Century America*. Berkeley: University of California Press.

Ong, Paul M. 1985. "The Central Pacific Railroad and Exploitation of Chinese Labor." *Journal of Ethnic Studies* 13: 119–124.

Saxton, Alexander. 1971. *The Indispensable Enemy: Labor and the Anti-Chinese Movement in California*. Berkeley: University of California Press.

Steiner, Stan. 1979. *Fusang: The Chinese Who Built America*. New York: Harper & Row.

Tsai, Shih-shan Henry. 1986. *The Chinese Experience in America*. Bloomington: Indiana University Press.

U.S. Congress. Joint Special Committee to Investigate Chinese Immigration. 1877. *Report of the Joint Special Committee to Investigate Chinese Immigration: February 27, 1877*. Washington, D.C.: Government Printing Office. https://archive.org/details/reportofjointspe00unit

Williams, John Hoyt. 1988. *A Great and Shining Road: The Epic Story of the Transcontinental Railroad*. New York: Times Books.

The Chinese Exclusion Act, 1882

Nathan Jung

Chronology

1848 Chinese immigration to California accelerates following the conclusion of the Mexican-American War and the discovery of gold in territories recently incorporated into the United States.

1850 On April 13, California's legislature passes the Foreign Miners' Tax Act. Signed into law by Governor Peter Hardeman Burnett, the law requires all miners in California who are not citizens of the United States to pay a tax of twenty dollars per month. While the tax technically applies to all foreign workers engaged in the mining industry, in practice, it specifically targets California's Chinese population.

1851 John McDougal assumes the governorship of California after Burnett resigns from the position. McDougal repeals the Foreign Miners' Tax Act over concerns about California's labor shortage.

1852 John Bigler defeats John McDougal in a general election for the governorship and reintroduces the Foreign Miners' Tax. Under the new law, all foreigners engaged in the mining trade in California are taxed at the starting rate of three dollars per month.

1852 Under Bigler's guidance, California passes a commutation tax that requires ship owners to list their foreign passengers and either post a $500 bond or pay a tax of up to fifty dollars per passenger.

1854 In the case of *People v. Hall*, California's Supreme Court sides with defendant George Hall, a white man sentenced to death after being convicted of murdering Chinese immigrant Ling Sing. On appeal, the Court decides that Chinese immigrants cannot testify in cases involving a white person. Their decision establishes precedent for the unequal legal status of Chinese persons.

1855 John Bigler signs a bill that taxes inbound ships fifty dollars for every foreign passenger deemed ineligible for citizenship. California's Supreme Court finds the bill unconstitutional on the grounds that only the federal government can legislate immigration policy.

1858 California's legislature passes "An Act to Prevent the Further Immigration of Chinese or Mongolians to This State," which explicitly prevents Chinese immigrants from entering California. The state's Supreme Court rules the act unconstitutional.

1862 Anti-Chinese laws pass at both the state and federal levels. In California, Chinese nationals have to pay two dollars and fifty cents a month to work in the state; nationally, U.S. citizens can no longer transport foreigners under penalty of fines and/or seizure of property. These laws are known as "Anti-Coolie Laws," after a derogatory term used for persons of Asian descent.

1875 The Page Act passes the U.S. Congress and is signed into law by President Ulysses S. Grant. This act is generally understood as the first restrictive immigration law issued by the federal government. In response to a number of racially motivated concerns, it bars "undesirable" foreigners (especially Chinese forced laborers and women) from entering the country.

1880   The United States and China sign the Angell Treaty on November 17, revising the previous 1868 Burlingame Treaty between the two countries. The Angell Treaty paves the way for the Chinese Exclusion Act by announcing the intention of the United States to suspend Chinese laborers from traveling to the country for a temporary period. The treaty allows entry for Chinese merchants and reaffirms the rights of the Chinese population already living in the United States.

1882   The Chinese Exclusion Act is signed into law on May 6 by President Chester Arthur. The law formally suspends the immigration of Chinese laborers to the United States for a period of ten years. It is widely seen as the first federal law to ban immigration by a specific race.

1888   The Scott Act adds further restrictions to the Chinese Exclusion Act. Under the law, laborers who travel back to China can no longer reenter the United States unless they have family or significant financial ties in the country. The Scott Act also nullifies 20,000 return certificates previously granted to Chinese laborers.

1892   The Geary Act extends the Chinese Exclusion Act for another ten years. It also makes burdensome new demands on Chinese residents in the United States, including the use of personal photographs to obtain now-mandatory identification papers and certificates of residence. Chinese residents are required to have these papers with them at all times.

1902   Congress extends the Chinese Exclusion Act for another ten years.

1904   Congress extends the Chinese Exclusion Act indefinitely.

1943   The Magnuson Act rescinds the Chinese Exclusion Act. Signed on December 17, the law allows some limited Chinese immigration to the United States and opens a path to citizenship for the Chinese community already residing in the country, while maintaining bans against Chinese business and property ownership.

Narrative

The Chinese Exclusion Act of 1882 initially barred the immigration of Chinese laborers to the United States for ten years but ended up lasting for over half a century. Building on anti-Chinese policies originating particularly in California, it is generally viewed as the first federal law to sweepingly restrict immigration based on race. In this respect, it led to the National Origins Act of 1924, which imposed upper limits on immigration in general and specifically barred persons of Asian descent from entering the country.

From its origins in racially discriminatory state laws to its own emendations and renewals, the Chinese Exclusion Act directly shaped decades of Chinese American life. It split Chinese families between continents, forced Chinese businesses to close, created a large surplus of Chinese bachelors in the American host state, and centralized Chinese communities in urban Chinatowns. In addition to its immeasurable impact on contemporary Chinese American demographics and identity, the Chinese Exclusion Act helped codify federal immigration enforcement and human trafficking as a trade.

The Gold Rush Era

The prehistory of the act begins with tensions between white and Chinese immigrant laborers, state politicians, and mining companies in California during the middle of the nineteenth century. Chinese workers began rapidly immigrating to California to fill labor shortages following the gold rush of 1848–1855. By 1852, the Chinese comprised one-tenth of the state's population and nearly one-third of the overall mining population (Dreyfus 2007, 201). While initially tolerated and even warmly welcomed in an 1852 speech to California's legislature by then-governor John McDougal, California's Chinese workers were soon faced with a growing nativist movement that sought to marginalize them through a series of racially exclusionary policies that eventually culminated in the federal Chinese Exclusion Act.

The racism underlying these policies is multifaceted; it is even seen in positive assessments of the Chinese community during this period, as in McDougal's statement that the Chinese are "peculiarly suited" to the "climate and character of these lands" (Yin 2000, 16). The primacy of race in laws that otherwise emphasize labor issues thus cannot be overstated. In response to the growing antagonism toward Chinese workers from California's white settlers, John Bigler (1805–1871) was nominated and elected governor in 1851, due largely to his anti-Chinese policies. Upon his becoming governor in January 1852, Bigler immediately proceeded to promote a legislative agenda designed to "check this tide of Asiatic immigration" (Ancheta 1998, 21).

Bigler quickly brought back the Foreign Miners' Tax, which was originally enacted by California's first governor, Peter Burnett, in 1850. The tax required foreign miners to pay twenty dollars per month for the right to work in the mines (Pfaelzer 2007, 469). While the tax technically applied to all foreigners employed in the mining industry, in practice it took aim at the Chinese workers who comprised a large portion of California's foreign mining labor. The act was repealed in 1851, but Bigler reintroduced it in 1852 with the lower base tax rate of three dollars per month. However, after the new Foreign Miners' Tax was emended to include annual increases, the rate eventually rose back up to the twenty-dollar mark, until the tax as a whole was declared unconstitutional by California's Supreme Court in 1870.

The appearance, disappearance, and reappearance of the Foreign Miners' Tax suggest a pattern followed by many of the anti-Chinese measures leading up to the Chinese Exclusion Act, as well as the act's own revisions and extensions. In this pattern, California's state legislature passes laws that stymie Chinese immigrants through indirect measures like taxes. The laws take effect until they are struck down by state courts or overridden by new state laws. In both cases, the laws are terminated not because they violate the rights of California's Chinese community, but because they exceed the legal jurisdiction of the state or threaten to do so. Ultimately, this pattern encourages federal action to blanketly restrict Chinese immigration and to circumvent the rights of Chinese persons living in the United States on the basis of race.

For example, along with the Foreign Miners' Tax, which forced Chinese workers out of a specific industry, Bigler instituted the Commutation Tax in the same year (1852). This tax sought to prevent Chinese immigration to California entirely. First, it required ship owners to list foreign passengers; second, for each foreign passenger listed, ship owners had to either post a $500 bond or pay a tax ranging from five to fifty dollars (Chang 2004, 42). California's Supreme Court ruled the tax unconstitutional in 1857, as it could not locate the state's legal authority to tax immigrants. In another example, the Supreme Court decided in the 1854 case of *People v. Hall* that Chinese immigrants could not testify in cases against a white person. This decision established an implicit precedent for using race to ascribe unequal legal status to Chinese persons.

While eventually rescinded, these and other precursors to the Chinese Exclusion Act had the practical effect of pushing the Chinese community out of California's mining industry and sanctioning its further marginalization in all areas of American life. It is important to note that this community, like others from Mexico and South America, did not passively accept such discriminatory measures. Instead, it developed sophisticated resistance tactics ranging from open protest to vigorous use of the court system at all levels (McClain 1984, 534).

John Bigler and Anti-Chinese Sentiment

John Bigler is best known as the third governor of California, serving in that capacity from 1852 to 1856. Bigler was the first governor in the state to complete a full term and the first to win a reelection. While known for establishing Sacramento as California's state capital, Bigler's tenure as governor was defined by his anti-Chinese actions, which eventually led to the passage of the Chinese Exclusion Act.

Born into a family with German roots near Carlisle, Pennsylvania, on January 8, 1805, Bigler and his younger brother William, who later became governor of Pennsylvania, started in the printing trade. They bought a newspaper, the *Centre County Democrat*, in 1831. Bigler served as editor of the newspaper for four years until leaving the position to study law in 1835. After earning his law degree and gaining admittance to the bar in Illinois, Bigler migrated to California following the gold rush of 1848, with the intention of practicing law.

However, after arriving in Sacramento in 1849, Bigler found fewer employment opportunities in the legal profession than he had anticipated. As a result, he turned to politics. That same year he was elected to the California state legislature, and in 1850 he became its speaker. Bigler's rise was fortuitously timed; in 1851, California's first governor, Peter Burnett, resigned due to his declining popularity after California's incorporation as a new state and to his opinions in favor of slavery. Lieutenant Governor John McDougal replaced him on January 9, 1851. McDougal held a favorable view of California's Chinese workers, but he was not re-nominated by the Democratic Party to run as its candidate in the 1852 general election. Instead, the party chose Bigler, who won against Whig opponent Pierson Reading by a slim margin.

Bigler's nomination and election were largely attributable to his protectionist attitude toward the mining industry and its white workers. In addition to ensuring that the mines stayed free from control by large monopolies, this attitude entailed regulating the mining labor pool to exclude immigrant labor, particularly Asian immigrant labor. Bigler's central argument was that Chinese laborers were inassimilable to American culture and therefore should not be allowed to work in the mines, as they had no intention of staying in or otherwise contributing to the country.

As a result, Bigler advanced anti-Chinese proposals early in his governorship. The first was to develop a "taxing power by the state as will check the present system of discriminate and unlimited Asiatic immigration" (Bigler 1997, 27). The second was "a demand by the State of California for the Prompt passage of an Act prohibiting 'Coolies' shipped from California under contracts, from laboring in the mines of the state" (Bigler 1997, 27). Bigler thus advanced a two-pronged local and national strategy to address the problem of Chinese immigration as he saw it. This strategy included direct state action in the form of taxes that targeted the Chinese minority in California and called for more sweeping interventions on the part of Congress, which controlled immigration policy overall.

Bigler's 1853 reelection went smoothly, as he coasted on the broad popularity of these policies. Their popularity was reiterated in 1855, when the state legislature passed a tax of fifty dollars per Asian immigrant based on a 1789 federal statute limiting naturalization to free white persons (Daniels 1988, 35). However, in some ways Bigler became a victim of the success of such policies. By succeeding in mainstreaming anti-Chinese sentiments, he could no longer appeal to voters on the basis of this specific issue, as other parties and candidates now advanced similar views.

As a result, Bigler faced difficult external challenges during the 1855 general election. At this time, California's economy was suffering. Gold had essentially disappeared in the Sierra Nevadas and had been found in Australia. The state's mounting debt was also an issue, especially in light of the perceived mismanagement of infrastructure and state finances on the part of Bigler's executive branch. Due to a general sense that his administration was too extravagant, Bigler lost the election to another nativist: the American Know-Nothing Party candidate, a former Democrat named Neely Johnson.

At the height of Bigler's popularity in 1854, the state legislature named a body of water in the Sierra Nevada "Lake Bigler" in honor of its then-governor. By 1862, however, "Lake Tahoe" was gaining traction as an alternative. In many ways this suggests the arc of Bigler's career: immensely well regarded during his governorship, he fell into disfavor due to his Confederate sympathies and, later, to his nativist policies. While Bigler immediately followed his governorship with a stint as ambassador to Chile from 1857 to 1861, he never regained political office, despite his best efforts. He ran as a Southern-friendly independent to Congress in 1863 but lost. In 1866, Andrew Jackson nominated him to be the Internal Revenue Service's Federal Assessor for the Sacramento district, but he was never confirmed due to conflicts between Jackson and Congress. On the heels of recurring political defeats, Bigler eventually returned to newspaper work, serving as editor of the *State Capital Reporter* for the remainder of his working life.

National and International Legislation

The influence of California's anti-Chinese laws resonated far beyond the borders of the state. As the Civil War wound down, the American economy contracted. In California, jobs and wages declined, while immigration continued to increase. Building on their successful efforts to control the demographics of California's mining industry, California's white-majority labor unions began reasserting their push to obstruct Chinese immigration on a national stage.

To this end, in 1875, the Page Act passed the U.S. Congress and was signed into law by President Ulysses S. Grant. The Page Act is often viewed as the first restrictive immigration law issued by the federal government. It encapsulates the two strands of labor protectionism and racism that wind through the history of the Chinese Exclusion Act. The Page Act barred entry of Chinese immigrants that fit into the category of "undesirable." This category included forced or "coolie" laborers, who were believed to take jobs away from whites and drive down wages. However, it also included Asian women who engaged in the prostitution trade. The designation of these women as "undesirable" stemmed not from labor concerns, but from racist fears of miscegenation arising from the notion that such women carried germs that could be transmitted to white men.

Having established a foothold at the national level through the Page Act, anti-Chinese measures soon expanded to direct negotiations with China itself. The U.S. government revisited the immigration-friendly Burlingame Treaty it had signed

The Workingmen's Party of California

The Workingmen's Party of California was founded in San Francisco in 1877. Expanding from its roots as an association of workers, the party became a major political force for anti-Chinese agitation under the guidance of the Irish immigrant Dennis Kearney.

California, and San Francisco in particular, suffered a severe economic downturn beginning around 1876. In response to the discontent following mass unemployment, Kearney delivered highly provocative orations around San Francisco's "Sand Lots" that codified a political party out of grassroots workers' associations. While the Workingmen's Party of California did push for progressive labor measures, such as an eight-hour work day and support for railroad strikers, it also increasingly adopted a nativist, anti-Chinese platform.

As the party expanded its political influence in San Francisco and beyond, Kearney's anti-Chinese speeches, which often led to riots against the Chinese community, became central to its platform. The party openly advocated for changes to the Burlingame Treaty and used its newly gained influential status as a viable opposition party to promote sympathetic politicians like Isaac Kalloch to local office and to enshrine its nativist views in all levels of law. For example, in 1879, California was drafting a new state constitution; the increased stature of Kearney's party prompted the legislature to adopt explicitly anti-Chinese measures like barring Chinese voting rights and making it illegal for corporations to hire them. These and other measures eventually became central features of the Chinese Exclusion Act.

with China in 1868, which established China as a most-favored nation in trade. Scuttling the Burlingame Treaty's allowance of free immigration by the Chinese to the United States, the Angell Treaty established the right of the United States to suspend travel by Chinese laborers to America for a temporary period. The treaty continued to allow for the entry of white-collar Chinese immigrants of the merchant class and nominally reaffirmed America's dedication to protecting the rights of the Chinese population already living in the country. The two countries signed the Angell Treaty on November 17, 1880.

The Angell Treaty allowed Congress to pass the Chinese Exclusion Act of 1882. Introduced to the House of Representatives by California's Horace Page (the namesake of the Page Act) on April 12, 1882, the Chinese Exclusion Act was quickly approved by both Houses of Congress in April and signed into law by President Chester Arthur on May 6, 1882. Building on the Page Act, the Chinese Exclusion Act restricted entry to the country by Chinese laborers, particularly those engaged in mining work, while welcoming merchants, Chinese officials, and their servants. The Chinese Exclusion Act also affected Chinese persons currently residing in the country, who were required to obtain reentry papers if they left the country and wished to return. Finally, it denied Chinese immigrants the possibility of attaining American citizenship through naturalization.

Despite its quick passage, the bill was not uncontroversial. In addition to open letters (Asing 1852, 32–35) and long-lasting court challenges from the Chinese community, opposition to the bill was seen from lawmakers like George Frisbie Hoar and labor unions such as the Industrial Workers of the World (Choi 1999, 1; Daniels 1988, 54). Criticism was also heard from the California region by figures like the poet Joaquin Miller, who explicitly challenged the claim on the part of nativist unions to represent the interests of "real" laborers, as distinct from Chinese workers (Miller 1901, 782).

Enforcement and Revisions

Despite such opposition, the Chinese Exclusion Act remained legally viable. However, its implementation proved difficult. Certain gaps in the language and conception of the original act required substantial revisions to ensure its effectiveness. The first gap pertained to enforcement. As originally written, the Chinese Exclusion Act did not provide for the personnel and institutional housing needed to maintain border security. As a result, the administration of the law was left to a motley crew of Treasury and Customs officials until enforcement authority was fully transferred to the newly created Immigration Bureau in 1903. Ultimately, the gradual evolution of the act's enforcement mechanisms changed America's approach to patrolling the Canadian and Mexican borders, albeit in different ways.

Chinese Labor and the Transcontinental Railroad

One of the largest employers of Chinese labor prior to the Chinese Exclusion Act was the transcontinental railroad, and especially the Central Pacific Railroad that connected California to the Utah Territory and beyond. Under construction beginning in the early 1860s, the Central Pacific project eventually brought over thousands of Chinese workers from southern China to do the dangerous work of connecting America by rail.

Most of the initial surge of Chinese immigration to California was due to the gold rush. However, when the gold mines dried up and initiatives such as the Foreign Miners' Tax pushed Chinese workers out of the mines, the Chinese population needed to find other sources of income. While some continued to work in the silver mines, many others found domestic work in restaurants and laundries in San Francisco and other areas. These occupations, however, were not abundant enough to employ the full pool of Chinese laborers.

The construction of the transcontinental railroads undertaken around 1862 brought with it the promise of jobs. Initially the railroad companies did not want to hire Chinese workers, due to racial prejudice. By the middle of the decade, though, these companies faced a labor shortage. The sheer scope of their project required many more workers than they could secure, and the railroad companies did not want to pay Irish laborers the higher wages they were increasingly demanding. In response, they hired fifty Chinese workers in 1865. These workers proved reliable and willing to work in harsh conditions. As a result, by 1869 the railroad companies had hired thousands of Chinese workers from the United States and began recruiting thousands of additional workers directly from China. By the time of the railroad's completion, Chinese labor comprised 90 percent of the railroad workforce.

The second gap pertained to the instability of the act's reliance on categories like "laborers" (who were not allowed entry) and "merchants" (who were allowed). As Kitty Calavita notes, the Chinese Exclusion Act presumed that there were two distinct varieties of Chinese immigrants (laborers and merchants) and that it would be easy for officials to tell the two apart. Instead, the original act failed to recognize that "the myriad occupations of aspiring entrants could not be so easily dichotomized, 'merchant' status was fluid and shifting, and inspectors repeatedly encountered difficulties discerning class status by its presumed physical markers" (Calavita 2000, 9). Such markers included rough hands, which were not absolute indicators of current class status. The language of the act also did not anticipate the difficulty of situating occupations like "doctor" into merchant/laborer dichotomies or the fact that Chinese immigrants would ingeniously exploit the ambiguities of merchant status by devising ways to "pass" as merchants.

These gaps were addressed in revisions of the Chinese Exclusion Act that often accompanied its extensions. An 1884 revision, for instance, imposed additional bureaucratic burdens on Chinese immigrants seeking to leave and return to the country and clarified that the return laws applied to all ethnic Chinese, regardless of their country of origin. The 1888 Scott Act imposed further restrictions, stipulating that laborers who had returned to China were now forbidden to reenter the United States unless they had either documented wives, children, or parents in the country or property and/or debts in excess of $1,000. The Scott Act thus nullified tens of thousands of return certificates that had already been granted to Chinese laborers in the United States, effectively stranding the landed Chinese population in the host state.

A Chinese immigrant with his son. This photo was archived by the United States Justice Department as part of an immigration investigation conducted around 1899, in relation to the Chinese Exclusion Act of 1882. (National Archives)

In 1889 the U.S. Supreme Court upheld the constitutionality of the Chinese Exclusion Act in *Chae Chan Ping v. United States*, even with these onerous race-based distinctions in effect. The Geary Act of 1892 extended the act for another ten years and introduced a number of further provisions. Under the Geary Act, the definition of "merchant" tightened significantly. In addition, beginning in 1893, the Geary Act required all Chinese persons in the United States to register with the federal government, which entailed furnishing a photograph to obtain an official certificate of residence. These certificates were necessary to avoid deportation, so Chinese persons were required to carry them at all times. The Geary Act also denied Chinese workers the right to post bail and to file habeas corpus complaints. With these new provisions in place, the Chinese Exclusion Act was once again renewed in 1902 and finally made indefinite in 1904, shuttering the doors to Chinese immigration and isolating the Chinese community already residing in the country for nearly four decades.

In 1943, two years after China allied with the United States in World War II, Warren Magnuson, a Democratic representative from Washington, introduced the Magnuson Act. Sometimes called the Chinese Exclusion Repeal Act of 1943, this law allowed for limited migration to the United States from China. It also provided a path to naturalization for Chinese persons already living in America. While the Magnuson Act did not address issues such as the bans on Chinese business and property ownership that had developed around the Chinese Exclusion Act and persisted for several decades, it did mark a crucial reopening of corridors between China and the United States. In so doing, it paved the way for the 1965 Immigration Act, which officially discarded race as a consideration in national immigration policy. With the 1965 law, Chinese immigration resumed in a significant way after roughly eighty years of Chinese American identity and population tallies being forcibly shaped by the Chinese Exclusion Act and its predecessors.

Biographies of Notable Figures
Wong Chin Foo (1847–1898)

Given the explosion of highly public anti-Chinese sentiments during the period of the Chinese Exclusion Act, it is important to highlight the many voices raised in opposition to the act, especially when these voices come from inside the Chinese community. One prominent and irreducibly complex voice belonged to Wong Chin Foo (1847–1898). Wong's writings, speeches, advocacy, and political organization helped forge a nascent sense of Chinese American identity that stood against the dominant trend of American nativism.

Wong was born Won Sa Kee in 1847 in Jimo, which is located in the Shandong Province of China. His once-prosperous family saw its fortunes decline during the Taiping Rebellion that lasted from 1850 to 1864. In 1861, the teenage Wong was taken in by the Baptist missionary Sallie Little Holmes and her husband Landrum. Under Holmes's tutelage, Wong became fluent in English, and in 1867 he was baptized. To prepare for his assumed future occupation in the Baptist ministry, Wong traveled to America in the same year of his baptism to further his religious education. While in the United States, he went to a preparatory school in Washington, D.C., and later to Lewisburg University (now Bucknell University) in Pennsylvania for a year, from 1869 to 1870.

After briefly traveling the country, Wong returned to China for a period of three tumultuous years. During this time, he married Liu Yu San, adopted the name Wong

Yen Ping, worked in the Imperial Maritime Customs Service and as an interpreter at a customs house, and finally was excommunicated from the Shanghai Baptist Church, allegedly for leading a dissolute life. He also engaged in political activism, ranging from cultural initiatives to efforts to prohibit the opium trade. Wong was ultimately forced to leave China in 1873 after he helped import foreign fighters and weapons to lead an unsuccessful overthrow of the Qing government.

Parting with his wife and child, Wong traveled first to Japan and then back to the United States. He was one of the first Chinese immigrants to become a naturalized U.S. citizen; upon arriving in the country, he adopted his adult name and began his career as a public lecturer who sought to defend the Chinese population against nativist attacks. These attacks increased after an economic contraction following the American Civil War and the completion of the transcontinental railroad in 1869, which dispersed the Chinese labor market into other occupations. When combined with depressed wages on the whole, this surplus of Chinese workers brought out racist tendencies in the progressive labor movement. The end result was a series of laws culminating in the Chinese Exclusion Act, which forced Chinese persons out of specific industries and increasingly out of civic life under the assumption that they were unassimilable to American culture.

Wong contested this assumption in his provocative writings and speeches. He wrote voluminous newspaper articles and essays on issues relating to Chinese life in America and started the first Chinese-language newspaper circulated east of the Rocky Mountains in 1883. The English title of this newspaper, *The Chinese American*, is the first recorded use of the term "Chinese American." Along with his print advocacy, Wong continued speaking on the lecture circuit, where he engaged nativist leaders such as Dennis Kearney, whom Wong was judged to have beaten in a public debate contest in 1887. With his strong religious training and sardonic sense of humor, Wong defended Chinese workers in several registers and in several venues, depending on the needs of the occasion. He could, for example, communicate the core values of Confucianism and/or Buddhism to white Christian Americans in ways that drew parallels between their faiths, although he was also capable of explicitly polemical writing that challenged dominant religious authorities in America, as seen in his most famous essay, "Why Am I a Heathen?"

Once the Exclusion Act passed in 1882, Wong found it more necessary than ever to politically organize the Chinese American community. To this end, he convened all the naturalized Chinese citizens in the New York area in 1884 to form the first-ever Chinese American civic association in American history. While this particular association didn't last long, Wong also founded the influential Chinese Equal Rights League, an organization that he represented in his testimony before the U.S. Congress against the renewal of the Chinese Exclusion Act in 1892. Although he also remained involved in mainland Chinese politics throughout his entire life abroad, the last period of Wong's work as a political agitator in the United States was based in Chicago, where he moved in the mid-1890s to found two newspapers and a Confucian temple.

In late 1896, Wong decided to return to China, purportedly in response to a letter from his son. After having his American passport issued and then rapidly rescinded on orders from the U.S. State Department while in Hong Kong, Wong eventually died in Weihai in 1898. While his militancy in favor of Chinese assimilation to American cultural standards presents some complications for contemporary readers, Wong's esteemed status as a civil rights advocate for the Chinese community at a volatile time in American history has remained rightfully durable.

DOCUMENT EXCERPTS

The Chinese Exclusion Act

Enacted on May 6, 1882, the Chinese Exclusion Act placed a ten-year ban on Chinese immigrants entering the United States or becoming naturalized U.S. citizens. Though he originally vetoed the act, President Chester A. Arthur eventually signed it into law after some minor revisions. The Chinese had been entering the country in record numbers for years, particularly in California, and were typically forced to work for low wages and to live in conditions of poverty. Many of them lived as near slaves while they were employed building railroad lines. They were victims of attacks by white workingmen and other immigrant groups who believed the Chinese were taking jobs away from them and bringing the wages and living standards down.

Chinese Exclusion Act (1882)

(Excerpts)

An act to execute certain treaty stipulations relating to Chinese.

WHEREAS, in the opinion of the Government of the United States the coming of Chinese laborers to this country endangers the good order of certain localities within the territory thereof: Therefore,

Be it enacted by the Senate and House of Representatives of the United States of America in Congress assembled, That from and after the expiration of ninety days next after the passage of this act, and until the expiration of ten years next after the passage of this act, the coming of Chinese laborers to the United States be, and the same is hereby, suspended; and during such suspension it shall not be lawful for any Chinese laborer to come, or, having so come after the expiration of said ninety days, to remain within the United States.

Section 2. That the master of any vessel who shall knowingly bring within the United States on such vessel, and land or permit to be landed, any Chinese laborer, from any foreign port or place, shall be deemed guilty of a misdemeanor, and on conviction thereof shall be punished by a fine of not more than five hundred dollars for each and every such Chinese laborer so brought, and may be also imprisoned for a term not exceeding one year.

Section 3. That the two foregoing sections shall not apply to Chinese laborers who were in the United States on the seventeenth day of November, eighteen hundred and eighty, or who shall have come into the same before the expiration of ninety days next after the passage of this act, and who shall produce to such master before going on board such vessel, and shall produce to the collector of the port in the United States at which such vessel shall arrive, the evidence hereinafter in this act required of his being one of the laborers in this section mentioned; nor shall the two foregoing sections apply to the case of any master whose vessel, being bound to a port not within the United States, shall come within the jurisdiction of the United States by reason of being in distress or in stress of weather, or touching at any port of the United States on its voyage to any foreign port or place: Provided, That all Chinese laborers brought on such vessel shall depart with the vessel on leaving port.

Section 4. That for the purpose of properly identifying Chinese laborers who were in the United States on the seventeenth day of November, eighteen hundred and eighty, or who shall have come into the same before the expiration of ninety days next after the passage of this act, and in order to furnish them with the proper evidence of their right to go from and come to the United States of their free will and accord, as provided by the treaty between the United States and China dated November seventeenth, eighteen hundred and eighty, the collector of customs of the district from which any such Chinese laborer shall depart from the United States shall, in person or by deputy, go on board each vessel having on board any such Chinese laborer and cleared or about to sail from his district for a foreign port, and on such vessel make a list of all such Chinese laborers, which shall be entered in registry-books to be kept for that purpose, in which shall be stated the name, age, occupation, last place of residence, physical marks or peculiarities, and all facts necessary for the identification of each of such Chinese laborers, which books shall be safely kept in the custom-house; and every such Chinese laborer so departing from the United States shall be entitled to, and shall receive, free of any charge or cost upon application therefor, from the collector or his deputy, at the time such list is taken, a certificate, signed by the collector or his deputy and attested by his seal of office, in such form as the Secretary of the Treasury shall prescribe, which certificate shall contain a statement of the name, age, occupation, last place of residence, personal description, and facts of identification of the Chinese laborer to whom the certificate is issued, corresponding with the said list and registry in all particulars. In case any Chinese laborer after having received such certificate shall leave such vessel before her departure he shall deliver his certificate to the master of the vessel, and if such Chinese laborer shall fail to return to such vessel before her departure from port the certificate shall be delivered by the master to the collector of customs for cancellation. The certificate herein provided for shall entitle the Chinese laborer to whom the same is issued to return to and reenter the United States upon producing and delivering the same to the collector of customs of the district at which such Chinese laborer shall seek to reenter; and upon delivery of such certificate by such Chinese laborer to the collector of customs at the time of reentry in the United States, said collector shall cause the same to be filed in the custom-house and duly canceled.

Section 5. That any Chinese laborer mentioned in section four of this act being in the United States, and desiring to depart from the United States by land, shall have the right to demand and receive, free of charge or cost, a certificate of identification similar to that provided for in section four of this act to be issued to such Chinese laborers as may desire to leave the United States by water; and it is hereby made the duty of the collector of customs of the district next adjoining the foreign country to which said Chinese laborer desires to go to issue such certificate, free of charge or cost, upon application by such Chinese laborer, and to enter the same upon registry-books to be kept by him for the purpose, as provided for in section four of this act. . . .

Section 8. That the master of any vessel arriving in the United States from any foreign port or place shall, at the same time he delivers a manifest of the cargo, and if there be no cargo, then at the time of making a report of the entry of the vessel pursuant to law, in addition to the other matter required to be reported, and before landing, or permitting to land, any Chinese passengers, deliver and report to the collector of customs of the district in which such vessels shall have arrived a separate list of all Chinese passengers taken on board his vessel at any foreign port or place, and all such passengers on board the vessel at that time. such list shall show the names of such passengers (and if accredited officers of the Chinese Government traveling on the business of that government, or their servants, with a note of such facts), and the names and other particulars, as shown by their respective certificates; and such list shall be sworn to by the master in the manner required by law in relation to the manifest of the cargo. Any willful refusal or neglect of any such master to comply with the provisions of this section shall incur the same penalties and forfeiture as are provided for a refusal or neglect to report and deliver a manifest of the cargo.

Section 9. That before any Chinese passengers are landed from any such vessel, the collector, or his deputy, shall proceed to examine such passengers, comparing the certificates with the list and with the passengers; and no passenger shall be allowed to land in the United States from such vessel in violation of law.

Section 10. That every vessel whose master shall knowingly violate any of the provisions of this act shall be deemed forfeited to the United States, and shall be liable to seizure and condemnation in any district of the United States into which such vessel may enter or in which she may be found. . . .

Section 12. That no Chinese person shall be permitted to enter the United States by land without producing to the proper office of customs the certificate in this act required of Chinese persons seeking to land from a vessel. And any Chinese person found unlawfully within the United States shall be caused to be removed therefrom to the country from whence he came, by direction of the President of the United States, and at the cost of the United States, after being brought before some justice, judge, or commissioner of a court of the United States and found to be one not lawfully entitled to be or remain in the United States.

Section 13. That this act shall not apply to diplomatic and other officers of the Chinese Government traveling upon the business of that government, whose credentials shall be taken as equivalent to the certificate in this act mentioned, and shall exempt them and their body and household servants from the provisions of this act as to other Chinese persons.

Section 14. That hereafter no State court or court of the United States shall admit Chinese to citizenship; and all laws in conflict with this act are hereby repealed.

Section 15. That the words "Chinese laborers," whenever used in this act, shall be construed to mean both skilled and unskilled laborers and Chinese employed in mining.

Source: Chinese Exclusion Act of 1882. *U.S. Statutes at Large* 22: 58.

See also: California Gold Rush, 1848–1855; Japanese American Internment, 1942–1946; 9/11 and Islamophobia, 2001–2018; *United States v. Wong Kim Ark*, 1898

Further Reading

Ancheta, Angelo. 1998. *Race, Rights, and the Asian-American Experience*. New Brunswick, NJ: Rutgers University Press.

Asing, Norman. 1852. "A Defense of Chinese Immigrants." In *Asian Americans: Opposing Viewpoints*, edited by William Dudley, Bruno Leone, and John C. Chalberg, 32–35. San Diego: Greenhaven Press. Reprinted 1997.

Bigler, John. 1997. "Asian Immigration Must Be Restricted." In *Asian Americans: Opposing Viewpoints*, edited by William Dudley, Bruno Leone, and John C. Chalberg, 26–31. San Diego: Greenhaven Press.

Calavita, Kitty. 2000. "The Paradoxes of Race, Class, Identity, and 'Passing': Enforcing the Chinese Exclusion Acts, 1882–1910." *Law & Social Inquiry* 25, no. 1: 1–40.

Chang, Iris. 2004. *The Chinese in America: A Narrative History*. New York: Penguin Books.

Choi, Jennifer Jung Hee. 1999. "The Rhetoric of Inclusion: The I.W.W. and Asian Workers." *Ex-Post Facto: Journal of the History of Students at San Francisco State University* 8, no. 4: 1–8.

Daniels, Roger. 1988. *Asian America: Chinese and Japanese in the United States since 1850.* Seattle: University of Washington Press.

Dreyfus, Philip Jacques. 2007. "California." In *Encyclopedia of U.S. Labor and Working-Class History.* Vol. 1, *A–F,* edited by Eric Arneson, 200–204. New York: Routledge Press.

McClain, Charles. 1984. "The Chinese Struggle for Civil Rights in Nineteenth Century America: The First Phase, 1850–1870." *California Law Review* 72, no. 4: 529–568.

Miller, Joaquin. 1901. "The Chinese and the Exclusion Act." *The North American Review* 173, no. 541: 782–789.

Pfaelzer, Jean. 2007. "Foreign Miners Tax." In *Encyclopedia of U.S. Labor and Working-Class History.* Vol. 1, *A–F,* edited by Eric Arneson, 468–469. New York: Routledge Press.

Saxton, Alexander. 1995. *The Indispensable Enemy: Labor and the Anti-Chinese Movement in California.* Berkley: University of California Press.

Yin, Xiao-huang. 2000. *Chinese American Literature since the 1850s.* Chicago: University of Illinois Press.

Hawaii Becomes a U.S. Territory, 1898

Laura Stanfield Prichard

Chronology

1350   Kalaunuiohua (ruled 1315–1345) nearly unites the Hawaiian islands, conquering all but Kauai.

1778   James Cook of the British Navy lands on Kauai, accurately locating it for Western maps.

1810   King Kamehameha I (ruled 1782–1819) unites Hawaiians into a single kingdom.

1819   King Kamehameha II (ruled 1819–1824), abolishes the kapu system after the Battle of Kuamo'o. In December, Protestant missionaries from Boston depart for Hawaii on a mission of Christian conversion.

1835   Ladd & Co. establish the first permanent sugar plantation in Koloa, Kauai.

1839   The Kingdom of Hawaii adopts its first bill of rights (Ke Kumukānāwai o ka Makahiki), establishing a constitutional monarchy under King Kamehamaha III (ruled 1825–1854). The *Baibala Hemolele* is published.

1848   Private property is established with the Buke Māhele (Division Book).

1874   Kalākaua defeats Queen Dowager Emma in a legislative election, and the nonjudicial foreclosure law passes.

1887   King Kalākaua (ruled 1874–1891) signs the "Bayonet Constitution," which restricts voting eligibility.

1891   Queen Liliʻuokalani (ruled 1891–1893) refuses to recognize the constitution of 1887 and restores the monarchy's traditional authority.

1893   The USS *Boston* sends sailors and Marines ashore to take up positions in Honolulu. A coup d'état led by the Committee of Safety places Queen Liliʻuokalani under arrest at ʻIolani Palace on January 17.

1894   The Republic of Hawaii is established on July 4, with Sanford B. Dole as president.

1898   The U.S. Congress passes the Newlands Resolution on August 12, annexing Hawaii. President William McKinley signs it into law, and Hawaii becomes a U.S. territory in 1900.

Narrative

The Hawaiian archipelago (formerly called the Sandwich Islands) was annexed as a territory of the United States in 1898 and became a state on August 21, 1959. This Pacific island chain is home to a variety of peoples, from native Polynesian founders to Asian immigrants and largely English-speaking Europeans and Americans. Recent scholarship, incorporating Hawaiian language sources and dissenting viewpoints, has provided us with new ways of looking at the events that led to Hawaii's annexation by the United States.

Hawaii is the only state to have been a royal kingdom: after King Kamehameha I unified the islands into one country in 1810, a centralized monarchy was in place for eighty-three years. In an attempt to maintain independence, kings and queens gradually introduced westernized economic and political ideas to the Hawaiian islands in order to identify themselves as a nation-state. These new systems created tension between the islands' natives and foreign residents. An independent republic was established from 1894 to 1898, and the annexation was seen by some as the culmination of a seventy-year relationship with the United States, brokered by Americans and Europeans living on the island (Bruce 2012, ii).

Background

Now known for its cultural pluralism, Hawaii is the northernmost group of islands settled by Pacific Polynesians and has a flourishing indigenous cultural heritage. Early ocean explorers began to arrive in Hawaii by outrigger canoe as early as 400

CE. Scholars have traced the origins of these first inhabitants to the Marquesas Islands, 2,000 miles away. From 1100 to 1400, a larger wave of Polynesian migration brought people from the Society Islands and Tahiti. Native Hawaiian people, or Kānaka Maoli, explored the central Pacific and developed a large repertoire of stories, songs, chants, and political prose in the Hawaiian language ('Ōlelo Hawaii) to record their history and define their place in the world.

Hawaii occupies a strategic position as a main crossroads of the Pacific. In 1778, Captain James Cook (1728–1779) of the British Navy landed in Hawaii, accompanied by a crew that included Chinese sailors. This event marked the beginning of an era of considerable change and led to Hawaii being placed under the Protectorate of Great Britain by Captain George Van-

A Statue of King Kamehameha I of Hawaii. King Kamehameha I united the islands and ruled Hawaii from the late eighteenth to the early nineteenth century. After unification, he established peace and laid the foundations for the islands' prosperity. (Library of Congress)

couver in 1794. During the same period, Hawaiian chiefs such as Ka'iana (known as Prince of Kauai, 1755–1795) sailed throughout the Pacific Rim and developed indigenous approaches to mapmaking (Chang 2016, 44).

After Hawaii's "discovery" and inclusion in late eighteenth-century European maps, colonial powers began to compete for control over the Pacific. Great Britain and Germany fought over New Guinea, the Bismarck Archipelago, Fiji, and Samoa; France and Great Britain clashed in continental southwest Asia. The United States was fighting the Spanish-American War, begun after Spanish troops tried to suppress the guerilla war in Cuba. The USS *Maine* was sunk in Havana's harbor on February 15, 1898, and by May the U.S. Asiatic Squadron had destroyed the Spanish Pacific Fleet in Manila Bay. The United States fought Spanish ground troops in Cuba and Puerto Rico during the summer and occupied Manila in August. On December 10, 1898, Spain and the United States signed an armistice: Spain relinquished its sovereignty over Cuba, ceding Puerto Rico, Guam, and the Philippine Islands to the United States after the Treaty of Paris in 1898.

Unification and Cultural Diversity

Early attempts were made by local kings to unify the Hawaiian island chain, such as the 1783 conquest of Oahu by Kahekili of Maui. By the 1810s, King Kamehameha I (from the "Big Island" of Hawaii) was able to conquer this large, unified area, rather than battling separately for each district or island. The year 1819 also marked another important moment of change: Kamehameha I's son, Liholiho, ascended to the throne as Kamehameha II. He abolished the ancient kapu code of conduct and ended formal worship at the stone platform temples (*heiaus*). At the urging of several powerful female chiefs, he removed many prohibitions, including the ʻaikapu, which restricted contact between men and women and limited women's diets. The 1819 Battle of Kuamoʻo (on the Big Island), led by the king's cousin, Kekuaokalani, was the only armed rebellion in favor of the old religion.

In December of the same year, Protestant missionaries departed Boston for Hawaii on a mission of Christian conversion. Christianity spread quickly due to the fall of the kapu system. Hawaii began a period of acculturation with the introduction of Protestant missionary songs and European secular music. The collection *Na himeni Hawaii* was published in 1823, and the first Western singing school opened the following year. The publication of the first edition of the *Baibala Hemolele* (1839) marked a crucial paradigm shift caused by Hawaii's rapidly growing literacy. From a sociological standpoint, this translation of the Bible (*Baibala* in Hawaiian) into the Hawaiian language marked the irreversible collision of an insulated native culture with Western influences. The *Baibala Hemolele* is the largest single volume ever printed in Hawaiian. Its 2012 edition consists of 1,400 pages, down from the publication's prior 2,300 pages (1837–1839). This tedious project was the most work-intensive literary body created since Hawaiian had become a written language. Roughly nine people regularly contributed to its creation (five native scholars and four American ministers) in addition to many others who contributed to the work over the course of a decade. The American participants were highly educated scholars with deep knowledge of ancient biblical languages. The Hawaiian participants included were among the highest-ranking *aliʻi* (chiefs) and *kākāʻōlelo* (advisors to the chiefs), who were also scholars in Hawaiian languages and oral literature (Lyon 2017).

The arrival of the first twelve companies of missionaries (1819–1848) marked the beginning of the struggle between indigenous culture and a (mostly) white culture. The children of missionaries had an outsized impact on nineteenth-century U.S. foreign policy, as they eventually alienated themselves from the Hawaiian monarchy and indigenous population. Almost none followed their parents into missionary work, and many rejected the Christian faith. Men such as Sanford Dole (1844–1926), Samuel Mills Damon (1845–1924), William Owen Smith (1848–1929), and Lorrin Thurston (1858–1931) secured disproportionate economic and political power and began a path toward political revolution: almost all supported the annexation of Hawaii, despite their parents' hope that the islands would remain independent.

Most early Asian immigrants to the United States went to Hawaii. Many came to work on the sugarcane, pineapple, and coconut plantations, including Filipinos (who originally came to play in the Royal Hawaiian Band and constituted 25 percent of Hawaii's total population in 2010), Chinese (most of whom were from the Cantonese Guangdong and intermarried with Hawaiian women), and Japanese (who first arrived in 1806 with a shipwreck). Between 1869 and 1885, Japan barred emigration to Hawaii in fear that Japanese workers would degrade the reputation of the Japanese race; the first official Japanese immigrants were not permitted to enter Hawaii until February 8, 1885. Until 2010, people of Japanese ancestry made up the majority of Hawaii's population, and at their height made up 42 percent in the 1920 census (1920 Federal Population Census, 65).

Musical acculturation shows how Hawaiians adapted Western sounds and instruments. Sailors and vaqueros (Spanish-speaking Mexican cowboys) imported by King Kamehameha III (1813–1854) introduced the guitar and falsetto singing to Hawaiian cowboys (paniolos) as early as 1832. Many generations of the Hawaiian royal family studied under Henri Berger (1844–1929), who was sent from Prussia in 1872 at the request of King Kamehameha V (1830–1872). Berger founded the Royal Hawaiian Band, the oldest municipal band in the United States, and became fascinated by Hawaiian folk music. He published many of the first articles about indigenous culture and instructed Hawaiian musicians in European styles. With the arrival of the *SS Ravenscrag* in 1879, Portuguese immigrants brought the braguinha and machête da braça, small, four-stringed variants of the cavaquinho, from Madeira, calling them "'ukulele." German singing societies (1880s–1990s) and small orchestras (1881–1884 and 1895–1902) were also active in Hawaii during this period. Hawaii's largest institution devoted to natural, historical, and cultural preservation is the Bernice Pauahi Bishop Museum in Honolulu, founded in 1889.

While Hawaii's royal rulers adopted Christianity and contracted workers from Asia, they also worked to preserve indigenous traditions. In native Hawaiian cultural practice, music and dance were used to show gratitude, communicate stories about family lineage and mythology, and accompany celebrations and numerous other secular events. Hawaiian rulers encouraged, translated, and composed several varieties of chanting (mele) and music meant for highly ritualized dance (hula). The Chicago Columbian Exposition of 1893 was the earliest mainland presentation of Hawaiian music. The poetry that accompanies all Polynesian mimetic dance is highly nuanced and complex, and many subtleties of vocal styles survive today, such as the rapid kepakepa and the carefully enunciated koihonua.

Economic Engines

Sugarcane cultivation in Hawaii began with the arrival of Polynesian settlers, expanded into a commercial venture in the mid-1800s, and became a leading economic and political force by the end of the nineteenth century. Ladd & Co. established the first permanent sugar plantation in Koloa, Kauai, in 1835. The move toward large-scale agricultural concerns concentrated wealth in the hands of a few, encouraged importation of foreign workers, and led to dramatic governmental evolution. As Hawaii's sugar industry became a world leader, enormous societal and environmental changes occurred due to its aggressive search for labor, land, and water.

In 1839, the Kingdom of Hawaii adopted its first bill of rights (*Ke Kumukānāwai o ka Makahiki*), laying the groundwork for a free enterprise system. The 1840 constitution established a constitutional monarchy with all of Hawaii's land under the management of the monarch. Britain, France, and the United States reaffirmed Hawaii's sovereignty in 1843 following the notorious Paulet Affair, which evolved from a land dispute to a five-month occupation of the islands by the British captain of *HMS Carysfort*. The 1848 Buke Māhele (Division Book) transformed Hawaii from communal land into private property but left many issues unresolved. One-third of the land was allocated to the mō'ī (monarch) Hawaiian Crown Lands, another third was reserved for the chiefs and managers, and the remaining third was given to the people, who could file land claims until 1852 under the Kuleana Act. The modern state of Hawaii still has a high percentage of government-owned lands (over 30 percent).

While intended to provide secure titles to Hawaiians, the Māhele would eventually separate many of them from their land, as few filed formal claims. Most of the land was sold by the government during the republic period (1894–1898) to U.S. mainlanders who favored annexation: this helped establish an oligarchy in territorial Hawaii dominated by the Big Five Hawaii sugar corporations. The wealth generated by these corporations came to symbolize the rise of foreign dominance in Hawaii, which continues today. The "Bayonet Constitution" (1887), the overthrow of the monarchy (1893), the establishment of the Republic of Hawaii (1894), annexation (1898), and even statehood (1959) were all responses to tariffs on sugar.

Political Upheaval

Paired with the end of the U.S. Civil War, the Alaska purchase, the increased importance placed on the Pacific states, and desires to have a duty-free market for

Hawaiian goods, Hawaii was drawn into the nation's rapid dreams of expansion. Beginning in 1866, the USS *Lackawanna* was assigned to cruise among the islands, surveying the islands and reefs northwest of the Sandwich Islands toward Japan and establishing U.S. claims to Midway. Congress appropriated $50,000 to deepen its harbor in 1869.

After the death of King Lunalilo, pro-American candidate David Kalākaua narrowly defeated the leading pro-British candidate, the Dowager Queen Emma, in the 1874 legislative election for monarch. Anti-American factions precipitated riots, and hundreds of American and British military forces intervened in the conflict, occupying Honolulu for a week. America's involvement in the upheaval led directly to the establishment of the first navy coaling and repair station in Pearl Harbor. In the same year, the government passed a law allowing for foreclosures without the supervision of a judge. This further contributed to an erosion of indigenous land ownership.

King Kalākaua sought to control the fraught but economically beneficial relationship between Hawaii's privileged native class and the king's elite foreign subjects. Property ownership was an essential element in being able to vote or join the legislature, and as such, most of the control was wielded by wealthy Americans and Europeans. Under pressure from U.S. investors, American sugar planters, the Reform Party (formerly called the Missionary Party), and the Hawaiian League (a secret society formed in 1887, privately called the Annexation Club), King Kalākaua was forced to sign the Bayonet Constitution in 1887, allowing for the formal establishment of a U.S. naval base at Pearl Harbor.

When Queen Lili'uokalani ascended to the throne upon her brother's death, she began a program of nativist legal revisions. By overturning or replacing the constitution of 1887, she hoped to restore the monarchy's traditional authority. This proposal would later been seen as a kind of "abdication" in the U.S. Congress' Morgan Report, and it led to the revolutionary actions of the thirteen-member Committee for Safety. The committee's members had strong political ties to U.S. Minister John L. Stevens and were supported by the Honolulu Rifles, a local, non-native militia of 200 who fought under the command of annexationist Colonel Volney Ashford.

On January 17, 1893, a policeman was shot while trying to stop a delivery of weapons to the Honolulu Rifles. The Committee for Safety requested that Stevens station heavily armed sailors and Marines from the USS *Boston* at U.S. government offices in Honolulu, marking under international law the illegal U.S. intervention in the domestic affairs of an allied sovereign state. The queen ordered her forces to surrender, and the Honolulu Rifles seized control of government buildings, disarmed the Royal Guard, and declared a provisional government. Japan refused to recognize this declaration, and concern grew that Japan might utilize their naval presence and opposition to the queen's overthrow to force Lili'uokalni to take the throne again, this time acting in Japan's interests. Independent of American foreign policies, this coup d'état resulted from multiple domestic conflicts but garnered international attention. Although the coup was not supported by the majority of the Hawaiian population, Queen Lili'uokalani was removed from the throne, tried following an unsuccessful 1895 rebellion, and held under house arrest for a year.

Annexation

The new provisional government immediately delivered a treaty of annexation to U.S. President Benjamin Harrison, then in the last month of his term (February 1893). Pro-annexationist propaganda began to appear in the *Pacific Commercial Advertiser*. Grover Cleveland, the new Democratic president, opposed colonialism and withdrew the treaty from the Senate in March 1893. Lili'uokalani began a series of appeals to Cleveland: following a confidential investigation by James Blount that considered the military support of the antiroyalist conspirators to have been improper, Cleveland unsuccessfully demanded that Dole dissolve Hawaii's provisional government and reinstate the queen.

After Dole refused, Cleveland referred the matter to the U.S. Congress, who produced the Morgan Report (February 26, 1894), concluding that the United States had no role in the Hawaiian Revolution. The Morgan Report concluded the congressional investigation into the overthrow of the Hawaiian Kingdom and Queen Lili'uokalani; it was led by Senator John Tyler Morgan, Democrat of Alabama and chairman of the U.S. Senate Committee on Foreign Relations.

Many witnesses were handpicked to make the best possible case for annexation. Under the guidance of firebrand Lorrin Thurston, who stated publicly that Hawaii should be ruled by whites, Morgan made the case against the queen and for annexation (supporting Stevens and the provisional government) and contradicting facts in Blount's earlier report. Senator George Gray was very opposed to annexation and enlisted witnesses whose testimonies were critical of the provisional government. Of the nine senators on the Morgan Committee, four Republicans and three Democrats indicated their support for annexation. The Turpie Resolution (May 31, 1894) ended any hope for further assistance in restoring the monarchy, and Lili'uokalani's appeals for help were rebuffed by the Cleveland administration.

The provisional government convened a constitutional convention limited to Hawaiians and taxpayers of "European" origin (excluding Asians). The Republic of Hawaii was established on July 4, 1894, creating a police state led by Dole. Since the royalists boycotted subsequent elections, all thirty legislative seats were won by the American Union Party. Voting rights were only extended to those who could demonstrate $1,500 in net worth (copied from the 1887 constitution) and to men who were naturalized or "natural-born" citizens, eliminating almost all Japanese, Chinese, Portuguese, and European immigrants. As a result, Polynesians held a two-thirds majority voting bloc, including Speaker of the House J. L. Kaulukou, and were the best-represented group in the Republic legislature. The 1897 election had the lowest turnout in Hawaii's history, with less than 1 percent of the population going to the polls. The Crown Lands were confiscated and sold off.

Due to the continued lobbying efforts of the Republic, strenuous floor debate concerning Hawaii's possible annexation continued in both houses of Congress after the inauguration of President William McKinley (March 4, 1897). Agriculture Secretary James Wilson testified that Hawaiian sugar "does not interfere with beet sugar," an important commercial consideration in favor of the annexation. Commodore George Melville submitted a report to Congress outlining the future control of the Pacific Ocean, the strategic value of Hawaii, and the importance of its annexation to the United States, stating, "Pearl Harbor is the sole key to the full defense of our western shore." Petitions signed by over 21,0000 native Hawaiians, the majority of the population, were gathered by a coalition of indigenous activists—the Hui Aloha ʻĀina for Women, the Hui Aloha ʻĀina for Men, and the Hui Kālaʻāina—and were presented to Congress to protest annexation in 1897. The first versions of the annexation proposal were defeated.

When the issue was revived in 1898, stirring speeches and debates in support of the annexation were contributed by Judge Harry Bingham (NH), Shelby Cullom (chairman of the Senate Committee on Hawaiian Annexation, IL), De Alva Alexander (House, NY), Daniel Mills (House, IL), Jacob Bromwell (House, OH), Charles Pearce (House, MO), James Davidson (House, WI), Galusha Grow (House, PA), Horace Packer (House, PA), Marion De Vries (House, CA), Thomas Ball (House, TX), Charles Henry (House, IN), and George Ray (House, NY).

Queen Liliʻuokalani's 1898 autobiography is seen by many in the Hawaiian sovereignty movement as a key source documenting this period of Hawaiian history, even though some assertions are contradicted by other primary sources, such as the Native Hawaiians Study Commission Report (1983). The Southern congressional delegation was opposed to Hawaiian reciprocity and annexation, supported by speeches from University of Chicago history professor Hermann von Holst, Hugh A. Dinsmore (House, AR), John Mitchell (Senate, WI), John Rixey (House, VA), Edgar Crumpacker (House, IN), James Richardson (House, TN), Augustus Bacon (Senate), Adolph Meyer (House, LA), John C. Bell (House, CO), Richard P. Bland (House, MO), and Stephen White (Senate, FL).

Pettigrew employed racially charged arguments on the Senate floor against annexation, stating, "No one for a moment pretends that we intend to admit the Asiatic people of Hawaii or of the Philippines into full citizenship" and "High civilization is only embraced by people who find it necessary to wear warm clothes and who feel the tingle of frost in their veins during a portion of the year" (Pettigrew 1898, 5). Justin Morrill (Senate, VT) agreed on the same racial grounds, stating that "the undesirable character of the greater part of their ill-gathered races of population, gathered by contract to long years of semi-slavery by sugar employers," made Hawaiians unsuitable for potential "admission into the Union" (Morrill 1898, 3).

In the wake of the Spanish-American War (1898) and the new interest in Hawaii shown by Japan and Britain, the Newlands Resolution was passed on July 4, 1898, with the Senate voting 42 to 21 and the House affirming by 209 to 91. President McKinley signed the bill accepting the Republic of Hawaii's treaty offer on July 7, 1898. Hawaii's flag was replaced by the Stars and Stripes at the former 'Iolani Palace on August 12, and Hawaii became an "organized, incorporated" U.S. territory in 1900.

Individual American imperialists used the country's increased nationalism during the Spanish-American War to appropriate the Hawaiian Islands as a military asset (Bruce 2012, ii). The true victim, as with most global historical narratives, remained the islands' neglected indigenous people, who were caught in the drive to enhance financial gains. One hundred years later, the U.S. Congress published a report to accompany U.S. Public Law 103-150 (1993), acknowledging the one-hundredth anniversary of the January 17, 1893, coup d'état and offering "an apology to Native Hawaiians on behalf of the United States for the overthrow of the Kingdom of Hawaii."

Biographies of Notable Figures

David Kalākaua (1836–1891)

Sometimes called The Merrie Monarch, David Kalākaua reigned as king of Hawaii from 1874 to 1891. He revived the hula (ceremonial dance) and the Kapu Ku'ailua (martial art), published traditional mele chants, and encouraged ukulele playing and surfing. Hawaii experienced a cultural and musical renaissance under his rule.

Fluent in both English and Hawaiian, Kalākaua studied law under Charles Coffin Harris, who later became chief justice of the Supreme Court of Hawaii. Kalākaua's professional work included serving in the army, as Postmaster General (1863), and as a member of the House of Nobles of the legislature (1863–1873). He was politically active throughout his life, opposing the ceding of any part of the Hawaiian Islands to foreign interests, and brought his nation to international attention through an 1881 trip circumnavigating the globe.

Under the 1864 constitution of the Kingdom of Hawaii, the legislature was responsible for appointing a new monarch after the death of King Kamehameha V in 1872. A popular election was held on January 1, 1873, and William Charles Lunalilio defeated Kalākaua to become the sixth monarch of Hawaii, ruling until February 3, 1874. Kalākaua was appointed as a colonel on the military staff of the king and held leadership roles among the Young Hawaiians movement and in the army. He was suspected to have incited the (native) Royal Guards to mutiny against their white officers at the ʻIolani Barracks, an event that resulted in Lunalilio disbanding Hawaii's standing army.

After Lunalilio's death, Kalākaua defeated the Queen Dowager Emma in a contentious election, causing a riot and the intervention of American troops. As king, he helped negotiate the Reciprocity Treaty (1875) and agreements allowing the United States to use Pearl Harbor, established the Education of Hawaii Youths Program (1880–1887), rebuilt and electrified the ʻIolani Palace (1879–1886), and restored Hawaii's standing army. His powers as monarch were severely curtailed by the 1887 Bayonet Constitution, but he remained a lifelong advocate of Hawaii's independence.

Liliʻuokalani (1838–1917)

Liliʻuokalani (born Lydia Kamakaʻeha) was the last monarch of the Kingdom of Hawaii, reigning from 1891 until the overthrow of the kingdom on January 17, 1893. An accomplished composer of songs such as "He Mele Lāhui Hawaii" (replacing "God Save the Queen" as the national anthem from 1866 to 1874) and "Aloha ʻOe," she played the organ, piano, guitar, and ukulele and led coached choirs. Her autobiography is the most important Hawaiian memoir from the turn of the last century.

The younger sister of David Kalākaua, Liliʻuokalani was informally adopted (hānai) and raised by Bernice Pauahi Bishop, attending the Royal School in Honolulu and Presbyterian worship services. She was briefly engaged to King Lunalilo (1857) and was a lady-in-waiting for Queen Emma (1856–1863), with whom she raised funds to build The Queen's Hospital. In 1862, she married her childhood friend, American-born John Owen Dominis, who served as governor of Oahu from 1868; the marriage was unhappy due to Dominis's infidelities, but she adopted three hānai children. In 1864, Liliʻuokalani and Pauahi Bishop helped Princess Victoria establish the female-led Kaʻahumanu Society, now the oldest Hawaiian civic organization, for victims of smallpox.

After the accession of her brother to the throne, Liliʻuokalani was given the title of princess (1874), proclaimed as heir apparent (1877), and served as regent twice (1881 and 1890–1891). As a result of her visit to the leper settlement on Molokai in 1881, she advocated for land to be set aside for a hospital in the Kakaʻako district of Honolulu. In 1887, she traveled as an official envoy to the United States and United Kingdom but cancelled her planned tour of Europe and returned to

Hawaii after the Bayonet Constitution was signed. Liliʻuokalani succeeded King Kalākaua as monarch on January 29, 1891.

Supported by the Hawaiian Supreme Court, the new queen forced Kalākaua's Cabinet to resign. She restored the governorships of the four main islands and worked to extend voting rights to Asians and disenfranchised Hawaiians. Both the Hui Kālaiʻāina and the National Reform parties (representing two-thirds of registered voters) petitioned her to rewrite the 1887 constitution, which she did with the aid of legislators Joseph Nāwahī and William Pūnohu White. As a result, Liliʻuokalani was deposed on January 17, 1893. U.S. President Grover Cleveland commissioned a report supporting her claim to the throne, but she refused to grant amnesty to those involved in the coup for several months; by the time she reconsidered, the provisional government refused to reinstate her. After a failed counter-revolution in 1895, she formally abdicated the throne and was confined to her palace for almost a year, during which time she worked on translating the Hawaiian creation chant (the Kumolipo).

After her pardon and release in late 1896, Liliʻuokalani composed and compiled songs (*The Queen's Songbook,* published in 1999) and wrote her autobiography. While lobbying in Washington, D.C., against the annexation of Hawaii, she met with more than 5,000 people. An advocate for freedom of religion, Liliʻuokalani was baptized by an Anglican bishop in Honolulu (1896) and a Mormon Elder in Salt Lake City, Utah (1901) and supported both Buddhism and Shintoism in Hawaii. In 1909, she brought an unsuccessful lawsuit against the United States seeking the return of the Hawaiian Crown Lands, which had been confiscated in 1900. Liliʻuokalani returned to Hawaii, finally receiving a lifetime pension, in 1911. Upon her death, most of her estate was put in trust for orphaned and destitute children. Numerous festivals, hula events, and races are regularly held in her memory.

Sanford Ballard Dole (1844–1926)

Sanford Ballard Dole was a legislative representative of Kauai (1884–1886), an associate justice of the Hawaii Supreme Court (1886–1893), and the first and only president of the Republic of Hawaii (1894–1900) after the monarchy was overthrown in 1893. He was born in Honolulu and raised on Oahu and Kauai, studying at Williams College for two years and later receiving an honorary LLD degree. He worked for one year in a Boston law office, was a notary public in Honolulu from 1880, and practiced law in Honolulu from 1869 to 1887. He was a cousin of James Dole, who came to Oahu in 1899 and founded the Dole Pineapple Company. An opponent of the policies of King Kalākaua, Dole became a Republican leader in the reform movement and helped draft the 1887 Bayonet Constitution, which curtailed voting rights and limited the powers of the Hawaiian monarchy. He also helped to draft the declaration of the Committee of Safety following the 1893 over-throw of Queen Lili'uokalani.

Dole was a successful diplomat: his lobbying efforts in Washington, D.C., resulted in the annexation of Hawaii in spite of native resistance, congressional find-ings, presidential requests, legal verdicts, and petition drives. He served as the first territorial governor of Hawaii (1900–1903). President Theodore Roosevelt appointed him to the second judgeship of the U.S. District Court for the District of Hawaii (1904–1915). After retirement from politics, Dole contributed to local civic life on Oahu by serving on commissions for parks and public archives.

DOCUMENT EXCERPTS

Protest against Hawaiian Annexation

The U.S. government formally annexed the Hawaiian Islands on July 7, 1898. This effort was a work in progress over the second half of the nineteenth century. Ameri-can sugar planters made significant financial investments in Hawaii and campaigned to undermine the native government. Hawaii was not admitted to the Union until 1959, when it officially became the fiftieth state long after its initial annexation. The following outlines Hawaiian Queen Lili'uokalani's official statements of pro-test against the annexation on June 17, 1897.

Queen Lili'uokalani's Official Protest against Hawaiian Annexation
June 17, 1897

I, Liliuokalani of Hawaii, by the will of God named heir apparent on the 10th day of April, A.D. 1877, and by the grace of God Queen of the Hawaiian Islands on the 17th day of January, A.D. 1893, do hereby protest against the ratification of a cer-tain treaty, which, so I am informed, has been signed at Washington by Messrs. Hatch, Thurston, and Kinney, purporting to cede the said islands to the territory and dominion of the United States. I declare such treaty to be an act of wrong toward the native and part-native people of Hawaii, an invasion of the rights of the ruling chiefs, in violation of international rights both toward my people and toward friendly nations with whom they have made treaties, the perpetuation of the fraud whereby the Constitutional Government was overthrown, and, finally, an act of gross injus-tice to me.

Because the official protests made by me on the seventeenth day of January, 1893, to the so-called Provisional Government was signed by me and received by said government with the assurance that the case was referred to the United States of America for arbitration.

Because that protest and my communications to the United States Government immediately thereafter expressly declares that I yielded my authority to the forces of the United States in order to avoid bloodshed and because I recognized the futility of a conflict with so formidable a power.

Because the President of the United States, the Secretary of State, and an envoy commissioned by them reported in official documents that my government was unlawfully coerced by the forces, diplomatic and naval, of the United States, that I was at the date of their investigations the constitutional ruler of my people.

Because such decision of the recognized magistrates of the United States was officially communicated to me and to Sanford B. Dole, and said Dole's resignation requested by Albert S. Willis, the recognized agent and Minister of the Government of the United States.

Because neither the above-named commission nor the Government which sends it has ever received any such authority from the registered voters of Hawaii, but derived its assumed powers from the so-called Committee of Public Safety, organized on or about the 7th day of January, 1893, said committee being composed largely of persons claiming American citizenship, and not one single Hawaiian was a member thereof or in any way participated in the demonstration leading to its existence.

Because my people, about 40,000 in number, have in no way been consulted by those, 3,000 in number, who claim the right to destroy the independence of Hawaii. My people constitute four-fifths of the legally qualified voters of Hawaii, and excluding those imported for the demands of labor, about the same proportion of the inhabitants.

Because said treaty ignores, not only the civic rights of my people, but, further, the hereditary property of their chiefs. Of the 4,000,000 acres composing the territory said treaty offers to annex, 1,000,000 or 915,000 acres, has in no way been heretofore recognized as other than the private property of the constitutional monarch, subject to a control in no way differing from other items of a private estate.

Because it is proposed by said treaty to confiscate said property, technically called the Crown lands, those legally entitled thereto, either now or in succession, receiving no consideration whatever for estates, their title to which has been always undisputed, and which is legitimately in my name at this date.

Because said treaty ignores not only all professions of perpetual amity and good faith made by the United States in former treaties with the sovereigns representing the Hawaiian people, but all treaties made by those sovereigns with other and friendly powers, and it is thereby in violation of international law.

Because by treating with the parties claiming at this time the right to cede said territory of Hawaii the Government of the United States receives such territory from the hands of those whom its own Magistrates (legally elected by the people of the

United States and in office in 1893) pronounced fraudulently in power and unconstitutionally ruling Hawaii; therefore I, Liliuokalani of Hawaii, do hereby call upon the President of that Nation to whom alone I yielded my property and my authority, to withdraw said treaty (ceding said lands) from further consideration, I ask the honorable Senate of the United States to decline to ratify said treaty, and I implore the people of this great and good Nation, from whom my ancestors learned the Christian religion, to sustain their representatives in such acts of justice and equity as may be in accord with the principles of their fathers, and to the Almighty Ruler of the universe, to him who judgeth righteously, I commit my cause.

Done at Washington, D.C., United States of America, this 17th day of June, in the year eighteen hundred and ninety-seven.

Liliuokalani
Joseph Heleluhe, Wekeki Heleluhe,
Julius A. Palmer, witnesses to signature.

Source: "Protest of Liliuokalani." *New York Times*, June 18, 1897.

See also: Asian/Pacific American Heritage Week Established, 1978; Daniel K. Inouye, First Asian American U.S. Senator, 1962; Gentlemen's Agreement between the United States and Japan, 1907

Further Reading

Bruce, Becky. 2012. "A Luscious Fruit: America's Annexation of Hawaii." PhD diss., University of Alabama.

Chang, David A. 2016. *The World and All the Things upon It: Native Hawaiian Geographies of World Exploration*. Minneapolis: University of Minnesota.

Chapin, Helen. 2000. *Guide to Newspapers of Hawaii, 1834–2000*. Honolulu: Historical Society.

Coffman, Tom. 2016. *Nation Within: The History of the American Occupation of Hawai'i*. Durham, NC: Duke University Press.

Committee on Foreign Relations 1789–1901 (vol. 6), S. Rep. No. 227 (1894).

Dole, Sanford. 1936. *Memoirs of the Hawaiian Revolution*. Honolulu: Advertiser.

Forbes, David W. 1998. *Hawaiian National Biography: 1780–1900*. 4 volumes. Honolulu: University of Hawaii Press.

Kame'eleihiwa, Lilikalā. 1992. *Native Land and Foreign Desires: Ko Hawai'i 'āina a Me Nā Koi Pu'umake a Ka Po'e Haole: A History of Land Tenure Change in Hawai'i from Traditional Times until the 1848 Māhele, Including an Analysis of Hawaiian Ali'i Nui and American Calvinists*. Honolulu: Bishop Museum Press.

Kuykendall, Ralph S. 1938–1967. *The Hawaiian Kingdom*. 3 volumes. Honolulu: University of Hawaii Press.

Lightner, Richard. 2004. *Hawaiian History: An Annotated Bibliography*. Westport, CT: Praeger.

Lili'uokalani. 1898. *Hawaii's Story by Hawaii's Queen*. Boston: Lothrop, Lee & Shepard. Rev. ed. annotated by David W. Forbes. Honolulu: Hui Hānai, 2013.

Lyon, Jeffrey. 2017. *No ka Baibala Hemolele: The Making of the Hawaiian Bible*. https:// scholarspace.manoa.hawaii.edu/bitstream/10125/43986/1/07_1lyon.pdf

Morrill, Justin. 1898. "Speech of Hon. Justin S. Morrill, of Vermont, in the Senate of the United States, on the Annexation of Hawaii." (Speech, U.S. Congress, June 20).

1920 Federal Population Census: A Catalog of National Archives Microfilm. 1991. Washington, D.C. National Archives Trust Fund Board.

Nogelmeier, M. Puakea. 2010. *Mai Pa'a i Ka Leo: Historical Voice in Hawaiian Primary Materials: Looking Forward and Listening Back*. Honolulu: Bishop Museum Press.

Okamura, Jonathan. 2008. *Ethnicity and Inequality in Hawai'i*. Philadelphia: Temple University Press.

Osborne, Thomas J. 1981. "Trade or War? America's Annexation of Hawaii Reconsidered." *Pacific Historical Review* 50, no. 3: 285–307.

Pettigrew, Richard Franklin. 1898. "Speech of Hon. Richard F. Pettigrew, of South Dakota, in the Senate of the United States, on the Annexation of Hawaii." (Speech, U.S. Congress, June 22 and 23).

Sai, David Keanu and Pū'ā Foundation. 2011. *Ua mau ke ea—Sovereignty Endures: An Overview of the Legal and Political History of the Hawaiian Islands*. Honolulu: Pū'ā Foundation.

Schmitt, Rovert. 1977. *Historical Statistics of Hawaii*. Honolulu: University of Press of Hawaii.

Siler, Julia Flynn. 2012. *Lost Kingdom: Hawaii's Last Queen, the Sugar Kings, and America's First Imperial Adventure*. New York: Atlantic Monthly Press.

Silva, Noenoe K. 2004. *Aloha Betrayed: Native Hawaiian Resistance to American Colonialism*. Durham, NC: Duke University Press.

Spickard, Paul, Joanne L. Rondilla, and Debbie Hippolite Wright. 2002. *Pacific Diaspora: Island Peoples in the United States and across the Pacific*. Honolulu: University of Hawaii Press.

Stauffer, Robert H. 2004. *Kahana: How the Land Was Lost*. Honolulu: University of Hawaii Press.

Stillman, Amy Ku'uleialoha. 1998. *Sacred Hula: The Hula 'Āla'apapa*. Honolulu: Bishop Museum Bulletins in Anthropology, Bishop Museum Press.

Takaki, Ronald. 1984. *Pau Hana: Plantation Life and Labor in Hawaii, 1835–1920*. Honolulu: University of Hawaii Press.

Vowell, Sarah. 2012. *Unfamiliar Fishes*. New York: Riverhead Books.

2
Citizenship and Community Building

United States v. Wong Kim Ark, 1898

William B. Noseworthy

Chronology

1790   The Naturalization Act restricts individuals eligible for citizenship to "any alien, being a free white person" who has been in the United States for two years.

1870   The Naturalization Act creates a system to control naturalization and penalties for fraudulent practices. It extends citizenship eligibility to persons of African nativity and descent.

1879   California Constitution Article XIX bars employment of Chinese or Mongolians in the state, except in the form of punishment for a crime. It delegates power to cities and towns for the removal of Chinese from city and town limits.

1882   The Chinese Exclusion Act is the first significant law restricting U.S. immigration. It bars all Chinese laborers and associated families from entering the United States.

1884   *In re Look Tin Sing* establishes that both the Fourteenth Amendment to the U.S. Constitution and the common law of the land provide that Look Tin Sing is a citizen, according to the California Circuit Court.

1886   *Yick Wo v. Hopkins* rules that even a law that is race-neutral on its face but is administered in a prejudicial manner infringes on the Equal Protection Clause of the Fourteenth Amendment.

1889 The Supreme Court recognizes Congress's plenary power over immigration and rules that immigration policy is the realm of the legislative and executive branches of government.

1891 The Immigration Act expands the classes of excludable aliens, includes new land and maritime policing procedures, creates an office to oversee enforcement, and broadens the penalties for immigration violations, including expanded powers of deportation.

1892 The Geary Act requires resident permits, a form of internal passport, for all resident Chinese and extends the Chinese exclusion acts for another 10 years, adding more provisions to restrict Chinese testimony in courts. Two white witnesses are required to testify on the matter of a Chinese person's immigration status to avoid an immigration violation. The act also punishes immigration violations with one year of hard labor and deportation.

1892 Grover Cleveland returns to the presidency. Cleveland has negotiated the passage of various immigration and citizenship restrictions, although his relationship with the labor movement proves tense during his second presidency.

1898 *United States v. Wong Kim Ark*, a landmark Supreme Court precedent case, provides for the citation of principles of *jus soli* citizenship, regardless of racial background, in the case of Chinese.

1917 The Asiatic Barred Zone Act extends the provisions of Chinese exclusion to an enormous swath of Asia. The zone affects all immigrants from southern, southeastern, and central Asia; the South Pacific; the Middle East; and much of China, Mongolia, and Kazakhstan. Only northeastern China, the Korean peninsula, the Philippines, and Japan are not included in the zone, being protected by other negotiations like the Gentlemen's Agreement of 1907, which regulates Japanese immigration.

1924 The Johnson-Reed Act includes the National Origins Act and Asian Exclusion Act. It limits the annual number of immigrants to 2 percent of the total population of individuals from the same national origins already living in the United States. The act outright bans Arabs and Asians.

1933 The Immigration and Naturalization Service (INS) merges two separate offices of administration into a single office.

1965 The Immigration and Naturalization Act abolishes the quota system. It holds that immigration cannot be discriminatory based on race or national origin, in theory, but also maintains per-country limits for immigration and creates a preference for skilled labor and those with families already in the United

States. Immediate relatives and "special immigrants" are ruled exempt from restrictions.

1982 In *Plyler v. Doe*, the Supreme Court strikes down a state statute that denies funding to children of undocumented immigrants. It also strikes down the charge of additional tuition fees for children of undocumented immigrants.

2003 The INS is disbanded and replaced by the Bureau of Citizenship and Immigration Services (BCIS), which is later renamed the U.S. Citizenship and Immigration Services (USCIS). Enforcement is re-regulated to the work of customs officers, under U.S. Immigration and Customs Enforcement (ICE). Border patrol and INS inspectors are merged with U.S. Customs inspectors to form U.S. Customs and Border Protection.

Narrative

United States v. Wong Kim Ark (1898) was a landmark U.S. Supreme Court decision that stated a person born in the United States is an American citizen, even when born to foreign parents ineligible for citizenship. In this case, the court ruled that it did not matter that Wong Kim Ark's parents were excluded from citizenship because they were Chinese (Brook 2007, 178). By implication, the Court's decision means that citizenship cannot be defined by the race or nationality of the parents, so long as the child is born on U.S. soil. The case was critical in that it set the only path to citizenship for individuals who were deemed ineligible for citizenship during the half-century of Chinese exclusion and, arguably, the harshest 50 years of anti-Asian sentiment in American history.

There are two ways of gaining citizenship in the United States: by birth and by naturalization. Birthright citizenship was established by the Fourteenth Amendment. Congress has the right to determine naturalization. The Naturalization Act of 1790 defined those eligible for naturalization as "any alien, being a free white person." *Dred Scott v. Sandford* (1857) ruled for the exclusion of slaves from citizenship rights, including the right to bring a lawsuit to the courts. But slaves were set free by the Emancipation Proclamation of 1863, and by 1868 almost all peoples of African descent living in the United States had been born there. Senator Charles Sumner, in an ensuing debate, attempted to strike the word "white" from the Naturalization Act of 1802. However, fears were raised that Chinese would be admitted as citizens. Hence, by 1870, citizenship rights were extended to "aliens of African nativity, and to persons of African descent," as a measure of practicality. In 1878, Chinese immigrant Ah Yup applied for naturalization and was denied, based on the argument that, scientifically, Ah Yup was a member of the "Mongolian" or

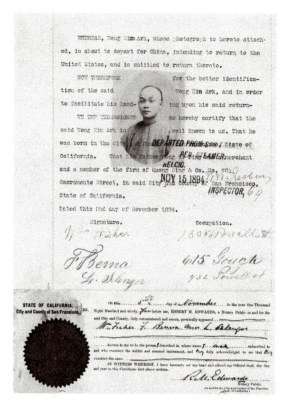

WHEREAS, Wong Kim Ark, whose photograph is hereto attached, is about to depart for China, intending to return to the United States, and is entitled to return thereto.

NOW THEREFORE ... for the better identification of the said ... Wong Kim Ark, and in order to facilitate his landing upon his said return.

WE THE UNDERSIGNED do hereby certify that the said Wong Kim Ark is ... well known to us. That he was born in the city ... State of California. That his father ... merchant and a member of the firm of Quong Sing & Co., No. 7... Sacramento Street, in said City and County of San Francisco, State of California.

Dated this 2nd day of November 1894.

A portrait of American-born Wong Kim Ark and his departure statement, composed when he was denied re-entry to the United States in 1894. *United States v. Wong Kim Ark,* decided in 1898, was a landmark Supreme Court case regarding citizenship. The court ruling stated that if a person was born in the United States, they were an American citizen. (National Archives)

"Asiatic" race and therefore did not meet the provisions of the definition of being white. Citizenship rights were not extended to persons of Chinese or Asian descent. A series of exclusion acts were a congressional ban on citizenship that applied specifically to the Chinese (Brook 2007, 180; Lyman 1991, 204; Ngai and Gjerde 2013, 182–83).

After the Chinese Exclusion Act was passed in 1882, cases were immediately filed to challenge it. A British subject, born in Hong Kong, submitted a petition to be included and allowed U.S. citizenship, based on the fact that he was a British subject, not a subject of China. But a circuit court ruling from 1883 reaffirmed the race-based nature of exclusion: since the individual was racially Chinese, he could not be granted citizenship (Brook 2007, 179). Before *Wong Kim Ark,* the 1886 case *Yick Wo v. Hopkins* established that the laws of an administration that is proven to be discriminatory may also be ruled biased. In *Yick Wo,* the court ruled that laws created as San Francisco safety ordinances were actually designed to harass Chinese laundry workers and business owners.

Chinese also continuously petitioned for admission. Between 1882 and 1890, 7,080 petitions were filed, and 85 to 90 percent of the cases received reversals. Between 1891 and 1905, 60,000 Chinese applied for admission into the United States. In 1892, William W. Morrow, the California District Court judge who was the critical California jurist on *Wong Kim Ark,* ruled in favor of three Chinese: Yeap Shee, Fong Yot Hing, and Fong Sam Toy. At least one of these individuals, Fong Yot Hing, had been born in the United States. It was on Fong Yot Hing's precedent that Wong Kim Ark's petition would later be successful (Salyer 1989, 91–95).

Chinese Exclusion Acts

The Chinese exclusion acts (1882, 1884, and 1888) were a series of anti-Chinese congressional acts that prevented Chinese laborers, their wives, and their children from China from being admitted into the United States or gaining citizenship between 1882 and 1943. They were based on pre-existing legislation in the state of California and enacted by drawing on the anti-Chinese sentiment that permeated a predominantly West Coast labor movement that had been co-opted for political gain. Similar acts were passed in New Zealand, Australia, and Canada during the same period.

The provisions were notably strict, as they extended to both legitimate and illegitimate offspring, to persons who were only half Chinese, and to Chinese aliens who had served in the U.S. armed forces. As per the *Wong Kim Ark* decision, the only way for Chinese to be both admitted into the United States and receive citizenship was to be born to Chinese families who had migrated before the passage of the exclusion acts. Even Chinese granted naturalization rights under the provisions of several states found that higher courts could potentially revoke their citizenship. Higher courts could also attempt to remove professional certifications, such as the certification to practice law, revoke passports, or prevent re-entry into the United States when Chinese traveled abroad. A federal judge also ruled that a foreign-born child of a Chinese person who was a U.S. citizen could not be made a U.S. citizen. It was only in 1943, by a wartime act of Congress, that these laws were removed for the sake of forging a stronger alliance with the Chinese government against the Japanese Empire during World War II (Lyman 1991, 204–06; Salyer 1989, 95–98).

Historical Background

Wong Kim Ark was born to Chinese parents in San Francisco in 1873. His parents lived legally in the United States but could not become citizens. According to the account of Justice Horace Gray, they returned to China in 1890, although other reports inaccurately suggest they remained in the United States (Brook 2007, 179; Young 2008, 20). Wong Kim Ark went to China in 1890 and returned to San Francisco on July 26, 1890. Collector Timothy Phelps admitted him as a citizen, presumably because he had been born in the United States well before the Chinese Exclusion Act had passed Congress. Having successfully returned to the United

States as a citizen in 1890, Wong Kim Ark left the United States again in 1894 to visit China. This time, when he returned in August 1895, an anti-Chinese collector, John H. Wise, claimed he was not a citizen and the existing Chinese Exclusion Act barred his entry (Young 2008, 20).

Wong Kim Ark hired Thomas Riordon, a prominent attorney, and they mounted the case that Wong Kim Ark was indeed a citizen under the terms of the Fourteenth Amendment. The passage that was most important to their argument reads: "All persons born or naturalized in the United States, and subject to the jurisdiction thereof, are citizens of the United States and of the state wherein they reside" (Young 2008, 20). They faced a fierce argument, however, as Wise's decision was backed by the U.S. District Attorney's (DA) office, based on the provision that matters of the state were the purview of the DA. The DA, Henry S. Foot, mounted the counter-argument that someone born of Chinese parents in the United States should be ruled a subject of China, not a U.S. citizen (Ngai and Gjerde 2013, 187–90).

By all established legal precedents, *Wong Kim Ark* should have been open and shut, but legal criteria cannot account for shifts in popular opinion and political pressure. In his campaign to win the 1892 presidential campaign, Grover Cleveland relied on the Democratic Party's allegiances. This meant gaining the support of major labor unions in the country, labor unions that had also become patently racist in their anti-Chinese sentiment. They had helped pass the Geary Act earlier that year. Illicit residence in the United States became a federal crime punishable by one-year imprisonment, during which time the prisoner could be forced into hard labor before facing subsequent deportation.

The purpose of the Geary Act was to prevent Chinese entry into the United States and extend the Chinese Exclusion Act for another 10 years. It also forced Chinese living in the United States to always carry identity cards. Photo identity was originally required, but many protested, including Tsui Kuo-yin, China's minister to the United States, and the photo requirement was removed. Representative Thomas Geary of California had argued that these provisions were designed to free immigrant Chinese from hassle, while at the same time he stoked xenophobic anti-Chinese sentiment and claimed that photos were necessary because all Chinese were too similar in appearance, and photography was the only means to distinguish them.

The Geary Act was challenged immediately on the premise that, through its provisions for detaining immigrants, it denied them due process under the Fifth Amendment. However, the Supreme Court ruled that the Fifth Amendment rights of due process were different for citizens and Chinese individuals, as this was a matter of immigration subject to congressional law (Brook 2007, 180–83). Ruling in favor of Wong Kim Ark would upset this piece of legislation, since the individuals supporting the Geary Act were not much concerned with anything other than ensuring Chinese were excluded from citizenship through a combination of anti-miscegenation and immigration law. Therefore, Foot argued that the birthright citizenship enshrined in the Constitution was intended to exclude Chinese and that including them would threaten the "very existence of our Country" (Brook 2007, 184). Foot lost his argument. Judge William Morrow relied on *In re Look Tin Sing* (1884) to reaffirm the Fourteenth Amendment.

Even after Morrow ruled in his favor, Wong Kim Ark's case was not dropped. Instead, a San Francisco lawyer, George D. Collins, led the appeal to the Supreme Court in 1898. He called the concept that Chinese born on U.S. soil were legally citizens "a most degenerate departure from the patriotic ideals of our forefathers" (Brook 2007, 184). At the time, the Geary Act had proved impossible to enforce. Hence, the Democratic Party and Cleveland's administration were widely criticized. This put pressure on the side supported by Collins's argument. The case received widespread attention and far outshone the famous *Plessy v. Ferguson* (1896). The issue facing the court was the nature of birthright. Wong Kim Ark argued the concept of birthright was territorial, which meant one born on U.S. soil received birthright citizenship. However, the opposition contended birthright was national, and therefore, the children of a U.S. citizen could become U.S. citizens, even when born abroad. Similarly, the children of Chinese parents were to be considered Chinese, even when born abroad. In other words, was citizenship determined by soil (*jus soli*) or was it by blood (*jus sanguinis*)? The court ruled in Wong Kim Ark's favor in a 6–2 decision authored by Gray.

Gray's decision was substantial. He determined that the U.S. Constitution uses two phrases: "citizen of the United States" and "natural-born citizen of the United States." In a turn toward common law, he followed the court's ruling in *Minor v. Happersett* (1875). A common law ruling by Justice Edward Coke (1608) claimed all persons born on the lands of the king were subjects of the king, so long as they were not children of occupying armies (foreign enemies) or children of foreign ambassadors. Because the common law was adopted by the United States, the Fourteenth Amendment didn't change the *jus soli* ruling. It merely overturned the verdict of *Dred Scott*, meaning citizenship was no longer limited to whites. He affirmed the court's decision in *Elk v. Wilkins* (1884), which held that one could not renounce tribal loyalty and become a citizen because tribal lands were not directly controlled as a territory of the United States, but were ruled through independent treaties with the federal government. The court suggested that John Elk, a member of the Winnebago tribe born on a reservation, could theoretically still be naturalized but could not become a citizen based on *jus soli*. This case, however, provided Gray the grounds to emphasize two forms of citizenship in the Court decision he authored. Furthermore, Gray argued that to deny *jus soli* in Wong Kim Ark's case would also imply that thousands of English, Scotch, Irish, German, and other European descendants born in the United States were not citizens. Hence, he argued, the only question was whether or not the clause of *jus soli* citizenship applied to Chinese or not. He suggested that Chinese persons born outside the United States still had due protections when they resided inside the United States, just as other aliens were, even after the Chinese Exclusion Act was passed. This opinion won the majority, and Wong Kim Ark was granted citizenship.

The dissent in *Wong Kim Ark*, authored by Chief Justice Melville W. Fuller and joined by Justice John Marshall Harlan, contended that common law had no place in American law when it came to matters of immigration. Fuller claimed that the rule of *jus soli* had not survived the French Revolution, and it should not have survived the American Revolution. But *jus soli* actually had survived in France, being extended to third-generation immigrants in a clarifying ruling in 1859 and again in 1889 to second-generation immigrants in positions similar to Wong Kim Ark's. Fuller's ignorance of French immigration law aside, the contention that the United States was a country that recognized expatriation was arguable. Congress recognized the right of expatriation with a July 27, 1868 law, which became the basis of several naturalization treaties, such as the 1870 treaty with Great Britain. The legislation ruled that persons born in the United States before the revolution were not necessarily subjects of the crown. To Fuller, this was a break from the common law system. However, the law also asserted *jus soli* citizenship for individuals born in territories that later became parts of the United States. To Fuller, the break from common law was the most important factor, and therefore, common law could not be cited as a legal precedent for U.S. law. Another issue was that common law applied to "subjects," whereas U.S. law was to apply to "citizens." Fuller further argued that there was a precedent for an emphasis on *jus sanguinis* in the 1866 Civil Rights Act, which provided that "all persons born in the United States and not subject to any foreign power" were to be citizens (Brook 2007, 188). Hence, in Fuller's understanding, if Wong Kim Ark was subject to a foreign power, he could not be a U.S. citizen. However, his citizenship would not necessarily be ruled invalid by a position supporting *jus sanguinis* alone.

Instead of relying entirely on a ruling of *jus sanguinis* or *jus soli*, Fuller's objection rested on his understanding that Chinese law had forbidden expatriation (Brook 2007, 188). Fuller's argument does not indicate he understood Chinese law well. Under Chinese law, expatriates could only be punished upon their return to China. So long as they remained abroad, they were not subject to Chinese law. Regardless, Fuller claimed that since expatriation was forbidden by China and U.S. law forbade naturalization, Chinese persons in the United States were not wholly subject to the laws of the United States (Brook 2007, 188). Indeed, Fuller's argument uses the widespread, racialized perception of Chinese immigrants in the 19th century: that they were permanent "pilgrims and sojourners" (Brook 2007, 188). Despite a waffling argument, Fuller was correct in his argument that if the U.S. government could deport parents but not children, then the government could break up families over matters of immigration. His appeal to the value of the family unit, as a closing argument, however, was not enough to sway the bench.

The existing evidence suggests that in Harlan's vision, citizenship could be extended to Native Americans based on his ruling in the *Elk* case, and that it could be extended to African Americans based on his decision in the *Plessy* case. But the Chinese were just "too different" for Harlan. In his *Plessy* dissent, he wrote, "There

---

Jus Soli Citizenship

Jus soli citizenship is a principle of nationality law that is derived from Roman law. In the Roman Empire, any free individual who was born on Roman soil was considered a Roman citizen. The principle was adopted in France after the French Revolution and among the independent, formerly English colonies in America. As migration became more and more common in the 19th and 20th centuries, the principle of *jus soli* spread throughout Western Europe as well as French and British colonial possessions. As more countries adopted the law, contestation between *jus soli* and citizenship by blood (*jus sanguinis*) became more popular, and it is common to find nations outside of the United States that have had similar debates over the principles of the two forms of citizenship.

India, for example, banned *jus soli* citizenship as recently as 2004 in reaction to fears of illegal migration from Bangladesh. In contrast to former British territories, simple comparisons with the United States are France and Germany. France is often characterized as a state of *jus soli* and Germany as a state of *jus sanguinis*. This condition may be an oversimplification, however. French law after the revolution did provide conditional *jus soli* citizenship in combination with *jus sanguinis*, although an 1851 revision of the French code provided that all third-generation immigrants were granted *jus soli*. Furthermore, an 1889 change allowed for second-generation immigrants to become French citizens. Hence, at the time of *Wong Kim Ark*, a parallel case in France would have, theoretically, granted the individual citizenship under the principles of the 1889 law (Brubaker 1992, 85–95).

is a race so different from our own that we do not permit those belonging to it to become citizens of the United States. Persons belonging to it are, with few exceptions, absolutely excluded from our country. I allude to the Chinese race" (Brook 2007, 191). During his time on the bench, Harlan appears to have been anti-Chinese. He often ruled against cases brought by Chinese individuals. He ruled with the Court to uphold the Scott Act of 1888, which denied Chinese laborers the right of return to the United States, including those with return certificates issued before the legislation was passed. He approved the Court's upholding of the Geary Act, allowing the deportation of Chinese with legal immigration papers. He supported giving immigration officials the power to exclude various Chinese. His view that Chinese could never be citizens of the United States is an essential caveat to his oft-misinterpreted "color blind" and "casteless" interpretation of the U.S. Constitution (Brook 2007, 192). He completely passed over the wording of the Fourteenth Amendment clauses on due process and equal protection, which refer to "persons," not "citizens." Ignoring this vital wording was well in keeping with Harlan's earlier political stance as a member of the anti-immigration Know-Nothing Party and an argument that he put forward as a law school lecturer when he proclaimed that Congress had the right to exclude any race.

Long-Term Impact and Current Status

Gray's opinion on the meaning of the Fourteenth Amendment had a substantial long-term impact on the Supreme Court and U.S. immigration policy. The amendment was designed to overrule the *Dred Scott* decision, but created thousands of cases like *Wong Kim Ark*. Wong Kim Ark's case came to the Court in 1895 and took more than two years to resolve. The petition of *habeas corpus* in the case was urgent, but the case was somewhat simple in that none of the facts were disputed. Gray's opinion was written in 56 pages, which are rarely read in their entirety. Gray's theoretical turn, to rely on English common law because there was no common law of the U.S. Constitution, stood against the principles of Roman law and *jus sanguinis*, which the council inaccurately argued was the standard across the Atlantic. Furthermore, Gray and Harlan flipped their previous positions on Native American citizenship, where Harlan had claimed "all meant all," and Gray had stated, "not in the case of tribal affiliations," as it were. Senator George F. Edmunds, chairman of the Senate Judiciary Committee on Immigration, backed Gray's decision. The Court had upheld the conclusion that certain classes of foreigners could be excluded (*Nishimura Ekiu v. the United States*) and that the U.S. government had the power of deportation even during times of peace (*Fong Yue Ting v. the United States*). Due process in deportation proceedings had been removed, although Fuller stood aside at the time and authored a vital opinion suggesting that it should not be removed. Hence, the same justice who argued that due process should extend to all, regardless of citizenship, also claimed that Chinese could never be considered citizens. These cases were typical in that the justices did not seem to follow a particular pattern of reasoning by 20th-century standards (Mitchell 1961, 141–68). Conscious or not, racialization was a pervasive factor in the rulings.

Thomas Brook (2007, 180) has argued that the way Americans have tended to racialize immigration began with the Chinese Exclusion Act of 1882. The facts show that Americans began to racialize immigration before the passage of the act, but the act solidified the principles of racialized reasoning as a basis for citizenship. Hence, popular anti-immigration sentiment led to its expansion. Except in cases of *jus soli* citizenship, like *Wong Kim Ark*, Congress barred all "natives of the 'Asiatic Zone,'" which was a broad swath of the continent stretching from Afghanistan to Japan (Brook 2007, 179). The act was removed in 1943 to help establish a Chinese alliance against the Japanese, but its influence lives on. For example, this act and others led to the founding of the Immigration and Naturalization Service (INS, 1933–2003), which polices immigration and controls visas, passports, registration cards, and all immigration documents necessary to establish citizenship for immigrants. In 2003, INS was divided into three agencies: U.S. Citizenship & Immigration Services (USCIS), U.S. Immigration and Customs Enforcement (ICE), and U.S. Customs and Border Protection (CBP).

A century after the Chinese Exclusion Act, *Plyer v. Doe* (1982) provided an argument for the extension of *jus soli* to children of undocumented immigrants. Twentieth- and 21st-century conservatives have argued against these extensions, particularly as racially charged anti-immigrant sentiment rose. For example, James R. Edwards Jr. of the Center for Immigration Studies has claimed that the *jus soli* precedent was an incentive for "illegal immigrants" to birth an "anchor baby" (Young 2008, 15).

A contemporary counterpoint to the xenophobia-infused conservative arguments of recent history has been provided by a former Supreme Court law clerk, James C. Ho. Ho argues, "Birthright citizenship is a constitutional right no less for the children of undocumented persons than for descendants of passengers of the Mayflower" (Young 2008, 15). Indeed, given that the concept of immigration enforcement is very much a 20th-century phenomenon, simple logic dictates that many of the white or European peoples who arrived in the United States in the 19th century and earlier were not necessarily fully legal under later immigration guidelines. In fact, being undocumented had little meaning until the 20th century. These complexities aside, the "anchor baby" argument has been widely accepted as logically unsound because there is no way to ensure government assistance funds without being documented. The claim that "anchor babies" have caused a drain on federal and state funds is therefore often ruled a nonfactor in contemporary legal debates (Young 2008, 15–16).

In the end, we should not overemphasize court rulings in favor of *jus soli*, since history has proven that all three branches of government have found ways to ensure that de facto racially biased immigration practices continue. After all, if all congressional, judiciary, and executive policy were genuinely nondiscriminatory, the United States would have become a much more diverse nation during the 20th century (Brook 2007, 195). At the same time, we should not underemphasize the importance of *jus soli* either, mainly as the principles debated in the case continue to be discussed today in the United States and many other countries. The ruling in *Wong Kim Ark* was a critical landmark, indicating that exclusion of individuals from U.S. citizenship based on their race was not a principle that could be upheld by the highest court in the land if the individual had been born on U.S. soil.

Biographies of Notable Figures

Horace Gray (1828–1902)

Born in 1828, Horace Gray was an associate justice for the U.S. Supreme Court (1882–1902) and author of the *Wong Kim Ark* (1898) decision, determining that all children born in the United States were automatically citizens of the nation under the common law principles of *jus soli*.

Gray graduated from Harvard in 1845 with a Bachelor of Arts degree when he was 17, and although he did not participate in commencement (indicating his place at the lower half of the class), it is notable that the average graduate at the time was 20 years of age. He was imposing even then, reaching his adult height of six feet, six inches as a 13-year-old, although he would not reach his adult weight of 250 pounds until he was 25 (Mitchell 1961, 1–55).

Gray had an advantage in that he came from a well-to-do family, with several Harvard graduates in the line. This presumably allowed him to be educated at a private preparatory school in Boston, although the record states that all his brothers attended Boston Latin and Gray's background before Harvard is unknown. Perhaps his early college record can be explained by his father's insistence that Gray maintain only a certain number of library hours as a young teenager and focus on improving his hunting skills on the family plot outside of Cambridge.

After graduation, Gray did not take up a profession immediately. He initially traveled to Europe, but fate took a turn when his father went bankrupt due to spreading his investments too thinly across the iron manufacturing industry. This forced Gray to return as the family attempted to maintain its shipping business.

Gray entered Harvard Law when he was 20 years old, in 1848. Joel Parker, former Chief Justice from New Hampshire, had just joined the faculty. The school was minuscule by modern standards: only three faculty members gave 10 lectures a week to 115 students, more than half of whom had no college degree. There was no standard curriculum, the library was decaying from lack of care, and all one had to do to graduate was paying the tuition bills for a total of a year and a half. Arguments performed in moot court before the faculty were the only testing method. It was in this venue that Gray set himself apart. He proved himself during a time when the case-based method was a newly introduced method of legal principle and legal history focused on accounts of the common law to suit the needs of the commonwealth system in Massachusetts (Mitchell 1961, 1–55).

Gray graduated from Harvard Law in 1849, held an apprenticeship at Sohier & Welch, and was admitted to the bar in 1851 before becoming a part-time court reporter just a few months later. In 1852 he co-authored the Practice Act (1852), which established modern plea procedures and did away with common law procedures of one written accusation and one written response. The Practice Act established that testimony could be taken as response and interpreted under multiple legal codes, first to acquiesce to the complexities of human actions, and second to democratize the process of legal testimony, since, under the Practice Act, one only needed to state the facts of the case as testimony. Hence, when Gray became the full-time reporter of decisions for the Supreme Judicial Court of the Commonwealth of Massachusetts in 1854, he already had a substantial reputation, one that earned him the position of unofficial counsel to Massachusetts war governor John A. Andrew in 1861 (Mitchell 1961, 32–55).

Meanwhile, Gray maintained a part-time practice, winning 24 of 31 cases before the Supreme Court between 1854 and 1864, while also researching legal history. In the volume of *Quincy's Reports* (1864) he had a 50-page report on the history of slavery law in New England states and another 150-page report on the John Otis writs of assistance. He also authored an essential note in the landmark *Commonwealth v. Roxbury* (1857) case, which established state authority over tidal flats bounding the shore. Furthermore, he took a critical stand against the *Dred Scott* decision in the *Monthly Law Review* in the same year, while his actions openly identified Gray with the Free-Soil contingent of the Republican Party. He lost the Republican nomination for attorney general in 1860, but his reputation earned him an elected post at the Massachusetts Historical Society (1861). From there, he would go on to serve on the governing standing committee for three terms (1863–1865). While he served on the standing committee, he was also appointed associate justice for the Supreme Court of Massachusetts (August 23, 1864). There, he served for nine years and authored 515 opinions before he was raised to chief of the court, where he authored another 852 opinions in just eight years and four months (Mitchell 1961, 32–60).

Gray was appointed to the Supreme Court in Washington in 1881, upon Chester Arthur's ascension to the presidency following the death of President James Garfield. A vacant seat had been left open on the bench, as Justice Nathan Clifford, also a New Englander, had recently passed away. Gray's nomination was unremarkable because he was put in place to maintain the balance of the bench, and his 51–5 confirmation vote was marked only by the opposition of Southern Democrats from the states of Texas, Louisiana, North Carolina, and Arkansas.

Gray's time in the Court was marked by debates over the Due Process Revolution after the passage of the Fourteenth Amendment, which in part framed his position on the *Wong Kim Ark* decision. His time on the Court was characterized in some ways by the field of legal scholarship on the Due Process Revolution, as scores of cases involving personal property were filed after the passage of the Fourteenth Amendment. The bench, however, established a precedent of due process of law that resisted individual pressure, substantiating the position that state restrictions on personal property did not violate the Fourteenth Amendment (Mitchell 1961, 60–141).

William W. Morrow (1843–1929)

William W. Morrow was born in Wayne County, Indiana, on July 15, 1843. When he was two years old, his parents moved to Adams County, Illinois, where he attended common school and also received private instruction. He helped his widowed mother on the family farm after the death of his father. At 16 years of age, he moved to Santa Rosa, California, where he explored the mining regions and taught school on his arrival.

In 1862, Morrow rode with a party of explorers from Santa Rosa to Oregon, and they became lost, wandering along the edges of the Day River. However, they discovered placers along the river at a site that later became Canyon City, Oregon. That same year, he traveled east, where he joined the Union Army in 1862 and served in the District of Columbia in the Army of the Potomac. He was then appointed special agent of the Treasury Department in 1865 and sent back to California, where he again studied law. By the end of his college career, Morrow had a degree in law from an unspecified "eastern college," as well as a doctor of law degree from the University of California. He received honors from presidents Harrison, McKinley, and Taft. The first two honors were granted to him in the form of judiciary appointments, whereas the honor from President Taft was awarded in recognition of Morrow's work with the Red Cross. He was given additional honors as a trustee for the Carnegie Foundation (Biographical Directory n.d.; Jury 1921, 1–7).

In addition to *In re Wong Kim Ark,* Morrow made so many important decisions that he was cited in 200 of 276 volumes of the *Federal Reporter,* a marker of his contributions to American law. His station in San Francisco made maritime law and business his primary purview, although he also made significant decisions regarding extradition of ex-military personnel, such as *In re Ezeta,* which stated that murders and robbery committed as actions of war were not grounds for extradition. Further, Morrow determined that charterers of goods due for Chilean ports were "liable for demurrage and there was no actual vis major within the exceptions of the charter party, including 'the act of God, political occurrences, fire'" (In *McLeod v. 1600 Tons of Nitrate of Soda,* quoted in Jury 1921, 3). He also authored the opinion in a case that determined parcels of land could be enjoined by a court authority in instances of flooding or injury caused by the diversion of waters from the Colorado River, as long as the tracts didn't extend across the border with Mexico. Finally, he extended the authority of the law in cases of conspiracy as a result of the Pullman Strike (July 1894). By Morrow's ruling, persons involved in the planning of "conspiracies" (strikes or other actions) could be held responsible even if they only played a small role, and even if their actions took place in a distant location. His thoughts can be found recorded throughout his studies of legal history, such as an entire history of the Nome cases that he wrote for the *California Law Review* and an introduction to *California Jurisprudence,* which was an exhaustive work of legal review in the history of state policy (Biographical Directory; Jury 1921, 1–7).

After he was admitted to the bar in 1869, Morrow was promoted to assistant U.S. attorney for California (1870). He organized the San Francisco Bar Association (1872) and served as its president (1892–1893). He served on the Republican State Central Committee (1877–1880), the State Board on Harbor Commissions (1880–1883), and as U.S. special attorney for the French and American Claims Commission (1881–1883) and the Alabama Claims Commission (1882–1885). He was elected as a Republican National Convention delegate (1884) and served in Congress (1885–1891). He then returned to California as Northern District judge (1891–1897) and was promoted to U.S. circuit judge for the Ninth District (1897–1922). He retired from the bench to reside in San Francisco one year before his death on July 24, 1929 (Biographical Directory; Jury 1921, 1–7).

On the surface, Morrow's time on the bench stands in contrast with his congressional career. He was involved in not just one, but several cases that granted

Chinese citizenship based on the principle of *jus soli*. But his time in Congress was spent as an advocate of Chinese exclusion. His opinions were nuanced. For example, he referred to a September 1885 massacre of Chinese in the Territory of Wyoming as "disgraceful in the extreme" (Morrow 1886, 1) and pointed to Article III of the November 17, 1880, U.S.-China treaty, which protected anyone on U.S. lands from harm, regardless of whether the crime had been committed by a U.S. citizen. Therefore, he argued, the United States owed China indemnity, but he offered this cancellation on the condition that Congress meets his "demand that the immigration of Chinese laborers into this country shall absolutely cease" (Morrow 1886, 2).

Morrow could not have been more transparent in his sentiments toward Chinese immigration in his recorded statements in Congress. He referred to Chinese immigration as "the cause of disease" and believed that Chinese were "slyly creeping in through the holes [their] cunning ha[d] discovered in the law" (Morrow 1886, 2–4). He believed that "[b]etween Asiatic labor and American labor there is an antagonism beyond the reach of arbitration, compromise, or judicial degree" (Morrow 1886, 3) and therefore excluding Chinese for 10 years was not enough. Instead he called, at first, for 20 years of exclusion, and, in the end, to make exclusion "permanent and perpetual," clarifying that the indemnity would be money well spent "if while discharging whatever moral obligation we may be under we can also make it do duty in paving the way to settlement of this vexed question of Chinese immigration" (Morrow 1886, 4). Two years later, he argued for strict tariffs on Chinese imports, citing the Chinese "invasion of our territory by treaty stipulations" and claiming that continued Chinese immigration "would degrade our own labor and be destructive to the best interests of the whole people" (Morrow 1888, 4). To him, Chinese labor was "cheap," and therefore duties admitted through the customs house would need to be subject to substantial tariffs, for the sake of the protection of American labor (Morrow 1888, 4). But these views did not trump his belief in the principle of *jus soli*.

DOCUMENT EXCERPTS

The key debate in United States v. Wong Kim Ark *was whether a child born in the United States was an American citizen if his or her parents were subjects to the emperor of China. The ruling on behalf of the Supreme Court was that the child was a U.S. citizen on the basis of the Fourteenth Amendment. This case and the court ruling set an important precedent to uphold the principle of* jus soli *citizenship. Today, a child born in the United States is a U.S. citizen regardless of the parents' nationality.*

United States v. Wong Kim Ark, 169 U.S. 649. 1898.
(Excerpts)

MR. JUSTICE GRAY, after stating the facts in the foregoing language, delivered the opinion of the Court.

The facts of this case, as agreed by the parties, are as follows: Wong Kim Ark was born in 1873, in the city of San Francisco, in the state of California and United States of America, and was and is a laborer. His father and mother were persons of Chinese descent, and subjects of the emperor of China. They were at the time of his birth domiciled residents of the United States, having previously established and are still enjoying a permanent domicile and residence therein at San Francisco. They continued to reside and remain in the United States until 1890, when they departed for China; and, during all the time of their residence in the United States, they were engaged in business, and were never employed in any diplomatic or official capacity under the emperor of China. Wong Kim Ark, ever since his birth, has had but one residence, to wit, in California, within the United States and has there resided, claiming to be a citizen of the United States, and has never lost or changed that residence, or gained or acquired another residence; and neither he, nor his parents acting for him, ever renounced his allegiance to the United States, or did or committed any act or thing to exclude him therefrom. In 1890 (when he must have been about 17 years of age) he departed for China, on a temporary visit, and with the intention of returning to the United States, and did return thereto by sea in the same year, and was permitted by the collector of customs to enter the United States, upon the sole ground that he was a native-born citizen of the United States. After such return, he remained in the United States, claiming to be a citizen thereof, until 1894, when he (being about 21 years of age, but whether a little above or a little under that age does not appear) again departed for China on a temporary visit, and with the intention of returning to the United States; and he did return thereto, by sea, in August, 1895, and applied to the collector of customs for permission to land, and was denied such permission, upon the sole ground that he was not a citizen of the United States.

. . .

The question presented by the record is whether a child born in the United States, of parents of Chinese descent, who at the time of his birth are subjects of the emperor of China, but have a permanent domicile and residence in the United States, and are there carrying on business, and are not employed in any diplomatic or official capacity under the emperor of China, becomes at the time of his birth a citizen of the United States, by virtue of the first clause of the fourteenth amendment of the constitution: "All persons born or naturalized in the United States, and subject to the jurisdiction thereof, are citizens of the United States and of the state wherein they reside."

I. In construing any act of legislation, whether a statute enacted by the legislature, or a constitution established by the people as the supreme law of the land, regard is to be had, not only to all parts of the act itself, and of any former act of the same lawmaking power, of which the act in question is an amendment, but also to the condition and to the history of the law as previously existing, and in the light of which the new act must be read and interpreted.

The constitution of the United States, as originally adopted, uses the words "citizen of the United States" and "natural-born citizen of the United States." By the original constitution, every representative in congress is required to have been "seven years a citizen of the United States," and every senator to have been "nine years a citizen of the United States"; and "no person except a natural-born citizen, or a citizen of the United States at the time of the adoption of this constitution, shall be eligible to the office of president." The fourteenth article of amendment, besides declaring that "all persons born or naturalized in the United States, and subject to the jurisdiction thereof, are citizens of the United States and of the state wherein they reside," also declares that "no state shall make or enforce any law which shall abridge the privileges or immunities of citizens of the United States; nor shall any state deprive any person of life, liberty, or property, without due process of law; nor deny to any person within its jurisdiction the equal protection of the laws." And the fifteenth article of amendment declares that "the right of citizens of the United States to vote shall not be denied or abridged by the United States, or by any state, on account of race, color, or previous condition of servitude."

. . .

VII. Upon the facts agreed in this case, the American citizenship which Wong Kim Ark acquired by birth within the United States has not been lost or taken away by anything happening since his birth. No doubt he might himself, after coming of age, renounce this citizenship, and become a citizen of the country of his parents, or of any other country; for by our law, as solemnly declared by congress, "the right of expatriation is a natural and inherent right of all people," and "any declaration, instruction, opinion, order or direction of any officer of the United States, which denies, restricts, impairs or questions the right of expatriation, is declared inconsistent with the fundamental principles of the republic." Rev. St. 1999, re-enacting Act July 27, 1868, c. 249, 1 (15 Stat. 223, 224). Whether any act of himself, or of his parents, during his minority, could have the same effect, is at least doubtful. But it would be out of place to pursue that inquiry, inasmuch as it is expressly agreed that his residence has always been in the United States, and not elsewhere; that each of his temporary visits to China, the one for some months when he was about 17 years old, and the other for something like a year about the time of his coming of age, was made with the intention of returning, and was followed by his actual return, to the United States; and "that said Wong Kim Ark has not, either by him-self or his parents acting for him, ever renounced his allegiance to the United States, and that he has never done or committed any act or thing to exclude him therefrom."

The evident intention, and the necessary effect, of the submission of this case to the decision of the court upon the facts agreed by the parties, were to present for determination the single question, stated at the beginning of this opinion, namely, whether a child born in the United States, of parents of Chinese descent, who, at the time of his birth, are subjects of the emperor of China, but have a permanent domicile and residence in the United States, and are there carrying on business, and are not employed in any diplomatic or official capacity under the emperor of China, becomes at the time of his birth a citizen of the United States. For the reasons above stated, this court is of opinion that the question must be answered in the affirmative.

Order affirmed.

Source: *United States v. Wong Kim Ark*, 169 U.S. 649 (1898).

See also: The Chinese Exclusion Act, 1882; Daniel K. Inouye, First Asian American U.S. Senator, 1962; The Immigration and Nationality Act, 1965; The Luce-Celler Act, 1946; *United States v. Bhagat Singh Thind*, 1923

Further Reading

Biographical Directory of the U.S. Congress. n.d. "Morrow, William W, (1843–1929)." http://bioguide.congress.gov/scripts/biodisplay.pl?index=M001006

Brook, Thomas. 2007. *Civic Myths: A Law and Literature Approach to Citizenship*. Chapel Hill: University of North Carolina Press.

Brubaker, Rogers. 1992. *Citizenship and Nationhood in France and Germany*. Cambridge, MA: Harvard University Press.

Jury, John G. 1921. "William W. Morrow." *California Law Review* 10, no. 1: 1–7

Kingston, Maxine Hong. 1980. *China Men*. New York: Alfred A. Knopf Press.

Lyman, Stanford. 1991. "The Race Question and Liberalism: Casuistries in American Constitutional Law." *International Journal of Politics, Culture and Society* 5, no. 2: 183–247

Mitchell, Stephen Robert. 1961. "Mr. Justice Horace Gray." PhD diss., University of Wisconsin-Madison.

Morrow, William W. 1886. "Chinese Indemnity." (speech, House of Representatives, Washington, D.C., May 12).

Morrow, William W. 1888. "The Tariff: Protection of American Labor." (speech, House of Representatives, Washington, D.C., May 8 and 9).

Ngai, Mae M. and Jon Gjerde. 2013. *Major Problems in American Immigration History: Documents and Essays*. Boston: Wadsworth.

Salyer, Lucy. 1989. "Captives of Law: Judicial Enforcement of the Chinese Exclusion Laws, 1891–1905." *Journal of American History* 76, no. 1: 91–117.

Young, Mitchell. 2008. *Immigration*. Issues on Trial series. Detroit: Greenhaven Press.

Gentlemen's Agreement between the United States and Japan, 1907

Yuki Obayashi

Chronology

June 1893	The San Francisco Board of Education attempts to segregate Japanese students from public schools, but it fails after receiving complaints from the Japanese consulate.
February 23, 1905	*The San Francisco Chronicle* launches an anti-Japanese campaign.
May 6, 1905	The San Francisco Board of Education announces Japanese segregation from public schools. This second attempt also fails.
May 1905	The Japanese and Korean Exclusion League is established in San Francisco.
April 18, 1906	A magnitude 7.9 earthquake hits San Francisco.
October 11, 1906	In a third attempt, the San Francisco Board of Education passes a resolution to segregate Japanese and Korean students from public schools, effective October 16.
October 22, 1906	The American ambassador in Tokyo, Luke E. Wright, informs Washington, D.C. of San Francisco's school segregation, foreseeing a potential diplomatic crisis between Japan and the United States.
October 25, 1906	Japanese Ambassador Viscount Shuzo Aoki and U.S. Secretary of State Elihu Root meet in Washington, D.C.
October 26, 1906	President Theodore Roosevelt announces he will send Secretary of Commerce and Labor Victor H. Metcalf to San Francisco for an investigation.
October 27, 1906	Roosevelt has a conference with Metcalf over San Francisco's school segregation.

October 29, 1906	Roosevelt authorizes Root to use armed forces to protect the Japanese.
October 31, 1906	Metcalf arrives in San Francisco.
December 3, 1906	In his annual message to Congress, Roosevelt delivers his first official speech concerning the San Francisco school segregation.
December 18, 1906	Metcalf reports his findings in San Francisco to Congress.
January 8, 1907	California Governor George Pardee states that Japanese are "unassimilable" like Chinese and criticizes Roosevelt.
February 3, 1907	Accepting Roosevelt's invitation, Superintendent Alfred Roncovieri and Board of Education President Lawrence F. Walsh leave for Washington, D.C. San Francisco Mayor Eugene Schmitz follows.
February 6, 1907	Foreign Minister Hayashi Tadasu informs Root through Ambassador Wright that the Japanese cabinet would support immigration restriction if San Francisco rescinds school segregation.
February 20, 1907	Congress passes "an act to regulate the immigration of aliens into the United States" that allows the president to ban immigration to the mainland United States via other countries, insular possessions, and the canal zone.
February 24, 1907	Japan agrees to stop issuing passports to Japanese who intend to migrate to the United States in search of work.
March 13, 1907	The San Francisco Board of Education rescinds school segregation.
March 14, 1907	Roosevelt issues Executive Order 589, following the February 20 immigration act. Japanese and Korean citizens who are laborers are prohibited from entering the mainland United States through Mexico, Canada, and Hawaii.
1924	The Immigration Act of 1924 bans further Japanese immigration. The Gentlemen's Agreement of 1907 is nullified.

Narrative

The United States and Japan negotiated to limit Japanese migration to the United States between late 1906 and early 1908 through exchanges of diplomatic notes between U.S. Secretary of State Elihu Root and Japan Foreign Minister Hayashi Tadasu. The decisions were collectively called the Gentlemen's Agreement because these were official but not written into federal law. Due to this ambiguity and the number of diplomatic stages that constitute it, scholars have delineated the Gentlemen's Agreement using various dates and years.

The bilateral negotiations began as a result of a local incident in San Francisco, where the Board of Education passed a resolution in October 1906 to segregate Japanese students from public schools. The news spread to Japan and caused diplomatic tensions between the two countries. Japan, as an emerging empire, won the Russo-Japanese War in 1905 and had increasing influence on international diplomacy. However, its citizens still faced racial inequality in the United States. President Theodore Roosevelt initiated an investigation to mitigate the tensions; he persuaded San Francisco to rescind the school segregation in exchange for limiting Japanese laborers' immigration to the United States.

Japan's Foreign Minister Hayashi Tadasu in 1905. United States Secretary of State Elihu Root exchanged diplomatic notes with Tadasu and negotiated to limit Japanese immigration to the United States between 1906 and 1908. The decisions made between them became known as the Gentlemen's Agreement. (Hulton Archive/Getty Images)

The Gentlemen's Agreement is an example of how a local incident on the West Coast could attract national and international attention and change the policies and patterns of immigration. In Asian American history, the Gentlemen's Agreement is a crucial instance in which another ethnic group was singled out for immigration restriction after the Chinese Exclusion Act of 1882. Furthermore, the Gentlemen's Agreement created a new immigration group, the so-called "picture brides" for Japanese bachelors who were already living in the United States because the agreement did not prohibit the entry of spouses. After the Gentlemen's Agreement, the Japanese immigrant community changed in gender demographics and familial status.

Racism and Segregation before the Gentlemen's Agreement

Japanese first began to migrate to Hawaii as plantation laborers in the late 19th century. The end of the Edo Era (1603–1867) not only opened the door to foreign countries for Japanese but also created an increase in the population. One of the major reasons why Japanese laborers were welcomed was the Chinese Exclusion Act of 1882, which caused labor shortages in Hawaii. Initially, Japanese labors were not allowed into the United States because of the bilateral agreement made in 1900. However, the U.S. annexation of Hawaii in 1898 allowed the Japanese to relocate to the mainland, especially California, for better wages and opportunities. The U.S. census shows the increase of Japanese population in California at the beginning of the early 20th century: 1,147 people in the 1890 census, 10,151 in 1900, and 41,356 in 1910 (Daniels 1962, 1).

The growth of the Japanese population in California caused fear and anger among white workers. The Japanese were regarded as threats because they were willing to work for lower wages and took jobs from the whites. In particular, San Francisco became a central stage for such exclusionist movements because it had strong labor unions. Racism in San Francisco prompted the first attempt to segregate Japanese students in June 1893, but strong objection from the Japanese consul turned it down. In the 1902 mayoral election, Eugene Schmitz's platform, "All Asiatics, both Chinese and Japanese, should be educated separately," won him the race. Anti-Asian sentiments further escalated in February 1905 when the *San Francisco Chronicle* launched an anti-Japanese campaign in its editorial series. Within three months, 67 organizations, including the Union Labor Party, established the Japanese and Korean Exclusion League, which later was renamed the Asiatic Exclusion League. In the midst of such anti-Asian sentiments, the San Francisco Board of Education made another attempt to segregate Japanese and Koreans in May 1905, announcing, "Our children should not be placed in any position where their youthful impressions may be affected by association with pupils of the Mongolian race" (Buell 1922, 623). However, it failed again for lack of organization and funding.

On April 18, 1906, a magnitude 7.9 earthquake hit San Francisco, and fires continued for three days. Of about 400,000 people in the city, it was estimated that 3,000 people died and 225,000 people lost their homes. Superintendent of Schools Alfred Roncovieri took the city's devastated situation as an opportunity to segregate Japanese and Korean students from public schools and proposed a resolution to the San Francisco Board of Education. The Chinese Primary School in Chinatown, which was built in 1885 as a segregation school for Chinese, was reopened six months after the earthquake, but with vacancies caused by Chinese families fleeing the city due to the devastation. On October 11, under pressure from the Japanese and Korean Exclusion League, the Board of Education voted for Roncovieri's proposal to use the vacancies for Japanese and Korean students and make it a segregation school for Chinese, Japanese, and Koreans. The new resolution became effective only five days after the vote. Japanese and Korean

The Asiatic Exclusion League

Sixty-seven organizations in San Francisco, including political parties and labor unions, launched the Japanese and Korean Exclusion League in May 1905. Two years later, in December 1907, it was renamed the Asiatic Exclusion League and existed until the end of World War II. The main purpose of the league was to prevent Asians, especially Japanese, from gaining economic power.

The Asiatic Exclusion League believed that only white people could assimilate into the United States. Its first president, Olaf Tveitmore, and other influential people in the organization were, in fact, immigrants from Europe. Their fear of Asian immigrants was incited by the belief that Asians took jobs from white Americans. Moreover, the organization promoted fear of interracial marriages between white women and Asian men. Thus, it was based on a racist agenda toward Asians.

In 1905, inspired by the organization, two Republican congressmen, Duncan E. McKinlay and Everis A. Hayes, brought a bill excluding Japanese from immigration to the Foreign Affairs Committee. Although the bill was ignored, it showed how influential the Asiatic Exclusion League was in California's politics. The organization's political agenda was further demonstrated in its pressuring the San Francisco Board of Education for school segregation in 1906.

The Asiatic Exclusion League accused Japanese immigrants of competing with white people by working for lower wages. Economic fear further incited people to boycott Japanese-owned shops and goods imported from Japan. The rhetoric of the Asiatic Exclusion League echoed what was used when Chinese immigrants were excluded in the late 19th century. The league's primal goal was in fact to apply the Chinese Exclusion Act of 1882 to other Asian immigrants.

students were ordered to transfer to the segregation school, which was renamed the Oriental Public School.

The San Francisco Board of Education explained that a lack of space after the earthquake required Japanese and Korean students to attend the same school as Chinese students. However, the official account did not match the reality. There were 93 Japanese and a few Korean students out of the total 28,000 students in the city. Furthermore, previously the Japanese and Korean students were not only spread across the 23 different public schools but also did not encounter or cause any racial tensions that the city anticipated ("Few Japanese Schools," 1906, 1).

Japan's Reactions

The Japanese government had strong ties with Issei (first-generation Japanese Americans) because they were ineligible for U.S. citizenship. The Japanese Association of America, which was organized under the Japanese consulate, took a role of liaison between the Japanese government and Japanese Americans. After the San Francisco Board of Education ordered the school segregation, the Japanese Association of American wired the news to Japan. On October 20, 1906, the media printed the story and incited waves of anger in Japan. For example, on October 22, the *Mainichi Shimbun* published, "Stand up, Japanese nation! Our countrymen have been HUMILIATED on the other side of the Pacific. Our poor boys and girls have been expelled from the public schools by the rascals of the United States, cruel and merciless like demons" (quoted in Kennedy and Bailey 2015, 513).

News of the school segregation reached Japan before Washington learned of it. The American ambassador in Tokyo, Luke E. Wright, telegrammed to Washington about the possible diplomatic crisis between the two countries. Having newly emerged as an empire after winning the Russo-Japanese War in 1905, Japan had international influence and too much national pride to submit to the school segregation (Bailey 1964, 46).

Japanese officials claimed that the school segregation violated the Treaty of Commerce and Navigation enacted in November 1894. In the treaty, American and Japanese citizens were mutually promised to receive "most-favored-nation treatment in the territories of the other." The Japanese consul in San Francisco, Kisaburo Uyeno, and the Japanese ambassador in Washington, Viscount Shuzo Aoki, filed an official complaint to Washington about the school segregation.

The Gentlemen's Agreement

As an emerging empire, Japan was humiliated by school segregation in San Francisco and agreed to immigration restriction to save face. Roosevelt admitted Japan's rising imperial power and even admired Japan's victory in the Russo-Japanese War. Sensing a potential war with Japan as the worst scenario, Roosevelt hastened his negotiations with Japan and San Francisco.

By the end of October 1906, Roosevelt had sent Secretary of Commerce and Labor Victor H. Metcalf to San Francisco to investigate the situation. Meanwhile, on December 3, Roosevelt delivered a speech at the annual meeting of Congress in which he criticized anti-Japanese sentiments and San Francisco's school segregation. He criticized California negatively and harshly, exposing the fundamental differences on the issue between the state and Washington. Two weeks after Roosevelt's speech, Metcalf reported his findings to Congress. He agreed with Japan, arguing that the school segregation in San Francisco violated the 1894 treaty guaranteeing the equal treatment of Japanese. Metcalf said that Japanese children should be protected under the U.S.-Japan alliance. However, because racial segregation was legal at the time, Roosevelt needed to negotiate with San Francisco to rescind the school segregation.

At the negotiation table, Roosevelt proposed to limit the entry of Japanese laborers to the mainland in favor of San Francisco if the city rescinded the school segregation. While waiting for responses from San Francisco and Japan, Roosevelt proposed a bill to empower the president to restrict immigration to the mainland United States via other countries, insular possessions, and the canal zone. On February 24, 1907, Japan agreed to stop issuing passports to Japanese who intended to migrate to the United States for work, but the agreement did not include Hawaii. Foreign Minister Hayashi Tadasu insisted that Japan would not stop Japanese relocation from Hawaii to the mainland, yet agreed that the United States could step up to prevent it. Following Japan's decision, the San Francisco Board of Education rescinded the school segregation on March 13. The next day, Roosevelt applied the newly passed bill to Japanese laborers and prohibited them from migrating to the United States from Hawaii, Mexico, and Canada.

Some scholars believe that the Gentlemen's Agreement occurred in a series of negotiations in 1907. Some include 1908 because the United States continued to pressure Japan not to issue passports to laborers. In 1908, Japanese laborers still migrated to the U.S. mainland: 150 people in March and 900 people in May. Furthermore, Japan had difficulty keeping track of these immigrants, who were scattered all over the West Coast. The United States negotiated with Japan to implement a registration system that identified legal residents. In February 1908, Japan accepted the U.S. proposal and eventually practiced the new registration system.

After the Gentlemen's Agreement

Japanese laborers were banned from immigrating to the U.S. mainland, but the Gentlemen's Agreement was applied only to new laborers. The Japanese who already resided in the United States were granted renewed passports. Additionally, merchants, students, and spouses were not included in the restriction. After the Gentlemen's Agreement, Japanese bachelors in the United States brought over their spouses, "picture brides" whom they married through matchmaking, which was not uncommon at that time in Japan. The United States did not expect the influx of picture brides, and the loophole was later closed by a ban in 1920.

After losing the opportunity of migrating to the U.S. mainland, Japan sought alternative paths for migration to Asia and the Pacific. Japan expanded its colonial territories, including Taiwan, Korea, and Manchuria. Following the end of World War I, Japan received Micronesia from the League of Nations in 1922 and eventually governed it as a colony. Japan also established a puppet state called Manchukuo (1932–1945) in the northeastern area of China and Inner Mongolia. Japanese politicians and intellectuals advocated these territorial expansions and migration to Asia and the Pacific when the United States shut down Japanese immigration in 1907 (the Gentlemen's Agreement) and 1924 (the Immigration Act).

On January 24, 2017, the San Francisco Board of Education passed a resolution to repeal school segregation, which had never been officially revoked. Although school segregation had not been practiced for many years, this move by the Board of Education symbolically marked an effort to acknowledge this negative part of San Francisco's history.

Biographies of Notable Figures

Theodore Roosevelt (1858–1919)

Theodore Roosevelt was the 26th president of the United States between 1901 and 1909. Before the presidency, he served as the Republican state assemblyman (1882–1884), the governor of New York (1899–1900), and vice president of the United States (1901). Roosevelt was regarded as a politician who led the Progressive Era in the early 20th century.

When Roosevelt was a student studying naval history at Harvard University, he began writing a scholarly work titled *The Naval War of 1812*, which was published in 1882. Although he continued to study at Columbia Law School, he decided to pursue a career in politics and was elected as the Republican state assemblyman. He built a reputation as a politician who worked against corruption.

Roosevelt was selected as assistant secretary of the U.S. Navy under President William McKinley's administration but decided to leave the post to serve in the Spanish-American War (1898). He served as a lieutenant colonel in the Rough Riders regiment, which fought at the battle of San Juan Hill in Cuba.

Returning as a war hero, Roosevelt moved back to politics. He was elected the vice president of McKinley's administration and became president after McKinley's assassination in 1901. At that point in U.S. history, Roosevelt became the nation's youngest president at the age of 42. In domestic policy, Roosevelt reinforced the Sherman Antitrust Act of 1890 and dismantled monopolies. One of the 43 cases that the Roosevelt administration sued was a railroad company called the Northern Securities Company. In 1904, the Supreme Court ordered the company to dissolve. In 1902, Roosevelt intervened in a strike by the United Mine Workers in Pennsylvania. With federal intervention, the coal miners won a wage increase and fewer labor hours after a 163-day strike. Roosevelt was the first president to intervene in a strike on behalf of the workers.

During his second term of the presidency, Roosevelt worked for food safety and enacted the Pure Food and Drug Act and the Meat Inspection Act in 1906. These acts enforced accurate food labeling. Furthermore, beginning in the first year of his presidency, he worked to conserve nature by establishing national parks, forests, and monuments. In 1906, he enacted the Antiquities Act, which was the first law to recognize the importance of preserving archaeological sites. In 1908, he set up the National Conservation Commission to compile an inventory for the preservation of the nation's natural resources. During his presidency, Roosevelt protected approximately 230 million acres.

In international diplomacy, Roosevelt adopted an imperialist agenda. Following the victory in the Spanish-American War, in which he served as a lieutenant colonel, the United States took over Cuba, Puerto Rico, the Philippines, and Guam, previously controlled by the Spanish Empire.

Roosevelt persisted in building a canal to connect the Atlantic and Pacific Oceans. After a failed attempt by England, the United States gained a license in 1901 to build a canal in Panama. In 1902, the United States negotiated with Colombia, which dominated Panama at that time, but failed to reach an agreement due to financial disagreements. Roosevelt took advantage of Panama's longing for independence from Columbia by sending warships to Panama City and Colón on both oceanic sides. Colombia succumbed to the pressure and gave up Panama. Soon after gaining independence, the Republic of Panama rewarded the United States by allowing it to construct the canal.

Roosevelt's pro-Japanese stance in San Francisco's school segregation did not mean that he did not have racial biases. In 1902, he renewed the Chinese Exclusion Act of 1882 and expanded restrictions on immigration to the newly acquired Hawaii and the Philippines. Indeed, he believed that a racial hierarchy existed in which Asians, Native Americans, and African Americans were inferior to civilized whites. However, his racial views were more complicated than they seemed. In 1901, Roosevelt invited American educator Booker T. Washington to dine with him and his family at the White House and received harsh criticism from Southern politicians and media. Although African Americans had joined meetings in the White House, a U.S. president dining with African Americans was unprecedented.

Roosevelt was acutely aware of Japan's emerging imperial power and attempted to avoid significant conflict over the school segregation in San Francisco. He became a mediator between Russia and Japan during the Russo-Japanese War. The Treaty of Portsmouth, which was enacted in 1905 under Roosevelt's arbitration, acknowledged southern Manchuria and Korea as Japan's territories and ceded the southern part of the island of Sakhalin from Russia to Japan. For this, he was awarded the Nobel Peace Prize in 1906, the first president of the United States to be so honored.

William Howard Taft succeeded to the presidency. Unsatisfied with Taft, Roosevelt pursued the Republican presidential nomination in 1912. Failing the attempt, Roosevelt founded the Progressive Party the same year. The party pressed onward with progressive policies and reforms but did not succeed and disappeared by 1918. After a two-year expedition in the Brazilian Amazon, Roosevelt returned to politics and challenged the 1920 presidential election. Although he was a front-runner for the Republican nomination, he passed away in 1919.

DOCUMENT EXCERPTS

President Theodore Roosevelt's Report of the Commissioner General of Immigration (1908)

Negotiated by President Theodore Roosevelt's administration, the Gentlemen's Agreement was an arrangement between the Japanese and U.S. governments to stop immigration from Japan to America. Leading up to the agreement, Japan had expressed concerns that many of its most valuable workers, particularly the young men it needed to support its growing military, had immigrated to America. The United States had its own concerns, namely the so-called "Yellow Peril" Americans felt, which centered on fears that the influx of Japanese immigrants was harmful to American culture and the workforce. As a result, both countries had motives to stop Japanese immigration. The agreement was initially approved by representatives from both countries on January 24, 1907, and became formalized on February 18, 1908. It remained in effect until the United States superseded the agreement with the Immigration Act of 1924, which continued the restrictive immigration policies.

Report of the Commissioner General of Immigration, 1908

In order that the best results might follow from an enforcement of the regulations, an understanding was reached with Japan that the existing policy of discouraging emigration of its subjects of the laboring classes to continental United States should be continued, and should, by co-operation with the governments, be made as effective as possible. This understanding contemplates that the Japanese government shall issue passports to continental United States only to such of its subjects as are non-laborers or are laborers who, in coming to the continent, seek to resume a formerly acquired domicile, to join a parent, wife, or children residing there, or to assume active control of an already possessed interest in a farming enterprise in this country, so that the three classes of laborers entitled to receive passports have come to be designated former residents, parents, wives, or children of residents, and settled agriculturists.

With respect to Hawaii, the Japanese government of its own volition stated that, experimentally at least, the issuance of passports to members of the laboring classes proceeding thence would be limited to former residents and parents, wives, or children of residents. The said government has also been exercising a careful supervision over the subject of emigration of its laboring class to foreign contiguous territory.

Source: "Report of the Commissioner General of Immigration." Washington, D.C.: Government Printing Office, 1908, 125.

President Theodore Roosevelt's Sixth Annual Message (1906)

In his sixth annual message, delivered to the Senate and House of Representatives on December 3, 1906, President Theodore Roosevelt highlighted the importance of treating all nations fairly and treating all immigrants who are "honest and upright in his dealings" with justice and goodwill. His speech particularly expressed his concerns about the hostility against Japanese immigrants in the United States, emphasized the important friendship between Japan and the United States, and asked for fair treatment for the Japanese.

Sixth Annual Message, 1906
(Excerpts)

To the Senate and House of Representatives:

As a nation we still continue to enjoy a literally unprecedented prosperity; and it is probable that only reckless speculation and disregard of legitimate business methods on the part of the business world can materially mar this prosperity.

. . .

Not only must we treat all nations fairly, but we must treat with justice and good will all immigrants who come here under the law. Whether they are Catholic or Protestant, Jew or Gentile; whether they come from England or Germany, Russia, Japan, or Italy, matters nothing. All we have a right to question is the man's conduct. If he is honest and upright in his dealings with his neighbor and with the State, then he is entitled to respect and good treatment. Especially do we need to remember our duty to the stranger within our gates. It is the sure mark of a low civilization, a low morality, to abuse or discriminate against or in any way humiliate such stranger who has come here lawfully and who is conducting himself properly. To remember this is incumbent on every American citizen, and it is of course peculiarly incumbent on every Government official, whether of the nation or of the several States.

I am prompted to say this by the attitude of hostility here and there assumed toward the Japanese in this country. This hostility is sporadic and is limited to a very few places. Nevertheless, it is most discreditable to us as a people, and it may be fraught with the gravest consequences to the nation. The friendship between the United States and Japan has been continuous since the time, over half a century ago, when Commodore Perry, by his expedition to Japan, first opened the islands to western civilization. Since then the growth of Japan has been literally astounding. There is not only nothing to parallel it, but nothing to approach it in the history of civilized mankind. Japan has a glorious and ancient past. Her civilization is older than that of the nations of northern Europe—the nations from whom the people of the United States have chiefly sprung. But fifty years ago Japan's development was still that of the Middle Ages. During that fifty years the progress of the country in every walk in life has been a marvel to mankind, and she now stands as one of the greatest of civilized nations; great in the arts of war and in the arts of peace; great in military, in industrial, in artistic development and achievement. Japanese soldiers and sailors have shown themselves equal in combat to any of whom history makes note. She has produced great generals and mighty admirals; her fighting men, afloat and ashore, show all the heroic courage, the unquestioning, unfaltering loyalty, the splendid indifference to hardship and death, which marked the Loyal Ronins; and they show also that they possess the highest ideal of patriotism. Japanese artists of every kind see their products eagerly sought for in all lands. The industrial and commercial development of Japan has been phenomenal; greater than that of any other country during the same period. At the same time the advance in science and philosophy is no less marked. The admirable management of the Japanese Red Cross during the late war, the efficiency and humanity of the Japanese officials, nurses, and doctors, won the respectful admiration of all acquainted with the facts. Thru the Red Cross the Japanese people sent over $100,000 to the sufferers of San Francisco, and the gift was accepted with gratitude by our people. The courtesy of the Japanese, nationally and individually, has become proverbial. To no other country has there been such an increasing number of visitors from this land as to Japan. In return, Japanese have come here in great numbers. They are welcome, socially and intellectually, in all our colleges and institutions of higher learning, in all our professional and social bodies. The Japanese have won in a single generation the right to stand abreast of the foremost and most enlightened peoples of Europe and

America; they have won on their own merits and by their own exertions the right to treatment on a basis of full and frank equality. The overwhelming mass of our people cherish a lively regard and respect for the people of Japan, and in almost every quarter of the Union the stranger from Japan is treated as he deserves; that is, he is treated as the stranger from any part of civilized Europe is and deserves to be treated. But here and there a most unworthy feeling has manifested itself toward the Japanese—the feeling that has been shown in shutting them out from the common schools in San Francisco, and in mutterings against them in one or two other places, because of their efficiency as workers. To shut them out from the public schools is a wicked absurdity, when there are no first-class colleges in the land, including the universities and colleges of California, which do not gladly welcome Japanese students and on which Japanese students do not reflect credit. We have as much to learn from Japan as Japan has to learn from us; and no nation is fit to teach unless it is also willing to learn. Throughout Japan Americans are well treated, and any failure on the part of Americans at home to treat the Japanese with a like courtesy and consideration is by just so much a confession of inferiority in our civilization.

Our nation fronts on the Pacific, just as it fronts on the Atlantic. We hope to play a constantly growing part in the great ocean of the Orient. We wish, as we ought to wish, for a great commercial development in our dealings with Asia; and it is out of the question that we should permanently have such development unless we freely and gladly extend to other nations the same measure of justice and good treatment which we expect to receive in return. It is only a very small body of our citizens that act badly. Where the Federal Government has power it will deal summarily with any such. Where the several States have power I earnestly ask that they also deal wisely and promptly with such conduct, or else this small body of wrong-doers may bring shame upon the great mass of their innocent and right-thinking fellows—that is, upon our nation as a whole. Good manners should be an international no less than an individual attribute. I ask fair treatment for the Japanese as I would ask fair treatment for Germans or Englishmen, Frenchmen, Russians, or Italians. I ask it as due to humanity and civilization. I ask it as due to ourselves because we must act uprightly toward all men.

I recommend to the Congress that an act be passed specifically providing for the naturalization of Japanese who come here intending to become American citizens. One of the great embarrassments attending the performance of our international obligations is the fact that the Statutes of the United States are entirely inadequate. They fail to give to the National Government sufficiently ample power, through United States courts and by the use of the Army and Navy, to protect aliens in the rights secured to them under solemn treaties which are the law of the land. I therefore earnestly recommend that the criminal and civil statutes of the United States be so amended and added to as to enable the President, acting for the United States Government, which is responsible in our international relations, to enforce the rights of aliens under treaties. Even as the law now is something can be done by the Federal Government toward this end, and in the matter now before me affecting the Japanese everything that it is in my power to do will be done, and all of the forces, military and civil, of the United States which I may lawfully employ will be so employed. There should, however, be no particle of doubt as to the power of the National Government completely to perform and enforce its own obligations to other nations. The mob of a single city may at any time perform acts of lawless violence against some class of foreigners which would plunge us into war. That city by itself would be powerless to make defense against the foreign power thus assaulted, and if independent of this Government it would never venture to perform or permit the performance of the acts complained of. The entire power and the whole duty to protect the offending city or the offending community lies in the hands of the United States Government. It is unthinkable that we should continue a policy under which a given locality may be allowed to commit a crime against a friendly nation, and the United States Government limited, not to preventing the commission of the crime, but, in the last resort, to defending the people who have committed it against the consequences of their own wrongdoing.

Source: Richardson, James D. *A Compilation of the Messages and Papers of the Presidents, 1789–1908 and Index.* Washington, D.C.: Bureau of National Literature and Art, 1908, 1181–1228.

See also: The Chinese Exclusion Act, 1882; Hawaii Becomes a U.S. Territory, 1898; Japanese American Internment, 1942–1946; The Webb-Haney Act Passed by California State Legislature, 1913

Further Reading

Bailey, Thomas A. 1964. *Theodore Roosevelt and the Japanese-American Crisis: An Account of the International Complications Arising from the Race Problem on the Pacific Coast.* Gloucester, MA: Peter Smith.

Buell, Raymond Leslie. 1922. "The Development of the Anti-Japanese Agitation in the United States." *Political Science Quarterly* 37, no. 4: 605–38. http://www.jstor.org /stable2142459

Daniels, Roger. 1962. *The Politics of Prejudice: The Anti-Japanese Movement in California and the Struggle for Japanese Exclusion.* Berkeley: University of California Press.

"Few Japanese in Schools." *New York Times.* December 8, 1906.

Ichioka, Yuji. 1988. *The Issei: The World of the First Generation Japanese Immigrants, 1885–1924.* New York: The Free Press.

Johnson, Herbert. 1971. *Discrimination against the Japanese in California: A Review of the Real Situation.* San Francisco: R and E Research Associates.

Kenney, David M. and Thomas A. Bailey. 2015. *The American Spirit: The United States History as Seen by Contemporaries.* 13th ed. Boston: Cengage.

Kitano, Harry H. L. 1969. *Japanese Americans: The Evolution of a Subculture.* Englewood Cliffs, NJ: Prentice-Hall.

Kurashige, Lon. 2017. "Transpacific Accommodation and the Defense of Asian Immigrants." In *Pacific America: Histories of Transoceanic Crossings,* edited by Lon Kurashige, 129–145. Honolulu: University of Hawaii Press.

Patterson, David S. 2011. "Japanese-American Relations: The 1906 California Crisis, the Gentlemen's Agreement, and the World Cruise." In *A Companion to Theodore Roosevelt,* edited by Serge Ricard, 391–416. Malden, MA: Blackwell Publishing Ltd.

Roosevelt, Theodore. 1926. *State Papers as Governor and President: 1899–1909.* Vol. 15 of *The Works of Theodore Roosevelt,* edited by Hermann Hagedorn. National edition. New York: Charles Scribner's Sons.

Spickard, Paul. 1996. *Japanese Americans: The Formation and Transformations of an Ethnic Group,* rev. ed. New Brunswick, NJ: Rutgers University Press.

Takaki, Ronald. 1990. *Strangers from a Different Shore: A History of Asian Americans.* New York: Penguin Books.

The USGS Earthquake Hazards Program. 2018. "The Great 1906 San Francisco Earthquake." https://earthquake.usgs.gov/earthquakes/events/1906calif/18april/index.php

Wollenberg, Charles M. 1976. *All Deliberate Speed: Segregation and Exclusion in California Schools, 1855–1975.* Berkeley: University of California Press.

Angel Island Opens in San Francisco Bay, 1910

Hayley Johnson and Sarah Simms

Chronology

Pre-1769	For thousands of years, the Coast Miwok Indians, a part of the Hookooeko group, utilize Angel Island as hunting and fishing grounds.
1769	Gaspar De Portola's expeditionary party becomes the first recorded group of Europeans to see San Francisco Bay.
1775	Juan Manuel de Ayala y Aranza sails to Angel Island on the *San Carlos.*
1839	The governor of California gives Antonio Maria Osio a land grant for Angel Island, where Osio establishes a cattle ranch.
1848	Mexico cedes California to the United States.
November 6, 1850	President Millard Fillmore issues an executive order that reserves Angel Island and surrounding islands for public purposes.

1870–1890	Camp Reynolds, on the west side of the island, is used by the U.S. Army as a headquarters, rest camp, and recruit depot for troops.
1891–1935	A quarantine station for ships entering San Francisco Bay opens on Angel Island's Ayala Cove. The steamship *China* becomes the first ship to be placed in quarantine at the Angel Island facility.
1900	The War Department changes the name of the post on Angel Island to Fort McDowell.
1905	Surveying and construction begin on the immigration station.
April 18, 1906	Earthquake decimates San Francisco and damages quarantine station on Angel Island.
January 22, 1910	Angel Island Immigration Station opens.
August 11, 1940	Fire breaks out in the administration building of the immigration station. This fire heralds the end of the immigration station and precipitates its move back to San Francisco.
1942	Angel Island returns to U.S. Army control and serves as a processing center for World War II prisoners of war and enemy aliens.
1946	U.S. Army declares Angel Island as surplus.
1954	U.S. Army engineers install Nike antiaircraft missile site on Angel Island.
1962	Nike missile battery is decommissioned.
1963	Angel Island (except for two U.S. Coast Guard areas) is turned over to the state of California to become a state park.
1970	California state park ranger Alexander Weiss discovers poems carved into the walls of the old detention barracks.
1976	Special legislation passes, providing $250,000 for the preservation and restoration of the detention barracks and Chinese poetry.
1997	Angel Island Immigration Station becomes a National Historic Landmark.

Narrative

Often referred to as the "Jewel of San Francisco Bay," Angel Island, located off California's coast, is the largest natural island in the San Francisco Bay and has a rich history as a Miwok Indian hunting ground, Mexican land grant, military fort,

A young immigrant was interviewed on Angel Island in 1923. The rigorous interview process was, at the time, designed to keep Asian immigrants out of the country. Some immigrants endured weeks, months, or even years of detainment and cross-examination. (National Archives)

quarantine station, immigration and detention station, and national park. The island consists of approximately 740 acres with 360-degree views of San Francisco Bay and the Golden Gate Bridge.

On January 22, 1910, Angel Island officially opened as an immigration station. Dubbed the "Ellis Island of the West," the Angel Island station was unique because most of the immigrants arriving there were Asian. The largest numbers came from China, Japan, Russia, and South Asia. Unlike Ellis Island's immigrant policy of inclusion and openness, Angel Island operated under policies of exclusion based on race that had been in operation since the 1880s. Even with a policy of exclusion, however, Angel Island was the point of entry for an estimated 1 million Asian and other immigrants. Between 1910 and 1940, an estimated 175,000 Chinese and 60,000 Japanese immigrants were processed through Angel Island. Many Asian Americans living in the United States today are deeply tied to Angel Island because it was the primary point of entry into the United States at the time.

Gold Mountain and the Chinese Exclusion Act

With the California gold rush in the 1850s came large-scale Chinese immigration into the United States. Chinese laborers came looking for work to support their families, who remained in China. From around 1850 until 1900, around 100,000 Chinese men, many from Guangdong Province in southern China, flooded into the United States in search of a better life. They were drawn to "Gam Saan" (literally meaning "Gold Mountain" and referring to the United States) and began working in the gold mines. Eventually, Chinese laborers moved into other areas of employment, such as construction labor for the Central Pacific Railroad's portion of the transcontinental railroad. Chinese immigrants were also recruited as agricultural laborers, who were in high demand in California at that time.

In the 1870s, however, the American economy found itself in a postwar decline. Economic crises began with the Panic of 1873 and continued, resulting in falling wages and rising unemployment. White laborers found themselves competing for scarce jobs with Chinese immigrants who would work for lower wages. This period in American history became rife with anti-Chinese sentiment as many Americans began to feel threatened by the widespread availability of cheap Asian immigrant labor. Chinese immigrants began to be painted as scapegoats for both declining wages and unemployment. Resentful white laborers began to see Chinese immigrants as morally corrupt and as a racial threat. Pressures from various entities, such as labor groups and political leaders, especially in California, resulted in Congress passing the Chinese Exclusion Act of 1882. This is the first and only time that federal legislation was passed to explicitly suspend immigration for a specific group based on race, nationality, and class.

The Chinese Exclusion Act prevented Chinese immigrants already in the country from becoming citizens and barred Chinese "skilled and unskilled laborers and Chinese employed in mining" from entering the country for 10 years. Though the act barred all Chinese laborers from entering the country, Chinese immigration to the United States did not come to a complete halt. The act allowed "exempt" classes consisting of non-laborers to enter the United States. These classes included merchants, diplomats, clergy, teachers, and students.

Anti-Chinese immigration legislation did not stop with the passage of the 1882 Exclusion Act. The Geary Act was passed May 5, 1892, extending the Exclusion Act for another 10 years and strengthening various procedures. On April 29, 1902, the act was extended "until otherwise provided by law." These laws were not repealed until the passing of the Magnuson Act in 1943, when President Franklin Roosevelt officially rescinded the Chinese Exclusion Act due to China's service as an American ally against the Japanese in World War II. Despite these legislative barriers, many Chinese found a way to circumvent the Exclusion Act. One way that was both costly and strenuous for Chinese immigrants was the advent of the "paper son."

1906 San Francisco Earthquake and Fire and the Rise of "Paper Sons"

At 5:12 a.m. on April 18, 1906, one of the most significant earthquakes in American history shocked San Francisco. Although the earthquake lasted mere minutes, major fires burned throughout the city for several days afterward. In these fires, municipal documentation that could verify citizenship was destroyed. As a result, Chinese residents of the city could claim they were born in the United States and were therefore American citizens.

This ability to claim native citizenship was important in circumventing the Exclusion Act. The Exclusion Act allowed for the naturalization of family members of U.S.-born citizens. This meant that U.S.-born citizens could consequently report the birth of a son or daughter to Chinese officials in order to get the proper paperwork for their offspring to enter the United States. These individuals often falsely reported giving birth to children and claimed the children (or grown children) still lived in China, typically listing the sex of the fictitious child as male. This newly registered Chinese individual provided an immigration "slot" that men wishing to immigrate could purchase, even though they had no true family relations in the United States. Merchant brokers would often act as intermediaries to facilitate the sale of these slots. Men who entered the United States through this process became known as "paper sons."

Proving that one was a child of an exempt class or native citizen to facilitate immigration to the United States was a challenge. Many immigrants spent weeks learning their new "family history" during the voyage to the United States so that they could pass the rigorous interviews they would face at Angel Island. Immigration officials had no way to tell paper sons from real sons, and this necessitated intense interrogations. Additionally, immigration officials at Angel Island actively worked to enforce the Exclusion Act, which was designed to prevent immigration rather than encourage it.

Immigrant Processing

The Angel Island Immigration Station opened its doors on January 22, 1910, and was the main processing center for all Asian immigrants entering the United States. In stark contrast to Ellis Island, Angel Island served as a barrier to entry for immigrants, beginning with the passage of the Chinese Exclusion Act in 1882 and continuing with rigorous interview processes designed to keep immigrants out of the country.

From 1910 to 1940, Angel Island served as the detention headquarters for immigrants awaiting decisions based on the outcomes of both their medical and immigration examinations. Whereas European immigrants on Ellis Island only received cursory examinations for a few hours or less, Asian immigrants at Angel Island endured weeks, months, or even years of detainment and cross-examinations testing every aspect of their familial and village history. All of these differences in treatment were geared toward implementing the Exclusion Act and rooting out what immigration inspectors suspected were phony family histories.

Chinese immigrants made up the single largest ethnic group entering San Francisco until 1915, when Japanese outnumbered Chinese for the first time. Russians,

South Asians, Mexicans, Central and South Americans, Australians, and New Zealanders all entered the United States through Angel Island. In total, approximately 80 countries utilized Angel Island as a point of entry.

Even though Angel Island processed large numbers of immigrants, it was widely recognized that the facilities there were substandard in terms of building construction and the facility's isolated location, which required the use of ferries. A 1920 report by the Commissioner General of Immigration noted the Bureau of Immigration had repeatedly requested that a facility be found on the mainland to process incoming immigrants. The report states, "Aside from the ever-present danger of fire, which is obvious in a series of framed buildings grouped in close proximity, as are those at Angel Island, the present hospital facilities are considerably below the requirements, and the detention barracks are generally over-crowded" (U.S.

Japanese Picture Brides

Japanese picture brides, or *shashin hanayome*, were part of a long tradition of arranged marriages originating in the Tokugawa period (1603–1868). In the early 20th century, this practice took the form of exchanging photographs between the prospective bride, still living in Japan, and the prospective groom, a Japanese immigrant man working in America or Hawaii. These were brokered by a matchmaker, an intermediary known as *nakōdo* or *baishakunin*, or, in Hawaii, *shimpai*. This matchmaker would set up meetings between the head of each respective family to discuss and negotiate the marriage proposal. Pictures of the groom were accompanied by information regarding his employment and achievements. Wealth, health, and family history were among the various criteria considered when negotiating these matches.

If both parties were found acceptable, then a marriage by proxy occurred. The name of the bride only needed to be entered into the groom's family registry for the marriage to be considered legal in Japan. The groom did not need to be present for this, and once the name was registered, the new bride was able to travel to the United States to meet her new husband. Because marriage by proxy was not considered legally binding in the United States, mass marriage ceremonies would be held upon the brides' arrival. Some brides were disappointed with their new husbands; some men fabricated or exaggerated their lives in America or sent photographs of themselves as younger men (or even photographs of different men). Although there were some cases of divorce, the majority accepted their fate. This practice came to an end with the Ladies Agreement of 1921 (Nakamura 2014).

Department of Labor 1920, 30). Despite the continued documentation of substandard facilities, Angel Island remained in operation until 1940, when a fire eventually damaged the structures.

Detention at Angel Island

After crossing the Pacific, vessels would first land in San Francisco. Some passengers were allowed to disembark there after undergoing medical exams and having their papers examined, but most were ferried to Angel Island to begin a much more extensive investigation. Most of these were Asian immigrants, especially Chinese and the poor or sick. Once on Angel Island, detainees were separated by gender; husbands and wives would not see or be able to communicate with each other for the duration of their detainment. Women were detained separately in the administration building. Children were put under the care of their mothers. Boys over the age of 12 were detained with other males. Further segregation by race was initially enforced within the dormitories, but with the heavy influx of immigrants, this proved difficult, and the practice was eventually abandoned. The dormitories were sparsely furnished and crowded with metal bunks stacked two or three high.

Upon disembarking, detainees were registered, and their bags were taken and fumigated for fear of possible diseases. Each endured a thorough medical examination the next day. Under the auspice of protecting Americans from perceived health threats carried by immigrants, this medical examination was one way of excluding people from entry into the United States. Contagious diseases such as tuberculosis, syphilis, leprosy, and a variety of parasitic diseases such as hookworm (*uncinariasis*) were considered grounds for exclusion.

Parasitic diseases, in particular, thrive in rural areas that lack proper sanitation, a description of many of the areas Asian immigrants originated from. Because of the high proportion of Asian immigrants carrying these parasitic diseases, exclusion based on this was hotly protested. Eventually, diseases born of parasites (hookworm, liver fluke, and threadworm, among others) were removed from the exclusion list, provided detainees were properly treated at the Angel Island medical facility. However, the afflicted detainees were responsible for the costs associated with their treatment (Yung and Lee 2015).

Inspectors were also on the lookout for other ailments or afflictions that could inhibit one's ability to work, such as hernias, pregnancy, nervous conditions, and eye afflictions. The point of this scrutiny was to guarantee the "model" immigrant—those able to work without the need of assistance from the government at any point. These medical examinations were very invasive: stool samples were taken and exams were done of the naked body at a time when cultural norms dictated the opposite.

Once through the medical exam, detainees were sent back to their barracks to await their interviews. For Asians, especially Chinese, detainment could be considered temporary imprisonment. Guards were located throughout the island to hinder escape and to ensure messages or coaching material was not being shared between fellow detainees or passed from the mainland. Until a case for entry had been heard, no visitors could be received. Women were sometimes allowed to walk around the camp accompanied by guards, whereas men were only allowed to venture into the gated yard outside their dormitory during scheduled exercise times.

To help Chinese immigrants pass the interview process, sponsors would often give them coaching booklets that might consist of dozens of pages (Angel Island 2004, 12). These booklets attempted to cover every possible question that an interviewer might typically ask. Both paper and real sons would study for these interviews, as the detailed questions could be difficult for anyone to answer. Paper sons were claiming a fraudulent past as real, and even real sons and fathers—many of whom had been separated for some time—often found it difficult to answer correctly (Angel Island 2004, 12). They studied these booklets for weeks as they voyaged across the ocean. Upon nearing the United States, they would throw the booklets overboard or otherwise destroy them, because possessing this contraband would result in automatic deportation.

Interviews were conducted by the Board of Special Inquiry, composed of two interrogators with one stenographer to record the questions and answers. A translator could be utilized, if necessary. Often, translators were not especially versed in the various spoken dialects, which could contribute to confusion during the interviews. Paper children would have to prove their relationships with fathers currently residing in the United States by answering specific questions, such as:

What is your living room floor made of?
Where is the rice bin kept?
Where is your village's temple?
How many houses are in your village lane?
What are the names of the neighbors who live in your village and what are their occupations?
What direction does your house in China face?
How many windows does your house in China have? (Angel Island 2004, 12)

The father, husband, or sponsor would also have to answer the same questions. The answers would be compared for discrepancies. If too many discrepancies were found, additional interviews could be deemed necessary, or entry could be denied. Denial of entry could be appealed but meant a lengthier stay on Angel Island. The longest recorded stay of a detainee on Angel Island was that of Quok Shee, a woman detained from September 1, 1916, to August 1918—over 600 days—before being allowed to join her merchant husband (Barde 2004, 28). Although hers was not the normal length of stay, detention for days, weeks, or months was common.

Feelings of desperation and hopelessness abounded, especially for those denied entry. Some on Angel Island attempted suicide. One such documented case is that of Soto Shee, who arrived at Angel Island with her seven-month-old son, Soon Din. She was also pregnant with her second child. She arrived just after the passing of the 1924 immigration act that exercised further bans on Chinese, specifically Chinese wives of U.S. citizens. After her hearing with the Board of Special Inquiry, she was denied entry. Soon Din died at the immigration station five days later, reportedly of gastroenteritis. Distraught, Soto Shee hanged herself in the women's bathroom but was found by Matron Grace McKeener, who cut her down. Soto Shee recovered and was eventually allowed into the country on bond, where she joined her husband and gave birth to their second child (Lee 2010, 101–2).

Throughout Angel Island's history as an immigration station, conditions were consistently reported as unsanitary, unsatisfactory, and unsafe. Because of the cramped living quarters, sickness and disease were of great concern. In 1920, for instance, there was an outbreak of meningitis due to the unsanitary conditions. The food served to detainees was a constant source of complaint because it was often served cold and inedible. Two riots protesting the food erupted at Angel Island, once in 1919 and again in 1925. Troops were called in each time to quell the disturbance. The buildings lacked fire escapes, and many of the windows were gated and locked. In 1915, complaints about fire safety were lodged with the Secretary of Labor. These same reports were lodged again in 1923, this time to the Immigration Commissioner. On August 12, 1940, the administration building caught fire and was destroyed. Soon after, detainees and officials were moved to San Francisco, as it was apparent that Angel Island could no longer serve as an adequate immigration station.

World War II and Beyond

In 1941, the facilities became the North Garrison of Fort McDowell. With the start of World War II, the immigration barracks were turned into a prisoner of war (POW) processing center. Here, German and Japanese POWs were processed before being sent to the mainland United States for detention. The first POW captured by American armed forces in World War II arrived at Angel Island in March 1942. Japanese

Navy Ensign Kazuo Sakamaki was brought to Angel Island from Pearl Harbor, Hawaii. He was the captain of one of the five midget submarines that were part of the attack on December 7, 1941, and was the sole survivor.

In addition to POWs, Fort McDowell housed Japanese enemy aliens during World War II. The men arrested were aliens who had been monitored before the war and classified into custodial detention lists, or ABC lists. The ABC lists designated those individuals whom the government viewed as potential threats, should war break out. Many of these men were arrested on the very same day as the bombing of Pearl Harbor. The men all held positions that could be seen as powerful within Japanese communities. They were community leaders, journalists, ministers (mostly of the Buddhist and Shinto denominations), people who worked with the Japanese consulates to help the adjustment of Japanese immigrants, shopkeepers, farmers, photographers, and others who were members of kendo and other martial arts clubs or contributed to organizations seen by the U.S. government as "pro-Japan" (Angel Island 2017). Around 600 of these men came from Hawaii, and around 98 men were mainland Japanese immigrants. Many of these men remained as internees under the control of both the U.S. Army and the Department of Justice and were held for the duration of the war.

The Poetry that Saved Angel Island

After the immigration station closed in 1940, the island was used as a military base. The buildings that constituted the station fell into disrepair and were scheduled for demolition. But in 1970, California state park ranger Alexander Weiss discovered poems carved into the wall of the detention center. He notified officials in the park system, but interest was lacking, and the demolition was slated to continue. Weiss next contacted a professor at San Francisco State University, Dr. George Araki. Araki and photographer Mak Takahashi visited the island and documented the carvings. Their findings gained the notice of the Asian American community in San Francisco, and the Angel Island Immigration Station Historical Advisory Committee (AIISHAC) was formed, led by Paul Chow. In 1976, the California state legislature allotted $250,000 to save the immigration station, including the poetry held within, and to designate Angel Island a state monument.

The poems that were saved were written exclusively by men, many from villages in the Pearl River delta region in Guangdong Province in southern China. Although many of the poems were written anonymously, they reflect the feelings of the men detained—defiance, anger, despair, and in some cases, hope. They provide a glimpse into the thoughts and experiences of Chinese immigrants at Angel

Island. These poems were written in the classical style that was popularized in the Tang Dynasty (618–907 CE). There are reports of poems written by women, but they were lost to history when the administrative building, where the women were housed, burned in 1940. Some of the men's poetry has subsequently been copied down and printed.

The act of carving into the walls of Angel Island to leave one's mark did not stop with the removal of Chinese immigrants. Japanese POWs and enemy aliens held at Angel Island left their mark just as the Chinese immigrants had before them. On the second floor of the detention barracks, Japanese prisoners produced a second set of wall carvings. In stark contrast to the Chinese poems, the Japanese carvings can be described as "little known, terse, and most unpoetic" (Soennichsen 2005, 138). One example of the Japanese carvings reads "November 7, 1945, at 12 o'clock. Headed for Yokohama in homeland—approximately 700 . . . from McCoy [Camp McCoy, Wisconsin] Internment Camp leaving San Francisco" (Soennichsen 2005, 138). Again, individuals felt the need to document their history on the walls of Angel Island as a means of expressing their plight, loneliness, and frustration.

Angel Island and Immigration Today

The Angel Island Immigration Station Foundation has worked in partnership with the California State Parks system to educate the public about immigration to the Pacific Coast and raise much-needed funds for the ongoing restoration and preservation of the immigration station. In 2008, the barracks building was reopened to the public as a museum where visitors can learn about the experiences of Asian immigrants during their journeys to new lives in America.

The plight of immigrants at Angel Island was created by the passage of laws designed to exclude based on race and a conceived inferiority bred by decades of anti-Chinese rhetoric and sentiment. Immigration laws did not bring immigrants onto equal footing until the passage of the Immigration and Nationality Act of 1965, also known as the Hart-Celler Act, which abolished the earlier quota system based on national origin and instituted a new immigration policy based on uniting families and attracting skilled labor into the United States.

Executive Order 13780, followed by Proclamation 9647 in 2017 (widely known as the Muslim travel bans), discriminates against minorities, separates families, and promotes intolerance based on both religion and country of origin. This targeted detention and banning of certain groups is a reminder of what Asian immigrants faced when coming to America in the 19th and 20th centuries. As of the writing of this entry, the Supreme Court has yet to rule on President Trump's ban, which bars entry into the United States for residents of six majority-Muslim countries. This is in direct conflict with the Immigration and Nationality Act of 1965.

Biographies of Notable Figures

Katharine Maurer (1881–1962), the "Angel of Angel Island"

Deaconess Katharine Maurer spent more than 20 years ferrying from San Francisco to Angel Island to minister and lend her support to detainees. Appointed in 1912 by the United Methodist Episcopal Church, Maurer was a source of comfort to the thousands who passed through Angel Island until its closing in 1940. In addition to supplying daily necessities like toiletries and clothing, she taught English and held classes in American customs, visited both men and women in the hospital, and was generally considered a comforting presence in stark contrast to the conditions on Angel Island. She became known as the "Angel of Angel Island."

Although not employed by immigration officials, Maurer was eventually given an office in the administration building that also included a library. She had the support and assistance of local community organizations, including the Daughters of the American Revolution, the YMCA, and the YWCA. Maurer is described in an article for a women's magazine: "So she sits, day after day, in the early morning with a group of Oriental girls about her, teaching them English; the first schooling they have in America. And the Methodist Episcopal Church ought to be happy that the first schooling and the first impressions these girls receive are from a great-souled Christian woman" (*Woman's Home Missions* 1920, 11).

See also: California Gold Rush, 1848–1855; The Chinese Exclusion Act, 1882; Japanese American Internment, 1942–1946

DOCUMENT EXCERPTS

Excerpts from Mary Bamford, Angel Island: The Ellis Island of the West (1917)

Together with other Baptist missionaries, Mary Bamford visited Angel Island frequently. They met with immigrants, distributed Bibles in their native languages, and offered English language lessons. Bamford's book Angel Island: The Ellis Island of the West *was first published in 1917 and now has been digitalized by California Historical Society and California Digital Library. As the excerpt below shows, her book describes the journey to Angel Island, the buildings, and the immigrants she met there. In their effort of spreading Christianity, missionaries like Bamford helped new immigrants settle in America.*

Chapter 1

Angel Island

When a vessel bearing immigrants to California sails into San Francisco Bay, through the Golden Gate, anchorage is made off Meiggs' wharf, the vessel signals by whistling, and the immigration officials go aboard. The vessel proceeds to its dock in San Francisco, where first-cabin passengers land, but all others are sent to Angel Island, which corresponds to Ellis Island of the Eastern Coast.

To visit Angel Island, we first obtain a pass from the Commissioner of Immigration. On a visiting day, Tuesday or Friday, we go to Pier No. 7, San Francisco, to take the Angel Island Immigration Service boat, which makes several trips a day. We wait, toward the end of the long covered shed, for the coming boat. The cry of sea-gulls is in the air, bells or whistles sound from different vessels, Chinese and Japanese wander about.

The immaculate white boat for Angel Island comes alongside with its American, Japanese, and Chinese passengers. As they are discharged, the other Americans, Japanese and Chinese, who have been waiting, pass up the gangway and start on their journey.

...

The Japanese. The Japanese girls with the Japanese young men in one section are "picture=brides," with their prospective bridegrooms and their friends. [...]

Our guide leads us from the main room of the Administration Building into a long curving passageway, made secure by wire netting on the side opening outdoors, and we are ushered into the large dining=room for immigrants. Long, clean rows of tables stretch parallel to one another across the width of the room.

The Chinese Detention Building.—Sometimes one may find here a group of little Chinese boys, eating with chopsticks. High above the first table is a notice in Chinese, warning the Chinese not to make trouble, nor to spill food on the floor. Off this dining-room, we pass into the fine kitchen that has cost many hundreds of dollars. Everything is cooked by steam-heat. Two shining copper boilers are for the ever-necessary tea of which the Oriental is so fond. The cooks are Chinese.

...

The Koreans.—Another and very interesting oriental race to be found in California, although in small numbers, is the Korean. As very few of them are now coming to this country, I have never seen them at Angel Island. I have often met them, however, in my work...

Source: Bamford, Mary. *Angel Island: The Ellis Island of the West.* Chicago: The Women's American Baptist Home Mission Society, 1917, 1, 15–16, 22.

Further Reading

Angel Island Immigration Station Foundation. 2004. "Angel Island Immigrant Journeys: Historical Background." https://static1.squarespace.com/static/5a81dadde9bfdff9a97b0da7/t/5a85d417e4966b2bd40d3595/1518720025581/Curriculum_Guide_Historical_Background.pdf

Angel Island Immigration Station Foundation. 2017. "Japanese American Detainees on Angel Island in World War II." https://www.aiisf.org/history

Angel Island Immigration Station Foundation. 2018. "History of Angel Island Immigration Station." https://www.aiisf.org/history

Barde, Robert. 2004. "An Alleged Wife: One Immigrant in the Chinese Exclusion Era." *Prologue: Quarterly of the National Archives and Records Administration* 36, no. 1: 25–35.

Barde, Robert Eric. 2008. *Immigration at the Golden Gate: Passenger Ships, Exclusion, and Angel Island.* Westport, CT: Praeger.

Barde, Robert. 2013. "Angel Island and the Control of Immigrant Entry at San Francisco." In *Transforming America: Perspectives on U.S. Immigration*, edited by Michael C. LeMay, vol. 2, *The Transformation of a Nation of Nations: 1865 to 1945*, 151–73. Santa Barbara, CA: Praeger.

Chan, Sucheng, ed. 1991. *Entry Denied: Exclusion and the Chinese Community in America, 1882–1943.* Philadelphia: Temple University Press.

Chinese American Museum. 2018. http://camla.org/chinese-exclusion-act

Daniels, Roger. 1997. "No Lamps Were Lit for Them: Angel Island and the Historiography of Asian American Immigration." *Journal of American Ethnic History* 17, no. 1: 3–18.

Lai, Him Mark. 1978. "Island of the Immortals: Angel Island Immigration Station and the Chinese Immigrants." *California History* 57, no. 1 (Spring): 88–103.

Lai, Him Mark, Genny Lim, and Judy Yung. 1980. *Island: Poetry and History of Chinese Immigrants on Angel Island 1910–1940.* San Francisco: History of Chinese Detained on Island.

Lau, Estelle T. 2006. *Paper Families: Identity, Immigration Administration, and Chinese Exclusion.* Durham, NC: Duke University Press.

Lee, Erika. 2003. *At America's Gates.* Chapel Hill: The University of North Carolina Press.

Lee, Erika. 2010. *Angel Island: Immigrant Gateway to America.* Oxford, UK: Oxford University Press.

Nakamura, Kelli. 2014. "Picture Brides." Densho Encyclopedia. http://encyclopedia.densho.org/Picture%20brides/

Natale, Valerie. 1998. "Angel Island: 'Guardian of the Western Gate.'" *Prologue: Quarterly of the National Archives and Records Administration* 30, no. 2: 125–135.

Sakovich, Maria. 2011. "Deaconess Katharine Maurer: 'A First-Class Favourite Anytime.'" *The Argonaut: Journal of the San Francisco Museum and Historical Society* 22, no. 1 (Spring 2011): 6–27.

Soennichsen, John. 2005. *Miwoks to Missiles: A History of Angel Island.* Tiburon, CA: Angel Island Association.

U.S. Department of Labor. 1920. Bureau of Immigration. *Annual Report of the Commissioner General of Immigration to the Secretary of Labor, Fiscal Year Ended June 30, 1920.* Washington, D.C.: Government Printing Office. https://hdl.handle.net/2027/uiug .30112004080088

Woman's Home Missions. 1920. Editorial: "Immigrants from the Far East." *Woman's Home Missions* 37, vol. 1, 10–11. https://books.google.com/books?id=c3bQAAAAMAAJ&dq =women%27s%20home%20mission%20volumes%2037-38&pg=PA10#v=onepage&q &f=false

Yu, Connie Young. 1977. "Rediscovered Voices: Chinese Immigrants and Angel Island." *Amerasia Journal* 4, no. 2: 123–139.

Yung, Judy. 1991. "Detainment at Angel Island: An Interview with Koon T. Lau." In *Chinese America: History and Perspectives, 1991*, 157–166. San Francisco: Chinese Historical Society of America.

Yung, Judy and Erika Lee. 2015. "Angel Island Immigration Station." *Oxford Research Encyclopedia of American History.* doi: 10.1093/acrefore/9780199329175.013.36. https:// apps.cla.umn.edu/directory/items/publication/338748.pdf

The First Sikh Gurdwara in the United States Established in Stockton, California, 1912

Harveen Sachdeva Mann

Chronology

1897   Soldiers of the Sikh Lancers and Infantry Division of the British army travel across Canada following their participation in Queen Victoria's Diamond Jubilee celebrations in London.

1899   Four Sikh soldiers of the British Royal Artillery are allowed to land in San Francisco.

1903–1906   Twenty Asian Indians immigrate to North America in 1903; 258 follow in 1904, and 150 more arrive in 1905. By 1906, approximately 600 Indians, most of them Sikhs from Punjab, have applied for entry to the United States from Vancouver.

1904   The *Guru Granth Sahib*, the holy book of the Sikhs, is brought to North America for the first time.

1905   Several hundred Sikhs work on the Western Pacific Railway in northern California. Over the next several years, 2,000 Sikhs build roads, tunnels, and bridges from Oakland, California to Salt Lake City, Utah. They also work on the Panama Canal.

1906	The first North American Sikh organization, the Khalsa Diwan Society, is established in Vancouver.
1906–1922	The "Hindoo Alley," including Hindus, Sikhs, and Muslims, is established in Astoria, Oregon.
1907	Anti-Hindu riots break out in Bellingham, Washington, where 500 white lumberjacks attack 250 Sikh mill workers and destroy their property. Many flee to Canada, where they are arrested.
1907	The Asiatic Exclusion League (AEL) is formed in San Francisco.
1908	The first Sikh gurdwara in North America opens in Vancouver.
1908	The Canadian government, in concert with the AEL, effectively bans the entry of Indians into Canada by passing the "continuous journey" council order.
1909	"The Awakening of the Sikhs" takes place, in which they refuse to wear British war medals or to hold British military ranks.
1911	Sardar Wasakha Singh and Bhai Jawala Singh head a meeting in Holt, near Stockton, California, to form a Sikhs unit, one of the first Sikh societies in the United States, and to raise funds to buy a gurdwara property.
1912	The Pacific Coast Khalsa Diwan Society is founded.
1912	Land is purchased on South Grant Street in Stockton, and the small frame house on the lot is inaugurated as the Pacific Coast Khalsa Diwan Society Gurdwara Sahib. The Guru Granth Sahib is installed with full honors, and the Nishan Sahib (the Sikh religious flag) is hoisted. Baba Wasakha Singh and Baba Jawala Singh Thathian (originally from Amritsar, India) serve as the first granthis (priests).
1913	The Webb-Haney Act, also known as the Alien Land Law of California, prohibits Asian Indian ownership and long-term leases of agricultural land.
1913	The first meeting of the Ghadar ("Revolutionary") Party is held in Astoria, Washington. Its international efforts to end British rule in India lead to the San Francisco "Hindu Conspiracy" trial in 1917–1918.
1914	The Japanese ship *Komagata Maru*, carrying mostly Sikh passengers, arrives in Vancouver on May 23. All but a handful of the passengers are turned away.
1915	Two new buildings of the Stockton gurdwara, designed by W. B. Thomas and built by A. J. McPhee, are dedicated. They are the earliest Indian religious buildings in the United States.

1917	The Asiatic Barred Zone and literacy test legislation discriminates against Asian Indians, with legal immigration coming to a virtual halt for the next 30 years. By this time, though, 6,000 to 7,000 Asian Indians have immigrated to the United States.
1920s	Sikhs lease more than 32,000 acres of land in Southern California's Imperial Valley. Prohibited from bringing wives from India, many of them marry Mexican women, giving rise to a sizable Mexican Sikh population.
1923	The Bhagat Singh Thind case, *United States v. Thind*, comes to trial.
1925	Pakhar Singh murders two white Americans who, under California's discriminatory Alien Land Law, had cheated him out of substantial payment for his leased land. Singh is, however, convicted only of second-degree murder because his action is deemed justified to an extent.
1929	The new Stockton gurdwara is built.
1946	The Luce-Celler Act is signed into law by President Harry S. Truman, giving Asian Indians the right to become naturalized U.S. citizens. The act sets a quota of 100 Indians and 100 Filipinos to immigrate to the United States per year.
1956	Dalip Singh Saund is elected the first Sikh, Indian, and Asian American member of Congress.
1965	President Lyndon B. Johnson signs the landmark immigration reform bill Hart-Celler Act. The act abolishes the 1924 quota system based on national origins, which directed nearly 70 percent of immigration slots to Northern Europeans. The act also gives preference to skilled workers and professionals from around the globe.
1965–1975	After 1965, highly educated Sikhs immigrate to the United States, and the U.S.-Sikh community increases fourfold in a single decade. By 1975, more than 8,000 Sikhs have become U.S. citizens.
1966–1969	New Sikh gurdwaras open apace in Los Angeles, San Francisco, New York, Chicago, Detroit, Houston, Palo Alto, Yuba City, Washington, D.C., and other U.S. cities.
1968	Yogi Bhajan (Harbhajan Singh Khalsa) founds the Sikh Dharma Brotherhood in Los Angeles. The movement, now known as 3HO (Healthy, Happy, Holy Organization), has more than 120 yoga and meditation centers around the globe.

1984   Indian troops, under orders from Prime Minister Indira Gandhi, attack Harmandir Sahib (Golden Temple), the Sikhs' holiest shrine in Amritsar, to rout Sant Jarnail Singh Bhindranwale's separatist Khalistani followers. In the wake of this devastation, the World Sikh Organization is established in the United States to protect the political, religious, and human rights of Sikhs worldwide. The newspaper *World Sikh News* begins publication in Stockton.

1988   The first Sikh Day Parade is held in New York City to celebrate Baisakhi, the Sikh New Year.

1996   The Sikh Mediawatch and Resource Task Force (SMART), later renamed the Sikh American Legal Defense and Education Fund (SALDEF), is founded. It is now the oldest Sikh civil rights and educational organization in the United States.

2001   Following the 9/11 attacks, U.S. Sikhs become targets of anti-Muslim hate crimes, mainly because observant Sikh males wear turbans and sport beards resembling those of conservative Muslims.

2004   The "Sikhs: Legacy of the Punjab" permanent exhibition opens at the Sikh Heritage Gallery in the National Museum of Natural History at the Smithsonian in Washington, D.C.

2004   The White House marks the 400th anniversary of the installation of the Guru Granth Sahib in the Golden Temple, Amritsar, India.

2009   Preet Bharara is appointed U.S. attorney for the Southern District of New York, a position he held until 2017.

2009   Kashmir Gill of Yuba City, California, is the first Sikh to be elected mayor in the United States, a post he is re-elected to in 2013.

2012   The Sikh History Museum, Library, and Heritage Center opens in the Gadri Baba Building of the Stockton gurdwara.

2012   The Punjabi American Heritage Society inaugurates its "Becoming American" exhibit in the Sutter County Museum in Yuba City.

2012   In August, a neo-Nazi and U.S. Army veteran gunman kills six congregants at the Oak Creek, Wisconsin, gurdwara and wounds four others before being killed.

2012   United Sikhs, a United Nations (UN)–affiliated nongovernmental organization (NGO) dedicated to protecting and advancing the civil rights and liberties of all Americans, hosts Sikh Summit 2012 in the wake of the gurdwara killings in Wisconsin and increasing hate crimes and xenophobia against Sikhs.

2012	The Sikh Journey in America Conference is hosted at the University of the Pacific in Stockton to mark the centennial celebration of the founding of the Stockton gurdwara.
2017	Nimrata "Nikki" Haley, nee Randhawa, born to an Indian American Sikh family, is sworn in as the U.S. ambassador to the UN. She previously served in the South Carolina House of Representatives and as governor of South Carolina.
2018	Gurbir Singh Grewal of New Jersey becomes the first Sikh to hold the position of attorney general in the United States.

Narrative

By 1912, a few thousand Sikhs had immigrated to North America. Their immigration started in 1897 as a way to escape harsh British colonial practices in their home state of Punjab. Later, they immigrated to escape fighting in Europe in World War I. They settled primarily in Vancouver, Canada; Bellingham, Washington; and the San Joachin and Imperial Valleys in central and southern California. The Stockton *gurdwara* ("a doorway to the guru"), the earliest permanent Sikh settlement built in the United States, first held services on October 24, 1912, a year that marked the 426th anniversary of the birth of the founder of Sikhism, Guru Nanak. That same year, Woodrow Wilson was elected U.S. president, New Mexico and Arizona were admitted as the 48th and 49th states, Alaska became incorporated as a U.S. territory, and Japan sent thousands of cherry trees to Washington, D.C., as a gift. Meanwhile, half a world away, India was still a British colony ruled by George V.

Working on the Western Pacific Railway and the lumber mills, Sikhs, along with other Asian immigrants, faced grave racism in the early 20th century, which culminated in the appalling 1907 Anti-"Hindu" riot in which 250 mill workers were beaten by some 500 white lumberjacks and driven out of Bellingham. This was followed by the formation of the Asiatic Exclusion League (AEL) in 1907, which advocated for the prohibition of Asian labor immigration in order to keep the United States a "white man's country." After this, Sikh migration shifted south to California. Taking naturally to farming, as they had done in their native Punjab, these early Sikh pioneers, as they have come to be known, began as farmhands, gradually leasing and even buying vast tracts of agricultural land.

To support the influx of Sikhs and Punjabis generally and to help them contend with rampant discrimination, the Pacific Coast Khalsa Diwan ("Free Divine Commission") Society was established in Stockton in 1912 under the leadership of Teja Singh. In cooperation with Jawala Singh and Wasakha Singh—who, having immigrated to the United States in 1908, had become successful farmers owning 500 acres on the Holt River and had already established the Sri Guru Gobind Singh Educational Scholarship for Indians to attend the University of California at Berkeley—Teja Singh also founded the Stockton gurdwara, with Jawala Singh and Wasakha Singh serving as the first granthis, or priests. (A more precise definition of the term granthi is "one who reads from the *Guru Granth*," the holy book of the Sikhs, and who is considered the caretaker of the gurdwara.) Even though at the time Sikhs could not buy land individually, they held title to the gurdwara property free and clear in the name of the Sikh sangat, or community. They continued to serve the sangat as the only U.S. gurdwara for the next three and a half decades until the El Centro, California, gurdwara opened in 1948.

The Ghadar Party

It is impossible to talk about the Stockton gurdwara as the spiritual home for Sikh immigrants without also talking about its involvement in the Indian independence movement as the home of the Ghadar ("Revolutionary") Party. Long before Mohandas "Mahatma" Gandhi appeared on the national scene, the Indians of the Pacific Coast, most of them Sikh, driven by the American founding fathers' vision of freedom from colonial rule, committed themselves to bringing an end to British colonialism in their natal country through armed conflict, if necessary. But as they themselves, ironically, faced harsh race- and religion-based discrimination in an anticolonial but racist United States, they soon realized that only as people from a free country could they fight for equality in the West and lead lives of dignity and self-respect. Whereas the Japanese government had come to the aid of its citizens and even received compensation and a promise of protection against racist policies from the U.S. government, the Indians could hardly turn to the British colonial government in India for protection and had no one to rely on but themselves.

Thus, in April 1913, Wasakha Singh and Jawala Singh, along with Santokh Singh and Sohan Singh Bhakna and a handful of Indian students at the University of California at Berkeley, convened the Ghadar Party in Astoria, Oregon. In November that year, 17-year old Kartar Singh Sarabha, a newly arrived student at Berkeley, published the first weekly copy of *The Ghadar*, the first Punjabi-language newspaper in the United States, with the financial support of the Stockton gurdwara. Later published in several other Indian languages, the newspaper had a global circulation, distributed as it was by other Ghadarites in gurdwaras as far afield as Vancouver, Shanghai, Hong Kong, and Singapore. While upholding the ideals of social justice, democracy, economic freedom and equality, and the peaceful coexistence of nations, *The Ghadar* did not hesitate to advocate a violent uprising against the British, while also providing practical guidance in the use of weapons and explosives to its audience.

Joined by leaders of other faiths from different parts of India—the Hindus Har Dayal, Rash Behari Bose, Tarak Nath Das, and Vishnu Ganesh Pingle, and the Muslims Mohamed Barakatullah and Husain Rahim, among others—the Ghadarites combined their ideological resistance to the race and class discrimination against Indians in the United States on one hand and the British colonial oppression of India as a nation on the other to initiate the first organized and militant resistance movement since India's First War of Independence in 1857. Known variously as the Sepoy/Indian Mutiny (by the British colonizers) and the First War of Independence (by contemporary Indians), the rebellion of 1857 was a major, though ultimately unsuccessful, uprising against the East India Company's oppressive system of land taxes, annexation of Hindu princely states, support of Christian missionary activity, and Western-style social reforms. As Maia Ramnath points out in her meticulously researched study of the Ghadar movement and global radicalism, "Much of the power of the [Indian] independence struggle was incubated outside the territory of British India in expatriate intellectual circles in London, Paris, Berlin, and San Francisco" (2011, 1), as well as in Gandhi's early career in South Africa and among members of the Pan-Islamic Khilafat and Communist International movements. But much of this power was "routed, sooner or later, along the channels of a circulatory system with its heart in California, headquarters of the Ghadar movement" (Ramnath 2011, 2), in which the Stockton gurdwara played a preeminent role.

The Komagata Maru *Incident*

Early in the 20th century, Canada accepted hundreds of thousands of North European immigrants, but to keep nonwhites (especially Indians) out, Canada's government passed an order-in-council prohibiting the immigration of persons who did not "come from the country of their birth or citizenship by a continuous journey." Since the sea voyage from India could not be made without stopovers, this effectively shut down Indian immigration to Canada. In an effort to keep Canada white, the government also attempted to resettle Indians in Honduras (then a British colony) but was unsuccessful in getting them to leave voluntarily.

In a plan conceived to circumvent the 1908 Canadian "continuous journey" legislation, Gurdit Singh, a supporter of the Ghadar rebels, arranged for 376 passengers, among them 340 Sikhs from Punjab, to set sail in summer 1914 from British Hong Kong via Shanghai and Yokohama to Vancouver. The Sikhs, many of whom had fought in China and Japan as conscripted British soldiers, were fleeing the oppression of agricultural colonization in Punjab. When their ship, the *Komagata Maru* (renamed the *Guru Nanak Jahaz*) reached Canada, 352 of the passengers were not allowed to disembark on the grounds of their alleged Ghadar sympathies. After two months and a violent standoff at Vancouver harbor, they were turned back to sea. The tragedy was compounded when, on their return to Calcutta, more than 20 of them were killed by British soldiers, while others were arrested and imprisoned or kept under house/village arrest until the end of World War I.

Using the *Komagata Maru* incident as a rallying point, the Ghadar leaders continued their fight for immigration and civil rights in Canada and the United States and for Indian independence by radicalizing students and workers. They drew their inspiration from eclectic sources, both Eastern and Western: from Guru Gobind Singh, the 10th Sikh guru, to George Washington, Rana Partap and Garibaldi, and Sivaji and the Fenians. Although the planned uprising in February 1915 was vanquished by the first Lahore Conspiracy Case trials—in which 42 of the 291 convicted conspirators were executed and most of the others imprisoned for life—the socialism and labor unionism they had embraced and propagated had ripple effects among later Indian as well as Irish and Egyptian revolutionists, reverberating beyond the nation-state and diaspora to rally for freedom around the world.

The 2012 Stockton Gurdwara Centennial Celebrations

In September and October 2012, the Stockton gurdwara marked its 100th anniversary with a weeks-long celebration, which paid homage to the Sikh pioneers who had lived and fought for immigration and citizenship rights, civil rights, family reunification, and land ownership, not only for Sikhs but also for South Asians and Asian Americans broadly, and who had launched India's first organized revolutionary campaign for independence from British colonialism. To honor the sacrifices and bravery of those heroes who paved the way for the approximately 500,000 Sikhs currently in the United States (of 25 million worldwide), the centennial celebrations were organized into four constituent parts: the Sikh Journey in America Conference on September 22; the inauguration of the Sikh History Museum, Library, and Heritage Center on September 22; the Voyage of the Ghadar: An Eastern Perspective Conference, held a week after the English-language Sikh Journey in America Conference; and the Community Centennial Celebration on the October 13–14 weekend.

Biographies of Notable Figures

Bhagat Singh Thind (1892–1967)

Dr. Bhagat Singh Thind's life and legacy are monumental in the history of Asian America not only because of his tireless and multiple attempts to secure U.S. citizenship but also because of his many other unparalleled achievements. Early in the

20th century, he earned a PhD in divinity from the University of California at Berkeley and went on to write and lecture widely in the United States. He served as the first turbaned Sikh soldier in the U.S. Army, and he worked as general secretary of the Ghadar Party from 1916 to 1917.

Born in the village of Taragarh in Amritsar District, Punjab, in colonial India in 1892, Thind sought higher education in the United States in 1913. He paid his way through Berkeley by working summers in lumber mills in Astoria, Oregon, in what was known as "Hindoo Alley." While still an Indian citizen, he joined the U.S. Army to fight in World War I. Promoted to the rank of acting sergeant, he received an honorable discharge at the end of the war and also received his U.S. citizenship certificate from the state of Washington in December 1918. However, the Immigration and Naturalization Service (INS) revoked his citizenship four days later on the grounds that he was not a "free white man."

Thind reapplied for citizenship from neighboring Oregon in May 1919 and was granted citizenship a second time in November 1920, over the objections of the same INS official who had revoked his earlier certificate based on his being an Indian "Hindoo" and therefore not white and his membership in the Ghadar Party, which advocated for Indian independence from Britain, a close ally of the United States. This time the INS appealed the ruling to the U.S. Supreme Court, which, on reconsideration of the "common man's" definition of "white" as not applying to Caucasians like Thind, as well as the retroactive application of the Asiatic Barred Zone Act of 1917, rescinded Thind's citizenship once more in 1923.

But again Thind persevered, and in 1936, he was finally granted U.S. citizenship through a law that allowed nonwhite veterans to retain citizenship. His case opened the door for more progressive immigration laws. Following this, he was ordained as a minister of the Builders of Aquarius Church and issued a certificate of ordination as a Sikh gyanee and parcharak (scholar and preacher) from the Stockton gurdwara, enabling him to write and to lecture on metaphysics until his death in 1967. Drawing on his knowledge of the Sikh scriptures and philosophy, as well as the Hindu Vedas, the 15th-century Indian mystic Kabir, and American transcendentalists Ralph Waldo Emerson, Walt Whitman, and Henry David Thoreau, Thind traveled the length and breadth of the country, addressing audiences in Boston, New York City, Philadelphia, and Washington, D.C., among others. In addition, he authored more than a dozen books, including the three-volume *Jesus, the Christ: In the Light of Spiritual Science* and *Divine Wisdom*, also in three volumes.

On the secular front, very soon after his arrival in the United States, Thind joined other Indian delegates from California, Oregon, Washington, and Canada as a member of the Hindu Association of the Pacific Coast, which eventually became the Ghadar movement and the Ghadar Party. In his role as general secretary of the organization, he delivered speeches across Oregon advocating India's independence from Britain. For this involvement, Thind was placed under surveillance by the British Intelligence Agency, an act that greatly complicated his application for citizenship.

In 1940, Thind married Vivian Davies of Toledo, Ohio, with whom he had two children, David and Rosalind. The Thinds visited India in 1963, where they were enthusiastically received by Prime Minister Jawaharlal Nehru. Thind also gave several high-profile lectures, such as those at Delhi University and Panjab University, where he spoke about "What America Means to Me."

Thind passed away in California in September 1967, remembered by the Hindustan (India) Ghadar Party Memorial Committee as "not just a man, but an institution . . . this great soul of piety and devotion, whose concern for his native country and countrymen is as deep as his faith in the teachings of the Sikh gurus . . . an outstanding patriot and humanitarian . . . with [whom] by our side . . . we shall overcome, we shall never fail" (*The Call of the Martyrs* 1967).

Thind's rich legacy lives on in multiple ways in both the United States and India. During his life, Thind paid for the higher education of 86 students, both in India and the United States (at Harvard, Stanford, and the University of Southern California), with many of his U.S.-educated mentees returning to India to become lawyers, doctors, and even members of Parliament. Following his death, his wife and many of his students and followers established the annual Dr. Bhagat Singh Thind Spiritual Science Foundation Scholarship at his alma mater in India, Khalsa College, Amritsar, to enable underprivileged students to obtain college educations. In 2006, the Punjabi American Festival in Yuba City, California, honored Thind for his tireless efforts on behalf of South Asians fighting for U.S. citizenship rights. And each year, the Sikh American Legal Defense and Education Fund gives the Bhagat Singh Thind Community Empowerment Award to a Sikh best demonstrating the Sikh spirit and tradition of Seva (selfless service).

Dalip Singh Saund (1899–1973)

Like Bhagat Singh Thind, Dalip Singh Saund was born near Amritsar, in Chhajulwadi village, in colonial India in 1899. Like Thind, he came to the United States in 1920 to study at the University of California at Berkeley, where he obtained a master's degree and a doctorate in mathematics. As with many other newly arrived Sikhs of his generation, while at Berkeley he lived in the Guru Nanak Khalsa Hostel, which was owned and run by the Stockton gurdwara and which also funded Saund's studies. It was at Berkeley too that Saund was first initiated into politics, becoming president of the Hindustani Association of America, an organization committed to Indian independence from Britain.

In 1930, the Stockton gurdwara commissioned Saund to write a response to American historian Katherine Mayo's 1927 polemic, *Mother India*, which declared India unfit for self-rule and independence on the grounds of its (purported) social backwardness rooted in the practices of Hinduism, especially as they related to the low status accorded to women and the plight of child wives. Saund's *My Mother India* (1930), which he dedicated to his "beloved friend Dr. Bhagat Singh Thind," went far beyond providing merely a "comprehensive reply" to Mayo's book, offering instead a "handbook on India for general use by the American public" (Saund 1930). Drawing on the works of Mohandas Gandhi, Rabindranath Tagore, and Sarojini Naidu, among others, Saund addressed not only the position of Indian women and the caste system—which he compared to racism in the United States and elsewhere—but also the civilization and ethics of India and the Hindu ideal of marriage, Gandhi and passive resistance, and colonial violence and Indian nationalism.

In 1928, Saund married Marian Kosa, daughter of Czech immigrants, with whom he raised three children and who was to remain a staunch supporter of his future political career. In the 1930s, Saund established himself as a major lettuce farmer and distributor of chemical fertilizers in California's Imperial Valley, as many Sikh Americans of the period did. At the same time, he was lecturing extensively at California civic organizations and churches about India's struggle for independence. In the 1940s, Saund was instrumental in persuading the U.S. Congress to pass the Luce-Celler Act of 1946, which granted immigration and naturalization rights to Indians and Filipinos. But even as he progressed in his political career, he never forgot his debt and commitment to the Stockton gurdwara, serving as general secretary from 1948 to 1950 and as a member of its executive committee until 1953.

In 1949, Saund was himself naturalized as a U.S. citizen, after which he was elected justice of the peace for Westmoreland Township, California, in 1952. In 1955, Saund ran as a Democratic candidate for the U.S. House of Representatives in 1956 and won in a district with very few ethnic voters, thereby also breaking racial barriers to become the first Sikh American, the first Indian American, and the first Asian American to serve in the U.S. Congress the same year that the United States passed the Civil Rights Act of 1957. Remarkable too for not "Americanizing" his name or changing his religion, Saund was reelected to his seat twice, serving almost three full terms before he suffered a major stroke that ended his political career. He died at his home in Hollywood, California in 1973.

In Congress, Saund lobbied for farm subsidies, a balanced national budget, free enterprise for small business owners, flood control and supplemental water for Southern California, and civil rights for immigrants and minorities alike. He served on the influential Foreign Affairs Committee and traveled abroad as a U.S. emissary to Mexico, India (where he was received jubilantly, especially in his ancestral village), Japan, Taiwan, Vietnam, Indonesia, Singapore, and the Philippines. Above all, he campaigned tirelessly for U.S. citizenship for Asian Americans.

Saund's 1960 book *Congressman from India* details what he describes as "the struggles, sorrows and joys, defeats and recoveries of a twenty-year native of India who came to the United States and, nearly two score years later, became a United States congressman" (Saund 1960). Inspired by Abraham Lincoln and Mohandas Gandhi, Saund combined the best of East and West and proved in his life and career to be that ideal American, an immigrant who worked hard, did fairly by others, and who politically "[found] comfort in the Declaration of Independence and hope for mankind in the great inalienable truths expressed in the Bill of Rights" (Saund 1960).

Saund was honored in 2012 in the California legislature's commemoration of the 100-year anniversary of the Sikh American community, and he was described by President Barack Obama as one of those American "trailblazers" who, in the face of hardship, racism, and even ridicule, still "didn't give up . . . didn't make excuses . . . kept forging ahead." "They kept building up America," Obama continued, because though most of them "didn't have belongings," what "they did have was an unshakeable belief that this country—of all countries—is a place where anybody can make it if they try" (Obama 2012).

DOCUMENT EXCERPTS

Dedication of Stockton's Gurdwara

The following document commemorates the dedication of the gurdwara in Stockton, California. It was published in the Stockton Record *on November 22, 1915, and was accompanied by a photo of the gurdwara taken by V. Covert Martin. The Stockton gurdwara was not only a spiritual home for Sikh immigrants but also an important community landmark among South Asian immigrants. It remained the only gurdwara in the United States for over 30 years. In 2012, the gurdwara celebrated its 100th anniversary.*

1915
Stockton Sikh Temple

The new Sikh Temple of the Pacific Coast Khalsa Diwan (free divine communion) Society was dedicated yesterday with impressive ceremonies. The day selected for the formal opening of the new temple, which is located at 1936 South Grant Street, was the 426th anniversary of the birth of Guru Nanak, founder of the faith.
Fully two hundred prominent Stocktonians, to whom special invitations were issued, attended the dedicatory services. No shoe-clad person is permitted to step within the sacred precincts of the Temple. The American residents in conformity with the

customs of the turbaned Hindus, removed their shoes before entering. They were provided with sandals but these were discarded at the door. The congregation sat upon the floor on costly rugs and carpets, facing the altar. There are no chairs or pews in the Sikh temple.

Great Gathering of Sikhs

In the morning services were conducted by priests of the temple in the Sikh language before a gathering of Hindus, about 400 of whom had come to Stockton from outside points to attend the opening. At 1 p.m. the services were resumed with the recitation of sacred hymns, which tell in the Hindu language of the life and teachings of Guru Nanak.

Following the above named service a meeting was held in the temple for Americans as well as Hindus and at this service a large number of Stockton residents as well as visitors from other cities were present. The Americans listed attentively to the explanation of the Sikh creed by Paradaman Singh who delivered an address.

Nand Singh presided as chairman of the meeting and outlined the objects of the society, which is incorporated for religious and educational propaganda in the United States. He explained the teachings of Guru Nanak and likened them to the teachings of the Puritans in the early days of New England.

Professor Pope Speaks

At the conclusion of the service in the temple proper, the American guests retired to the lecture rooms on the first floor of the temple, where several addresses were delivered and a musical program was rendered.

Professor Arthur U. Pope, of the philosophical department of the University of California, delivered the chief address on the meaning and significance of the Sikh movement. The Sikhs are a small minority of the total population of India, but their teachings have wrought a profound influence upon the life of that country. India has a total population of more than 300,000,000, and of these but 5,000,000 are adherents of this faith.

Sikh Opposes Idolatry

The Sikh believes, said Professor Pope, in a pure and lofty Monotheism. And when it is remembered that India has long been a country of many gods, the importance of such teaching can readily be seen. The adherents of this faith are strongly opposed to idol worship as well as to the use of an elaborate ritual.

This rejection of idol worship and the substitutions of the worship of one God which is a Spirit, bids fair to revolutionize the religious life of India, according to Professor Pope.

No Caste

With the rejection of idolatry goes also the repudiation of caste. The Sikh teaches the brotherhood of man and spurns all practice that places one individual above his fellows. This branch of the Hindu race endeavors to carry out this principle of equality by sharing property in common.

Tolerance is another principle of the Sikh religion, said Professor Pope. The Sikh is willing to read and study the religious principles of any other creed, and the scriptures of other sects are always found on their tables.

Based upon these religious principles, the moral teachings of the Sikhs are of a higher order, explained the speaker. In common with Christianity they teach that a man's life should be lived for the benefit of the world. They teach that one should contend for the oppressed even unto death and this principle has made of the Sikh a brave and valiant soldier in time of war.

Equality of Sex

Nand Singh, who presided over the exercises in the lecture room, explained that the Sikhs stand for the equality of the sexes in marked contrast to the ancient belief in the inferiority of woman, held in India.

Professor W.G. Everett, of Brown University, Providence, R.I., was present in the audience, and was called upon for an address. He spoke briefly and informally of the significance of the gathering and bespoke not only toleration but sympathy as well for the efforts being made by the Hindu people.

Other brief addresses were made by members of the Hindu race, and the exercises were concluded with a prayer in the Sikh language by Nand Singh.

The new temple is two stories in height, the temple proper being on the second floor. This is beautifully furnished and carpeted with very fine rugs. The first floor is fitted up with chairs and is arranged as a place for lectures and social gatherings.

It is the hope of the Sikhs to build a larger and finer structure when the time arrives that it shall be needed.

Free Dining Room for Poor

Nand Singh asked the *Record* today to call attention to the fact that the *Pacific Khalsa Diwan Society* maintains a free dining room in connection with its temple on South Grant Street.

"We do not permit our people to become charges on public charity," said Nand Singh. "If a man is hungry and out of funds, we feed him. Our dining room is open at all hours of the day, and is closed only for a few hours during the night. The unfortunate hungry American will be as welcome as our own people. We provide coffee, bread and cake and such other things as possible."

Source: "Stockton Sikh Temple." *Stockton Record,* November 22, 1915.

See also: The Luce-Celler Act, 1946; *United States v. Ghagat Singh Thind,* 1923; 9/11 and Islamophobia, 2001–2018

Further Reading

Backhaus, Bhira. 2012. "A Sikh Temple's Century." *New York Times*, August 7. https://www.nytimes.com/2012/08/08/opinion/a-sikh-temples-proud-history.html

Barrier, N. Gerald and Verne Dusenbery, eds. 1989. *The Sikh Diaspora: Migration and the Experience beyond Punjab.* Columbia, MO: South Asia Publications.

Bhatt, Amy and Nalini Iyer. 2013. *Roots and Reflections: South Asians in the Pacific Northwest.* Seattle: University of Washington Press.

Cahn, David. 2008. "The 1907 Bellingham Riots in Historical Context." University of Washington: Seattle Civil Rights and Labor History Project. http://depts.washington.edu/civilr/bham_history.htm

The Call of the Martyrs: The Bulletin of the Hindustan Gadar Party Memorial Committee, 3, no. 10 (August 1967). https://www.saada.org/item/20110806-291

Coulson, David. 2017. *Race, Nation, and Refuge: The Rhetoric of Race in Asian American Citizenship Cases.* Albany, NY: SUNY Press.

Gould, Harold A. 2006. *Sikhs, Swamis, Students, and Spies: The India Lobby in the United States, 1900–1946.* Thousand Oaks, CA: Sage.

Harvard University. 2018. "The Pluralism Project: Sikhism in America." http://pluralism.org/timeline/sikhism-in-america

La Brack, Bruce. 1988. *The Sikhs of Northern California, 1904–1975.* New York: AMS Press.

Nayar, Kamala Elizabeth. 2004. *The Sikh Diaspora in Vancouver: Three Generations amid Tradition, Modernity, and Multiculturalism.* Toronto: University of Toronto Press.

Nayar, Kamala Elizabeth. 2010. "The Making of Sikh Space: The Role of the Gurdwara." In *Asian Religions in British Columbia*, edited by Larry DeVries, et al., 43–63. Vancouver: UBC Press.

Obama, Barack. 2012. "Remarks by the President at the 18th Annual Gala for the Asian Pacific American Institute for Congressional Studies" (speech, Ritz Carlton, Washington, D.C., May 8). https://obamawhitehouse.archives.gov/the-press-office/2012/05/08/remarks-president-18th-annual-gala-asian-pacific-american-institute-cong

Ramnath, Maia. 2011. *Haj to Utopia: How the Ghadar Movement Charted Global Radicalism and Attempted to Overthrow the British Empire.* Berkeley: University of California Press.

Regents of the University of California. 2016. "Pioneering Punjabis Digital Archive: A New Resource Documenting the History of the South Asian Pioneers in California, 1899-Present." https://pioneeringpunjabis.ucdavis.edu

Saund, Dalip Singh. 1930. Preface to *My Mother India*. Stockton, CA: Pacific Coast Khalsa Diwan Society (Sikh temple). http://www.saund.org/dalipsaund/mmi/my-mother-india.pdf

Saund, Dalip Singh. 1960. Preface to *Congressman from India*. New York: E. P. Dutton. http://www.saund.org/dalipsaund/cfi/cfi.html

Shani, Giorgio. 2008. *Sikh Nationalism and Identity in a Global Age*. London: Routledge.

Sidhu, Gurmel Singh. 2015. *Another Aspect of the Ghadar Movement: The Struggle for American Citizenship and Property Ownership*. Anaheim, CA: Shri Guru Granth Sahib Foundation.

Sikh Foundation International. 2018. www.sikhfoundation.org

Sikh Journey in America Conference. 2012. "'Sikh Journey in America': Abstracts of 19 Scholarly Papers on the Centennial Celebration of Pacific Coast Khalsa Diwan Society, Gurdwara Sahib, Stockton, CA, USA." Stockton, CA: Pacific Coast Khalsa Diwan Society.

Sikh Pioneers. 2018. "Preserving the Sikh Pioneers Journey to North America." https://www.sikhpioneers.org

Singh, Nirvikar. 2016. "Cosmopolitanism, Tradition and Identity: Framing the Sikh Experience in California." *Sikh Research Journal* 1, no. 5: 1–16. http://www.sikhfoundation.org/sikh-research-journal

Singh, Pashaura and N. Gerald Barrier. 1996. *The Transmission of Sikh Heritage in the Diaspora*. New Delhi: Manohar Publishers.

Sohi, Seema. 2014. "Sites of 'Sedition,' Sites of Liberation: Gurdwaras, the Ghadar Party, and Anticolonial Mobilization." *Sikh Formations* 10, no. 1: 5–22.

Tatla, Darshan Singh. 1991. *Sikhs in North America: An Annotated Bibliography*. New York: Greenwood Press.

Thind, Bhagat Singh. n.d. *DOCTORJI: The Life, Teachings, & Legacy of Dr. Bhagat Singh Thind*. www.bhagatsinghthind.com

U.S. Department of Homeland Security. 1996–2016. "Yearbook of Immigration Statistics." https://www.dhs.gov/immigration-statistics/yearbook

U.S. Department of Justice, Immigration and Naturalization Service. 1978–2001. "Statistical Yearbook of the Immigration and Naturalization Service." https://catalog.hathitrust.org/Record/002973860?type%5B%5D=title&lookfor%5B%5D=%22Yearbook%20of%20immigration%20statistics%22&ft

Zhao, Xiaojian and Edward J. W. Park, eds. *Asian Americans: An Encyclopedia of Social, Cultural, Economic, and Political History* (3 vols.). Santa Barbara, CA: Greenwood, 2014.

The Webb-Haney Act Passed by California State Legislature, 1913

Kaori Mori Want

Chronology

1868 The first Japanese immigrants, or "Gannen Mono," come to Hawaii without government permits to work on the sugarcane plantations.

1870 The Naturalization Act of 1870 is passed. This act limits citizenship to white and black people and prohibits Asians from becoming U.S. citizens.

1881 King of Hawaii Kingdom Kamehameha visits the Meiji Emperor of Japan, and they agree to send Japanese immigrants to Hawaii.

1884 The Meiji Japanese government opens a consulate in Hawaii and starts issuing official permits for citizens to travel abroad. The Japanese laborers who go abroad with the government permit are called "Kanmin Imin" (official immigrants).

1893 The San Francisco Board of Education makes its first attempt to segregate Japanese American children from public schools but withdraws the measure following protests by the Japanese government.

1901 California and Nevada send a request to the federal government to halt Japanese immigration.

1905 The Asiatic Exclusion League (AEL) is organized in San Francisco, California. The main body of the league is white labor union leaders. Feeling threatened by the increase of Japanese laborers and their families, the league launches anti-Japanese movements and spreads anti-Japanese sentiments among Americans on the West Coast.

1906 The San Francisco Board of Education again attempts to exclude Japanese school children from public schools and to relocate them to Chinese schools, but President Theodore Roosevelt intervenes.

1908 Responding to anti-Japanese sentiments in the States, the Gentlemen's Agreement is made between Japan and the United States. The agreement aims to stop the migration of Japanese laborers to the United States, but Japanese women, mainly picture brides, are allowed to immigrate as wives of Japanese men already residing there.

1911 Arizona bans the leasing of land to aliens ineligible for citizenship.

1913 The Webb-Haney Act, also known as the California Alien Land Act, is enacted. The act bans all aliens ineligible for citizenship (mainly Japanese immigrants) from purchasing and leasing land for more than three years.

1920 The Japanese government stops issuing passports to Japanese women, mainly picture brides.

1920 The Alien Land Act of 1920 bans the purchase and lease of land to the offspring of aliens ineligible for citizenship.

1922 *Ozawa v. the United States.* Takao Ozawa applies for naturalized citizenship, but the U.S. Supreme Court denies the application on the condition that Japanese are aliens ineligible for naturalization.

1924 Congress passes the Immigration Act of 1924, which halts Japanese immigration to the United States.

1929 The Japanese American Citizens League is founded to protect the Japanese immigrant community from the anti-Japanese social environment.

1941 The Japanese navy bombs the U.S. naval base at Pearl Harbor in Hawaii. The United States declares war against Japan, and the Pacific theater of World War II begins.

1942 After the Pearl Harbor attacks, President Franklin Roosevelt signs Executive Order 9066, which orders the incarceration of Japanese immigrants on the West Coast and their American offspring for the sake of national security. Approximately 120,000 Japanese immigrants and their children are forced to abandon their property in less than a week and are detained in 10 incarceration camps.

1943 The 100th Infantry Battalion and the 442nd Regimental Combat Team, both all-Japanese American Nisei (second-generation) military units, are organized. The U.S. government starts drafting young male Japanese internees, who swear their loyalty to the United States. The units consist of only Japanese because of the persistent prejudice against Japanese. The units are assigned to rescue a Texas military unit surrounded by Germans in Italy. The units save 211 Texan soldiers with the sacrifice of 216 Japanese soldiers. For their courage, the Japanese soldiers are awarded more Purple Heart medals than any other unit in previous U.S. history.

1948 *Oyama v. California.* The lands of Fred Oyama, a United States–born American citizen, are confiscated by the state of California. He sues the state on the grounds that his rights as a citizen are violated. The case is brought to the federal Supreme Court, and the Court rules in Oyama's favor. This ruling overturns the Alien Land Act of 1920.

1952 The Immigration and Nationality Act, also known as the McCarran-Walter Act, eliminates the category of "immigrant ineligible for citizenship," which was used as a legal reason for passing the Alien Land Acts.

1952 *Fujii v. California.* Japanese immigrant Sei Fujii fights for his right to possess land. The California Supreme Court rules that the Alien Land acts violate the Equal Protection Clause of the Fourteenth Amendment to the Constitution and therefore are unconstitutional.

1956 The California Alien Land Act is repealed.

1988 President Ronald Reagan signs the Civil Liberties Act of 1988. It offers an apology and reparation payments of $20,000 to each surviving Japanese American person incarcerated during World War II.

2010 President Barack Obama signs legislation to grant the Congressional Gold Medal, one of the highest civilian awards in the United States, to all servicemen of the 100th Infantry Battalion and the 442nd Regimental Combat Team for their dedicated service during World War II.

Narrative

Japanese immigrants came to the United States for the first time in 1868, when the Meiji government began in Japan. It was the first year ("Gannen" in Japanese) of the Meiji period, and the immigrant group ("Mono" in Japanese) is referred to as "Gannen Mono." The Japanese social system at the time was a primogeniture system, under which only first-born sons could inherit their parents' property, and its main economy was agriculture. Many Japanese were farmers, and under the primogeniture system, Japanese men who were ineligible to inherit land from their parents usually had no way of making a living. Thus, some of these men sought their fortunes overseas and went to Hawaii to work as plantation laborers. They traveled to the United States without official government permits.

The United States were regarded as a country of gold by some Japanese in the 19th century. They dreamed of finding fortune there. When the Japanese government began issuing official permits in 1884, more and more Japanese moved to the United States. These immigrants planned to return to Japan after saving money, but most ended up becoming poor laborers. They settled in the United States permanently and raised their families here. Because Japanese men were not allowed to marry white women due to anti-miscegenation acts, they sought their future wives back in Japan through the "picture bride" system. They exchanged pictures with Japanese women and brought those women to the United States if both parties agreed to marry. These early immigrants worked hard and started families. Some of them purchased their own land and settled down. Some Japanese, such as George Shima, became successful farmers and land owners.

While the number of Japanese was increasing in the United States by the end of the 19th century, Japan was emerging as a powerful nation in the international landscape. The Japanese victory in the Russo-Japanese War (1904–1905) surprised many Western nations, and they came to see Japan as a threat. The increase and success of Japanese immigrants and and Japan as an emerging world power, convinced some white Americans of the early 20th century that the Japanese had become part of the "Yellow Peril." The term represented the notion that Asians were taking over the wealth of white Americans and therefore needed to be eliminated from the United States. This mentality led to anti-Japanese sentiments and the establishment of organizations such as the Asiatic Exclusion League of San Francisco (AEL).

The Asiatic Exclusion League

The increase of Japanese immigrants and their success in agriculture and business offended some white Americans. The anti-Asian sentiment at the beginning of the 20th century led to the establishment of the Asiatic Exclusion League in San Francisco in 1905. The league's members consisted of a wide range of individuals and organizations. In 1908, the league had approximately 100,000 members and 238 affiliated bodies, such as the Native Sons (and Daughters) of the Golden West, the American Legion, the California State Federation of Labor, and agriculture-related organizations, for example: the California State Grange. The main body of the league was composed of labor unions.

"Keeping California White" was the league's slogan. Members of the league felt that Japanese immigrants threatened their labor opportunities. They claimed that Japanese were unassimilable to American culture and believed that for the preservation of the Caucasian race upon American soil, it was necessary to adopt all possible measures to prevent or minimize Japanese immigration to the United States.

The Asiatic Exclusion League took several extreme actions to oppress Japanese immigrants. For example, they penalized anyone hiring Japanese workers, boycotted Japanese businesses, and demanded the school board segregate Japanese students. San Francisco's Board of Education twice tried to relocate Japanese students from public schools to Chinese schools, first in 1893 and again in 1906. The first attempt was successfully protested by the Japanese government, and the second was renounced by President Theodore Roosevelt, who was worried about the worsening relationship between Japan and the United States. There were only 93 Japanese students among 29,000 public school students in San Francisco at the time of the second attempt. The school board eventually repealed its segregation order, but that did not halt rising anti-Japanese sentiments among some white Americans.

The league's lobby against Japanese immigrants culminated in a demand for the passing of the Webb-Haney Act, also known as the Alien Land Act of 1913. The league pressured California's state legislature to pass the act, which did not allow Japanese to possess land or to settle down in the state.

Immigration Policies

The Japanese government was watching over the well-being of overseas Japanese, and its officials were concerned about the intensifying anti-Japanese sentiment in the United States. As early as 1890, Sutemi Chinda, the Japanese consul in San Francisco, wrote a letter to Shuzo Aoki, the Japanese minister of foreign affairs.

Juichi Soyeda of the Associated Chambers of Commerce of Japan and the Japanese American Society of Tokyo and Tadao Kamiya, chief secretary of the Tokyo Chamber of Commerce, visited the United States in 1913. Soyeda and Kamiya lobbied against proposed anti-Japanese legislation in California. In the same year, the California Alien Land Act banned all aliens ineligible for citizenship from purchasing or leasing land for more than three years. (Library of Congress)

Chinda wrote that Japanese in the States were becoming targets of discrimination because the Japanese government issued passports to prostitutes and other Japanese who tarnished the reputation of all Japanese immigrants. Chinda pressed the Japanese government to stop issuing passports temporarily. Following Chinda's proposal, the Japanese government decided to no longer issue passports to Japanese

---

Picture Brides

In the late 19th century, Japanese men went to Hawaii to work on the sugarcane plantations as cheap laborers. Some of them later moved to the mainland United States to look for better job opportunities. These men originally planned to leave plantation work and go back to Japan after saving some money. Between the years of 1886 and 1924, 199,564 Japanese entered Hawaii and 113,362 returned to Japan.

However, some men could not make enough money to go back home, and in 1908, the Gentlemen's Agreement prohibited the migration of Japanese laborers from Hawaii to the United States. Thus, their mobility was limited, and they had to make either Hawaii or the mainland United States their home.

In order to settle down in the States, these Japanese men needed families. Some of them asked their friends, relatives, or matchmakers in Japan to find wives for them. Intermediaries selected possible brides usually from the same villages as the men. After a series of photo exchanges and final agreements between the families, Japanese brides would undergo the traditional marriage ceremony, record their names in their spouses' family registers, and apply for U.S. passports. When passports were issued, they would finally cross the Pacific Ocean by ship to meet their husbands.

Picture brides only knew their future husbands through pictures, and some were shocked when they arrived in the United States because the men were sometimes older than they had appeared in their pictures. Many of the men were poor laborers, rather than the rich husbands some of the wives had been led to expect. Some picture brides left their husbands, but most stayed, mainly because they had no other way of surviving in this new land. They took root and raised families, increasing the visibility of Japanese immigrants along the West Coast and spurring anti-Japanese sentiments among some white Americans.

These white Americans concluded that halting the issue of passports to picture brides could prevent the increase of Japanese in the United States. Under such pressure, the Japanese government decided to stop issuing passports to picture brides in 1920.

who hoped to immigrate to the United States in 1900. But Japanese who had already immigrated to Hawaii were still able to move to the mainland, so the Japanese government's attempt to temporarily halt Japanese emigration to the States ultimately failed. As a result, the number of Japanese immigrants kept increasing in California and further fueled rising anti-Japanese sentiments.

Fearing the rising animosity would have repercussions on relations between the two countries, the Japanese and American governments decided not to issue passports to new Japanese immigrants in 1908. This was called the Gentlemen's Agreement. However, since the Gentlemen's Agreement allowed the immigration of Japanese picture brides, the number of Japanese did not decrease. Some white Americans who felt threatened by the increasing Yellow Peril demanded the state legislature enact a law to prevent Japanese from taking over their land.

The Webb-Haney Act and the Alien Land Act

The Webb-Haney Act, also known as the California Alien Land Law, was passed in 1913. Its implementation led to protests from the Japanese government. Japanese government sent a letter to the United States Secretary of State, stating that the act jeopardized the friendly relationship between Japan and the United States and deprived Japanese immigrants of their livelihood. Despite the protest, the act went into effect in California.

The Webb-Haney Act prohibited aliens ineligible for citizenship from owning land or leasing land for more than three years. It did not explicitly refer to Japanese, but because Japanese immigrants were not eligible for naturalization, it is obvious that the act targeted them.

The act was a terrible blow to the many Japanese immigrants engaged in agriculture in California because it attempted to strip them of their means of making a living. They tried to find other ways of securing land for farming, such as purchasing land through white intermediaries and creating corporations to purchase land on behalf of Japanese immigrants. They also found a loophole in the act, which allowed Japanese children born in the United States to possess and lease land. These second-generation Japanese Americans were called Nisei.

This loophole was legally admitted by the case of *California v. Harada* in 1918. The Harada family bought a house in Riverside, California, under their minor Nisei sons' names. The legality of their purchase was fought in California's Supreme Court. The court ruled that the Webb-Haney Act could not prevent United States–born citizens from possessing land. After the case, many Japanese immigrants purchased land in their Nisei children's names. In fact, even after the implementation of the Webb-Haney Act, Japanese immigrants kept coming to the United States, and they extended their possession of land in California.

Japanese resilience, however, fueled the anger of anti-Japanese whites, and anti-Japanese activists lobbied the state legislature to tighten the provisions of the Webb-Haney Act. Under this pressure, the state legislature closed the loopholes in the act in 1920. The revised Alien Land Act prohibited even short-term leases of land to Japanese. It also prohibited stock companies owned by Japanese from purchasing agricultural lands and prohibited the Nisei from possessing land as proxies for their parents. Thus, the revised act completely stymied Japanese immigrants' attempts to possess land.

Some Japanese challenged the Alien Land Act of 1920. For example, in the 1922 case of the Yano family, the California Supreme Court defended the Nisei child's rights to purchase and possess land and the alien parents' right to guardianship over that land. Hayao Yano purchased land in California in the name of his Nisei daughter, Tetsubumi. The state saw that the purchase of land under his daughter's name was a violation of the Alien Land Act and attempted to escheat the land. Yano filed against the state, and the state Supreme Court ruled that Yano's daughter had a right to possess the land.

On the other hand, two cases that fought the constitutionality of the Alien Land Act in the federal Supreme Court, *Terrace v. Thompson* and *Porterfield v. Webb* in 1923, had the opposite result. The Court ruled that the act did not violate the Equal Protection Clause of the Fourteenth Amendment of the Constitution. Along with the enactment of the Immigration Act of 1924, which completely halted Japanese immigration to the United States, the Webb-Haney Act and the Alien Land Act of 1920 succeeded in discouraging Japanese from immigrating to the United States.

Inevitably, land possession by Japanese dropped after the Webb-Haney Act. In 1900, Japanese owned 4,698 acres of land. This number increased to 99,254 acres by 1910 and reached 321,276 acres by 1920 but then dropped to 191,427 acres by 1930. Japanese immigrants were surrounded by racial hostility and effectively discouraged from working in the United States.

The 1941 attack on Pearl Harbor, Hawaii, by the Japanese navy resulted in the incarceration of approximately 120,000 Japanese Americans on the West Coast the following year. Regarded as enemy aliens, they were forced into 10 concentration camps and lost most of their property, including land that some had toiled upon for decades. During World War II, other states enacted alien land laws, exacerbating the plight of Japanese. But racism did not daunt Japanese Americans.

After World War II, some Japanese revived their challenge of the constitutionality of the Alien Land Act. For example, Fred Oyama sued the state of California in 1946. His father, Kajiro Oyama, bought land in California in 1934 under Fred's name. Because the family was incarcerated during the war and ordered not to return home, the state tried to escheat Oyama's land. The California Supreme Court ruled in favor of the state, but Oyama brought his case to the federal Supreme Court. His case was taken up by the American Civil Liberties Union, and the Court ruled the Alien Land Act unconstitutional. The ruling said the act infringed upon the Equal Protection Clause of the Fourteenth Amendment of the Constitution, and it deprived Fred Oyama of the equal protection of the Constitution and of his privilege as an American citizen. The ruling, however, did not go as far as striking down the Alien Land Act.

The Alien Land Act was again ruled unconstitutional in 1952's *Fujii v. California*. Sei Fujii immigrated to the United States in 1903 and studied law at the University of South California, but because he was not an American citizen, he was not allowed to practice law in the United States. Before the war, Fujii had challenged discriminatory laws with Marion Wright, a lawyer and classmate at the university. Like other Japanese immigrants, he was incarcerated during World War II. After he was released, Fujii and Wright resumed Fujii's challenge to discriminatory laws targeting Japanese.

In order to challenge California's Alien Land Act, Fujii bought land in Los Angeles, fully aware that he was not qualified to do so under the provisions of the act. Fujii and Wright filed suit so Fujii could build a house there. They brought the case to the California Supreme Court, and the Court finally ruled that the act was unconstitutional, admitting that it violated the Equal Protection Clause of the Fourteenth Amendment of the Constitution. As a result of this ruling, the Alien Land Act was struck down and Japanese immigrants were once again allowed to possess land.

The late 19th century and early 20th century saw unprecedented anti-Japanese hysteria in California. This hysteria resulted in the enactment of one racist law after another, including the Webb-Haney Act of 1913. Japanese Americans fought bravely against xenophobia in California. Some individuals challenged the act in court. Many simply endured patiently and survived. Nisei soldiers fought in World War II and dedicated their lives to the United States to prove that Japanese Americans were not the enemy, as some white Americans insisted. They all struggled to prove their loyalty to the United States despite harsh anti-Japanese sentiments and convinced mainstream American society that Japanese Americans were worthy of trust. In the process, they contributed to creating a racially just society in the United States.

Biographies of Notable Figures

George Shima (1864–1926)

George Shima is a renowned figure in the history of Japanese Americans. He made his fortune through agriculture by producing about 85 percent of the potato crop in California in the early 20th century, earning the nickname "Potato King." He was not only a successful entrepreneur but also served the Japanese immigrant community as the first president of the Japanese Association of America. Shima was born Ushijima Kinji in Kurume, Fukuoka prefecture, Japan, in 1864. His family members were landowners and farmers. Shima went to Tokyo with the dream of becoming a Chinese classics scholar. He took an entrance exam at the Tokyo Commercial School (now Hitotsubashi University) but failed the exam due to his lack of English-language skills. In response to this failure, young Shima decided to go to the United States to study English.

Shima arrived in San Francisco in 1889, when he was 26. Shima first worked as a schoolboy who completed household chores for host families in exchange for room and board. Shima noticed that many white Americans could not pronounce his Japanese name, so he changed it to George Shima. Then he moved to the Stockton-Sacramento delta and engaged in farm labor. He later started a management company to supply Japanese farm workers to white farmers. As a labor contractor, Shima noticed that large areas of the Stockton-Sacramento delta were not used for agriculture because of the periodic flooding of the Sacramento and San Joaquin Rivers. The price of land in these areas was just three to five dollars per acre, which was affordable to Shima. He bought acreage in the delta and started growing potatoes. It took him almost 10 years of trial and error to learn how to grow potatoes there. Many Japanese farmers hesitated to work with him because they had to compete with white farmers, but Shima continued his endeavor. He found the potato business profitable because potatoes were an essential staple for Americans and would grow in the delta, where other crops tended to fail.

By the late 1890s, Shima had bought more swampland in the San Joaquin River delta, which white American farmers considered unsuitable for farming. He cultivated the land and invented his own potato, called "Shima Fancy." By 1913, he owned 28,000 acres in production. By 1920, he had 85 percent of the market share with his Shima Fancy and had gained more than $18 million.

While his potato business grew in California, Shima returned to Japan in 1900 at the age of 37 to visit his deceased mother's tomb. During this visit, he met Shimeko Shimamura, whom he married and brought to the United States. They had four children together.

Shima's life reached its peak in 1905. He expanded his farm and gained a tremendous fortune. It was during this period that people started calling him Potato King. In 1909, Shima was chosen as the first president of the Japanese Association of America, which consisted of 50 umbrella Japanese immigrant communities. He was an active president and community member. Since Japanese immigrants were discriminated against because of their heritage, Shima promoted the Americanization of Japanese, such as encouraging immigrants to improve their English and to acquire American customs.

However, Shima's business success and commitment to the Americanization of Japanese immigrants did not protect him from anti-Japanese hysteria in California. Rather, his success fueled white Americans' hostility against Japanese immigrants. In 1909, he tried to buy a house in a campus town, Berkeley, but real estate agents and neighbors opposed the sale. Shima bought the house and his family moved in anyway, but the harassment of the Shima family continued. Neighbors demanded the Shima family move out, and the media joined the harassment by writing vicious gossip news about Shima. Shima built high walls around his house to avoid confrontations with his neighbors but that did not lessen their hatred. The Berkeley community only accepted Shima in their neighborhood after he donated a large sum of money to the University of California.

Such deep-rooted white American resentment against Japanese entrepreneurs like Shima, who were perceived as being too successful, persisted. The emergence of Meiji Japan as a modern nation also augmented some white Americans' view of Japanese immigrants as the Yellow Peril. The white community was alarmed by Shima's success as an agricultural entrepreneur and his possession of a large area of land. White Americans' jealousy and fear of Japanese like Shima contributed to the passing of the Webb-Haney Act of 1913. Before the act was passed, Shima wrote to California Governor Hiram Johnson in 1911, claiming that possession of land by Japanese was minimal compared to the whites' possession of land and that the fear of whites against Japanese was an overreaction. However, Shima's plea did not convince Johnson, and the act was passed.

When the state legislature moved to close the loophole in the act that allowed Nisei children to purchase and lease land as a proxy of their parents, Shima wrote a pamphlet called "An Appeal to Justice." In this pamphlet, Shima tried to tell white Americans that Japanese were assimilating and contributing to the United States, and therefore the act should not be revised. Again, Shima's effort failed, and the revised Alien Land Act of 1920 was passed.

Two years after the enactment of the Immigration Act of 1924, which prohibited the emigration of Japanese to the United States, Shima had a stroke and passed away. He was 63. He had dedicated his life to the development of the Japanese American community and experienced both acceptance and rejection by American society. Though his efforts were not rewarded in his lifetime, Shima worked hard to build trust between Japanese communities and their white American neighbors.

Kyutaro Abiko (1865–1936)

Kyutaro Abiko was born the son of Ishiko and Tokushiro Kobayashi in 1865 in Suibara, Niigata prefecture, Japan. His mother died after delivering him, and he was adopted and raised by his maternal grandfather, Hikoichiro Abiko. When Abiko was

14 years old, a British Christian missionary opened a school in Suibara. Abiko joined the school, where he encountered Christianity. In 1882, he went to Tokyo with his friends to study English. He was baptized by Pastor Masatsuna Okuno and converted to Christianity in 1883.

With Okuno's recommendation, Abiko immigrated to the United States in 1884 as a student of the Gospel Society in San Francisco. While he studied English at Lincoln Grammar School, he actively served the Gospel Society. He attended the University of California at Berkeley, in 1897, but there is no record that he graduated from the school. In his early years in the United States, Abiko further developed his English-language skills, which enabled him to become a leader and advocate of the Japanese immigrant community.

About the time he entered the university, Abiko, who was in his thirties, emerged as a leader of the San Francisco's Japanese Christian community. He was one of the founding members of the Japanese Methodist Church in San Francisco, and he was also appointed president of the Gospel Society. As a leader of the Japanese Christian community, Abiko assisted his peers in many ways. For example, after the famous 1906 San Francisco earthquake, Abiko and other leaders of the Japanese Christian community helped Japanese immigrants recover from their losses.

Abiko was active not only in his commitment to the Japanese Christian community but also in business. He first ran a restaurant and a laundromat. In 1899, after taking over two Japanese newspapers, he published a newspaper for Japanese immigrants called the *Nichibei*. The *Nichibei* soon became the leading newspaper for Japanese immigrants. In the same year, Abiko also founded Nichibei Kinyusha, which later became the Japan-American Bank, with his business partners. In 1902 Abiko helped found the Japanese American Industrial Corporation of San Francisco. Through this organization, Abiko connected Japanese immigrant laborers with various industries such as sugar, mining, and railways in Utah, Idaho, Wyoming, and Nevada. While he was a president of this company, he managed more than 3,000 Japanese laborers.

Utilizing his profits from his businesses, Abiko founded the American Land and Produce Company in California in 1906. He purchased undeveloped land and sold it to Japanese immigrants seeking land for farming. He divided the land into 40-acre plots and encouraged Japanese farmers who bought his land to live in the United States permanently. This land was called the Yamato Colony. In this colony, Abiko tried to create a space for the Japanese immigrant community where Japanese farmers could settle down in American society.

In 1908, Abiko returned to Japan to raise funds for the Yamato Colony. People held a welcome-back party for Abiko, and one of the party guests was Yonako Sudo, his future wife. Yonako was a younger sister of Umeko Tsuda, a founder of a women's college in Japan. Her parents were Christians, and they had networks with influential Americans and Japanese. Yonako was a highly educated woman and active in society. They married in 1909 and went to the United States together the same year. Because of her upbringing, Yonako believed that Japanese immigrants should not be ashamed of their ethnic roots. Rather, she believed they should be proud of their Japanese roots while simultaneously respecting and assimilating into American culture. Sharing the same vision, Abiko furthered his dedication to the improvement of Japanese immigrants' lives.

While Abiko ascended as a leader in the Japanese immigrant community, the anti-Japanese movement in San Francisco was becoming more intense. Abiko believed that some white Americans' hostility toward Japanese could be overcome by improving Japanese immigrants' behavior and attitudes. He thought white Americans resented Japanese immigrants' reluctance to assimilate in the United States. In fact, the participation of some Japanese immigrants in problematic behaviors such as gambling and prostitution concerned Abiko, so he started the 1915 "keihatsu undo" (moral education campaign). This campaign was intended to discourage Japanese immigrants from engaging in such problematic behaviors. Abiko launched several attempts to better assimilate the community, such as improving Japanese immigrants' English-language skills and encouraging them to settle permanently in the United States.

Abiko fought against injustice. For example, when the Japanese government decided to stop issuing passports to picture brides in 1919, Abiko protested the decision in the *Nichibei*. Abiko believed that picture brides enabled male Japanese immigrants to settle in the United States and that their existence brought stability to Japanese immigrant communities. Abiko protested the Webb-Haney Act, too. Although he understood that the act had many loopholes, he supported court cases such as the 1922 Yano case. In the *Nichibei,* he defended Japanese people who filed against the state to protect the rights of Japanese immigrants. Abiko did not hesitate to challenge authority, whether it was the Japanese or American government. He expressed his opinions, which he believed to be politically correct, without hesitation.

Abiko's vision for the development of the Japanese community extended to the United States–born Nisei children. With his wife, Yonako, Abiko started "Nisei Kengakudan," a tour to take the Nisei to Japan to instill pride in their ethnic roots. Abiko and Yonako found hope in the Nisei as a bridge between Japan and the United States. The couple believed that the Nisei who exhibited ethnic pride could convince hostile white Americans that Japanese Americans were worthy of equal treatment in the United States. For this purpose, they sponsored the Nisei tour to Japan and encouraged participants to take on the task of enabling peaceful relationships between the two countries.

Due to intensifying anti-Japanese sentiments in California, Abiko's efforts to improve the living conditions of Japanese Americans were not fully successful. Abiko passed away in 1936, but his contribution to the development of the Japanese

American community has had a lasting impact. Furthering Abiko's vision that Japanese Americans would prosper on U.S. soil through simultaneously assimilating American culture and maintaining Japanese ethnic pride, Japanese Americans are active in many areas of American society today. They pass Abiko's legacy to following generations.

DOCUMENT EXCERPTS

Statutes of California; Chapter 113

Anti-Asian prejudice in California, particularly against Japanese immigrants, was growing in the early 20th century. The Webb-Haney Act (also known as the California Alien Land Law of 1913) prohibited "aliens ineligible for citizenship" from purchasing and owning land. It also limited land leases to no more than three years. Although it affected Chinese, Korean, Indian, and other immigrants who were not eligible to become naturalized U.S. citizens at the time, its main target was Japanese immigrants. The Japanese government protested against the act.

An act relating to the rights, powers and disabilities of aliens and of certain companies, associations and corporations with respect to property in this state, providing for escheats in certain cases, prescribing the procedure therein, and repealing all acts or parts of acts inconsistent or in conflict herewith.
May 19, 1913
[Approved May 19, 1913.]
The people of the State of California do enact as follows:
SECTION 1. All aliens eligible to citizenship under the laws of the United States may acquire, possess, enjoy, transmit and inherit real property, or any interest therein, in this state, in the same manner and to the same extent as citizens of the United States, except as otherwise provided by the laws of this state.
SEC 2. All aliens other than those mentioned in section one of this act may acquire, possess, enjoy and transfer real property, or any interest therein, in this state, in the manner and to the extent and for the purposes prescribed by any treaty now existing between the Government of the United States and the nation or country of which such alien is a citizen or subject, and not otherwise, and may in addition thereto lease lands in this state for agricultural purposes for a term not exceeding three years.
SEC 3. Any company, association or corporation organized under the laws of this or any other state or nation, of which a majority of the members are aliens other than those specified in section one of this act, or in which a majority of the issued capital stock is owned by such aliens, may acquire, possess, enjoy and convey real property, or any interest therein, in this state, in the manner and to the extent and for the

purposes prescribed by any treaty now existing between the Government of the United States and the nation or country of which such members or stockholders are citizens or subjects, and not otherwise, and may in addition thereto lease lands in this state for agricultural purposes for a term not exceeding three years.

SEC 4. Whenever it appears to the court in any probate proceeding that by reason of the provisions of this act any heir or devisee cannot take real property in this state which, but for said provisions, said heir or devisee would take as such, the court, instead of ordering a distribution of such real property to such heir or devisee, shall order a sale of said real property to be made in the manner provided by law for probate sales of real property, and the proceeds of such sale shall be distributed to such heir or devisee in lieu of such real property.

SEC 5. Any real property hereafter acquired in fee in violation of the provisions of this act by any alien mentioned in section two of this act, or by any company, association or corporation mentioned in section three of this act, shall escheat to, and become and remain the property of the State of California. The attorney general shall institute proceedings to have the escheat of such real property adjudged and enforced in the manner provided by section 474 of the Political Code and title eight, part three of the Code of Civil Procedure. Upon the entry of final judgment in such proceedings, the title to such real property shall pass to the State of California. The provisions of this section and of sections two and three of this act shall not apply to any real property hereafter acquired in the enforcement or in satisfaction of any lien now existing upon, or interest in such property, so long as such real property so acquired shall remain the property of the alien, company, association or corporation acquiring the same in such manner.

SEC 6. Any leasehold or other interest in real property less than the fee, hereafter acquired in violation of the provisions of this act by any alien mentioned in section two of this act, or by any company, association or corporation mentioned in section three of this act, shall escheat to the State of California. The attorney general shall institute proceedings to have such escheat adjudged and enforced as provided in section five of this act. In such proceedings the court shall determine and adjudge the value of such leasehold, or other interest in such real property, and enter judgment for the state for the amount thereof together with costs. Thereupon the court shall order a sale of the real property covered by such leasehold, or other interest in the manner provided by section 1271 of the Code of Civil Procedure. Out of the proceeds arising from such sale, the amount of the judgment rendered for the state shall be paid into the state treasury and the balance shall be deposited with and distributed by the court in accordance with the interest of the parties therein.

SEC 7. Nothing in this act shall be construed as a limitation upon the power of the state to enact laws with respect to the acquisition, holding or disposal by aliens of real property in this state.

SEC 8. All acts and parts of acts inconsistent, or in conflict with the provisions of this act, are hereby repealed.

Source: The Webb-Haney Act (Alien Land Act of 1913). *The Statutes of California and Amendments to the Codes Passed at the Fortieth Session of the Legislature, 1913.* Sacramento: Superintendent of State Printing, 1913.

See also: Gentlemen's Agreement between the U.S. and Japan, 1907; Japanese American Internment, 1942–1946; The Murder of Vincent Chin, 1982; *United States v. Bhagat Singh Thind*, 1923

Further Reading

Azuma, Eiichiro. 2005. *Between Two Empires: Race, History, and Transnationalism in Japanese America.* New York and Oxford: Oxford University Press.

Bailey, Thomas. 1934. *Theodore Roosevelt and the Japanese-American Crises: An Account of the International Complications Arising from the Race Problem on the Pacific Coast.* Stanford, CA: Stanford University Press.

Chan, Sucheng. 1991. *Asian Americans: An Interpretative History.* Boston: Twayne Publishers.

Chuman, Frank. 1976. *The Bamboo People, the Law and Japanese Americans.* Del Mar, CA: Publishers.

Daniels, Roger. 1966. *The Politics of Prejudice: The Anti-Japanese Movement in California and the Struggle for Japanese Exclusion.* Gloucester, MA: Peter Smith.

Ferguson, Edwin. 1947. "The California Alien Land Law and the Fourteenth Amendment." *California Law Review* 35, no. 1: 61–90.

Glenn, Evelyn Nakano.1986. *Issei, Nisei, War Bride: Three Generations of Japanese American Women in Domestic Service.* Philadelphia: Temple University Press.

Hata, Donald. 1979. *Undesirables: Early Immigrants and the Anti-Japanese Movement in San Francisco, 1892–1893.* New York: Ayer.

Ichioka, Yuji. 1988. *The Issei: The World of the First Generation Japanese Immigrants, 1885–1924.* New York: The Free Press.

Kawakami, Barbara. 2016. *Picture Bride Stories.* Honolulu: University of Hawaii Press.

Matsumoto, Valerie. 1993. *Farming the Home Place: A Japanese American Community in California, 1919–1982.* Ithaca, NY: Cornell University Press.

Spickard, Paul. 2008. *Japanese Americans: The Formation and Transformations of an Ethnic Group.* New Brunswick, NJ: Rutgers University Press.

Takaki, Ronald. 1998. *A History of Asian Americans: Strangers from a Different Shore.* New York: Back Bay Books.

3

Conflicts and Politics

United States v. Bhagat Singh Thind, 1923

Philip Deslippe

Chronology

1892 Bhagat Singh Thind is born in the village of Taragarh Talawa, near the city of Amritsar, in the Indian state of Punjab.

1913 Thind arrives in Seattle, Washington, just shy of his twentieth birthday. He later attends the University of California at Berkeley to further his education.

1913 The Hindustan Association of the Pacific Coast, commonly known as the Ghadar Party, is formed.

1917 The 1917 Immigration Act, also known as the Asiatic Barred Zone Act, is passed, restricting immigration from much of Asia and the Middle East.

1917 The Hindu-German Conspiracy Trial begins in San Francisco.

1918 Thind is inducted into the U.S. Army.

1918 Thind receives American citizenship in the state of Washington, only to have it revoked four days later.

1918 Thind is honorably discharged from the U.S. Army.

1919 Thind applies for American citizenship for a second time in the state of Oregon.

1920 Thind receives citizenship from the state of Oregon. The Immigration and Naturalization Service (INS) appeals the ruling. It goes to the Ninth Circuit Court of Appeals and, eventually, the Supreme Court.

1922   The U.S. Supreme Court hears the case of Takao Ozawa, a Japanese American who was found ineligible for naturalization.

1923   In *United States v. Bhagat Singh Thind*, the U.S. Supreme Court unanimously rules against Thind.

1923   Thind marries Inez Marie Pier Buelen in Spokane, Washington.

1924   Thind begins a career as a traveling metaphysical lecturer and author that will continue for more than four decades.

1925   Thind publishes *Divine Wisdom*, the first of many books.

1926   Sakharam Ganesh Pandit co-authors and publishes a pamphlet protesting the *Thind* decision titled "An Examination of the Opinion of the Supreme Court of the United States Deciding against the Eligibility of Hindus for Citizenship."

1926   A resolution to grant Thind citizenship is introduced by Senator David Reed but is ultimately tabled.

1936   Thind is granted American citizenship after the passage of the Nye-Lea Act (1935), which allowed for the naturalization of "any alien veteran of the World War heretofore ineligible to citizenship because not a free white person."

1940   Thind marries Vivian Davies in a Presbyterian church in Toledo, Ohio. They later raise a son and a daughter together.

1952   The Immigration and Nationality Act of 1952, or the McCarran-Walter Act, is passed and establishes small, token quotas for Asian immigrants.

1963   Thind returns to India for the first time in more than half a century.

1965   The Immigration and Nationality Act of 1965, also known as the Hart-Celler Act, is passed by the eighty-ninth U.S. Congress, abolishing the national origins quota system along with racial and national barriers for immigrants.

1967   Thind passes away in Los Angeles.

Narrative

United States v. Bhagat Singh Thind was a 1923 case heard by the Supreme Court of the United States, which ruled that an immigrant from the Punjab region of India was ineligible for American citizenship because he did not qualify as a "free white person." The *Thind* decision was not only significant for Asian Americans but was also a major part of what the historian John Higham has referred to as the "Tribal

Twenties," a period of intense nativism and restricted immigration in the United States. *United States v. Thind* was preceded by the Asiatic Barred Zone Act of 1917, which admitted no immigrants from nearly all of Asia and the Pacific Islands. It was followed by the Johnson-Reed Act of 1924, which began a restrictive national origins quota and numerical limit on immigration that lasted until the Immigration Act of 1965.

The man at the center of the case, Bhagat Singh Thind, was born on October 3, 1892, in the village of Taragarh Talawa, close to the city of Amritsar in the Punjab region of modern-day western India and eastern Pakistan. Thind graduated from Khalsa College in 1912 and then left for the United States, arriving in

Indian American Sikh writer and war veteran Bhagat Singh Thind, date unknown. (Courtesy of David Thind and the South Asian American Digital Archive)

Seattle, Washington, on July 4, 1913. He attended the University of California at Berkeley and supported himself in the summers by working with other Punjabi immigrants in the lumber mills of the Pacific Northwest. In 1918, at the onset of World War I, Thind enlisted in the U.S. Army and was stationed at Camp Lewis in the state of Washington. While enlisted, he successfully petitioned for American citizenship, only for it to be cancelled four days later by the Immigration and Naturalization Service (INS) due to the claim that Thind was racially ineligible for citizenship. The next year, he petitioned for citizenship in the state of Oregon, only for the INS to object once again. His appeal went to the United States Court of Appeals for the Ninth Circuit in San Francisco and then to the Supreme Court of the United States.

When immigrants from India arrived in significant numbers in America at the turn of the century, they did not fit neatly into preexisting racial categories. South Asians were referred to during this time as "Hindus," a geographical and racial marker, not a religious designation. For xenophobic and nativist groups on the

Pacific Coast, such as the Asiatic Exclusion League, immigrants from India could be grouped together with previous Chinese and Japanese migrants as a source of cheap labor that would undercut white American workers. There were also theories of common ancestry between Europeans and South Asians, such as those espoused by the German philologist Friedrich Max Müller and others, which classified people from India as Aryan and Caucasian, and thereby white. South Asians in the United States were usually thought of as being nonwhite and were at times grouped with African Americans and subject to the same laws and policies of racial segregation.

The right to become a naturalized American citizen was bracketed by two laws: the Naturalization Law of 1790, which limited it to "free white persons," and an amendment to that law passed in 1870 during Reconstruction, which extended it to "aliens being free white persons, and to aliens of African nativity and to persons of African descent." In short, nearly all immigrants to America seeking to naturalize needed to prove that they were white and racially eligible for citizenship. The confusion inherent in the 1870 amendment—that race could be determined by either ethnicity or geographic origin—was only heightened by the indeterminate racial classification of South Asians. Prior to *Thind*, a series of confused and conflicting legal battles for citizenship ensued, in which South Asians used a wide array of criteria, from common sense to linguistics, to prove that they were white. South Asians were compared to everyone from Syrians to hypothetical space aliens from Mars in these debates, and they often found themselves eligible in one court and ineligible in the next.

United States v. Bhagat Singh Thind is nearly inseparable from the preceding case of a Japanese man named Takao Ozawa, who similarly sought to naturalize. The case of *Ozawa v. United States* was decided by the Supreme Court in mid-November 1922, less than two months before it began to hear arguments in *Thind*. Scholars and historians usually mention the cases in tandem, either within the same argument or by combining the two cases together as "*Ozawa* and *Thind*" (Gross 2008, 240–44; López 1996, 79–109; Snow 2007, 111–42). *Ozawa* did not challenge the racial restrictions placed on naturalization but instead argued that the Japanese qualified as "free white persons," supported by anthropological evidence and the light skin tone of many Japanese that made them "whiter than the average Italian, Spaniard or Portuguese" when not exposed to the sun.

Ozawa further qualified his eligibility for citizenship by his character and the extent to which he was assimilated, noting that he was college educated, he spoke English at home, his children went to American schools, and his family attended American Christian churches. The court ruled unanimously against Ozawa. The opinion rendered by Justice George Alexander Sutherland (1862–1942) stated that the case was not a matter of individual worth or skin tone but was instead a matter of qualifying as a "free white person," and that was dependent on being classified as part of the Caucasian race, which he ruled that Ozawa was not.

Similar to the *Ozawa* case, the two main questions before the Supreme Court in *United States v. Bhagat Singh Thind* were whether Thind, "a high-caste Hindu of full Indian blood, born in Amritsar, Punjab, India" was a "white person" and eligible for citizenship under the law and if the possible racial ineligibility of South Asians disqualified those who had naturalized prior to the passing of the Immigration Act of 1917. It is usually assumed that the strategy on behalf of Thind in 1923 was based on the outcome of the *Ozawa* case, that Thind buttressed his claims to being Caucasian with anthropological and ethnographic evidence because Ozawa was denied by so many "numerous scientific authorities" that the Supreme Court found them unnecessary to review. There is, however, a strong similarity between Thind's arguments in Washington State in 1918 and those in Washington, D.C., in 1923, in which he used evidence from anthropology, linguistics, and racial science that fixed northern Indians as Aryan, and thus Caucasian and white. Thind repeatedly qualified his racial identity through geography (northern rather than southern India) and caste (both his being of high caste and pointing to the caste system's injunctions against intermarriage, which kept his ancestry definitive).

Like Ozawa, Thind lost in a unanimous decision. A simple explanation is that the Court granted supremacy to a commonsense understanding of race and that the phrase "free white persons" was "words of common speech, to be interpreted in accordance with the understanding of the common man, synonymous with the word 'Caucasian' only as that word is popularly understood" (*United States v. Thind*). On closer scrutiny, the argument of the government and the decision of the Court in *United States v. Thind* were more complex and conflicted, and in places were at odds with evidence they relied upon only two months earlier in the *Ozawa* case (Coulson 2017, 52–54). The government countered Thind's argument with scientific evidence of its own that suggested India was too diverse and mixed to support Thind's claim of purity. It also sidestepped racial science and defined the crucial phrase "free white persons" as a "composite type, a combination of color, race, and social institutions." Sutherland offered the possible truth of shared ancestry in antiquity among those from India and Scandinavia, but at different points suggested that it was secondary to the characteristics possessed by groups in the present and not as important as what the original framers of the statute envisioned in 1790.

Factors *within* United States v. Thind

Relatively little attention has been given the role played by Sutherland, the justice who delivered the opinion of the Court for its unanimous verdicts in both *Thind* and *Ozawa*. Biographies of Sutherland give little consideration to the two racial eligibility cases, and in studies of *Ozawa* and *Thind*, Sutherland is usually presented without background and as a figure who "seems to arrive out of nowhere" (Jew 1997, 555).

British-born Sutherland moved to the Utah Territory with his family when he was a child. He practiced law in Provo, Utah, then represented the state in both the House (1901–1903) and the Senate (1905–1917) and was nominated to the Supreme Court in 1922, where he heard the oral arguments in *Takao Ozawa v. United States* after having taken his seat only a day earlier.

Many scholars have noted that from what we can surmise about Sutherland, himself an immigrant, he seems to have used different reasoning for Asian immigration and citizenship than for Anglo-Europeans. One historian has highlighted a 1907 speech by Senator Sutherland in defense of his then-fellow senator from Utah, Reed Smoot, who was subjected to four years of heated Senate proceedings over his suitability for the office on account of his being a Mormon and leader in the Church of Jesus Christ of Latter-day Saints (Jew 1997). In defending Smoot and the Mormons, who were labeled "alien enemies and outlaws" by Stephen Douglas decades earlier, Sutherland argued that they were not essentially or permanently different from the majority of Americans, that their perceived difference was a product of the historical moment, and that the military service of Mormons in the Spanish-American War showed them to be patriotic and worthy of inclusion. None of these arguments were applied to Thind fourteen years later.

One key difference between Sutherland's treatment of Mormons in 1907 and his opinion for *Thind* in 1923 is that he saw Mormons, beyond any differences with American society at large, as white. Thind and many of his South Asian contemporaries also saw themselves as white and cited the claimed Aryan origins of Indic people as evidence. Dr. Kesha Deva Shastri, a physician from India who traveled within the United States in the late 1910s, took this logic to its furthest ends in his book, *India in Scandinavia*, in which he claimed that Scandinavia was settled by Aryans from India five millennia earlier. Several of these theories, including those cited and used in *United States v. Thind*, positioned South Asians as more white than Anglo- and European Americans through claims that the rigidity of the caste system in India maintained a purity of Aryan blood among the highest castes of northern India. Often this was done with explicit and favorable comparisons to racial segregation in the United States. Thind's side argued in front of the Supreme Court that "[t]he high-caste Hindu regards the aboriginal Indian Mongoloid in the same manner as the American regards the Negro, speaking from a matrimonial standpoint."

To many contemporary observers who are aware of the details of the case, Thind's racial positioning of himself is unsettling and does not comport with the now-standard portrayal of him as a victim of discriminatory laws and policies who fought for the rights of Asian Americans. Many who are unaware of the Aryan-origins theory among South Asian elites see Thind's assertion of whiteness as simply a pragmatic legal strategy to gain citizenship. The 2017 short dramatic film about Thind's legal battles, titled *All Quiet on the Homefront* and directed by Harjus Singh, imagined Thind as having to be forced by his attorney to adopt a tactic Thind found odious. Perhaps the best evidence that Thind sincerely believed in the racial claims that he made before the Supreme Court comes from Omaha, Nebraska, in 1926. Thind was in the city to deliver lectures, and his first wife, Inez Pier Buelen (whom he married in 1923 and separated from less than a year later), came up from Houston to counter any false impressions he may have given audiences about her. A reporter for the local *World-Herald* covered the spat, and in separate interviews, the couple showed that racial categories were at the heart of their split. Buelen said that Thind was "Oriental to the core" and "his subtle Oriental ways were unbearable to me." Thind countered by telling the reporter, "I am white" and that although his citizenship was revoked because he was Asiatic, "it was not because my blood is not white" ("Wife of Dr. Thind" 1926).

In addition to questions of racial classification and skin tone, there is the possibility that the Court's decision was a matter of Thind's religious identity and appearance. Thind was a Sikh, who, as a matter of his faith, left his hair uncut and wore a turban. The large majority of South Asian immigrants to America in the early twentieth century were Sikh men from the Punjab, and the turban was a constant fixture in written descriptions and photographs of newly arrived "Hindus" in American newspapers and magazines. The sharpest connection between the two was from Herman Scheffauer's 1910 article for *Forum* titled "The Tide of Turbans," which described the turban as an indelible and unalterable part of Indian immigrants. "Always the turban remains," wrote Scheffauer, "the badge and symbol of their native land, their native customs and religion" (Scheffauer 1910, 616–18).

Sutherland's decision focused strongly on appearance and visual recognition, evidenced by his use of phrases such as "familiar observation" and "readily distinguishable." Sutherland stated that "the children of . . . European parentage quickly merge into the mass of our population and lose the distinctive hallmarks of their European origin," but "it cannot be doubted that the children born in this country of Hindu parents would retain indefinitely the clear evidence of their ancestry." For the former, it is likely that Sutherland and the Court had in mind the various forms of native dress worn by European immigrants to Ellis Island—preserved in photographs by Augustus Sherman and made known through their publication in *National Geographic* magazine—and for the latter, the perceived connection between the turban and South Asian immigration. If this was the case, then ironically the qualities assumed by Thind to exemplify him as a desirable citizen—his education, his command of English, his military service—when combined with his turban would instead have highlighted in the mind of the Court his ultimate inability to assimilate and blend in.

Another thread within the *Thind* decision is Thind's involvement with the Ghadar Party, a group of South Asians in the United States that attempted to foment rebellion and overthrow British colonial rule in India. In Judge Charles E. Wolverton's earlier opinion, he discussed Thind's alleged connections to the Ghadar Party at length, including his friendship with prominent members such as Bhagwan Singh and Ram Chandra. Wolverton believed that these ties and Thind's strong belief in "India for the Indians" was outweighed by his "genuine affection for the Constitution, laws, customs, and privileges of this country" and the testimony of "disinterested" American citizens who testified to Thind's character and suitability.

Thind, the Sikh

Although he was referred to as a "Hindu"—a racial and geographic designation of the time—Bhagat Singh Thind was a Sikh, a member of a monotheistic faith founded in the late fifteenth century by Guru Nanak in the Punjab region of modern-day eastern Pakistan and northwestern India. It would be difficult to understand the person behind the Supreme Court case without referring to the Sikh tradition. Thind's writings during his metaphysical career were filled with references to the Sikh gurus and their teachings, and he would often lecture on the topic of the "Soulful Science of the Sikh Saviors." He was the principal speaker when the first *gurdwara*, or Sikh temple, in the United States was rebuilt in 1930 in Stockton, California. The Stockton *gurdwara* also certified Thind as a *gyanee* (teacher) and *parcharak* (preacher) of the Sikh faith later that year, and he performed funerary services for a Punjabi Sikh man who passed away in Texas after a workplace accident. Thind also served as a spokesperson for the Sikh faith at 1933 and 1938 gatherings of the interreligious group known as the World Fellowship of Faiths. During the decades of the exclusion era, when there was a small number of Sikh immigrants in the United States, few Sikh institutions, and little public awareness of Sikhs, Thind was one of the few and most visible representatives of the Sikh tradition.

Although Wolverton could set aside Thind's involvement with the Ghadar Party, the years between his decision and the Supreme Court case—the height of the First Red Scare—saw a much more highly charged atmosphere in America against those perceived to be foreign radicals (Coulson 2017, 56–60). There was the lingering memory of the Hindu-German Conspiracy Trial, in which several members of the Ghadar Party were put on trial and imprisoned for conspiring with the Germans to create an armed revolt against the British in India. There was also a series of bombings carried out by anarchists in 1919, including one on the home of Attorney General A. Mitchell Palmer. These resulted in a wave of arrests and deportations of radical leftists, known as the Palmer Raids. Lothrop Stoddard referenced Ghadar with a mention of "Hindu extremists" who "hatched terroristic plots and welcomed German aid" in his 1921 racist tirade *The Rising Tide of Color against White World-Supremacy*. While Sutherland does not mention Ghadar or Thind's political activities and sentiments in his opinion, Sutherland certainly read Wolverton's earlier ruling.

Thind himself believed that the British were behind the Supreme Court's decision. In a speech given at the World Fellowship of Faiths in Chicago in 1933, he said that "America . . . sided with perfidious Albion (a derogatory term for England) to insult India in the matter of citizenship, we being the only Aryans excluded" (quoted in de la Garza 2010, 20–21). There is a wealth of evidence that Thind was under surveillance by British intelligence for decades starting as early as 1916, when he worked in the lumber mills of Oregon and circulated pamphlets published by the Ghadar press. British agents continued to monitor him during his career as a traveling lecturer, attending his talks, taking notes on his speeches, and keeping copies of his materials. Thind was included in lists of "Indian Extremists" and was referred to on one occasion as "the notorious Indian seditionist."

The Aftermath of United States v. Thind

There were major consequences in the wake of the decision in *United States v. Thind*, not just for Thind himself, but across the United States and throughout the world. The Court's ruling in *Thind* was retroactively applied to Asian Americans who had been rendered "ineligible" for citizenship. When combined with various laws on the Pacific Coast that excluded "aliens ineligible for citizenship" from owning land, *Thind* led to the disenfranchisement of large numbers of Asian American farmers and forced many into precarious arrangements in which they had to lease land or own it through white proxies (Park 2004, 127). The INS swiftly moved through local U.S. attorneys to denaturalize other South Asian immigrants who had previously gained citizenship, leaving an estimated forty-two to sixty-nine South Asian immigrants stateless by 1926 (Jacoby 1958, 2). Women who had married naturalized

Asian Americans also became suddenly vulnerable to becoming stateless after *Thind*, since the Cable Act of 1922 had removed guarantees of citizenship to any woman who married an "alien eligible to naturalization." Roughly 3,000 South Asians returned to India between the First and Second World Wars, a massive percentage of their total numbers. Doubtlessly, the *Thind* decision and the changes that resulted from it were a major cause of this mass exodus of immigrants, who saw little hope for themselves to become citizens or landowners in the United States.

In 1926, Sakharam Ganesh Pandit, the first Indian-born attorney in the United States, authored a pamphlet with Roy E. Chase entitled "An Examination of the Opinion of the Supreme Court of the United States Deciding against the Eligibility of Hindus for Citizenship," in which he pointed out the inconsistencies of the Court's opinion, argued against its retroactive application, and gave a summary of "the consensus of scientific opinion . . . that Hindus are Caucasians and therefore of the white race." Pandit and Chase ended the pamphlet by raising the specter of the threat posed by imperial Japan and a hypothetical pan-Asian alliance. They suggested that through the *Thind* decision, the United States was cutting itself off from a natural ally in India, with its people of Aryan descent and "a considerable degree of Anglo-Saxon culture." Pandit was not incorrect in seeing international consequences stemming from the *Thind* decision. Several resolutions and enactments by Indian legislative bodies explicitly responded to *United States v. Thind*, as well as reports of related restrictions placed on American missionaries and business interests within India (Hess 1969, 67–68).

Some of the most significant domestic agitation came from the Bengali-born scholar and activist Taraknath Das and his wife, Mary, who made numerous attempts to pass legislation in America that would validate the citizenship of those Indian immigrants who naturalized before the *Thind* decision (Hess 1969, 69–70). In 1926, they were supported by Senator David Reed, who introduced a resolution to this end. Although Reed's measure was sidelined and never enacted, there is evidence that while it was pending, it was one of the main factors that motivated American author Katherine Mayo to go to India and write her book, *Mother India*, a scathing polemical work that sought to undercut opposition to British colonial rule of India by presenting an array of social ills there as the result of Hinduism (Jha 1971, 51–52, 53n). Mayo's book was widely read, and it created an uproar across three continents that resulted in a series of significant unintended political consequences (Sinha 2006).

In the year following the Supreme Court's decision, Thind, along with several of his South Asian American peers, began a career as a traveling metaphysical lecturer and spiritual teacher that would continue for more than four decades and take him to scores of cities across the United States (Deslippe 2016, 103–04; Deslippe

2018). Relying on his learned background, Thind would usually offer dozens of lectures in any given city and complement them with classes on healing and breathing exercises. He also authored several books, including *Divine Wisdom* and *Radiant Road to Reality*, as well as several pamphlets and booklets. Many of his lectures were collected and published in book form. Thind was also an exponent of *Sant Mat* (literally "path of the saints") and the *Radhasoami* movement, and some have viewed Thind's career as a spiritual journey consisting of two main acts: the first fifteen years as a metaphysical lecturer, during which he combined various threads into his teaching (his Sikh background, the proto-positive thinking movement of New Thought, Western psychology), and a second period from the late 1930s onward, in which he more openly espoused *Sant Mat*, initiated students in the tradition, and made his own claims to being of *Radhasoami* lineage (Diem-Lane 2008, 49–53).

In 1935, the Nye-Lea Act was passed by Congress. It granted American citizenship to any veteran of the First World War who had served honorably and was "heretofore ineligible to citizenship because not a free white person or of African

---

Yogis, Swamis, and Lecturers

Thind's career as a metaphysical lecturer and spiritual teacher was a surprisingly common and logical choice for dozens of South Asian Americans during the interwar decades of the 1920s and 1930s. The Indian-born Christian missionary Theodore Fieldbrave felt it necessary to include the category of "The Hindu Swamis and Yogis" alongside farmers, students, and merchants in his 1934 survey of "East Indians in the United States." While Americans were generally opposed to immigration from South Asia, there was also a widespread curiosity about India and an acute interest from metaphysical seekers who saw the land as a source of ancient, mystic truths. The *Thind* decision and resulting wave of denaturalization proceedings left many educated Indian immigrants unable to travel, ineligible to own land, and underemployed. Many of them were able to make a living by catering to an interested American public and pulled from their respective backgrounds to recast themselves as yogis, swamis, and rishis. Most would travel the country, stay in a given city for a week to several months, and give a series of free public lectures to draw interest, which would then lead to a series of smaller private courses of instruction for a fee. Some engaged in this livelihood temporarily for several months or years, and others, like Thind, did so for decades.

nativity or of African descent." Thind once again applied for citizenship in 1936, and on this, his third attempt, it finally held. He married Vivian Davies in March 1940, and they raised a son and a daughter at a home in Los Angeles. More than half a century after his first arrival in the United States, Thind made a return trip to India with his wife in the summer of 1963. He was met by the prime minister and president, honored in Delhi and the Punjab, and gave lectures at several universities. Thind passed away in mid-September 1967, just shy of his seventy-fifth birthday.

United States v. Thind stands as a landmark moment and is referred to often as a critical event in the history of race and immigration in America. As one of the most notable figures within a relatively tiny number of immigrants from India in the early twentieth century, Bhagat Singh Thind, along with Congressman Dalip Singh Saund, is an honored and often-remembered pioneer among South Asian, Punjabi, and Sikh Americans. In recent years, Thind's legacy has been significantly bolstered by his son, David, who has reprinted many of his books; commissioned a biography and documentary film; and collected and digitized a host of documents, photographs, and ephemera related to his father. Thind himself is largely remembered for his Supreme Court case and efforts to gain citizenship, often at the expense of the complexities of those efforts, an intricate understanding of Thind as an individual, and his later life as a teacher.

DOCUMENT EXCERPTS

U.S. v. Bhagat Singh Thind *Ruling (1923)*

The Supreme Court ruling in the case of U.S. v. Bhagat Singh Thind *was delivered by Justice George A. Sutherland on February 19, 1923. The excerpts included here show that the key element of the case was Thind not being "a white person" and therefore not being eligible for naturalization. The Court decision against Thind echoes and reflects the widespread nativism and restrictive immigration policies at the time, especially those against immigrants from Asian countries and regions.*

United States v. Bhagat Singh Thind, 1923

If the applicant is a white person, within the meaning of this section, he is entitled to naturalization; otherwise not. In Ozawa v. United States, 260 U.S. 178, 43 Sup. Ct. 65, 67 L. Ed., decided November 13, 1922, we had occasion to consider the application of these words to the case of a cultivated Japanese and were constrained to hold that he was not within their meaning. As there pointed out, the provision is not that any particular class of persons shall be excluded, but it is, in effect, that only white persons shall be included within the privilege of the statute. "The intention was to confer the privilege of citizenship upon that class of persons whom the fathers knew as white, and to deny it to all who could not be so classified. It is not enough to say that the framers did not have in mind the brown or yellow races of Asia. It is necessary to go farther and be able to say that had these particular races been suggested the language of the act would have been so varied as to include them within its privileges"—citing Dartmouth College v. Woodward, 4 Wheat. 518, 644. Following a long line of decisions of the lower Federal courts, we held that the words imported a racial and not an individual test and were meant to indicate only persons of what is popularly known as the Caucasian race. But, as there pointed out, the conclusion that the phrase "white persons" and the word "Caucasian" are synonymous does not end the matter. It enabled us to dispose of the problem as it was there presented, since the applicant for citizenship clearly fell outside the zone of debatable ground on the negative side; but the decision still left the question to be dealt with, in doubtful and different cases, by the "process of judicial inclusion and exclusion." Mere ability on the part of an applicant for naturalization to establish a line of descent from a Caucasian ancestor will not ipso facto to and necessarily conclude the inquiry. "Caucasian" is a conventional word of much flexibility, as a study of the literature dealing with racial questions will disclose, and while it and the words "white persons" are treated as synonymous for the purposes of that case, they are not of identical meaning-idem per idem.

In the endeavor to ascertain the meaning of the statute, we must not fail to keep in mind that it does not employ the word "Caucasian," but the words "white persons," and these are words of common speech, and not of scientific origin. The word "Caucasian," not only was not employed in the law, but was probably wholly unfamiliar to the original framers of the statute in 1790. When we employ it, we do so as an aid to the ascertainment of the legislative intent, and not as an invariable substitute for the statutory words. Indeed, as used in the science of ethnology, the connotation of the word is by no means clear, and the use of it in its scientific sense as an equivalent for the words of the statute, other considerations aside, would simply mean the substitution of one perplexity for another. But in this country, during the last half century especially, the word, by common usage has acquired a popular meaning, not clearly defined to be sure, but sufficiently so to enable us to say that its popular, as distinguished from its scientific application is of appreciably narrower scope. It is in the popular sense of the word, therefore, that we employ is as an aid to the construction of the statute, for it would be obviously illogical to convert words of common speech used in a statute into words of scientific terminology when neither the latter nor the science for whose purposes they were coined was within the contemplation of the framers of the statute or of the people for whom it was framed. The words of the statute are to be interpreted in accordance with the understanding of the common man from whose vocabulary they were taken.

. . .

It does not seem necessary to pursue the matter of scientific classification further. We are unable to agree with the District Court, or with other lower federal courts, in the conclusion that a native Hindu is eligible for naturalization under section 2169. The words of familiar speech, which were used by the original framers of the law, were intended to include only the type of man whom they knew as white. The immigration of that day was almost exclusively from the British Isles and Northwestern Europe, whence they and their forebears had come. When they extended the privilege of American citizenship to "any alien being a free white person" it was these immigrants—bone of their bone and flesh of their flesh—and their kind whom they must have had affirmatively in mind. The succeeding years brought immigrants from Eastern, Southern and Middle Europe, among them the Slavs and the dark-eyed, swarthy people of Alpine and Mediterranean stock, and these were received as unquestionably akin to those already here and readily amalgamated with them. It was the descendants of these, and other immigrants of like origin, who constituted the white population of the country when section 2169, re-enacting the naturalization test of 1790, was adopted, and, there is no reason to doubt, with like intent and meaning.

What, if any, people of Primarily Asiatic stock come within the words of the section we do not deem it necessary now to decide. There is much in the origin and historic development of the statute to suggest that no Asiatic whatever was included. The debates in Congress, during the consideration of the subject in 1870 and 1875, are persuasively of this character. In 1873, for example, the words "free white persons" were unintentionally omitted from the compilation of the Revised Statutes. This omission was supplied in 1875 by the act to correct errors and supply omissions. 18 Stat. c. 80, p. 318. When this act was under consideration by Congress efforts were made to strike out the words quoted, and it was insisted upon the one hand and conceded upon the other, that the effect of their retention was to exclude Asiatics generally from citizenship. While what was said upon that occasion, to be sure, furnishes no basis for judicial construction of the statute, it is, nevertheless, an important historic incident, which may not be altogether ignored in the search for the true meaning of words which are themselves historic. That question, however, may well be left for final determination until the details have been more completely disclosed by the consideration of particular cases, as they from time to time arise. The words of the statute, it must be conceded, do not readily yield to exact interpretation, and it is probably better to leave them as they are than to risk undue extension or undue limitation of their meaning by any general paraphrase at this time.

What we now hold is that the words "free white persons" are words of common speech, to be interpreted in accordance with the understanding of the common man, synonymous with the word "Caucasian" only as that word is popularly understood. As so understood and used, whatever may be the speculations of the ethnologist, it does not include the body of people to whom the appellee belongs. It is a matter of familiar observation and knowledge that the physical group characteristics of the Hindus render them readily distinguishable from the various groups of persons in this country commonly recognized as white. The children of English, French, German, Italian, Scandinavian, and other European parentage, quickly merge into the mass of our population and lose the distinctive hallmarks of their European origin. On the other hand, it cannot be doubted that the children born in this country of Hindu parents would retain indefinitely the clear evidence of their ancestry. It is very far from our thought to suggest the slightest question of racial superiority or inferiority. What we suggest is merely racial difference, and it is of such character and extent that the great body of our people instinctively recognize it and reject the thought of assimilation.

It is not without significance in this connection that Congress, by the Act of February 5, 1917, 39 Stat. 874, c. 29, 3, has now excluded from admission into this country all natives of Asia within designated limits of latitude and longitude, including the whole of India. This not only constitutes conclusive evidence of the congressional attitude of opposition to Asiatic immigration generally, but is persuasive of a similar attitude toward Asiatic naturalization as well, since it is not likely that Congress would be willing to accept as citizens a class of persons whom it rejects as immigrants.

It follows that a negative answer must be given to the first question, which disposes of the case and renders an answer to the second question unnecessary, and it will be so certified.

Source: *United States v. Bhagat Singh Thind*, 261 U.S. 204 (1923).

See also: The First Sikh Gurdwara in the United States Established in Stockton, California, 1912; The Luce-Celler Act 1946; The Webb-Haney Act Passed by California State Legislature, 1923

Further Reading

Coulson, Doug. 2017. *Race, Nation, and Refuge: The Rhetoric of Race in Asian American Citizenship Cases*. Albany: State University of New York Press.

de la Garza, Amanda. 2010. *Doctorji: The Life, Teachings, and Legacy of Dr. Bhagat Singh Thind*. Los Angeles: Dr. Bhagat Singh Thind Spiritual Science Foundation.

Deslippe, Philip. 2016. "Rishis and Rebels: The Punjabi Sikh Presence in Early American Yoga," *Journal of Punjab Studies* 23, no. 1–2, 93–129.

Deslippe, Philip. 2018. "The Swami Circuit: Mapping the Terrain of Early American Yoga," *Journal of Yoga Studies* 1, no. 1, 5–44.

Diem-Lane, Andrea. 2008. *The Guru in America: The Influence of Radhasoami on New Religions in America*. Walnut, CA: Mt. San Antonio College Philosophy Group.

Gross, Ariela J. 2008. *What Blood Won't Tell: A History of Race on Trial in America*. Cambridge, MA: Harvard University Press.

Hess, Gary. 1969. "The 'Hindu' in America: Immigration and Naturalization Policies and India, 1917–1946." *Pacific Historical Review* 38, no. 1, 55–79.

Jacoby, Harold S. 1958. "More Thind against than Sinning." *The Pacific Historian* 2, no.1–2, 8.

Jew, Victor. 1997. "George Sutherland and American Ethnicity: A Pre History to 'Thind' and "Ozawa.'" *The Centennial Review* 41, no. 3: 553–564.

Jha, Manoranjan. 1971. *Katherine Mayo and India*. New Delhi: People's Publishing House.

López, Ian F. Haney. 1996. *White by Law: The Legal Construction of Race*. New York: New York University Press.

Park, John S. W. 2004. *Elusive Citizenship: Immigration, Asian Americans, and the Paradox of Civil Rights*. New York: New York University Press.

Scheffauer, Herman. 1910. "The Tide of Turbans." *The Forum* 43, June, 616–618.

Sinha, Mrinalini. 2006. *Specters of Mother India: The Global Restructuring of an Empire*. Durham, NC: Duke University Press.

Snow, Jennifer C. 2007. *Protestant Missionaries, Asian Immigrants, and Ideologies of Race in America, 1850–1924*. New York: Routledge.

Sohi, Seema. 2014. *Echoes of Mutiny: Race, Surveillance and Indian Anticolonialism in North America*. Oxford, UK: Oxford University Press.

"Wife of Dr. Thind Says in City to See If He's Talking about Her." 1926. *World-Herald* (Omaha, Nebraska), April 29.

Gong Lum v. Rice, 1927

Michael S. Rodriguez

Chronology

1896   *Plessy v. Ferguson* upholds the "separate but equal" doctrine in public transportation and asserts the authority of the government to determine the racial classification of individuals.

1882   Chinese Exclusion Act (Immigration Act of 1882) excludes Chinese laborers from entering the United States and bars re-entry for Chinese returning to America. Reauthorized in 1892 and repealed in 1943, the act instigates early forms of illegal immigration— Chinese immigrants entering the United States through Canada or Mexico, some settling in the Mississippi delta.

1898   *United States v. Wong Kim Ark* affirms the constitutional rights that any person born in the United States is a citizen, regardless of their parents' citizenship status or eligibility for naturalization.

1899	*Cumming v. Richmond County Board of Education* upholds a state law that allows separate high schools for black and white students.
October 12, 1927	The *Gong Lum v. Rice* case is argued before the U.S. Supreme Court.
April 25, 1938	*United States v. Carolene Products Co.* establishes the framework for heightened judicial scrutiny, a key development for subsequent civil rights cases.
1944	Supreme Court notes in *Korematsu v. United States* that limiting the civil rights of a specific racial group invokes a suspect classification but that not all such classifications are unconstitutional. A dissenting opinion characterizes the internment of Japanese Americans during World War II as the "legalization of racism."
1950	*Sweatt v. Painter* and *McLaurin v. Oklahoma* effectively end the *Plessy* doctrine of "separate but equal" in graduate and professional schools.
1954	The U.S. Supreme Court in *Brown v. Board of Education of Topeka* invalidates the *Plessy* doctrine of "separate but equal" in public education.

Narrative

Supreme Court Justice Robert Jackson famously observed that a pillar of American constitutionalism is that the government cannot prescribe matters of individual conscience and expression for individuals (*West Virginia*, 642). Generations of Asian Americans confronted and challenged a racialized political order that classified them as either incompatible with American identity or as a threat to national security. Despite an abiding faith in America, foreign-born Chinese Americans were rendered categorically ineligible for naturalization under the Chinese Exclusion Act, and Japanese Americans were classified as a subversive "fifth column" that warranted forcible relocation to internment camps during World War II. The historical experience of Asian Americans in the United States exemplifies a racial paradigm that hindered the constitutional democracy until the civil rights movement of the twentieth century.

Though not well known, the Supreme Court case *Gong Lum v. Rice* (1927) challenged the classification of Chinese Americans in the Mississippi delta as "colored," thereby segregating them into nonwhite public schools. *Gong Lum* highlights three critical, underlying assumptions of America's racial paradigm: the government, not the individual, is the final arbitrator of defining and assigning racial identity and racial classification; it is the proper role of the government through policy making and statutory and constitutional interpretation to confer racial privileges on the group that occupies the dominant position in a racialized society; and majoritarian politics, as distinguished from basic and universal constitutional guarantees, was the *sine qua non* of America's racial paradigm. *Gong Lum* falls squarely within a line of constitutional interpretation, since the *Dred Scott v. Sanford* (1857) case placed the scope and nature of social and political rights for nonwhites entirely in the hands of white majoritarian politics.

Martha and Berda Lum were removed from Rosedale Consolidated High School in Mississippi during their lunch period on the first day of the academic term (September 15, 1924) because the school superintendent classified them as members of the "colored race" and therefore ineligible to attend the whites-only high school. The Lum family hired a former governor of Mississippi, Earl Brewer, and secured an order from a trial court in Bolivar County, Mississippi, mandating that the school readmit the Lum children. However, on appeal to the Supreme Court of Mississippi and ultimately to the United States Supreme Court in 1927, the Lum family's challenge to the racial classification and segregation was unsuccessful. The outcome left the Lums no choice but to uproot the family in an act of self-exile and abandon their home in Rosedale. The Court decision imposed an impossible choice on Chinese Americans of the Mississippi delta: surrender to the racial indignities of Jim Crowism or move to other parts of the country. Many Chinese families opted for the latter (Berard 2016, 141).

In the historical trajectory of American constitutionalism, the importance of a case is not always the court decision but what it clarifies and reveals about people. Another case involving Chinese Americans, *United States v. Wong Kim Ark* (1898), affirmed the constitutional guarantee that any person born in the United States is a citizen, regardless of their parents' citizenship status or eligibility for naturalization. The legacy of *Wong Kim Ark* is evident in contemporary debates on birthright citizenship and immigration. In contrast, *Gong Lum*'s contribution is that it exposed the underlying racialized assumptions that impeded the fulfillment of constitutional democracy in the United States until the second half of the twentieth century.

The Lums of the Mississippi Delta

The arrival of the Lum family in the Mississippi delta is tied to the racialized economic and political systems of the South in the late nineteenth and early twentieth centuries. The Thirteenth Amendment abolished private, chattel slavery. However, it did not completely end slavery and indentured servitude, providing for their continuance through the amendment's qualifying phrase "except as a punishment for crime." Convict labor, through racially targeted vagrancy laws in the South, helped to resuscitate the racialized economic order that was temporarily decimated by the Civil War and Reconstruction. The failure of the state-sponsored, forced labor system to fully meet the needs of Southern labor created the conditions for Chinese immigrants to come to the Mississippi delta. Chinese immigrants were recruited and transported to the United States or entered the country illegally over the Canadian and Mexican borders and subsequently became embroiled in a system of peonage labor that replaced slave labor. A similar pattern unfolded in other regions of the hemisphere and the Caribbean (Berard 2016, 24).

Like thousands of Chinese immigrants who settled in the post–Civil War South, the Lum family occupied a racially precarious position between whites and African Americans during a period of virulent racism, nativism, and anti-immigrant sentiment. The harsh and demeaning working conditions, as well as poor pay, compelled many delta Chinese to abandon peonage labor for entrepreneurial opportunities, opening groceries and laundromats that primarily served African Americans (*Gong Lum v. Rice*). The Lum family owned a grocery store and secured a measure of economic mobility that was tethered to the fluctuations of the sharecropping agrarian economy of the Mississippi delta. When Martha and Berda Lum, along with two other Chinese students, were summarily prohibited from attending Rosedale Consolidated High School, the Lum family secured legal counsel and sued the school district. The Lum family was initially victorious at the trial court level, where a writ of mandamus was issued ordering the school district to readmit Martha and Berda to the high school. The school district immediately filed an appeal to the Supreme Court of Mississippi, thereby preventing the return of the Lum children to Rosedale Consolidated. The practical and symbolic implication of keeping the case in litigation was that the determination of the social status, race, and identity of the Lum children, and all other Chinese children in Mississippi, was reserved for the state's judiciary (Berard 2016, 100).

The Mississippi constitution of 1890 expressly provided for racially separated schools for white and colored students. Chinese children were considered members of a distinct race (Mongolian) but for the purpose of state-sponsored segregation were classified under the general term of "colored races." The delta Chinese rejected being amalgamated into a category under which all members were simply nonwhite. They did not want their children to attend under-resourced schools for African Americans, nor did they wish to accept the notion that the referent group for their pathway to assimilation was blacks, not whites (Quan 1982, 45).

Racial Kratocracy and Constitutional Democracy

The *Gong Lum* case provides an opportunity for us to understand how, for much of its history, the United States operated under a dual system of constitutional democracy and racial kratocracy. The term "kratocracy" relates to the social Darwinist belief that it is right and legitimate for the strong to impose their will on the weak. A dimension of American racial kratocracy that bears prominently on the significance of the *Gong Lum* case is how ideology functions to legitimatize the power relations in racial hierarchy. In its most straightforward formulation, an ideology is how a culture structures and understands the meaning of the social reality it has constructed for itself. While that meaning is understood as being produced and reproduced through social action and negotiation, a racial kratocracy limits participation in shaping ideology to members of the dominant racial group. Ideology is not value-neutral; the power and privilege of dominant groups are simultaneously embedded and veiled in the very structure of an ideology. *Gong Lum* highlights the ideological elements of America's racial kratocracy that had to be discredited and abandoned for a fuller, more inclusive, constitutional democracy to emerge through the civil rights movement. Regarding the three ideological assumptions that undergird the racial paradigm that legitimized the political order of racial kratocracy, America's racial paradigm rationalized the denial of basic guarantees, rights, immunities, and privileges of citizenship to vast segments of the American populace (i.e., people of color).

A paradigm is a useful framework for understanding and deliberating the social and political reality a polity constructs for itself. Thomas Kuhn observes that a paradigm represents a way of organizing knowledge that allows a community of scholars to achieve consensus on the most comprehensive explanation of natural and social phenomena. A paradigm remains ascendant until anomalies arise that it cannot explain; this "problem" creates the possibility for a new paradigm to emerge—hence, a paradigm shift occurs. A new paradigm eclipses a previous one if it is more comprehensive, that is, if it accounts for the same phenomena but can also explain the previously anomalous phenomena. Racial kratocracy and constitutional democracy can be described as competing and incompatible paradigms for organizing American society. Both paradigms coexisted and vied for dominance from the country's founding to the civil rights revolution. The paradigm shift represents the long-standing clash between two paradigms—racial kratocracy and constitutional democracy—that was ultimately resolved in favor of the latter during the second half of the twentieth century.

The sustained political mobilization in the streets, legislatures, and courts of America by civil rights activists and organizations precipitated the kind of crisis that could not be accommodated by the paradigm of racial kratocracy. Ultimately, a string of landmark Supreme Court decisions, most notably *Brown v. Board of Education of Topeka* (1954); statutes like the Civil Rights and Voting Rights acts of 1964 and 1965, respectively; and a moral consensus on the urgency of racial equality ultimately laid the groundwork for the (formal) demise of racial kratocracy and the ascendancy of constitutional democracy.

Racial Classification, Racial Privilege, and Majoritarian Politics

The identity and classification of the Lum children were initially defined in terms of national origin or ancestry—being Chinese. The conflation of race and national origin calls to mind *Westminster v. Mendez*, a 1947 case that challenged California's racially segregated public education system as it applied to Mexican Americans. The state used national origin as a proxy for race, though Mexican Americans were legally categorized as white. Since California law did not expressly provide for segregation based on national origin, two federal courts ruled in favor of the Mendez family. A year later, California enacted legislation that desegregated the state's public education system. The governor who signed the law, Earl Warren, authored the unanimous *Brown* decision seven years later as chief justice of the U.S. Supreme Court.

The attorney for the Lum family advanced a multipronged argument: first, it was incorrect to classify Martha as a member of the "colored race"; second, the school officials had no authority to deny the Lum children admission to the school based on a misapplication of the colored racial classification; and third, since the school district did not provide a separate educational institution for the Mongolian race, the decision to attend either the white or colored school should devolve to the Lum family. School officials argued that as a member of the "Mongolian or yellow race," Martha was ineligible to attend schools established exclusively for white children; her only choice was to either attend the colored school or enroll in a private institution (Berard 2016, 99).

The trial court issued a writ of mandamus and ordered Rosedale Consolidated to readmit Martha and her sister; the school district immediately appealed to the Supreme Court of Mississippi. Brewer, the Lum family counsel, argued that racial classifications are matters of degree, not kind. Instead of a binary polarity between two mutually exclusive racial categories that are organized hierarchically, Brewer offered an understanding of racial difference that is based on a racial continuum, not categorically distinct racial categories. He argued that both Chinese and Japanese evince some of the same virtuous qualities as whites, that is, they are intelligent, entrepreneurial, and somehow between whites and blacks on the racial continuum (Berard 2016, 103).

The state Supreme Court summarily rejected Brewer's theory of a racial continuum and ruled against the Lum family by predicating its ruling on a state constitutional provision that expressly provided for segregated schools for white and colored children (Berard 2016, 12). The state Supreme Court reasoned that since Martha was not imbued with the purity of the white race, she could not be classified as white. The Court rejected Brewer's argument and embraced the opposing counsel's argument that it was left to Mississippi to define the only viable choice for the Lum family: attending the colored school or opting for a private school (Berard 2016, 107).

The U.S. Supreme Court reinforced the Supreme Court of Mississippi's codification of a binary classification between a pure white or Caucasian race and an amalgamation of races consolidated under the generic category of colored races (Berard 2016, 137). The court deferred to Mississippi's binary school system. Chief Justice William Howard Taft observed in *Gong Lum* that most of the segregation cases cited, in the Court's opinion, only involved separation of whites and blacks. Therefore, he asserted that the Court could not think of any reason not to treat Chinese Americans the same as African Americans for purposes of deciding the constitutionality of racial segregation (Berard 2016, 137). His reasoning rejected the view of the Lum family's counsel before the Mississippi Supreme Court that Chinese were closer in the racial continuum to whites than blacks. Taft clearly preferred the binary and hierarchical construction of racial categorization that renders an individual either white or nonwhite.

The legal arguments for the Rosedale Consolidated School before both the Mississippi and United States Supreme Courts were explicitly predicated on this link between racial classification and state-sponsored, racial privilege. The school district advanced three arguments for the proposition that it was the explicit purpose of Mississippi, through its statutes and constitution, to confer an exclusive racial privilege to whites. First, it was the state that determines the legislative classification for each group, not members of a racial group. The legislature determined that the racial status of Chinese was essentially the same as that of African Americans (Berard 2016, 103). Second, segregation was established by the state's legislature for the express purpose of protecting whites from all other races, including the Chinese (Berard 2016, 107). Third, the state's legislature, through majority rule, had determined that the exclusive beneficiary of preventing intermingling was the Caucasian race, and consequently, the intermingling among nonwhite races was not a legislative concern. Chinese could therefore be classed with African Americans. The central organizing principle of segregation in Mississippi was that a legislative majority intended the exclusive beneficiary of segregation to be whites. Nonwhite races could therefore not enjoy the state-sponsored privilege of having the preservation of their racial essence rise to the level of legislative and constitutional recognition.

The exclusive nature of that privilege meant that political authority would insulate the racial purity of the dominant racial group from perceived corruption through association, especially miscegenation, with racial groups deemed as colored and thereby inferior. The reification of racial purity occurs when political authority confers this state-sponsored privilege in a racial kratocracy to one group, while denying it to others. The ideological logic of race purity, or essence, has three elements: each distinct racial group has an essence, or purity; there is no moral equivalence among the various racial groups—that is, the purity of the racially superior white race is understood to be worthier of protection from intermingling with other groups; and segregation is not merely the de facto separation of the races, but an expression of the white majority's will that the exclusive racial privilege should be enforced through legislative enactment.

The logic of exclusive racial privilege was clear in the legal reasoning of *Gong Lum*. The U.S. Supreme Court's unanimous opinion acknowledged this privilege and categorically asserted that the privilege of invoking state power to protect a group's racial purity belongs exclusively to the white race. Nonblack people of color (like the Chinese of the Mississippi delta) who occupied the racially amorphous spaces between whites and blacks were denied access to the same exclusive racial privilege of not mixing with blacks. The value of the privilege lay in its exclusivity, which was authoritatively allocated to invoke the famous definition of politics through majoritarian politics and constitutional interpretation.

Brewer did not challenge the constitutionality of racial classifications, the racial privilege of protecting the purity of a racial group, or the appropriateness of government to enact the assumptions of racial kratocracy through majoritarian politics. Brewer's litigation strategy was based, quite simply, on the equal protection argument that the logical implication of these assumptions would be that the Lum children could attend the school of their choice, if the assumptions were applied fully and universally to all racial groups. The fallacy in Brewer's equal protection reasoning in *Gong Lum* became apparent in subsequent civil rights cases (*Sweatt v. Painter* [1950] and *McLaurin v. Oklahoma* [1950]) in which the Supreme Court rejected the notion that a literal and precise application of the *Plessy* doctrine of separate but equal was possible.

Taft's opinion in *Gong Lum* embraced an alternative definition of equal protection, one that would be satisfied if the state of Mississippi, at a minimum, provided a common education to all children of the state. The manner in which that obligation was met did pose an equal protection concern and consequently did not justify scrutiny by the federal judiciary. The U.S. Supreme Court would not object if Mississippi chose to provide a common education by creating school systems based on a binary, racial classification that gave one race—but not all races—the state-sponsored privilege of being educated in a manner that preserved its racial purity. The Lum family's counsel largely embraced this same racialized logic but argued that equal protection demanded that if the state-sponsored privilege of not intermingling with undesirable races was to be extended to one race, it was a constitutional violation of equal protection to not extend it to all races. The idea that government can classify Americans on the basis of race and extend the exclusive privilege of preserving racial purity to only one racial group through legislation was astonishingly unproblematic to the supreme courts of both Mississippi and the United States.

Paradigm Shift: United States v. Carolene Products *and* Brown v. Board of Education of Topeka

Although *Gong Lum* did not trigger the paradigm shift from racial kratocracy to constitutional democracy, it revealed the ideological assumptions that had to be dismantled for the latter paradigm to eclipse the former. That shift entailed discrediting the constitutional doctrine that racial classifications, as well as the exclusive privilege extended to one but not all racial groups, are so problematic that they should be deemed presumptively invalid. Subsequent cases that signaled this critical paradigm shift were *United States v. Carolene Products* (1938) and the *Brown* decision. *Carolene Products* undercut the first (racial classifications) and third (majoritarian politics) assumptions of racial kratocracy. *Brown* discredited the second assumption (exclusive racial privilege).

The primacy of majoritarian politics within the ideological framework of racial kratocracy, and affirmed by *Gong Lum,* was subsequently undermined eleven years later by what has come to be known as the famous footnote #4 in *Carolene Products.* The case is profoundly significant in modern constitutional interpretation because it outlined a framework for the judicial review of federal and state legislative enactments. The facts of the case were entirely unrelated to racial segregation. The case turned on the authority of Congress under the Commerce Clause to regulate milk with a substitute for milk fat (coconut oil). In the opinion's footnote #4, the Court articulated a framework for reviewing challenges to economic regulations. Henceforth, it would adopt a deferential posture to legislative majorities—if economic regulations contained a plausible and discernible rational basis. The decision was a significant departure from decades of imposing more exacting scrutiny on economic regulations, from the laissez-faire theory of constitutionalism of the Lochner period to the evisceration of New Deal programs by the Supreme Court. The conservative judicial activism of the Supreme Court had previously imposed a skeptical view of economic regulations that limited property and contractual rights, or it rejected an overly expansive view of governmental authority to regulate interstate commerce. While *Carolene Products* marked a retreat from the controversial invalidations of crucial New Deal economic legislation, the Court signaled that heightened scrutiny would be reserved for legislation that restricted the capacity of political processes to democratically rectify problematic public policies.

The third element of the footnote is especially crucial for the paradigm shift from racial kratocracy to constitutional democracy. It articulated a standard of review for social legislation that imposed heightened judicial review of legislation that placed special burdens on "insular and discrete" groups based on religion, national origin, or race. When prejudice against minorities diminishes the capacity of democratic political processes to function properly in protecting them, the Court argued that heightened judicial scrutiny would be warranted; indeed, it would be imperative (*United States v. Carolene Products*, 155).

The protection of insular and discrete minorities became the doctrinal underpinning of the Court's approach to "suspect classifications," a standard of judicial review that yielded landmark civil rights victories in the federal judiciary for a generation. The standard reserved the Court's strictest scrutiny for legislative enactments that proceeded from racial, national origin, or religious classifications. Henceforth, the Court would begin its analyses of challenged legislation with the presumption that such (suspect) classifications are facially invalid. The burden of proof fell to the government to overcome that presumption by demonstrating a compelling governmental purpose for the challenged classifications. Additionally, the legislative enactments had to be narrowly tailored to accomplish the stated legislative goals. The noted constitutional scholar Gerald Gunther characterized this standard of review (strict scrutiny) as "'strict' in theory but fatal in fact" (Winkler 2006, 794). The *Carolene Products* footnote was instrumental in providing the Supreme Court a rigorous standard of review that no longer simply deferred to legislative majorities that imposed burdens on specific minority groups through classifications based on facially unconstitutional grounds like race, national origin, religion, language, and sexual orientation.

The second ideological assumption of racial kratocracy was undermined by the reasoning of the unanimous Supreme Court decision in *Brown*, which at first glance is only incidentally related to *Gong Lum*. Chief Justice Earl Warren's unanimous decision in *Brown* cited *Gong Lum* only to note the difference between the two cases: the latter did not challenge the doctrine of separate but equal but merely argued its misapplication to the Lum family (*Brown v. Board*, 491). Warren also incorrectly referred to the child in *Gong Lum* (Martha) as a male. However, the *Brown* decision failed to appreciate how an underlying link in both cases illuminated the pathway through which a paradigm shift from racial kratocracy to constitutional democracy would unfold. A significant portion of that link lies in the state-sponsored, exclusive privilege outlined in *Gong Lum* and the notion of "intangibles" in the Supreme Court's reasoning in *Brown*.

The Warren court abandoned the doctrinal cornerstone of separate but equal by asserting that for purposes of constitutional interpretation, the crucial test was not solely an empirical analysis, namely whether the state in question created separate educational facilities that were, in objective terms, "substantially equal" (*Brown v. Board*, 488). Warren's pronouncement that separate but equal is inherently unequal, and therefore a violation of the Fourteenth Amendment, was not that the metric for establishing substantial equality was impossible to achieve. Nor was he asserting that the doctrine is a non sequitur, that is, that equality can ever be achieved through separateness. States that were the most adamant defenders of America's racial kratocracy could have erected educational institutions that were equal in terms of physical plant, per-student expenditures, quality of faculty, libraries, etc. However, such an approach would have belied, on two levels, the hierarchical order of social and political relations in America's racial kratocracy. The first is that absolute equality in public benefits, like a common education, would have implied that whites and nonwhites shared formal equality before the law. Second, separating the various races to maintain their racial purity through separate but equal educational systems would have connoted a certain moral equivalence in the worth of each group's racial essence. Both scenarios were incompatible with a central feature of racial kratocracy, that is, that the worth of the dominant racial group justified using state authority to protect it from the consequences of intermingling with races that whites deemed undesirable. If this state-sponsored, exclusive privilege denoted racial superiority for whites, its converse connoted racial inferiority for nonwhite races who were categorically excluded from the privilege.

The *Brown* decision cited previous cases, *Sweatt* and *McLaurin*, for the proposition that even though educational facilities were seemingly equal, the intangible benefits of studying at white institutions vastly surpassed those at the institutions designated for African Americans. The remedy in both cases was limited to the petitioners without fully invalidating the doctrine of separate but equal. Both cases strengthened the paradigm of constitutional democracy by making the relative distribution of intangible benefits and burdens matters of constitutional cognizance. However, the primary point of reference for intangible factors in the *Sweatt* and *McLaurin* cases was the quality of the educational resources at segregated institutions, and only derivatively the beneficiaries of those resources (i.e., whites). *Brown* expanded the framework of analysis by focusing on another intangible factor: the "effect" of segregation on the children of color, who were deemed inferior on racial grounds and treated accordingly through segregation. If *Sweatt* and *McLaurin* established the proposition that segregation allocated certain intangible benefits to the dominant group and denied them to subordinated groups, *Brown* turned on the converse implication—namely that the denial of intangible benefits on racial grounds was not without effect. The flipside of intangible benefits is intangible burdens, and both convey symbolic expressions of individual and group worth.

Warren's opinion advanced the paradigm of constitutional democracy by expanding the scope of the Fourteenth Amendment's Equal Protection Clause to encompass the effect of the racial burden segregation imposes on students of color. He concluded that segregation imposes a potentially irreparable mark of inferiority in the hearts and minds of members of the community (*Brown v. Board*, 494). Racially based educational segregation conveyed to students of color a clear message of lesser worth, a psychological injury further compounded in Warren's reasoning by the sanction of law.

Warren signaled the demise of the paradigm of racial kratocracy by expressly rejecting any reasoning in *Plessy v. Ferguson* (1896) contrary to the *Brown* decision. The discredited racial logic was the infamous aphorism in *Plessy* that if racial segregation stamped the colored race with a "badge of inferiority," it was not a function of legislative enactment, but a freely chosen, yet fallacious, construction that people of color placed on segregation. To reinforce its point, the *Plessy* majority asserted that if African Americans were to assume a legislative majority and subordinate whites, a not-too-veiled reference to contemporaneous white perceptions of Reconstruction, the latter would simply not accept the assumption of inferiority (*Plessy v. Ferguson*, 559). The *Plessy* decision undercuts its own point in this regard. It conceded that the badge of inferiority indeed attached to the power of the state to classify people racially and to treat them accordingly, but simply asserted that it is an assumption that whites would not accept. The objection by the plaintiffs in both *Plessy* and *Brown* was not that they were forced to accept the assumption of inferiority but that the assumption was enforced through the force of law. Racialized assumptions of superiority/inferiority were also present in *Gong Lum*, but the Lum family's counsel asserted it was left to Martha Lum and her parents, not the government, to define their association with the groups that corresponded to those assumptions.

The second element in *Plessy* that *Brown* rejected was that government had the authority to racially classify individuals as it deemed appropriate. The *Plessy* majority argued that the power to assign races to a coach obviously implied the power to determine to which race the passenger belonged, as well as the power to determine the metric by which a particular state would deem an individual either white or colored. Like the Lum family years later, *Plessy* did not challenge the authority of government to establish racial classifications but asserted that the determination of assigning individuals to one classification or the other was left to the individual and not a governing authority. Indeed, Plessy himself claimed that he had a property interest in making that determination (i.e., maintaining his reputation for passing as white based on his creole features). The Court rejected Plessy's argument by ruling that the designation of Plessy as either white or colored was to be made not by him but by the laws of his state. That the power to establish racial classifications, as well as the metric for assigning individuals to them, was reserved for governmental authority and not individual autonomy was understood in *Plessy* as self-evident. That metric in *Plessy* was defined biologically in terms of the proportion of colored blood. However, the opinion simultaneously undercut its own racial logic by asserting that the relative mixture of white and colored blood was not self-determining but had to be constructed politically and legislatively through majoritarian sensibilities that varied from one state to the other, from an individual's mere physical appearance in some states to more formulaic ratios of black to white blood in other states.

Current Status and Influence

The well-known dissent by Justice John Marshall Harlan in *Plessy* is a vivid reminder that the Constitution does not interpret itself, notwithstanding the appeal in some quarters of textualist theories of constitutional interpretation. His dissent understood well the underlying assumptions of the paradigm of constitutional democracy. He articulated a nascent formulation of the presumptive invalidity of suspect classifications by arguing government is constitutionally prohibited from being cognizant of race in the protection and disbursement of rights and benefits. He declared that America's constitutional democracy is blind to caste, color, and racial classifications (*Plessy v. Ferguson*, 559). Harlan's dissent would also resonate with contemporary views that defining one's racial identity and consciousness is a matter of personal liberty, not governmental authority. His reasoning also categorically precluded state-sponsored, exclusive privileges that connote racial superiority/inferiority. Harlan also anticipated footnote #4 in *Carolene Products*, namely that the Fourteenth Amendment contains a positive immunity especially for people of color against legislation that targets them solely on the basis of race (*Plessy v. Ferguson*, 556). Perhaps the most prescient comments in Harlan's dissent are that the seeds of racial hatred are planted when a dominant majority imposes legislative enactments on minorities that are based on the assumption that the excluded racial groups are of such inferior worth that they should be precluded by public authority from intermingling with other races (*Plessy v. Ferguson*, 560).

If America can now be genuinely described as a fully developed constitutional democracy, it was not a foreordained conclusion that racial kratocracy would be eclipsed. W.E.B. Du Bois identified the "color line" as the essential challenge of the twentieth century, but it was also a question of which paradigm would emerge ascendant. Decades of civil rights protest and landmark victories in the federal judiciary facilitated the paradigm shift from racial kratocracy to constitutional democracy. However, less celebrated cases, like *Gong Lum v. Rice*, performed the indispensable role of bringing into sharp relief the ideological assumptions of racial kratocracy that had to be dismantled. The Lum family was ultimately unsuccessful in its challenge to racial segregation in Mississippi's public school system, but the enduring legacy of their case is that it illuminated the signposts along the path to a mature constitutional democracy.

DOCUMENT EXCERPTS

Gong Lum v. Rice *Ruling (1927)*

Gong Lum v. Rice *is a Supreme Court case in which the practice of sending Asian American children to segregated schools with African American children was upheld as constitutional. Although the case is little known among general public, it is of significance regarding equal rights, education, and the racial classification of white and "colored." A Chinese American living in Mississippi, Gong Lum sued the school superintendent in his district after his daughter, Martha, was sent to a segregated school attended only by African American students. Lum claimed that the school board had violated his daughter's rights of equal protection under the Fourteenth Amendment. The Supreme Court ruled in a unanimous decision that classifying Martha as "of the yellow race" and thus "colored" allowed the school board to send her to a segregated school. Chief Justice William Howard Taft wrote the Court's opinion.*

MR. CHIEF JUSTICE TAFT delivered the opinion of the Court.

This was a petition for mandamus filed in the state circuit court of Mississippi for the First judicial district of Bolivar county.

Gong Lum is a resident of Mississippi, resides in the Rosedale consolidated high school district, and is the father of Martha Lum. He is engaged in the mercantile business. Neither he nor she was connected with the consular service, or any other service, of the government of China, or any other government, at the time of her birth. She was nine years old when the petition was filed, having been born January 21, 1915, and she sued by her next friend, Chew How, who is a nativeborn citizen of the United States and the state of Mississippi. The petition alleged that she was of good moral character, between the ages of 5 and 21 years, and that, as she was such a citizen and an educable child, it became her father's duty under the law to send her to school; that she desired to attend the Rosedale consolidated high school; that at the opening of the school she appeared as a pupil, but at the noon recess she was notified by the superintendent that she would not be allowed to return to the school; that an order had been issued by the board of trustees, who are made defendants, excluding her from attending the school solely on the ground that she was of Chinese descent, and not a member of the white or Caucasian race, and that their order had been made in pursuance to instructions from the state superintendent of education of Mississippi, who is also made a defendant.

The petitioners further show that there is no school maintained in the district for the education of children of Chinese descent, and none established in Bolivar county where she could attend.

The Constitution of Mississippi . . . requires that there shall be a county common school fund, made up of poll taxes from the various counties, to be retained in the counties where the same is collected, and a state common school fund to be taken from the general fund in the state treasury, which together shall be sufficient to maintain a common school for a term of four months in each scholastic year, but that any county or separate school district may levy an additional tax to maintain schools for a longer time than a term of four months, and that the said common school fund shall be distributed among the several counties and separate school districts in proportion to the number of educable children in each, to be collected from the data in the office of the state superintendent of education in the manner prescribed by law; that the Legislature encourage by all suitable means the promotion of intellectual, scientific, moral, and agricultural improvement, by the establishment of a uniform system of free public schools by taxation or otherwise, for all children between the ages of 5 and 21 years, and as soon as practicable, establish schools of higher grade.

The petition alleged that, in obedience to this mandate of the Constitution, the Legislature has provided for the establishment and for the payment of the expenses of the Rosedale consolidated high school, and that the plaintiff, Gong Lum, the petitioner's father, is a taxpayer and helps to support and maintain the school; that Martha Lum is an educable child, is entitled to attend the school as a pupil, and that this is the only school conducted in the district available for her as a pupil; that the right to attend it is a valuable right; that she is not a member of the colored race, nor is she of mixed blood, but that she is pure Chinese; that she is by the action of the board of trustees and the state superintendent discriminated against directly, and denied her right to be a member of the Rosedale school; that the school authorities have no discretion under the law as to her admission as a pupil in the school, but that they continue without authority of law to deny her the right to attend it as a pupil. For these reasons the writ of mandamus is prayed for against the defendants, commanding them and each of them to desist from discriminating against her on account of her race or ancestry, and to give her the same rights and privileges that other educable children between the ages of 5 and 21 are granted in the Rosedale consolidated high school.

The petition was demurred to by the defendants on the ground, among others, that the bill showed on its face that plaintiff is a member of the Mongolian or yellow race, and therefore not entitled to attend the schools provided by law in the state of Mississippi for children of the white or Caucasian race.

The trial court overruled the demurrer and ordered that a writ of mandamus issue to the defendants as prayed in the petition.

The defendants then appealed to the Supreme Court of Mississippi, which heard the case. . . . In its opinion, it directed its attention to the proper construction of section 207 of the state Constitution of 1890, which provides:

Separate schools shall be maintained for children of the white and colored races.

The court held that this provision of the Constitution divided the educable children into those of the pure white or Caucasian race, on the one hand, and the brown, yellow, and black races, on the other, and therefore that Martha Lum, of the Mongolian or yellow race, could not insist on being classed with the whites under this constitutional division. The court said:

The Legislature is not compelled to provide separate schools for each of the colored races, and unless and until it does provide such schools, and provide for segregation of the other races, such races are entitled to have the benefit of the colored public schools. Under our statutes a colored public school exists in every county and in some convenient district, in which every colored child is entitled to obtain an education. These schools are within the reach of all the children of the state, and the plaintiff does not show by her petition that she applied for admission to such schools. On the contrary, the petitioner takes the position that, because there are no separate public schools for Mongolians, she is entitled to enter the white public schools in preference to the colored public schools. A consolidated school in this state is simply a common school conducted as other common schools are conducted; the only distinction being that two or more school districts have been consolidated into one school. Such consolidation is entirely discretionary with the county school board, having reference to the condition existing in the particular territory. Where a school district has an unusual amount of territory, with an unusual valuation of property therein, it may levy additional taxes. But the other common schools under similar statutes have the same power.

If the plaintiff desires, she may attend the colored public schools of her district, or, if she does not so desire, she may go to a private school. The compulsory school law of this state does not require the attendance at a public school, and a parent under the decisions of the Supreme Court of the United States has a right to educate his child in a private school if he so desires. But plaintiff is not entitled to attend a white public school.

As we have seen, the plaintiffs aver that the Rosedale consolidated high school is the only school conducted in that district available for Martha Lum as a pupil. They also aver that there is no school maintained in the district of Bolivar county for the education of Chinese children, and none in the county. How are these averments to be reconciled with the statement of the state Supreme Court that colored schools are maintained in every county by virtue of the Constitution? This seems to be explained, in the language of the state Supreme Court, as follows: By statute it is provided that all the territory of each county of the state shall be divided into school districts separately for the white and colored races; that is to say, the whole territory is to be divided into white school districts, and then a new division of the county for colored school districts. In other words, the statutory scheme is to make the districts, outside of the separate school districts, districts for the particular race, white or colored, so that the territorial limits of the school districts need not be the same, but the territory embraced in a school district for the colored race may not be the same territory embraced in the school district for the white race, and vice versa, which system of creating the common school districts for the two races, white and colored, do not require schools for each race as such to be maintained in each district; but each child, no matter from what territory, is assigned to some school district, the school buildings being separately located and separately controlled, but each having the same curriculum, and each having the same number of months of school term, if the attendance is maintained for the said statutory period, which school district of the common or public schools has certain privileges, among which is to maintain a public school by local taxation for a longer period of time than the said term of four months under named conditions which apply alike to the common schools for the white and colored races.

We must assume, then, that there are school districts for colored children in Bolivar county, but that no colored school is within the limits of the Rosedale consolidated high school district. This is not inconsistent with there being at a place outside of that district and in a different district, a colored school which the plaintiff Martha Lum may conveniently attend. If so, she is not denied, under the existing school system, the right to attend and enjoy the privileges of a common school education in a colored school. If it were otherwise, the petition should have contained an allegation showing it. Had the petition alleged specifically that there was no colored school in Martha Lum's neighborhood to which she could conveniently go, a different question would have been presented, and this, without regard to the state Supreme Court's construction of the state Constitution as limiting the white schools provided for the education of children of the white or Caucasian race. But we do not find the petition to present such a situation.

The case then reduces itself to the question whether a state can be said to afford to a child of Chinese ancestry, born in this country and a citizen of the United States, the equal protection of the laws, by giving her the opportunity for a common school education in a school which receives only colored children of the brown, yellow or black races.

The right and power of the state to regulate the method of providing for the education of its youth at public expense is clear. In Cumming v. Richmond County Board of Education . . . persons of color sued the board of education to enjoin it from maintaining a high school for white children without providing a similar school for colored children, which had existed and had been discontinued. Mr. Justice Harlan, in delivering the opinion of the court, said: Under the circumstances disclosed, we cannot say that this action of the state court was, within the meaning of the Fourteenth Amendment, a denial by the state to the plaintiffs and to those associated with them of the equal protection of the laws, or of any privileges belonging to them as citizens of the United States. We may add that, while all admit that the benefits and burdens of public taxation must be shared by citizens without discrimination against any class on account of their race, the education of the people in schools maintained by state taxation is a matter belonging to the respective states, and any interference on the part of federal authority with the management of such schools cannot be justified, except in the case of a clear and unmistakable disregard of rights secured by the supreme law of the land.

The question here is whether a Chinese citizen of the United States is denied equal protection of the laws when he is classed among the colored races and furnished facilities for education equal to that offered to all, whether white, brown, yellow, or black. Were this a new question, it would call for very full argument and consideration; but we think that it is the same question which has been many times decided to be within the constitutional power of the state Legislature to settle, without intervention of the federal courts under the federal Constitution. . . .

In Plessy v. Ferguson, . . . in upholding the validity under the Fourteenth Amendment of a statute of Louisiana requiring the separation of the white and colored races in railway coaches, a more difficult question than this, this court, speaking of permitted race separation, said:

The most common instance of this is connected with the establishment of separate schools for white and colored children, which has been held to be a valid exercise of the legislative power even by courts of states where the political rights of the colored race have been longest and most earnestly enforced.

The case of Roberts v. City of Boston, . . . in which Chief Justice Shaw, of the Supreme Judicial Court of Massachusetts, announced the opinion of that court upholding the separation of colored and white schools under a state constitutional injunction of equal protection, the same as the Fourteenth Amendment, was then referred to, and this court continued: Similar laws have been enacted by Congress under its general power of legislation over the District of Columbia . . . , as well as by the Legislatures of many of the states, and have been generally, if not uniformly, sustained by the courts'—citing many of the cases above named.

Most of the cases cited arose, it is true, over the establishment of separate schools as between white pupils and black pupils; but we cannot think that the question is any different, or that any different result can be reached, assuming the cases above cited to be rightly decided, where the issue is as between white pupils and the pupils of the yellow races. The decision is within the discretion of the state in regulating its public schools, and does not conflict with the Fourteenth Amendment.

The judgment of the Supreme Court of Mississippi is affirmed.

Source: *Gong Lum v. Rice*, 275 U.S. 78 (1927).

See also: The Chinese Exclusion Act, 1882; *Lau v. Nichols*, 1974; *United States v. Bhagat Singh Thind*, 1923; *United States v. Wong Kim Ark*, 1898

Further Reading

Berard, Adrienne. 2016. *Water Tossing Boulders: How a Family of Chinese Immigrants Led the First Fight to Desegregate Schools in the Jim Crow South.* Boston: Beacon Press.

Brown v. Board of Education of Topeka, 347 U.S. 483 (1954). https://supreme.justia.com/cases/federal/us/347/483/case.html

Dred Scott v. Sanford, 60 U.S. 393 (1857). https://www.law.cornell.edu/supremecourt/text/60/393

Gong Lum v. Rice: The Forgotten Case for Equal Education in the Jim Crow South. n.d. "Mississippi Delta after the Civil War." http://www.gonglumvrice.com/mississippi-after-the-cival-war.html

Huntington, Samuel P. 1993. "The Clash of Civilizations?" *Foreign Affairs* 72, no. 3 (Summer): 22–49.

Kuhn, Thomas S. 1964. *The Structure of Scientific Revolutions.* Chicago: University of Chicago Press.

Plessy v. Ferguson, 163 U.S. 537 (1896). https://www.law.cornell.edu/supremecourt/text/163/537

Quan, Robert S. 1982. *Lotus among the Magnolias: The Mississippi Chinese.* Jackson: University Press of Mississippi.

United States v. Carolene Products Co., 304 U.S. 144. https://www.law.cornell.edu/supremecourt/text/304/144

United States Constitution, Section 1, 13th Amendment. https://www.law.cornell.edu/constitution/amendmentxiii

United States v. Wong Kim Ark, 169 U.S. 649 (1898). https://www.law.cornell.edu/supremecourt/text/169/649

West Virginia State Board of Education v. Barnette, 319 U.S. 624. https://www.law.cornell
.edu/supremecourt/text/319/624

Winkler, Adam. 2006. "Fatal in Theory and Strict in Fact: An Empirical Analysis of Strict
Scrutiny in Federal Courts." *Vanderbilt Law Review* 59, no. 3: 793–872.

Japanese American Internment, 1942–1946

Ann Matsuuchi

Chronology

May 6, 1882   The Chinese Exclusion Act is signed by President Chester A.
Arthur, barring immigration from China. It becomes the first federal law to target immigration from a specific ethnic group, and it
remains in effect until the passage of the Magnuson Act in 1943.

May 24, 1924   The Immigration Act of 1924 is signed into law by President Calvin
Coolidge. The law places limits on immigration visas based on a
national origins quota that results in barring all immigrants from Asia.

**March 17,
1941**   The Western Defense Command is established, headed by Lt. Gen.
John L. DeWitt.

**November 7,
1941**   The Report on Japanese on the West Coast of the United States,
also known as the Munson Report, is sent to President Franklin
Delano Roosevelt to provide intelligence information regarding
the security threat of Japanese Americans on the West Coast.
Despite its clearly stating that "[t]here is no Japanese 'problem'
on the coast" and recommending community self-policing, the
report's findings are not acknowledged.

**December 7,
1941**   The Pearl Harbor naval base in Hawaii is attacked, resulting in
more than 2,000 deaths. War is declared between the United
States and Japan the next day. In the following weeks, the Federal
Bureau of Investigation (FBI) begins arresting Japanese American community leaders and raiding homes based on a "Custodial
Detention List."

**December 14,
1941**   Secretary of the Navy Frank Knox reports to Roosevelt and to the
press that the Pearl Harbor attack is due to fifth-column sabotage
by Japanese Americans, despite lacking military intelligence to
back this claim.

February 19, 1942	Roosevelt signs Executive Order 9066, which authorizes the mass removal and imprisonment of all Japanese Americans on the West Coast. The order allows military commanders to remove designated populations from specified areas with justification of "military necessity."
February 25, 1942	Military postings give the Japanese American community of Terminal Island in California forty-eight hours to prepare for mass removal into government custody. The justification is the proximity of the island to a U.S. shipyard.
March 2, 1942	DeWitt issues Public Proclamation No. 1 defining areas of the U.S. West Coast (including Washington, Oregon, California, and Arizona) as military areas from which all persons of Japanese ancestry could be "excluded."
March 11, 1942	The Wartime Civil Control Administration (WCCA), part of the Western Defense Command, is established to plan and engineer the removal and relocation of Japanese American citizens and noncitizens.
March 18, 1942	The War Relocation Authority (WRA), a civilian agency, is established via Executive Order 9102 to oversee and administer the relocation of Japanese Americans who live on the West Coast into temporary detention centers until permanent "camps" are built.
March 24, 1942	DeWitt issues the first of more than 108 civilian exclusion orders that set the template for how the relocation is communicated and facilitated. Postings entitled "Instructions to All Persons of Japanese Ancestry" give people one week to prepare for relocation under threat of criminal penalties. These orders are issued from March until August 1942.
March 27, 1942	DeWitt issues Public Proclamation 4, effectively ending the possibility of "voluntary evacuation," or moving away from West Coast areas to avoid imprisonment in detention centers. Approximately 5,000 Japanese Americans flee to other U.S. states in response.
March 28, 1942	Minoru "Min" Yasui (1916–1986) breaks the curfew law in Portland, Oregon, and is arrested in his challenge of it. Yasui becomes one of four Japanese Americans who appeal their convictions all the way to the U.S. Supreme Court.

April 11, 1942	Community newspaper *Manzanar Free Press* begins publication in the detention center in Manzanar, California.
May 16, 1942	Gordon Hirabayashi (1918–2012) turns himself in to the FBI in Seattle, Washington, as a test case against the legality of curfew and exclusion orders. His case also goes up to the U.S. Supreme Court, with the backing of the American Civil Liberties Union (ACLU). As with the Yasui case, his challenge is denied.
June 2, 1942	The Manzanar Relocation Center in California becomes the first of ten WRA permanent incarceration centers, with a peak population of 10,046. The other sites are Gila River, Granada, Heart Mountain, Jerome, Minidoka, Poston, Rower, Topaz, and Tule Lake.
July 12, 1942	Mitsuye Endo (1920–2006) becomes the plaintiff in the Supreme Court case that challenges the constitutionality of imprisoning loyal U.S. citizens. The 1944 *Ex parte Endo* decision leads to the closing of the detention centers.
July 27, 1942	Two men, Toshio Kobata and Hirota Isomura, are shot by a guard at the Lordsburg, New Mexico, detention center, allegedly during an escape attempt. Five other cases of similar homicides at other detention centers are also witnessed.
March 23, 1943	The War Department organizes a segregated Japanese American Army unit, the 442nd Regimental Combat Team, calling for volunteers from Hawaii (where Japanese Americans were not relocated) and from those in mainland detention centers. The 442nd, together with the 100th Infantry Battalion, become the most decorated unit in U.S. military history to date for its size and length of service.
July 15, 1943	The Tule Lake detention center in California is designated a "segregation center" where more than 12,000 Japanese Americans whose answers to a problematic "loyalty questionnaire" are transferred in another removal as means of political suppression.
December 17, 1943	The Magnuson Act (Chinese Exclusion Repeal Act of 1943) permits limited immigration from China, and in some states naturalization becomes possible. Prohibition is not completely overturned until the Immigration Act of 1965.
January 20, 1944	Japanese American men in the ten detention centers are drafted into compulsory military service, although several hundred resist in various ways. Most draft resisters are tried and sentenced in respective state federal courts, with sentences ranging from several months to three years.

December 18, 1944	The U.S. Supreme Court decides the *Ex parte Endo* case unanimously, ruling that the incarceration of loyal citizens was unconstitutional.
August 15, 1945	Japan surrenders after the Hiroshima and Nagasaki atomic bombs.
March 20, 1946	The Tule Lake facility becomes the last of the ten WRA detention centers to close.
June 2, 1948	The Japanese American Evacuation Claims Act is passed by the Senate and is signed into law by President Harry S. Truman. Although nearly $38 million in compensation is paid, coverage of many claims of losses of property and business goes unawarded.
June 27, 1952	Despite a presidential veto from Truman, the Immigration and Nationality Act of 1952 (the McCarran-Walter Act) is passed by Congress. While it again allows immigration from Japan and naturalization of Japanese Americans, its basis on race rather than national origins and anti-Communist provisions for targeting potential subversives make the act controversial.
October 4, 1965	The Immigration Act of 1965 (the Hart-Celler Act), signed by President Lyndon B. Johnson, changes U.S. immigration policies, removing quotas that served as a near-total barrier to immigrants from Asia.
March 6, 1968	The last of the cases started by lawyer Wayne M. Collins in 1945 to restore citizenship to nearly 5,000 Japanese Americans from Tule Lake, who became stateless due to a negative response on the 1943 loyalty questionnaire, ends successfully.
July 1970	At the Japanese American Citizens League (JACL) national convention in Chicago, activist Edison Uno's redress resolution is passed. This campaign is met with community disagreement about how these demands should be articulated. In 1978, the JACL unanimously votes for monetary reparations.
February 19, 1976	President Gerald Ford rescinds Executive Order 9066 via Proclamation 4417.
November 25, 1978	Based on an idea from writer and playwright Frank Chin, the first Day of Remembrance is staged in Seattle, in the hopes of moving forward the redress movement. This event is duplicated and held annually in cities across the country to call attention to the continuing significance of the signing of Executive Order 9066, with a date moved to reflect this on February 19.

July 31, 1980 The Commission on Wartime Relocation and Internment of Civilians (CWRIC), a bipartisan federal commission, is established by Congress to investigate the justifications and the constitutionality of Executive Order 9066.

February 24, 1983 The CWRIC issues a report, *Personal Justice Denied*, presenting findings that "internment" was not justified by military necessity, and the decisions to do so were based on "race prejudice, war hysteria, and a failure of political leadership." The commission goes on to recommend redress and a national apology.

November 10, 1983 Fred Korematsu's criminal conviction for evading internment is overturned. Two weeks later, petitions are filed for Yasui and Hirabayashi. In January 1984, Yasui's conviction for violating curfew is overturned. In September 1987, Hirabayashi's convictions for refusing the evacuation order and violating curfew are overturned.

August 10, 1988 Based on CWRIC recommendations, President Ronald Reagan signs the Civil Liberties Act of 1988 into law, resulting in a formal apology and redress of $20,000 to every surviving U.S. citizen or legal resident immigrant of Japanese ancestry who was incarcerated during World War II.

October 9, 1990 In a Washington, D.C., ceremony, Attorney General Richard Thornburgh presents the first group of Japanese American internees a written apology signed by President George H. W. Bush and redress payments of $20,000 each. These redress payments are issued to 82,250 surviving internees in the years following, until 1999.

March 3, 1992 The Manzanar incarceration facility is designated a National Historic Site, managed by the National Park Service. Other facilities such as Minidoka, Tule Lake, and Honouliuli are similarly utilized as memorial sites.

June 10, 1998 *Mochizuki v. United States*, a class action lawsuit on behalf of more than 2,000 incarcerated Japanese in Latin America who were citizens of thirteen countries such as Peru and Panama, is settled. Reparations of $5,000 and an apology from President Bill Clinton are granted to individuals who previously were not covered by the Civil Liberties Act of 1988.

December 21, 2006	The Japanese American Confinement Sites (JACS) grant program is established by Congress, providing up to $38 million for the preservation of incarceration sites, as well as educational programs that support related activities. Projects such as the Densho Encyclopedia online resource are examples of supported work.
September 23, 2010	California passes a law establishing January 30 as the Fred Korematsu Day of Civil Liberties and the Constitution, the first statewide day honoring an Asian American. Other states such as Hawaii, Utah, Illinois, Georgia, Virginia, and New York follow.

Narrative

From the start of the U.S. government's plans for Japanese American communities during World War II, euphemistic language was employed to shape public perception. The forced removal of Japanese Americans on the West Coast was referred to in neutral, sanitized ways: "evacuation centers," "relocation centers," "assembly centers," "exclusion" rather than "eviction," and "detention" rather than "imprisonment." Prior to World War II and the discovery of the atrocities in Nazi concentration camps, the descriptive term "concentration camp" did not have the connotations that it later gained, and both U.S. military agents' and incarcerated Japanese Americans' use of the term was common parlance. Today, out of respect for the objections of Holocaust survivors who warned against conflating levels of crime—genocide versus a lessened violation of human rights—the usage of "internment" and "internment camps" have become the most frequently used terms.

For example, in 1998, an Ellis Island museum exhibit on Japanese American internment was entitled "America's Concentration Camps: Remembering the Japanese-American Experience," referring to the sites in a way that has fallen into disuse due to its near-exclusive association with the Holocaust and genocide. Although the facilities were called concentration camps by both American military personnel and internees up until contemporary times, there was concern that the dramatic revival might cause confusion or unintentional offense to Jewish communities. Negotiations that followed allowed for the exhibit to use this title, accompanied by clear statements about its use. What this highlighted was how the government's use of euphemism to refer to controversial acts—"relocation" and "internment"—has operated both in the past and present.

Furthermore, it can be argued that the continued usage of "concentration camps" to describe what were "extermination camps" or "death camps" is itself a problematic lessening that should be corrected. The shortened form of many of these terms, "camps," that was frequently used also led to public relations softening. Photos of

A store owned by a Japanese American displays a sign reading "I am an American" the day after the Pearl Harbor attack in December 1941. This store in Oakland, California, like many others on the West Coast, was closed following the orders that all Japanese Americans must be evacuated to internment camps during World War II. (National Archives)

incarcerated Japanese Americans involved in leisure activities were captioned in governmental reports with the description "happy campers," suggesting summer holiday camps rather than prison facilities. Historians such as Roger Daniels have objected to the continued usage of "internment" and advocated instead for more historically accurate terms such as "incarceration" (Daniels 2005). The following essay attempts to reflect this advocacy.

On December 7, 1941, Japan bombed the Pearl Harbor naval base in Hawaii, spurring the United States to enter World War II. The government then decided that the incarceration of its Japanese American population was justified by wartime security concerns. On February 19, 1942, President Franklin Delano Roosevelt signed Executive Order 9066, authorizing the military's mass removal and imprisonment of all Japanese Americans on the West Coast. From 1942 to 1946, more than 110,000 Japanese American citizens and permanent residents who lived on the West Coast, as well as a smaller number of Japanese Latin Americans, German and Italian immigrants, and Native Americans, were either forcibly relocated into military-run incarceration sites or deported. In 1982, the Commission on Wartime Relocation and Internment of Civilians (CWRIC), appointed by President Jimmy Carter and Congress, described these events as an injustice that was not justified by necessity, but rather based on "race prejudice, war hysteria and a failure of political leadership" (U.S. National Archives 1992, 459).

In the post-9/11 era, Japanese American and Muslim American communities have worked similarly to address historically familiar threats of profiling, detention, and deportation in response to fears of terrorism and espionage. The Japanese American Citizens League (JACL), one of the oldest Asian American civil rights organizations, has issued statements and enabled coalitions utilizing the slogan "Never Again" in efforts to avert government measures that justify racist actions for reasons of military convenience and public safety (Japanese American Citizens League 2015).

Film and television actor George Takei has become one of the most visible social media commentators for the Japanese American community. His family's imprisonment at the Rohwer site in Arkansas informed his activism about the historical significance of incarceration, his support of institutions such as the Japanese American National Museum in Los Angeles, and his work in the production of the 2015 Broadway musical *Allegiance*.

Before World War II

In 1941, President Roosevelt appointed a journalist named John Franklin Carter to provide an intelligence report on the potential threat of Japanese Americans on the West Coast (Ringle 1981). Carter hired Curtis B. Munson, an independent investigator, to conduct the fieldwork and submit a formal report on Japanese American communities. Munson's November 7, 1941, report was based on interviews and consultations with local FBI and naval intelligence officers such as Kenneth Ringle, concluding that, due to a "remarkable, even extraordinary degree of loyalty" among Japanese Americans, the government should not "want to throw a lot of American citizens into a concentration camp of course, and especially as the almost unanimous verdict is that in case of war they will be quiet, very quiet" (Ringle 1981). Ringle's report to naval intelligence in January 1942 also reinforced the lack of evidence of any security threat and opposed any mass removal.

The December 7, 1942, surprise attack on Pearl Harbor by the Japanese navy, coupled with public outcry exacerbating preexisting racial tension and distrust of Japanese Americans, called into doubt Japanese Americans' loyalty to the United States. Japanese American noncitizens (first-generation Issei) were named enemy aliens, and American-born citizens (second-generation Nisei) were enemy non-aliens. Fear that locations on the West Coast would be targeted was compounded by a belief that Japanese Americans would secretly aid Japan. Seemingly to placate criticism about the legality of mass incarceration, justifications were made that mass removal was necessary to protect the Japanese American population from mob violence. Carter and Munson reported to Roosevelt that anti-Japanese sentiments led them to believe that violence directed at, rather than originating from, Japanese Americans was the greater concern (Robinson 2001, 66).

Several groups campaigned for this removal, including military officials who sought to contain potential threats, opportunistic regional businesses and farmers who thought that the removal of Japanese competitors would be beneficial, and a general populace fueled by alarmist and racist messages in the media. The historical context is rife with increasing anti-Asian sentiments, frequently described as the "Yellow Peril." This historical, anti-Asian sentiment most visibly resulted in the Chinese Exclusion Act of 1882, signed by President Chester A. Arthur during a time marked by numerous cases of lynching of Chinese Americans. The act was the first federal law designed to specifically ban immigration from a specific ethnic group, and it remained in effect until the passage of the Magnuson Act in 1943. The Immigration Act of 1924, which extended immigration visas based on a national-origins quota, resulted in barring all immigrants from Asia.

After the Pearl Harbor attack, President Roosevelt sent Secretary of the Navy Frank Knox to investigate, and the press widely reported his untrue remarks about Japanese American "fifth column" espionage. Roosevelt's subsequent decisions were guided by a growing number of military and political actors such as Knox, Secretary of War Henry Stimson, and the commanding general of the Western Defense Command, Lt. Gen. John L. DeWitt, all of whom strongly pushed for mass incarceration of Japanese Americans due to military necessity.

Mass Incarceration of Japanese American Communities on the West Coast

On February 19, 1942, President Roosevelt signed Executive Order 9066 authorizing the secretary of war and designated military commanders to define large geographic areas as zones of exclusion from which categories of people could be forcibly removed. No specific groups of people, states, or regions were named in the order, but the purpose was clear. In *Korematsu v. United States*, DeWitt described "all individuals of Japanese descent as 'subversive,' as belonging to 'an enemy race' whose 'racial strains are undiluted.'" The order granted the military the authority to carry out its plans, without hindrance from other agencies and with the support needed to rapidly relocate and house large numbers of people, with the entire process policed by armed military personnel. DeWitt went on to issue more than 108 military exclusion orders that applied to all persons of Japanese ancestry from areas designated Military Areas 1 and 2, with no exceptions for American-born citizens or young children. These zones included most of the West Coast region from Washington State in the north, through California, and extending inland to Arizona. Although Hawaii would seem like the first choice of location to prevent further attack, the removal of Japanese Americans there was deemed impossible, since they composed nearly a third of the state's population. Furthermore, Hawaiian politicians and businesses interpreted removal as being harmful to their economy. Other areas like New York City largely remained "free zones" and attracted an influx of Japanese Americans, who were received at locations such as hostels run by local religious groups like the Quakers. Even in New York, there were at least 440 Japanese "enemy aliens" who were incarcerated at a wartime prison at Ellis Island (Pegler-Gordon 2017, 379). Other Japanese Americans were kept under close surveillance in their homes, obliged to report their daily activities to authorities.

At first, the exclusion orders called for "voluntary evacuation" from Military Area 1 to Area 2. The difficulty, or even impossibility, of the immediate move and resettlement of entire communities to new areas where they were largely unwelcome was compounded by numerous factors, such as the freezing of Issei bank accounts. After Congress enacted Executive Order 9066 on March 21, 1942, these additional exclusion orders made disobeying removal procedures punishable by fines of up to $5,000 and imprisonment for one year.

Two agencies were created by the Western Defense Command to facilitate this large-scale removal and incarceration: the Wartime Civil Control Administration (WCCA) and the War Relocation Authority (WRA). On March 27, 1942, the WCCA began organizing the forcible removal and confinement of Japanese Americans in these areas, enabled by illegal contributions of demographic data from the Census Bureau. Despite many years of denial, in 2007, the Census Bureau confirmed suspicions that there was a breach of confidentiality terms in 1943. Researchers had uncovered papers proving that names and addresses were provided in response to a request from the Treasury Department. All Japanese Americans on the West Coast were given notice to report to locations where they would first be transported to temporary "assembly centers" before being transferred to ten long-term WRA incarceration facilities, referred to as "relocation centers." Under short notice, in some cases as little as a few days, individuals and families could only bring whatever possessions they could carry by hand. Attempts to sell businesses, farms, crops, possessions, and homes at fair values were rarely successful. Overall property loss has been estimated to be about $1.3 billion.

The assembly centers were constructed hastily on public spaces such as racetracks, sporting arenas, and fairgrounds. The conditions in some locations were worse than those found in permanent prisons, such as the Tanforan and Santa Anita centers in California, where people were housed in horse stalls. The duration of

The Mochida family waited for transportation in Hayward, California, in May 1942. The bus that they waited for would eventually take them to one of the evacuation centers. Every member of their family wore an identification tag. (National Archives)

this temporary detention was as long as several months. Although families were permitted to stay together in most cases, individuals were transferred to specific WRA incarceration facilities based on factors both random and geographic, as well as on perceived loyalty to the United States. The facilities were built on federally owned land, including some on Native American reservations, recalling an earlier precedent of forced removal of indigenous peoples. The harsh conditions due to climate, inadequate construction, and lack of privacy in the makeshift barracks erased any illusion of normal community life, with incarcerated individuals assigned labor tasks like farming and construction.

The WRA incarceration facilities were located in remote inland locations. On June 2, 1942, the WRA began transition of the Manzanar, California, site from an assembly center into one of the ten main detention sites that housed imprisoned Japanese Americans until the conclusion of World War II in 1945. The other nine WRA sites were Poston and Gila River in Arizona, Jerome and Rohwer in

Arkansas, Tule Lake in California, Amache in Colorado, Minidoka in Idaho, Topaz in Utah, and Heart Mountain in Wyoming. American photographers Dorothea Lange and Ansel Adams documented this history with images that capture both the desolation of the locations and the despair and endurance of the people of all ages who attempted a semblance of normal community life while surrounded by barbed wire fences and armed guard towers.

Some incarceration facilities were located in areas so remote that security was less visible. The Poston facility was built on desert land within the Colorado River Indian Reservation and was initially run jointly by the federal Office of Indian Affairs (OIA) and the WRA. The leaders of the Colorado River Indian Tribes did not agree to this use of their land, given historical memories of forced removal, resettlement, and uncompensated takeover of Native American communities (Franco 1999, 106). The OIA saw the location choice as a convenient avenue for needed land and agricultural development and newly justified federal funding that allowed construction of roads, bridges, and a major irrigation system (Fujita-Rony

Executive Order 9066

The program of removal of Japanese Americans began on February 19, 1942, when President Franklin D. Roosevelt signed Executive Order 9066, giving the secretary of war and designated military commanders the power to define large geographic areas as zones of exclusion from which categories of people could be forcibly removed. Essentially, this granted the military broad authority over civilians in specific places. The stated purpose of the order was to support national defense by preventing espionage and sabotage. Despite its contradiction to the Fourth, Fifth, and Fourteenth Amendments to the Constitution, which protect property from unwarranted seizure and guaranteed the right to due process, only limited official opposition came from the Department of Justice and the FBI. Congress enacted the order on March 21, 1942, and added fines and prison terms for resistance to military demands. In the following months, more than 110,000 citizens and noncitizens were forcibly removed from their homes and properties on the West Coast and incarcerated in ten relocation facilities. The order was rescinded in 1945. The 1944 Supreme Court case *Korematsu v. United States* challenged the constitutionality of the order, but the Court ruled 6–3 in favor of the government. In his dissent, Justice Frank Murphy called this ruling a "legalization of racism." On February 19, 1976, President Gerald Ford rescinded Executive Order 9066 via Proclamation 4417.

2018). When Poston reached its maximum population of 17,814 in September 1942, it became the third largest city in Arizona and the largest incarceration site until Tule Lake outsized it as a segregation center (Burton, Farrell, Lord, and Lord 2003, 216).

Demonstrations of Loyalty and Americanness

While limited self-governance was permitted in some incarceration sites, the communities were fractured along generational and cultural lines, mirroring the WRA imposition of assimilation and "Americanization" tactics. Only American-born Nisei were allowed to take up leadership positions in incarceration site governance. The largest and most influential Japanese American community organization from 1929 to the present, the Japanese American Citizens' League (JACL), was led by Nisei, many of whom pushed for demonstrations of loyalty over organized resistance as a means of lessening suspicion and proving patriotism. The JACL was known to have collaborated with governmental entities before and after the start of World War II and largely opposed the legal test cases attempted by citizens to contest curfew and exclusion. In addition to this, the JACL pushed for allowing Japanese American citizens to be eligible for military service, in the hopes of producing unquestioned evidence of Japanese American patriotism and possible restoration of other citizenship rights. In March 1943, the War Department allowed for a segregated Japanese American army unit, the 442nd Regimental Combat Team, which consisted of volunteers from Hawaii and the mainland detention facilities. The decorated and revered soldiers of the 442nd and the 100th Infantry Battalion from Hawaii proceeded to supply stories of heroism that supported later efforts to restore justice. However, military service prompted the WRA to administer "loyalty questionnaires" to those incarcerated as a means of identifying and segregating those deemed loyal or disloyal. Most questions related to "Americanness" or "Japaneseness," but two in particular caused a wave of protest in some of the facilities. Question 27 asked if Nisei would agree to serve in the military, and question 28 asked if individuals would swear unqualified allegiance to the United States and forswear any form of allegiance to the emperor of Japan. Despite the complexities and contradictions that made these questions confusing, answering incorrectly—no—was deemed a sign of disloyalty. The epithet "no-no boy" originated with such negative responses.

Some respondents who answered no to question 27 feared that they would be separated from parents who needed care; others refused to serve because their families were unjustly imprisoned. Adequate clarification was not provided when inquiries were made, and any qualifications that they wrote alongside their answers were ignored. Respondents who answered no to question 28 also did so for a variety of reasons. Some thought it was a trick question posed with the intent of providing evidence that they had previously acted as agents for the Japanese government. Others thought answering "yes" would render them effectively without a state, since those born in Japan were barred from U.S. citizenship. John Okada's 1957 novel *No-No Boy* centers on a young Nisei man who is imprisoned for answering no to both questions and describes his conflicts with those in the community who answered yes and volunteered to serve in the U.S. military. Those who answered no were labeled disloyal troublemakers. Consequently, they and their families were transferred to the Tule Lake Segregation Center, the largest and most heavily guarded incarceration site. This solution for separating designated "troublemakers" was supported by the JACL.

In 1944, a mandatory draft was imposed on male Japanese American citizens. Given the context of the loss of citizenship rights, it was unsurprising that army recruitment was low in the incarceration facilities. Resistance was not supported widely, but at the Heart Mountain and Poston sites there were public discussion and statements issued about the legality of this obligation. Three hundred and fifteen men from eight of the ten facilities did not comply with draft orders and faced federal charges. Most were convicted and served from six months to more than three years in prison. In December 1947, President Harry S. Truman pardoned all draft resisters.

The Renunciation Act of 1944 was passed to enable the deportation of disloyal Nisei along with Issei who agreed to be repatriated. In Tule Lake, some internees were misled into renunciation under the belief that this was required in order to remain in detention until the end of the war. In 1945, Wayne Collins, a San Francisco American Civil Liberties Union (ACLU) attorney, delayed a mass deportation of voluntary and involuntary "native American aliens," arguing that their renunciations were made under duress. Cases for the restoration of citizenship to nearly 5,000 Japanese Americans went through the courts in the years following, as late as 1968.

Throughout all this, the JACL continued to denounce those labeled disloyal at Tule Lake, draft resisters, and plaintiffs in cases against the government, creating a sense of marginalization among those who chose to protest rather than accommodate. These conflicting views of Japanese American community leaders and activists remained problematic in the campaign for redress in the second half of the twentieth century. In 1989, the JACL commissioned a historical analysis, written by legal scholar Deborah Lim, to investigate the organization's actions during World War II. Despite being suppressed for several years after it was submitted in 1990, the analysis later allowed for necessary re-examination and supported some chapters' calls for acknowledging the heroism of dissidents as well as soldiers.

Resettlement

The WRA's plans involved resettlement in areas outside of the West Coast from the start, although local resistance was expected. Limited options for placement of Japanese Americans as college students and seasonal farm workers offered some Japanese Americans an alternative to continued detainment. In 1944, Seabrook Farms in New Jersey saw this as an opportunity to address their farm labor shortage and, through advertising better living conditions, it attracted enough migrants to establish it as a known Japanese American community. By 1946, it had around 2,500 residents. However, this became a temporary destination for many, as one worker described it as a "town of chain-linked fences." By the 1970s, the Japanese American population was 530 (Nakamura 2018).

In mid-January 1945, the WRA announced it would begin closing all detainment sites, with the exception of Tule Lake, which remained open until March 1946. After the atomic bombings in Hiroshima and Nagasaki, Japan surrendered on September 2, 1945. WRA director Dillon Myer believed that policies encouraging Americanization would ease anti-Japanese hysteria, and he pushed for integration over preservation of Japanese American communities and cultures. Influential nativist groups like the Native Sons of the Golden West led popular campaigns calling for stripping Japanese Americans of citizenship and mass deportation (Rego 2018, 87).

Postwar communities were not easily reestablished at first on the West Coast. The WRA established field offices to enable post-internment migrations, assisting with employment, housing, and social services. Many Japanese Americans were dispersed to various locations in the Midwest and along the East Coast, including Denver, Salt Lake City, Chicago, and New York. Many were given only twenty-five dollars and a bus ticket upon their departure, to establish new lives in locations without the support of preexisting Japanese American communities to ameliorate a host of challenges (Yamamoto 2013, 193). Some of these designated resettlement areas objected to federal placement of relocated Japanese Americans, often using racist language in their justifications. In New York, Mayor Fiorello La Guardia, in both public statements and in private correspondence with Secretary of the Interior Harold L. Ickes (whose office directed the WRA), actively opposed the arrival of Japanese Americans as a potential security threat and suggested the influx would antagonize the Chinese American community in New York (Levine 2012). These politically expedient decisions had repercussions for the development of Asian American communities all across the United States. Gradually, by the 1950s, the Japanese American population on the West Coast approached prewar levels. The nature of the communities changed significantly, with occupations shifting away from farming to jobs like domestic service and gardening.

The phrase "shikata ga nai" ("it cannot be helped") was the name of a chapter in Jeanne Wakatsuki Houston's 1973 memoir *Farewell to Manzanar* and was pointed to as an explanation for Japanese American compliance with military orders and the self-imposed silence of many of the formerly incarcerated. This attitude was also referred to as a demonstration of obedient loyalty by the WRA, which sought to facilitate the assimilation of detainees into what was presented as mainstream Americanness. This community reaction could too easily be painted as one of overall cultural passivity and conformity, as well as one of the factors that caused divisiveness among Japanese Americans about resistance during the experience and later demands for justice and restitution (Shimabukuro 2015, 73). While there were many postwar Japanese Americans whose politics echoed those of some conservative JACL voices that advocated loyalty, others were motivated to become civil rights activists working toward a realization of social justice for all. Yuri Kochiyama in New York became an ally of Malcolm X, and Roy Aoki became one of the founding members of the Black Panthers in California. These activities reactivated earlier calls for official restitution of rights, widespread acknowledgment of past injustices, and a more urgent need to prevent the possibility of its recurrence.

Historians, writers, and artists have sought to preserve the memory of these events in contemporary discourse, and discussions about Japanese American incarceration are of particular importance in both legal classes and Asian American studies. Literary texts such as Okada's *No-No Boy* and Wakatsuki Houston's *Farewell to Manzanar* are frequently chosen for study. Julie Otsuka's 2002 novel *When the Emperor Was Divine* also details one family's experience of incarceration. Mine Okubo's 1946 graphic novel memoir, *Citizen 13660*, provides a detailed, affected account of her experiences at the Tanforan and Topaz facilities. George Takei, a social media celebrity best known for playing one of the most prominent Asian American roles in history on the hit television show *Star Trek*, produced a musical entitled *Allegiance*, also about a family's experience during incarceration, which debuted in San Diego in 2012 and on Broadway in 2015.

Redress Movement

Efforts to grant reparations for losses began prior to the end of the war. Even with the support of Myer and Ickes, negotiations were difficult and resulted in compromises that negated meaningful compensation. An evacuation claims bill was submitted to Congress that would decide on claims made for losses of personal property or assets suffered by internees. Mike Masaoka and the JACL Anti-discrimination Committee lobbied government officials for a lump-sum payment of $1,000 instead, believing that passage of any claims bill was unlikely. Masaoka then assisted Truman's Committee on Civil Rights in its 1947 report, *To Secure These Rights*, which, along with advocating for protections of African Americans, denounced the incarceration of Japanese Americans based on race and called for a commission to further investigate the issue. On June 2, 1948, the Japanese American Evacuation Claims Act was passed by the Senate and was signed into law by Truman. Although nearly $38 million in compensation was paid, the coverage of many claims of losses of property and business went unawarded. Many claims required receipts and paperwork that internees had lost during their abrupt removals from their homes and businesses. The bill also did not provide for an official acknowledgement of a violation of civil rights of citizens and legal residents.

Afterward, JACL lobbied for the Immigration and Nationality Act of 1952 (McCarran-Walter Act), which, despite a veto from Truman, was passed by Congress on June 27, 1952. Along with granting naturalization rights to Issei and other Asians, it formally ended racial exclusion from Asia and paved the way for the Immigration and Nationality Act of 1965. However, the act employed race-based, rather than national-origin, quotas that served to limit Asian immigration and also included anti-Communist provisions for targeting potential subversives.

In the 1960s, activists started campaigning for redress, which involved formal apologies from the state and reparations to surviving individuals who lived through incarceration. At the JACL national convention in Chicago in July 1970, activist Edison Uno called for a redress resolution inclusive of financial restitution. This was opposed by some JACL leaders, such as Masaoka and journalist Bill Hosokawa, who saw this as diminishing the efforts for seeking a formal apology. The redress campaign met with community disagreement about how demands should be articulated. A JACL redress committee was formed in 1978, and the following year, Japanese American politicians called for a federal commission to investigate the causes and justification for detainment.

In 1980, Congress created the Commission on Wartime Relocation and Internment of Civilians (CWRIC) to investigate the civil rights violations experienced by Japanese Americans who were also forcibly removed during World War II. The CWRIC report, entitled *Personal Justice Denied*, determined that the government's decision to support the program was not based on any legitimate national threat, but rather "race prejudice, war hysteria and a failure of political leadership." Based on the CWRIC's findings, on August 10, 1988, President Ronald Reagan signed the Civil Liberties Act of 1988 into law, providing a formal apology and redress of $20,000 to every surviving U.S. citizen or legal resident immigrant of Japanese ancestry who was incarcerated during World War II. On October 9, 1990, Attorney General Richard Thornburgh presented the first group of Japanese American internees a written apology signed by President George H. W. Bush, with redress payments of $20,000 each. These redress payments were issued to 82,250 surviving internees in the years following until 1999.

Legal Challenges

The portrayal of Japanese Americans during these events as passive or obedient can be contested with the mention of numerous actions, including protests and legal challenges. That said, there remained vocal dissent concerning these challenges within the community before and after. The challengers were not widely celebrated as activist heroes until the ends of their lives. Four cases led by Nisei plaintiffs, Minoru Yasui, Gordon Hirabayashi, Fred Korematsu, and Mitsuye Endo, challenged the constitutionality of military actions and were brought before the Supreme Court.

The 1943 *Yasui v. United States* and *Hirabayashi v. United States* challenged the military curfew and relocation orders. The Court chose to focus on the military decision to institute curfews during wartime and upheld the legality of these orders.

The 1944 *Ex parte Endo* tested the constitutionality of incarcerating loyal citizens and was the only decision ruled in favor of the plaintiff. On December 18, 1944, the U.S. Supreme Court decided the *Ex parte Endo* case unanimously, ruling that the incarceration of loyal citizens was unconstitutional. The case resulted in Roosevelt's revoking the exclusion orders via Public Proclamation No. 21. Japanese Americans would be allowed to return to West Coast military areas, and the closing of most detention centers was announced.

However, in a decision announced the same day, the Court upheld the government's actions in imprisoning a class of Americans for reasons of military necessity in *Korematsu v. United States*. This case challenged the constitutionality of Executive Order 9066, but the Court ruled 6–3 in favor of the government. In his dissent, Justice Frank Murphy called this ruling a "legalization of racism" and went on to state, "Racial discrimination in any form and in any degree has no justifiable part whatever in our democratic way of life."

On November 10, 1983, based on *coram nobis* (a legal order that can be used to challenge convictions if there is evidence of errors that affected court decisions), U.S. District Court Judge Marilyn Hall Patel overturned Korematsu's criminal conviction for evading incarceration. Two weeks later, petitions were filed for Yasui and Hirabayashi. In January 1984, Yasui's conviction for violating curfew was overturned, but any further challenge to the case was unsuccessful. In September 1987, Hirabayashi's convictions for refusing the evacuation order and violating curfew were overturned.

On September 23, 2010, California passed a state law establishing January 30 as the Fred Korematsu Day of Civil Liberties and the Constitution, the first statewide day honoring an Asian American. Other states, such as Hawaii, Utah, Illinois, Georgia, and Virginia, followed, as well as New York City in 2017. In 2017, some of the children of these activists, Jay Hirabayashi, Karen Korematsu, and Holly Yasui, filed an amicus brief in federal court against President Donald Trump's

Executive Order 13769, known as the Muslim travel ban. In 2018, the Supreme Court officially overruled the Korematsu decision in its support of an entry ban on travelers from several Muslim-majority countries (Bump 2018).

Biographies of Notable Figures

Gordon Kiyoshi Hirabayashi (1918–2012)

In May 1942, Gordon Kiyoshi Hirabayashi, a twenty-three-year-old University of Washington student, protested the violation of his civil rights by disobeying military curfew and exclusion orders. All Japanese Americans on the West Coast were subject to curfew restrictions, which stipulated they had to remain in their homes from 8 p.m. to 6 a.m. Exclusion orders entailed compliance with relocation proceedings, since they could not be freely present in these geographic areas. Hirabayashi turned himself in to the authorities, stating that his defiance was based on his belief in his constitutional rights as an American citizen. Hirabayashi was imprisoned and tried in a state court five months later. He was found guilty and given two concurrent ninety-day sentences. The decision was appealed and sent to the Supreme Court, but in 1943 the Court decided against Hirabayashi, primarily based on the curfew violation.

DOCUMENT EXCERPTS

Japanese Internment Essay by Herbert Yoshiwaka

On February 19, 1942, President Roosevelt signed Executive Order 9066 and authorized the mass relocation and internment of Japanese Americans on the West Coast. From 1942 to 1946, more than 110,000 Japanese Americans, including citizens and permanent residents, were forced to leave their home and properties behind and were transported to a number of relocation camps. Many were sent to temporary assembly centers first, as Herbert Yoshiwaka's essay here documents.

Chieko Hirata
Period II, English I

My Last Day At Home

The month of May when I was attending school, all the residents of Hood River county, as well as the people of the whole western coast was surprised to receive such an unexpected order of evacuation.

Promptly after hearing about the order I with my folks went to register and then for a brief physical examination. Then I helped my folks pack and prepared to leave my dear home on May 13, 1942.

On May 8, 1942 I withdrew from Parkdale Grade School, where all my friends and teachers bid me farewell with sorrowful face and tears. Our packing never seem to cease, we kept on packing then finally we were finished. Then came May 13th, my most dreaded day which I shall never forget the rest of my life. On the afternoon of the 13th, I board the train headed for Pinedale, California.

On the night of the 15th we arrived. The weather was pretty hot. In Pinedale I lived in the D-section which had forty barracks, which had vie apartments to a barrack.

I stayed at the Pinedale Assembly Center about two months. Then around July 15, 1942 we received our order to evacuate for Tule Lake. Then on July 18th we evacuated for Tule Lak and spent a night on the train. I arrived in Tule Lake. At present I am living in Block 58. The residents of this block is most Tacoma folks which I am not very much acquainted with as yet. Being that my cousin lives in Block 57 I am always visiting them.

I am always hoping that this war will end, so that I will be able to go back to Parkdale, my home town and see all my old friends, and live to my dying days in my old home in Parkdale, Oregon.

Herbert Yoshiwaka

Source: Yoshiwaka, Herbert. "My Last Day at Home." n.d. National Archives.

See also: Gentlemen's Agreement between the United States and Japan, 1907; The Murder of Vincent Chin, 1982; The Webb-Haney Act Passed by California Legislature, 1923

Further Reading

Bump, Philip. 2018. "How a 1944 Decision on Japanese Interment Affected the Supreme Court's Travel Ban Decision." *The Washington Post*, June 26. https://www.washingtonpost .com/news/politics/wp/2018/06/26/how-a-1944-decision-on-japanese-internment -affected-the-supreme-courts-travel-ban-decision/?utm_term=.3c9539cfd86d

Burton, Jeffery F., Mary M. Farrell, Florence B. Lord, and Richard B. Lord. 2003. *Confinement and Ethnicity: An Overview of World War II Japanese American Relocation Sites*. Seattle: University of Washington Press.

Daniels, Roger. 1989. *American Concentration Camps: A Documentary History of the Relocation and Incarceration of Japanese Americans, 1942–1945*. New York: Garland.

Daniels, Roger. 2005. "Words Do Matter: A Note on Inappropriate Terminology and the Incarceration of the Japanese Americans." In *Nikkei in the Pacific Northwest: Japanese Americans and Japanese Canadians in the Twentieth Century*, edited by Louis Fiset and Gail Nomura, 183–207. Seattle: University of Washington Press. https://www.nps.gov /tule/learn/education/upload/RDaniels_euphemisms.pdf

Franco, Jere B. 1999. *Crossing the Pond: The Native American Effort in World War II*. Denton: University of North Texas Press.

Fujita-Rony, Thomas. 2018. "Poston (Colorado River)." Densho Encyclopedia. https://encyclopedia.densho.org/Poston%20(Colorado%20River)/

Hayashi, Brian Masaru. 2008. *Democratizing the Enemy: The Japanese American Internment.* Princeton, NJ: Princeton University Press.

Howard, John. 2008. *Concentration Camps on the Home Front: Japanese Americans in the House of Jim Crow.* Chicago: University of Chicago Press.

Irons, Peter H. 1993. *Justice at War: The Story of the Japanese American Internment Cases.* Berkeley: University of California Press.

Japanese American Citizens League. 2015. "JACL Stands with Asian American Leaders to Rally against Anti-Muslim Hate." https://jacl.org/jacl-stands-with-asian-american-leaders-to-rally-against-anti-muslim-hate

Jones, Jennifer Locke, ed. 2001. *A More Perfect Union: Japanese Americans & the U.S. Constitution.* Washington, D.C.: Smithsonian National Museum of American History. http://amhistory.si.edu/perfectunion/experience/index.html

Levine, Steven A. 2012. "Mayor La Guardia, Japanese Internment and World War II: 70 Years Later." La Guardia and Wagner Archives. http://laguardiawagnerarchives.blogspot.com/2012/02/mayor-la-guardia-japanese-internment.html

Library of Congress. "Collection: Japanese-American Internment Camp Newspapers, 1942 to 1946." https://www.loc.gov/collections/japanese-american-internment-camp-newspapers

Murray, Alice Yang. 2008. *Historical Memories of the Japanese American Internment and the Struggle for Redress.* Stanford, CA: Stanford University Press.

Nakamura, David. 2011. "Japanese Americans: House Hearings on Radical Islam 'Sinister.'" *Washington Post,* March 8. http://www.washingtonpost.com/wp-dyn/content/article/2011/03/08/AR2011030802876.html

Nakamura, Kelli Y. 2018. "Seabrook Farms." Densho Encyclopedia. https://encyclopedia.densho.org/Seabrook%20Farms/

Ng, Wendy L. 2002. *Japanese American Internment during World War II: A History and Reference Guide.* Westport, CT: Greenwood Press.

Pegler-Gordon, Anna. 2017. "'New York Has a Concentration Camp of Its Own': Japanese Confinement on Ellis Island during World War II." *Journal of Asian American Studies* 20, no. 3: 373–404. https://muse.jhu.edu/article/673368/pdf

Phelps, Shirelle and Jeffrey Lehman, eds. 2005. "Japanese American Evacuation Cases." In *West's Encyclopedia of American Law* 6: 1–6. Detroit: Thompson Gale. https://gpreview.kingborn.net/184000/b830eeef86724a5dbb3492565f414b62.pdf

Rego, David Alan. 2018. "Native Sons of the Golden West." In *Japanese Americans: The History and Culture of a People,* edited by Jonathan H. X. Lee, 86–88. Santa Barbara, CA: ABC-CLIO.

Ringle, Ken. 1981. "What Did You Do Before the War, Dad?" *The Washington Post,* December 6. https://www.washingtonpost.com/archive/lifestyle/magazine/1981/12/06/what-did-you-do-before-the-war-dad/a80178d5-82e6-4145-be4c-4e14691bdb6b

Robinson, Greg. 2001. *By Order of the President: FDR and the Internment of Japanese Americans.* Cambridge, MA: Harvard University Press.

Robinson, Greg. 2009. *A Tragedy of Democracy: Japanese Confinement in North America*. New York: Columbia University Press.

Shimabukuro, Mira. 2015. *Relocating Authority: Japanese Americans Writing to Redress Mass Incarceration*. Boulder: University Press of Colorado.

Takai, Barbara. 2018. "Tule Lake." Densho Encyclopedia. http://encyclopedia.densho.org /Tule_Lake/#As_.22Segregation_Center.22

U.S. National Archives and Records Administration. United States. 1992. *Personal Justice Denied: Report of the Commission on Wartime Relocation and Internment of Civilians: Report for the Committee on Interior and Insular Affairs*. Washington, D.C.: U.S. G.P.O. http://www.archives.gov/research/japanese-americans/justice-denied

Yamamoto, Eric K. 2013. *Race, Rights, and Reparation: Law and the Japanese American Internment*. New York: Wolters Kluwer Law & Business.

Yang, Alice. 2018. "Redress Movement." Densho Encyclopedia. https://encyclopedia.densho .org/Redress%20movement/

The Luce-Celler Act, 1946

Lan Dong

Chronology

1790	The Nationalization Act restricts citizenship to "free white persons" who reside in the United States for five years and renounce their allegiance to their country of origin.
1870	The Naturalization Act limits citizenship to "white persons and persons of African descent," excluding Asians from becoming citizens.
1875	The Page Act prohibits the immigration of Asian subjects who are convicts in their own countries or would become forced laborers in America, as well as Asian women who would become prostitutes.
1882	The Chinese Exclusion Act is passed, prohibiting immigration of all Chinese laborers.
1898	At the end of the Spanish-American War, the Philippines becomes a U.S. territory.
1906	The Hawaii Sugar Planters Association (HSPA) begins recruiting Filipino workers.
1907	The Expatriation Act declares that an American woman who marries a foreign national will lose her citizenship.

1907	The Japanese and Korean Exclusion League is renamed the Asian Exclusion League (AEL) to oppose immigration from India and other parts of Asia.
1914–1918	Many Asian Americans serve in World War I.
1917	The Immigration Act of 1917 restricts immigration from the Asiatic Barred Zone, with the exception of Filipinos. Since the Philippines is an American territory, Filipinos are American nationals.
1923	The U.S. Supreme Court rules that Bhagat Singh Thind and other Indians are not white, even though they are Caucasians, and finds them ineligible for citizenship in *United States v. Bhagat Singh Thind*.
1924	The Johnson-Reed Immigration Act creates a quota system based on national origins that limits the number of immigrants by countries of origin and excludes all immigrants from Asia.
1934	The Tydings-McDuffie Act grants independence for the Philippines, to take effect on July 4, 1946, after a ten-year transitional period, thereby removing Filipinos' status as U.S. nationals.
1941	The Imperial Japanese Navy Air Service attacks the U.S. naval base at Pearl Harbor in Hawaii on December 7.
1943	The Chinese Exclusion Act is repealed.
1946	The Philippines becomes independent from the United States.
1946	The Luce-Celler Act is signed into law. It allows 100 Filipinos and 100 Indians to immigrate to the United States per year. It also allows Filipino Americans and Indian Americans to become naturalized U.S. citizens.
1948–1965	Nearly 7,000 Asian Indians immigrate to the United States.
1952	The McCarran-Walter Act (also known as the Immigration and Nationality Act of 1952) eliminates the Asiatic Barred Zone and allots each Asian country a minimum of 100 visas annually. This act affirms the national-origins quota system of 1924 and limits the total annual quota of immigrants to one-sixth of 1 percent of the population of the continental United States in 1920. It exempts spouses and children of U.S. citizens and people born in the Western Hemisphere.
1956	Dalip Singh Saund becomes the first Asian American elected to Congress.
1965	The Hart-Celler Act (also known as the Immigration and Nationality Act of 1965) abolishes the national-origins quota system and replaces

it with a preference system based on skills and family ties to U.S. citizens and permanent residents.

1980   The Refugee Act grants asylum to politically oppressed refugees.

1986   The Immigration Reform and Control Act allows undocumented persons who have resided in the United States continuously since January 1, 1982, to apply for legal status.

1990   The Immigration Act of 1990 increases the annual visa cap to 700,000 for the next three years and 675,000 annually after that.

2001   The Development, Relief, and Education for Alien Minors Act, commonly known as the DREAM Act, is first introduced in the U.S. Senate. It has been reintroduced several times since then but so far has failed to pass.

2007   The Secure Borders, Economic Opportunity, and Immigration Reform Act of 2007 (also known as the Comprehensive Immigration Reform Act) is discussed in Congress but not voted on. The last vote on cloture fails. This bill would have granted legal status and a path to citizenship for approximately twelve million undocumented immigrants and increased border security.

2012   Asians surpass Hispanics to become the largest group of new immigrants in the United States.

2017   Executive Order 13769, titled "Protecting the Nation from Foreign Terrorist Entry into the United States" (also known as the Muslim Ban or the Travel Ban), is issued by President Donald J. Trump on January 27. It lowers the number of refugees to be admitted into the United States; suspends the U.S. Refugee Admissions Program; suspends the entry of Syrian refugees; and suspends entry of those from Iran, Iraq, Libya, Somalia, Sudan, Syria, and Yemen.

2017   Executive Order 13780 is issued by President Donald J. Trump on March 6, replacing Executive Order 13769. It sets limits on travel to the United States from certain countries and by refugees who do not possess a visa or valid travel documents.

Narrative

Proposed by Republican Clare Boothe Luce and Democrat Emanuel Celler in 1943, the Luce-Celler Act was signed into law by President Harry Truman in 1946. The act allowed a quota of 100 Filipinos and 100 Indians to immigrate to the

Four Filipino plant sprayers in the Pacific Islands in 1945. The following year, the Philippines became independent and the Luce-Celler Act was signed into law. This act allowed 100 Filipinos and 100 Indians to immigrate to the United States each year. It also allowed Filipino Americans and Indian Americans to become naturalized U.S. citizens. (Eliot Elisofon/The LIFE Picture Collection/Getty Images)

United States per year. It also allowed Filipino Americans and Indian Americans to become naturalized citizens. Filipino Americans would otherwise have lost their eligibility for naturalization in 1946 when the Philippines gained independence from the United States. Indian Americans were not eligible for naturalization following the *United States v. Bhagat Singh Thind* Supreme Court ruling in 1923. Although not well known to general readers, this act has had an important impact on Asian American communities and American immigration history and policies. It was a step toward changing discriminatory and restrictive regulations, policies, and practices against immigrants from Asian countries. It was also of significance to Indian nationalism at a time when Indian nationalists worked toward gaining independence from the British Commonwealth and establishing a unified Indian government.

Historical Context: Anti-Asian Sentiment and Laws

In the late nineteenth and early twentieth centuries, anti-Asian sentiment began to manifest in political campaigns and violence in America. Between 1882 and 1924, U.S. legislation passed a series of laws restricting Asians from immigrating to the United States, beginning with the Chinese Exclusion Act of 1882 that banned Chinese laborers from entering the country. This act and its many amendments not only have had a long-lasting impact on Chinese immigration but also set the precedent for discriminatory immigration policies and regulations based on race, ethnicity, and country of origin.

The 1907 Bellingham riots were among the first incidents along the Pacific Coast in which immigrant workers from India were driven out of town by white men. A mob attacked the boarding houses and mills in Bellingham, Washington, and expelled Indian immigrant workers from the milling town. Similar violent incidents also happened in California, Oregon, and Vancouver, Canada, not long after. The Japanese-Korean Exclusion League, a national labor organization, was the driving force behind the riots in Bellingham. The league had a mission "to guard the gateway of Occidental Civilization against Oriental invasion" (Seattle Civil Rights and Labor History Project 2007) and was later renamed the Asiatic Exclusion League (AEL) to oppose immigration from Asia in general. Such racism and hostility continued for the next few decades, culminating in a series of immigration policies and laws excluding Asians, denying them entry to the United States and the rights to become naturalized citizens.

Organizations such as the AEL played important roles in promoting anti-Asian sentiment, agitating violence against immigrant workers living in the United States and campaigning for restrictive immigration laws at the time. The AEL was a North American organization founded in the early twentieth century whose main goal was to prevent Asian immigrants from entering the United States and Canada. Its predecessor, the Japanese and Korean Exclusion League, was founded in May 1905 in San Francisco, California. Members attending the first meeting included labor organization leaders such as Patrick Henry McCarthy (from the Building Trades Council of San Francisco) and Andrew Furuseth and Walter McCarthy (from the International Seamen's Union). League members accused immigrant workers of stealing their jobs and driving down wages and shared exclusionist views of immigration. In December 1907, the organization was renamed the Asiatic Exclusion League. Led by the Trades and Labour Council, a sister organization with the same name was founded in Vancouver, British Columbia, in August 1907. The AEL's main agenda was to spread anti-Asian propaganda and advocate for legislation to restrict and prevent labor immigration from Asian countries. AEL had branches up and down the Pacific Coast in the United States and Canada.

A series of anti-immigration actions and laws in the early twentieth century were influenced by AEL and its widespread campaigns. Among others, an executive order issued by President Theodore Roosevelt in 1907 ended immigration of Japanese laborers from Hawaii and Mexico; the Webb-Haney Act signed by California Governor Hiram Johnson in 1913 (commonly known as the Alien Land Law of 1913) and its 1919 and 1920 amendments limited land leases by "aliens ineligible to citizenship," and the Johnson-Reed Immigration Act of 1924 signed by President Calvin Coolidge restricted Japanese immigration to the United States.

The 1917 and 1924 immigration acts created the Asiatic Barred Zone and resulted in Asians becoming "aliens ineligible to citizenship." As a U.S. protectorate, the Philippines was exempted from these exclusions until 1934, when the Tydings-McDuffie Act granted independence for the Philippines, stripped Filipinos of their status as U.S. nationals, and put in place an entry restriction of fifty persons annually. During World War II, as part of the United States' efforts to build an alliance with China, the Magnuson Act finally repealed the Chinese Exclusion Act in 1943, serving as an inspiration for the bill and the passage of the Luce-Celler Act a few years later.

Republican Clare Boothe Luce and Democrat Emanuel Celler proposed their bill in 1943. The act would allow a quota of 100 Filipinos and 100 Indians to immigrate to the United States per annum and grant naturalization rights to Filipino and Indian immigrants. According to the South Asian American Digital Archive's website, the bill earned widespread support from higher education institutions; churches; corporations; community organizations; and well-known individuals such as W.E.B. Du Bois, Albert Einstein, Pearl S. Buck, and Upton Sinclair. Sirdar J. J. Singh, president of the India League of America (ILA) and a proponent of the bill, wrote about the proposed bill in a memorandum: "Democratic and freedom loving Americans are certainly not shedding their blood for the continuance of racial discrimination, racial intolerance, [or] racial superiority, which are Hitlerian theories" (South Asian American Digital Archive 2018).

On July 2, 1946, President Harry Truman signed the Luce-Celler Act into law. According to the Public Broadcasting Service (PBS), several community leaders and officials were present at the signing, including Antonio Gonzales, director of the Filipino Community Center in Chicago in the late 1930s and elected president of the Filipino Inter-Community Organizations of America in 1949; Juan Dionisio, director of the Philippine Resident Commissioner's Office of the Pacific Coast from 1945, part of the Diplomatic Corps of the new Philippine Republic in 1946, and the Philippine ambassador to Pakistan and later Iran in the 1960s; Anoop Singh of New York, later elected to the Indian Parliament; and Singh, ILA president, Washington, D.C.,–area businessman, and son of the deputy commissioner in his home district of Peshawar, Punjab (PBS 2000).

The Bellingham Race Riots, 1907

A small town in the Pacific Northwest, Bellingham, Washington, experienced an economic boom in the early twentieth century. A few hundred Asian immigrants, mostly from India, resided in Bellingham at the time. Many of them worked in the lumber mills. On September 4, 1907, a few hundred white men, many of them members of the Japanese-Korean Exclusion League (later renamed the Asiatic Exclusion League), broke into the lumber mills, drove away Indian immigrant workers, looted their valuables, and destroyed properties. The Indian immigrant community was essentially wiped out overnight. Several Indians were hospitalized. In the end, no one was prosecuted. Headlines in local newspapers at the time indicated bias, racism, and sympathy for the rioters, for example: "Millmen Will Fight for Rights," "Scared Hindus in Hurry to Go," and "Dwellings of Hindus Are Dens of Dirt," among others (Seattle Civil Rights and Labor History Project 2007). Such anti-Asian and anti-immigration sentiment would have a lasting impact in the town. As a result of the riots, there are few traces of the Indian immigrant community left in Bellingham.

The Bellingham riots were among the first anti-Asian incidents along the Pacific Coast. Similar violent riots also took place in California, Oregon, and Vancouver, Canada, during this period. Such racism, violence, and exclusion were echoed by a series of anti-immigration and anti-Asian legislations at the federal and state levels in the United States.

On its one hundredth anniversary, University of Washington's Seattle Civil Rights and Labor History Project created a special section on the 1907 Bellingham race riots. It featured David Cahn's historical essay "The 1907 Bellingham Riots in Historical Context," Andrew Hedden and Ian Morgan's video documentary *Present in All That We Do*, and a collection of newspaper reports from 1907 and commemorative articles from 2007 (Seattle Civil Rights and Labor History Project 2007). This project hopes to bring awareness to this little-known incident and its historical significance.

On the international stage, the Philippines gained independence from the United States in 1946, and India from Great Britain in 1947. Despite the seemingly small quota specified, this act is of unique significance not only to Filipino and Indian communities in the United States but also to Asian American history in general.

Filipinos in America

The Philippines has a long history of colonization. It was under Spanish rule from the sixteenth century until 1898, under American rule from 1898 to 1946, and under Japanese occupation during World War II. The recorded earliest presence of Filipinos in America dates back to October 1587 around Morro Bay, California (Bonus 2000, 191). They arrived with Spanish ships. Filipino settlements were established in Louisiana in the 1800s, most likely by sailors from Spanish galleons. Filipinos in sizeable numbers began to arrive in the United States in the early 1900s.

After the Spanish-American War (1898), the Philippines became a U.S. territory and Filipinos became U.S. nationals, thus exempted from the anti-Asian immigration laws put in place in the late nineteenth century and early twentieth century. At the time, agricultural laborers from the Philippines mainly lived in Hawaii and California. From 1903 until World War II, groups of Filipino students entered the United States on government scholarships. They were known as the *pensionados*. After completing their study in the United States, some of them returned to the Philippines; others stayed. The Tydings-McDuffie Act of 1934 (also known as the Philippine Commonwealth and Independence Act) granted independence for the Philippines, to take effect on July 4, 1946, after a ten-year transitional period, and thus removed Filipinos' status as U.S. nationals. Only fifty persons from the Philippines were allowed entry per year, with the exception of U.S. Navy recruits. The 1945 War Brides Act allowed veterans to bring their fiancées, wives, and children into the United States. The Luce-Celler Act increased the quota to 100 per year in 1946. After the 1965 Immigration and Nationality Act, the number of immigrants from the Philippines increased substantially. Nowadays Filipino Americans make up the second-largest Asian American group in the United States, after Chinese Americans.

Indians in America

Possibly the earliest recorded presence of an individual from India in the United States dates back to 1790, when an Indian national from Madras was spotted in Salem, Massachusetts. It was believed that he may have accompanied a British merchant ship to the United States. In 1851, six Indians participated in the Fourth of July Independence Day parade in Salem (Chandrasekhar 1982, 12). The first groups of Indian immigrants seeking economic opportunities in the United States arrived in California around the end of the nineteenth century and the beginning of the twentieth century. In addition to joining the workforce, Indian students sought admission to American colleges and universities. Their presence, however, provoked hostility from exclusionary groups and organizations such as the Asiatic Exclusion League.

A series of laws from the late nineteenth century to the early twentieth century further prevented Indian immigrants from entering the country and restricted their rights in the United States. The Emigration Act of 1883 passed by the British government of India regulated the emigration of Indian laborers. The U.S. Contract Labor Law of 1885 forbade companies and individuals from bringing foreign subjects into the country in order to contract them for labor. As a result, most of the Indian immigrants entering the country at the end of the nineteenth century were merchants and students. Farmers and working-class Indians in sizable numbers began to arrive in the United States in the early twentieth century and soon faced hostility and discrimination. Their number remained small. The 1913 Alien Land Law prevented "aliens ineligible for citizenship" from owning property in California. The Immigration Act of 1917 prohibited immigrants from the Asiatic Barred Zone from entering the country or taking up permanent residence, Indians included. The Cable Act of 1922 stripped an American woman of her citizenship if she married an alien ineligible for citizenship. Given the fact that early Indian immigrants were mostly men, this act limited their marriage prospects.

In 1910, the lower federal court held that Asian Indians were Caucasians and therefore eligible for U.S. citizenship in *United States v. Balsara*. In 1920, U.S. Army veteran Bhagat Singh Thind was granted citizenship by an Oregon District Court. However, in 1923, the Supreme Court ruled that Thind and other Indians were not white, even though they were Caucasians, and thus found them ineligible for citizenship in *United States v. Bhagat Singh Thind*. Until the Luce-Celler Act in 1946 granted them the right to naturalize, Indian immigrants were not allowed to become U.S. citizens.

In 1924, Congress imposed a quota system that limited immigration for people of any nationality to 3 percent of that nationality reported living in the United States in 1910 and an annual limit of 356,000 immigrants in total. This national-origins system reduced immigration from eastern and southern Europe and excluded immigration from Asia. The Johnson-Reed Act of 1924 legalized the anti-immigrant violence found in Bellingham and other riots along the Pacific Coast in the early twentieth century. By 1946, there were fewer than 4,000 Indians living in the United States, most of them Punjabi farmers in California and Oregon and a small number of students and businessmen in major cities such as New York and Philadelphia (Hing 1993, 294–95).

Dalip Singh Saund and His Contribution

Dalip Singh Saund (1899–1973) was an influential figure during this time. He was born in Punjab, India, to a Sikh family, came to the United States in 1920, and became a naturalized citizen in 1949. He received his bachelor's degree in mathematics from the University of Punjab in 1919 and an MA and PhD in mathematics from the University of California at Berkeley, in 1922 and 1924, respectively. He worked as a farmer after graduation and became a community leader among South Asian Americans before entering the political arena. In the 1940s, he helped mobilize Indian communities in California and New York to lobby for Indians' citizenship rights. His campaign organization later turned into the India Association of America, and Saund became its leader. After Truman signed the Luce-Celler Act into law, Saund was one of the earliest to apply for naturalization (Patterson 1992).

Saund served as a judge of Justice Court, Westmoreland Judicial District, County of Imperial, from 1952 to 1957. He was elected as a Democrat to the U.S. Congress and served from 1957 to 1962, becoming the first Asian American, the first Indian American, and the first Sikh to be elected to the U.S. House of Representatives. Even though his political career was cut short due to a stroke in 1962, his activism and public service became inspirations for others to follow. Saund published his autobiography, *Congressman from India*, in 1960. Columnist Tom Patterson published "Triumph and Tragedy of Dalip Saund" in *California Historian* in 1992. Endorsed by the National Council for the Social Studies (NCSS), the Heritage Series released a documentary short film—*Dalip Singh Saund: His Life, His Legacy*—that pieces together his remarkable life, despite widespread discrimination and other challenges of his time, through oral histories, family photos, and other narratives.

Impact and Current Conditions

The Luce-Celler Act has had significant impact on Filipino and Indian immigrants and their communities in the United States. Having the right to become naturalized American citizens means they can own and lease land, participate in elections, run for public office, and bring their spouses and minor children to the United States. More importantly, this act marks a turning point in the history of U.S. immigration legislation. After its passage in 1946, immigration laws underwent several modifications, leading to the Immigration and Nationality Act of 1965, which ended the discriminatory immigration regulations and resulted in the unprecedented increase of the number of Filipino, Indian, and other Asian immigrants arriving in the United States. The act also implicitly recognizes India as an independent nation. According to the 2010 census, there are 3,416,840 Filipinos and 3,183,063 Asian Indians living the United States (U.S. Census 2010). They continue to make contributions in various ways to American society.

Recent years have witnessed much debate on immigration, particularly about undocumented immigrants and immigrants and refugees from Muslim-majority countries. Since the 2016 presidential election, anti-immigration rhetoric and policies seem to be on the rise. One such example is Executive Order 13769, "Protecting the Nation from Foreign Terrorist Entry into the United States" (commonly known as the "Travel Ban"), issued by President Donald J. Trump on January 27, 2017. This proclamation suspends and limits the immigration of nationals of seven Muslim-majority countries—Iran, Iraq, Libya, Somalia, Sudan, Syria, and Yemen—with exceptions and case-by-case waivers.

Biographies of Notable Figures

Clare Boothe Luce (1903–1987)

Born Ann Clare Boothe in New York on March 10, 1903, Clare Boothe Luce was an American writer, playwright, journalist, politician, and public figure. Her parents separated when she was a child; her mother later married Albert Austin, who served in the Connecticut state legislature and the U.S. House.

Luce attended private schools in New York and pursued acting in her early years. In 1923, she married George Tuttle Brokaw, wealthy heir of a clothing manufacture business. The couple had a daughter, Ann Clare Brokaw, and divorced in 1929. She later married Henry R. Luce, publisher of *Time*, *Fortune*, and *Life* magazines, in 1935. After her daughter's death in a tragic car accident in 1944, Luce went through a difficult period and converted to Roman Catholicism in 1946. The power couple stayed together until Henry's death in 1967.

Luce had a rather successful career as a fiction writer, playwright, and journalist before she entered politics. In the 1930s, she worked as a writer and editor for *Vogue* and *Vanity Fair*. Her collection of satirical stories, *Stuffed Shirts*, was published in 1931. She wrote several plays: *Abide with Me* (1935), *The Women* (1936), *Kiss the Boys Goodbye* (1938), and *Margin for Error* (1939). The last three plays were adapted into films. The Broadway production of *The Women* in 1936 was a huge success. This play has been staged widely both in the United States and abroad. Luce also wrote the screenplay for a feature film, *Come to the Stable* (1949). During World War II, she toured Great Britain, Belgium, Italy, China, and other places, publishing articles and interviews as a war correspondent for *Life* magazine. She wrote about her experience and observations during the war in *Europe in the Spring* (1940).

Luce was an influential figure in politics, known for her conservative and anti-communist views. She was appointed to serve on the House Military Affairs Committee in the early 1940s. A Republican and a conservative, she was elected a member of the U.S. House of Representatives from Connecticut's Fourth District, serving from 1943 to 1947. During her terms, she advocated for the repeal of the

1882 Chinese Exclusion Act and for aids for war victims abroad, played an instrumental role in creating the Atomic Energy Commission, supported the Equal Rights Amendment on the twentieth anniversary of its introduction in the House, endorsed the development of the Women's Army Auxiliary Corps, and co-sponsored the Luce-Celler Act of 1946. She delivered speeches at the 1944 and 1948 Republican National Conventions.

Luce held prominent positions related to foreign affairs and diplomacy. She served as the U.S. ambassador to Italy from 1953 to 1956, the first American woman appointed to a major ambassadorial post abroad. As ambassador to Italy, she played an important role in the negotiation of a peaceful solution for the Trieste Crisis (1953–1954). In 1959, President Dwight Eisenhower nominated Luce to be the U.S. ambassador to Brazil. Her appointment was confirmed, but she resigned from the position days later. She served on the President's Foreign Intelligence Advisory Board in the 1970s and 1980s under presidents Richard Nixon, Gerald Ford, and Ronald Reagan.

Luce passed away in Washington, D.C., on October 9, 1987, at the age of eighty-four. Several biographies of her life and work have been published, including Stephen C. Shadegg's *Clare Booth Luce: A Biography* (1970), Ralph G. Martin's *Henry and Clare: An Intimate Portrait of the Luces* (1991), and Sylvia Jukes Morris's two-volume work *Rage for Fame: The Ascent of Clare Boothe Luce* (1997) and *Price of Fame: The Honorable Clare Boothe Luce* (2014).

Luce's contributions have been recognized widely. She received the Sylvanus Thayer Award from the U.S. Military Academy at West Point in 1979, the first woman to be awarded this honor. President Reagan awarded her the Presidential Medal of Freedom in 1983, the first congresswoman to receive this honor. She was posthumously inducted into the National Women's Hall of Fame in 2017. Her legacy continues to influence American society today. Run by the Henry Luce Foundation, the Clare Boothe Luce Program (CBL) has been a significant private source in supporting women in science, mathematics, and engineering in the United States since 1989. Founded in 1993, the Clare Boothe Luce Policy Institute (CBLPI) helps prepare young women for leadership and promotes conservative values. Established in 1991, the Heritage Foundation's Clare Boothe Luce Award recognizes distinguished contributions to the conservative movement.

Emanuel Celler (1888–1981)

Emanuel Celler (1888–1981) was an American politician from New York. He was a member of the U.S. House of Representatives from New York from 1923 to 1973, chairman of the House Judiciary Committee from 1949 to 1953 and from 1955 to 1973, and dean of the U.S. House of Representatives from 1965 to 1973. One of its longest-serving members, he served in the House of Representatives for almost half a century. Richard Lyons's article for *The Washington Post* upon Celler's death praises his long career in public service, during which he helped draft and pass four constitutional amendments, all of the major civil rights bills of the twentieth century, and around 400 laws (Lyons 1981). Celler was a strong opponent of the Johnson-Reed Immigration Act of 1924 and the immigration restriction of national-origins quotas. He played an important role during the process of proposing and passing the Hart-Celler Act in 1965, which finally eliminated national origin as a restriction for immigration.

Born in Brooklyn, New York, on May 6, 1888, Celler was the grandson of immigrants from Europe. Three of his grandparents were Jewish; his maternal grandfather was Catholic. He graduated from Columbia College in 1910 and from Columbia University Law School in 1912. Celler began a successful career as a lawyer in New York City in 1912. During World War I, he worked as a government appeal agent on the draft board. He ran for Congress in 1922 in a district that had never elected a Democrat before and won. In 1914, he married Stella B. Barr, who passed away in 1966. The couple had a daughter, Jane Wertheimer.

Celler was a strong advocate for immigrants and an opponent of restrictive immigration policies and laws based on national origin. In 1921, Congress imposed a quota that limited immigration for persons of any nationality to 3 percent of that nationality present in the United States in 1920 and the annual admission of immigrants to 356,000. Celler spoke against the Johnson-Reed Immigration Act of 1924, which further restricted immigration by reducing the total number of immigrants using the national-origins quota system. Although the Johnson-Reed Act passed in Congress and was signed into law, Celler continued to advocate for eliminating the national-origins quota system for the next few decades. His efforts led to the Luce-Celler Act of 1946 and culminated in the passage of the Hart-Celler Act in 1965 that eliminated national origins as the base for immigration.

During his long political career, Celler also campaigned in favor of civil rights and against Prohibition. As chairman of the House Judiciary Committee, he played an important role in drafting and passing the Civil Rights Act of 1964, the Civil Rights Act of 1968, and the Voting Rights Act of 1965. Because of his association with a number of progressive causes, he was criticized by Joseph McCarthy in the 1950s. Celler defended himself at the Democratic National Convention in 1952.

After unexpectedly losing the Democratic primary in 1972, Celler retired from his political career in 1973 and went back to practicing law in New York City. He passed away in Brooklyn on January 15, 1981, at the age of ninety-two. His autobiography, *You Never Leave Brooklyn*, was published in 1953.

DOCUMENT EXCERPTS

Luce-Celler Act, 1946

Signed into law by President Harry Truman in 1946, the Luce-Celler Act allowed a quota of 100 Filipinos and 100 Indians to immigrate to the United States per year. Although these numbers seem small, the act was important to Filipino and Indian communities in the United States. It suggested a change in the restrictive immigration policies and regulations against Asian immigrants. The act also allowed Filipino Americans and Indian Americans to become naturalized U.S. citizens. Filipino Americans would have lost their eligibility for naturalization in 1946 when the Philippines gained independence from the United States.

The Luce-Celler Act

[CHAPTER 534]

AN ACT

To authorize the admission into the United States of persons of races indigenous to India, and persons of races indigenous to the Philippine Islands, to make them racially eligible for naturalization, and for other purposes.

Be it enacted by the Senate and House of Representatives of the Nationality Act of United States of America in Congress assembled, That section 303 of the Nationality Act of 1940, as amended (54 Stat. 1140; 57 Stat. 601; 8 U. S. C., Supp. 703), be amended to read as follows:

"SEC. 303 (a) The right to become a naturalized citizen under the provisions of this Act shall extend only to-

"(1) white persons, persons of African nativity or descent, and persons who are descendants of races indigenous to the continents of North or South America or adjacent islands and Filipino persons or persons of Filipino descent;

"(2) persons who possess, either singly or in combination, a preponderance of blood of one or more of the classes specified in clause (1);

"(3) Chinese persons and persons of Chinese descent, and persons of races indigenous to India; and

"(4) persons who possess, either singly or in combination, a preponderance of blood of one or more of the classes specified in clause (3) or, either singly or in combination, as much as one-half blood of those classes and some additional blood of one of the classes specified in clause (1).

"(b) Nothing in the preceding subsection shall prevent the naturalization of former citizens of the United States who are otherwise 54 8 U.S. stat. C. 1146. § 717. eligible to naturalization under the provisions of section 317."

SEC. 2. The Nationality Act of 1940 (54 Stat. 1137; 8 U. S. C. 907) is hereby amended by adding a new section, to be known as "SEO. 321A", and to read as follows:

"SEO. 321A. Certificates of arrival or declarations of intention shall not be required of Filipino persons or persons of Filipino descent who are citizens of the Commonwealth of the Philippines on the date of the enactment of this section, and who entered the United States prior to May 1, 1934, and have since continuously resided in the United States. The term 'Filipino persons or person of Filipino descent' as used in this Act shall mean persons of a race indigenous to the Philippine Islands and shall not include persons who are of as much as one-half of a race ineligible to citizenship."

SEC. 3. Section 324 (a) (54 Stat. 1149; 8 U. S. C. 724) of such Act, as amended is amended by striking out after the word "person" the words "including a native-born Filipino".

SEC. 4. With the exception of those covered by subsections (b), (d), (e), and (f) of section 4, Immigration Act of 1924 (43 Stat. 155; 44 Stat. 812; 45 Stat. 1009; 46 Stat. 854; 47 Stat. 656; 8 U. S. C. 204), all persons of races indigenous to India entering the United States annually as immigrants shall be allocated to the quota for India computed under the provisions of section 11 of the said Act. A preference up to 75 per centum of the quota shall be given to Indians and other aliens racially eligible to naturalization, born and resident in India or its dependencies.

SEC. 5. (a) For the purposes of section 2 of this Act, the term "persons of races indigenous to India" shall mean any person who is as much as one-half of the blood of a race indigenous to India and who is eligible to naturalization under section 303 of the Nationality Act of 1940, as amended by section 1 of this Act.

(b) For the purposes of section 2 of the Act of December 17, 1943 (57 Stat. 601; 8 U. S. C., Supp. 703), the term "Chinese person" shall mean any person who is as much as one-half Chinese blood and who is eligible to naturalization under section 303 of the Nationality Act of 1940 as amended by section 1 of this Act.

(c) Notwithstanding the two preceding subsections, any quota immigrant who is of one-half Chinese blood and one-half the blood of a race indigenous to India shall, if born in India, be chargeable to the quota for India; if born in China, to the quota for the Chinese or if born in neither of those countries, to whichever of the said quotas has the least applications for visas against it at the time the application for visa is made.

Approved July 2, 1946.

Source: The Luce-Celler Act, H.R. 3517; Public Law 483 (1946).

See also: The Immigration and Nationality Act, 1965; *United States v. Bhagat Singh Thind*, 1923

Further Reading

Bayor, Ronald. 2011. *Multicultural America: An Encyclopedia of the Newest Americans.* Santa Barbara, CA: ABC-CLIO.

Bonus, Rick. 2000. *Locating Filipino Americans: Ethnicity and the Cultural Politics of Space.* Philadelphia: Temple University Press.

Chandrasekhar, Sripati. 1982. *From India to America.* La Jolla, CA: Population Review Publications.

Daniels, Roger. 2004. *Guarding the Golden Door: American Immigration Policy and Immigrants since 1882.* New York: Hill and Wang.

Gotanda, Neil. 1996. "Towards Repeal of Asian Exclusion." In *Asian Americans and Congress: A Documentary History*, edited by Hyung-chan Kim, 309–336. Westport, CT: Greenwood.

Hing, Bill Ong. 1993. *Making and Remaking Asian America through Immigration Policy: 1850–1990.* Stanford, CA: Stanford University Press.

Jensen, Joan M. 1988. *Passage from India: Asian Indian Immigrants in North America.* New Haven, CT: Yale University Press.

Karnow, Stanley. 1989. *In Our Image: America's Empire in the Philippines.* New York: Random House.

Leonard, Karen Isaksen. 1997. *The South Asian Americans.* Westport, CT: Greenwood.

Lyons, Richard L. 1981. "Former Rep. Emanuel Celler Dies," *Washington Post*, January 16. https://www.washingtonpost.com/archive/local/1981/01/16/former-rep-emanuel-celler -dies/330902c8-30df-4ada-a150-09f2ab58bc3e/?noredirect=on&utm_term=.5d 12e3cacbde

Okihiro, Gary Y. 2005. *The Columbia Guide to Asian American History.* New York: Columbia University Press.

Patterson, Tom. 1992. "Triumph and Tragedy of Dalip Saund." *California Historian,* June. http://www-tc.pbs.org/rootsinthesand/dalip.pdf

PBS. 2000. "The Luce-Celler Act of 1946." http://www.pbs.org/rootsinthesand/a_lucecellar .html

Seattle Civil Rights and Labor History Project, University of Washington. 2007. "1907 Bellingham Riots." http://depts.washington.edu/civilr/bham_intro.htm

South Asian American Digital Archive. 2018. http:// www.saada.org/

Stern, Jennifer. 1989. *The Filipino Americans.* New York: Chelsea House.

Trinh Võ, Linda. 2004. *Mobilizing an Asian American Community.* Philadelphia: Temple University Press.

U.S. Census Bureau. 2010. "The Asian Population: 2010." https://www.census.gov/prod /cen2010/briefs/c2010br-11.pdf

Korean War, 1950–1953

Kimberly McKee

Chronology

August 22, 1910	The Treaty of Annexation results in Japan's annexation of Korea, resulting in thirty-five years of colonization.
March 1, 1919	Nationwide peaceful protests occur as citizens demand independence.
1931	Japan imposes military rule on the Korean peninsula.
December 1, 1943	The Cairo Declaration released by the United States, Great Britain, and Republic of China pledges to continue war against Japan and agrees Korea would gain freedom and independence in due course, as Japan would become stripped of all territories acquired after World War I.
February 1945	American President Franklin D. Roosevelt suggests to Soviet Premier Joseph Stalin that a four-power trusteeship—United States, Great Britain, Soviet Union, and Republic of China—for Korea be implemented following the war. A formal agreement to the proposition is not made.
July 1945	The Potsdam Declaration reiterates the statement released in the Cairo Declaration concerning Korea's future independence.
September 1945	Imperial Japan officially surrenders to the Allies on September 2, ending World War II.
1945	The Soviet Union and United States divide the Korean peninsula at the thirty-eighth parallel, resulting in the Soviet Union stationing troops in the north and the United States in the south.
1947	The United Nations (UN) assumes responsibility for the southern part of the Korean peninsula, with the U.S. military nominally in control.
August 1948	The Republic of Korea (South Korea) is established, and Syngman Rhee is elected president.
August 1948	The Democratic People's Republic of Korea (North Korea) is established, with Kim Il Sung as president.

June 25, 1950	North Korea crosses the thirty-eighth parallel and launches an offensive toward Seoul. The UN Security Council unanimously condemns North Korea's invasion of South Korea. The Soviet Union has been boycotting the UN since January 1950 and is not present for the vote.
June 27, 1950	Resolution 83 is adopted by the UN Security Council, authorizing UN member states to provide military assistance to South Korea.
June 28, 1950	The Korean People's Army (North Korea) enters Seoul, and the Republic of Korea Army (South Korea) moves south of the Han River in Seoul.
July 1950	U.S. troops arrive in South Korea and assume operational command over UN forces, including South Korea's army.
September 30, 1950	South Korea units enter North Korea. By this time, the war has resulted in 111,000 South Korean deaths, 106,000 wounded, and 57,000 missing.
October 1950	China enters the Korean War as a North Korean ally.
July 27, 1953	Armistice ends the Korean War, declaring a demilitarized zone (DMZ) that roughly follows the thirty-eight parallel. An estimated three million Koreans, one million Chinese, and 54,000 Americans were killed during the fighting.

Narrative

The Korean War marked a shift in the Cold War as the United States and the Soviet Union found their adversarial relationship turning toward military warfare vis-à-vis their support of the Republic of Korea (South Korea) and the Democratic People's Republic of Korea (North Korea), respectively. Prior to the start of the Korean War, many Americans were unfamiliar with Korea. In fact, many Americans' understandings of the war are rooted in popular culture's portrayal of Korea in the television show *M*A*S*H*, which premiered in 1972 and remains in syndication today. This reflects how the war is commonly referred to as the Forgotten War and underscores Americans' limited engagement with Korea and Koreans in the mid-twentieth century. Yet the Korean War remains a significant event in Cold War history and present-day politics because it exemplifies the schism between democracy and communism and has come to signal broader differences in the contemporary political climate.

An anti-communist North Korean, a newly-released prisoner of war, holds up the flag of the Republic of South Korea in Seoul around 1953–1954. The Korean War ended with the demarcation between North Korea and South Korea. (National Archives)

Korean migration to the United States was limited not only due to Korea's status as a Japanese colony but also to restrictive American immigration legislation that effectively curtailed any entry of persons of Asian descent. From 1875 to 1924, a series of immigration laws halted migration from Asia. As a result, by the end of World War II, the number of Koreans in the United States was negligible compared to the total American population of 139.9 million. This small Korean American population includes an estimated 7,000 Koreans who migrated to Hawaii to labor on sugar plantations between 1903 and 1905, as well as Korean students and diplomats who came to the United States. Following Japanese aggression and then colonization, these Koreans in the states were joined by "approximately one thousand picture brides from 1910 to 1924 and some nine hundred political exiles, students, and intellectuals during and after this period" (Abelmann and Lie 1995, 53). The term "picture bride" stems from the way men and women selected their spouses using photographs, as men lived in Hawaii and women lived in Korea.

Additionally, migration was profoundly shaped by the role of Christian missionaries. One of the earliest missionaries to Korea was Horace Newton Allen, who arrived in November 1884. Allen served as an envoy to the first Korean delegation sent to the United States in 1887. The experience of early Korean immigrants is recorded in the writings of Younghill Kang (*The Grass Roof*, 1931; *East Goes West: The Making of an Oriental Yankee*, 1937) and Mary Paik Lee (*Quiet Odyssey: A Pioneer Korean Woman in America*, 1990).

Emigration to the United States was spurred by the conclusion of war on the Korean Peninsula. Women married to U.S. servicemen composed the largest group of immigrants at the time. An estimated 6,400 women arrived in the immediate postwar period (1951–1964) (Kim 2002, 13). Those women entering the United States prior to the revision of U.S. immigration law in 1952 entered through "special acts of Congress that established temporary windows of opportunity through which American soldiers could bring home their Asian wives" (Yuh 2002, 2). Joining these women were war orphans and adoptees, which started the pattern of migration for an estimated 130,000 Korean adoptees who entered the United States and another 70,000 Korean adoptees who entered other countries in the West. From 1953 to 1965, an estimated 5,800 children were sent abroad for adoption. The majority of these were considered "abandoned" or children of "unwed mothers." An estimated 79.6 percent of all adoptees from 1958 to 1970 fall into these two categories (Hübinette 2018).

Restrictions to the migration of persons of Asian descent were not lifted until the 1952 Immigration and Naturalization Act and the subsequent 1965 Immigration Act (Hart-Celler Act). This combined legislation resulted in the removal of racist and xenophobic immigration legislation that began in 1882. As a result of the legislative changes, which included the abolishment of national-origins quotas and emphasized family reunification, the number of Korean immigrants grew rapidly, increasing threefold from 11,200 in 1960 to 38,700 in 1970. This wave of

Singing Korean Children in the Postwar Period

The postwar period found Americans entertained by the Korean Children's Choir, sponsored by the American-Korean Foundation, who first arrived in the United States in 1954. The Korean Children's Choir contributed to shifting cultural understandings of Korea following the Korean War. Susie Woo notes, "For the first time, Americans saw Korean children in an American context, a juxtaposition that deepened sentimental connections and allowed many to imagine what it might be like to have the children here permanently" (2015, 26). Traveling to over fifty cities from April to June 1954, the Korean Children's Choir performed at the Statue of Liberty and for First Lady Mamie Eisenhower in the White House. After this initial tour, the interdenominational organization World Vision, Inc., sponsored five tours of the Korean Orphan Choir between 1958 and 1968. Unaffiliated with the Korean Children's Choir, the Korean Orphan Choir drew its troupe of children under the age of sixteen from Korean orphanages. The Korean Orphan Choir reflected the interconnected nature of Christianity and adoption in Korea in the post–Korean War period. The Korean children captured American hearts and became embedded in the American public's consciousness.

immigrants included individuals sponsored by family members already living in the United States, as well as those eligible for entry following the lifting of previous restrictions. This exponential growth of the Korean population persisted, and the numbers increased from 290,000 in 1980 to 864,000 in 2000. Peak immigration occurred from 1985 to 1987, when more than 35,000 Koreans arrived annually. Approximately 1.8 million Koreans lived in the United States by 2015.

The war haunts the Korean diaspora in the United States, as many of these initial immigrants personally experienced the tragedies of war, which resulted in more than three million casualties. Internal Korean migration also occurred as families from North Korea migrated south, and many families found themselves divided at the end of the war as a result. Nancy Abelmann and John Lie note, "It is widely appreciated among Korean Americans that northern exiles are overrepresented in the United States. Their earlier displacement contributes to their decision to emigrate" (1995, 51–52). Such displacements as a result of war have been featured in fictional accounts of the Korean War and its legacies on Koreans and

Intergenerational Trauma in Fiction

Min Jin Lee's debut novel, *Free Food for Millionaires* (2007), introduces Casey Han, a second-generation Korean American, who grew up in a small apartment with her immigrant parents, Joseph and Leah, and sister, Tina, in Queens, New York. The novel follows Casey as she strives to attain success in Manhattan upon graduating from Princeton. Readers witness the complexities of intergenerational trauma and struggles between immigrants and their children as Korean and American cultural norms conflict with one another. Exemplifying the chasm between the generations is Casey's ruminations over her father's stories of the Korean War and life in Busan, a port city on South Korea's southwest coast, after escaping from his family estate near Pyongyang and leaving his civil servant family behind at the age of sixteen. In many ways, the Han family is emblematic of Korean Americans who migrated in the 1970s and 1980s whose lives were touched by the Korean War. Sponsored by Leah Han's brother, the family arrived and moved into a Korean immigrant enclave as the family settled in the United States. *Free Food for Millionaires* captures the nuances of interpersonal family dynamics shaped within Korean American practices, ideologies, and institutions. Lee captures the ways in which the Korean War haunts members of the Han family and the older generation of Korean immigrants and the effect of this haunting on their family dynamics.

Korean Americans, as seen in Chang-Rae Lee's novels *A Gesture Life* (1999) and *The Surrendered* (2008).

The Korean War deeply affected the lives of generations of Korean immigrants and Korean Americans. A silence exists where the chasm of war is not breached, what Grace M. Cho terms a haunting. For those who lived through the Korean War, Cho notes, "Memories of civilian massacres perpetrated by the U.S. military reveal a hidden history and thus instigate a radical rupturing of the fantasy of the American dream and of friendly U.S.-Korea relations" (2008, 19). To engender a richer conversation concerning the loss and devastation of war, psychology professor Ramsey Liem co-curated an interactive media exhibit, *Still Present Pasts: Korean Americans and the "Forgotten War,"* which has been on national tour since 2005. Discussing the exhibit, Liem notes:

> More than anything else, *Still Present Pasts* is about claiming voice, breaking six decades of silence about how ordinary people experienced the Korean War in Korea and the United States. The people whose oral histories inspired our exhibit challenged the culture of silence in the U.S. that shrouds the Korean War, risked becoming targets of political and ideological conflict in their own communities, and were willing to relive personal traumas and expose them to other family members as well as strangers. (2009, 11)

The public testimony of Koreans and Korean Americans featured in *Still Present Pasts* captures the ways in which the Korean American community navigates memory and the act of remembering. To share the stories of everyday Koreans' experiences of the war means revisiting buried histories and disrupting a generalized narrative of U.S. benevolence on the Korean Peninsula, whereby Americans helped stop the spread of communism and rescued vulnerable orphaned waifs. The exhibit resulted in *Memory of a Forgotten War* (2013), a documentary centered on the experiences of four Korean American survivors.

Military Camp Towns in South Korea

The Korean War devastated the Korean Peninsula. Not only were families separated as the country found itself officially divided at the thirty-eighth parallel by the armistice agreement signed on July 27, 1953, but the military presence shaped the rebuilding of South Korea. Part of this military presence included the rise of military camp towns. Many Koreans lived near the U.S. military bases, and work related to the military encampments was one of the more reliable forms of employment in the postwar period.

One of the first camp towns appeared at the end of 1950 in Bupyong, a town near Incheon. Stationed at Incheon, soldiers sought recreation through liquor and girls. Poverty-stricken women engaged in sex work as a method of economic survival, and some of these women were former "comfort women" forced into sex work under Japanese occupation. Other camp towns emerged in Seoul and Busan (Yuh 2002, 21). Informal economies arose. Often those Koreans living in camp towns were from lower classes, seeking out a living in areas that garnered a reputation as "stigmatized twilight zones fraught with prostitution, crime, and violence and were characterized by substandard community infrastructure" (Moon 2010, 54).

Following the armistice that formally ended the war in 1953, camp towns flourished, and as Ji-Yeon Yuh notes, "The 1960s were the heyday of the camptowns, when more than thirty thousand women earned their living entertaining some sixty-two thousand U.S. soldiers stationed in virtually every corner of South Korea" (2002, 21). It is critical to recognize that women engaged in sex work as a means of economic survival. These women made constrained choices as a means to support their families, but in many cases, they remain shameful family secrets (Cho 2008, 100). Often these women moved from rural to urban areas in search of work. Grace M. Cho writes, "By some estimates, over one million Korean women worked as prostitutes for the U.S. military between the early 1950s and the mid-1990s, but this number is likely to be conservative" (2008, 96). Monitored by the Korean government and U.S. military, these camp towns were regulated with "decades-long collaboration to regulate camptown women and their behavior" (Yuh 2002, 25).

Military camp towns deeply affected the restructuring of South Korea's economy, as well as the way in which Koreans and Korean Americans understood the sexual labor of women who worked in clubs and bars that serviced members of the U.S. military. These women encountered stigma. Even though their labor supported the economic development of a rebuilding South Korea and the survival of their own families, their means of employment resulted in shame. Further, the negative association attached to Korean women involved with non-Korean men followed those women who participated in consensual relationships with U.S. servicemen and those who married them and migrated to the United States.

Military Brides in the United States

Married to U.S. servicemen, Korean War brides often paved the way for other family members to leave South Korea and migrate. Korean War brides arrived outside of existing immigration quotas, in some ways similar to the war brides of World War II from Japan and China. An estimated 28,000 women entered the United States from 1950 to 1972, representing the largest group of Korean immigrants entering the United States since the end of World War II. This growth contributed to a skewed sex ratio of Korean immigrants—an estimated 82 percent were women and represented half of the Koreans naturalized as Americans from 1965 to 1981 (Abelmann and Lie 1995, 58).

Korean War brides typically found themselves subjected to classism and racism. Unlike the diplomats and students who emigrated earlier, this new wave of immigrants possessed lower levels of education and came from lower-class backgrounds. At the same time, they faced stigma as a result of their association with potential military prostitution, given their marriages to U.S. servicemen, even if they met their husbands in locales other than U.S. military bases.

Marriages between Korean women and American servicemen did not end immediately after the Korean War. These relationships continued as the United States maintained involvement on the Korean Peninsula. Well-known Korean military bride communities emerged throughout the United States in cities such as New York, Chicago, Los Angeles, San Diego, Atlanta, and Washington, D.C., as well as in more rural communities in Kansas. The association with military camp towns, and by extension prostitution, continued after the Korean War.

Even as these women encountered assumptions concerning their lives immediately prior to migration, they were instrumental in changing the demographics of Korean Americans in the United States. For many families, they were the start of the chain migration of other relatives. In many ways, these women were pioneers in reshaping the Korean American community from the mid-twentieth century onward.

International Adoption Participation

The Korean War signaled a shift in how the Korean Peninsula and Koreans were understood by Americans. Young Korean boys became military mascots to U.S. troops stationed on the peninsula. These children not only performed household tasks but also held a symbolic position, forging deep friendships with the men in the units they served. Arissa Oh notes, "*Stars and Stripes* published images and carried stories of servicemen doing fatherly things like giving a mascot a bath, teaching him to manage his money, and administering spankings" (2015, 34). Some of these children were adopted as part of the initial wave of Korean adoptions. For example, U.S. Navy Chief Boatswain's Mate Vincent J. Paladino adopted Kyung Soo Lee, a four-and-a-half-year-old boy, in 1953 and brought the child (renamed Lee James Paladino) home to New Rochelle, New York. The public interest garnered by these initial adoptions humanized Korean War orphans. Stories like the adoption of Kyung Soo Lee or the role of Korean boys as mascots for the U.S. military demonstrated how Korean children could seamlessly become Americans and adopt an American way of life.

The plight of war orphans greatly affected Americans' understandings of the devastation on the Korean Peninsula. Christian missionary organizations and international relief organizations also promoted supporting Korean children through sponsorship plans. Sponsorship programs, along with films such as the World Vision, Inc.–produced *The Other Sheep* (1955), spurred families to consider adoption. For example, moved by *The Other Sheep*, Harry Holt and his wife, Bertha Holt, adopted eight mixed-race orphans and founded the Holt Adoption Project (now known as Holt International). The Holts' efforts affected the rapid growth of adoption. This is not to say that they were the sole adoption agency facilitating Korean adoptions; rather, they skillfully employed the media to raise awareness of orphanage conditions and the economic precarity facing Korean children at the time.

Prospective adoptive parents sometimes wrote to their adoption agencies with a deep interest in formally adopting the children they sponsored. Heartwarming stories of these children's entry into their new families accompanied the adoption of Korean children in American media outlets at the time (e.g., *Life*, *Saturday Evening Post*, and *Time*). In contrast, modern documentaries such as *First Person Plural* (2000) and *In the Matter of Cha Jung Hee* (2010) highlight the complexities of such programs in their focus on the experiences of Deann Borshay Liem and her adoption into the Borshay family.

International adoption from South Korea continues today. Although the numbers of children entering the West are lower than the peak in the 1970s and 1980s, the legacy of a post–Korean War project to aid orphaned children and mixed-race children is seen in the continued placement of full-blooded Korean children with families in Europe, North America, and Australia. And the reverberations of decisions to place children for adoption affect Koreans today, as birth mothers seek restorative justice (H. Kim 2016). These women frequently found themselves being forced to choose adoption, or their children were sent for adoption without their consent.

Biographies of Notable Figures

Deann Borshay Liem (1957–)

Adopted by the Borshay family in March 1966 and taken to the United States, Deann Borshay Liem became one of the most notable Korean American adoptees as a result of the popularity of her autobiographical documentaries—*First Person Plural* (2000) and *In the Matter of Cha Jung Hee* (2010). These films found a home at the Public Broadcasting Service (PBS), where they were screened as part of its Point of View (POV) series. They are part of the vanguard of Korean adoptees' experiences entering into broader cultural conversations.

Like hundreds of other Americans, the Borshays were moved by the plight of Korean orphans that populated news in the post–Korean War period. They sponsored Cha Jung Hee, who resided at Sun Duck Orphanage, through the Foster Parents Plan before seeking to adopt the child. Donating fifteen dollars a month, the Borshays also mailed letters and, occasionally, clothing. Unbeknownst to the Borshay family, the child who arrived—the one who would become Deann Borshay—was not the original Cha Jung Hee. The child who was adopted was originally named Kang Ok Jin. Her mother placed her youngest children in the orphanage due to the family's economic precarity.

Kang Ok Jin was forever lost to her Korean family when it was determined by orphanage workers that she would replace Cha Jung Hee for adoption following Cha Jung Hee's return to a family member. By the age of eight, Liem was three people—Kang Ok Jin born June 14, 1957; Cha Jung Hee born November 5, 1956; and Deann Borshay born March 3, 1966, as she stepped off the airplane in San Francisco. Only in May 1981 did Deann confirm that she was Kang Ok Jin, after she received a letter from her biological Korean brother—a response to her letter to her orphanage. While *First Person Plural* documents her reunion with her Korean family, *In the Matter of Cha Jung Hee* explores the deceit that led to her adoption. Part of this examination includes dismantling the narrative she believed to be true about her origins: that her mother died in childbirth and her father died during the Korean War. This seemed plausible to Borshay as a child and young adult. Yet after careful consideration, she realized it was a fabrication because she was born four years following the war's end.

Deann Borshay Liem's films call into question widely held beliefs of Korean international adoption as an act of humanitarian rescue. She centers on adoptee voices, which is particularly evident in her forthcoming documentary, *Geographies of Kinship*. At the same time her documentaries examine the legacies of the Korean War on South Korea's adoption participation. She connects histories of U.S. militarism on the Korean Peninsula with adoption and explores how the adoptee immigrants reshape how we understand the Korean American community.

Liem's work is not limited to focusing on Korean adoption. She partnered with her brother-in-law, Ramsey Liem, to co-produce and co-direct the documentary *Memory of Forgotten War* (2013), which captures the voices of four Korean American survivors of the military conflict. She is also working on *Crossings*, a film documenting thirty women peacemakers who seek to cross the demilitarized zone (DMZ) from North to South Korea. Featuring Nobel Peace laureates Leymah Gbowee (Liberia) and Mairead Maguire (Northern Ireland), women's rights pioneer Gloria Steinem, and Korean American peace activist Christine Ahn, *Crossings* explores the legacies of war and women's role in the peacemaking process.

DOCUMENT EXCERPTS

The War Brides Act

The War Brides Act allowed alien spouses and dependents of the United States Armed Forces members to enter the United States. Their entry was not included in the nationality-based immigration annual quota at the time. As a result, an estimated 28,000 Korean women entered the United States from 1950 to 1972, representing one of the large groups of Korean immigrants entering the United States since the end of World War II. A 1947 amendment of the act removed the term "if admissible" so that Japanese and Korean spouses of American troops could immigrate. The Alien Fiancées and Fiancés Act of 1946 extended the privileges to fiancées and fiancés of war veterans as well.

The War Brides Act

[CHAPTER 289]
AN ACT
To amend the Act approved December 28, 1945 (Public Law 271, Seventy-ninth Congress), entitled "An Act to expedite the admission to the United States of alien spouses and alien minor children of citizen members of the United States armed forces."
Be it enacted by the Senate and House of Representatives of the United States of America in Congress assembled, That the Act approved December 28, 1945 (Public Law 271, Seventy-ninth Congress, ch.591, first session) (59 Stat. 659; 8 U. S. C. 232–236), is amended by adding a new section thereto, to be known as section 6, and to read as follows:
"SEC. 6. The alien spouse of an American citizen by a marriage occurring before thirty days after the enactment of this Act, shall not be considered as inadmissible because of race, if otherwise admissible under this Act."
Approved July 22, 1947.

Source: The War Brides Act, H.R. 31491, Public Law 213 (July 22, 1947).

Settlement Proposal by Zhou Enlai

Truce talks began at Kaesong near the thirty-eighth parallel in July 1951. However, the Korean War did not end until July 1953. The talks later moved to Panmunjom and came to a deadlock in October 1952. The negotiation resumed in 1953. Chinese Foreign Minister Zhou Enlai made the following statement, proposing that upon a cease-fire, those prisoners of war (POWs) who wished to be exchanged should be returned home, with the remainder handed over to a neutral state. His proposal broke the deadlock in the negotiation process. On July 27, 1953, the UN,

North Korea, and China signed an armistice agreement, continuing the division of Korea. This armistice ended the Korean War, declaring a demilitarized zone (DMZ) that roughly follows the thirty-eighth parallel.

Zhou Enlai POW Settlement Proposal

The Central People's Government of the People's Republic of China and the Government of the Democratic People's Republic of Korea, having jointly studied the proposal put forward by Gen. Mark W. Clark, Commander in Chief of the United Nations Command, on Feb. 22, 1953, concerning the exchange of sick and injured prisoners of war of both sides during the period of hostilities, are of the common opinion that it is entirely possible to achieve a reasonable settlement of this question in accordance with the provision of Article 109 of the Geneva Convention of 1949.

A reasonable settlement of the question of exchanging sick and injured prisoners of war clearly has a very significant bearing upon the smooth settlement of the entire question of prisoners of war. It is, therefore, our view that the time should be considered ripe for settling the entire question of prisoners of war in order to insure the cessation of hostilities in Korea and to conclude the armistice agreement.

The Government of the People's Republic of China and the Government of the Democratic People's Republic of Korea hold in common that the delegates of the Korean People's Army and the Chinese People's Volunteers to the armistice negotiations and the delegates of the United Nations Command to the armistice negotiations should immediately start negotiations on the question of exchanging sick and injured prisoners of war during the period of hostilities, and should proceed to seek an over-all settlement of the question of prisoners of war.

The Korean armistice negotiations in the past one year and more have already laid the foundation for the realization of an armistice in Korea. In the course of the negotiations at Kaesong and Panmunjom, the delegates of both sides have reached agreement on all questions except that of prisoners of war.

In the first place, on the question of a ceasefire in Korea, about which the whole world is concerned, both sides have already agreed that "the Commanders of the opposing sides shall order and enforce a complete cessation of all hostilities in Korea by all armed forces under their control, including all units and personnel of the ground, naval, and air forces, effective twelve hours after this Armistice Agreement is signed" (Paragraph 12 of the draft Korean armistice agreement).

Secondly, both sides have further reached agreement on the various important conditions for an armistice. On the question of fixing a military demarcation line and establishing a demilitarized zone, both sides have already agreed that the actual line of contact between both sides at the time when the armistice agreement becomes effective shall be made the military demarcation line and that "both sides shall withdraw two kilometers from this line so as to establish a demilitarized zone between the opposing forces . . . as a buffer zone to prevent the occurrence of incidents which might lead to a resumption of hostilities" (Paragraph 1 of the draft armistice agreement).

On the question of supervising the implementation of the armistice agreement and settling violations of the armistice agreement, both sides have already agreed that a military armistice commission, composed of five senior officers appointed jointly by the Supreme Commander of the Korean People's Army and the commander of the Chinese People's Volunteers, and five senior officers appointed by the Commander in Chief of the United Nations Command, shall be set up to be responsible for the supervision of the implementation of the armistice agreement, including the supervision and direction of the committee for the repatriation of prisoners of war, and the settling through negotiations any violations of the armistice agreement (Paragraphs 19, 20, 24, 25 and 56 of the draft armistice agreement); both sides have also agreed that a neutral nation's supervisory commission shall be set up, composed of two senior officers appointed as representatives by Poland and Czechoslovakia, neutral nations nominated jointly by the Supreme Commander of the Korean People's Army and the Commander of the Chinese People's Volunteers, and two senior officers appointed as representatives by Sweden and Switzerland, neutral nations nominated by the Commander in Chief of the United Nations Command, and that under this commission there shall be provided neutral nations inspection teams composed of officers appointed as members to the teams by the aforementioned nations.

These inspection teams shall be stationed at the following ports of entry in North Korea: Sinuiju, Chongjin, Hungnam, Manpo, Sinanju, and at the following ports of entry in South Korea: Inchon, Taegu, Pusan, Kangnung and Kunsan, to supervise and inspect the implementation of the provisions that both sides cease the introduction into Korea of reinforcing military personnel and combat aircraft, armored vehicles, weapons, and ammunition (except for rotation and replacement as permitted by these provisions), and may conduct special observations and inspections at those places outside the demilitarized zone where violations of the armistice agreement have been reported to have occurred, so as to ensure the stability of the military armistice (Paragraphs 36, 37, 40, 41, 42 43 of the draft armistice agreement).

In addition, both sides have reached agreement that "the military commanders of both sides hereby recommend to the governments of the countries concerned on both sides that, within three months after the armistice agreement is signed and becomes effective, a political conference of a higher level of both sides be held by representatives appointed respectively to settle through negotiations the questions of the withdrawal of all foreign forces from Korea, the peaceful settlement of the Korean question, etc." (Paragraph 60 of the draft armistice agreement).

As stated above, in the course of the Korean armistice negotiations one question alone—the question of prisoners of war—blocks the realization of an armistice in Korea. And even with respect to the question of prisoners of war, both sides have reached agreement on all the provisions in the draft armistice agreement on the arrangements relating to prisoners of war, except on the question of the repatriation of prisoners of war. Had the Korean armistice negotiations not been interrupted for more than five months, a solution might long since have been found to this issue of the repatriation of prisoners of war.

Now inasmuch as the United Nations Command has proposed to settle, in accordance with Article 109 of the Geneva Convention, the question of exchanging sick and injured prisoners of war during the period of hostilities, we consider that subsequent upon the reasonable settlement of the question of sick and injured prisoners of war, it is entirely a matter of course that a smooth solution to the whole question of prisoners of war should be achieved, provided that both sides are prompted by real sincerity to bring about an armistice in Korea in the spirit of mutual compromise.

Regarding the question of prisoners of war, the Government of the People's Republic of China and the Government of the Democratic People's Republic of Korea have always held and continue to hold that a reasonable solution can only lie in the release and repatriation of war prisoners without delay after the cessation of hostilities in accordance with the stipulations of the 1949 Geneva Convention, particularly those of Article 118 of the convention.

However, in view of the fact that the differences between the two sides on this question now constitute the only obstacle to the realization of an armistice in Korea, and in order to satisfy the desire of the people of the world for peace, the Government of the People's Republic of China and the Government of the Democratic People's Republic of Korea, in pursuance of their consistently maintained peace policy and their position of consistently working for the speedy realization of an armistice in Korea and striving for a peaceful settlement of the Korean question, thus to preserve and consolidate world peace, are prepared to take steps to eliminate the differences on this question so as to bring about an armistice in Korea.

To this end, the Government of the People's Republic of China and the Government of the Democratic People's Republic of Korea propose that both parties to the negotiations should undertake to repatriate immediately after the cessation of hostilities all those prisoners of war in their custody who insist upon repatriation and to hand over the remaining prisoners of war to a neutral state so as to insure a just solution to the question of their repatriation.

Source: Department of State Bulletin. April 13, 1953, 526–527.

See also: The Immigration and Nationality Act, 1965; The Los Angeles Riots, 1992; Vietnam War and Refugee Migration from Southeast Asia, 1965–1975

Further Reading

Abelmann, Nancy and John Lie. 1995. *Blue Dreams: Korean Americans and the Los Angeles Riots*. Cambridge, MA: Harvard University Press.

Cho, Grace M. 2008. *Haunting the Korean Diaspora: Shame, Secrecy, and the Forgotten War*. Minneapolis: University of Minnesota Press.

Hübinette, Tobias. 2018. "Korean Adoption/Adoptees Statistics 1953–2004." http://www.tobiashubinette.se/korean_adoptions.pdf

Kim, Hosu. 2016. *Birth Mothers and Transnational Adoption Practice in South Korea: Virtual Mothering*. New York: Palgrave Macmillan.

Kim, Sang Jo. 2010. "'We Shouldn't Be Forgotten': Korean Military Brides and Koreans in Kansas." PhD diss., University of Kansas. https://kuscholarworks.ku.edu/bitstream/handle/1808/10252/Kim_ku_0099D_12209_DATA_1.pdf;sequence=1

Lee, Jin-Kyung. 2010. *Service Economies: Militarism, Sex Work, and Migrant Labor in South Korea*. Minneapolis: University of Minnesota Press.

Liem, Ramsey. 2009. "The Korean War, Korean Americans and the Art of Remembering." *The Asia-Pacific Journal* 7, no. 41.4: 1–14. https://apjjf.org/-Ramsay-Liem/3235/article.pdf

Moon, Katharine H. S. 1998. "Prostitute Bodies and Gendered States in U.S.-Korea Relations." In *Dangerous Women: Gender & Korean Nationalism*, edited by Elaine H. Kim and Chungmoo Choi, 141–174. New York: Routledge.

Moon, Seungsook. 2010. "Regulating Desire, Managing the Empire: U.S. Military Prostitution in South Korea, 1945–1970." In *Over There: Living with the U.S. Military Empire from World War Two to the Present*, edited by Maria Höhn and Seungsook Moon, 39–77. Durham, NC: Duke University Press.

Oh, Arissa. 2015. *To Save the Children of Korea: The Cold War Origins of International Adoption*. Stanford, CA: Stanford University Press.

Pate, Soojin. 2014. *From Orphan to Adoptee: U.S. Empire and Genealogies of Korean Adoption*. Minneapolis: University of Minnesota Press.

Woo, Susie. 2015. "Imagining Kin: Cold War Sentimentalism and the Korean Children's Choir." *American Quarterly* 67, no. 1: 25–53.

Yuh, Ji-Yeon. 2002. *Beyond the Shadow of Camptown: Korean Military Brides in America*. New York: New York University Press.

4

Activism and the Post-1965 Era

Daniel K. Inouye, First Asian American U.S. Senator, 1962

Katelind Ikuma

Chronology

1924   Daniel K. Inouye is born on September 7 in Honolulu, Hawaii.

1941   Pearl Harbor in Hawaii is bombed by the Japanese, prompting the United States to enter World War II.

1942   Inouye graduates from McKinley High School and enrolls at the University of Hawaii.

1943   President Franklin D. Roosevelt creates an act creating the 442nd Regimental Combat team, which is composed entirely of Japanese American men. Inouye enlists in the 442nd, making him one of its youngest members.

1945   Inouye loses an arm in an attack against a German bunker in northern Italy.

1947   Inouye is discharged from the Army as a captain. He returns home with a Distinguished Service Cross, Bronze Star Medal, two Purple Hearts, and twelve other medals and citations.

1950   With the help of the GI Bill, Inouye graduates from the University of Hawaii.

1952   Inouye graduates from the George Washington University of Law in Washington, D.C.

1954   Inouye returns to Hawaii, where he is elected into the Territorial House of Representatives as a Democrat. He then moves on to the Territorial Senate. During the same period, Hawaii goes through a political upheaval, making the Democratic Party of Hawaii the majority party.

1959 Hawaii becomes the fiftieth state of the United States, and Inouye is sworn in as Hawaii's first representative to the U.S. House.

1962 Inouye is elected into the U.S. Senate, becoming the first Japanese American senator. He is the first Asian American in such a high position.

1964 President Lyndon Johnson signs the Civil Rights Act, banning racial discrimination.

1968 Inouye is the first person of color to deliver the keynote address at the Democratic National Convention in Chicago. He is not afraid to address the lingering racism in America and the complexity of the Vietnam War.

1969 Inouye uses his political power to call for an end to the American military involvement in the Vietnam War.

1973 Inouye serves as a member of the Senate Watergate Committee, which is nationally televised and leads to the resignation of President Nixon.

1976 After a fifteen-month investigation into abuses by the nation's intelligence agencies, Inouye serves as the first chairman of the Senate Select Committee on Intelligence.

1987 Inouye serves as chairman of the Senate Select Committee investigating the Iran-Contra affair, which investigates the alleged arms-for-hostages program. He is also named the chairman of the Senate Committee on Indian Affairs, where he leads the enactment of landmark legislation affecting almost every Native American.

1989 Inouye serves as chairman of the Appropriations Subcommittee on Defense. He eventually serves on this committee three different times as Senate control shifts from Democratic to Republican.

2000 The Distinguished Service Cross, given to twenty-two Asian American soldiers, is upgraded to the Medal of Honor by President Bill Clinton.

2003 The United States invades Iraq.

2007 Inouye serves as the chairman of the Senate Commerce Committee.

2008 Inouye serves as the chairman of the Senate Appropriations Committee. He focuses on aiding national security, while making sure the armed forces are fully equipped and have the best training.

2010 Inouye serves as the appointed present pro tempore of the Senate (third in line of presidential succession). As such, he again becomes the highest-ranking public official of Asian descent in U.S. history.

2012 On December 12, Inouye passes away at eighty-eight years old.

2013 Inouye is awarded the Presidential Medal of Freedom by President Barack Obama.

Narrative

On November 6, 1962, Daniel K. Inouye was elected into the U.S. Senate and became the first Japanese American senator. When Hawaii became a state in August 1959, Inouye became the first person from Hawaii elected to the U.S. House of Representatives. He also became the first Japanese American to serve in the U.S. Congress. In 1962, he was elected to the Senate and became the first Asian American in such a high position. He had a runaway victory over his Republican opponent, Benjamin F. Dillingham, by more than two to one and replaced Senator Oren E. Long. Without a doubt, Inouye paved the way for future Asian Americans in politics.

Early Life

Inouye was born on September 7, 1924, in Honolulu, Hawaii. His parents, Hyotaro Inouye and Kama Imanaga Inouye, were Japanese immigrants. Daniel was the first of four children. He grew up in an area of Honolulu known as Chinese Hollywood,

Senator Daniel K. Inouye inspected the joint services honor guard assembled on the Pentagon parade field during the observance of National POW/MIA Recognition Day on September 4, 2004. He was the guest of honor and the featured speaker at the ceremony. Senator Inouye served in the armed forces during World War II. (R. D. Ward/Department of Defense)

and he went through the Hawaii public school system. The Inouyes raised their children with a mixture of American and Japanese traditions. Inouye went to an American high school, McKinley High School, but also went to a Japanese school afterward. During high school, Inouye wanted to become a surgeon and volunteered at the local Red Cross aid station.

But December 7, 1941, changed Inouye's life course entirely. He was only seventeen at the time. That particular morning caused a chain reaction in Inouye's life and the lives of many other second-generation Japanese Americans. "It was a bright Sunday morning in December nearly six decades ago when aircraft bearing the symbol of the rising sun on their wings flew over my home in Hawaii" (Inouye 2001). Because of Inouye's Red Cross training, during and after the attack he volunteered his time at his local school, helping the sick and wounded. He did not go home for five days. This tragic event in his hometown would turn Inouye's world upside down. On February 19, 1942, ten weeks after the attack on Pearl Harbor, President Franklin D. Roosevelt signed Executive Order 9066, which led to the mass incarceration of all West Coast Japanese Americans in concentration camps. But in Hawaii, only those who seemed suspicious, dangerous, or disloyal to the United States were detained. Inouye and his family were not among them, but their house was searched for suspicious materials, and the authorities destroyed the Inouyes' family radio. But the Inouyes still petitioned the government to give them a chance to prove their loyalty because being American was not based on skin color but the passion within a person (Daniel K. Inouye Institute 2014).

Inouye at War

In January 1943, the government announced that the War Department had decided to accept Japanese American volunteers to join in the fight and form a full-fledged combat team. Inouye immediately volunteered but was turned down at first. Because of his first-aid training, he was considered essential as a worker at the medical aid station. So Inouye withdrew from his pre-med courses at the university and was then ordered to report for active duty. A year after Pearl Harbor, 2,686 Japanese American volunteers from Hawaii sailed out for war. Inouye was number 2,685. This group of Japanese American volunteers became the 442nd Regimental Combat Team, which went on to become the most decorated unit in history.

Inouye quickly attained the rank of sergeant and became a combat platoon leader. In the fall of 1944, Inouye participated in the dramatic rescue of the "Lost Battalion." A U.S. Army unit had become stranded in the mountains of France and was under siege by surrounding German forces. Inouye's unit broke through German lines and rescued the other American soldiers. Inouye survived being shot in the chest because the bullet bounced off two silver dollars he carried in his chest pocket for good luck. He was awarded a Bronze Star and earned a battlefield commission as second lieutenant.

Unfortunately, Inouye did not endure the next attack so well. Inouye and his men were preparing to attack a heavily defended ridge near Terenzo, Italy, when he realized he had lost his lucky silver dollars. Inouye's unit came under fire from three different locations. Inouye was shot in the stomach, but he continued forward. He was throwing hand grenades toward the enemy machine guns when his right arm was almost completely severed by an enemy blast. Firing his machine gun with his left hand, Inouye pressed on until he was shot in the leg and lost consciousness. He awoke but refused medical evacuation until he knew all his men were safe. Once at the field hospital, he convinced the surgeons to operate, even though they believed he would not survive. Inouye had to undergo surgery without anesthesia because he had already received so much morphine. Although the doctors managed to repair his other wounds, they were unable to save his right arm. After nearly two years of recovery in army hospitals, Inouye was discharged with the rank of captain on May 27, 1947. He received a Distinguished Service Cross, a Bronze Star, two Purple Hearts, and twelve other medals and citations for valor.

Political Beginnings

As Inouye was recovering from his injuries, he knew could not go back home to the same Hawaii because of the majority ruling party, which consisted of mainly Caucasian Americans. After the war, Inouye went on to finish his education. While Inouye was completing his bachelor's degree in government and economics from the University of Hawaii, he learned of a man named John Burns. At that time, Burns was running for delegate to the U.S. Congress against popular Republican, Joseph Farrington. Burns, an ex-police officer, knew the votes of the young Nisei generation (second-generation Japanese Americans) and unsatisfied Hawaiian voters could catapult the Democratic Party into office. Inouye agreed that the potential power of the Japanese ethnic vote would be significant. So Inouye contacted Burns and asked him if he needed help in his campaign. Over coffee and buns, Inouye and Burns discussed the future of the Democratic Party. Inouye spread word of Burns through the 442nd Veterans Club. He argued to his comrades that this was a man who was going to change Hawaii because Burns wanted to help them to a better life, a life different from anything their parents could ever dream of. Thus began Inouye's long association with the Democratic Party, most importantly during its rise to power in Hawaii.

When Inouye convinced Dan Aoki, Nisei president of the 442nd Veterans Club, that the energies of the club could be used to improve the social and political status of the Japanese in Hawaii, the foundations of the powerful Democratic Party were

Revolution of 1954

The "Revolution of 1954" was a time of great change in Hawaiian politics. Until 1954, Hawaii's government was controlled by the primarily Caucasian government. However, this government did not accurately represent the state's rapidly changing and growing population. Many immigrants had come to Hawaii from all over the Pacific to work in the sugarcane fields. The Nisei generation was coming of age. Many of these Nisei key players of the "revolution" went on to become major figures in Hawaiian politics for the next few decades.

The revolution gained traction for several reasons. First, a generation of American-born Japanese, Filipino, and Chinese were coming of age alongside native Hawaiians. These groups were most likely to favor Democrats because of the injustice they felt from the ruling Republican party (Niiya 1993, 349). Second, the International Longshoremen's and Warehousemen's Union (ILWU) had great power because dock and plantation workers in Hawaii were well organized. Third, World War II veterans, including those of the all-Nisei 100th Infantry Battalion and 442nd Regimental Combat Team, felt that, having fought for their country, they should have equal opportunities to participate in all aspects of American society.

The Nisei generation of immigrants did not care for the misrepresentation within their vastly white government. After World War II, the Nisei veterans craved change in their homeland of Hawaii. This was illustrated in the rising ambitions of Hawaii's growing middle class; resentments of Hawaii's nonwhite groups against the patterns of the past; and increasing pride in the articulate and youthful leadership of Japanese and Hawaiian lawyers, Chinese businessmen, and Filipino union officials. Even though there was great support for Democrats in 1948, the Democrats could not overcome the Republicans because of the competing factions within the Democratic Party at the time. By 1952, a more moderate faction of the party, led by former police captain John Burns and a core of Nisei veteran supporters led by 442nd Veterans Club president Dan Aoki, had gained control.

The 1954 election was indeed a revolution. Democrats won two-thirds of the seats in the territorial House and nine out of fifteen seats in the Senate. Almost half of these legislators were Nisei, whereas just ten years earlier there had been none. These legislators included Daniel K. Inouye, Sakae Takahashi, and Spark M. Matsunaga. The Democrats also emerged with control over local politics on the islands of Oahu, Kauai, and Maui. The power of the Democrats came full circle in 1970, when the governor of Hawaii was George Ariyoshi (John Burns's protégé) and the two U.S. senators were Inouye and Matsunaga.

laid. All of this was the start of the Democratic Party's rise to power in Hawaii, known as the "Revolution of 1954." The Democratic Party took control of the territorial legislature and finally became a major party. In 1954, Inouye—who had graduated in 1952 from the George Washington University Law School in Washington, D.C.—served as majority leader in the Territorial House of Representatives. Later, from 1958 to 1959, he served as a member of the Territorial Senate.

U.S. Senator of the Fiftieth State of America

When Hawaii became a state in 1959, Inouye became the first person from Hawaii to be elected to the U.S. House of Representatives. He also became the first Japanese American to serve in the U.S. Congress. Then, in 1962, Inouye became a U.S. senator, the first Asian American in such a high position. This signified the beginning of his political career, during which he served in a number of highly influential positions. He would become one of the longest-serving senators in the history of the U.S. Congress.

Inouye chaired the Select Committee on Intelligence, which was formed to investigate the abuse of power by the Central Intelligence Agency and the Federal Bureau of Investigation. He served on the Senate Appropriations Subcommittee on Defense, which is responsible for the allocation of federal funding to government agencies. Inouye concentrated on strengthening national security while ensuring our armed forces had the best equipment and training. He also served on the Senate Commerce, Science and Transportation Subcommittee on Surface Transport and Merchant Marine. There he served Hawaii well with jurisdiction over aviation, maritime, telecommunications, tourism, science, and technology. Inouye also served on the Committee on Indian Affairs, where he led landmark legislation affecting almost every aspect of life for Native Americans. He also served on the Select Committee on Secret Military Assistance to Iran and the Nicaraguan Opposition.

But Inouye is best known for serving on congressional committees investigating both the Watergate and Iran-Contra scandals. The Senate Watergate Committee was set up in the early 1970s to investigate charges of illegal activities by officials of the administration of President Richard M. Nixon during his 1972 re-election campaign. This investigation was televised all over America, and Inouye's patient but determined questioning impressed the huge national television audience (Daniel K. Inouye Institute 2014). Inouye also served on the special committee to investigate the Iran-Contra scandal. The committee found that U.S. government officials had secretly sold weapons to Iran and used the profits to support Contra rebels who were trying to overthrow the Nicaraguan government.

Inouye was also a key player in securing the passage of the Civil Liberties Act of 1988. Under this act, the U.S. government issued an official apology and redressed payments to Japanese Americans who were involuntarily detained during World War II. On June 21, 2000, President Bill Clinton awarded Inouye the Medal of Honor, which is the United States' highest award for military valor. This prestigious award had been previously denied to Japanese American veterans of the 442nd Regimental Combat Team. Twenty-two Japanese American veterans of the 442nd Regimental Team were awarded the Distinguished Service Cross, which was eventually upgraded to the Medal of Honor.

In June 2010, Inouye became the president pro tempore of the Senate, putting him third in line of succession to the presidency (following the vice president and the Speaker of the House). Once again, Inouye had become the highest-ranking public official of Asian descent in American history.

Inouye's Legacy

Inouye was a widely recognized figure during his lifetime. In 1962, he was selected as "One of the 100 Most Important Men and Women in the United States" by *Life* magazine. His autobiography, *Journey to Washington*, was published in 1967.

Inouye's five-decade career in public service ended with his death on December 17, 2012, at Walter Reed National Military Medical Center in Bethesda, Maryland. Inouye's body lay in state at the U.S. Capitol rotunda on December 20, 2012, to allow people to pay their respects. Remarkably, Inouye was only the thirty-first person to receive this honor, and the first Asian American to be honored in this manner as well. President Obama, former President Clinton, Vice President Joe Biden, and House Speaker John Boehner spoke at Inouye's funeral service at the Washington National Cathedral on December 21. Two days after the service, Inouye's body lay in state at the Hawaii State Capitol. The following day, a second funeral was held at the National Memorial Cemetery of the Pacific in Honolulu, where he was laid to rest. Inouye was posthumously awarded the Presidential Medal of Freedom by President Barack Obama, thus becoming the first senator to receive both the Medal of Freedom and the Medal of Honor.

In his foreword to Susan Wels's *Pearl Harbor: December 7, 1941: America's Darkest Day*, Inouye states his observation of himself in relation to this tragic day in history. Pearl Harbor was a catalyst for Inouye's political career, yet it is an experience he is forever grateful for because it shaped his master plan as a politician:

> It is ironic that if Japan had not attacked Pearl Harbor, I might never have become a member of the U.S. Senate, where I have fought to avert war, maintain peace, promote racial harmony, and enhance diplomatic relations. . . . I will never forget that Sunday morning, and I hope that my fellow Americans will remember Pearl Harbor and its many lessons forever.

To forget Pearl Harbor is to forget the good and evil that human beings are capable of in times of crisis. Without a vivid memory of this event, we may lack the fortitude and the preparedness to withstand future assaults on our country and its democratic ideals. (Inouye 2001)

Biographies of Notable Figures

Patsy Matsu Takemoto Mink (1927–2002)

In 1965, Patsy Takemoto Mink became the first Asian American woman elected to the U.S. Congress. But during her lifetime, Mink had many firsts and was a notable public servant of Hawaii in Washington, D.C. During her political career, Mink was well known for fighting to improve education and woman's rights.

Patsy Matsu Takemoto was born and raised in Paia, Maui, Hawaii. She began her political career very early in life, serving as the president of her student body at Maui High School. She went on to graduate from the University of Hawaii, Honolulu, in 1948 and then attended the University of Chicago School of Law. During law school, she met John Mink, whom she married in 1951. She came back to Hawaii as the first Japanese American woman lawyer, but no firm was willing to hire her. So she opened her own private practice.

Mink began her long association with the Democratic Party during its rise to power. She founded the Oahu Young Democrats and then was the Hawaiian delegate to the Young Democratic National Convention. Her first elected position was to the Hawaii House of Representatives in 1956 and 1958. She was elected to the Hawaii senate and served from 1958 to 1959. During a second term on the Hawaii state senate, from 1962 to 1964, she chaired the Education Committee.

When Mink ran for Congress, she did it the old-fashioned way, with a grassroots campaign. Her husband was her voluntary campaign manager, and her friends and co-workers volunteered their time for free. She ran without the support of the state Democratic Party leadership, so she raised campaign funds through small, individual contributions. She easily beat the Republican candidate. In 1964, Mink was elected to Congress.

Once in Congress, she did not waste any time. She immediately began to fight for much-needed legislation for school construction in the U.S. Pacific territories and for education and child welfare. She was against the Vietnam War and argued that money for the war could be better spent on improving the lives of the neediest Americans. During her twelve years in Congress, Mink served on the Education and Labor Committee, the Interior and Insular Affairs Committee, and the Budget Committee. In 1970, she became the first Democratic woman to deliver a State of the Union response. She even made a bid for the Democratic presidential nomination in 1972, her primary focus being women's rights and her opposition to the Vietnam War.

Throughout her career, Mink had never had a warm relationship with the state leaders of her party because of her unwillingness to allow the party to influence her political agenda. In her subsequent five campaigns for re-election, Mink faced a number of difficult primaries in which the local Democratic Party tried to oust her, twice by running women candidates to dilute Mink's gender issues.

Her most important contribution to American legislation was when she co-authored the Title IX Amendment of the Higher Education Act, which was renamed the Patsy T. Mink Equal Opportunity in Education Act in 2002 by President George W. Bush (Keene 2018). The amendment prohibits gender discrimination by federally funded institutions: "No person in the United States shall, on the basis of sex, be excluded from participation in, be denied the benefits of, or be subjected to discrimination under any education program or activity receiving federal financial assistance" (Seaman and Eldridge 2012). Many believed this piece of legislation would only make changes in school activities, specifically sports, but it went on to include housing, health care, and even academic programs that had quota systems to keep women out when they should have been admitted. Mink pushed for this legislation because of the discrimination she experienced in college (Keene 2018).

Mink also introduced the Early Childhood Act and authored the Women's Educational Equity Act. The Women's Educational Equity Act passed as part of an education bill in 1974. The act provided $30 million a year in educational funds for programs to promote gender equity in schools, increasing educational and job opportunities for women, and excising sexual stereotypes from textbooks and school curricula. Many of these legislations that Mink wrote were later considered great accomplishments in American history because of how they furthered equal rights for Americans beyond what could have been imagined at the time (Keene 2018).

In 1976, Mink had an unsuccessful run for Senate, so she served her final year in the House, where she remained active in politics by serving as assistant secretary of state for Oceans and International Environmental and Scientific Affairs. Afterward, she moved back to Hawaii and served on the Honolulu city council from 1983 to 1987. In the city council, she consistently butted heads with Honolulu's controversial mayor at the time, Frank Fasi. But in 1990, after the death of Senator Spark Matsunaga, Mink accepted a seat back in Congress, in the House of Representatives. Mink once again served on the Education and Labor Committee and was also assigned to the Government Operations Committee. Mink continued to pursue legislative reform in health care and education.

Mink combined two of her long-standing interests when she co-sponsored the Gender Equity Act in 1993. Mink asserted that targeting gender bias in elementary and secondary education would help reduce inequalities between the sexes. Mink continued to crusade for women's rights, organizing and leading the Democratic Women's Caucus in 1995.

Mink was reelected for another term in 2000 and, in September 2002, she won the Democratic primary election for her seat in the U.S. House of Representatives. She was seventy-four years old when she died of viral pneumonia on September 28 in a hospital in Honolulu. Because Mink passed away a week before the general election, it was too late to remove her name from the ballot. Consequently, she was posthumously re-elected to Congress on November 5, 2002.

Patsy Matsu Takemoto Mink was an honored leader who fought for women's issues, family and medical leave, workplace fairness, and universal health care. She was also a professor at the University of Hawaii Law School and an accomplished writer, with many published articles about the law. She also received a posthumous Presidential Medal of Freedom from President Barack Obama.

Dalip Singh Saund (1899–1973)

In 1956, Dalip Singh Saund became the first Asian to be elected to the U.S. Congress. He represented California's 29th Congressional District, composed of Riverside and Imperial Counties. Saund was taught early in life to respect education. His parents, who were uneducated, made sure Saund was very well educated, and he set his goals very high. He rejected the ideology of India's tradition-bound civil service. His mentors were American presidents Abraham Lincoln and Woodrow Wilson. When he moved to the United States, his goal was to become "a living example of American democracy in practice" (Sinnott 2003, 107).

Saund was born in northern India's Punjab Province, where he began his education very early. Saund attended a local college before traveling to the University of the Punjab. In 1920, he continued his education in America, where he enrolled in the graduate program in mathematics at the University of California, Berkley. In 1924, he earned his PhD. After Berkley, he fell in love with America's democratic system and vowed to stay in America instead of going back to India. But there were little opportunities for an immigrant from India, so he did the only conceivable job: he became a farmer, more specifically a lettuce farmer. He lived in a clubhouse maintained by a Sikh temple group in Stockton, California. Most of the Sikhs were refugees who had moved to California during World War I as agricultural laborers. Home to many refugees, Stockton was the intellectual and political center of the Hindu community. The Hindustani Association of America was active in Berkley, and after two years, young Saund was elected as its national president.

As president, Saund had a number of opportunities in which he could make speeches about India and meet with other groups as a representative of Indian students at the university. Saund was a nationalist and was eager to share his beliefs with others about India's rights to self-government, and did so by participating in debates and speaking to a number of organizations. After he moved to Imperial Valley, California, he continued to seek opportunities in which he could speak, debate, and present India's side for democracy and humanity.

In 1928, Saund married Marian Kosa, born of immigrant Czech parents. Saund met Marian through his friend, Emil J. Kosa, Marian's brother. As a friend of the Kosa family, Saund was a frequent visitor to their home and soon fell in love with Marian, a nineteen-year-old University of California, Los Angeles (UCLA) student. He was unsure if they could marry because he was a foreigner in a country where the laws prevented him from becoming a citizen or even owning a home. Saund was an immigrant without a secure job and no clear future. Still, he eventually married Marian, and they had three children.

Because of U.S. immigration laws at the time, Saund and his fellow Hindus could not become citizens. So he organized the India Association of America and went to Washington, D.C., to fight to change the current laws. The organization's primary objective was to galvanize the Indian community in an effort to help Indian nationals gain citizenship. Saund understood that persuading elected officials to introduce a bill in Congress was an enormous feat, but he continued to travel through California, raise money for the cause, mail letters written in Punjabi, and arrange financial assistance to help pro-Indian groups lobby.

His efforts helped Indians in the country to organize in new ways as they attempted to gain citizenship rights. They were able to convince a couple of congressmen to write up a bill, but the group kept running into roadblocks, such as convincing the majority of Congress members, who believed this bill would open the door to other Asian immigrants demanding citizenship. But in 1946, President Truman took special interest in the legislation, and finally Congress passed an amendment to the immigration law to allow Asian Indians to become American citizens. It was a great triumph for Saund and his organization. Thus, July 3, 1946, is an "Independence Day" for all Indians in the United States.

There were very few Indian Americans registered to vote in Saund's district. In fact, there were not many ethnic voters at all; the large majority were Caucasians. Saund had completely assimilated with mainstream America while maintaining his heritage. While living in America, he had not modified his name or changed his religious beliefs to become more "American," which helped make him a target of criticism by opponents who wished to discredit him.

But in 1955, Saund ran for the U.S. House of Representatives and won, beating a very popular Republican candidate. Saund's slogan was that a vote for him would show there was no true prejudice in the United States. In Congress, he was appointed to the House Foreign Affairs Committee, where he continued to concern himself with Asian (particularly Indian) matters. He made a well-publicized tour of India, addressed a joint session of India's House of Parliament, and forcefully advocated increasing cultural and educational exchanges between the two countries. He actively participated in Democratic Party activities and rose to be a delegate in three conventions, starting in 1952. He represented grassroots philosophies and voiced his support for what were considered to be middle-class values. Saund was reelected twice, but during his third campaign, he suffered a massive stroke from which he never fully recovered. He died in his home in Hollywood in 1973.

Today, many Indian Americans who aspire to become involved in politics still bring up Saund, which is similar to ways in which Saund drew comparisons to Gandhi and others he admired during his speeches.

DOCUMENT EXCERPTS

Senator Daniel Inouye's Statements on Asian Pacific American Heritage Month

The following is one of the late Senator Daniel Inouye's congressional statements attributed to Asian Pacific American Heritage Month that was established in 1992 to recognize and celebrate the contributions that Asian Americans and Pacific Islanders have made to the United States. His statement praised Asian American and Pacific Islander communities' cultural values, heritage, and commitment, as well as well-known individuals in sciences, arts, literature, entertainment, sports, military service, politics, and other fields. He also called the audience's attention to current issues and underserved communities.

Statement on Asian Pacific American Heritage Month

Mr. INOUYE. Mr. President, I rise today in recognition of Asian Pacific American Heritage Month. In 1992, President Bush signed into law legislation designating May as Asian Pacific American Heritage Month to celebrate the contributions the Asian American and Pacific Islander communities have made to our country.

Asian Americans and Pacific Islanders have been instrumental in the development of the American landscape for more than a century. The diversity within the Asian American and Pacific Islander communities exemplifies the richness of our multicultural country, celebrated through Asian Pacific American Heritage Month.

Valuing family, cultural heritage, and commitment to society, Asian Americans and Pacific islanders have built strong communities contributing to our dynamic society and adding strength to the foundation of our country. With strong values, Asian Americans and Pacific Islanders have succeeded in many facets of life including science where Dr. David Ho was celebrated as *Time Magazine's* 1996 Man of the Year;

the arts, with fashion designer Vera Wang, writer Amy Tan, and actress Ming Na-Wen; sports with ice skaters such as Kristi Yamaguchi and Michelle Kwan and football legend Junior Seau; in the military where General Eric Shinseki is the Chief of Staff for the U.S. Army; and politics where there are two Pacific Islander Governors and where I am joined by six other Asian Americans and Pacific Islanders serving in Congress, and where a record number of Asian American and Pacific Islanders are serving as Administration appointees in some of the highest offices of government. This list is by no means exhaustive, it only scratches the surface of the contributions Asian American and Pacific Islanders have made to our country. Asian Pacific American Heritage Month allows us to pay tribute to the commitment and contributions these men and women have made to their communities and to our country.

The growth of the Asian American and Pacific Islander communities, along with the achievements we have gained, have brought Asian American and Pacific Islander issues to the forefront of American politics. Last June, President Clinton signed Executive Order 13125 establishing the White House Asian and Pacific Islander Initiative seeking to improve the quality of life for Asian Americans and Pacific Islanders through increased participation in federal government programs where they are most likely to be under-served. I commend the President for this Initiative and optimistically look forward to the progress this commission will achieve, under the chairmanship of Mr. Norman Mineta, to highlight and challenge issues pertinent to Asian Americans and Pacific Islanders.

Asian Americans and Pacific Islanders have made considerable contributions to our nation. I am pleased that through Asian Pacific American Heritage Month the various histories, cultures, triumphs, and hardships of all Asian Americans and Pacific Islanders can be celebrated, honored, and remembered.

Source: *Congressional Record*, Vol. 146, No. 59. May 15, 2000.

See also: Asian/Pacific American Heritage Week Established, 1978; The First Asian American Studies Program Established at San Francisco State College, 1969; Hawaii Becomes a U.S. Territory, 1898

Further Reading

Becker, Peggy Daniels. 2014. *Japanese-American Internment during World War II*. Detroit: Omnigraphics.

Daniel K. Inouye Institute and Hawaii Community Foundation. 2014. "Daniel K. Inouye Institute." https://dkii.org

Davidson, Sue. 1994. *A Heart in Politics: Jeannette Rankin and Patsy T. Mink*. Women Who Dared Series, Book 2. Seattle: Seal Press.

Fuchs, Lawrence H. 1992. *Hawaii Pono: Hawaii the Excellent: An Ethnic and Political History*. Honolulu: Bess Press.

Hamilton, Lee H., Daniel K. Inouye, and United States Congress and House of Representatives. Select Committee to Investigate Covert Arms Transactions with Iran. 1987. *Report of the Congressional Committees Investigating the Iran-Contra Affair: With Supplemental, Minority, and Additional Views*. Washington, D.C.: Government Printing Office.

Inouye, Daniel K. 2001. Foreword to *Pearl Harbor: December 7, 1941: America's Darkest Day*, by Susan Wels, 16–19. San Diego: Time Life Books.

Keene, Ann T. 2018. "Mink, Patsy (1927–2002), US Congresswoman." American National Biography. https://doi.org/10.1093/anb/9780198606697.article.0700812

Kotani, Roland and Oahu Kanyaku Imin Centennial Committee. 1985. *The Japanese in Hawaii: A Century of Struggle*. Honolulu: Hawaii Hochi.

Niiya, Brian and Japanese American National Museum. 1993. *Japanese American History: An A-to-Z Reference from 1868 to the Present*. New York: Facts on File.

Ogawa, Dennis M. and Glen Grant. 1978. *Kodomo No Tame Ni: For the Sake of the Children: The Japanese American Experience in Hawaii*. Honolulu: University Press of Hawaii.

Seaman, Barbara and Laura Eldridge. 2012. *Voices of the Women's Health Movement*. New York: Seven Stories Press.

Singh, Inder. "Dalip S. Saund, the First Asian in U.S. Congress." Global Organization of People of Indian Origin. http://www.gopio.net/pio_corner/saund.htm

Sinnott, Susan. 2003. *Extraordinary Asian Americans and Pacific Islanders*, rev. ed. Extraordinary People series. New York: Children's Press.

The Delano Grape Strike and Boycott, 1965–1970

Maharaj Desai, Karen Buenavista Hanna, and Teresa Hodges

Chronology

1587   First contact of Filipina/os with the Americas occurs when a group of Indios from Luzon aboard the galleon *Nuestra Senora de Esperanza* stops at Morro Bay, Alta, California.

Late 1700s   Indios arrive on galleons in Acapulco, make their way to Louisiana, **and early**   and establish coastal communities, such as the Saint Malo **1800s**   settlement.

1898   Spanish-American War/Cession and Battle of Manila Bay.

1899–1913   Philippine-American War. While the war is documented as formally ending in 1902, some scholars cite 1913 as the end of the war against the American military by the Moro people in Mindanao.

1903   The Pensionado Act of the Philippines is passed.

1904	Philippine pavilion exhibits are featured at the World's Fair in St. Louis, Missouri.
1906	The first *sakadas* from the Philippines arrive at Hawaii sugarcane plantations.
1906	The first nursing school is established in the Philippines.
1924	The Hanapepe Massacre occurs in Hawaii.
1930	The Watsonville riots take place in California.
1934	The Tydings-McDuffie Act is passed, creating provisions for the eventual sovereignty of the Philippines after a ten-year "grooming" period.
1935	The Filipino Repatriation Act is passed.
1942	Manila falls to the Japanese Imperial Army.
1944	U.S. Army Gen. Douglas MacArthur returns to Leyte to help "liberate" the Philippines from Japanese occupation.
1945	The Battle of Manila takes place.
1945	World War II ends, and many Filipino servicemen are granted U.S. citizenship.
1945	The War Brides Act is passed.
1946	Formal independence is granted to the Republic of the Philippines by the United States.
1946	Carlos Bulosan publishes his landmark work, *America Is in the Heart*.
1946	The Bell Trade Act is passed.
1955	The Laurel Langley Agreement is approved to replace the Bell Trade Act.
1965	The Immigration and Nationality Act (also known as the Hart-Celler Act) is passed, leading to a wave of Filipina/o professionals arriving in the United States and drastically changing the class demographic of Filipina/o Americans.
1965	The Delano Grape Strike and Boycott begins.
1966	The United Farm Workers Organizing Committee is formed.
1970	The Delano Grape Strike and Boycott ends.

1971	The first Filipino Young People's Far West Convention is held in Seattle, Washington.
1972	Philippines President Ferdinand Marcos declares martial law in the Philippines. During this time, Marcos issues numerous labor codes, merges government agencies, and pushes manufacturing export programs leading to the Overseas Foreign Worker (OFW) phenomenon.
1973	The national organization Katipunan ng mga Demokratikong Pilipino (KDP), or Union of Democratic Filipinos, is formed.
1974	The Laurel Langley Agreement expires.
1976	Leonora Perez and Filipina Narciso, two Filipina immigrant nurses, are charged by the Federal Bureau of Investigation (FBI) with the murders of patients at the Ann Arbor Veterans Administration Hospital, despite "highly circumstantial evidence" and prosecutorial misconduct.
1977	Elderly tenants, many of whom are Filipino agricultural workers, are evicted from the International Hotel in San Francisco after an almost decade-long fight by the Asian American community to save them from eviction.
1981	Marcos ends martial law. Filipino American labor and anti–martial law activists Gene Viernes and Silme Domingo are murdered in Seattle.
1982	The Filipino American National Historical Society (FANHS) is founded.
1983	Ninoy Aquino is assassinated.
1986	Marcos is ousted during the People Power (EDSA) Revolution.
1991	The Philippine Senate refuses to approve a United States–Philippines bases treaty.
1992	U.S. military bases are removed from the Philippines.
1999	The Little Manila Foundation is created to preserve Stockton, California's Little Manila as a historical site and to provide education to the Filipina/o community. The Philippine Senate ratifies the Philippines–United States Visiting Forces Agreement.
2005	The International Hotel is rebuilt on its former site as low-income senior housing.

2009   Congress votes to issue a $15,000 lump-sum payment to each eligible Filipino World War II veteran.

2011   Congress officially recognizes October as Filipino American History Month.

Narrative

The Delano Grape Strike and Boycott in California began on September 8, 1965, and lasted more than five years. It was a major event in Asian American, Mexican American, Chicana/o, and American labor history. It marks a defining moment when Filipina/o Americans not only united to fight for their rights as workers but also challenged employers' approaches to divide and conquer, which had historically pitted them against Mexican American farm laborers. As used by the historians such as Dorothy Fujita-Rony (2003) and Dawn Bohulano Mabalon (2013), "Filipina/o" refers to women and men of Filipina/o ancestry who lived in the past and contests the historical absence of women in written history.

The Delano Grape Strike and Boycott was initiated by the primarily Filipino Agricultural Organization Workers Committee (AWOC), led by Larry Itliong, Philip Vera Cruz, Ben Gines, Pete Velasco, and others, and consisting of mostly Filipino farm workers (Mabalon 2013, 261). The Filipina/os of AWOC went on strike after Itliong and Velasco helped organize wage increases for grape workers in the Coachella Valley (Mabalon 2013, 261). Knowing that the growers would hire Mexican workers to replace them during the strike, Itliong approached Cesar Chavez and Dolores Huerta, leaders of the Mexican American National Farmworkers Association (NFWA), and tried to persuade them to have their organization join the strike. Itliong stated that Filipina/os would be the "scabs" (replacement labor during a strike) that would break up NFWA's future strikes if Chavez and Huerta declined (Mabalon 2013, 261). Itliong's invitation to Chavez, Huerta, and the NFWA echoes the words of Lilla Watson, an Australian Aboriginal artist, scholar, and activist, who argues, "If you have come here to help me you are wasting your time, but if you have come because your liberation is bound up with mine, then let us work together" (Riggs 2004).

On September 16, 1965, the NFWA joined the AWOC's grape strike. Their unity led to the formation of the United Farm Workers Organizing Committee (UFW) in 1966, headed by Chavez and Itliong, who served as assistant director (Kim 2017; Mabalon 2013, 262). During the strike's five years, women cooked food for the men on the picket lines, who were evicted from their camps for organizing.

In tandem with the strike, the UFW urged the public to stop buying grapes without a union label. Itliong, the national coordinator of the grape boycott, traveled

A Filipino retiree in his room at Agbayani Village in Delano, California, around 1975. The United Farm Workers Union (UFW) opened Agbayani Village, a retirement community for Filipino farm workers, in 1974. The village was named in honor of Paulo Agbayani, a Filipino farm worker and UFW member who died of a heart attack while picketing during the Delano Grape Strike. (Cathy Murphy/Getty Images)

throughout the country, organizing communities to support the boycott (Mabalon 2013, 262). Union volunteers created boycott centers nationwide to encourage unions, churches, community organizations, and other allies to stop buying grapes and help publicize the boycott (Kim 2017).

The Delano Grape Strike and Boycott succeeded in 1970 when the grape growers accepted the union's proposed contracts. In the end, the action led to higher wages, a health plan, and a union-run hiring hall, which ended discrimination and favoritism by labor contractors. According to Inga Kim, the Delano Grape Strike and Boycott organized the most members ever represented by a union in California's agriculture history (2017). By 1970, however, most of the Filipino veteran leaders of the UFW had left the union, partly due to differences between the leadership, rank and file, organizing styles, priorities, philosophies, and strategy (Mabalon 2013, 262). Despite the eventual fracturing of the UFW, the merging of the Filipina/o AWOC and the Mexican American NFWA into the UFW was the beginning of a momentum-building movement for farm laborer rights that crossed racial lines. The strike was a pivotal victory for the UFW and a significant event for work-ers' rights in America. Furthermore, its success cemented the presence of Fili-pina/os in the United States as a militant labor force. In fighting for fair wages and better working conditions, Filipina/os asserted the value of their labor and dignity as humans.

The Filipina/o strikers' actions reflected their active resistance against the ste-reotype of Asians as "perpetual foreigners." Indeed, Asians have been in the United States for well over a century. While some Asian groups have migrated to the United States in more recent decades, the long history of Filipina/os in the country has been enduring. The United States colonized the Philippines in 1898 and facili-tated Filipina/os' migration to the country, which strikes many as emphasizing the irony of the "perpetual Asian foreigner" stereotype. Yen Le Espiritu names this irony as an example of "differential inclusion," or the process through which "a group of people is deemed integral to the nation's economy, culture, identity, and power—but integral only or precisely because of their designated subordinated standing" (2003, 47). In other words, even though Filipina/os' labor contributions have been essential to U.S. society, society nonetheless discriminates against them. The history of the Delano Grape Strike and Boycott demonstrates that Filipina/os refused to passively accept differential inclusion and their resulting subjugated position on a racialized hierarchy.

The history of the Delano Grape Strike and Boycott also reveals the myth of meritocracy and false rewards of the model minority stereotype. The model minor-ity stereotype upholds the notion of a successfully assimilated Asian American who participates in U.S. political and economic systems through hard work. Yet Fili-pina/os' hard work and talent in the fields did not bring them success. Instead it brought increased hostility and anti-Filipina/o sentiments. It was militant resistance, rather than assimilation, that helped Filipina/os obtain dignity and fair treatment from their employers.

A History of United States–Philippine Relations

Although Filipina/os had been in various parts of the Americas since 1587, it was not until 1898 that the United States and the Philippines established a formal politi-cal connection. That year, the United States officially expanded its borders beyond the shores of North America and asserted itself as an international power by claim-ing colonies in the Pacific and Caribbean.

In 1898, both Cuba and the Philippines were embroiled in separate rebellions against their shared colonizer, Spain. When the battleship USS *Maine* exploded and sank in Havana Harbor, the United States initiated war against Spain, initially sid-ing with the native populations of Cuba and the Philippines in their revolts to oust their colonial oppressor. On May 1, 1898, U.S. Commodore George Dewey sailed into Manila Bay and quickly defeated the Spanish fleet, capturing Manila Bay and marking an end to the Philippines' Spanish colonial period. But it was the "mock" Battle of Manila on August 13, 1898, that ended the Spanish-American War, occurring the day after the United States and Spain signed a cease-fire treaty in Washington, D.C. American occupation of the walled city of Intramuros in Manila prevented the Filipina/o forces of the Katipunan from claiming the last Spanish stronghold on the islands. Later that year, on December 10, Spain and the United States signed the Treaty of Paris, through which Spain ceded Cuba, Puerto Rico, Guam, and the Philippines to the United States in exchange for $20 million. Many activists and scholars view this exchange as a betrayal of Filipina/o revolutionaries who became allies of the United States during the Spanish-American War.

Other Filipina/o revolutionaries refused to submit to the United States and continued to fight for the national liberation of the Philippines. The result was the Philippine-American War, which began in 1899. While 1902 is the "official" end of the Philippine-American War, armed conflict continued between the American military and Filipina/o citizens until 1913. The United States recognized the Philippines as an important component of their military, economic, and political strategy and used the war to "perfect" methods of torture. Some scholars refer to the Philippine-American War as the "first Vietnam War," an imperial bloodbath instigated by the United States to quell Filipina/o revolutionary forces; it resulted in over one million dead Filipina/os. As Howard Zinn comments, "American firepower was overwhelmingly superior to anything the Filipino rebels could put together. . . . Dead Filipinos were piled so high that the Americans used their bodies for breastworks" (2003, 230).

It was through racist and satirical political cartoons promoting and critiquing U.S. President William McKinley and the new American imperial agenda in the Philippines that the Philippines entered mainstream American consciousness (De la Cruz, Emmanuel, Ignacio, and Toribio 2004, 36). In creating and disseminating racist cartoons that depict Filipina/os as "savage" people whom the United States infantilized, these cartoons served to uphold justification for Filipina/os as designated low-wage labor, in particular, "low-skilled" stoop labor for which growers would later claim Filipina/os were built (Baldoz 2011, 69). Americans split as to whether the United States should become an empire or remain a republic and support other nations in their revolutionary struggles.

The Philippine-American War was a very significant event for the relationship between Filipina/os and the United States, yet it is largely forgotten. Scholars argue that one reason for this forced historical amnesia was the American-instilled schooling system in the Philippines. This schooling system, which outlasted the official American colonial presence in the Philippines, taught Filipina/o children to idealize America and look down upon their own history, cultures, and languages. Filipino scholar Renato Constantino has argued:

> The most effective means of subjugating a people is to capture their minds. Military victory does not necessarily signify conquest. As long as feelings of resistance remain in the hearts of the vanquished, no conqueror is secure. . . . The molding of men's minds is the best means of conquest. Education, therefore, serves as a weapon in wars of colonial conquest. (1970, 2–3)

Given the history of U.S. education in the Philippines, it is no surprise that for the majority of Filipina/os, the American colonial period is looked upon with nostalgia as a time of progress, infrastructure development, and allyship. Forgotten was the brutality of the U.S. military, as well as "the entry of American monopoly capital" that benefited the most elite families and American business interests while deteriorating the agricultural economy for the majority of Filipina/os (Mabalon 2013, 59). This "push" factor, combined with the allure of America's promises of "milk and honey," led many Filipina/os to the United States to become agricultural workers. They soon realized that America was not all they had dreamed it would be.

On July 4, 1946, the United States granted the Philippines independence. This meant the Philippines was responsible for repairing the damages of World War II, which left Manila and many other places in the Philippines physically and economically devastated. Two days before, on July 2, the U.S. Congress had passed the Bell Trade Act, also known as the Philippine Trade Act, which governed trade between the Philippines and the United States and solidified a neocolonial relationship between the two countries that continues today. The act placed preferential tariffs on U.S. goods imported to the Philippines, fixed the exchange rate between the U.S. dollar and the Philippine peso, and allowed U.S. citizens equal rights with Filipina/os involving ownership of utilities and natural resources. While the Laurel Langley Agreement revised the Bell Trade Act in 1955, the imbalance of power between the United States and the Philippines remained, both politically and economically. Anti-imperialist activists in the Philippines protested the Laurel Langley Agreement, leading to its expiration in 1974. These activists also fought for agrarian reform, decreased dependence on foreign (especially American) goods, and greater autonomy for the Philippine government and economy.

Some scholars argue that growing anti-imperialism was one of the reasons that Philippines President Ferdinand Marcos declared martial law in 1972. During the martial law period, Marcos issued numerous labor codes, merged government agencies, pushed manufacturing export programs, and established Overseas Contract

Worker (OCW) agreements with other nations to provide employment opportunities for Filipina/os that were limited or unavailable domestically. These developments led to the Overseas Filipino Worker (OFW) phenomenon we see today, in which, at any given point in time, 10 percent of the Philippines' population is working abroad in order to survive and sustain its economy.

Thus, the relationship between the Philippines and the United States, which actualized formally during the Philippine-American War, was one that became increasingly entrenched in structural policies binding a reciprocal connection between the two nations. Equally significant is the creation of narratives and characterizations of Filipina/os that were used to justify U.S. domination and Filipina/o subjugation. These tropes, embedded especially through legislation, solidified the United States–Philippine relationship. Structural policies enabled opportunities for migration and labor from the Philippines to the United States that colored the treatment of Filipina/o agricultural workers in the country before, during, and after the Delano Grape Strike and Boycott.

Filipina/o Migration to the United States

Necessary for understanding the social, political, and economic context of Filipina/o farm workers (*manangs*/*manongs*) is the history of Filipina/o migration to the United States during and after the American colonial period. Filipina/os comprised the bulk of immigrants coming from Asia from the early twentieth century through World War II. Their status as U.S. nationals allowed them to immigrate to the States despite anti-immigrant legislation that prevented immigration from most of Asia. On August 26, 1903, the Philippine Commission, under Governor General William H. Taft, passed the Pensionado Act, which granted scholarships for Filipina/o students to study in U.S. universities. The aim of this program was to instill American ideals and understanding of U.S. politics and government and create a self-governing Philippine government that mimicked the U.S. system (Mendoza 2015, 172). The first batch of pensionados consisted of 103 students derived primarily from the wealthy classes.

The year following the Pensionado Act, 1904, was the year of the World's Fair in St. Louis, Missouri. Displayed were people from newly acquired U.S. territories. The Philippine pavilion was one of the biggest and most popular attractions of the fair, comprising forty-seven acres, forty tribes, six villages, and over 1,200 people. Filipina/os from different class backgrounds and ethnic communities were put on display for the American public. These different groups were strategically positioned to show the evolutionary progression of the Filipina/o from savage, tribal headhunter, to semi-civilized Moro, to Catholic Hispanicized mestizo, to civilized Americanized pensionado (Mendoza 2015, 93). The delineation of savage versus civilized Filipina/os at the World's Fair is similar to the way the Spanish separated Igorot and Moro communities from Christianized lowlander communities into different racial categories. Some scholars describe this moment of history as the creation of American stereotypes that affect Filipina/o American identities and communities today. One such example is the stereotype of dog eating, which entered American consciousness at the 1904 World's Fair. An American audience expected Filipina/os from an Igorot village to hunt, cook, and eat dogs as a spectacle.

The imagery from the World's Fair helped justify America's benevolent assimilation of savage Filipinos through American education. Choy (2003) describes how the contemporary phenomenon of Filipina/o nurses actually begins with American imperialism and the establishing of nursing schools in the Philippines in 1906. These early nursing schools taught English language and American practices around health and science as a way to sanitize, civilize, and educate Filipina/os, thereby reinforcing American colonial dominance. Exchange programs were established through which Filipina/o nurses could work in U.S. hospitals—usually under white administrators and supervisors. This pre-1965 wave of Filipina/o nurses experienced unfair labor practices and exploitation in hospitals just like the *manongs/manangs* did in the sugarcane plantations of Hawaii, the fields of California, and the canneries of Alaska.

While most Americans in the continental United States had barely begun to hear about the Philippines at the beginning of the twentieth century, the Hawaii Sugar Planters Association (HSPA) on the newly acquired U.S. territory of the Pacific campaigned to bring Filipina/os from the Ilocos and Visayas regions to work as skilled laborers in sugarcane fields. These men, known as *sakadas*, first arrived in the islands in 1906. In only thirty years, Filipina/os would become the largest ethnic group in Hawaii's sugar plantations by the 1930s.

Although they were the largest ethnic groups on plantations, Filipina/os were the lowest-paid workers and were housed in the worst conditions on the plantations. After living the realities of American structural racism on the plantations and witnessing their stark contrast to the American ideals being touted in the Philippines as superior to indigenous Philippine practices, *sakadas* joined together to organize and advocate for greater equity on the plantations as early as 1918. In fact, from 1924 to 1925, Filipina/os held strikes on multiple plantations on Oahu, Kauai, Maui, and Hawaii.

From the late 1910s through the 1930s, Filipina/o labor was in demand in Hawaii, California, Washington, and Alaska. Some industries, like sugar in Hawaii, asparagus in California's Central Valley, and salmon canneries in Alaska, specifically targeted Filipina/os as a source of cheap labor. As in Hawaii, Filipina/os in California, Washington, and Alaska collaborated inter- and intra-ethnically to form unions to advocate for fair wages and humane labor practices. The result was severe anti-Filipina/o sentiment during the Great Depression, which heightened competition for the few available jobs and positioned Filipina/os against whites and other ethnic groups.

Anti-Filipina/o racism thus led to the passing of the Tydings-McDuffie Act in 1934, which curbed migration of Filipina/os to the United States (previously limitless) to only fifty individuals per year. The act stated that the United States would grant full return of sovereignty and autonomy to the Filipina/o people after a period of ten years, during which time the United States would "groom" the Filipina/o people and set up Philippine infrastructure to mimic that of the States. When the United States passed the Tydings-McDuffie Act, it renamed the U.S. territory of the Philippines as the Commonwealth of the Philippines. Meanwhile, Filipina/os in the States went from being "nationals" to "aliens" ineligible for citizenship. The following year, 1935, saw another act passed in Congress: the Philippine Repatriation Act. This legislation offered to pay for the return voyage of any Filipina/o wishing to go back to the Philippines, as long as they signed a contract stating they would not attempt to return to the United States.

The United States enacted the War Brides Act in 1945, a few months after the end of World War II. This legislation allowed spouses and children of U.S. military personnel to immigrate, regardless of quota restrictions or countries of origin. As a result, many Filipina/o veterans were able to bring home with them the brides they had met and married in the Philippines during and immediately after the war.

In 1965, President Lyndon B. Johnson's administration passed the Hart-Celler Immigration Act in response to the controversy over the Vietnam War and the civil rights movement. The act created the preference system for determining visa eligibility and changed the demographics of American immigration by increasing immigration quotas from Asia, Africa, and southern and eastern Europe. This change had a direct and significant impact on the Filipina/o American community. First, it enabled what some scholars call "chain migration," as U.S. citizens and permanent residents of Filipina/o descent became able to petition family members, including siblings, unmarried and married adult children, and their families to come to the United States. To position the United States in contrast to the Soviet Union, the Hart-Celler Act also created provisions for the immigration of skilled workers, particularly those in fields that were underemployed in the United States, such as health care, engineering, science, and education. The act led to a wave of Filipina/o professionals arriving in the United States, drastically changing the class demographic of Filipina/os there. As a result, new generations of Filipina/o immigrants are unfamiliar with the history of the earlier communities that helped make their present communities possible. The difference in pre- and post-1965 Filipina/o immigration lies in the shifted composition of immigrants, their relationship to family, and their social class.

The Tydings-McDuffie Act

The Tydings-McDuffie Act was marketed to Filipina/os as a step toward the independence for which they had been fighting since they were first colonized by Spain in the late sixteenth century. In reality, the act served American domestic interests, as it limited Filipina/o migration to the United States by changing Filipina/o status from nationals to aliens. The U.S. government passed the act amid mainstream American discourse featuring racist stereotypes of Filipina/os as a source of cheap labor and a threat to white American jobs during the Great Depression. At the same time, many American businesses were wary of Filipina/os who had been heavily involved in labor organizing since the early 1920s. Immigration restrictions limited growth within the community and caused Filipina/os to build interethnic alliances. This led to the Filipina/o American unity displayed in the initiation of the Delano Grape Strike and Boycott.

Anti-Filipina/o Sentiment

To understand the historical significance of Filipina/os initiating the Delano Grape Strike and Boycott, it is vital to know the history of anti-Filipina/o sentiment in the United States. In the opening of Filipino writer and labor organizer Carlos Bulosan's *America Is in the Heart*, Carey McWilliams writes, "'It is hard to be a Filipino in California,' a countryman sadly warned Carlos Bulosan shortly after his arrival in Seattle from the Philippines. But Carlos, of course, had to find this out for himself. 'I came to know afterwards,' he wrote, 'that in many ways it was a crime to be a Filipino in California' (121)" (McWilliams in Bulosan 1973, vii). Dawn Mabalon states that the experience of Filipino farm laborers in Stockton in the 1920s is first and foremost predicated under the reality that "they learned that race, more than class, ethnicity, dialect, or regional origin, shaped one's opportunities and social status in Stockton" (Mabalon 2013, 102). Signs indicating "No dogs or Filipinos allowed" hung in commercial establishments, echoing the Jim Crow era that prohibited blacks from co-mingling and co-existing equally with white people. In January 1930, California experienced the Watsonville riots, inflamed by headlines of a love affair between a Filipino man, Perfecto Bandalan, and a white woman, Esther Schmick (who turned out to be engaged with consent from her mother) (Baldoz 2011, 124–28). Not only did white U.S. society frown upon this relationship, but laws against miscegenation ruled that interracial marriage between whites and nonwhites was illegal at the time. Whites accused Filipina/os, like other Asian immigrants, of stealing jobs from them, leading whites to work for less pay. Mobs of white people stormed taxi dance halls frequented by Filipina/os, labor camps where Filipina/o laborers lived, and other public sites, violently terrorizing them. In some situations, whites harassed Filipina/os to the point of death, such as in the murder of Fermin Tobera, a Filipino laborer (Baldoz 2011, 139–41).

Anti-Filipina/o sentiment was so virulent that the Tydings-McDuffie Act ultimately actualized racism against Filipinos. Scholars of Filipina/o American studies recognize that Filipina/o laborers filled a labor gap created when the U.S. government barred Chinese (1882) and Japanese (1907 and 1924) laborers from immigrating to the United States due to anti-Asian sentiment. This legislation would eventually lead the U.S. government to pass the 1934 Tydings-McDuffie Act, which imposed quotas on Filipina/os entering the United States.

Filipina/o American identity became crucial, not only for resisting racism inflicted by others and for organizing under the farm labor movement but also in countering the internalized racism that Filipina/os themselves believed—a manifestation of what scholars call "colonial mentality." David and Okazaki describe colonial mentality, or "internalized colonialism," as manifesting in the following ways for Filipina/os: "denigration of the Filipino self; denigration of the Filipino culture or body; discriminating against less-Americanized Filipinos; and tolerating historical and contemporary oppression of Filipinos and Filipino Americans" (2006, 241–42). An example of colonial mentality can be seen in the way many Filipina/os valorize American soldiers who bravely fought side by side to defeat the Japanese in World War II and either deny, forget, or never learn about the atrocities of the Philippine-American War.

Despite the pervasive colonial mentality that still affects many today, there were many ways in which being Filipina/o was an uplifting source of identity and community through experiences of Filipina/o Americans in the United States, especially surrounding the communities of laborers during the 1930s. Mabalon writes:

> Moreover, community organizations, the boxing matches, the Little Manila neighborhood, and their labor unions . . . [in Stockton] . . . became places for Ilocanas/os, Visayans, and Tagalogs to find solidarity and common ground and imagine themselves as Filipina/o Americans whose lives were open to many possibilities. In these spaces, they rejected the identity of the debased, exploited, faceless laborer hunched over endless miles of asparagus, celery, or beets. (2013, 147)

Here, not only did Filipina/os reject colonial mentality, but they also (re-)created Filipina/o American identity.

Struggle and Resistance in the United States Post-Delano Grape Strike and Boycott

Overlapping with Filipina/o Americans' labor union participation and civil-rights organizing was the arrival of activist exiles from the Philippines during President Ferdinand Marcos's dictatorship in the late 1960s. On September 21, 1972, Marcos signed Proclamation 1081, declaring martial law in the Philippines. Leading up to Marcos's declaration was a rise in mass protest over the Philippines' deteriorating economic and political situation. To quell his opposition, Marcos began a fourteen-year dictatorship, which led to over 3,000 extrajudicial killings, 35,000 torture victims, 70,000 incarcerations, and at least 750 missing activists, who have not been found to this day (McCoy 1999). Americans divided over whether to support or oppose Marcos, who was popular among many U.S.-based and professional Filipina/o immigrants from Marcos's Ilocos Norte Province. Such divisions were pervasive enough to affect the UFW. In 1977, Philip Vera Cruz resigned from his position as UFW vice president, partially in protest over UFW President Cesar Chavez's decision to visit the Philippines as a guest of Marcos (Gaerlan 2003, 26).

The dangerous climate of martial law compelled an undetermined number of young activists to move to the United States in the 1970s and 1980s. These exiled activists converged with Filipina/os and non-Filipina/os to form several organizations dedicated to educating Americans about Marcos's human rights violations. One organization created was the Union of Democratic Filipinos, or KDP (*Katipunan ng mga Demokratikong Pilipino*), founded in July 1973 in the Santa Cruz Mountains, almost one year after Marcos declared martial law. An openly Marxist organization, KDP's program took a "dual-line," supporting "national democracy" in the Philippines by bringing an end to Marcos's martial law government and promoting socialism in the United States. It organized chapters in more than ten cities, extending its reach from New York City to Guam, with its national executive board based in California's Bay Area. Throughout its existence of more than thirteen years, KDP also created numerous solidarity groups like CAMD (Coalition against the Marcos Dictatorship). KDP attracted members from various social, class, and political positions, including "the Civil Rights, anti-war, and student movements, the Third World, Asian American, and New Communist movements, and the liberal-progressive Christian churches" (Toribio 1998, 156). Its members were inspired by Filipino American communists from the generation that preceded them, including labor leaders Chris Mensalves, Phillip Vera Cruz, and UFW retirees at the UFW's Agbayani Village.

Groups like the Friends of the Filipino People (FFP), the Movement for a Free Philippines (MFP), and KDP sought to pressure the U.S. government into cutting military and economic aid to the Philippines until civil liberties for Filipinos abroad were restored (Fuentecilla 2013, viii). KDP also organized around domestic issues, such as bilingual education and labor reforms for medical professionals. KDP's other work included advocating for justice for immigrant nurses, labor reform in the Alaska Cannery Workers Association Local 37 in Seattle, and stopping forced evictions of elderlies in the International Hotel in San Francisco (Choy 2003; Domingo 2010; Habal 2007). Through all of these campaigns, KDP weathered government surveillance, intimidation, and the murders of two members linked to the Marcos regime, Silme Domingo and Gene Viernes, in 1981. When the EDSA People Power Revolution ousted Marcos from power in 1986, the KDP continued to work in solidarity with the Philippine struggle for self-determination until its disbandment in the late 1980s, albeit with difficulty, given its split with the Communist Party of the Philippines.

In the early 1980s, some ex-KDP members united with other U.S.-based Filipina/os to continue supporting the National Democracy Movement (NDM) in the Philippines in groups like the Alliance for Philippine Concerns (APC), an umbrella group of progressive organizations spread throughout the country. In 1989, the Gabriela Support Network (which later became GabNet and is now AF3irm, a transnational feminist organization) was formed to support national democracy in the Philippines, "removal of foreign control" of the country, and the "distinct and specific concerns of women" (Enrile and Levid 2009, 97, 101). In 1991, the Philippine Senate voted to remove the U.S. military based in the Philippines, which was an enormous win for groups that had been organizing for its removal for decades.

KDP clashed with some Filipina/o American activists who were not comfortable with KDP's militant stance and preoccupation with Marcos's martial law, arguing that it had interrupted momentum behind a burgeoning Filipino American civil rights movement. However, what some call the "Filipino American Identity Movement" lived on through groups such as Filipino Youth Activities (FYA) in Seattle and the Search to Involve Pilipino Americans (SIPA) in Los Angeles, both of which still exist today. In 1982, the Filipino American National Historical Society (FANHS) was created to document and promote Filipino American history through its archives, conferences, books, programs, films, art, and other programs. It has thirty-three chapters throughout the United States. October has formally been recognized as Filipino American History Month since 2011, a result of the decades-long work of FANHS and its founders, Dr. Fred Cordova and Dr. Dorothy Cordova.

In 1999, the Little Manila Foundation was founded to advocate for the historic preservation of the Little Manila Historic Site in Stockton and provide leadership and education to revitalize the Filipina/o American community (The Little Manila Foundation 2018). The Justice for Filipino American Veterans (JFAV), a broad alliance of veteran, youth, student, and community organizations, was also formed to advocate for Filipino American World War II veterans' equal rights under the law. In 2009, Congress voted to issue a $15,000 one-time payment to each eligible Filipino veteran, a payment some felt was insulting in its implication that the veterans were mercenaries instead of loyal soldiers serving their commonwealth and country. A small victory occurred on October 25, 2017, when the U.S. government presented approximately 25,000 Filipino World War II veterans the Congressional Gold Medal during a ceremony at the U.S. Capitol. Unfortunately, most of those veterans had already passed away.

Filipina/o American organizations today are diverse and vibrant. Many are committed to education, leadership development, cultural arts, and advocacy. For example, groups like Filipino Advocates for Justice (FAJ) in the Bay Area, Filipino Community of Seattle (FCS), CIRCA Pintig and Alliance of Filipinos for Immigrant Rights and Empowerment (AFIRE) in Chicago, Migrante in Washington, D.C., and Damayan Migrant Workers Association in New York City work with the Filipina/o immigrant community to educate, organize, and mobilize them toward social justice goals. Organizations like Af3irm and GABRIELA USA advocate for women's rights and liberation. Some groups have educational aims. Founder Allyson Tintiangco-Cubales describes Pinay/Pinoy Educational Partnerships (PEP), for example, as "a Filipina/o American Studies curriculum and teaching apprenticeship program. More importantly, PEP is a pipeline. PEP is a spatial and curricular intervention of decolonizing pedagogical praxis" (2007, 2). Other organizations help by identifying health services members can use, provide case management when needed, support survivors of domestic violence, organize clinics to provide legal aid, and provide pro bono consultation for workers. Through various methods, they address violence against women, militarization, trafficking, and systemic racism, among other issues. While some continue to support "national democracy" in the Philippines and the removal of foreign control from the Philippines' self-determination as an autonomous nation, others are "homegrown" and focus on politics in the United States. Some groups take a hybrid approach.

Above all, Filipina/o American organizations continue to be a vital source of support, strength, and resistance for countless workers, women, and immigrants and are inspired by a long legacy of Filipina/o labor organizing in the United States and in the Philippines. In 2017 and 2018, a number of Filipina/o American organizations, scholars, and activists have led community and online protests against U.S. President Donald Trump's administration's travel ban, immigration policy, and educational and health care budget cuts. Likewise, Filipina/o Americans have initiated campaigns denouncing Philippines President Rodrigo Duterte's administration for massive numbers of extrajudicial killings of the urban poor and indigenous activists in the Philippines.

Biographies of Notable Figures

Carlos Bulosan (1913–1956)

Carlos Sampayan Bulosan was born on November 23, 1913, in the barrio of Mangus-mana in the town of Binalonan in Pangasinan, Philippines. After struggling with the poverty and limited socioeconomic mobility faced by many farmers in the Philippines, Bulosan immigrated to Seattle, Washington, on July 22, 1930. He struggled to find work in many of the same occupations that other Filipina/os found themselves in: service work in hotels along the West Coast, farm labor in California and Washington, and working in the canneries in Alaska. While working and traveling among these various Filipino American communities, Bulosan experienced economic hardships, unjust labor practices, and racial discrimination. Due to these experiences, Bulosan became heavily involved with other Filipinos in the labor movement, especially in California and Washington. His work with labor unions resulted in him becoming blacklisted as a communist during the McCarthy era. Although unable to finish high school, Bulosan was a prolific writer and poet. In fact, his novel, *America Is in the Heart*, published in 1946, was the first novel to be published by an Asian American author in the United States. Some of Bulosan's other well-known works include the novel *The Laughter of My Father* and the essay "Freedom from Want," which was published in the *Saturday Evening Post* in 1942. Bulosan died from complications related to pneumonia on September 11, 1956, at the age of forty-two in Seattle. He is buried at the Mount Pleasant Cemetery in Seattle's Queen Anne Hill.

Larry Itliong (1913–1977)

Modesto "Larry" Itliong was born on October 25, 1913, in the town of San Nicolas in Pangasinan Province in the Philippines. With only a sixth-grade education, Itliong came to the United States in 1929 at the age of fourteen. In the United States, he worked in the canneries in Alaska, as well as on farms in Washington, California, South Dakota, and Montana. Itliong was a skillful organizer who also spoke nine different Philippine dialects. Nicknamed "Seven Fingers" due to a salmon cannery accident in Alaska that claimed three of his fingers, Itliong founded and organized several unions and union events, including the Alaska Cannery Workers Union, the Cannery Workers in the sardine industry in San Pedro, the 1948–1949 Local 7 asparagus strikes in Stockton, and the Filipino Farm Labor Union of Stockton. He held several leadership positions, including president, in the Filipino community of Stockton, as well as Local 37. After World War II, Itliong got married and raised a family in Stockton. They later moved to Delano, where he began organizing the mostly Filipino grape workers. He died of Lou Gehrig's disease in February 1977 in Delano.

Philip Vera Cruz (1904–1994)

Philip Vera Cruz was born in 1904 in the Philippines and immigrated to the United States in 1926. He went on his first strike in 1939 with the Filipino Agricultural Labor Association (FALA) in Stockton, California. Dawn Mabalon references Vera Cruz's autobiography in saying, "I was so naive I didn't even know the name of the union organizing the strike, but I knew it was a part of the CIO [Congress of Industrial Organizations] and the leaders were Filipino" (Mabalon 2013, 255). Hailing from Delano, Vera Cruz became increasingly more involved in labor organizing and later became a part of the Agricultural Organization Workers Committee (AWOC) leadership along with Pete Velasco, Ben Gines, Larry Itliong, and Rudy Delvo (Mabalon 2013, 260).

DOCUMENT EXCERPTS

Delano Grape Workers' Boycott Day Proclamation

In September 1965, grape workers in Delano, California, under the guidance of the National Farm Workers Association, went on strike for a higher wage. The grape workers were fighting against the giant corporate farming enterprises of the state. The American Federation of Labor and Congress of Industrial Organizations (AFL-CIO) came in on the side of the farm workers. As the strike went on, the grape workers sought to elicit national support by calling for a consumer boycott of grapes. As the strike went into its sixth year, some of the smaller growers signed contracts with the unions, but the larger corporations still held back until July 1970, when contracts were finally signed. The corporations benefited from several factors: the great majority of farm workers were not yet union members, the federal government awarded large amounts of subsidies to the growers, and the U.S. Defense Department increased purchases of grapes enormously in an effort to offset the effects of the consumer boycott. The excerpts reprinted below are from the Boycott Day Proclamation issued by the grape workers on May 10, 1969.

Delano Grape Workers' Boycott Day Proclamation
May 10, 1969

We, the striking grape workers of California, join on this International Boycott Day with the consumers across the continent in planning the steps that lie ahead on the road to our liberation. As we plan, we recall the footsteps that brought us to this day and the events of this day. The historic road of our pilgrimage to Sacramento later branched out, spreading like the unpruned vines in struck fields, until it led us to willing exile in cities across this land. There, far from the earth we tilled for generations, we have cultivated the strange soil of public understanding, sowing the seed of our truth and our cause in the minds and hearts of men.

We have been farm workers for hundreds of years and pioneers for seven. Mexicans, Filipinos, Africans and others, our ancestors were among those who founded this land and tamed its natural wilderness. But we are still pilgrims on this land, and we are pioneers who blaze a trail out of the wilderness of hunger and deprivation that we have suffered even as our ancestors did. We are conscious today of the significance of our present quest. If this road we chart leads to the rights and reforms we demand, if it leads to just wages, humane working conditions, protection from the misuse of pesticides, and to the fundamental right of collective bargaining, if it changes the social order that relegates us to the bottom reaches of society, then in our wake will follow thousands of American farm workers. Our example will make them free. But if our road does not bring us to victory and social change, it will not be because our direction is mistaken or our resolve too weak, but only because our bodies are mortal and our journey hard. For we are in the midst of a great social movement, and we will not stop struggling 'til we die, or win!

We have been farm workers for hundreds of years and strikers for four. It was four years ago that we threw down our plowshares and pruning hooks. These Biblical symbols of peace and tranquility to us represent too many lifetimes of unprotesting submission to a degrading social system that allows us no dignity, no comfort, no peace. We mean to have our peace, and to win it without violence, for it is violence we would overcome—the subtle spiritual and mental violence of oppression, the violence subhuman toil does to the human body. So we went and stood tall outside the vineyards where we had stooped for years. But the tailors of national labor legislation had left us naked. Thus exposed, our picket lines were crippled by injunctions and harassed by growers; our strike was broken by imported scabs; our overtures to our employers were ignored. Yet we knew the day must come when they would talk to us, *as equals.*

We have been farm workers for hundreds of years and boycotters for two. We did not choose the grape boycott, but we *had* chosen to leave our peonage, poverty and despair behind. Though our first bid for freedom, the strike, was weakened, we would not turn back. The boycott was the only way forward the growers left to us. We called upon our fellow men and were answered by consumers who said—as all men of conscience must—that they would no longer allow their tables to be subsidized by our sweat and our sorrow: They shunned the grapes, fruit of our affliction. We marched alone at the beginning, but today we count men of all creeds, nationalities, and occupations in our number. Between us and the justice we seek now stand the large and powerful grocers who, in continuing to buy table grapes, betray the boycott their own customers have built. These stores treat their patrons' demands to remove the grapes the same way the growers treat our demands for union recognition—by ignoring them. The consumers who rally behind our cause are responding as we do to such treatment—with a boycott! They pledge to with-hold their patronage from stores that handle grapes during the boycott, just as we withhold our labor from the growers until our dispute is resolved.

Grapes must remain an unenjoyed luxury for all as long as the barest human needs and basic human rights are still luxuries for farm workers. The grapes grow sweet and heavy on the vines, but they will have to wait while we reach out first for our freedom. The time is ripe for our liberation.

Source: U.S. Congress. *Congressional Record*, Proceedings and Debates of the 91st Congress, First Session, May 12, 1969.

Grape Boycott Proclamation by Hon. James G. O'Hara

Charismatic labor activist Dolores Huerta (1930–) was born in New Mexico and grew up in Stockton at the northwest end of California's San Joaquín Valley. Huerta had been an organizer with the Community Service Organization (CSO) and worked as a teacher. She left these secure jobs to join labor activist César Chávez (1927–1993) to organize farmworkers. Huerta became the most prominent Chicana labor leader in the United States. Huerta was a seasoned organizer who lobbied in Sacramento, California, traveled the country organizing boycott committees, and spoke to workers. Speaking for the farmworkers' union, Huerta called for an international grape boycott, which eventually became an international cause with supporters refusing to eat grapes until the growers signed contracts with the union. The following is a resolution by the Hon. James G. O'Hara of Michigan, which includes the call for the Delano Grape Boycott.

Remarks of Hon. James G. O'Hara of Michigan about the
Proclamation of the Delano Grape Workers for International
Boycott Day to House of Representatives

Two years ago, the farmworkers of California called upon consumers to boycott grapes in an effort to force the growers to recognize the rights of the workers and to bargain collectively with them. The boycott has been more and more effective as the public has become more and more aware of the plight of the farmworkers. By boycotting grapes, consumers tell growers that they will not purchase their product until they know that the workers who harvest it are assured of a just wage, humane working conditions, job security, and other employee benefits taken for granted by most working men and women in America.

Mr. Speaker, I insert the proclamation of the Delano grape workers for International Boycott Day at this point in the Record:

. . .

Source: *Congressional Record*, 91st Cong., 1st sess. May 17, 1969.

See also: The First Asian American Studies Program Established at San Francisco State College, 1969; The Luce-Celler Act, 1946; Vietnam War and Refugee Migration from Southeast Asia, 1965–1975

Further Reading

Baldoz, Rick. 2011. *The Third Asiatic Invasion: Empire and Migration in Filipino America, 1898–1946.* New York: New York University Press.

Bulosan, Carlos. 1973. *America Is in the Heart: A Personal History.* Seattle: University of Washington Press.

Chew, Ron. 2012. *Remembering Silme Domingo and Gene Viernes: The Legacy of Filipino American Labor Activism.* Seattle: University of Washington Press.

Choy, Catherine Ceniza. 2003. *Empire of Care: Nursing and Migration in Filipino American History.* Durham, NC: Duke University Press.

Constantino, Renato. 1970. "The Mis-Education of the Filipino." *Journal of Contemporary Asia* 1, no. 1: 20–36.

David, Eric John Ramos and Sumie Okazaki. 2006. "The Colonial Mentality Scale (CMS) for Filipino Americans: Scale Construction and Psychological Implications." *Journal of Counseling Psychology* 53, no. 2: 241–252.

De la Cruz, Enrique, Jorge Emmanuel, Abe Ignacio, and Helen Toribio. 2004. *The Forbidden Book: The Philippine-American War in Political Cartoons.* San Francisco: T'Boli Publishing and Distribution.

Domingo, Ligaya Rene. 2010. "Building a Movement: Filipino American Union and Community Organizing in Seattle in the 1970s." PhD diss., University of California, Berkeley.

Enrile, Annalisa V. and Jollene Levid. 2009. "GAB[riela] NET[work]: A Case Study of Transnational Sisterhood and Organizing," *Amerasia Journal* 35:1, 92–107.

Espiritu, Yen Le. 2003. *Home Bound: Filipino American Lives across Cultures, Communities, and Countries.* Berkeley: University of California Press.

Garcia, Matt. 2001. *A World of Its Own: Race, Labor, and Citrus in the Making of Greater Los Angeles, 1900–1970.* Chapel Hill: University of North Carolina Press.

Fuentecilla, Jose. 2013. *Fighting from a Distance: How Filipino Exiles Helped Topple a Dictator.* Urbana: University of Illinois Press.

Fujita-Rony, Dorothy. 2003. *American Workers, Colonial Power: Philippine Seattle and the Transpacific West, 1919–1941.* Los Angeles: University of California Press.

Gaerlan, Barbara. 2003. "The Movement in the United States to Oppose Martial Law in the Philippines, 1972–1991: An Overview." Unpublished manuscript.

Habal, Estella. 2007. *San Francisco's International Hotel: Mobilizing the Filipino American Community in the Anti-Eviction Movement.* Philadelphia: Temple University Press.

Kim, Inga. 2017. "The Rise of the UFW." UFW Website, April 3. http://ufw.org/the-rise-of-the-ufw

Lawsin, Emily Porcincula. 1996. "Hanggang Pier Na Lamang: Filipina War Brides of Seattle." *Filipino American National Historical Society Journal* 4: 50A–50G.

Lawsin, Emily Porcincula. 1996. "Pensionados, Paisanos and Pinoys: An Analysis of the Filipino Student Bulletin, 1922–1939." *Filipino American National Historical Society Journal* 4: 33A–33P.

The Little Manila Foundation. 2018. http://www.littlemanila.org

Mabalon, Dawn Bohulano. 2013. *Little Manila Is in the Heart: The Making of the Filipina/o American Community in Stockton, California*. Durham, NC: Duke University Press.

McCoy, Alfred. 1999. "Dark Legacy: Human Rights under the Marcos Regime." Paper presented at the "Legacies of the Marcos Dictatorship" conference, Ateneo de Manila University, September 20.

McWilliams, Carey. 1973. Introduction to *America Is in the Heart: A Personal History,* by Carlos Bulosan. Seattle: University of Washington Press.

Mendoza, Victor. 2015. *Metroimperial Intimacies: Fantasy, Racial-Sexual Governance, and the Philippines in U.S. Imperialism, 1899–1913*. Durham, NC: Duke University Press.

Ocampo, Anthony Christian. 2016. *The Latinos of Asia: How Filipino Americans Break the Rules of Race*. Stanford, CA: Stanford University Press.

Riggs, Damien. 2004. "'We Don't Talk about Race Anymore': Power, Privilege and Critical Whiteness Studies." *Borderlands eJournal* 3, no. 2. http://www.borderlands.net.au/vol3no2_2004/riggs_intro.htm

Schulze-Oechtering, Michael. 2016. "The Alaska Cannery Workers Association and the Ebbs and Flows of Struggle: Manong Knowledge, Blues Epistemology, and Racial Cross-Fertilization." *Amerasia Journal* 42, no. 2: 23–48.

Tintiangco-Cubales, Allyson. 2007. *Pin@y Educational Partnerships: A Filipina/o American Studies Sourcebook Volume 1*. Quezon City, the Philippines: Phoenix Publishing House International.

Toribio, Helen. 1998. "We Are Revolution: A Reflective History of the Union of Democratic Filipinos (KDP)." *Amerasia Journal* 24, no. 2: 155–177.

Zinn, Howard. 2003. *A People's History of the United States*. Abridged teaching edition. New York: The New Press.

Vietnam War and Refugee Migration from Southeast Asia, 1965–1975

Khoi Nguyen

Chronology

1870–1872   Bui Vien, seeking support in the fight for independence from France, is perhaps the first Vietnamese to travel to the United States.

1887–1954   Officially, France colonized Southeast Asia for almost a century. In reality, modern-day Vietnam, Cambodia, and Laos comprised French Indochina, a French colony in Southeast Asia that lasted approximately two and a half centuries.

1946–1954 The First Indochina War—also known as the Anti-French Resistance War in Vietnam—takes place. France decolonizes Vietnam, Cambodia, and Laos. The war ends with the Geneva Conference dividing Vietnam at the seventeenth parallel to allow the country to reunify and rebuild itself.

1951 At the Refugee Convention, the United Nations defines refugees as people who reside outside of their country due to fear of persecution based on ethnicity, race, religion, or politics.

1954 Approximately one million northern Vietnamese refugees migrate to South Vietnam at the end of the French occupation.

1954–1975 The Second Indochina War—also known as the American War in Vietnam or the Vietnam War—takes place. The United States tries to stop the "domino effect" of communism spreading in the area by increasing its military presence in Southeast Asia.

November 1963 President John F. Kennedy is assassinated; Lyndon B. Johnson becomes president of the United States.

January 1968 The Tet Offensive becomes the turning point of the Vietnam War.

April 30, 1975 The Fall of Saigon marks the end of the Vietnam War.

1975 The first wave of Vietnamese refugee migration consists mostly of people who belong to the middle class, are Catholic, are affiliated with the U.S. government, and have some knowledge of the English language. The United States accepts approximately 130,000 refugees after the war in 1975 and 17,000 more refugees over the next two years.

1975–1991 The Third Indochina War takes place. Approximately sixteen years of interconnected conflicts occur between various communist countries seeking to control Southeast Asia after the U.S. withdrawal.

1979–1980s The second wave of the Vietnamese refugee migration consists of mostly oceanic refugees, pejoratively and commonly known as boat people, seeking political asylum in neighboring countries (Malaysia, Indonesia, the Philippines, and Thailand). The total population of Vietnamese and Vietnamese Americans in the United States in 1980 is approximately 230,000. The United States accepts approximately 166,700 political refugees in 1980 and another 123,350 in 1981 due to international pressures and domestic guilt.

March 17, 1980	The Refugee Act of 1980 eases restrictions on Vietnamese and Southeast Asian refugees entering the United States.
Late 1980s	The third wave of the Vietnamese refugee migration consists mainly of ethnically Chinese Vietnamese escaping due to ethnic and political persecutions. Approximately 40,000 political asylum seekers enter the United States each year throughout the 1980s.
1987–1990s	The fourth wave of the Vietnamese refugee migration consists mostly of biracial children who were left behind in Vietnam after the Vietnam War. The Amerasian Homecoming Act of 1987 admits approximately 23,000 mixed-race Vietnamese, along with 70,000 of their family members.
1994	President Bill Clinton lifts the U.S. trade embargo against Vietnam, which started in 1964.
1989–1999	The fifth wave of the Vietnamese refugee migration consists mainly of political prisoners and their families. The Humanitarian Operation (HO) program admits over 70,000 political refugees into the United States. As of the year 2000, the total population of Vietnamese and Vietnamese Americans recorded in the United States is two million.
2016	The population of Vietnamese and Vietnamese Americans in the United States is recorded as 2,067,527.

Narrative

April 30, 1975, marked the end of the Vietnam War (also known as the American War in Vietnam). This date signifies the reunification of North and South Vietnam, the mass exodus of Vietnamese (and Southeast Asian) refugees to the United States, and the genesis of a new Vietnamese nation-state. This catastrophic day is also known as the Fall of Saigon to many South Vietnamese (or the Liberation of Saigon to many North Vietnamese), when the North Vietnamese military force seized control of Saigon, the former capital of South Vietnam—later renamed Ho Chi Minh City (HCMC). South Vietnamese civilians and military personnel had been evacuating the city months prior to the final day. It was one of the largest helicopter evacuations in history.

Today, the legacy of the American War in Vietnam continues to haunt the United States as what many argue is its only failed war. Contemporary Vietnam exists as a unified nation-state. Since more than half of its current population was born after 1990, few personal memories of the war survive. In an attempt to forget the war,

Vietnamese refugees fled Tet Offensive attacks in 1968. The attacks marked an important turning point in the Vietnam War. Even though North Vietnam suffered heavy casualties, it achieved a strategic victory; the attacks led to American withdrawal from the region. (National Archives)

the United States and Vietnam have reestablished their international relationship in the interest of increasing globalized development.

It is nearly impossible to summarize the American War in Vietnam without discussing the colonial history of Vietnam and Southeast Asia. Riddled with colonial occupations—Chinese, French, and Japanese—Vietnam is a geopolitically important country located near the South China Sea, bordering Cambodia, Laos, and southern China. It plays a key role in the trading routes between China and India. After Chinese colonial rule of more than a thousand years, Vietnam fell under French colonial rule in the nineteenth century and remained so for nearly a century. However, Vietnam also participated in its own colonial occupation and displacement of indigenous populations (for example, the Khmers and Chams kingdom). During World War II, France lost its colonial stronghold in Vietnam, which led to the Japanese military occupation that lasted until the end of the war. After a short period of reoccupation, France later decolonized Vietnam, Cambodia, and Laos as a result of the first Indochina War (1946–1954). The war ended with the Geneva Conference dividing Vietnam at the seventeenth parallel to allow the country to reunify and rebuild itself. The end of World War II in Europe further spread the decolonialization movement throughout Asia and Africa.

Disassociated from the European colonial project, the United States utilized liberal antiracist discourse to establish a moral legitimacy as a world superpower championing global liberal democracy through the logic of capitalism. Emerging as the victor of World War II, the United States equated its victory over Nazism to its democratic values, which embraced diversity and multiculturalism. But historically, the United States has participated in racist and xenophobic imprisonment of Japanese Americans in internment camps during World War II, centuries of enslavement and racial segregation, the removal and displacement of native communities, and countless unjust treatments of people of color. As part of the modernization and anticommunist project, the U.S. government increased its military support of the South Vietnamese government as a humanitarian mission to secure its geopolitical grip on Southeast Asia. This resulted in the Second Indochina War (1954–1975), also known as the Vietnam War or the American War in Vietnam. The U.S. military justified its intervention in Vietnam, along with Cambodia and Laos, to prevent the "domino effect" of communism. The Third Indochina War (1975–1991) was fought over who would govern Cambodia. As a political project, the American War in Vietnam became a proxy for the Cold War between the Soviet Union and the United States, an ideological war between capitalism and communism. As its first and only failed war, the United States justified the military occupation in South Vietnam near the end of the war as a humanitarian project to liberate South Vietnamese allies, and later to rescue the abandoned war victims as refugees. To this end, the Vietnamese/Southeast Asian refugee crisis in the United States (1975–1990s) legitimized future U.S. military interventions on any foreign nation-state on the basis of human rights through the spreading of liberal democracy (i.e., the U.S. occupation in the Middle East).

Refugees have existed throughout history. Significantly, within the twentieth century, the homogenization of citizenship and migration created the categorization of the refugee subject. In 1951, the United Nations (UN) defined refugees as people who reside outside of their country due to fear of persecution based on ethnicity, race, religion, or politics. After Saigon fell, many South Vietnamese left the country as refugees in fear of persecution by the Northern Vietnamese government. Later in the 1980s, many Chinese Vietnamese (ethnic Chinese in/from Vietnam), along with a large number of South Vietnamese, escaped the country as oceanic refugees (pejoratively known as boat people) due to ethnic and political persecutions. Over the span of two decades, the United States saw five major waves of Vietnamese—Southeast Asian—refugees entering the country.

Immigrants from Vietnam

Problematically, the genesis of the Vietnamese American subject often starts with the fall of Saigon on April 30, 1975, after which the first major wave of Vietnamese refugees arrived in the United States. However, Vietnamese had already been immigrating to the United States for decades as scholars, students, war brides, diplomats, and others, albeit in insignificant numbers. This temporal division of pre- and post-1975 separates the Vietnamese American experience based on socioeconomic and immigration status. On one hand, in addition to being Catholic, most of the Vietnamese immigrants who came to the United States before 1975 (and immediately after April 30, 1975) had financial means, educational background, and language skills due to previous affiliation with the U.S. government. These advantages helped them better adapt to a new culture. On the other hand, Vietnamese refugees and immigrants who arrived in the United States after 1975 (years, if not decades, later) as prolonged victims of war had little to no financial assets, had a wide range of educational levels and language skills, and came from a diverse religious background. However, with both the threat of communism via the Cold War and the failure of the American War in Vietnam, these relocated Vietnamese in the United States could only exist as war victims who needed to be rescued from the failed totalitarian communist regime. Therefore, the construction of the Vietnamese American subject often starts and ends on April 30, 1975, as part of a liberating and liberalizing project, rooted in capitalism, which justified the destructive war in Southeast Asia.

An overview of the migration experience and the identity formation of the Vietnamese (Southeast Asian) American subject in the United States post-1975 is important to understanding the relationship between the Vietnamese (and Southeast Asian) American and the United States population at large. In a matter of hours, marked by the official handover of Saigon, millions of South Vietnamese went from being U.S. allies against communism to being a threat against the new nation-state of the Socialist Republic of Vietnam. As the last remnant of U.S. aid departed Vietnamese soil, the U.S. military temporarily relocated approximately 125,000 Vietnamese refugees to nearby countries: the U.S. territory of Guam, Thailand, the Philippines, and Indonesia. Significantly, the United States converted Anderson Air Force Base in Guam—a location 1,500 miles east of Saigon that had housed B-52 bombers during the war—to be a processing center and temporary shelter for Vietnamese refugees before legally permitting them to enter the States. However, the overwhelming number of refugees caused a backlog that required the U.S. government to create makeshift immigration camps in the Philippines and Thailand. Guam received approximately 4,000 Vietnamese daily, but only 3,000 people left the island per day due to the unclear migration policies pertaining to refugee status.

While the UN defined refugees as victims of persecution, U.S. officials still screened immigrants for history of personal crime, mental and physical health, and subversive activities to determine admission status. Further, these Vietnamese refugees required a U.S.-based sponsor to ensure a smooth assimilation process to prevent another migration crisis like that involving Cuba. By mid-May 1975, four domestic refugee camps were set up in the United States: Camp Pendleton, California; Fort Chafee, Alaska; Fort Indiantown Gap, Pennsylvania; and Eglin Air Force Base, Florida (Zhou and Bankston 1999, 27–29). These refugee camps served as transitional spaces for U.S. government officials to conduct interviews to determine sponsorship and redistribution of the first wave of Vietnamese refugees—the largest group of Southeast Asian migrants at that point. Additionally, under Operation New Life and Operation Baby Lift, approximately 111,919 Vietnamese refugees and orphans left the country that year, and over 90,000 resettled in the United States. Paradoxically, the Vietnamese refugees saw these camps as reminders of their lost country and representations of a hopeful new beginning in a foreign land. This structure of feelings continues to inform the identity of many first-generation Vietnamese and Vietnamese Americans, who see their placement in diaspora as temporary before they get to return to Vietnam. Many of the camp residents bonded over their trauma and loss (Kelly 1977, 2–3; Liu, Lamanna, and Murata 1979, 8–10). These five camps (Guam and four U.S. mainland-based camps) closed between September and December 1975, as the refugee population integrated into local U.S. communities.

The mass exodus from Vietnam and Southeast Asia did not stop after the U.S. military withdrawal in 1975. Immediately after end of the American War in Vietnam, the Khmer Rouge came to power in Cambodia and committed the first and only auto-genocide over the next four years by killing approximately two million Khmers who might have had a connection to the West. These included but were not limited to politicians, doctors, lawyers, scholars, artists, and even those who simply wore glasses. This caused a major influx of Cambodian refugees exiting Southeast Asia. Additionally, as Vietnam began to rebuild itself, the new nationalistic government aggressively targeted ethnically Chinese Vietnamese as foreigners who posed a threat to the country's closed economy. Significantly, these two ethnic groups were mostly identified through their socioeconomic class status rather than their racial identity—ethnic Chinese Vietnamese occupied the upper middle class as small business owners, and educated Khmers signified wealth and education. Over the next two years, 17,000 more Vietnamese and Southeast Asians continue to illegally and dangerously escape the country through any means necessary, often by boat, to seek political asylum in Thailand, Indonesia, Malaysia, and the Philippines. Often resulting in death by drowning or other causes, millions would rather risk their lives at sea than remain in the country. By 1979, the UN High

Commissioner on Refugees responded to the outrageously high death toll and released a comprehensive plan by Western nation-states (primarily the United States, France, Germany, and Australia) to accept undocumented refugees escaping Vietnam through the South China Sea. Driven by guilt, the United States finally opened its borders to accept another major wave of oceanic refugees as part of the second wave: in 1979, 80,700 people; in 1980, 166,700 people; and in 1981, 123,250 people. Years later, the U.S. and Vietnam governments came to an agreement, developing the Orderly Departure Program to ensure a safer and legal passage to reunite families. By 1981, the total number of Vietnamese refugees and immigrants had reached 230,000 within the United States alone.

Addressing the large population influx, the U.S. government implemented the Refugee Dispersion Policy to deal with the political and financial constraints created by the refugees. The policy had four primary goals: 1) relocate and establish financial independence for the refugees as soon as possible; 2) ease the refugees' impact on local communities; 3) make it easier for refugees to find sponsors; and 4) avoid the development of an ethnic ghetto (Liu et al. 1979, 20). Ruben Rumbaut stated that the U.S. government wanted to "avoid another Miami" with hundreds of thousands of unregistered Cubans taking over the city (2006; 29, 51–52); therefore, the plan was to disperse the Vietnamese and Southeast Asian refugees throughout the country. However, due to the lack of available resources and preparations, many Vietnamese refugees created an informal network and social strata to address the needs within their own communities. As the Vietnamese refugee network grew larger, the needs of the newly settled immigrant communities also grew. The United States witnessed a second (or an internal) migration within the Vietnamese community, known as the resettlement. In 1984, Beth Baldwin's survey found that a third of the Vietnamese refugees who embarked on a secondary migration to Orange County, California, came from other states in search of better job opportunities; a more conducive, warmer climate; and a greater sense of Vietnamese community. Furthermore, the 1990 census shows a national pattern of Vietnamese relocating to metropolitan areas such as Houston, Los Angeles, San Jose, San Diego, Seattle, New Orleans, Boston, Washington, D.C., and many other cities to seek a better support network. As the Vietnamese migrants integrated into local U.S. communities, they started to witness racial tension, ranging from microaggression to full-blown racism, originating in white communities, communities of color, and even Asian American communities.

Throughout the 1980s, the United States saw a third wave of Vietnamese migrants entering the country that amounted to approximately 40,000 people per year. Almost all of the refugees admitted into the United States entered as political asylum refugees. Unlike the first two waves of Vietnamese refugees, the third wave consisted of both oceanic refugees and Orderly Departure Program participants;

financial resources separated the two groups. Even though the application did not cost anything to the Vietnamese applicants, the cumulative expenses, such as the cost of traveling to the embassy from small towns, the cost of living in the city while waiting for the paperwork, and even the cost of translation services, added up to a huge price tag. Due to the complexity of the formal application process, which led to endless scams, many people would rather gamble their lives at sea in hopes of a faster and more reliable result. Boat escape still posed similar problems such as fraud (fake boat trips), imprisonment (being caught by local police), or robbery (piracy). Furthermore, with limited financial means, the third-wave migrants faced other problems upon arriving in the United States. The clear division between the different waves of immigrants and refugees started to become more noticeable as governmental social programs and assistance began to disappear.

With no language skills or marketable professional trades, this wave of new-comers faced yet another layer of discrimination from within the Vietnamese com-munity. As the informal Vietnamese networks begin to solidify in major cities, a hierarchical structure started to take shape that placed the first-wave population (pre-1975 and immediately after) at the top, followed by the second-wave population (those with financial means and connection). The newly emigrated population remained at the bottom (with the least amount of preparation). In like manner, the established Asian American (Chinese, Japanese, and some Filipino and Korean) communities hesitated to incorporate the new Southeast Asian migrants because their political and ideological agendas did not align. The Southeast Asian popula-tion, as new migrants, gravitated toward ethnicity and community-oriented inter-ests, rather than historical and socioeconomic issues rooted in earlier Asian American communities. Geographically, government agencies and social services regularly placed newly arrived Southeast Asian migrants in city ghettos or underdeveloped neighborhoods inhabited by people of color due to affordability. Academically, it was not until the late 1990s that comparative literature departments in the United States started to engage in conversations with Southeast Asian scholars.

In 1987, the United States started another initiative—the Amerasian Homecom-ing Act—to bring the abandoned biracial children of U.S. soldiers and Vietnamese mothers home from Vietnam. As a political project, these children symbolized the lives of U.S. soldiers who died on the battlefield finally coming home. However, aside from the short attempt of Operation Baby Lift to extract more than 10,300 infants and children immediately before the Fall of Saigon (April 3–26, 1975), children remained absent from most of the migration narratives. After the war, a number of U.S. soldiers left their partners and biracial children in Vietnam when they returned to their lives in the States. Under the new Vietnamese regime, the Amerasian population—predominately children born between 1962 and 1976—remains as a bitter reminder of the U.S. military occupation. The newly forgotten single mother often mistreated or discarded her biracial child(ren) due to the stigmatization of being a traitor for having sexual relations with a Westerner. In the case of the fortunate few, grandparents or distant relatives adopted and brought them to the countryside to live. Those with no familial ties remained on the streets as beggars to fend for their own survival and were given the name *bụi đời*—"dust of life." Overall, these biracial children grew up receiving little to no formal education due to discrimination and harassment from local communities, even within school walls.

Significantly, the Amerasian Homecoming Act admitted 23,000 mixed-race children along with over 70,000 family members, marking the fourth major wave of Vietnamese migration to the United States. Overnight, these abandoned children became the golden ticket for many Vietnamese who failed to escape the country by other means. The commodification of these Amerasian individuals can be traced in different exploitive acts, such as estranged family members who tried to re-establish lost kinship, family members and caretakers who sold Amerasian individuals, and/ or strangers who bought or kidnapped previously abandoned individuals. Furthermore, upon arriving in the United States, the accompanying "families" would once again sever ties with the "adopted" individuals to focus on assimilating their true family members into the new country. Due to the lack of formal education, a large number of the Amerasian population remained illiterate, with no proper skilled trades with which to enter the job market. Despite an easier path to citizenship, the Amerasian population did not qualify for most of the government assistances designed for newly arrived immigrants. Nevertheless, by 1990, the Vietnamese population in the United States had reached 500,000, establishing strong niche communities around the country.

The fifth and last major wave of Vietnamese migrants entered the United States through the Humanitarian Resettlement Program, a joint agreement between the U.S. and Vietnamese governments. Colloquially known as the Humanitarian Operation (HO) program, a derivative of the Orderly Departure Act, thousands of middle-aged Vietnamese political prisoners and their families arrived in the States as political refugees. Once again, the admission of this final wave reaffirmed the liberal humanitarian project of the United States, which justified the war in Vietnam and in larger Southeast Asia. Unbeknownst to many Vietnamese applicants, the acronym "HO" never stood for "humanitarian operation" but was a derivative of the alphabetical order in which the "H" program comes after the "F" and "G" programs. The "O" was actually a zero and part of a numerical sequence of the H program—H-zero one (H01), H-zero two (H02), up to H-ten (H10).

To qualify for the program, the Vietnamese applicants had to serve at least one year within the Vietnamese reeducation camp in addition to being trained by, or working for, the U.S. government prior to April 30, 1975; widower applicants also qualified. Many HO refugees saw this opportunity as their last chance to escape the economically and politically repressed country in hope of a better life in the United States. Media coverage in the States often portrayed these refugees as tragic survivors of communism via the reeducation camp, which disassociated the individuals from the problematic war that caused their initial displacement. Arriving during the economic recession of the 1990s, many refugees ended up competing against a much younger, Spanish-speaking migrant population for entry-level manual labor jobs. Regardless of their struggles, the newly arrived population did not express any ingratitude toward the U.S. government, as this was their second chance for a new life in the West. The Vietnamese population in the United States continued to grow exponentially, and the U.S. Census Bureau recorded approximately two million Vietnamese living in the States by 2017.

Soon after 1975, the federal government funded a number of research projects to better understand, and later assimilate, the newly arrived refugee population. The

Southeast Asian Population in the United States

According to the 2010 census, more than 6.4 million Southeast Asians reside in the United States, making up about 2 percent of the total population. Southeast Asians did not enter the U.S. national populist consciousness until the 1970s, when the not-so Cold War got heated over Vietnam and forced this geopolitical country to the global center stage. The southeast region of Asia encompasses Brunei, Cambodia, East Timor and Indonesia, Laos, Malaysia, Myanmar (Burma), the Philippine Islands, Singapore, Thailand, and Vietnam. The region is composed of a vast collection of languages, cultures, religions, and histories. These Southeast Asian countries have had very different experiences of postwar migrations into the United States. Yet contemporary academic and popular discourses often privilege a particular populist narrative to recount a more universal and singular story: the Vietnamese—a stand-in for all Southeast Asians—were rescued by the United States from communism. This process erases the complex history of Southeast Asia intra- and inter-colonialism, rendering the region ahistorical until the discovery of European colonialism, or more recently, the American War in Vietnam. Upon arriving in the States, Southeast Asians faced further challenges not shared with the larger Asian American community. The Southeast Asian population, as new migrants, organized around ethnicity and community-oriented interests, rather than racial and socioeconomic issues faced by early Asian American communities—predominantly Chinese, Japanese, and Filipino members.

literature commonly reduced the Vietnamese migrant population to both passive objects to be studied and to docile refugees waiting to be rescued. As a political and a restorative project, scholar Yến Lê Espiritu argues that it is necessary to look at the "refugee" not only as "a legal classification" but also as an *idea* to explain the U.S. perception of Vietnam and the Vietnamese (2014, 4). Historically, scholarship on Vietnamese subjects has centered on American exceptionalism, immigration, and transnationalism that does not always engage in critical conversations with American imperialism and racism. Problematically, the economic success story of Vietnamese refugees over the decades gets integrated into the Asian American "model minority" myth that further divided the different communities of color. Emphasizing cultural differences, mass media and social scientists accredited the refugees' assimilation to preexisting traditional core values. In other words, the "good refugee" who embodied a strong work ethic—grounded on Confucianism— was able to escape the inequitable racial barriers and achieve upward mobility through capitalism. Therefore, the admission of the "good refugee" is not only

Vietnamese and Southeast Asian Women in the Workforce

Within the American workforce, Vietnamese and Southeast Asian women regularly have an advantage over their male counterparts in gaining employment due to the high number of cheap and exploitative jobs. By participating in the labor economy, these women gain the financial freedom that was not always available to them prior to migration. However, according to a study conducted by Nazli Kibria (1993), Vietnamese women continue to straddle an "ideological tightrope" to maintain traditional Vietnamese cultural practices while also providing for the family as the primary source of income. Moreover, these women cannot be completely independent from their male counterparts due to the limitations of low-wage income. Though their work is often hazardous and arduous, these immigrant women see it as a sacrifice and an opportunity for the betterment of their whole family, in contrast to the individualized upward mobility that is emphasized within the Western feminist movement. In other words, their labor is an extension of their familial responsibilities as wives and mothers, and less so a personal gain or liberation. These newly arrived Vietnamese and Southeast Asian women take pride in the ability to financially provide for their families and maintain the traditional family structure (Espiritu 1992, 22; 2014, 12; Nguyen 2002, 8–82; Pelaud, 2011, 33–35; Rumbaut 2006, 19; Võ 2004, xii; Zhou and Bankston 1999, 34).

needed to justify the war in Vietnam but is also necessary to normalize the existing racism and capitalism in the United States.

Contemporarily, Vietnamese Americans occupy multiple spaces and identities that often do not include memory of the American War in Vietnam. Many Vietnamese Americanists have articulated that Vietnam is not a war, but a country. As the later generations of Vietnamese Americans (1.5, second, and third) come to political consciousness, their social activism shifts away from the traditional anticommunist narratives to a broader racial framework accounting for their personal experience. Nicole Waligora-Davis (2011) offers a critical lens to look at the refugee through the racial articulation of statelessness that historically delimits citizenship for African Americans and black Americans. Others propose viewing the Vietnamese refugee as a site of struggles to move beyond the conventional analysis grounded in American exceptionalism, thus engaging in a larger conversation at the intersection of race, class, and gender analysis.

Asian Women in Modern Pop Culture

Two modern figures in American pop culture embody the "American dream" pursued by a number of Vietnamese and Southeast Asian American individuals today.

Kelly Marie Tran (1989–) is an actress who starred in the 2017 film *Star Wars: The Last Jedi* as a rebel mechanic who joins forces with the film's main characters to fight against the First Order. Tran is the first Asian American woman to play a leading role in the Star Wars franchise. Her appearance in the feature film highlights the lack of representation of Asian American characters on the silver screen, along with the endless exploitation of "yellow-face." Tran is scheduled to appear in the second season of *Star Wars: Forces of Destiny*, a web series that focuses on female characters from previous installments.

Another Asian American on American screens is Jujubee (1984–), a pop icon and a drag queen contestant on the award-winning reality television show *RuPaul's Drag Race*. Jujubee, whose legal name is Airline Inthyrath, is a vibrant drag queen who embodies charisma, uniqueness, nerve, and talent— all of the qualities needed to be a "Ru-girl." As the first Laotian Thai American drag queen to be featured on national television, she often uses her cultural heritage to challenge gender norms and deconstruct stereotypes surrounding Asian Americans. Local to the Boston area, Jujubee remains a prominent figure within the local gay bar scene.

Since 1975, Vietnamese Americans and Southeast Asians have continued to make great contributions to the larger U.S. society as artists, politicians, athletes, actors, scholars, filmmakers, designers, and countless other professions. Through their personal achievements, Southeast American refugees, predominantly Vietnamese Americans, embodied the capitalist American dream that further reinforced the ideology of American exceptionalism.

Biographies of Notable Figures

Viet Thanh Nguyen (1971–)

Viet Thanh Nguyen is a Vietnamese American author and scholar whose debut novel, *The Sympathizer*, won the 2016 Pulitzer Prize for Fiction, the Dayton Literary Peace Prize, the Center for Fiction First Novel Prize, and three other awards. He was also the recipient of the MacArthur Genius Grant in 2017. Nguyen is currently the Aerol Arnold Chair of English and professor of English and American Studies and Ethnicity at the University of Southern California. His first book, *Race and Resistance: Literature and Politics in Asian America* (2002), examines different sites of resistance to argue that literature can still be an important space for political interventions. His family first arrived in one of the four camps in the United States, Fort Indiantown Gap, Pennsylvania, where his wife and her family also relocated. He serves on the board of the Diasporic Vietnamese Artists Network, an art nonprofit based in California.

Jacqueline H. Nguyen (1965–)

Jacqueline H. Nguyen is a U.S. circuit judge of the U.S. Court of Appeals for the Ninth Circuit, appointed by President Barack Obama. Born in Da Lat, Vietnam, and immigrating to the United States at the age of ten after the Fall of Saigon, Nguyen grew up in Los Angeles, where she attended Occidental College for her undergraduate degree and UCLA for law school. She is the first Asian American female to serve as a federal appellate judge and the first Vietnamese American federal judge. In 2016, the *New York Times* identified Nguyen as one of the potential judges to fill the vacant seat in the U.S. Supreme Court.

Trinh T. Minh-ha (1952–)

Trinh T. Minh-ha is an avant-garde filmmaker, composer, writer, and postcolonial feminist. Trinh immigrated to the United States in 1970 to attend the University of Illinois, Urbana-Champaign, studying French literature, music, and ethnomusicology. She started as an associate professor of cinema at San Francisco

State University and is currently professor of Gender and Women's Studies and Rhetoric at the University of California at Berkeley. She has published numerous well-recognized theoretical and critical texts: *Woman, Native, Other: Writing Postcoloniality and Feminism* (1989); *When the Moon Waxes Red* (1991); *Elsewhere, Within Here: Immigration Refugeeism and the Boundary Event* (2010); and *Lovecidal* (2016). Trinh has also established herself as a renowned filmmaker: *Reassemblage* (1982), *Naked Spaces—Living Is Round* (1985), *Surname Viet Given Name Nam* (1989), *Shoot for the Contents* (1991), *A Tale of Love* (1995), *The Fourth Dimension* (2001), *Night Passage* (2004), and *Forgetting Vietnam* (2015).

Mee Moua (1969–)

Mee Moua is a Hmong American who served in the Minnesota state legislature from 2002 to 2011. In 1978, her family migrated to the United States after the American War in Vietnam, with a short period of residence in Thailand. She attended Brown University for her undergraduate degree, the University of Texas for her master's, and finally the University of Minnesota for law school. Moua was the first Hmong American to be elected to state legislature, where she chaired the Judiciary Committee. After three terms, she announced her retirement from public office to focus on her family. Minnesota houses one of the two largest Hmong populations in the United States.

DOCUMENT EXCERPTS

Refugee Act of 1980

The long title of the Refugee Act of 1980 states its purposes: "An Act to amend the Immigration and Nationality Act to revise the procedures for the admission of refugees, to amend the Migration and Refugee Assistance Act of 1962 to establish a more uniform basis for the provision of assistance to refugees, and for other purposes." The act was signed into law by President Jimmy Carter on March 17, 1980, and became effective on April 1, 1980. It eases restrictions on Vietnamese and other Southeast Asian refugees entering the United States and led to the third wave of the Vietnamese refugee migration in the 1980s. The following is a selection of excerpts from this act.

Refugee Act of 1980
Public Law 96-212—MAR. 17, 1980
(Excerpts)

An Act
Immigration and Nationality Act to revise the procedures for the admission of refugees, to amend the Migration and Refugee Assistance Act of 1962 to establish a

more uniform basis for the provision of assistance to refugees, and for other purposes.

Be it enacted by the Senate and House of Representatives of the Refugee Act of United States of America in Congress assembled, That this Act may be cited as the "Refugee Act of 1980"

TITLE I—PURPOSE

Sec. 101. (a) The Congress declares that it is the historic policy of the United States to respond to the urgent needs of persons subject to persecution in their homelands, including, where appropriate, humanitarian assistance for their care and maintenance in asylum areas, efforts to promote opportunities for resettlement or voluntary repatriation, aid for necessary transportation and processing, admission to this country of refugees of special humanitarian concern to the United States, and transitional assistance to refugees in the United States. The Congress further declares that it is the policy of the United States to encourage all nations to provide assistance and resettlement opportunities to refugees to the fullest extent possible.

(b) The objectives of this Act are to provide a permanent and systematic procedure for the admission to this country of refugees of special humanitarian concern to the United States, and to provide comprehensive and uniform provisions for the effective resettlement and absorption of those refugees who are admitted.

TITLE II—ADMISSION OF REFUGEES

Sec. 201. (a) Section 101(a) of the Immigration and Nationality Act (8 U.S.C. 1101(a)) is amended by adding after paragraph (41) the following new paragraph: "Refugee." "(42) The term 'refugee' 5 means (A) any person who is outside any country of such person s nationality or, in the case of a person having no nationality, is outside any country in which such person last habitually resided, and who is unable or unwilling to return to, and is unable or unwilling to avail himself or herself of the protection of, that country because of persecution or a well-founded fear of persecution on account of race, religion, nationality, membership in a particular social group, or political opinion, or (B) in such special circumstances as the President after appropriate consultation (as Post, p. 103. defined in section 207(e) of this Act) may specify, any person who is within the country of such person's nationality or, in the case of a person having no nationality, within the country in which such person is habitually residing, and who is persecuted or who has a well-founded fear of persecution on account of race, religion, nationality, membership in a particular social group, or political opinion. The term 'refugee' does not include any person who ordered, incited, assisted, or otherwise participated in the persecution of any person on account of race, religion, nationality, membership in a particular social group, or political opinion.

(b) Chapter 1 of title II of such Act is amended by adding after section 206 (8 U.S.C. 1156) the following new sections:

ANNUAL ADMISSION OF REFUGEES AND ADMISSION OF EMERGENCY SITUATION REFUGEES

Sec. 207. (a)(1) Except as provided in subsection (b), the number of refugees who may be admitted under this section in fiscal year 1980, 1981, or 1982, may not exceed fifty thousand unless the President determines, before the beginning of the fiscal year and after appropriate consultation (as defined in subsection (e)), that admission of a specific number of refugees in excess of such number is justified by humanitarian concerns or is otherwise in the national interest.

(2) Except as provided in subsection (b), the number of refugees who may be admitted under this section in any fiscal year after fiscal year 1982 shall be such number as the President determines, before the beginning of the fiscal year and after appropriate consultation, is justified by humanitarian concerns or is otherwise in the national interest.

(3) Admissions under this subsection shall be allocated among refugees of special humanitarian concern to the United States in accordance with a determination made by the President after appropriate consultation.

(b) If the President determines, after appropriate consultation, that (1) an unforeseen emergency refugee situation exists, (2) the admission of certain refugees in response to the emergency refugee situation is justified by grave humanitarian concerns or is otherwise in the national interest, and (3) the admission to the United States of these refugees cannot be accomplished under subsection (a), the President may fix a number of refugees to be admitted to the United States during the succeeding period (not to exceed twelve months) in response to the emergency refugee situation and such admissions shall be allocated among refugees of special humanitarian concern to the United States in accordance with a determination made by the President after the appropriate consultation provided under this subsection.

(c)(1) Subject to the numerical limitations established pursuant to subsections (a) and (b), the Attorney General may, in the Attorney General's discretion and pursuant to such regulations as the Attorney General may prescribe, admit any refugee who is not firmly resettled in any foreign country, is determined to be of special humanitarian concern to the United States, and is admissible (except as otherwise provided under paragraph (3)) as an immigrant under this Act.

. . .

ASYLUM PROCEDURE

Sec. 208. (a) The Attorney General shall establish a procedure for 8 use 1158 an alien physically present in the United States or at a land border or port of entry, irrespective of such alien's status, to apply for asylum, and the alien may be granted asylum in the discretion of the Attorney General if the Attorney General determines that such alien is a refugee within the meaning of section 101(a)(42)(A).

(b) Asylum granted under subsection (a) may be terminated if the Attorney General, pursuant to such regulations as the Attorney General may prescribe, determines that the alien is no longer a refugee within the meaning of section 101(a) (42) (A) owing to a change in circumstances in the alien's country of nationality or, in the case of an alien having ho nationality, in the country in which the alien last habitually resided.

(c) A spouse or child (as defined in section 101(b)(1) (A), (B), (C), (D), or (E)) of an alien who is granted asylum under subsection (a) may, if not otherwise eligible for asylum under such subsection, be granted the same status as the alien if accompanying, or following to join, such alien.

. . .

TITLE III—UNITED STATES COORDINATOR FOR REFUGEE AFFAIRS AND ASSISTANCE FOR EFFECTIVE RESETTLEMENT OF REFUGEES IN THE UNITED STATES

Part A—United States Coordinator for Refugee Affairs

Sec. 301. (a) The President shall appoint, by and with the advice and consent of the Senate, a United States Coordinator for Refugee Affairs (hereinafter in this part referred to as the "Coordinator"). The Coordinator shall have the rank of Ambassador-at-Large.

(b) The Coordinator shall be responsible to the President for—(1) the development of overall United States refugee admission and resettlement policy; (2) the coordination of all United States domestic and international refugee admission and resettlement programs in a manner that assures that policy objectives are met in a timely fashion; (3) the design of an overall budget strategy to provide individual agencies with policy guidance on refugee matters in

. . .

TITLE IV—SOCIAL SERVICES FOR CERTAIN APPLICANTS FOR ASYLUM

Sec. 401. (a) The Director of the Office of Refugee Resettlement is 8 use 1522 note, authorized to use funds appropriated under paragraphs (1) and (2) of section 414(a) of the Immigration and Nationality Act to reimburse Ante, p. 116. State and local public agencies for expenses which those agencies incurred, at any time, in providing aliens described in subsection (c) of this section with social services of the types for which reimburse were made with respect to refugees under paragraphs (3) through (6) of section 2(b) of the Migration and Refugee Assistance

. . .

Source: Refugee Act of 1980. Public Law 96-212, March 17, 1980.

See also: Angel Island Opens in San Francisco Bay, 1910; Asian/Pacific American Heritage Week Established, 1978; Korean War, 1950–1953

Further Reading

Aguilar-San Juan, Karin. 2009. *Little Saigons: Staying Vietnamese in America*. Minneapolis: University of Minnesota Press.

Baldwin, Beth. 1984. *Patterns of Adjustment: A Second Look at Indochinese Resettlement in Orange County*. Orange, CA: Immigrant and Refugee Planning Center.

Espiritu, Yen Le. 1992. *Asian American Panethnicity: Bridging Identities and Institutions*. Philadelphia: Temple University Press.

Espiritu, Yen Le. 2014. *Body Counts: The Vietnam War and Militarized Refuge(es)*. Berkeley: University of California Press.

Kelly, Gail Paradise. 1977. *From Vietnam to America: A Chronicle of the Vietnamese Immigration to the United States*. Boulder, CO: Westview Press.

Kibria, Nazli. 1993. *Family Tightrope: The Changing Lives of Vietnamese Americans*. Princeton, NJ: Princeton University Press.

Liu, William Thomas, Mary Ann Lamanna, and Alice K. Murata. 1979. *Transition to Nowhere: Vietnamese Refugees in America*. Nashville: Charter House.

Nguyen, Mimi. 2012. *The Gift of Freedom: War, Debt, and Other Refugee Passages*. Durham, NC: Duke University Press.

Nguyen, Phuong Tran. 2017. *Becoming Refugee American: The Politics of Rescue in Little Saigon. Asian American Experience*. Urbana: University of Illinois Press.

Nguyen, Viet Thanh. 2002. *Race & Resistance Literature & Politics in Asian America*. New York: Oxford University Press.

Pelaud, Isabelle. 2011. *This Is All I Choose to Tell: History and Hybridity in Vietnamese American Literature*. Philadelphia: Temple University Press.

Pelaud, Isabelle, Lan Duong, Mariam B. Lam, and Kathy L. Nguyen. 2014. *Troubling Borders: An Anthology of Art and Literature by Southeast Asian Women in the Diaspora*. Seattle: University of Washington Press.

Pham, Vu Hong. 2002. "Beyond and before Boat People: Vietnamese American History before 1975." PhD diss., Cornell University.

Rumbaut, Ruben G. 2006 "Vietnamese, Laotian and Cambodian Americans." In *Asian Americans: Contemporary Trends and Issues*, edited by Pyong Gap Min, 232–270. Thousand Oaks, CA: Sage Publications.

Tang, Eric. 2015. *Unsettled: Cambodian Refugees in the New York City Hyperghetto*. Philadelphia: Temple University Press.

Trinh, T. Minh-Ha. 1989. *Woman, Native, Other: Writing Postcoloniality and Feminism*. Bloomington: Indiana University Press.

Võ, Linda Trinh. 2003. "Vietnamese American Trajectories: Dimensions of Diaspora." *Amerasia Journal* 29, no. 1: ix–xviii.

Võ, Linda Trinh. 2004. *Mobilizing an Asian American Community*. Philadelphia: Temple University Press.

Waligora-Davis, Nicole. 2011. *Sanctuary: African Americans and Empire*. New York: Oxford University Press.

Zhou, Min and Carl L. Bankston III. 1999. *Growing Up American: How Vietnamese Children Adapt to Life in the United States*. New York: Russell Sage Foundation.

The Immigration and Nationality Act, 1965

Philip Q. Yang

Chronology

Before 1882 The United States has an open immigration system.

1882 The Chinese Exclusion Act of 1882, signed by President Chester Arthur on May 6, begins a selective immigration system that excludes certain ethnic groups from immigration. The Chinese become the first ethnic group excluded from immigration in U.S. history.

1917 The Immigration Act of 1917 establishes the Asiatic Barred Zone, which bans most Asian laborers from immigration.

1921 The Emergency Quota Act of 1921 launches a new system of numerical restrictions to immigration. It sets the annual quota of immigration from any country at 3 percent of the foreign-born population from that country already residing in the United States, as determined by the U.S. Census of 1910.

1924 The National Origins Act of 1924 replaces the stopover Emergency Quota Act of 1921 and establishes the national-origins quota system. It reduces the annual quota of immigration from any country to 2 percent of the foreign-born population from that country already residing in the United States, as determined by the U.S. Census of 1890.

1952 The Immigration and Nationality Act of 1952, also known as the McCarran-Walter Act, lifts the ban on immigration from the "Asian-Pacific Triangle" (including most countries in East Asia, Southeast Asia, and the Indian subcontinent) and repeals naturalization exclusions against Asians but still retains most of the discriminatory features of the National Origins Act of 1924.

1964 Congress enacts the Civil Rights Act of 1964, which bans discrimination based on race, color, religion, sex, or national origins.

1965	The Immigration and Nationality Act of 1965, also known as the Hart-Celler Act, abolishes the national-origins quota system (in operation since 1924) that favored immigration from northwestern European countries while discriminating against immigration from other countries. President Lyndon Johnson signs it into law on October 3.
1968	The Immigration and Nationality Act of 1965 takes effect on July 1.
1970	The Asian American population totals 1.4 million.
1972	The number of legal Asian immigrants surpasses the number of legal European immigrants for the first time.
1983–1985	The number of legal Asian immigrants exceeds the number of legal Latino immigrants for three years in a row.
2016	The Asian American population reaches 21.4 million.

Narrative

The Immigration and Nationality Act of 1965, also known as the Hart-Celler Act, has had an enormous and far-reaching impact on Asian immigration and Asian Americans. Despite no dearth of description of this act, its significance pertinent to Asian Americans has yet to be adequately articulated and communicated. This essay seeks to fill in this gap by depicting the U.S. immigration system prior to this act, analyzing the context in which the act was enacted, highlighting the major provisions of the act, discussing the significance of the act, and examining the effects of the act on Asian Americans.

U.S. Immigration Systems Prior to the Act

Before 1882, the United States had an open immigration system, although restrictions and discrimination occurred at the state and local levels (Yang 1995). The Chinese Exclusion Act of 1882, signed by President Chester Arthur on May 6 of that year, began an immigration system that selectively excluded certain ethnic groups from immigration. The Chinese were the first ethnic group excluded from immigration in U.S. history (Yang 2011). This was followed by the exclusion of Japanese laborers as a result of the Gentlemen's Agreement of 1907–1908 and the exclusion of Asian Indian laborers and other Asian laborers by the Immigration Act of 1917.

However, a new system of numerical restrictions to immigration did not commence until 1921. This new U.S. immigration system, right before the Immigration and Nationality Act of 1965, is often referred to as the national-origins quota system. This system was launched by the temporary Emergency Quota Act of 1921 and made permanent by the Immigration Act of 1924, also known as the National Origins Act of 1924. The national-origins quota system set annual immigration quotas for each country based on the foreign population of each country already residing in the United States in 1890. Countries in western and northern Europe received large quotas. For example, for fiscal year 1924–1925, the annual immigration quotas for the United Kingdom, Germany, Ireland, and Sweden were 34,007, 51,227, 28,567, and 9,561, respectively. Countries in southern and eastern Europe got smaller quotas. For instance, during the same period, the quotas for Italy, Russia, and Poland were 3,845, 2,248, and 5,982,

President Lyndon B. Johnson spoke after signing the Immigration and Nationality Act of 1965 into law below the Statue of Liberty on October 3, 1965. This act abolished the national quota system, in place since 1924, that favored European immigrants and discriminated against immigrants from Asia. (Lyndon B. Johnson Library/Yoichi R. Okamoto)

respectively. Each African country received a quota of 100. Asian countries were allocated a quota of 100 apiece. Prior to the 1965 Act, the Immigration and Nationality Act of 1952, also known as the McCarran-Walter Act, rescinded the ban on immigration from the "Asian-Pacific Triangle" (including most countries in East Asia, Southeast Asia, and the Indian subcontinent) and naturalization exclusions against Asians, but this law still preserved most of the discriminatory features of the National Origins Act of 1924.

Passage of the Act

One factor pivotal to the enactment of the Immigration and Nationality Act of 1965 was the fact that the national-origins quota system proved to be flawed (Yang 1995). Between 1952 and 1965, only 61 percent of the system's quota visas were used, but tens of thousands of prospective immigrants waiting for immigration were unqualified because they fell into the "wrong" countries (Briggs 1984). Congress had to pass a series of temporary special legislation measures to bypass the existing immigration laws. Most immigrants admitted under this special legislation were refugees from western Europe and China or escapees from various communist countries of eastern Europe. They came as non-quota immigrants and comprised the bulk of immigration growth during this period. Approximately two-thirds of the immigrants did not come under the terms of the national-origins quota system.

Meanwhile, American society had undergone tremendous transformations by the 1960s. Attitudes of Americans toward ethnic minorities had become increasingly tolerant by the early 1960s. The civil rights movement had climaxed in the enactment of the landmark Civil Rights Act of 1964, which banned discrimination based on race, color, religion, sex, or national origins. Not only was discrimination against fellow citizens no longer acceptable, but discrimination against foreign immigrants to the United States was increasingly rejected by the American people. Additionally, continuing post–World War II prosperity had substantially reduced opposition to immigration. A combination of these conditions led to Americans' growing rejection of the discriminatory national-origins quota system that favored immigration from northwestern Europe and subsequently to the passage of the Immigration and Nationality Act of 1965. This act was signed into law by President Lyndon Johnson on October 3, 1965, at the foot of the Statue of Liberty (Yang 1995, 15).

Provisions of the Act

The Immigration and Nationality Act of 1965 abolished the national-origins quota system while trying to keep immigration at a manageable level. This act set an annual ceiling of 170,000 for the Eastern Hemisphere with a maximum of 20,000 quotas for each country, regardless of the population size of the sending country. It imposed for the first time an annual ceiling of 120,000 for the Western Hemisphere but with no numerical limit for each country. The combined total annual worldwide ceiling was set at 290,000, and applicants would be admitted on a first-come, first-served basis. To determine the eligibility of applicants from the Eastern Hemisphere, a seven-category preference system, including a category for refugees, was created (Table 1), but this system would not apply to the Western Hemisphere. Seventy-four percent of the visas were reserved for the family preference categories. Furthermore, in addition to these quota immigrants, non-quota immigrants (i.e., immediate relatives of U.S. citizens over twenty-one years old, including spouses,

Table 1. Immigration Preference System Created by the Immigration and Nationality Act of 1965, in Effect until 1980

Preference	Provision	Percentage of Total Visas
First	Unmarried adult sons and daughters of U.S. citizens	20%
Second	Spouses and unmarried sons and daughters of permanent resident aliens	20%[1]
Third	Members of the professions of exceptional ability in sciences or arts and their spouses and children	10%
Fourth	Married sons and daughters of U.S. citizens and their spouses and children	10%[1]
Fifth	Brothers and sisters of U.S. citizens aged twenty-one or older and their spouses and children	24%[1]
Sixth	Skilled or unskilled workers in occupations in which labor is in short supply and their spouses and children	10%
Seventh	Refugees	6%
Nonpreference	Other qualified applicants	Numbers unused in the earlier categories
Total		100%
Worldwide ceiling		290,000[2]
Per-country ceiling		20,000[3]

[1] Numbers not used in higher preferences may be used in these categories.
[2] Varied in years.
[3] Applicable to the Eastern Hemisphere since 1968 and to the Western Hemisphere since 1976.
Source: U.S. INS (1987, 126–28 and xv).

minor children, and parents) would not be counted as part of either the hemispheric or the per-country ceiling. As evidenced from the preference system and the stipulation for non-quota immigrants, family reunification became the cornerstone of U.S. immigration policy (Yang 1995). Only a small percentage of visas (6 percent or 17,400) was reserved for refugees from both hemispheres. This 1965 act was set to take effect on July 1, 1968.

Significance of the Act to Asian Americans

The Immigration and Nationality Act of 1965 is an epoch-making piece of legislation in the history of U.S. immigration. It underlies the current immigration system and is shaping the United States, present and future. Its impact on U.S. immigration, population growth, and racial and ethnic transformations is so wide-ranging and long-lasting that it goes far beyond the scope of this essay, which only addresses its significance to Asian Americans. It is no exaggeration to say that for Asian Americans, the importance of the 1965 act, especially in positive terms, will outshine that of any other U.S. immigration legislation. Three important aspects of the act relate directly to Asian Americans.

First, by repealing the national-origins quota system, the 1965 act provides an equal opportunity for Asians to immigrate to the United States. From 1882 to 1965, Asians experienced exclusions or severe restrictions in immigration to the United States. Recall that the annual immigration quota allocated for each Asian country stood at 100 as a result of the national-origins quota system. However, the 1965 act removed the restrictions to Asian immigration, as all Asian countries, regardless of population sizes, received an annual quota of 20,000 and could send non-quota immigrants in addition to the per-country quota. Asians were no longer discriminated against in their right to immigrate and began to enjoy the same numerical opportunities for immigration as people of other ethnicities or origins.

Second, the 1965 act is arguably the single most important factor contributing to the substantial increases in Asian immigration to the United States since 1965. Before the passage of the 1965 act, Asian immigration was a trickle compared to the influx from Europe, Latin America, and North America. In contrast, since 1965, Asian immigration numbers have surpassed those of European nations and are rivaled only by Latinos. Many factors have played a role in the massive growth of post-1965 Asian immigration, including large economic, political, and social disparities between many Asian countries and the United States; military, political, economic, and cultural connections between the United States and Asian countries; existing Asian immigrant social networks; and changes in emigration policies of some Asian countries (Yang 2011). However, it was the changes in U.S. immigration policy enacted by the 1965 act that made increasing Asian immigration possible (Yang 2011). Without it, the substantial growth of Asian immigration to the United States since 1965 simply would not have begun, even with the presence of other conditions.

Finally, the 1965 act set in motion "chain migration," a process through which U.S. citizens or permanent residents sponsor their immediate family members and extended family members (e.g., siblings and married adult children) for immigration. Those thus sponsored can then sponsor their own immediate and extended family members for immigration in a chain-like fashion conducive to the growth of Asian American communities. Before 1965, various Asian communities in the United States were typically small, included some so-called "bachelor's societies" due to serious imbalances in gender ratios, and tended to be dominated by people of farming or other working-class backgrounds. The immigration preference system instituted by the 1965 act not only favored family reunification but also provided opportunities for those with more diverse occupational skills. So chain migration has not only multiplied the sizes of Asian communities but has also led to more balanced gender ratios and more diverse and higher-class backgrounds in Asian communities.

All of these have paved the way for Asian Americans to grow into a major racial group and play a more important role in American society. Asian Americans are now widely recognized as one of the major racial categories in the United States and are expected to approach the proportion of African Americans (15 percent) at 13 percent by the end of this century, based on a Census Bureau projection (Yang 2006). Post-1965 Asian immigration spurred by the 1965 act has improved the quality of the U.S. labor force because post-1965 Asian immigrants tend to be college-educated and professional and managerial workers (Yang 2011). Post-1965 Asian immigration has also led to burgeoning Asian restaurants across the nation, popularized traditional Oriental medicines (e.g., acupuncture, herbology, Qigong, and yoga), contributed to the growth of science and technology, and strengthened American sport power in traditionally weak events (e.g., diving, ping pong, and badminton) due to an influx of Asian athletes (Yang 2011).

Impact of the Act on Asian Americans

The increase in Asian immigration since 1965 has been substantial. Except for immigrants from Middle East countries located in Asia (whom the United States does not qualify as Asian Americans), Asian immigration increased significantly right after the act was passed in 1965. In 1972, it surpassed the level of European immigration and later exceeded the level of immigration from Latin America in the early to mid-1980s. Since then, it has almost paralleled the level of Latino immigration except for the period of 1989–1991, when about three million undocumented Latino immigrants became legalized as a result of the Immigration Reform and Control Act of 1986.

Driven by these substantial increases in Asian immigration, the Asian American population has witnessed phenomenal growth since 1965. Available data indicate that the Asian American population has increased from 980,337 in 1960 to 1.4 million in

1970, 3.3 million in 1980, 6.9 million in 1990, 10.2 million (Asian alone) or 11.9 million (Asian alone or in combination with two or more races) in 2000, nearly 14.7 million (Asian alone) or 17.3 million (Asian alone or in combination) in 2010, and 21.4 million in July 2016 (Carter, Gartner, Haines, Olmstead, Sutch, and Wright 2006; Hoeffel, Rastogi, Kim, Shahid, and United States 2012; U.S. Bureau of the Census 2017; Yang 2011). If current demographic trends continue, the Asian American population is projected to reach 75 million by 2100 (Yang 2006).

Size is only one of the new demographic elements resulting from the 1965 act. More diverse Asian American communities are also springing up, including Chinese,

---

Surge in Asian Immigration Was an Unintended Consequence of the Immigration and Nationality Act of 1965

Surges in total immigration, Asian immigration, and Latino immigration since 1965 have been well documented and publicized. Less well known is that these surges were not the intended outcomes of the Immigration and Nationality Act of 1965. The lawmakers in 1965 truly believed that the act would not lead to a big increase in immigration or shifts of immigration sources to non-European countries (Reimers 1983). The original bill preferred immigrants with education and occupational skills. However, some of the key legislators, such as Chairman of the House Judiciary Subcommittee on Immigration Michael Feighan (D-OH) and subcommittee members Harold Donahue (D-MA), Jacob Gilbert (D-NY), and Peter Rodino (D-NJ) represented districts that were dominated by southern and eastern European immigrants. In the last minute, they won concession to prioritize admission of immigrants based on family reunifications. The notion was that through chain migration by family reunification, the bill would mainly benefit southern and eastern Europeans.

There were large immigration flows from southern and eastern Europe at the turn of the nineteenth to twentieth century, but southern and eastern European countries had received relatively small quotas under the national-origins quota system. In 1960, southern and eastern Europeans made up 40 percent of the migrant stock and were considered the main beneficiaries of the 1965 act. But demand for immigration from Europe declined because post–World War II prosperity reduced motivations to immigrate to the United States (Yang 1995). On the other hand, demand for immigration from Asia and Latin America soared, leading to substantial growth in Asian and Latino immigration since 1965.

Asian Indians, Filipinos, Vietnamese, Koreans, and Japanese, with at least a million people each. There are also growing Asian communities of Pakistanis, Bangladeshis, Thais, Cambodians, Laotians, Sri Lankans, Nepalese, and Indonesians in America. Because of the family reunification provisions, gender ratios have become more balanced since 1965 for many Asian communities (Yang 2011). The arrival of many educated, professional, middle-class immigrants since 1965 has transformed the class composition of many Asian American communities and positioned them well for future social mobility.

Biographies of Notable Figures

Lyndon Baines Johnson (1908–1973)

Lyndon B. Johnson (often referred to as "LBJ") was the thirty-sixth U.S. president who signed the milestone Immigration and Nationality Act of 1965 into law on October 3 of that year. LBJ was born on August 27, 1908, in a small central Texas farming community called Stonewall (near Johnson City) to Samuel Ealy Johnson, Jr. and Rebekah Baines Johnson. He was the oldest of their five children. His father was a farmer, businessman, and Texas state legislator who lost the family farm during LBJ's early teens because of financial difficulties.

LBJ graduated from Johnson City High School in 1924 and Southwest Texas State Teachers College (now Texas State University San Marcos) in 1930. After graduation, he taught predominantly Mexican American students in high school for a short period. In 1931 Johnson became the legislative secretary to Texas Democratic Congressman Richard M. Kleberg of Corpus Christi and moved to Washington, D.C. Being energetic, diligent, competent, and ambitious, LBJ was recognized as a young standout congressional aide.

LBJ attended the Georgetown University law school in Washington, D.C., in 1934. The same year, LBJ met twenty-one-year-old Claudia Alta Taylor, nicknamed "Lady Bird," and they were married three months later. Lady Bird soon became his top aide and ran his office for several years. In 1935, LBJ was appointed the Texas director of the National Youth Administration, a federal youth-employment program.

Funded by his wife's modest inheritance and her increasing wealth as the owner of a local radio station, LBJ was elected to the House of Representatives in Texas's Tenth Congressional District special election in 1937 at the age of twenty-eight, after Congressman James Buchanan of his home district died earlier that year, and he served in the House until 1949. In 1948, LBJ won a close and controversial primary election by a margin of just eighty-seven votes. He later won the general election and became a Texas senator (1949–1961).

In the Senate, LBJ ascended to power speedily. In two years, he was named the Democratic Senate minority whip. In 1953, because of the Republican victory in the Senate elections, his Democratic superiors were ousted, and LBJ became the youngest minority leader in Senate history. In 1954, as Democrats regained control of the Senate, LBJ was elected the Senate majority leader (1955–1961).

In 1960, LBJ sought the nomination of his party for the presidency. However, his chief rival, John F. Kennedy (JFK), a young and charismatic senator from Massachusetts, outcampaigned LBJ and won the nomination for presidency on the first ballot at the Democratic Convention. Recognizing that he could not win the presidency without the support of traditional Southern Protestant Democrats, most of whom had backed LBJ, JFK tapped the Texas senator as his running mate. The JFK/LBJ ticket won the general election against a skilled and compelling Republican candidate, Vice President Richard Nixon, by a slim margin. LBJ became the vice president of the United States in 1961.

In his role as vice president, LBJ was charged with the space program, negotiations on the nuclear test ban treaty, and equal opportunity legislation for minorities. He also played a key role in military policy. Nevertheless, LBJ overall felt frustrated because he was not in JFK's inner circle and lacked influence, especially on legislative issues.

In a trip to Texas to boost support for his reelection bid, JFK was assassinated in a traveling motorcade in Dallas on November 22, 1963. LBJ was only two cars behind JFK when the bullets hit the president. Just a few hours later, LBJ took the oath of office aboard Air Force One before its return to Washington, D.C.

A major legislative accomplishment after LBJ assumed the presidency was the passage of the landmark Civil Rights Act of 1964, signed by LBJ on July 2. The enactment of a civil rights bill had been part of JFK's platform during his election campaign. As vice president, LBJ was charged by JFK to chair the Committee on Equal Employment Opportunities. After JFK's death, LBJ carried on the torch to bring the bill to fruition.

In 1964, LBJ defeated Republican Senator Barry Goldwater of Arizona to become the U.S. president for the next four years. He won in a landslide with 61 percent of the popular vote, the largest margin of victory in U.S. presidential election history to date. Using his election mandate, LBJ pushed his "Great Society" agenda in the United States and waged war on communism in Southeast Asia.

LBJ's ambitious, wide-ranging Great Society legislative agenda got underway in January 1965. Great Society programs included the war against poverty, attack on disease, Medicare, urban renewal, beautification, environmental conservation, development of depressed regions, aid to education, crime and delinquency control and prevention, and guarantees for voting rights. With strong bipartisan support, Congress passed scores of bills, including but not limited to the Medicare

Act of 1965, the Medicaid Act of 1965, the Water Quality Act of 1965, the Motor Vehicle Air Pollution Control Act of 1965, the Voting Rights Act of 1965, and the Elementary and Secondary Education Act of 1965. The Immigration and Nationality Act of 1965 was also one of the laws passed that year. In later years of the Johnson presidency, Congress also passed the Child Protection Act of 1966, the Fair Housing Act of 1968, the Wild and Scenic Rivers Act of 1968, the Omnibus Crime Control and Safe Streets Act of 1968, the Juvenile Delinquency Prevention and Control Act of 1968, and the Gun Control Act of 1968, among others.

LBJ's legislative success was tarnished by his administration's handling of the Vietnam War. As U.S. casualties continued to rise, antiwar protests erupted across college campuses and major cities. By 1968, over half a million U.S. troops had been sent to Vietnam. The war showed no sign of ending. As the next election approached, there were deep divisions of four factions among Democrats, threatening LBJ's control over the party. His approval rating dropped to 36 percent. Ultimately, on March 31, 1968, LBJ announced that he would neither seek nor accept his party's renomination for the presidency.

After the end of his presidency in January 1969, LBJ retired to his ranch in Texas to work on his presidential library and to write his memoirs. In January 1973, LBJ died of a heart attack at the age of sixty-five. He was survived by his wife, Lady Bird Johnson, and his two daughters, Lynda Bird Johnson Robb and Luci Baines Johnson Turpin.

DOCUMENT EXCERPTS

Immigration and Nationality Act

Signed into law on October 3 by President Lyndon Johnson, the Immigration and Nationality Act of 1965, also known as the Hart-Celler Act, is a landmark piece of legislation in U.S. immigration history. The act abolishes the national-origins quota system established in 1924. The 1965 act has had far-reaching and long-lasting impact on Asian Americans. Since 1965 Asian immigration has increased substantially, the Asian American population in this country has grown, and Asian American communities have become more diverse.

Public Law 89-236 [*Excerpts*]
An ACT

To amend the Immigration and Nationality Act, and for other purposes.
Be it enacted by the Senate and House of Representatives of the United States of America in Congress assembled, That section 201 of immigration and the

Immigration and Nationality Act (66 Stat. 176; 8 U.S.C. 1151) be amended to read as follows:

"SEC. 201. (a) Exclusive of special immigrants defined in section 101(a) (27), and of the immediate relatives of United States citizens specified in subsection (b) of this section, the number of aliens who may be issued immigrant visas or who may otherwise acquire the status of an alien lawfully admitted to the United States for permanent residence, or who may, pursuant to section 203(a) (7) enter conditionally, (i) shall not in any of the first three quarters of any fiscal year exceed a total of 45,000 and (ii) shall not in any fiscal year exceed a total of 170,000.

(b) The 'immediate relatives' referred to in subsection (a) of this section shall mean the children, spouses, and parents of a citizen of the United States: Provided, That in the case of parents, such citizen must be at least twenty-one years of age. The immediate relatives specified in this subsection who are otherwise qualified for admission as immigrants shall be admitted as such, without regard to the numerical limitations in this Act.

(c) During the period from July 1, 1965, through June 30, 1968, the annual quota of any quota area shall be the same as that which existed for that area on June 30, 1965. The Secretary of State shall, not later than on the sixtieth day immediately following the date of enactment of this subsection and again on or before September 1, 1966, and September 1, 1967, determine and proclaim the amount of quota numbers which remain unused at the end of the fiscal year ending on June 30, 1965, June 30, 1966, and June 30, 1967, respectively, and are available for distribution pursuant to subsection (d) of this section.

(d) Quota numbers not issued or otherwise used during the previous fiscal year, as determined in accordance with subsection (c) hereof, shall be transferred to an immigration pool. Allocation of numbers from the pool and from national quotas shall not together exceed in any fiscal year the numerical limitations in subsection (a) of this section. The immigration pool shall be made available to immigrants otherwise admissible under the provisions of this Act who are unable to obtain prompt issuance of a preference visa due to oversubscription of their quotas, or subquotas as determined by the Secretary of State. Visas and conditional entries shall be allocated from the immigration pool within the percentage limitations and in the order of priority specified in section 203 without regard to the quota to which the alien is chargeable.

(e) The immigration pool and the quotas of quota areas shall terminate June 30, 1968. Thereafter immigrants admissible under the provisions of this Act who are subject to the numerical limitations of subsection (a) of this section shall be admitted in accordance with the percentage limitations and in the order of priority specified in section 203."

Sec. 2. Section 202 of the Immigration and Nationality Act (66 Foreign states. Stat. 175; 8 U.S.C. 1152) is amended to read as follows:

(a) No person shall receive any preference or priority or be discriminated against in the issuance of an immigrant visa because of his race, sex, nationality, place of birth, or place of residence, except as specifically provided in section 101(a) (27), section 201(b), and section 203: Provided, That the total number of immigrant visas and the number of conditional entries made available to natives of any single foreign state under paragraphs (1) through (8) of section 203(a) shall not exceed 20,000 in any fiscal year: Provided further, That the foregoing proviso shall not operate to reduce the number of immigrants who may be admitted under the quota of any quota area before June 30, 1968.

(b) Each independent country, self-governing dominion, mandated territory, and territory under the international trusteeship system of the United Nations, other than the United States and its outlying possessions shall be treated as a separate foreign state for the purposes of the numerical limitation set forth in the proviso to sub section (a) of this section when approved by the Secretary of State. All other inhabited lands shall be attributed to a foreign state specified by the Secretary of State. For the purposes of this Act the foreign state to which an immigrant is chargeable shall be determined by birth within such foreign state except that (1) an alien child, when accompanied by his alien parent or parents, may be charged to the same foreign state as the accompanying parent or of either accompanying parent if such parent has received or would be qualified for an immigrant visa, if necessary to prevent the separation of the child from the accompanying parent or parents, and if the foreign state to which such parent has been or would be chargeable has not exceeded the numerical limitation set forth in the proviso to subsection (a) of this section for that fiscal year; (2) if an alien is chargeable to a different foreign state from that of his accompanying spouse, the foreign state to which such alien is chargeable may, if necessary to prevent the separation of husband and wife, be determined by the foreign state of the accompanying spouse, if such spouse has received or would be qualified for an immigrant visa and if the foreign state to which such spouse has been or would be chargeable has not exceeded the numerical limitation set forth in the proviso to subsection (a) of this section for that fiscal year; (3) an alien born in the United States shall be considered as having been born in the country of which he is a citizen or subject, or if he is not a citizen or subject of any country then in the last foreign country in which he had his residence as determined by the consular officer; (4) an alien born within any foreign state in which neither of his parents was born and in which neither of his parents had a residence at the time of such alien's birth may be charged to the foreign state of either parent.

(c) Any immigrant born in a colony or other component or dependent area of a foreign state unless a special immigrant as provided in section 101(a) (27) or an immediate relative of a United States citizen as specified in section 201(b), shall be chargeable, for the purpose of limitation set forth in section 202(a), to the foreign state, except that the number of persons born in any such colony or other component or dependent area overseas from the foreign state chargeable to the foreign state in any one fiscal year shall not exceed 1 per centum of the maximum number of immigrant visas available to such foreign state,

(d) In the case of any change in the territorial limits of foreign states, the Secretary of State shall, upon recognition of such change, issue appropriate instructions to all diplomatic and consular offices."

SEC. 3. Section 203 of the Immigration and Nationality Act (66 Stat. 175; 8 U.S.C. 1153) is amended to read as follows:

"SEC. 203. (a) Aliens who are subject to the numerical limitations specified in section 201(a) shall be allotted visas or their conditional entry authorized, as the case may be, as follows:

1) Visas shall be first made available, in a number not to exceed 20 per centum of the number specified in section 201(a) (ii), to qualified immigrants who are the unmarried sons or daughters of citizens of the United States.

(2) Visas shall next be made available, in a number not to exceed 20 per centum of the number specified in section 201(a) (ii), plus any visas not required for the classes specified in paragraph (1), to qualified immigrants who are the spouses, unmarried sons or unmarried daughters of an alien lawfully admitted for permanent residence.

(3) Visas shall next be made available, in a number not to exceed 10 per centum of the number specified in section 201(a) (ii), to qualified immigrants who are members of the professions, or who because of their exceptional ability in the sciences or the arts will substantially benefit prospectively the national economy, cultural interests, or welfare of the United States.

(4) Visas shall next be made available, in a number not to exceed 10 per centum of the number specified in section 201(a) (ii), plus any visas not required for the classes specified in paragraphs (1) through (3), to qualified immigrants who are the married sons or the married daughters of citizens of the United States.

(5) Visas shall next be made available, in a number not to exceed 24 per centum of the number specified in section 201(a) (ii), plus any visas not required for the classes specified in paragraphs (1) through (4), to qualified immigrants who are the brothers or sisters of citizens of the United States.

(6) Visas shall next be made available, in a number not to exceed 10 per centum of the number specified in section 201(a) (ii), to qualified immigrants who are capable

of performing specified skilled or unskilled labor, not of a temporary or seasonal nature, for which a shortage of employable and willing persons exists in the United States.

(7) Conditional entries shall next be made available by the Attorney General, pursuant to such regulations as he may prescribe and in a number not to exceed 6 per centum of the number specified in section 201(a) (ii), to aliens who satisfy an Immigration and Naturalization Service officer at an examination in any non-Communist or non-Communist-dominated country, (A) that (i) because of persecution or fear of persecution on account of race, religion, or political opinion they have fled (I) from any Communist or Communist-dominated country or area, or (II) from any country within the general area of the Middle East, and (ii) are unable or unwilling to return to such country or area on account of race, religion, or political opinion, and (iii) are not nationals of the countries or areas in which their application for conditional entry is made; or (B) that they are persons uprooted by catastrophic natural calamity as defined by the President who are unable to return to their usual place of abode. For the purpose of the foregoing the term 'general area of the Middle East' means the area between and including (1) Libya on the west, (2) Turkey on the north, (3) Pakistan on the east, and (4) Saudi Arabia and Ethiopia on the south: Provided, That immigrant visas in a number not exceeding one-half the number specified in this paragraph may be made available, in lieu of conditional entries of a like number, to such aliens who have been continuously physically present in the United States for a period of at least two years prior to application for adjustment of status.

(8) Visas authorized in any fiscal year, less those required for issuance to the classes specified in paragraphs (1) thorough (6) and less the number of conditional entries and visas made available pursuant to paragraph (7), shall be made available to other qualified immigrants strictly in the chronological order in which they qualify. Waiting lists of applicants shall be maintained in accordance with regulations prescribed by the Secretary of State. No immigrant visa shall be entries. 914 PUBLIC LAW 89-236-OCT. 3, 1965 [79 STAT. issued to a nonpreference immigrant under this paragraph, or to an immigrant with a preference under paragraph (3) or (6) of this subsection, until the consular officer is in receipt of a determination made by the Secretary of Labor pursuant to the provisions of section 212(a) (14).

(9) A spouse or child as defined in section 101(b) (1) (A) (B), shall, if not otherwise entitled to an immigrant under paragraphs (1) through (8), be entitled to the same status, and the same order of consideration provided in subsection (b), if accompanying, or following to join, his spouse or parent.

(b) In considering applications for immigrant visas under subsection (a) consideration shall be given to applicants in the order in which the classes of which they are members are listed in subsection

(c) Immigrant visas issued pursuant to paragraphs (1) through (6) of subsection (a) shall be issued to eligible immigrants in the order in which a petition in behalf of each such immigrant is filed with the Attorney General as provided in section 204.

(d) Every immigrant shall be presumed to be a nonpreference immigrant until he establishes to the satisfaction of the consular officer and the immigration officer that he is entitled to a preference status under paragraphs (1) through (7) of sub-section (a), or to a special immigrant status under section 101 (a) (27), or that he is an immediate relative of a United States citizen as specified in section 201(b). In the case of any alien claiming in his application for an immigrant visa to be an imme-diate relative of a United States citizen as specified in section 201(b) or to be entitled to preference immigrant status under paragraphs (1) through (6) of subsec-tion (a), the consular officer shall not grant such status until he has been authorized to do so as provided by section 204.

(e) For the purposes of carrying out his responsibilities in the orderly administra-tion of this section, the Secretary of State is authorized to make reasonable esti-mates of the anticipated numbers of visas to be issued during any quarter of any fiscal year within each of the categories of subsection (a), and to rely upon such estimates in authorizing the issuance of such visas. The Secretary of State, in his discretion, may terminate the registration on a waiting list of any alien who fails to evidence his continued intention to apply for a visa in such manner as may be by regulation prescribed.

(f) The Attorney General shall submit to the Congress a report containing com-plete and detailed statement of facts in the case of each alien who conditionally entered the United States pursuant to subsection (a) (7) of this section. Such reports shall be submitted on or before January 15 and June 15 of each year.

(g) Any alien who conditionally entered the United States as a refugee, pursuant to subsection (a) (7) of this section, whose conditional entry has not been terminated by the Attorney General pursuant to such regulations as he may prescribe, who has been in the United States for at least two years, and who has not acquired perma-nent residence, shall forthwith return or be returned to the custody of the Immigra-tion and Naturalization Service and shall thereupon be inspected and examined for admission into the United States, and his case dealt with in accordance with the provisions of sections 235, 236, 8 use 1225- and 237 of this Act.

(h) Any alien who, pursuant to subsection (g) of this section, is found, upon inspec-tion by the immigration officer or after hearing before a special inquiry officer, to be admissible as an immigrant under this Act at the time of his inspection and exam-ination, except for the fact that he was not and is not in possession of the docu-ments required by section 212(a) (20), shall be regarded as lawfully admitted to the United States for permanent residence as of the date of his arrival.

. . .

Approved October 3, 1965, 3:25 p.m.

Source: Immigration and Nationality Act. Public Law 89-236, October 3, 1965.

See also: The First Sikh Gurdwara in the United States Established in Stockton, California, 1912; The Luce-Celler Act, 1946; *United States v. Bhagat Singh Thind*, 1923; *United States v. Wong Kim Ark*, 1898

Further Reading

Biographical Directory of the U.S. Congress. 2017. "Johnson, Lyndon Baines, (1908–1973)." http://bioguide.congress.gov/scripts/biodisplay.pl?index=j000160

Briggs, Vernon, Jr. 1984. *Immigration Policy and the American Labor Force*. Baltimore: Johns Hopkins University Press.

Califano, Joseph A., Jr. 2008. "Seeing Is Believing—The Enduring Legacy of Lyndon Johnson." Keynote address, Centennial Celebration for President Lyndon Baines Johnson, Washington, D.C., May 19. http://www.lbjlibrary.org/lyndon-baines-johnson/perspectives-and-essays/seeing-is-believing-the-enduring-legacy-of-lyndon-johnson

Carter, Susan, Scott Gartner, Michael Haines, Alan Olmstead, Richard Sutch, and Gavin Wright. 2006. *Historical Statistics of the United States: Earliest Times to the Present*. Vol. 1. New York: Cambridge University Press.

Congressional Record. 1965. "Congressional Record-House." August 25. Washington, D.C.: Government Publishing Office. https://www.gpo.gov/fdsys/pkg/GPO-CRECB-1965-pt16/pdf/GPO-CRECB-1965-pt16-5.pdf

Hoeffel, Elizabeth M., Sonya Rastogi, Myoung Ouk Kim, Hasan Shahid, and United States. 2012. *The Asian Population: 2010*. 2010 Census Briefs, C2010br-11. Washington, D.C.: U.S. Department of Commerce, Economics and Statistics Administration, U.S. Census Bureau.

Johnson, Lyndon B. 1965. "Remarks at the Signing of the Immigration Bill." Speech, Liberty Island, New York, October 3. http://www.lbjlibrary.org/lyndon-baines-johnson/timeline/lbj-on-immigration

Reimers, David M. 1983. "An Unintended Reform: The 1965 Immigration Act and Third World Immigration to the United States." *Journal of American Ethnic History* 3, no. 1: 9–28.

U.S. Census Bureau. 2017. "The Nation's Older Population Is Still Growing, Census Bureau Reports." https://census.gov/newsroom/press-releases/2017/cb17-100.html

Yang, Philip Q. 1995. *Post-1965 Immigration to the United States: Structural Determinants*. Westport, CT: Praeger.

Yang, Philip Q. 2006. "Future Prospects of Asian Americans." In *Contemporary Trends and Issues*. 2nd ed., edited by Pyong Gap Min, 292–316. Thousand Oaks, CA: Pine Forge Press.

Yang, Philip Q. 2011. *Asian Immigration to the United States*. Cambridge, UK: Polity Press.

The First Asian American Studies Program Established at San Francisco State College, 1969

Rosie Kar

Chronology

June 12, 1963   Civil rights activist and NAACP member Medgar Evers is assassinated by white supremacist Byron de La Beckwith in Jackson, Mississippi.

September 15, 1963   The 16th Street Baptist Church bombing occurs in Birmingham, Alabama. Four black girls—Addie Mae Collins, Cynthia Wesley, Carole Robertson, and Carol Denise McNair—are murdered in the attack by white supremacist terrorists.

November 22, 1963   President John F. Kennedy is assassinated by Lee Harvey Oswald in Dallas, Texas.

February 21, 1965   Malcom X is assassinated in Manhattan, New York.

March 1966   San Francisco State College's (SFSC) Negro Students Association is renamed the Black Student Union (BSU).

September 1966   Dr. John Summerskill is hired as the seventh president of SFSC. As a liberal-minded, young, white administrator, he is reputed to be in good standing and friendly with students, staff, and faculty.

October 15, 1966   Bobby Seale and Huey Newton found the Black Panther Party in Oakland, California.

May 2, 1967   Sixty students stage a sit-in at Summerskill's office in protest of SFSC's practice of providing students' academic records and standing to the selective service office, funneling them into the U.S. armed services.

June 22, 1967   Faculty and students protest SFSC's administrative offices following Chancellor Glenn S. Dumke's campus proclamation to continue providing academic standing records to the selective service office as a means of recruiting members to the U.S. armed services.

June 22, 1967   The Carnegie Corporation in New York secretly invites SFSC to apply for funds to develop programs for teaching black history, art, and culture on campus. This confidential information is revealed during a discussion of BSU activities on campus in spring 1967.

November 6, 1967   James Vaszko, white undergraduate editor of SFSC's campus newspaper *The Gater,* publishes an op-ed revealing that he had written to the Carnegie Corporation demanding they stop any plans they had to grant money to the campus' service programs, which included BSU-sponsored programs. Vaszko is confronted by students of color.

November 11, 1967   Six black students who confronted Vaszko are arrested and booked on felony charges.

November 17, 1967   BSU members hold a press conference to discuss their educational programs, which center on black community interests, awareness, and consciousness.

November 18, 1967   SFSC's Board of Appeals and Review holds a closed hearing on the suspension of students jailed for assaulting Vaszko. Protestors who sympathize with the students gather outside.

November 29, 1967   Summerskill appoints ten faculty members to an investigatory committee to report on causes of campus tension that resulted in the Vaszko attack.

December 2, 1967   The campus literary paper, *Open Process,* comes under administrative attack for publishing work deemed "offensive" and "sexually suggestive." Two undergraduate writers are suspended, and 450 students protest Summerskill's performative allyship and the Vietnam War.

December 6, 1967   Students protest the punishment of the black students involved in the Vaszko incident and break into the administration building. Summerskill opts to shut the campus down rather than summon the police.

December 10, 1967   Chairman of the Academic Senate Dr. Walcott Beatty says that campus demonstrations and disturbances will not end, due to concerns including the Vietnam conflict and racial tensions.

February 22, 1968   Summerskill submits his resignation, effective in September, even though the trustees of the California State College system support his leadership.

February 29, 1968   Sociology professor Dr. Juan Martinez invites 300 high school and junior college students of color to come to SFSC to ask for waivers of admission requirements for the fall semester. Dean of Admissions Dr. Charles Stone claims that he does not have power to grant waivers.

March 8, 1968   Black Panther Party Minister of Defense Bobby Seale speaks at SFSC and tells the mostly white audience that the only power blacks have is with a gun.

March 23, 1968   The Third World Liberation Front (TWLF; composed of the BSU, La Raza, the Intercollegiate Chinese for Social Action [ICSA], the Philippine American Collegiate Endeavor [PACE], the Student Kouncil of Intertribal Nations [SKINS], and the Asian American Political Alliance [AAPA]) occupies the YMCA office on campus.

March 26, 1968   Several white SFSC student leaders demand that California State Superintendent of Schools Max Rafferty protest campus activities of the BSU and the hiring by the student government of controversial black playwright and visiting professor LeRoi Jones.

March 31, 1968   Summerskill demands the TWLF leave the occupied YMCA offices. Martinez has not been rehired for the following year, enraging students and faculty alike.

April 4, 1968   Dr. Martin Luther King, Jr. is assassinated by white supremacist James Earl Ray in Memphis, Tennessee.

May 21, 1968   Police are summoned to remove students from the SFSC administration building after a nine-hour sit-in. Twenty-six people are arrested. Approximately 400 students participate in the protest, demanding an end to Air Force ROTC on campus, which was predominantly recruiting men of color; the rehiring and retention of sociology professor Martinez; the establishment of programs to admit 400 students from socioeconomically disadvantaged cities in the fall semester; and the hiring of nine faculty members of color to advise vulnerable student populations.

May 23, 1968   Students protest for campus reform. Demonstrations are led by Students for a Democratic Society (SDS) and the TWLF.

May 24, 1968   Dumke requests that Summerskill resign immediately, instead of waiting until September.

June 1, 1968	Professor of Education Dr. Robert Smith becomes president of SFSC.
June 6, 1968	New York Senator Robert F. Kennedy is assassinated by Sirhan Sirhan in Los Angeles, California.
September 10, 1968	SFSC English graduate student and Black Panther Minister of Education George Mason Murray is rehired as a teaching assistant. His role is to teach English classes for 400 newly admitted students of color.
September 18, 1968	Smith announces the creation of a Black Studies Department. Dr. Nathan Hare is named acting chair.
September 26, 1968	California State College trustees vote to ask Smith to reassign Murray to a nonteaching position. Smith refuses the trustees' demands.
October 9, 1968	Black Panther Party member Eldridge Cleaver addresses SFSC students.
October 31, 1968	Dumke demands that Smith suspend Murray after Smith refuses to carry out the trustees' request. Smith delays. The BSU and TWLF threaten a strike on November 6 and present fifteen demands.
November 1, 1968	Smith suspends Murray for allegedly advocating students of color to arm themselves to protect against the campus's racist administration.
November 6, 1968	Students strike, led by BSU and TWLF members, as a protest for creating ethnic studies departments and for Murray's reinstatement. Most students attend classes. Police are summoned to campus after students march on the administration building.
November 13, 1968	Campus closes after a week of violent confrontations between students and police. During the week, striking students cause widespread but minor damage all over the campus. Some faculty members consider striking.
November 14, 1968	At a faculty meeting in the SFSC auditorium, English professor Dr. Samuel Ichiyé Hayakawa urges the faculty to lend their support for Smith. Smith appeals to Dumke in an attempt to reinstate Murray. The academic senate debates the issues and demands Dumke's resignation.

November 15, 1968   SFSC faculty and administration meet again to discuss campus tensions. Smith asks them to conceive plans for how the campus may reopen.

November 18, 1968   California Governor Ronald Reagan and the trustees demand that Smith reopen the campus immediately. Smith wants the students to return for discussion, not formal classes. A faculty grievance committee agrees that Murray was suspended without due process.

November 19, 1968   Campus administration and faculty do not want to reopen the campus but desire a convocation to discuss the issues.

November 20, 1968   Approximately 10 percent of the students return to campus for departmental discussions. Convocation commences, and only a few classes are held.

November 26, 1968   Convocation continues. BSU leaders confront the faculty panel and Smith. BSU leader Jerry Varnardo calls Smith a pig and is chastised by the audience. Smith resigns. Reagan appoints Hayakawa acting president. Hayakawa's first official act is to shut the campus down.

December 2–3, 1968   SFSC campus reopens. Protesting students park a truck fitted with microphones and speakers on 19th and Holloway Avenue to urge other students to continue the strike. Hayakawa climbs on the truck, destroys microphones, and disconnects the speakers, and the crowd pulls his cap off his head. "Bloody Tuesday" ensues, with SFSC seeing some of the most violent attacks committed against protestors by police.

December 10, 1968   University of Michigan faculty member and labor arbitrator Dr. Ronald Haughton is hired to mediate the strike. San Francisco Mayor Joseph Alioto organizes a citizens' committee to help settle the strike.

December 11, 1968   The campus chapter of the American Federation of Teachers (AFT) seeks a strike sanction from the San Francisco Labor Council. Over fifty AFT members organize a picket line around the campus, urging the trustees to negotiate with the students.

December 13, 1968   Campus is closed for winter holidays one week early; administrative offices remain open.

December 15, 1968   Trustees meet with AFT representatives to hear their grievances. Alioto's citizens' committee attempts mediation.

January 4, 1969	Hayakawa declares a state of emergency and bans all meetings and gatherings on the campus and hints at possible acquiescence to BSU and TWLF demands if the campus remains quiet. He proclaims that no unauthorized persons will be allowed to set foot on the premises and orders that protests be limited to the external perimeters of the campus until April 11, 1969.
January 6, 1969	Campus reopens. The San Francisco State chapter of the AFT strikes, forming a picket line around the campus, with nearly 400 teachers involved. They demand the removal of police from campus, a collective bargaining agreement for California State college educators, acquiescence to student demands, and far-reaching educational reform.
January 8, 1969	San Francisco Superior Court Judge Edward O' Day orders the AFT teachers to halt the strike, but it persists.
January 19–20, 1969	Striking students, including some student library workers, start a "book-in" at the library, removing books from shelves, bringing them to the circulation desk, and leaving them there to slow down library operations.
February 3, 1969	In Washington, D.C., Hayakawa testifies to campus violence before the House of Representatives at a meeting for the Subcommittee of the House Education Committee.
February 4, 1969	San Francisco Superior Court Judge Henry Rolph orders the San Francisco State AFT local to halt their strike, but it continues.
February 24, 1969	The San Francisco State AFT declares a possible strike settlement.
February 29, 1969	Murray and Hare are not rehired for the following year, so the strike continues.
March 5, 1969	SFSC freshman Tim Peebles detonates a bomb in the creative arts building. It explodes prematurely, and his eyes, hands, and face are injured. He and junior William Pulliam are arrested.
March 20, 1969	The strike ends. An agreement is reached between TWLF, BSU, and campus administration concerning the fifteen demands of the students. The College of Ethnic Studies is established, with classes to commence in fall 1969. The Department of Black Studies, Department of Asian American Studies, Department of American Indian Studies, and Department of Latino/a Studies are the first of their kind on college campus. Hayakawa claims the campus "state of emergency" is still in effect until March 27, 1969.

Narrative

The Department of Asian American Studies at San Francisco State University was established in 1969. It was the first of its kind in the United States. During the late 1960s, political and social upheaval resulted in massive educational reforms across the United States and the world. Major strikes led by student organizers took place in California and elsewhere in the United States. The initial strike catalyzing momentum occurred at San Francisco State College (SFSC), known since 1974 as San Francisco State University (SFSU). The duration of the strike was November 6, 1968–March 20, 1969.

These efforts sought to address institutional racism and inequality and restructure educational opportunities for students of color. Violent clashes between the student strikers and police resulted in national news, highlighting the realities of police brutality committed against students and people of color. SFSC students, Bay Area community organizers, teachers, activists, and faculty demanded equal access for working-class students and people of color to public institutions of higher education. They wanted increased hiring of faculty of color and inclusive new curricula centering the perspectives of those historically marginalized communities. This

Teachers demonstrated in support of the student strike at San Francisco State College (now San Francisco State University),1968, while the San Francisco Police Department's tactical squad stood by. As a result of the strike, the country's first College of Ethnic Studies was established. (Garth Eliassen/Getty Images)

led to the creation of the College of Ethnic Studies, home to the Department of Black Studies, Department of American Indian Studies, Department of Latino/a Studies, and the Department of Asian American Studies at SFSC in 1969. Other institutions across the nation followed suit, establishing departments of Asian American studies. The Association of Asian American Studies was founded in 1979, rooted in interdisciplinarity and providing space for scholars of the field to connect through pedagogy, research, activism, and mentorship.

The SFSC strike holds significance for several reasons. It is seen as the higher education counterpart to the *Westminster School District v. Mendez* decision of 1947 and the *Brown v. Board of Education* decision of 1954 desegregating schools in the United States. The desires were for nonhierarchical, non-Eurocentric, community-specific models of public education. The collaborative efforts resulted in new fields of academic study, centering the long-silenced and long-erased histories of people of color. The result was the establishment of the nation's first ethnic studies programs, which served as models for other educational institutions, universities, and high schools. They were also examples of solidarity, moments where people of color, across racial and ethnic backgrounds, stood in allyship with each other, conscious of their shared connections as vulnerable and oppressed people. This was also significant in connecting the local with the global; student movements were happening across the world, taking place in historically colonized lands, including the global South.

SFSC's strikes were led by the Black Student Union (BSU) and the Third World Liberation Front (TWLF). The work of the TWLF is historically significant. Under the slogan of self-determination, African American, Asian American, Native American, Chicano/a, and Latino/a students called for departments of ethnic studies and open admissions to all applicants of color. SFSC students were conscious of their social locations and geographical position in the echelon of higher education, as the campus was historically populated by commuters, working-class people from urban areas, and people of color. TWLF's labor has been rendered invisible by the hegemonic narratives of the second wave of the women's movement and free speech and antiwar movements. According to William Wei, most histories of the strike "make only passing reference" to Asian American political involvement with TWLF, but those involved with the strike were militant and committed to solidarity in action (Wei 1993, 19).

Asian American participation in the strikes has also been invisible, despite Asian American communities' long and sustained tradition of political engagement, but the 1960s were when these efforts were rendered publicly visible. The strike and a "non-negotiable" list of demands from the BSU and TWLF resulted in major victories for public education. SFSC established the nation's first School of Ethnic Studies, carving a pathway for other institutions to follow. They were able to secure twenty-two faculty positions and create the Department of Black Studies, Department of Asian American Studies, Department of Latino/a Studies, and Department of American Indian Studies, grounded in the College of Ethnic Studies. The university also promised a commitment to increase percentages of admission slots to vulnerable and marginalized communities, and increased student input and participation in campus governance. Attention to social justice and commitments to addressing inequality remain, catalyzing new fields of study. Despite persistent, almost annual, attempts by critics to undermine the importance of ethnic studies, these fields thrive at academic institutions across the United States.

Currently, San Francisco State University's Department of Asian American Studies is the largest in the nation, employing nearly fifty faculty members, including tenure/tenure track, lecturers, adjuncts, and emerita. It offers many courses to undergraduates and graduate students. It is currently authorized to grant minors, BA, and MA degrees. Course offerings include freshmen surveys, introductions to critical thinking centering on Asian Americanness, history, media studies, composition, literature, music, community arts, photography, environmental justice, gender and sexuality studies, postcolonial theory, public health, social justice, community education, adoption, mixed-race people, and foci on diasporic specificities, including Chinese Americans, Japanese Americans, Korean Americans, Filipino/a Americans, Vietnamese Americans, Cambodian Americans, South Asian Americans, and Asian Americans in California. The department is committed to community service, teaching, and research, with interdisciplinarity at its core.

On Strike

November 6, 1968, is when SFSC students began one of the most significant strikes in U.S. history, over the duration of five months. Mainstream news coverage of the event reported on it as violent, painting students as militant and unruly. This reporting was tinged with racist overtones of white supremacist capitalist patriarchy. During its most turbulent moments, nearly 85 percent of classes were cancelled. Bay Area community members, some faculty, and many undergraduate and graduate students were angry about rapidly declining enrollment numbers for students of color. One attempt at establishing a Black Studies Department at SFSC had been disrupted by administrators.

Couched in racist and sexist terminology, U.S. President Richard Nixon's and California Governor Ronald Reagan's political rhetoric targeted liberal thinkers and students, people of color, and women. Tensions had been brewing for several years prior to the strike. The world saw youth uprisings questioning war and capitalism and pushes for decolonization profoundly affecting those in the United States. Agitations for civil rights; protests against capital punishment and the prison industrial complex; the work of the Freedom Riders; lunch counter sit-ins; the work of Students for a Democratic Society (SDS; the assassinations of Medgar Evers, John F. Kennedy, Malcolm X, Robert F. Kennedy, Martin Luther King Jr.; the murders of four black girls at an Alabama church; the murders of members of the Student Nonviolent Coordination Committee (SNCC); the second wave of the women's movement; and escalating tensions surrounding the Vietnam War all served as contemporaneous moments for campus strikes.

After World War II and the Korean War, the desire for higher education increased, and university application and enrollment numbers in California boomed. This was buttressed by the survival and aging of the baby boomer generation and the advantageous effects of the GI Bill, which created pathways to higher education for many Americans. The state passed "The California Master Plan for Higher Education" in 1960. According to San Francisco attorney and future federal judge William H. Orrick III, this was done in an effort to "manage increasing enrollment numbers" (Orrick 1969, 7). The plan outlined a three-tier program for the state's investment in higher education. This established the University of California (UC) system, the California State University (CSU) system, and the junior/community college system.

Socially conscious students suspicious of "The Master Plan" asserted that it was meant to appear altruistic in nature, to welcome all students. But they argued that the reality was that decision-making power lay in the hands of only a few, tied to dominant, hegemonic corporate investment structures and power-hungry politicians. The plan was financially beneficial to the national economy. The criteria for admission into the ranks of the UC and CSU were strenuous, resulting in the funneling of wealthy students from prominent families to be trained in professional fields. Applicants from working-class communities and communities of color were encouraged to enroll at community/junior colleges, specializing in vocational and technical disciplines.

This resulted in people of color taking up low-skill, low-wage factory work or conscription into the U.S. armed services. Monetarily, California saved on cost. The state budget allocated six dollars for every UC student and one dollar for every CSU or junior-college student. Deterred by impossible standards for admission and high tuition costs, excessive enrollment at the expensive UC declined. Funding for community colleges was supplemented by local state taxes. Working-class students and students of color were tracked into junior colleges, and their enrollment in top-tier UC and CSU institutions evaporated. The number of professionals produced by UC was far less than the number of technicians produced by community colleges. At SFSC, the sharp numerical decline of students of color, particularly black students, was one of the strike's catalysts. According to the California Newsreel's 1969 film report *San Francisco State on Strike*, black student enrollment decreased from 12 percent in 1960 to 3 percent in 1968.

Students of color at SFSC began to express their concerns about numerical disparity, pedagogical inequity, and conscription for the Vietnam War en masse. Racial divisiveness began to manifest itself, disrupting any notions of liberal idealism. Some white students began to express their hostility to the use of student funds for activities and education catering to the needs of black students. One of these was James Vaszko, an undergraduate editor of the student newspaper, *The Gater*. Vaszko wrote an op-ed vocalizing vehement opposition toward external funding for SFSC's special programs, including those created by the BSU. Several students of color confronted him, demanding he retract his words. They were arrested, jailed, and booked on felony charges. The offices of the paper were destroyed, and campus tensions escalated.

The BSU and the TWLF at SFSC were the purveyors of the strike, buttressed by interethnic allyship, support, solidarity, and advocacy from the Bay Area community. The labor of the Black Power movement and key players in the Black Panther Party were also crucial to the effort. These organizing moments centered on claiming agency, self-determination, and community-based classroom and campus programming. During spring 1968, the BSU reached out to other student organizations on campus to forge interethnic solidarity. As Karen Umemoto's "On Strike! San Francisco State College Strike, 1968–1969: The Role of Asian American Students" details, Asian American students' political activism was crucial to the successful efforts of the movement. The SFSC chapter of the TWLF was composed of the BSU, La Raza, the Intercollegiate Chinese for Social Action (ICSA), the Philippine American Collegiate Endeavor (PACE), the Student Kouncil of Intertribal Nations (SKINS), and the Asian American Political Alliance (AAPA). Umemoto details the chronology of Asian American student organizing efforts, starting with the ICSA's formation in 1967, which initially focused on community, social, and cultural activities and later turned to political interests. PACE was formed in 1968, centered on the interests of Filipino/a students for self-determination. SFSC took up a conversation with UC Berkeley, starting a chapter of the political and militant AAPA.

Yen Le Espiritu argues in *Asian American Panethnicity* that the term "pan-Asian solidarity" emerged and "Third World Unity" formation took hold after World War II, and people across the world, particularly in the global South, were throwing off the yoke of colonial hegemony. The discourse of pan-Asian narrative was inherently political. Those in the Asian American movement recognized that by encouraging interethnic solidarity and connecting local issues in the United States to those happening transnationally, the global majority was that of people of color. To develop a Third World identity meant to connect with struggles across Asia, as well as global social justice movements spearheaded by black and brown people. The slogan "Yellow Peril Supports Black Power" emerged with the recognition that antiblackness was the fulcrum for white supremacy. Asian American activists refuted the model minority image. Circulated in 1966, this was the same moment that the Black Power slogan made its debut and the Black Panther Party made its headquarters in Oakland, California. It was also a crucial moment for allyship, and Asian American activists like Richard Aoki, Grace Lee Boggs, and Yuri Kochiyama were highly visible curators of solidarity.

Political Efficacy and the Model Minority

The model minority narrative lauded the appearance of upward mobility for Asian Americans, vis á vis William Petersen's work in *The New York Times* and *U.S. News & World Report.* Pushed forth in 1966, the image rendered Asian Americans as apolitical; silent; committed to aspirational whiteness as a means to socioeconomic upward mobility; sutured to filial piety; and successful through hard work and frugality, community isolationism, and self-reliance. The notion of Asian Americans as exceptional was dangerous, as it perpetuated the myth of their existence as entirely separate from black and brown struggles. Amy Uyematsu details this labor in "The Emergence of Yellow Power in America," part of *Gidra* magazine's October 1969 issue, produced by Japanese American activist students at UCLA. Uyematsu asked for Asian Americans to hold themselves accountable; to claim political power and recognize interlocking, interconnected vulnerabilities and oppressions with other people of color; and to recognize and call out anti-black sentiment in Asian American communities.

Together, the BSU and TWLF produced a list of strike demands. The rhetoric of these demands mirrors the rhetoric posited by the Black Panther Party, the Chicano Student Movement, the Brown Berets, the Young Lords, the Asian American Movement, and the American Indian Movement, happening contemporaneously. The BSU's list of ten strike demands included:

- Establishment of an autonomous and formally designated department of black studies, to be
- Vested with the power of granting degrees and
- Headed by Dr. Nathan Hare as department chairperson,
- With full professorship and a salary commensurate to his colleagues;
- Creation of twenty academic positions for black scholars;
- Increasing admission numbers of black students;
- Hiring of a black person to determine financial need and disperse funds to students of color;
- An assurance of protection that no person affiliated with SFSC participating in the strike would be punished;

- An assurance that black-centered campus programming would be protected; and
- Job security for George Mason Murray (a graduate student and instructor in the English Department, Black Panther Party minister of education, and community organizer who was fired from his job before the strike began). (Litwak and Wilner 1971, 85–87; Orrick 1969, 151)

The TWLF's list of demands included:

- Establishment of ethnic studies departments centering the histories and experiences of what was then called the Third World, with
- The administrative, hiring, and determination of curricula powers in the hands of students of color, and
- Creation of fifty academic faculty positions for those departments;
- Granting admission to all student of color applicants in the following year (1969); and
- The selection/hiring/retention of faculty members, including Murray, for respective teaching positions in those departments, to be determined by people of color.
  (Orrick 1969, 151)

Discursively, the organizations were aligned. The BSU outlined these goals: "to educate our people that the only culture we have is revolutionary (directed toward our freedom and a complete change in our living conditions) and that this will never be endorsed by our enemy," "to educate ourselves to the necessity of relating to the collective and not the individual," and "to redistribute the wealth, the knowledge, food, land, housing, and all the material resources necessary for a society and its people to function" (Umemoto 1969, 22).

The TWLF advocated for self-determination, rooted in the agency of students of color to regulate the hiring and firing of faculty in their departments. They conceived of education as part of human rights discourse, demanding open admissions for all student applicants of color. And they sought to ensure that communities controlled their own narratives, vis á vis developing their own curricula, not just replicated by Eurocentric models of colonization. They wanted to center the lenses, voices, and experiences of historically vulnerable populations and rethink power structures, bringing in community-based curricula. The purpose of a "relevant education" was to listen to the needs of communities, across class, socioeconomic, and racial lines, and not simply cater to the needs of corporate entities.

Students of color viewed campus administration as uncaring, authoritarian, and bigoted, composed of ineffectual leaders complicit in upholding white supremacy by relying on police brutality to maintain power over students. They were seen as subservient to the whims of corporations and wealthy trustees in Los Angeles and controlled by disinterested, power-hungry politicians in Sacramento and Washington, D.C.

Over the course of 1968–1969, SFSC had three presidents, Dr. John Summerskill and Dr. Robert Smith, who both resigned, and Dr. Samuel Ichiyé Hayakawa. Hayakawa was a linguistics/semantics professor in the Department of English, appointed acting president by the trustees and Governor Ronald Reagan. Canadian-born Hayakawa was of Japanese ancestry, and students were suspicious of his appointment, as it appeared to be a mysterious circumvention of usual faculty governance structures. Prior to his appointment as acting president, Hayakawa was reportedly well liked, visiting the students at the BSU offices daily to chat with them. Upon rising in the ranks of power, however, he changed. He was vehemently opposed to the strike, openly militant in his tactics, and visibly furious at protesting students. He banned public gathering on campus and endorsed police violence against students. The urge to contain the strike shifted to a desire to crush student protest. His first line of defense was to summon police and Tactical Air Command (TAC) forces, who were totally indiscriminate about whom to assault. This further radicalized the students.

Curbing Status

On December 2, 1968, Hayakawa stormed out of his office, joined the crowd, and jumped atop a truck that aided in amplifying the sounds of protesters. Dodging objects thrown at him, he destroyed the wires of the amplifier, screamed at the crowd, and threatened to summon more police. His moments atop the truck were captured on camera and televised nationally. On December 3, 1968, designated as "Bloody Tuesday," police forces advanced on the campus cafeteria and commons, injuring students with batons. Many were beaten within inches of their lives. Bloody and injured, they were stuffed into ambulances shuttling back and forth to hospitals.

This new Hayakawa was widely considered to be controversial, colorful, and reportedly despised by many students. He received praise from conservative, older, white politicians and was highly favored by Nixon and Reagan. He was notorious for his performance of political hegemony and support of military presence. He drew the ire of the campus population through his curtailing of free speech and assembly, ignoring faculty procedures, and unabashed rage toward striking students. During a news conference, his intentions supporting law and order and police presence were rendered explicit. He praised the police for their "restraint and professionalism" and told the news cameras and reporters, "This has been the most exciting day of my life since my tenth birthday, when I rode on a roller coaster for the first time" (Karagueuzian 1971, 168–172). He and campus administrators eventually came to an agreement with TWLF and BSU, outlining the steps for creating the College of Ethnic Studies.

Hayakawa's presence was indicative of other tensions at the university. SFSC faculty and the campus chapter of the American Federation of Teachers (AFT) went on strike as well, long after the students did, but ended theirs earlier. Parents, community organizations, civic leaders, and religious leaders supported the cause. Violence and tensions between students of color, antiracist white allies, and white students became more visible. There were bombing attempts on campus by protestors, student occupation of administrative offices, and student beatings and bloodshed at the hands of police. There were internal divisions within BSU and TWLF. However, the net result of five months was productive. The summation of students' non-negotiable demands, the clashing with university administration, violent police brutality committed against students, and a reframing of university resources resulted in victory. SFSC created the nation's first College of Ethnic Studies, establishing the first Department of Asian American Studies, and catalyzing other institutions to do the same. Ethnic studies departments and student activism at UC Berkeley, San Jose State, UCLA, UC San Diego, California State University Long Beach, and other academic institutions occurred soon after. Commitment to social justice, community service, respect for differences, and attention to inequality remain on the forefront of these programs, and Asian American Studies remains an important interdisciplinary academic field.

Biographies of Notable Figures

Samuel Ichiyé Hayakawa (1906–1992)

Samuel Ichiyé Hayakawa was born on July 18, 1906, in Vancouver, British Columbia, Canada, and raised in Winnipeg, Cranbrook, British Columbia, and Calgary. He was the eldest of four children, and all attended public schools. His father owned a floundering export business and was a labor contractor. Hayakawa earned his undergraduate degree from the University of Manitoba, Winnipeg, in 1927, and a master's degree from McGill University in Montreal. He supported himself through graduate school by driving a taxi. When he was twenty-one, his family decided to relocate to Japan. Hayakawa opted to remain in Canada with one of his younger brothers, living with their uncle, Saburo, in Montreal. He matriculated to the University of Wisconsin, earning another master's degree at twenty-three in 1928 and a PhD in 1935. His dissertation was on the work of the poet Oliver W. Holmes.

In 1937, Hayakawa married a white woman, Margedant Peters. The couple had two sons and one daughter, Alan, Mark, and Wynne, and five grandchildren. By 1939, Hayakawa was named professor of English at the Armour Institute of

Technology and moved the family to Chicago, Illinois. He also taught at the University of Chicago. Hayakawa became renowned for his expertise in rhetoric and semantics, writing the textbook *Language in Action*. Published in 1938, 1941, and 1949, the book sold well and received national accolades. It is currently in its fifth edition. From 1943 to 1947, he wrote for the black newspaper, *The Chicago Defender.*

Although he was Nisei, he vociferously advocated that he would not be limited by his ethnicity and avoided discussions of specific racist institutional discrimination. Though he supported the abolition of Jim Crow laws and equal rights for the black community, Hayakawa was reluctant to comment on anti-Asian sentiment and was highly supportive of assimilationist practices, remarking that participation in politics promoted success. A strong supporter of political efficacy, he lobbied the Canadian government to grant Japanese Canadians voting rights but was unsuccessful. During World War II and later, his relationships to Issei, Nisei, and Sansei communities were trepidatious.

Hayakawa believed in using racially neutral, color-blind language to address issues. Because he was a Canadian citizen and did not live on the West Coast, he and his family avoided the forced internment put into place by President Franklin D. Roosevelt's Executive Order 9066, passed on February 19, 1942. Even though Hayakawa claimed to empathize with the plights of Issei, Nisei, and Sansei, all victims of national institutional discrimination, he remained faithful to practices of assimilation. Hayakawa was a vocal critic of the 1952 McCarran-Walter Immigration Act, which would carve a pathway to citizenship for people of Asian ancestry who had previously been barred from that privilege.

He had a fiery, contentious relationship with the Japanese American Citizens League (JACL), which supported this law; the irony was that Hayakawa himself could not be naturalized as a U.S. citizen until it was passed. In 1955, he was hired at SFSC in the English Department and was an editor of the linguistics journal *Etc.* During the 1968 campus strike, he rose to prominence for his militant opposition to the students' demands and his proclivity to calling in police forces. He earned the ire of students after firing six black faculty members in 1970. His hardline stances on power earned him praise from conservative white politicians and unwavering support from President Richard M. Nixon and California Governor Ronald Reagan.

After retiring from SFSC in 1973, he wrote for the *Register & Tribune Syndicate* newspaper and was elected a Republican senator in 1976, one of three Asian Americans in the chamber. While in the Senate, Hayakawa angered the JACL again by refusing to support federal apologies and reparations for wartime internment. Hayakawa was also a proponent of making English the official language of the United States, stoking the rage of progressives and other people of color.

He spent the remainder of his years in Mill Valley, California, enjoying political debate and becoming a jazz aficionado. He died on February 27, 1992, in Greenbrae, California. He is remembered as a divisive, controversial, and complicated figure in relation to SFSC and U.S. politics.

DOCUMENT EXCERPTS

Report to the National Commission on the Causes and Prevention of Violence

The following excerpts are from the report to the National Commission on the Causes and Prevention of Violence. The report reviews the strike at San Francisco State College from October 1968 to April 1969. It includes information about the California system of higher education and San Francisco State College; the situation before the strike; description of the strike, the Black Student Union, and some of the reasons behind the actions of the student strike leaders; and the outlook for the future. The appendices of the report contain ten demands of the Black Students Union, five demands of the Third World Liberation Front, a comment on the police, board of trustees of the California State colleges, a conceptual proposal for a Department of Black Studies, and San Francisco Examiner *and* Chronicle *accounts of the student strike settlement.*

Shut It Down! A College in Crisis
San Francisco State College
October, 1968-April, 1969
A Staff Report to the National Commission on the Causes and Prevention of
Violence Prepared by William H. Orrick, Jr.
(Excerpts)
The White House
June 10, 1968

EXECUTIVE ORDER #11412
ESTABLISHING A NATIONAL COMMISSION ON THE CAUSES
AND PREVENTION OF VIOLENCE

By virtue of the authority vested in me as President of the United States, it is ordered as follows:

SECTION 1. Establishment of the Commission, (a) There is hereby established a National Commission on the Causes and Prevention of Violence (hereinafter referred to as the "Commission").

(b) The Commission shall be composed of:

Dr. Milton Eisenhower, Chairman

Congressman Hale Boggs	Senator Roman Hruska
Archbishop Terence J. Cooke	Albert E. Jenner, Jr.
Ambassador Patricia Harris	Congressman William M. McCulloch
Senator Philip A. Hart	*Dr. W. Walter Menninger
Judge A. Leon Higginbotham	*Judge Ernest William McFarland
Eric Hoffer	*Leon Jaworski

SECTION 2. Functions of the Commission. The Commission shall investigate and make recommendations with respect to:

(a) The causes and prevention of lawless acts of violence in our society, including assassination, murder and assault;

(b) The causes and prevention of disrespect for law and order, of disrespect for public officials, and of violent disruptions of public order by individuals and groups; and

(c) Such other matters as the President may place before the Commission.

SECTION 4. Staff of the Commission.

SECTION 5. Cooperation by Executive Departments and Agencies.

(a) The Commission, acting through its Chairman, is authorized to request from any executive department or agency any information and assistance deemed necessary to carry out its functions under this Order. Each department or agency is directed, to the extent permitted by law and within the limits of available funds, to furnish information and assistance to the Commission.

SECTION 6. Report and Termination. The Commission shall present its report and recommendations as soon as practicable, but not later than one year from the date of this Order. The Commission shall terminate thirty days following the submission of its final report or one year from the date of this Order, whichever is earlier.

S/Lyndon B. Johnson

*Added by an Executive Order June 21, 1968

The White House
May 23, 1969

EXECUTIVE ORDER #11469
EXTENDING THE LIFE OF THE NATIONAL COMMISSION ON THE
CAUSES AND PREVENTION OF VIOLENCE

By virtue of the authority vested in me as President of the United States, Executive Order No. 11412 of June 10, 1968, entitled "Establishing a National Commission on the Causes and Prevention of Violence," is hereby amended by substituting for the last sentence thereof the following: "The Commission shall terminate thirty days following the submission of its final report or on December 10, 1969, whichever is earlier."

S/ Richard Nixon

STATEMENT ON THE STAFF STUDIES

The Commission was directed to "go as far as man's knowledge takes" it in searching for the causes of violence and the means of prevention. These studies are reports to the Commission by independent scholars and lawyers who have served as directors of our staff task forces and study teams; they are not reports by the Commission itself. Publication of any of the reports should not be taken to imply endorsement of their contents by the Commission, or by any member of the Commission's staff, including the Executive Director and other staff officers, not directly responsible for the preparation of the particular report. Both the credit and the responsibility for the reports lie in each case with the directors of the task forces and study teams. The Commission is making the reports available at this time as works of scholarship to be judged on their merits, so that the Commission as well as the public may have the benefit of both the reports and informed criticism and comment on their contents.

Dr. Milton S. Eisenhower, Chairman

PREFACE

From the earliest days of organization, the Chairman, Commissioners, and Executive Director of the National Commission on the Causes and Prevention of Violence recognized the importance of research in accomplishing the task of analyzing the many facets of violence in America. As a result of this recognition, the Commission has enjoyed the receptivity, encouragement, and cooperation of a large part of the scientific community in this country.

Because of the assistance given in varying degrees by scores of scholars here and abroad, these Task Force reports represent some of the most elaborate work ever done on the major topics they cover.

The Commission was formed on June 10, 1968. By the end of the month, the Executive Director had gathered together a small cadre of capable young lawyers from various Federal agencies and law firms around the country. That group was later augmented by partners borrowed from some of the Nation's major law firms who served without compensation. Such a professional group can be assembled more quickly than university faculty because the latter are not accustomed to quick institutional shifts after making firm commitments of teaching or research at a particular locus. Moreover, the legal profession has long had a major and traditional role in Federal agencies and commissions.

In early July a group of 50 persons from the academic disciplines of sociology, psychology, psychiatry, political science, history, law, and biology were called together on short notice to discuss for 2 days how best the Commission and its staff might proceed to analyze violence. The enthusiastic response of these scientists came at a moment when our Nation was still suffering from the tragedy of Senator Kennedy's assassination.

It was clear from that meeting that the scholars were prepared to join research analysis and action, interpretation, and policy. They were eager to present to the American people the best available data, to bring reason to bear where myth had prevailed. They cautioned against simplistic solutions, but urged application of what is known in the service of sane policies for the benefit of the entire society.

Shortly thereafter the position of Director of Research was created. We assumed the role as a joint undertaking, with common responsibilities. Our function was to enlist social and other scientists to join the staff, to write papers, act as advisers or consultants, and engage in new research. The decentralized structure of the staff, which at its peak numbered 100, required research coordination to reduce duplication and to fill in gaps among the original seven separate Task Forces. In general, the plan was for each Task Force to have a pair of directors: one a social scientist, one a lawyer. In a number of instances, this formal structure bent before the necessities of available personnel but in almost every case the Task Force work program relied on both social scientists and lawyers for its successful completion. In addition to our work with the seven original Task Forces, we provided consultation for the work of the eighth "Investigative" Task Force, formed originally to investigate the disorders at the Democratic and Republican National Conventions and the civil strife in Cleveland during the summer of 1968 and eventually expanded to study campus disorders at several colleges.

Throughout September and October and in December of 1968 the Commission held about 30 days of public hearings related expressly to each of the Task Force areas. About 100 witnesses testified, including many scholars, Government officials, corporate executives as well as militants and activists of various persuasions. In addition to the hearings, the Commission and the staff met privately with scores of persons, including college presidents, religious and youth leaders, and experts in such areas as the media, victim compensation, and firearms. The staff participated actively in structuring and conducting those hearings and conferences and in the questioning of witnesses.

As Research Directors, we participated in structuring the strategy of design for each Task Force, but we listened more than directed. We have known the delicate details of some of the statistical problems and computer runs. We have argued over philosophy and syntax; we have offered bibliographical and other resource materials, we have written portions of reports and copy edited others. In short, we know the enormous energy and devotion, the long hours and accelerated study that members of each Task Force have invested in their labors. In retrospect we are amazed at the high caliber and quantity of the material produced, much of which truly represents, the best in research and scholarship. About 150 separate papers and projects were involved in the work culminating in the Task Force reports. We feel less that we have orchestrated than that we have been members of the orchestra, and that together with the entire staff we have helped compose a repertoire of current knowledge about the enormously complex subject of this Commission.

That scholarly research is predominant in the work here presented is evident in the product. But we should like to emphasize that the roles which we occupied were not limited to scholarly inquiry. The Directors of Research were afforded an opportunity to participate in all Commission meetings. We engaged in discussions at the highest levels of decision making, and had great freedom in the selection of scholars, in the control of research budgets, and in the direction and design of research. If this was not unique, it is at least an uncommon degree of prominence accorded research by a national commission.

There were three major levels to our research pursuit: (1) summarizing the state of our present knowledge and clarifying the lacunae where more or new research should be encouraged; (2) accelerating known ongoing research so as to make it available to the Task Forces; (3) undertaking new research projects within the limits of time and funds available. Coming from a university setting where the pace of research is more conducive to reflection and quiet hours analyzing data, we at first thought that completing much meaningful new research within a matter of months was most unlikely. But the need was matched by the talent and enthusiasm of the staff, and the Task Forces very early had begun enough new projects to launch a small university with a score of doctoral theses. It is well to remember also that in each volume here presented, the research reported is on full public display and thereby makes the staff more than usually accountable for their products.

One of the very rewarding aspects of these research undertakings has been the experience of minds trained in the law mingling and meshing, sometimes fiercely arguing, with other minds trained in behavioral science. The organizational structure and the substantive issues of each Task Force required members from both groups. Intuitive judgment and the logic of argument and organization blended, not always smoothly, with the methodology of science and statistical reasoning. Critical and analytical faculties were sharpened as theories confronted facts. The arrogance neither of ignorance nor of certainty could long endure the doubts and questions of interdisciplinary debate. Any sign of approaching the priestly pontification of scientism was quickly dispelled in the matrix of mutual criticism. Years required for the normal accumulation of experience were compressed into months of sharing ideas with others who had equally valid but differing perspectives. Because of this process, these volumes are much richer than they otherwise might have been.

Partly because of the freedom which the Commission gave to the Directors of Research and the Directors of each Task Force, and partly to retain the full integrity of the research work in publication, these reports of the Task Forces are in the posture of being submitted to and received by the Commission. These are volumes published under the authority of the Commission, but they do not necessarily represent the views or the conclusions of the Commission. The Commission is presently at work producing its own report, based in part on the materials presented to it by the Task Forces. Commission members have, of course, commented on earlier drafts of each Task Force, and have caused alterations by reason of the cogency of their remarks and insights. But the final responsibility for what is contained in these volumes rests fully and properly on the research staffs who labored on them.

In this connection, we should like to acknowledge the special leadership of the Chairman, Dr. Milton S. Eisenhower, in formulating and supporting the principle of research freedom and autonomy under which this work has been conducted.

We note, finally, that these volumes are in many respects incomplete and tentative. The urgency with which papers were prepared and then integrated into Task Force Reports rendered impossible the successive siftings of data and argument to which the typical academic article or volume is subjected. The reports have benefited greatly from the counsel of our colleagues on the Advisory Panel, and from much debate and revision from within the staff. It is our hope, that the total work effort of the Commission staff will be the source and subject of continued research by scholars in the several disciplines, as well as a useful resource for policymakers. We feel certain that public policy and the disciplines will benefit greatly from such further work.

To the Commission, and especially to its Chairman, for the opportunity they provided for complete research freedom, and to the staff for its prodigious and prolific work, we, who were intermediaries and servants to both, are most grateful.

James F. Short, Jr. and Marvin E. Wolfgang
Directors of Research

. . .

APPENDIX 1
TEN DEMANDS OF THE BLACK STUDENTS UNION

1. That all black studies courses being taught through various other departments be immediately part of the black studies department and that all instructors in this department receive full time pay.
2. That Dr. Hare, chairman of the black studies department, receive a full professorship and a comparable salary according to his qualifications.
3. That there be a department of black studies which will grant a bachelor's degree in black studies; that the black studies department chairman, faculty, and staff have the sole power to hire and fire without the interference of the racist administration and the chancellor.

4. That all unused slots for black students from fall 1968 under the special admissions program be filled in spring 1969.

5. That all black students who wish to, be admitted in fall 1969.

6. That 20 full-time teaching positions be allocated to the department of black studies.

7. That Dr. Helen Bedesem be replaced in the position of financial aid officer and that a black person be hired to direct it and that Third World people have the power to determine how it will be administered.

8. That no disciplinary action will be administered in any way to any students, workers, teachers, or administrators during and after the strike as a consequence of their participation in the strike.

9. That the California State College Trustees not be allowed to dissolve any black programs on or off the San Francisco State College campus.

10. That George Murray maintain his teaching position on the campus for the 1968–69 academic year.

FIVE DEMANDS OF THE THIRD WORLD LIBERATION FRONT

1. That schools of ethnic studies for the ethnic groups involved in the Third World be set up, with students for each particular organization having the authority and the control of the hiring and retention of any faculty member, director, and administrator, as well as the curricula.

2. That 50 faculty positions be appropriated to the schools of ethnic studies, 20 of which would be for the black studies program.

3. That in the spring semester the college fulfill its commitments to the nonwhite students in admitting those that apply.

4. That in the fall of 1969, all applications of nonwhite students be accepted.

5. That George Murray and any other faculty members chosen by nonwhite people as their teachers be retained in their positions.

. . .

Source: Orrick, William H., Jr. "Shut It Down!: A College in Crisis: San Francisco State College, October 1968–April 1969: A Report to the National Commission on the Causes and Prevention of Violence." Washington D.C.: Government Printing Office, 1969.

See also: Asian/Pacific American Heritage Week Established, 1978; The Delano Grape Strike and Boycott 1965–1970; The Murder of Vincent Chin, 1982

Further Reading

Agents of Change. 2016. Directed by Abby Ginzberg and Frank Dawson. California Newsreel.

Black Panther/San Francisco State on Strike. 1969. California Newsreel.

Espiritu, Yen Le. 1992. *Asian American Panethnicity: Bridging Institutions and Identities*. Philadelphia: Temple University Press.

Fujino, Diane. 2015. "Black Militants and Asian American Model Minorities." *Kalfou* 2, no. 1: 96–116.

Haslam, Gerald and Janice Haslam. 2011. *In Thought and Action: The Enigmatic Life of S. I. Hayakawa*. Lincoln: University of Nebraska Press.

Ishizuka, Karen L. and Jeff Chang. 2016. *Serve the People: Making Asian America in the Long Sixties*. London: Verso.

J. Paul Leonard Library. "SF State College Strike Collection." https://library.sfsu.edu/sf-state -strike-collection

Karagueuzian, Dikran. 1971. *Blow It Up! The Black Student Revolt at San Francisco State College and the Emergence of Dr. Hayakawa*. Boston: Gambit.

Litwak, Leo and Herbert Wilner. 1971. *College Days in Earthquake Country: Ordeal at San Francisco State: A Personal Record*. New York: Random House.

On Strike! Ethnic Studies 1969–1999. 1999. Directed by Irum Shiekh. Center for Asian American Media.

Orrick, William H., and United States. National Commission on the Causes and Prevention of Violence. 1969. *Shut It Down! A College in Crisis: San Francisco State College, October 1968-April 1969; A Report to the National Commission on the Causes and Prevention of Violence*. NCCPV Staff Study Series; 6. Washington, D.C.: Government Printing Office.

Pulido, Laura. 2006. *Black, Brown, Yellow, and Left: Radical Activism in Los Angeles*. Berkeley: University of California Press.

Smith, Robert, Richard Axen, and DeVere Edwin Pentony. 1970. *By Any Means Necessary: The Revolutionary Struggle at San Francisco State*. Jossey-Bass Series in Higher Education. San Francisco: Jossey-Bass.

Umemoto, Karen. 1989. "'On Strike!' San Francisco State College Strike, 1968–69: The Role of Asian American Students." *Amerasia Journal* 15, no. 1: 3–41.

Uyematsu, Amy. 1969. "The Emergence of Yellow Power." *Gidra* (October): 8–11.

Wei, William. 1993. *The Asian American Movement*. Philadelphia: Temple University Press.

5

Heritage and Legacy

Lau v. Nichols, 1974

Rachel Endo and Verna Wong

Chronology

1969 The San Francisco Unified School District (SFUSD) publishes a report about the academic performance of Limited English Proficient (LEP) Chinese American students. The report states that students who do not receive a culturally and linguistically relevant K–12 education have higher dropout rates.

1970 In March, a class-action lawsuit is filed against SFUSD on the basis that the district discriminated against LEP Chinese American students by not providing them with bilingual education services. California attorney Edward Steinman represents Kinney Kinmon Lau and 1,856 other LEP Chinese American K–12 students who were enrolled in SFUSD schools.

1970 In May, the federal district court acknowledges that LEP Chinese American students have been significantly disadvantaged in U.S. public schools due to language barriers but rules that the SFUSD has no legal obligation to provide these students with additional accommodations, as long as they receive the same materials and services as the other students.

1971 In *Lee v. Johnson,* a group of Chinese immigrant parents oppose a measure by the SFUSD to desegregate its public schools out of fear that it will push their children out of neighborhood schools. The parents argue that by integrating their children into regular public schools with white students, their daughters and sons will not have access to the bilingual and culturally responsive education that they have been receiving in ethnocentric spaces.

1971 The *Lee v. Johnson* case is appealed to the Ninth Circuit Court of Appeals, where there is a ruling against the parents. The Court rules that the *Brown v. Board of Education* 1954 ruling for desegregation applies to students of all racial backgrounds, not just those who are black and white.

1973 Lau plaintiffs appeal the federal district court's 1970 decision to the U.S. Court of Appeals for the Ninth Circuit. Two of the three judges vote to uphold the federal district court's decision that the SFUSD is only legally required to provide its LEP students with the same materials and resources as native English-speaking students. Shortly after this decision, Steinman presents the case again to the U.S. Supreme Court in December 1973.

1974 *Lau v. Nichols U.S. 563*

Overturning a lower court order, the U.S. Supreme Court votes unanimously that SFUSD's practice of English-only instruction and the lack of supplemental education for LEPs violate the Fourteenth Amendment's Equal Protection Clause, Section 601 of the Civil Rights Act of 1964, and provisions of the California Education Code.

1974 Section 105(a)(1), Title VII, of the Elementary and Secondary Education Act of 1965 is amended as Section 701, or the Bilingual Education Act for public schools, to provide bilingual education support to all LEP students.

1975 In May, the U.S. Commission on Civil Rights releases a nationwide report titled, "A Better Chance to Learn: Bilingual Bicultural Education." The report provides a comprehensive overview of the experiences and needs of language minorities in public schools, including highlighting promising developments in bilingual education programs.

1998 With the passage of California Proposition 227 (the English Language in Public Schools Statute), California's voters decide to eliminate bilingual education programs in the public schools, thus undoing the wide-scale impact that the *Lau* decision has had for LEP students.

Narrative

In May 1970, California attorney Edward Steinman filed a class-action lawsuit against the San Francisco Unified School District (SFUSD) on behalf of eight-year-old Kinney Kinmon Lau and 1,856 other Chinese American students who were classified as Limited English Proficient (LEP). The suit alleged that the school district was denying LEP Chinese American students access to an equal education by not teaching them in a language that they understood. Steinman argued that the lack of linguistically appropriate education for LEP students perpetuated disproportionate academic gaps because these students had few opportunities to learn during the school day because of not understanding the English-based lessons. He said that as a result, students were engaging in delinquent activities and had higher dropout rates than their peers. Not graduating from high school would have long-term effects on LEP students' adult lives, including the lack of career and social opportunities. The lower federal court and the Ninth Circuit Court of Appeals in California both initially rejected the lawsuit.

However, when *Lau v. Nichols* was decided in 1974, the U.S. Supreme Court overturned the lower-court decisions. The Supreme Court noted that the lack of bilingual education programs in the SFUSD for its ethnically and linguistically diverse K–12 student populations violated Section 601, which prohibits discrimination under any program that receives federal funding. It also violated Title VI of the Civil Rights Act of 1964, which outlawed discrimination on the basis of color, national origin, race, religion, and sex. The ruling made clear that public schools that receive federal funding are required to provide their LEP students with appropriate and meaningful bilingual education services. Justice William Douglas wrote: "[T]hose who do not understand English are certain to find their classroom experiences wholly incomprehensible and in no way meaningful" (Walsh 2009, 9). As a result of the *Lau* outcome, the SFUSD was required to provide special language assistance and support to its LEP students.

The *Lau* decision is one of the most significant examples of a civil rights remedy in U.S. education policy. The outcome of the case occurred only twenty years after the landmark *Brown v. Board of Education* decision in 1954. It was also decided shortly after the 1968 Bilingual Education Act was implemented. The act was the first federally recognized legislation specifying that limited English-speaking ability (LESA) students have unique academic needs that are different from native speakers of English. The *Lau* case shaped how U.S. public schools serve bilingual and multilingual children by providing a rationale for how and why bicultural and bilingual education programs are necessary. While there was scant research on the topic at the time when *Lau* was decided, Asian Americans and other advocates in the months following argued that bilingual programs improved the academic performance of LEP students because they provided targeted support to help students acquire fluency in English more rapidly (Salomone 2010, 131).

Professor of education John Baugh (2009) notes that the *Lau* decision provides one of the strongest legal arguments for associating education risk to one's limited English language proficiency. According to Baugh, if students like Lau cannot understand English well but are held to the same academic standards as their native English-speaking peers, then the public schools are clearly setting up conditions that disadvantage and discriminate against LEP learners. This, however, does not mean researchers have agreed with one another on the impacts and implications of the *Lau* decision. Indeed, the case has become "a lightning rod for divided views about the appropriate education of students who were not proficient in English" (Gándara, Moran, and Garcia 2004, 29). As Peter Roos notes, the *Lau* decision was also a recognition that requiring uniformity may go against equality in education for students with diverse linguistic and cultural backgrounds (1978, 115). In this sense, the case fueled contested debates about the ethical and legal obligations that U.S. public schools have to provide a high-quality and rigorous education to an ethnically, linguistically, and racially diverse K–12 population.

Lau v. Nichols *in Relation to Asian American and Chinese American History*

The *Lau* case is by no means an isolated event in Asian American history. It is closely tied to Asian Americans' experience in the United States, particularly Chinese Americans' history in San Francisco. Chinese immigrants first arrived to San Francisco in the 1840s. They experienced intense racial discrimination that prevented them from finding jobs and housing. Consequently, the early Chinese in San Francisco were concentrated in low-wage industries and resided in an area called Chinatown. Anti-Asian sentiment in California and elsewhere in the United States prevented generations of Chinese immigrants and their descendants, as well as other Asian American families and communities, from accessing equal opportunities for over a century after their arrival. In 1882, President Chester Arthur signed the Chinese Exclusion Act, which became the first formalized race-based exclusion law in the United States. It placed a moratorium on Chinese immigration for a decade and, moreover, prevented Chinese immigrants from obtaining naturalization.

The Tape family, including Joseph, Emily, Frank, Mamie, and Mary, in 1884. The Tape family won the right for their daughter Mamie to attend public school in the California Supreme Court case *Tape v. Hurley*, a major turning point for Chinese Americans in the history of civil rights. (Smith Collection/Gado/Getty Images)

Even during times where they had few legal rights and were considered second-class citizens, Chinese immigrants actively found ways to demand equal rights, especially for their children's education. In the 1885 landmark case *Tape v. Hurley*, Chinese immigrants Joseph and Mary Tape sued the San Francisco Board of Education because their eight-year-old daughter, Mamie Tape, was denied entry at a public elementary school due to her Chinese ancestry. Basing their decision on the Fourteenth Amendment, the California Supreme Court ruled that it was unconstitutional for the district and school to deny Mamie, an American citizen, entry into a public school because of her heritage and nationality. Yet despite this legal victory, the district continued to exclude and segregate Chinese American students for several more decades, which led to disparate academic outcomes and low morale among many Chinese American youth.

Despite a steady decline in San Francisco's general population, the Chinese population continued to grow from the 1950s through the 1970s. Throughout this time, many Chinese Americans were in need of language instruction in schools, but the school district offered little financial commitment and gave limited services to a small number of students (Wang 1976, 59). With the busing efforts to desegregate schools, the Chinese community pushed back to preserve the little resources they had to maintain their cultural and linguistic identity (Moran 2008). By the 1960s, increased rates of criminal activities and delinquent behaviors among many Chinese American youth in San Francisco became a significant point of concern, which community members associated with the lack of a culturally and linguistically appropriate K–12 education. Since Chinese Americans were grouped into classrooms by age and not by their fluency in English, there was no differentiation in instruction to support those who had different levels of English-language proficiency. Advocates for linguistically appropriate education argued that because LEP students did not understand English well, they likely felt bored, confused, and disengaged with school and, worse yet, were mocked and ridiculed by their peers and teachers for not being fluent in English. Thus, LEP students had few incentives to attend school in a learning environment that was not supportive of their needs. Moreover, more out-of-school time for disengaged Chinese American LEP students meant greater opportunities to engage in criminal activities or to leave school entirely.

The implementation of the monumental Hart-Celler Act, or the Immigration Act of 1965, together with the rising concern about Asian Americans' academic and economic achievements in the United States, created a social environment leading to the *Lau* case. The 1965 act eliminated the long-standing national-origins quotas that previously excluded several subgroups of Asian nationals from entering the United States. This act marked the beginning of a new era in contrast to the social climate created by the passing and implementation of the Chinese Exclusion

Act of 1882. Since 1965, a greater number of Asian nationals, including those from affluent and middle-class backgrounds, have come to the United States under more liberal immigration laws. Many Asian immigrants, regardless of their educational attainment in their motherlands, found themselves working in low-wage industries due to ongoing discrimination in the mainstream U.S. labor sector. The post-1965 era could be described as representing a more ethnically and generationally diverse Asian American population, including four generations of Chinese American communities with varied needs. The *Lau* case also came during the zenith of the

---

Lau v. Nichols: Impact on Asian American Education

Asian American English-language learners (ELLs) represent a culturally, generationally, and linguistically diverse subgroup that is a fast-growing segment in K–12 schools. Of the estimated 4.7 million ELLs in the United States, 21 percent are of Asian American or Pacific Island descent, including a demographically diverse mix of foreign-born and U.S.-born students who have varying levels of English-language proficiency (Zong and Batalava 2015). While the *Lau* case specifically focused on Chinese American LEP students in the SFUSD, it also raised awareness about academic gaps that Asian American students experience in general. One challenge when analyzing the academic needs of Asian American K–12 students are that educational disparities within certain subgroups are often overlooked.

Currently, bilingual and ESL programs face significant challenges in closing equity gaps because K–12 students who receive ESL support are often arbitrarily tracked into less rigorous coursework (Umansky 2016). Whereas the *Lau* decision mandated that all ELLs gain access to language services in their native tongues, current models of English-language development in U.S. schools continue to perpetuate academic disparities, given that they still privilege English as the primary language of instruction. Thus, despite the challenges the Lau family encountered during and after a long ordeal to demand a linguistically relevant education for their son, the *Lau* case raised public awareness of multiple concerns that affect many Asian American families. Foremost, the *Lau* case reiterated that LEP students have distinct academic needs that cannot be remedied by simply treating them the same as native speakers of English. Finally, since 1974, the *Lau* case has galvanized other ethnic and racialized communities, families, and parents to continue challenging inequitable policies and practices in public schools, especially around language and literacy education.

pan-ethnic Asian American movement, including the Third World Liberation Front strikes at San Francisco State College and the University of California at Berkeley. All of these efforts focused on promoting the advancement and protecting the civil rights of ethnically diverse Asian American communities, families, and individuals.

Lau v. Nichols: *A Last Resort*

After the *Brown* ruling in 1954 and prior to the *Lau* decision in 1974, U.S. public schools were prohibited from engaging in blatantly discriminatory practices such as segregating students by national origin or race. However, the law did not address the consequences or impacts of more subtle forms of discrimination or unintentional acts that led to disparate outcomes for certain groups of students. For example, at the time, there were no formal legal protections available for students who were systemically disadvantaged in the public schools such as LEP students. In the case of LEP students, while public schools were required to provide them with the same resources as other students, they were not legally obliged to offer additional resources or differentiated services to provide them with the support they needed to catch them up with their peers who were fluent in English.

L. Ling Chi Wang points out that the *Lau* case materialized after Chinese Americans endlessly fought for their rights (1976). Under the leadership of board president Alan Nichols in the late 1960s, the SFUSD was, at the time, serving one of the most ethnically and linguistically diverse K–12 student populations in the nation. One key graduation requirement mandated by the state was that all of California's students were to be proficient in English upon graduating from high school to succeed in their careers and postsecondary pursuits. However, Steinman argued that since the SFUSD was not providing adequate language services to Chinese American LEPs to help them attain this graduation requirement, the students were ultimately being denied opportunities to succeed academically. To exacerbate the problem, many Chinese American LEP students were also inappropriately placed into a Chinese bilingual education program that did not provide them with much-needed English as a Second Language (ESL) support services to gain proficiency in English. Moreover, most of SFUSD's bilingual programs were inadequate to meet the needs of LEP students because they were not funded well and were also primarily taught by teachers who themselves were not bilingual or had no fluency in the students' first languages.

The Chinese American community and parents of LEP students made multiple attempts to resolve their concerns with the SFUSD. Their principal concern was not allegations of intentional discrimination, but the overall failure of SFUSD leaders to take active and timely steps to rectify the situation in collaboration with the community. Initially, the creation of a citizens' task force was recommended to present a program remedy to the courts, although it ended up exacerbating frustration and mistrust because there was no input from the community or SFUSD teachers (Wang 1976). After several failed attempts to resolve their differences with school administrators, the community finally took their grievances to the courts under Steinman's counsel. While no specific program or remedy was requested, the request to the court was simple: for the SFUSD school board to use its best judgment to address and remedy the situation to meet the needs of LEP students, and to do so in a timely manner.

Lau v. Nichols was argued in December 1973, and a unanimous ruling was decided approximately six weeks later in January 1974. In its ruling, the U.S. Supreme Court ruled that the SFUSD had illegally discriminated against Lau and other LEP Chinese American students by failing to provide them with appropriate bilingual education instruction and services. Justice Potter Stewart wrote that even if the SFUSD did not engage in intentionally discriminatory practices, the district was inherently negligent because it failed to produce concrete actions or remedies after district leaders became aware of the inequity, and therefore it did not respond to the needs of its LEP students. Justice Harry Blackmun, joined by Chief Justice Warren Burger, concurred with Justice Steward and further commented that the *Lau* case was significant because of the large number of students who were affected by this negligence versus just one student or a small group of language-minority students: "I stress the fact that the children with whom we are concerned here number about 1,800. This is a very substantial group that is being deprived of any meaningful schooling because they cannot understand the language of the classroom" ("Text of the Court's Decision" 1984). In his written opinion, Justice Blackmun also noted that other immigrant Americans and their descendants were largely able to overcome language barriers through assimilation and parental effort. However, his primary concern was that LEP Chinese American children were not able to assimilate and integrate as rapidly as European American children from immigrant families. Chinese American children were involuntarily concentrated in Chinatown because of discriminatory housing practices that excluded Chinese immigrants from integrating into white neighborhoods and thus were disadvantaged at a larger scale compared to European American children whose families were not subjected to these racist laws and practices.

While the U.S. Supreme Court ruling addressed the discrimination that LEP Chinese American students experienced in terms of the lack of equitable access to appropriate language instruction as a direct a violation of their civil rights, the Court did not identify any specific programs that would best benefit all language-minority students and instead left it up to the school district to make those determinations. Following the *Lau* ruling in 1974, the SFUSD school board was directed to provide a comprehensive and detailed plan that would better identify and serve the language-minority students in the district. The Chinese for Affirmative Action (CAA) formed a coalition and partnered with community organizations to urge the SFUSD school board to set up a task force consisting of a diverse group of parents and community members to develop recommendations for an effective bilingual education program.

The SFUSD school board delayed responding to the demands of the coalition and instead was hoping to design a program that would require minimal resources. The board was also accused of not proceeding with community input. After learning of these allegations, the coalition brought together several of San Francisco's African American, Asian American, Latina/o, and white families to address the issue, as well as the needs of language-minority students (Salomone 2010, 129). As a result of the attention brought to SFUSD's actions, or inactions, by the CAA's coalitional efforts and from the media, the school board finally agreed to the creation of the Citizens Task Force for Bilingual Education, which was composed of members of the coalition along with the Center for Applied Linguistics to develop a master plan, which resulted in a 700-page report that detailed the content of a bilingual education program that was brought forth by the community-led task force. The SFUSD board eventually approved the plan that took effect a year later in 1975 (Wang 1976).

Ultimately, the *Lau* decision clarified the key conceptual differences between the notions of educational equality versus educational equity. The *Lau* case established a legal understanding that treating all students equally (the equality definition) is not only inadequate for closing academic and equity gaps but often perpetuates academic disparities by failing to provide certain disadvantaged subgroups of students with the extra resources and support needed to succeed academically. In contrast, an equity-based approach and definition to education promoted by the *Lau* plaintiffs acknowledge that certain groups of learners like LEP students require additional support to succeed in English-only environments. Moreover, *Lau* created accountability expectations for public schools to help LEP students succeed academically beyond simply meeting baseline legal requirements of providing all students with the same type of materials and resources such as course offerings and textbooks. Patricia Gándara, Rachel Moran, and Eugene Garcia note that the *Lau* decision promoted "the view that Congress has the power to ban harmful practices that do not amount to constitutional violations" (2004, 33). That is, the *Lau* case also raised questions about the responsibility of public schools in terms of their ethical and legal obligations to level an uneven playing field for students considered disadvantaged, including LEP students. Significantly, the American public continues to view appropriate and fair treatment from an equality definition and from a lens of meritocracy, which has led to ongoing debates and legal challenges about the ultimate value of providing underserved learners with accessible and equitable opportunities.

Lau v. Nichols: Negative Impacts and Tracking of ELLs

For decades, education specialists and policy makers have debated what constitutes "best practices" that effectively serve ELLs and LEP learners. The development of standards-based instruction has framed recent legislation to emphasize English proficiency rather than maintaining bilingualism among ELLs (Gándara, Moran, and Garcia 2004, 39). Traditional ESL program models provide remedial language support to ELLs as a means for them to access the content learned in the classroom. However, this model assumes that ELLs bring little knowledge to the learning environment, as it does not capitalize on the foundation they have attained through their home language. The dominant perception of heritage languages other than English as deficits fails to acknowledge the complexity of one's linguistic capabilities, as well as the many forms of knowledge and ways of knowing ELLs bring to the learning environment (Callahan 2005). Ultimately, the traditional ESL model privileges English as the dominant language while devaluing other languages.

Significantly, during this shift away from bilingual education, language-immersion programs increased throughout the country by prioritizing the enrollment of native speakers of English from more affluent communities to learn a second language. For example, Mandarin immersion schools currently represent the third-largest immersion program in the United States (Valdez, Freire, and Delavan 2016). Though dual-language immersion programs are growing more popular for second-generation and interracial Chinese American families, they do not prioritize the demands of LEP students from lower-income backgrounds ("Asian Immersion Schools Surge" 2014). LEP students are often racialized and stigmatized for speaking in their heritage languages in mainstream schools, while affluent native English-speaking students are usually rewarded for learning another language because doing so helps them develop a cosmopolitan identity as Americans who embrace cross-cultural relations in a global world.

Lau also had a significant impact on educational policies pertaining to bilingual and ESL education, and since 1974, additional lawsuits, particularly among communities of color, have followed. For example, in 1981 only seven years after *Lau* was decided, the *Castañeda v. Pickard* case led to a suit against the Raymondville Independent School District (RISD) in Texas for discriminating against Mexican American children by segregating and tracking them because of their heritage. Moreover, the district was accused of denying bilingual Mexican American students access to bilingual education programming. There are other examples of bilingual education initiatives to support LEP students since the *Lau* case was decided, especially in states where ELLs are heavily served, including in California, Florida, and Texas.

In 1998, California's Proposition 227 eradicated bilingual instruction in the state's public schools and mandated English as the official language of instruction. The negative perceptions of bilingual education in recent cases have caused a number of districts and states to close down such programs (Crawford 2007). Due to Proposition 227, California's public school teachers are now required to teach LEP students in English only and in separate courses. The goal is for LEP students to acquire fluency in English as quickly as possible. While many claimed that Proposition 227 was needed to encourage California's increasingly diverse K–12 student population to quickly learn English to close academic gaps, many community members viewed it as having racially tinged motives for denying diverse students access to a culturally and linguistically appropriate education.

Biographies of Notable Figures

Kinney Kinmon Lau (1964–)

Kinney Kinmon Lau was the primary subject of the *Lau* case. At the age of five, Lau and his mother left Hong Kong to join his father, who was living in San Francisco at the time. While the young Lau became the official face for bilingual education during the 1970s, there has been very little documented and publicly known about his life and the experiences of his family after the case was decided. Lau represented twelve plaintiffs and the other Chinese-speaking children in San Francisco who were not receiving bilingual and culturally appropriate K–12 education services. The ultimate decision by the Lau family to work with Steinman and sue the SFUSD ignited a coalition-building movement for immigrant families to claim or reclaim their cultural identity and heritage language within public education. Since the case was decided, the Lau family has been very silent about their involvement before, during, and after the case (Soloman 2010, 130). Moreover, little is known about what happened to the remaining plaintiffs since 1974.

In 1969, Mrs. Lau visited the Chinatown Neighborhood Legal Services to seek legal advice on behalf of her family regarding a housing dispute. Like many Chinese-speaking immigrants in San Francisco, the Laus worked in low-paying jobs and could not afford to retain a lawyer on their own. Yet, by chance, Mrs. Lau met Steinman, who then was a recent graduate of Stanford University's Law School and also received a fellowship to address poverty needs in the community. During the time of his fellowship, Steinman had met with a number of Chinese American families who expressed concerns about their children's inability to access a quality education because the SFUSD was not providing them with adequate support. Through a translator, Mrs. Lau shared with Steinman the story of her son Kinney, who had struggled in school because he did not understand English well. From Steinman's perspective, Kinney's story was an opportunity to represent the multiple Chinese American families who had expressed similar concerns that had also gone unnoticed by the American public for decades (Moran 2008, 117).

Moreover, for Steinman, the translated narrative communicated to him from Mrs. Lau about her son's situation made him believe that Kinney was the best child to serve as the public face in the case against the SFUSD. Kinney was a young Asian immigrant in elementary school, and because he was not receiving help or services in his native language, he was struggling academically. Steinman also inaccurately believed that Kinney was a birthright citizen and that Mrs. Lau was a widow, both of which were pieces of the Lau narrative that later were proven false. Although there were higher populations of Mexican American K–12 students who were also not receiving appropriate bilingual programs and services through the SFUSD, Steinman specifically requested that the case solely address the needs of the Chinese immigrant populations, who he believed were subjected to less harsh biases from the public because of the general belief that Asian Americans are high-achieving model minorities who rarely make racial grievances (Burke 2002). In contrast, Latina/o communities, particularly generations of Mexican Americans, have long been subjected to negative stereotypes, including the inaccurate belief harbored by a majority-white public that they receive preferential treatment— including what is seen as unnecessary services in bilingual education. While Asian Americans and Latina/os in the United States have similarly been racialized as perpetual foreigners who do not assimilate to white-dominant norms through their language and literacy practices, the latter has been more harshly constructed as undeserving of extra services and support because of derogatory stereotypes that they do not make efforts to assimilate or work hard.

The U.S. Supreme Court victory and settlement from the *Lau* case made a lasting impact on the future of bilingual education for all students who were speakers of languages other than English. However, Lau was never able to receive the full benefits of this victory in terms of gaining access to bilingual services because of the lag time to design and implement these programs. By the time bilingual programs were implemented in SFUSD schools, the Lau family had moved out of San Francisco's Chinatown. Lau reportedly struggled throughout his K–12 schooling years, but he eventually learned English at school through full immersion. Lau attended San Francisco State University and graduated with a degree in Computer Programming in 1984 (Burke 2002). Though his name will continue to be associated with an important part of bilingual education in U.S. history, Lau is not fully literate in his heritage language. He is said to take pride in his ability to navigate his corporate career while still being able to communicate with his parents in their native language.

In a 2002 *Boston Globe* interview, Lau, who now goes by the American name of "Ken" instead of "Kinney," shared his perspectives of what he remembers about the case as a young boy in the 1970s. He saw his role as being the public face of the case and representing the many Chinese American families and organizations that rallied around the suit: "Whoever told the story wanted to tell it in their way, is my feeling," he says three decades later. "I don't remember much about it other than taking a trip to New Orleans a few years later—they invited us for a dinner, and they presented us with a plaque. I remember going up to the stage and saying thank you" (Burke 2002). Over time, the Lau family is said to have distanced themselves from Steinman and removed themselves from public attention. However, due to the influence that the Lau family had on bilingual education policy, other families across ethnic and racial lines, particularly Latina/o communities, continued a battle with the SFUSD to advocate for bilingual education programs and services for their children (Wang 1976). Community advocates also continued to testify to the U.S. Congress to influence federal policy. Thus, whether Lau and his family were anticipating it or not, their faces and legacy had a lasting impact on SFUSD and U.S. education policies, particularly in the areas of bilingual education and ESL education. The *Lau* case is also discussed in many U.S. teacher-preparation bilingual education programs, as well as in multicultural education courses.

Ling-chi Wang (1938–)

The *Lau* case was set during a time of active community organizing and significant momentum among the Asian American community during the 1960s and 1970s, especially from activists in San Francisco. The U.S. civil rights movement and anti-war protests during this era brought the masses to speak against a litany of social injustices that were affecting American Indians and communities of color in areas such as education, employment, political participation, and public housing. Asian American activists spoke about the specific needs of their own communities, including why their children required culturally relevant language and literacy education (Moran 2008, 115). Among one of the most notable Asian American activists during this time was Ling-chi Wang. Born in 1938 in the Xiamen, Fujian Province in China, a young Wang traveled to the United States to study music at Hope College in Michigan, where he earned his BA in 1961. In college, he learned about African American activists, including Malcom X and Martin Luther King, Jr., and was inspired by the civil rights movement led by these and other prominent African

Americans. Wang eventually earned his doctorate in Semitic Languages from the University of California at Berkeley (UC Berkeley).

At UC Berkeley, Wang was actively involved in organizing for the creation of an Asian American Studies Department alongside other ethnic studies programs. His bilingual skills in Chinese and English garnered credibility and respect from both the Chinese immigrant community and white American officials as he advocated for ethnic studies (Moran 2008, 115). In 1969, Wang and other UC Berkeley activists founded the Chinese for Affirmative Action (CAA). The CAA addressed the systemic ways that Chinese Americans were denied equal opportunities in various education institutions and society due to the intersection of their ancestry, national origin, and race. Wang also served on the faculty of the Asian American Studies Department at UC Berkeley and became a nationally acclaimed scholar of Asian American education and history. In addition to his scholarship, Wang was an activist who committed his life to tirelessly advocating for the social betterment of Chinese American and other Asian American communities.

In 1970, Wang began working in the same office as Steinman, the attorney who worked closely with the Lau family. Wang helped Steinman recruit fourteen Chinese American families to sign on with the Lau family as plaintiffs to the case against the SFUSD, many of whom represented the working poor (Moran 2008, 117). The CAA, with Wang's leadership, helped organize numerous events leading up to and following the U.S. Supreme Court decision in *Lau*. Wang's leadership in San Francisco also led him to collaboratively develop education policies and guidelines to uphold the *Lau* case with other education specialists. A number of community activists, including Wang, testified before the U.S. Congress to provide guidelines for the content and scope of bilingual education programs and helped draft the Bilingual and Bicultural Act of 1976 (Soloman 2010, 132). As a result of Wang's efforts, other states across the United States followed suit and also implemented guidelines in developing effective bilingual education programs.

For more than forty years following the *Lau* legal victory, Wang has been pivotal in advocating for culturally responsive education and language-education rights through promoting bilingual education and language immersion programs. He has advocated for including Asian languages in Educational Testing Service assessments and worked with the San Francisco community to provide working-class adults in Chinatown with access to ESL class offerings. In the 1980s, during the height of national battles over race-conscious affirmative-action initiatives, Wang uncovered several admission policies within the University of California system that appeared to discriminate against Asian American applicants. Until his retirement in 2006, Wang remained active in leading and participating in Asian American studies and other ethnic studies programs at UC Berkeley. Ultimately, Wang's unwavering support of the Lau family during the 1970s propelled his career-long commitment for advancing causes for Asian American communities, particularly in the areas of bilingual and ESL education.

DOCUMENT EXCERPTS

Lau v. Nichols *Ruling*

Twenty years before Lau v. Nichols, Brown v. Board of Education *(1954) struck down the "separate but equal" concept and found that racially segregating students was inherently unequal under the Equal Protection Clause of the Fourteenth Amendment. In* Lau v. Nichols, *the Supreme Court ruled that non–English-speaking students of Chinese ancestry in San Francisco were given instruction in English and therefore were not receiving an equal educational opportunity. The case ended in a unanimous decision in favor of bilingual instruction. While the Court ruling required school districts to provide supplemental instruction, it did not specify how and to what extent. The Court reached its conclusion using the California Education Code in the San Francisco Unified School District (SFUSD) Handbook and Section 601 of the Civil Rights Act of 1964.*

Lau v. Nichols

1974

MR. JUSTICE DOUGLAS delivered the opinion of the Court.

The San Francisco, California, school system was integrated in 1971 as a result of a federal court decree. See *Lee v. Johnson.* The District Court found that there are 2,856 students of Chinese ancestry in the school system who do not speak English. Of those who have that language deficiency, about 1,000 are given supplemental courses in the English language. About 1,800, however, do not receive that instruction.

This class suit brought by non-English-speaking Chinese students against officials responsible for the operation of the San Francisco Unified School District seeks relief against the unequal educational opportunities, which are alleged to violate, inter alia, the Fourteenth Amendment. No specific remedy is urged upon us. Teaching English to the students of Chinese ancestry who do not speak the language is one choice. Giving instructions to this group in Chinese is another. There may be others. Petitioners ask only that the Board of Education be directed to apply its expertise to the problem and rectify the situation.

The District Court denied relief. The Court of Appeals affirmed, holding that there was no violation of the Equal Protection Clause of the Fourteenth Amendment or of 601 of the Civil Rights Act of 1964, which excludes from participation in federal financial assistance, recipients of aid which discriminate against racial groups. One judge dissented. A hearing en banc was denied, two judges dissenting.

We granted the petition for certiorari because of the public importance of the question presented.

The Court of Appeals reasoned that "[e]very student brings to the starting line of his educational career different advantages and disadvantages caused in part by social, economic and cultural background, created and continued completely apart from any contribution by the school system." Yet in our view the case may not be so easily decided. This is a public school system of California and 71 of the California Education Code states that "English shall be the basic language of instruction in all schools." That section permits a school district to determine "when and under what circumstances instruction may be given bilingually." That section also states as "the policy of the state" to insure "the mastery of English by all pupils in the schools." And bilingual instruction is authorized "to the extent that it does not interfere with the systematic, sequential, and regular instruction of all pupils in the English language."

Moreover, 8573 of the Education Code provides that no pupil shall receive a diploma of graduation from grade 12 who has not met the standards of proficiency in "English," as well as other prescribed subjects. Moreover, by 12101 of the Education Code (Supp. 1973) children between the ages of six and 16 years are (with exceptions not material here) "subject to compulsory full-time education."

Under these state-imposed standards there is no equality of treatment merely by providing students with the same facilities, textbooks, teachers, and curriculum; for students who do not understand English are effectively foreclosed from any meaningful education.

Basic English skills are at the very core of what these public schools teach. Imposition of a requirement that, before a child can effectively participate in the educational program, he must already have acquired those basic skills is to make a mockery of public education. We know that those who do not understand English are certain to find their classroom experiences wholly incomprehensible and in no way meaningful.

We do not reach the Equal Protection Clause argument which has been advanced but rely solely on 601 of the Civil Rights Act of 1964, to reverse the Court of Appeals. That section bans discrimination based "on the ground of race, color, or national origin," in "any program or activity receiving Federal financial assistance." The school district involved in this litigation receives large amounts of federal financial assistance. The Department of Health, Education, and Welfare (HEW), which has authority to promulgate regulations prohibiting discrimination in federally assisted school systems, in 1968 issued one guideline that "[s]chool systems are responsible for assuring that students of a particular race, color, or national origin are not denied the opportunity to obtain the education generally obtained by other students in the system." In 1970 HEW made the guidelines more specific, requiring school districts that were federally funded "to rectify the language deficiency in order to open" the instruction to students who had "linguistic deficiencies."

By 602 of the Act HEW is authorized to issue rules, regulations, and orders to make sure that recipients of federal aid under its jurisdiction conduct any federally financed projects consistently with 601. HEW's regulations, 45 CFR 80.3 (b) (1), specify that the recipients may not

(ii) Provide any service, financial aid, or other benefit to an individual which is different, or is provided in a different manner, from that provided to others under the program;

 . . .

(iv) Restrict an individual in any way in the enjoyment of any advantage or privilege enjoyed by others receiving any service, financial aid, or other benefit under the program.

Discrimination among students on account of race or national origin that is prohibited includes "discrimination . . . in the availability or use of any academic . . . or other facilities of the grantee or other recipient."

Discrimination is barred which has that effect even though no purposeful design is present: a recipient "may not . . . utilize criteria or methods of administration which have the effect of subjecting individuals to discrimination" or have "the effect of defeating or substantially impairing accomplishment of the objectives of the program as respect individuals of a particular race, color, or national origin."

It seems obvious that the Chinese-speaking minority receive fewer benefits than the English-speaking majority from respondents' school system which denies them a meaningful opportunity to participate in the educational program—all earmarks of the discrimination banned by the regulations. In 1970 HEW issued clarifying guidelines, which include the following:

Where inability to speak and understand the English language excludes national origin-minority group children from effective participation in the educational program offered by a school district, the district must take affirmative steps to rectify the language deficiency in order to open its instructional program to these students.

Any ability grouping or tracking system employed by the school system to deal with the special language skill needs of national origin-minority group children must be designed to meet such language skill needs as soon as possible and must not operate as an educational dead end or permanent track.

Respondent school district contractually agreed to "comply with title VI of the Civil Rights Act of 1964 . . . and all requirements imposed by or pursuant to the Regulation" of HEW which are "issued pursuant to that title . . ." and also immediately to "take any measures necessary to effectuate this agreement." The Federal Government has power to fix the terms on which its money allotments to the States shall be disbursed. *Oklahoma v. CSC.* Whatever may be the limits of that power, *Steward Machine Co. v. Davis*, they have not been reached here. Senator Humphrey, during the floor debates on the Civil Rights Act of 1964, said: Simple justice requires that public funds, to which all taxpayers of all races contribute, not be spent in any fashion which encourages, entrenches, subsidizes, or results in racial discrimination.

We accordingly reverse the judgment of the Court of Appeals and remand the case for the fashioning of appropriate relief.

Reversed and remanded.

Source: *Lau v. Nichols.* 414 U.S. 563 (1974).

See also: The Chinese Exclusion Act 1882; *Gong Lum v. Rice*, 1927; *People v. Hall*, 1854

Further Reading

"Asian Immersion Schools Surge in Popularity to Meet Demand." 2014. *NBC News*. https://www.nbcnews.com/news/asian-america/asian-immersion-schools-surge-popularity-meet-demand-n142751

Baugh, John. 2009. "Linguistic Diversity, Access, and Risk." *Review of Research in Education* 33: 272–282.

Burke, Garance. 2002. "Ambivalent in Any Language Subject of Landmark Bilingual Case Uncertain of Role." *Boston Globe*, July 22.

Callahan, Rebecca. 2005. "Tracking and High School English Learners: Limiting Opportunity to Learn." *American Educational Research Journal* 42: 305–328.

Crawford, James. 2007. "Hard Sell: Why Is Bilingual Education So Unpopular with the American Public?" In *Bilingual Education: An Introductory Reader*, edited by Ofeila García and Colin Baker, 145–161. Tonawanda, NY: Multilingual Matters.

Gándara, Patricia, Rachel Moran, and Eugene Garcia. 2004. "Legacy of Brown: Lau and Language Policy in the United States." *Review of Research in Education* 28: 27–46.

Moran, Rachel. 2008. "The Story of Lau v. Nichols: Breaking the Silence in Chinatown." In *Education Law Stories*, edited by Michael Olivas and Ronna Schneider, 110–157. New York: Foundation Press.

Roos, Peter. 1978. "Bilingual Education: The Hispanic Response to Unequal Educational Opportunity." *Law and Contemporary Problems* 42: 111–140.

Salomone, Rosemary C. *True American: Language, Identity, and the Education of Immigrant Children*. Cambridge, MA: Harvard University Press, 2010.

"Text of the Court's Decision in Lau v. Nichols." 1984. *Education Week* (January 24): 14–15. https://www.edweek.org/ew/articles/1984/01/25/05300021.h03.html

Umansky, Ilana. 2016. "Leveled and Exclusionary Tracking: English Learners' Access to Academic Content in Middle School." *American Educational Research Journal* 53: 1792–1833.

Valdez, Veronica, Juan Freire, and Garrett Delavan. 2016. "The Gentrification of Dual Language Education." *The Urban Review* 48: 601–627.

Walsh, Mark. 2009. "ELLs and the Law: Statues, Precedents." *Education Week*: 8–9.

Wang, L. Ling Chi. 1976. "Lau v. Nichols: History of a Struggle for Equal and Quality Education." In *Counterpoint,* edited by Emma Gee, 240–259. Los Angeles: UCLA Asian American Studies Center.

Zong, Jie and Jeanne Batalova. 2015. "The Limited English Proficient Population in the United States." July 8. https://www.migrationpolicy.org/article/limited-english-proficient-population-united-states

Asian/Pacific American Heritage Week Established, 1978

William B. Noseworthy

Chronology

Eighteenth century	Since California was once part of Mexico, and Mexico was connected to the transpacific silver trade, as well as the Philippines, it is probable that Chinese first arrived in what is now the United States during this period. Chinese also arrived in East Coast port cities via Guangzhou and the Cape of Good Hope by the late eighteenth century.
Nineteenth century	Edo Japan has an explicitly anti-European trade policy, leading Americans and Europeans to interpret Japan as "closed," although in reality trade with Asian partners was common.
May 7, 1841	The first known Japanese immigrant arrives in the United States, one of five rescued by Captain Whitfield after a shipwreck. Four of the five disembark at Hawaii, then an independent kingdom. One, Manjiro, becomes the first known Japanese on U.S. soil and the first to be educated in the United States.
1852	After a wave of immigration, there are approximately 25,000 Chinese in the United States.
March 31, 1854	Manjiro is the lead translator of the Treaty of Kanagawa. De facto, he was the first ambassador to negotiate between the United States and Japan.
1854	Yung Wing graduates from Yale, the first Chinese American to graduate from a U.S. university.

May 10, 1869	"Golden Spike Day." The transcontinental railroad project is completed, with thanks to the significant aid of Chinese laborers, especially those who cut through the steepest part of the Sierra Nevada, the greatest and most difficult incline the project faced.
1870s	Riding an economic downturn after the decline of the mining industry in California and the American West, anti-Chinese sentiment spreads. Political figures such as Denis Kearney and John Bigler argue that Chinese exclusion is "pro-labor."
1879	Chinese are barred from certain terms of employment under the constitution of the state of California, supported in part by the anti-Chinese politics of John Bigler.
1880	After subsequent waves of migration, there are now 300,000 Chinese in the United States.
1882	The U.S. federal government bans Chinese immigration to the United States.
1892	The Geary Act extends the ban on Chinese immigration for an additional ten years.
1895	The queen of Hawaii is forced to abdicate, and Hawaii subsequently becomes a U.S. territory, one that would later become home to a significant Japanese-minority population.
1917	The Immigration Act of 1917 creates the Asiatic Barred Zone. For a brief period, only Japanese and Koreans are allowed to migrate to the United States. All other Asians are essentially barred.
1924	The National Origins Act bans immigration from East Asia as a whole.
1927	Kinjiro Matsudaira becomes the first Japanese American mayor of a U.S. city (Edmonston, Maryland).
1941–1943	The Japanese Empire's attack on Pearl Harbor leads to the internment of most of the West Coast Japanese American and Japanese population. Those who remain on Hawaii make up a significant portion of the 100th Battalion of the U.S. Army, specifically the all-volunteer 442nd Combat Team, the most decorated team of its size in U.S. military history.
1943	The Magnuson Act makes discrimination based on race illegal. The quota system of national origins remains, leading to de facto discrimination based on race.

1959	Daniel K. Inouye, a member of the 442nd Combat Team, becomes the first Japanese American to serve in Congress.
1963	Spark M. Matsunaga replaces Inouye, as Inouye moves to the Senate.
1966	*The New York Times* and *U.S. News & World Report* introduce the term "model minority," a term that will be quickly critiqued as divisive racist rhetoric by student leaders from the Asian American community.
1968	The founding of the Asian American Political Alliance (AAPA) is a turning point in the Asian American movement in the 1960s and 1970s. The AAPA participates in the longest student strikes in U.S. history as part of the Third World Liberation Front (TWLF) coalition.
1971	Matsunaga moves to the First District when Hawaii receives a second House district, and Norman Y. Mineta becomes the first Japanese American mayor of a major American city (San Jose, California).
1974	Mineta joins the U.S. House of Representatives.
January 1977	Matsunaga joins Inouye in the Senate.
June 1977	Representatives Mineta and Frank Horton introduce a House resolution to establish "Pacific/Asian American Heritage Week."
July 1977	Senators Inouye and Matsunaga introduce a Senate resolution to establish "Asian/Pacific American Heritage Week."
October 5, 1978	House Joint Resolution 1007 is signed into law, establishing Asian/Pacific American Heritage Week.
May 9, 1990	Congressional law expands Asian/Pacific American Heritage Week to a month-long observance.

Narrative

Asian/Pacific American Heritage Week originated as a means to commemorate Asian contributions to the United States. The week would later expand into a month, although it began quite simply. In June 1977, Representatives Norman Y. Mineta of California and Frank Horton of New York introduced a House resolution to establish the week in the first ten days of May. Following this introduction, in July 1977, two senators from Hawaii, Daniel K. Inouye and Spark M. Matsunaga, led a group

A musician from the Japanese Buddhist group Soh Daiko performed at the 32nd Asian American and Pacific Islander Heritage Festival in Union Square, New York, in 2011. Since the establishment of Asian/Pacific American Heritage Week in 1978, a number of yearly festivals are held, and some of them have become annual traditions. (Lei Xu/Dreamstime.com)

of co-sponsors on a similar resolution. While Horton had been a lawyer previously, it seems significant that Mineta, Inouye, and Matsunaga had all served in various organizations in the U.S. Army. Furthermore, Mineta's family had been detained in a Japanese internment camp during World War II, prior to his military service, while Inouye and Matsunaga both served in the U.S. Army during World War II. Despite their service and the relative simplicity of the resolutions, neither one passed, although the Senate resolution did muster additional bipartisan co-sponsors: Senator James A. McClure (R-ID), Senator E. J. "Jake" Garn (R-UT), Senator Pete Domenici (R-NM), Senator Richard S. Schweiker (R-PA), and Senator Birch Bayh (D-IN). Because neither resolution passed, Horton introduced Joint House Resolution 1007 in June 1978. That resolution passed and was signed into law on October 5, 1978 (Lee 2017, 159–61).

The text of the legislation, Public Law 95-419, authorized the request of the president to proclaim a seven-day period beginning May 4, 1979, as Asian/Pacific American Heritage Week, "calling upon the people of the United States, especially the educational community, to observe such week with appropriate ceremonies and activities" (House Joint Resolution 1007, 1978). The only notable difference between the original proposals and the legislation that passed was the timing of the week. The initial House resolution proclaimed the first ten days in May. The initial Senate resolution narrowed the time to a week, which was to include the seventh and the tenth of the month, during the first ten days in May. Hence, the final legislation only differed in that it assigned a specific start to the proclamation of the week. For the next twelve years, the American president would pass an annual declaration of the week, until an act of Congress simply expanded the period to a month, approved on May 9, 1990, as Public Law 101-283.

The congressional act that turned the week into a month-long veneration of the contributions of Asian Americans and Pacific Islanders specifically clarified the import of the seventh and tenth of May, highlighting the purposes of the earlier proposed authorizations for declarations in 1977. First, the seventh of May 1841 was the day that the first recorded Japanese immigrants came to the United States. Second, May 10, 1869, was "Golden Spike Day," the day that the last railroad tie completed the transcontinental railroad with "significant contributions from Chinese pioneers" (House Resolution 5572, 1992). The legislation furthermore clarified that the purpose of the initial week was to "recognize the history, concerns, contributions and achievements of Asian and Pacific Americans." One additional provision of this legislation was that it called upon federal, state, and outlying territories' levels of the executive branch of government to make proclamations in line with the ideals of the program.

Historical Background

Understanding the historical background of Asian/Pacific American Heritage Week requires an examination of the milestones of May 7, 1841, and May 10, 1869, in addition to the context of Asian exclusion policy in the United States and Asian contributions through the 1970s. In the early nineteenth century, Edo Japan maintained a relative position of isolationist policies, which was at least in part motivated by a pacifist approach to international relations. Northern Americans had great difficulty understanding this, however, since the policies were mostly motivated by stabilizing East Asian politics by terms of relations with Qing China. Americans were more struck, perhaps understandably, by the apparent policy of putting nonpermitted foreigners to death for setting foot on Japanese soil. Regardless, during this period it was not uncommon for sailors of various nationalities to rescue one another. As it would happen, Captain Whitfield rescued five Japanese sailors in 1841 (Kawada 2003).

Four sailors departed Whitfield's vessel at Honolulu—then part of the Kingdom of Hawaii, which was only annexed by the United States after the queen was forced to abdicate in 1895—but the fifth, a sixteen-year-old boy named Manjiro, remained on board until he reached Bedford, Massachusetts. He would eventually return to Japan, after living and studying in New England, whereupon he became the translator of the Treaty of Kanagawa. The Treaty of Kanagawa was signed on March 31, 1854, and normalized trading relations with the United States. Although it is credited as being the "treaty that opened Japan to the world," it is important to note that it is actually just the first normalization of relations with a government that was either predominantly European or European-descended. Regardless, Manjiro's contributions are wildly under-celebrated. De facto, he was the first ambassador negotiating between the United States and Japan and the first Japanese immigrant to the United States. Japanese continued to arrive in New England and, in the 1860s, in the gold hills of California. They also created significant communities in coastal California and Hawaii by the 1890s and 1900 (Kawada 2003).

The 17.6-karat gold final spike of the transcontinental railroad, which was driven into the ground on May 10, 1869, punctuates the long trajectory of Chinese migration to North America. First, it is well accepted that Chinese were already living in the Philippines in the sixteenth century when the transpacific silver trade stretched from the Americas to China. However, it is likely that much of these early populations would have been limited to Mexico, although some have argued that the first Chinese to arrive in what is now the United States would have arrived in California in the eighteenth century. However, just after the Revolutionary War, transpacific trade also meant that Chinese were arriving in ports in New England via Guangzhou and the Cape of Good Hope by the early eighteenth century. Populations were small, although occasionally upwardly mobile. The first Chinese student to graduate from any American university, for example, was Yung Wing, who graduated from Yale in 1854. By the middle of the nineteenth century, the number of Chinese immigrants began to increase dramatically, in part due to an economic crisis in southern China. There were 25,000 Chinese in America in 1852 and 300,000 by 1880. They worked in a wide variety of industries, including on Southern plantations during the Civil War, in fisheries on the West Coast, in the western U.S. mining industry, and on the first transcontinental railroad. In fact, the Central Pacific Railroad (CPRR) preferred to hire Chinese laborers, and consequentially, Chinese laborers were responsible for most of the manual labor of the CPRR, including cutting through the Sierra Nevada, the steepest and most difficult incline of the transcontinental project (Azuma and Yoo 2016, 301–06; Lee 2004; Lee 2016, 72–95).

Despite the successes of the transcontinental project, the contributions of Chinese labor were quickly scapegoated with an economic decline tied to the conditions of the mining industry in the 1870s. Denis Kearney of the Workingmen's Party led a pseudo–pro-labor movement that excluded the interests of any nonwhite labor.

The Democratic governor of California, John Bigler, had already supported explicitly anti-Chinese taxes in the 1850s. By 1879, California adopted a new constitution, which banned Chinese from certain terms of employment within the state. Just three years later, the federal government banned all immigration from China for a period of ten years, forced those who left to obtain reentry permits, and barred resident aliens from citizenship. Two years later, reentry provisions were banned, and in 1888 the Scott Act prohibited reentry altogether. The following year, the Chinese Exclusion Act and the Scott Act were upheld by the U.S. Supreme Court. The Geary Act of 1892 renewed the exclusion provisions for another ten years, and in 1902, they were renewed indefinitely. In 1917, another immigration "reform" created the Asiatic Barred Zone, which barred all immigrants from Asia except those from Japan, Korea, and parts of Russia. Later, in 1924, the National Origins Act banned immigration from East Asia as a whole (Azuma and Yoo 2016, 154–65; Lee 2004; Lee 2016, 94–103).

In effect, by 1924, it was illegal for Asians and Pacific Islanders to immigrate to the United States. Although Kinjiro Matsudaira became the first Japanese American mayor of a U.S. city (Edmonston, Maryland) in 1927, persecution of the Japanese continued. A 1913 law in California barred Japanese from purchasing land. Furthermore, when Japanese imperial forces attacked Pearl Harbor in 1941, Japanese community leaders were arrested and detained by federal authorities by simple provision of their ethnicity. Then, with the signing of Executive Order 9066, Japanese Americans were forcibly removed from their homes and put into prison camps along the West Coast, where the majority of Japanese at the time lived. However, the population of Hawaii was not interred, since Japanese Americans were one-third of the population of the state, and it was decided that moving them to a prison camp would create a substantial security threat (Azuma and Yoo 2016, 135–52; Nakanishi and Lai 2003, 39–80; Lee 2004; Lee 2016, 94–103).

Notably, three of the four drafters of the Asian/Pacific American Heritage Week legislation experienced World War II in different ways. The senators from Hawaii, Inouye and Matsunaga, served in the U.S. Army. In fact, the Japanese American soldiers who formed the 100th Infantry Battalion became a famous division in key engagements in Europe beginning in September 1943. Only one Japanese American, Ben Kuroki, served in the U.S. Air Force during the war. Meanwhile, more than 120,000 Japanese were put in prison camps, like the young Norman Y. Mineta and his family.

Furthermore, their experiences after the war also varied. While those Japanese Americans who served in the all-volunteer 442nd Regimental Combat Team joined the 100th Army Battalion in 1944, by 1945, the 442nd became the most decorated single military unit of its size in U.S. military history (Masuda 2015, 3–9,

271–77). For some, military service was never repaid, although they suffered mutilations, mental trauma, and economic ruin. For others, military service became a means of upward mobility. Inouye became the first Japanese American to serve in Congress in 1959, when he was elected Hawaii's House of Representatives at-large district member. When Inouye moved to the U.S. Senate four years later, Matsunaga served as his successor until 1971, when the representative seat district was split into two and Matsunaga took the First District. He would later join Inouye in the Senate in January 1977. The year 1971 was also pivotal in that Mineta became the first mayor of a major city in the United States, when he was elected to the office in San Jose, California. He joined the House of Representatives in 1974 and held his seat for a staggering ten reelections (Azuma and Yoo 2016, 426–31; Lee 2017, 159–61).

It would be fair to state that, in combination with the specific experiences of Japanese American congressional leaders, part of the broader context of the Asian/Pacific American Heritage Week proclamation in 1978 was a growing sense of pan–Asian American solidarity in the twentieth century. While it is true that with the passage of the Magnuson Act in 1943, the United States revised immigration policy to no longer bar Asians based on national security interests, naturalization was still relatively restricted until the subsequent passage of the Immigration and Nationality Act of 1952 and the Immigration and Nationality Act of 1965. Furthermore, domestic redlining—essentially keeping suburban neighborhoods as white as possible—was a broad discriminatory practice that affected Asian Americans, regardless of origins, as did discrimination in matters of employment and education.

Despite the fact that *The New York Times* and *U.S. News & World Report* described Asian Americans, and specifically Chinese Americans, respectively, as the "model minority," this idea was a myth, and most Asian American communities were not as upwardly mobile as they were perceived to be (Chan 2003, 70–85). In 1968, in a stunning moment of solidarity, the Black Students Union and a number of Asian American student associations participated in a student-led strike at San Francisco State University. The strike spread to Berkeley, where it was supported by the Asian American Political Alliance (AAPA), the first widely visible pan–Asian American political association, founded by Yuji Ichioka and Emma Gee. Subsequently, in part because of the success of the student strikes, the Asian American movement became a grassroots, community-based political force in California, New York City, and Hawaii. Therefore, it is not a surprise that when Mineta, Inouye, and Matsunaga pushed for congressional recognition of Asian Americans writ large, they were addressing the concerns of their political base, a political base that had yet to see the full promise of the civil rights movement (Azuma and Yoo 2016, 182–92; Lee 2016, 304–05; Lee 2017, 159–61; Maeda 2012).

Asian American Political Alliance

The Asian American Political Alliance (AAPA) was arguably the first nationally known pan-Asian political group in the United States. The organization was formed as a group of students at Berkeley University in 1968. Founded by Yuji Ichioka and Emma Gee, the organization was an effort to collectively organize student protesters into a coalition bloc, after the model of other ethnic solidarity organizations, and bringing the disparate groups of Japanese, Filipino, and Chinese American students together. Most of the organizers already had experience working with the civil rights movement in various coalitions, with the Black Panther Party, the Black Students Union, the United Farm Workers, the Peace Movement, or some combination thereof. The AAPA specifically recruited students from the Chinese Students Club, the Nisei Students Club, and other Asian student associations. As they formed meetings and reading groups, members became influenced by the ideas of Franz Fanon and the Black Panthers, as well as by Third World Liberation Front (TWLF) politics (Lee 2016, 304–05; Maeda 2012).

AAPA joined with the TWLF in organizing the longest student strikes in American history at Berkeley and San Francisco State University, which resulted in the formation of the first ethnic studies programs in the United States. Internationally, they looked toward the symbolism of the Bandung Movement in its opposition to American imperialism. The AAPA also specifically argued against the "model minority myth" presented by 1966 publications of *The New York Times* and *U.S. News & World Report*. AAPA held that this myth was created to divide minority groups in an "us–them," divide-and-conquer form of rhetoric, as well as to paint Asians broadly as docile and obedient. In a moment of pan–Asian American sentiment, founding member Richard Aoki highlighted solidarity with other minorities, including "Afro American people, the Chicanos, and the American Indians" in the AAPA's opposition to imperialism. Although the Congress members who went on to create Asian/Pacific American Heritage Week would likely have opposed the radicalism of the AAPA at the time, they created it in a move that addressed the popular pan–Asian American sentiment that the AAPA's movement successfully sparked (Lee 2016, 304–05; Maeda 2012; Nakanishi and Lai 2003, 158–68).

Current Status and Long-Term Impact

The long-term impact of Asian/Pacific American Heritage Week can almost certainly be measured by the subsequent transformation of the initial policy into a month-long series of nationwide events in the 1990s. From the 1980s through the 2000s, a number of local events were also inspired by the link to the Asian/Pacific American Heritage Week program. For example, the Asian/Pacific American Heritage Festival began in New York City in 1981, and a related film festival began in Los Angeles in 1983. An Asian Festival began in Dallas, Texas, in 1990, and a Pacific Rim Fest began in Sacramento, California, in 1992. Another Asian Festival began in Columbus, Ohio, in 1995. By the 2000s, these events spread locally across the country, from Penn State campus; Brandeis, Massachusetts; and Pittsburgh on the East Coast to San Diego, Oakland, San Francisco, and Seattle on the West Coast; to University of Florida Gainesville, Florida State University Tallahassee, and Houston, Texas, in the South; to the University of Illinois Urbana-Champaign, Cleveland, Ohio, and universities across the Midwest. In addition to this particular educational impact, the works of the bill's original authors continued to have substantial impacts on the United States. For example, Mineta, along with Republican Alan K. Simpson, became a major force behind House Resolution 442, also known as the Civil Liberties Act of 1988, which included a formal apology for the injustices endured by Japanese Americans during World War II and measures to redress those grievances (Maeda 2012).

Biographies of Notable Figures

Norman Y. Mineta (1931–)

When Norman Y. Mineta was born in November 1931 in San Jose, California, his Japanese first-generation parents could not become citizens of the United States under the provisions of the Asian Exclusion Act. Furthermore, during World War II, as a result of Japanese internment, his family was forcibly moved to a prison camp at Heart Mountain in Cody, Wyoming. While he was at the camp, Mineta became friends with Alan K. Simpson. Both were Boy Scouts, and Simpson visited the camp often. They remained close friends and political allies later in life; for instance, both were behind the Civil Liberties Act of 1988.

When Mineta's family was released, they eventually returned to California. He attended the University of California, receiving a degree in business administration in 1953, before he joined the U.S. Army, whereupon he served in the military intelligence corps unit in Japan and Korea and was known widely to his peers as "Norm." After he left the U.S. Army, Mineta joined his father at the Mineta

Insurance Agency for several years, before he began his political career (Azuma and Yoo 2016, 415–29; Lee 2017, 159–61).

This career began in 1967, when he was appointed to a vacant seat on the San Jose City Council. Two years later, Mineta was elected to the council seat and then to vice mayor by fellow council members. Two years later, he was elected to the office of mayor to replace Ron James, the former city council member. He beat fourteen other candidates in the election and took every precinct with more than 60 percent of the total vote. He then spent only three years as mayor before he ran for California's Thirteenth Congressional District, defeating his opponent with 52 percent of the vote and winning the Democratic nomination. After he began in 1975, he served in Congress for twenty years, winning re-election ten times and never dipping below a 57 percent margin of victory. He was not only instrumental in the establishment of Asian/Pacific American Heritage Week but also in the passage of House Resolution 442, which officially redressed some of the grievances of the Japanese American population that had resulted from their internment during World War II. However, his most influential moment was probably founding the Congressional Asian Pacific American Caucus and serving as its first chair (Azuma and Yoo 2016, 415–29; Lee 2017, 159–61).

After Mineta left Congress in 1995, he spent a brief period in the private sector before returning to politics in 2000 as the first Asian American to hold a post in a presidential cabinet. Mineta had resigned to take a position with Lockheed Martin in 1995 before chairing the National Civil Aviation Review Commission in 1997, which recommended provisions to make air travel safer. The Clinton administration was impressed with his work in this position, and he was then appointed secretary of commerce in 2000. Clinton originally offered him secretary of transportation in 1993, but he declined. Regardless, Mineta was moved to this post by President George W. Bush in 2001. He was put in the difficult position of issuing the emergency order to ground all air traffic on September 11, 2001. Mineta's testimony on the events of 9/11 were not included in the 9/11 Commission Report, although he later reported that he had heard Vice President Cheney stating that orders to shoot down American Airlines Flight 77 remained the same as the flight approached the Pentagon. Mineta said that the orders were not specified, and he did not know what orders Cheney was referring to at the time. In the end, the report was neither able to confirm nor discredit the accusations made by others against Cheney using Mineta's account (Azuma and Yoo 2016, 415–29; Lee 2017, 159–61).

Following the events of September 11, 2001, Mineta continued to be influential. On September 21, he issued an order to forbid all America-based airline companies from racial profiling or discrimination against Muslim passengers. The order stated that it was illegal to discriminate against anyone based upon their race, color, national or ethnic origins, or religion. In November 2001, in recognition of his accomplishments, San Jose International Airport was renamed in his honor.

Mineta left the Bush administration to join the firm Hill & Knowlton, a global public relations consulting company, in 2006, the same year he was awarded the Presidential Medal of Freedom. Mineta remained influential in the Democratic Party in 2008 through his endorsement of Barack Obama in a quite close Democratic primary in California. The same year, he joined the National Academy of Public Administration, where he worked for two years before he was named co-chair of the Joint Ocean Commission Initiative, a bipartisan group focused upon ocean policy reform.

Ultimately, Mineta's career may well have been one of the most influential in Japanese American and Asian American political history (Azuma and Yoo 2016, 415–29; Lee 2017, 159–61).

Daniel K. Inouye (1924–2012)

Daniel K. Inouye was born on September 7, 1924, to Japanese parents, Hyotaro and Kame Inouye, in Honolulu, Hawaii. He was raised in the Chinese American Bingham Tract, an enclave community in the mostly Japanese area of Moʻiliʻili. A recent high school graduate, he tried to become a medical volunteer during the Japanese Empire's attack on Pearl Harbor in 1941, but the U.S. Army had banned Japanese from joining the service as volunteers, so he entered premedical studies at the University of Hawaii. When the ban was dropped in 1943, Inouye promptly enlisted in the all-volunteer, Japanese American, 442nd Regimental Combat Team. This combat team became the most decorated unit in the history of the American military. The unit served in Italy and France. Reportedly, Inouye's life was saved by two silver dollars that he kept in his shirt pocket, which stopped a bullet, and he consequentially carried the same two silver dollars with him as good luck charms. The charms apparently worked. He led an assault on three machine gun positions in April 1945 and was shot in the stomach. However, he only collapsed from blood loss after leading the assault and personally taking out two of the three machine guns. His hand was then severed with a grenade still in it, as he dragged himself into position to attack the third machine gun. Inouye pried his severed hand open to remove the grenade with his other hand, then taking additional wounds to the leg. A field hospital amputated the rest of his right arm. In 1947, two years after the amputation, he was honorably discharged from the military (Azuma and Yoo 2016, 415–29; Huang 2001, 141–47; Lee 2017, 131–33; Masuda 2015).

Having lost his arm, Inouye was forced to abandon his planned medical career. He had hoped to become a surgeon, but instead returned to college to study political science at the University of Hawaii Manoa. After graduating in 1950, he went on to earn a law degree from George Washington University Law School in 1953, whereupon he was elected to the territorial House of Representatives in Hawaii. After two terms he was elected to the territorial Senate in 1957. When Hawaii was promoted to statehood in 1959, the fledging state needed a representative and senators. Inouye became Hawaii's first representative and was re-elected in 1960. Two years later, he was elected to the U.S. Senate, where he served as chairman of the Senate Intelligence Committee between 1976 and 1979, during the period when Asian/Pacific American Heritage Week was established. He served as chairman of the Senate Indian Affairs Committee from 1987 to 1995 and from 2001 to 2003. In addition to his work on Asian/Pacific American Heritage Week, he introduced the National Museum of the American Indian Act in 1984, which led to the establishment of the National Museum of the American Indian in 2004 (Azuma and Yoo 2016, 415–29; Huang 2001, 141–47; Lee 2017, 131–33).

In total, Inouye was elected eight times to the U.S. Senate, never with less than 57 percent of the vote, and only once with less than 69 percent. He was, in the minds of his constituents, incredibly popular by the standards of that post. He was an early voice in Congress on the environmental movement, citing environmental concerns in 1981 regarding the types of goods that Americans could ship overseas. That same year, he and Senator Spark M. Matsunaga offered the opening statements in a federal commission regarding the treatment of Japanese Americans during World War II. While he first appeared to oppose reparations for the families of Japanese who were forced into prison camps, in 1989 Inouye cited reparations to hostages of the Iran-Contra scandal during his speech on the subject. Also in the 1980s, he opposed constitutional amendments to create periods of organized prayer in public schools and periods of possible silent prayer in public schools (Azuma and Yoo 2016, 415–29; Huang 2001, 141–47; Lee 2017, 131–33).

After Inouye served his second term as chair of the Senate Indian Affairs Committee, he went on to three additional posts, in part due to his dedication toward service and in part due to his popularity in the U.S. Senate. He chaired the Senate Commerce Committee between 2007 and 2009, as well as the Senate Appropriations Committee from 2009 to 2012. He was also president pro tempore of the Senate from 2010 to 2012, serving in case of the absence of Vice President of the United States and President of the Senate Joe Biden. He remained in this post until his death on December 17, 2012. He was posthumously awarded the Presidential Medal of Freedom by President Barack Hussein Obama on August 8, 2013, and Honolulu International Airport was renamed Daniel K. Inouye International on April 27, 2017.

DOCUMENT EXCERPTS

Proclamation 4650 (1979)

Public Law 95-419 authorized the request of the president to proclaim a seven-day period as Asian/Pacific American Heritage Week, beginning May 1979, to recognize and celebrate the contributions of Asian Americans and Pacific Islanders. For the next twelve years, the American president would pass an annual declaration of the week until Public Law 101-283 expanded the period to a month in 1990, thus making it Asian/Pacific American Heritage Month. Since then a number of cultural events have been organized to celebrate the heritage week and month across the country, such as film festivals, lecture series, parades, and other activities.

Proclamation 4650 of March 28, 1979

Asian/Pacific American Heritage Week, 1979
By the President of the United States of America
A Proclamation

America's greatness—its ideals, its system of government, its economy, its people—derives from the contribution of peoples of many origins who come to our land seeking human liberties or economic opportunity. Asian-Americans have played a significant role in the creation of a dynamic and pluralistic America, with their enormous contributions to our science, arts, industry, government and commerce.

Unfortunately, we have not always fully appreciated the talents and the contributions which Asian-Americans have brought to the United States. Until recently, our immigration and naturalization laws discriminated against them. They were also subjected to discrimination in education, housing, and employment. And during World War II our Japanese-American citizens were treated with suspicion and fear. Yet, Asians of diverse origins—from China, Japan, Korea, the Philippines, and Southeast Asia—continued to look to America as a land of hope, opportunity, and freedom.

At last their confidence in the United States has been justified. We have succeeded in removing the barriers to full participation in American life, and we welcome the newest Asian immigrants to our shores—refugees from Indochina displaced by political, and social upheavals. Their successful integration into American society and their positive and active participation in our national life demonstrates the soundness of America's policy of continued openness to peoples from Asia and the Pacific.

The Ninety-fifth Congress has requested the President by House Joint Resolution 1007, approved October 5, 1978, to designate the seven-day period beginning on May 4, 1979, as "Asian/Pacific American Heritage Week."

NOW, THEREFORE, I, JIMMY CARTER, President of the United States of America, declare the week beginning on May 4, 1979, as Asian/Pacific American Heritage Week. I call upon the people of the United States, especially the educational community, to observe this week with appropriate ceremonies and activities.

IN WITNESS WHEREOF, I have hereunto set my hand this twenty-eighth day of March, in the year of our Lord nineteen hundred seventy-nine, and of the Independence of the United States of America the two hundred and third.

JIMMY CARTER

Source: Carter, Jimmy. Proclamation 4650, March 28, 1979. Washington, D.C.: Government Printing Office, 1979.

See also: Daniel K. Inouye, First Asian American U.S. Senator, 1962; The First Asian American Studies Program Established at San Francisco State College, 1969; The Murder of Vincent Chin, 1982

Further Reading

Azuma, Eiichiro and David Yoo. 2016. *The Oxford Handbook of Asian American History*. New York: Oxford University Press.

Chan, Sucheng. 2003. *Remapping Asian American History*. Walnut Creek, CA: Roman Altamira.

House Joint Resolution 1007, Pub. L. No. 95-419 (1978).

House Resolution 5572, Pub. L. No. 102-450 (1992).

Huang, Guiyou. 2001. *Asian American Autobiographers: A Bio-Bibliographical Critical Sourcebook*. Westport, CT: Greenwood.

Kawada, Shoryo. 2003. *Hyoson Kiryaku: Drifting Toward the Southeast: The Story of Five Japanese Castaways*. New Bedford, MA: Spinner Publications.

Lee, Erika. 2004. *At America's Gates: Chinese Immigration during the Exclusion Era, 1882–1943*. Chapel Hill: University of North Carolina Press.

Lee, Erika. 2016. *The Making of Asian America: A History*. New York: Simon and Schuster.

Lee, Jonathan H. X. 2017. *Japanese Americans: The History and Culture of a People*. Santa Barbara, CA: ABC-CLIO.

Maeda, Daryl J. 2012. *Rethinking the Asian American Movement*. New York: Routledge.

Masuda, Minoru. 2015. *Letters from the 442nd: The World War II Correspondence of a Japanese American Medic*. Seattle: University of Washington Press.

Nakanishi, Don T. and James S. Lai. 2003. *Asian American Politics: Law, Participation, and Policy*. Lanham, MD: Rowman and Littlefield.

Ng, Franklin. 1998. *The History and Immigration of Asian Americans*. New York: Garland.

Okihiro, Gary Y. 2005. *The Columbia Guide to Asian American History*. New York: Columbia University Press.

Yenne, Bill. 2007. *Rising Sons: The Japanese American GIs Who Fought for the United States in World War II*. New York: Macmillan.

Wei, William. 1993. *The Asian American Movement*. Philadelphia: Temple University Press.

The Murder of Vincent Chin, 1982

Martin Kich

Chronology

1955	Vincent Chin is born in Guangdong Province in China and spends his early childhood in an orphanage.
1961	Vincent Chin is adopted by Bing Hing Chin, a Chinese American veteran of World War II, and his Chinese wife, Lily.
1960s	The family lives in Highland Park, Michigan.
1971	The family moves to Oak Park, Michigan.
1973	Vincent Chin graduates from Oak Park High School.
After 1973	Vincent Chin studies drafting at the Control Data Institute. He is then employed as an industrial draftsman at Efficient Engineering, an auto-parts supplier.
June 19, 1982	Ronald Ebens and Michael Nitz beat Vincent Chin with a baseball bat outside the Fancy Pants Lounge in Highland Park, Michigan.
June 23, 1982	Vincent Chin dies from his injuries.
June 27, 1982	The day on which Vincent Chin is supposed to be married.
March 17, 1983	Ebens pleads guilty and Nitz pleads no contest to manslaughter charges, and Judge Kaufman sentences them to three-year suspended sentences and fines them each $3,780.
June 1983	Judge Kaufman refuses to reconsider his sentencing of Ebens and Nitz. Lily Chin files a civil suit against Ebens.
June 19–23, 1983	Days of Remembrance of Vincent Chin are declared in Detroit, prompting Asian American communities across the country to participate.
June 21, 1984	The federal trial of Ebens and Nitz, each on two charges that they violated Vincent Chin's civil rights, begins.
June 28, 1984	Ebens is convicted of one of the two charges he faced, but Nitz is acquitted on both charges.
September 19, 1984	Ebens receives a twenty-five-year sentence, but he remains free on $20,000 bond while his attorneys appeal the conviction.

September 13, 1986	A federal appeals court reverses Ebens's conviction and vacates his sentence.
September 20, 1986	Federal prosecutors announce that they will retry Ebens for violating Vincent Chin's civil rights.
April 23, 1987	Ebens's second federal trial begins in Cincinnati.
May 2, 1987	The jury acquits Ebens on the charge that he violated Vincent Chin's civil rights.
August 1, 1987	The family of Vincent Chin reaches an out-of-court settlement of the civil suit filed against Ebens.
March 1988	*Who Killed Vincent Chin?*, a film directed by Christine Choy and Renee Tajima, premieres at the 17th New Directors/New Films Festival, the annual collaboration between the Film Society of Lincoln Center and the Museum of Modern Art.
1990	*Who Killed Vincent Chin?* receives a Peabody Award.
1991	*Who Killed Vincent Chin?* receives a Silver Baton from the Alfred I. Dupont-Columbia University Awards for broadcast journalism.
1998	The Contemporary American Theatre Festival commissions *Carry the Tiger to the Mountain* by Cherylene Lee.
2002	Shortly before the twentieth anniversary of the murder of her son, Lily Chin passes away in a nursing home in the Detroit suburb of Farmington Hills.
2010	Curtis Chin's documentary film, *Vincent Who?*, is released.
2017	Helen Zia, the executor of Vincent Chin's estate, files an $8 million lawsuit against Ebens over his failure to comply with the terms of the settlement of the original civil suit.

Narrative

In 1982, Vincent Chin was murdered by Ronald Ebens and Michael Nitz outside of a strip club in Highland Park, Michigan, a northwest suburb of Detroit. Ebens and Nitz were auto workers who mistakenly thought that Chin was Japanese. Because the crime was racially motivated and, moreover, based on mistaken racial identity, it attracted national attention. That attention intensified significantly when Ebens and Nitz were allowed a lenient plea deal on the murder and then were not even successfully prosecuted on the federal level for violating Chin's civil rights.

A devastated Lily Chin left Detroit's City County Building in 1982. The two white men who brutally clubbed her son, Vincent Chin, to death in June 1982 were sentenced to only three years probation after plea bargaining agreements. (Bettmann/Getty Images)

This case became one of the earliest catalysts in promoting a much more nuanced awareness of Asian American identity and a greater sense of the need for political activism among Asian Americans themselves.

Vincent Chin (1955–1982) was a Chinese American who worked for an auto-parts supplier. Born in China in 1955, Chin was adopted from a Chinese orphanage in 1961 by a Chinese American veteran of World War II and his Chinese wife. After graduating from high school and attending the Detroit center of the Control Data Institute, a chain of vocational-technical schools, Chin found employment as an industrial draftsman for an auto-parts supplier. At the time of his murder, he was also working part-time as a waiter at the Golden Star restaurant in Ferndale, Michigan. In June 1982, several weeks before Chin was to be married, three of his friends held a bachelor party for him at the Fancy Pants Lounge, a strip club in the Highland Park suburb of Detroit. During the party, an argument escalated into a physical confrontation when the group was challenged by Ronald Ebens and his stepson, Michael Nitz. Ebens was employed as a supervisor at a Chrysler plant, and Nitz had been laid off from an assembly-line job with Chrysler. Assuming that Chin and his friends were Japanese, Ebens and Nitz began to berate them for the loss of U.S. auto-plant jobs because of increasing imports of Japanese automobiles into the United States.

Boyce Maxwell, the owner of the Fancy Pants Lounge, and Eddie Hollies, the doorman, separated the two groups of men inside the club. But after the fight was stopped inside the club, Ebens and Nitz again confronted Chin in the parking lot outside the club. Chin and one of his friends, Jimmy Choi, were willing to fight until Ebens took a baseball bat out of his trunk. Chin and Choi then fled and sought shelter in a McDonald's restaurant several blocks away. Ebens and Nitz drove around looking for them and even picked up an acquaintance, whom they paid $20 to help them find Chin. When Chin and Choi decided that it was safe to leave the McDonald's, Ebens and Nitz spotted them and caught up with them in a parking lot of a grocery store. Choi managed to escape, but Nitz held Vincent Chin while Ebens beat him into a bloody state of unconsciousness with a baseball bat. Chin was taken by ambulance to the Henry Ford Hospital, where he died from his injuries four days later. He was twenty-seven years old. One of the eyewitnesses to the crime was Michael Gardenhire, an off-duty Highland Park police officer, who had been eating with another off-duty officer at the McDonald's. He detained Ebens and Nitz and called for the ambulance. Because he had witnessed it firsthand, there was no doubt that Ebens and Nitz had committed the murder.

Although he was never interviewed by police or the prosecutor's office, or put on the stand to testify at Nitz and Ebens's trial, Boyce Maxwell went on the record with reporters, saying that Nitz and Ebens had confronted Chin about issues of race. "We got 16 percent unemployment in town. . . . There's lots of hard feelings. In my opinion, these people come in, they see a man, supposedly Japanese. They look at this guy and see Japan—the reason all my buddies are out of work," he said (Cummings 1983). Ebens admitted in court that he had shouted at Chin as he was killing him, using a racial slur as he blamed the unemployment issues on the Japanese.

The Wayne County prosecutor, William Cahalan, initially charged the two men with second-degree murder. Conviction on that crime would have carried a sentence up to life in prison. Ultimately, Ebens and Nitz were allowed to plead guilty to manslaughter, which carried a maximum sentence of fifteen years in prison. But Ebens and Nitz were given three-year suspended sentences and put on probation, and they were each fined $3,780. The chief judge of the Wayne County Circuit Court, Charles Kaufman, justified the final sentence in this way:

We're talking here about a man who's held down a responsible job with the same company for 17 or 18 years, and his son who is employed and is a part-time student. These men are not going to go out and harm somebody else. I just didn't think that putting them in prison would do any good for them or for society. You don't make the punishment fit the crime; you make the punishment fit the criminal. (Cummings 1983)

As much as the murder itself, this widely reported statement brought the Chin case to national attention.

At the time, there were only 30,000 to 35,000 Asian Americans in the greater Detroit metro area. But the obvious, glaring injustice of this sentence galvanized many of the Asian Americans in the community. Kin Yee, president of the Detroit Chinese Welfare Council, was on the forefront of these initial protests, declaring that the sentence that Kaufman imposed was tantamount to "a license to kill for $3,000, provided you have a steady job or are a student and the victim is Chinese" (Cummings 1983). Due to his outspokenness, Yee was elected to head the newly formed Asian American civil rights organization, American Citizens for Justice.

Liza Chan, an attorney retained by the group, attempted to intercede with Cahalan to petition to have Ebens and Nitz's sentencing vacated and a more just sentence imposed. When she pointed out that no one from the prosecutor's office had even been present at the sentencing hearing, Cahalan responded that such a presence was not required and that his office was overstretched and understaffed. But some months later, Cahalan announced that his office would no longer accept pleas reducing second-degree murder charges to manslaughter—and then denied that this change in policy was related to the sentencing in the Chin case. Because all statements and actions related to the Chin case were now receiving greater scrutiny, it was revealed that Cahalan's office had accepted similar plea deals in which second-degree murder charges had been reduced to manslaughter and the killers had been released on probation: one case involved a woman who had stabbed her husband eighteen times; another, a police officer who had beaten to death a prisoner in his custody; and a third, a grocer who had killed an eight-year-old who had stolen grapes.

The journalist and activist Helen Zia played a major role in ensuring that the case remained in the public eye. At the last of the hearings on the case before Kaufman, more than 500 people had protested outside the courthouse. After failing in court to convince Kaufman to consider resentencing Ebens and Nitz, Yee's group not only decided to appeal Kaufman's decision but also succeeded in getting the FBI to open an investigation into whether Vincent Chin's civil rights had been violated. The FBI investigation led to a federal grand jury being impaneled to consider whether charges should be brought in the case. One of the major obstacles to bringing the case was that, to this point, civil rights protections per se had never been legally extended to Asian Americans. In fact, groups such as the Michigan branches of the American Civil Liberties Union and National Lawyers Guild questioned whether there was a firm legal basis for extending those protections to any group other than African Americans. In the meantime, as the case was being presented to the grand jury, Lily Chin, Vincent Chin's mother, filed a $6 million civil suit against Ebens and Nitz.

The media attention to the murder of Vincent caused Asian Americans across the country to take note of the escalating animosity toward Asian Americans, reflected in the public stigmatizing of Asian American entrepreneurship and in other race-related killings in cities such as Houston, Boston, and Davis, California. For the first time, Asian American ethnic groups began to put aside long histories of animosity toward each other in order to present a more united front against racism that, as in the murder of Vincent Chin, often ignored the distinctions in their ethnicities. The city of Detroit declared June 19–23, 1983, to be Days of Remembrance of Vincent Chin, and Asian American communities throughout the country participated in their own ways. In 1985, Paul M. Igasaki, the Asian American liaison for the Chicago Commission on Human Rights, recalled Vincent Chin's murder and observed, "They see us basically as one race, and that's what racism is all about" (Butterfield 1985).

In June 1984, Ebens and Nitz were tried on two counts each for violating Vincent Chin's civil rights. After a five-day trial, the jury deliberated for twelve hours over three days. Ebens was convicted on one charge and acquitted on the other, while Nitz was acquitted on both charges. In September 1984, Federal District Judge Anna Diggs Taylor sentenced Ebens to twenty-five years in prison. But following his conviction, he was released on $20,000 bond, and that arrangement continued while his attorneys appealed the sentence. Federal prosecutor S. Theodore Merritt described Chin's murder as "a lynching with a bat instead of a rope," but Ebens now denied that the killing was racially motivated. Ebens's attorney, Frank Eaman, contended that the prosecution had failed to establish such a motivation ("Jury Debates . . ." 1984). Eaman also argued that if Ebens had received a two-year sentence on the manslaughter charge, there would not have been such a public uproar about the sentence and he never would have faced the federal charges for which he received the twenty-five-year sentence.

In September 1986, a federal appeals court for the Sixth Circuit reversed Ebens's conviction and vacated his sentence. Ebens's attorney, Frank Eaman, successfully argued that the federal trial judge had erred in not permitting them to introduce evidence that several witnesses damaging to Ebens's case had been coached by the prosecution. One week later, federal prosecutors announced that they would retry Ebens for violating Vincent Chin's civil rights.

One of the many ironies in these events is that while the case was making its way through the judiciary, attitudes toward Asian Americans began to shift rather dramatically in metro Detroit. Mazda refurbished an auto plant in the Detroit suburb of Southfield that had been closed by Ford. The groundbreaking ceremony included the blessing of the site by a Shinto priest. The plant brought an immediate infusion of about 2,000 Japanese into metro Detroit, and although that number represented a negligible percentage of the total population, the immigrants had a conspicuous cultural impact, with the sudden establishment or expansion of groceries and restaurants specializing in Japanese foods, the inclusion of many more

Japanese films in the stock of video rental stores, and the announcement of cross-cultural noncredit courses at Detroit colleges and universities.

On April 23, 1987, Ebens's second federal trial began in Cincinnati. The site had been moved because of the intense publicity that the case had received in the Detroit area. On May 2, after deliberating for eight hours over two days, the jury, which consisted of ten white and two African American jurors, announced its verdict, acquitting Ebens of violating Vincent Chin's civil rights. Shortly after the verdict, Mr. Ebens told reporters: "I'm very sorry about what happened. But you've got to realize how relieved I am (. . . .) It was a street crime that turned into a civil rights case because it served the purposes of a local Asian group." Speaking for Detroit's American Citizens for Justice, James Shimoura said, "Every American of Asian descent has shed a tear as a result of this case" (Wilkerson 1987).

In early August 1987, the family of Vincent Chin agreed to an out-of-court settlement with Ebens and Nitz in the $30 million civil suit filed against them. Ebens agreed to pay $200 each month to Mr. Chin's estate for two years and then to pay 25 percent of his net pay until his total payments to the estate amounted to $1.5 million. But Ebens indicated that he had no assets and claimed to be earning less than $500 per month from whatever irregular employment he could get. Over the next ten years, however, Nitz would pay $50,000 to the Chin estate.

In March 1988, the documentary film *Who Killed Vincent Chin?* premiered at the 17th New Directors/New Films Festival, the annual collaboration between the Film Society of Lincoln Center and the Museum of Modern Art. Directed by Christine Choy and produced by Renee Tajima, the film was selected to open the festival. As Choy and Tajima have frequently acknowledged, they initially conceived of the film as a fifteen-minute advocacy film, emphasizing the injustices of the murder and of the trials, as well as the activists who mobilized to seek justice. But they quickly saw that the subject offered the opportunity to explore a great many more nuances and complexities than the relatively straightforward message that they initially intended to communicate.

Into the film's eighty-seven minutes, the filmmakers fit a great deal: the details of the murder and the subsequent trials, interviews with some of the principal figures including Lily Chin and Ronald Ebens, the exposition of not just the economic dislocation becoming endemic in greater Detroit but of the social and cultural consequences of the collapse of American industrialism, and an examination of how justice and race intersect or collide across so very many aspects of contemporary American life. In sum, the film's title suggests the thematic ambiguities that it explores because there was never any question about who literally killed Vincent Chin. The film is not simply an indictment of Ronald Ebens and Michael Nitz or of the criminal justice system that did not punish them in any meaningful way for killing Vincent Chin. But the killers are not characterized as victims to the extent that they are in any way exonerated. Two of the film's most unsettling moments occur when Ebens says of the murder, "'It's not something you plan on happening, but it happens" and "'It was just like this was preordained to be." And when he says of the trials, "I think the system worked the way it should have worked, right down the line." But the most unsettling may be when Judge Kaufman, in effect, adds insult to injury when he states, in trying to justify the light sentence that he imposed, "The victim lingered for four days which . . . was indicative to me that they attempted to administer a punishment. They did this too severely, in careless disregard of human life, which is what manslaughter is. . . . Had it been a brutal murder, of course these fellas would be in jail right now." Such a statement cannot diminish the fact that the victim was brutally murdered by being struck repeatedly in the head with a baseball bat.

Who Killed Vincent Chin? was nominated for an Academy Award for Best Documentary Film. It was also featured in the PBS series *P.O.V.*, which provides a national audience for selected, independently produced documentary films. In 1990, the film received a Peabody Award, and in 1991, it was honored with a Silver Baton from the Alfred I. Dupont-Columbia University Awards for broadcast journalism.

In 1995, an exhibition at Atlanta's High Museum of Art included a work by Mel Chin (no relation to Vincent Chin) titled "Fan Club," in which a baseball bat and a Japanese flag are the main components of a giant folding fan. Seeking to honor Vincent Chin's memory, Mel Chin reportedly used his own blood to create the red sun symbol on the Japanese flag. Also in 1995, Ping Chong included the story of Vincent Chin's murder in his musical play *Chinoiserie*, which opened at the Majestic Theater in New York. In 1996, Dan Kwong included commentary on Vincent Chin's murder in his one-man show *Monkhood in 3 Easy Lessons*. Provocatively, while talking about the crime, he hit baseballs off a bat into the back curtain. In 1998, the Contemporary American Theatre Festival commissioned *Carry the Tiger to the Mountain*, by Cherylene Lee, an agitprop treatment of the murder of Vincent Chin. The play was subsequently presented by the Pan Asian Repertory Theater in New York, as well as by other theater groups around the country. In 2010, Curtis Chin's documentary *Vincent Who?* was released. Curtis Chin grew up in Detroit and was a contemporary of Vincent Chin; in fact, the two were casually acquainted. He made the documentary to focus less on the specific issues related to the murder itself than to explore its very significant impact on the development of Asian American identity and of Asian American political, social, and cultural activism. In 2017, Peter Ho Davies's novel *The Fortunes* was published. It includes four sections focusing on four different characters. The third section, "Jade," is told from the viewpoint of a friend of Vincent Chin who ran away as he was being murdered.

In 2002, about a week before the twentieth anniversary of her son's murder, Lily Chin passed away in a nursing home in the Detroit suburb of Farmington Hills. In 2017, on the thirty-fifth anniversary of the murder, Helen Zia, now the executor of Chin's estate, filed suit in federal court against Ebens, citing his failure to live up to the terms of the settlement of the civil suit brought against him and Michael Nitz and asking for a new judgment of $8 million. Zia said, "It's not about the money. It's about him being able to live his life outside of jail for all these years and him never taking full responsibility for what's he's done" (Aguilar 2017). As permitted by law, the estate had been filing suits for escalating claims against Ebens every ten years after the settlement.

On the twentieth, twenty-fifth, thirtieth, and thirty-fifth anniversaries of Vincent Chin's death, Asian American groups across the United States have held screenings of the film by Choy and Tajima, panel discussions, and other events not only to commemorate the tragedy but also to sustain the activism in the Asian American community that the senseless murder provoked and inspired. On the thirtieth anniversary of the murder in 2012, Frank H. Wu, chancellor and dean of the Hastings College of the Law, University of California, and the author of *Yellow: Race in America Beyond Black and White*, wrote a very widely read article for *The New York Times* titled "Why Vincent Chin Matters." Among its many very perceptive and nuanced insights about Asian American history and identity, the article includes this simple but profound observation: "Vincent Chin has lived longer in memory than reality."

Biographies of Notable Figures

Ronald Ebens (1939–)

Born in 1939 in Dixon, Illinois, Ronald Ebens served two and a half years in Army Defense School. In 1965, he got a job at the Chrysler plant in Belvidere, Illinois. Within three months, he was promoted to a salaried position as a foreman. In the early 1970s, he transferred to the Warren Truck Assembly Plant in suburban Detroit, and he owned a bar, called Ron's Place, for part of the decade. He had been briefly married when he was eighteen, but in 1971, he married for a second time, and this second marriage to Juanita Ebens proved to be more enduring—lasting even through all of the notoriety that followed his murdering Vincent Chin.

After the murder, Ebens was fired by Chrysler and lost a lawsuit claiming wrongful termination. He has claimed that his notoriety has prevented him from getting steady employment. Most recently, he and his wife were living in Nevada.

In the interviews of him included in *Who Killed Vincent Chin?*, he comes across as self-justifying and unfeeling, talking about the murder as if he bears only very limited responsibility for it and as if he has been as much a victim of race hysteria as Vincent Chin was a victim of racism at his hands. In 2012, he finally apologized for the murder but couched the apology by calling the murder "the only wrong thing I ever done in my life" (Asian American Legal Defense Fund 2018).

Charles Kaufman (1920–2004)

Charles Kaufman, the judge who imposed the astonishingly light sentence on Ebens and Nitz for the murder of Vincent Chin, was born in 1920. During the Second World War, he served with the Army Air Corps in the Pacific Theater. He completed twenty-seven missions before his plane was shot down and he became a prisoner of war of the Japanese army.

After the war, Kaufman enrolled in the Wayne State University School of Law, graduating in 1948. For a decade, he worked in his father's law firm. In 1959, he was elected as a common pleas court judge, and in 1965 he was elected as a judge with the Wayne County Third Circuit Court of Michigan. He would serve in that capacity for the next thirty years. In 1968, 1976, and 1982, he sought higher judicial positions on the Michigan Court of Appeals and the Michigan Supreme Court, but he lost those elections. After the controversy that surrounded the sentencing of Ebens and Nitz, his notoriety put him, in the words of one commentator, in the "political graveyard" ("Kaufman" 2015).

Defenders of Kaufman often cite the sentence that he gave to a young gang member—to complete his G.E.D. in six months to avoid a jail sentence on a concealed weapons charge. That defendant, Greg Mathis, went on to become the youngest judge elected to the 36th District Court in Detroit—and to star in the eponymous very popular and long-running reality-television series *Judge Mathis*.

But critics have attributed his leniency toward Ebens and Nitz to anti-Asian bias rooted in his experiences as a prisoner of war. They have also cited a number of cases in which he imposed rather draconian sentences on defendants who defied his rulings in cases having to do with local government and union activism.

Kaufman died in 2004. Interviewed for the film *Vincent Who?*, his daughter acknowledged that his decision in the Chin case was "immoral," but she could not bring herself to admit that her father had been motivated by racism.

Helen Zia (1952–)

A prominent activist on Asian American and LGBTQ issues, Helen Zia was born in 1952 in Newark, New Jersey. Her parents were the children of immigrants from Shanghai, China. She graduated in 1973. At Princeton, she was a founding member of the Asian American Students Association and a recognized activist on issues related to the Vietnam War, feminism, and racial identity and race relations. In 1974, Zia entered the Tufts University Medical School, but she left in 1976 without completing her MD.

Relocating to Detroit, Zia worked at a variety of jobs, including being an auto worker, before she discovered her true vocation as a writer. Not surprisingly, it was her work as a community activist that led her in this direction. Her activism in seeking justice for Vincent Chin and her reporting on the case brought her to not just regional but national prominence. Her contributions are recognized in the documentary *Who Killed Vincent Chin?*, and she was subsequently profiled as part of Bill Moyer's documentary series for PBS *Becoming American: The Chinese Experience*.

From 1989 to 1992, Zia served as the executive editor of *Ms. Magazine*. She has also served on the board of directors for the Women's Media Center. Her writing has appeared in such newspapers and periodicals as *Ms.*, *The New York Times*, *The Washington Post*, *The Advocate*, *Essence*, *The Nation*, and *OUT*.

Zia's most significant publications include *Asian American Dreams: The Emergence of an American People* (2000), which was a finalist for the Kiriyama Pacific Rim Book Prize; *My Country Versus Me* (2002), co-authored with Wen Ho Lee, the Los Alamos scientist who was falsely accused of being a spy for the People's Republic of China; and the essay "Reclaiming the Past, Redefining the Future: Asian American and Pacific Islander Women," which was included in *Sisterhood Is Forever: The Women's Anthology for a New Millennium* (2003), edited by Robin Morgan. In 2008, Zia married Lia Shigemura in San Francisco.

Renee Tajima (1958–)

The producer of *Who Killed Vincent Chin?*, Renee Tajima was born in 1958 in Chicago, Illinois. Her family relocated to the Los Angeles area, and she graduated from John Muir High School in Altadena. She then attended Radcliffe College of Harvard University, graduating cum laude with a degree in East Asian Studies and Sociology. While studying at Harvard, she chaired the United Front against Apartheid.

The first paid director at Asian Cine-Vision in New York, Tajima was a founder of both the Asian American Center for Media and the Asian American International Video Festival. She wrote reviews for the *Village Voice*, served as a commentator for National Public Radio, and edited the periodical *Bridge: Asian American Perspectives*.

Tajima was the graduate director of the Master's Program in Social Documentation as a professor of Film and Digital Media at the University of California,

Santa Cruz. In 2013, Tajima was appointed Professor of Asian American Studies and the Alumni and Friends of Japanese American Ancestry Endowed Chair at the University of California at Los Angeles. She also directs the Center for Ethno-Communications at UCLA. She is currently working on several transmedia projects.

Tajima has directed or produced more than a dozen documentary films, which have been featured at prominent film festivals and have been aired on television networks worldwide. For these films she has received numerous recognitions.

DOCUMENT EXCERPTS

Remembering Vincent Chin

The murder of Vincent Chin has become an important moment in the Asian American and Pacific Islander (AAPI) community and civil rights history. His brutal death and the legal process afterwards helped rally Asian American communities in their efforts to fight for justice and equal protection. But its influence goes well beyond Asian American communities. Racially motivated hate crimes remain prevalent in many communities across the country, especially since 9/11.

Remembering Vincent Chin

Thomas E. Perez

Thirty years ago this week, a 27 year-old Chinese-American named Vincent Chin was brutally murdered. Two assailants beat him with a baseball bat, matching their physical violence with a stream of racial epithets. He died four days later, shortly before what would have been his wedding day. Despite the heinous nature of the crime, the state court imposed lenient sentences, so the Civil Rights Division of the U.S. Department of Justice charged the assailants under the federal hate crimes law on the books at the time. One of the two was convicted, and although his conviction was overturned, the story of Vincent Chin serves as an important moment in the Asian American and Pacific Islander (AAPI) community and civil rights history.

Hate crimes enforcement is among the earliest of our responsibilities in the Civil Rights Division. Regrettably, hate crimes remain all too prevalent in communities across the country today. I have seen firsthand the devastating impact of hate crimes—and not only on victims and their families. Acts of bigotry can tear entire communities apart. Hate crimes are an unconscionable reminder that we have not yet achieved the ideal of equal justice for all.

In 2009, President Obama signed into law the Matthew Shepard and James Byrd, Jr. Hate Crimes Prevention Act. This landmark law was named in the memory of two men who, like Vincent Chin, were brutally murdered by assailants filled with hate. James Byrd, Jr. was a 49-year-old African-American man living in Jasper, Texas, who accepted a ride home from three men on June 7, 1998. They did not take him home. Instead, they drove him to the remote edge of town where they beat him severely, urinated on him, chained him by the ankles to the back of a pickup truck, and then drove the pickup truck for three miles, dragging him to his death. Matthew Shepard was a 21-year-old gay man studying at the University of Wyoming, when he went to a local bar and met two men who offered him a ride home on October 6, 1998. Instead of taking him home, they drove him to a remote area outside of town, where he was tortured, tied to a fence, and left to die.

While the men responsible for the Byrd and Shepard murders were convicted of murder, none of them were prosecuted for committing a hate crime. Neither state had a hate crimes law at the time the murders occurred, and federal law did not apply. A now two-year-old federal law, 18 U.S.C. Section 249 enables the Justice Department to prosecute cases involving hate crimes motivated by the actual or perceived race, color, national origin, gender, sexual orientation, gender identity, religion, or disability of the victim. Crucially, for particular cases the law removes the requirement that the Department show that the defendant was engaged in a "federally protected activity," which was required under the previous hate crimes statute, 18 U.S.C. Section 245, passed shortly after the assassination of the Reverend Martin Luther King, Jr.

In a diverse, democratic nation like ours, we all must be able to live and work in our communities without fear of being attacked because of how we look, what we believe, where we are from, or who we love. Despite our nation's great progress in advancing civil rights, brutal assaults made more vicious by racial epithets still occur in big cities and small towns. Crosses are still burned on the lawns of people minding their own business. Mosques, synagogues and churches still are desecrated and sometimes destroyed. Incidents that belong only in our history books still appear in the pages of our newspapers.

The prosecution of hate crimes must be one element in a broader effort of community engagement and empowerment. We need prevention, intervention and reporting strategies to move communities forward in a meaningful way. We have had to battle these acts of bigotry for too long, and in the 21st century, we must focus on eradicating hate from our communities altogether, stopping these acts before they occur.

Prosecuting hate crimes therefore is a top priority for the Attorney General and the Civil Rights Division, and we have expanded our efforts to prosecute hate crimes. So far, the Division has indicted 10 cases and charged 35 defendants under the Shepard-Byrd law.

Vincent Chin, James Byrd, Jr., and Matthew Shepard remain powerful reminders of why, in 2012, we continue to stand beside those in our nation who cannot make their voices heard alone. We will continue to enforce these essential laws to ensure that all individuals can realize the promise of equal justice under the law.

Source: Perez, Thomas E. "Remembering Vincent Chin." The White House, September 22, 2012. https://obamawhitehouse.archives.gov/blog/2012/06/22/remembering-vincent-chin

See also: Japanese American Internment, 1942–1946; 9/11 and Islamophobia, 2001–2018; *People v. Hall*, 1854; The Webb-Haney Act Passed by California State Legislature, 1913

Further Reading

Aguilar, Lewis. 2017. "Estate of Vincent Chin Seeks Millions from His Killer." *Detroit News*, June 24. http://www.detroitnews.com/story/news/local/oakland-county/2017/06/24/vincent-chin-th-anniversary/103167672

Asian American Legal Defense Fund. 2018. http://aaldef.org/blog/ronald-ebens-the-man-who-killed-vincent-chin-apologizes-30-years-later.html

Butterfield, Fox. 1985. "Violent Incidents against Asian Americans Seen as Part of Racist Pattern." *New York Times*, August 31.

Canby, Vincent. 1988. "New Directors/New Films; *Who Killed Vincent Chin?*: Answer Is Complex." *The New York Times*, March 11.

Carroll, John. 1991. "A Measure of Prejudice." *Daily Yomiuri*, March 16.

Collins, Monica. 1989. "A Chilling Glimpse of a Killing on *P.O.V.*" *USA Today*, July 18.

Cummings, Judith. 1983. "Detroit Asian Americans Protest Lenient Penalties for Murder." *New York Times*, April 26.

Haslett, John. 1989. "Film Questions U.S. Justice System." *Globe and Mail*, July 22.

Holusha, John. 1983. "Two Fined in Detroit Slaying Are Indicted by Federal Jury." *The New York Times*, November 3.

"Jury Debates the Guilt of Two in Detroit Slaying." 1984. *The New York Times*, June 27.

Kaplan, David A. 1989. "Film about a Fatal Beating Examines a Community." *The New York Times*, July 16.

"Kaufman." 2015. *The Political Graveyard: Index to Politicians*. December 20. http://politicalgraveyard.com/bio/kaufman.html

Mizui, Yoko. 1997. "Who Killed Vincent Chin?" *Daily Yomiuri*, March 2.

Quill, Greg. 1989. "A Very Ugly Story Beautifully Told." *Toronto Star*, July 23.

Shales, Tom. 1989. "Vincent Chin: The Wounds of a Dream Betrayed." *The Washington Post*, July 18.

"The $3,000 License to Kill." 1983. *The Washington Post*, April 30.

Wilkerson, Isabel. 1987. "For Asian Americans, Acquittal in Rights Case Arouses Outrage and Fear." *The New York Times*, May 6.

Wu, Frank H. 2012. "Why Vincent Chin Matters." *The New York Times*, June 23.

The Los Angeles Riots, 1992

Nancy Kang

Chronology

October 24, 1871	The Chinatown Massacre of 1871 is the first major racially motivated riot in Los Angeles. The event transpires in a disreputable area known as Calle de los Negros (colloquially, "Negro Alley" or a vulgar variation, "N—r Alley"). A mob of primarily white Los Angeles citizens converges on Chinatown, angry over an accidental killing of a white man. Approximately seventeen to twenty immigrant Chinese residents are viciously murdered, making for the largest mass lynching in U.S. history. Eight men are convicted but never serve time, as the ruling is overturned on a technicality. Among the dead is respected physician Dr. Gene Tong.
August 11–16, 1965	The five days of civil unrest known as the Watts Riots are triggered by a traffic stop by California Highway Patrol of a young African American man on suspicion of reckless driving. The event escalates into larger civil strife. The fighting, looting, burnings, and killings result in thirty-four deaths, over 1,000 injuries, nearly 3,500 arrests, and over $40 million in property damage. Damaged businesses are primarily white-owned. The scale of the event arguably sets the scene for the LA riots decades later.
March 3, 1991	Four Los Angeles Police Department (LAPD) officers are filmed by a civilian beating motorist Rodney King (b. April 2, 1965) with batons after a high-speed chase in Los Angeles County. The officers are white; King is a young African American parolee. Once on the ground, King is hit fifty-six times with batons. A number of other officers, largely from the LAPD, do not intervene as King suffers multiple fractures. This violent exchange becomes known as "the King incident." The policemen involved are Stacey C. Koon, Laurence M. Powell, Theodore J. Briseno, and Timothy E. Wind. They are charged with assault with a deadly weapon and excessive use of force.
March 16, 1991	Long-simmering tensions between African Americans and Korean merchants in South Central Los Angeles reach a flashpoint with the shooting death of Latasha Harlins, a fourteen-year-old African

American girl who got into a physical altercation over suspicion of theft at the Empire Liquor store with owner Soon Ja Du, a fifty-one-year-old Korean immigrant. Du shot Harlins in the head after being hit repeatedly by the teen. In *People v. Soon Ja Du*, the defendant is tried for first-degree murder. She is convicted of manslaughter but ultimately does not serve jail time. African American activist groups unleash a targeted campaign against Du and other Korean American business owners, including rigorous demonstrations and boycotting.

October 19, 1991	The near-fatal shooting of nine-year-old Juri Kang, child of Korean immigrants, occurs during a robbery of her parents' Shell gas station and mini mart by a (still unknown) black perpetrator, precipitating some interracial community discussion between blacks and Koreans. Kang's parents' business is looted and burned a few months later during the LA riots.
April 29, 1992	Verdicts are delivered in the police brutality case of the *People v. Stacey Koon et al.* The primarily white jury, which includes one Asian American and one Latino, acquits the four officers of criminal misconduct against King.
April 29-May 4, 1992	The *People v. Stacey Koon et al.* decision prompts surprise, disbelief, and outrage from the public, especially local African Americans. A day known as *Sa-i-gu* ("4-2-9" in Korean cardinal letters, signifying April 29) marks the start of a period of massive civil disturbance in Los Angeles. Burning, looting, vandalism, and other forms of unrest ensue.
April 30, 1992	Edward ("Eddie") Song Lee, an eighteen-year-old Korean American, is shot and killed in an exchange of gunfire, having been mistaken as a looter by other Koreans guarding their property from looters and arsonists.
May 1, 1992	King makes his famous appeal for calm: "People, I just want to say, can we all get along? Can we get along?" The rampant violence, theft, property damage, and lawlessness continue.
April 1993	A federal jury convicts Koon and Powell, sentencing the men to thirty months in prison each for violating King's civil rights. Briseno and Wind are acquitted. No similar civil furor erupts as it did in April 1992.

April– June 1994	After suing the city of Los Angeles, King is awarded $3.8 million in compensatory damages from the U.S. District Court in Los Angeles. In June, King does not receive any payout in his separate lawsuit against the officers.
April– June 17, 2012	In April, King publishes his autobiography *The Riot Within: My Journey from Rebellion to Redemption*, co-authored with Lawrence J. Spagnola. In June, King dies at the age of forty-seven at home in his swimming pool. The cause of death is a cardiac condition combined with alcohol and drug intoxication.

Narrative

For many Korean Americans, the fifth-largest Asian American subgroup in the United States, it is difficult to hear the Los Angeles riots described with epithets such as "urban uprising," "rebellion," "resistance," and "uncivil disobedience." These and other euphemistic terms often attempt to capture—and sometimes even justify—the violent events that transpired in the spring of 1992. Because Koreans and Korean Americans were not differentiated during the riots, the term "Korean American" is used to encompass immigrants from Korea and their American-born descendants (Oh 2002, 46). The six-day period between April 29 and May 4 witnessed a veritable detonation of tensions that had steadily risen from long unresolved racial, political, and socioeconomic inequalities. Los Angeles may be fabled for its sun-kissed palm trees, posh gated communities, and Hollywood mystique, yet the enduring reality of racism is far less frequently acknowledged, manifesting in urban ghettos, abject poverty, gang violence, crime, and limited economic and social opportunities, especially for communities of color. A number of Korean Americans were victims of racism during the Los Angeles riots.

Even before the riots, the mainstream U.S. news media often portrayed Koreans as un-American aliens whose opinions were either unimportant or inaccessible due to presumed cultural and language barriers. Immigrants tended not to be differentiated from second- and third-generation Korean Americans. Some non-Asian community activist groups (who were also people of color) adopted nativist and bigoted rhetoric, accusing Koreans of invading "their" neighborhoods and stealing "their" jobs and opportunities. Small business owners of Korean ancestry who ventured into low-income neighborhoods were sometimes viewed as parasitical, rude, and categorically disrespectful to other people of color. These proprietors often struggled financially, worked long hours, and felt fearful for their safety given the

A shopping center in Koreatown, Los Angeles, burned during the 1992 Los Angeles Riots. According to Professor Ed Chang of the University of California, Riverside, the riots caused $400 million in damages to more than two thousand Korean American owned stores. (Hyungwon Kang/Los Angeles Times via Getty Images)

high rate of crime in their neighborhoods. Aware of the vulnerability that stemmed from being seen as "outsiders" by other communities of color in locations that suffered from precarious police presence or protection, Korean business owners often experienced feelings of fear and alienation. Korean Americans generally lacked the activist infrastructures found within many other minority groups, which used activism to combat prejudice. They also lacked the high-profile and rhetorically aggressive commentators that some groups employed to disseminate their empowerment-focused platforms. Lacking direct political representation in municipal and state governments, as well as in the legal system, Korean small business owners often felt alienated. Many Koreans endured dismissal and disrespect in their communities and felt like they were portrayed by others as generally being aggressive, money-minded, exploitative, and even racist.

The destruction beginning on April 29, 1992, was the result of complex racial relationships in Los Angeles. Underlying causes of the riots' civil disaster included many feeling that there was a lack of accountability and responsibility for racism at the hands of white citizens, corruption within the police force, and a lack of municipal preparation. Black-, white-, and Latino-owned businesses also suffered damage and destruction during the riots, as did hundreds of businesses owned by Chinese, Japanese, Filipino, Thai, Indian, and Cambodian shopkeepers (Hata and Hata 2006; Zia 2000). However, Korean American small-business owners sustained more damage than any other ethnic group during that period (Kim 1993, 1).

The riots were not the first racially motivated incident of major civil disorder in the city. The largest mass lynching in U.S. history was of Chinese immigrants in Los Angeles's Chinatown on October 24, 1871, when a primarily white racist mob attacked small Chinese-owned businesses and homes, attacking and killing an estimated seventeen to twenty members of this group as retaliation for the unintended death of one white man. There were eight criminal convictions, but these were all overturned on a technicality, so no one served any jail time. The business losses, harassment, and murder of Chinese residents are a part of Southern Californian's history that many do not know about (Johnson, Jr. 2011; Zesch 2012). Asian Americans are often left out of discussions and educational curricula regarding lynchings in U.S. history, which many feel is part of a larger pattern of erasure of hate crimes against Asian people in the country. The anti-Korean violence was a large factor of the LA riots, but many are not as familiar with that as they might be with other events such as the Snake River Massacre of 1887 (which killed thirty-four Chinese miners in Oregon), Japanese internment during World War II, the beating death of Detroit native Vincent Chin in 1982, Islamophobic acts across the United States after the attacks on September 11, and the Oak Creek mass shooting of six Sikh temple-goers in 2012.

Similar racial strife between white Americans and African Americans occurred during the Watts Riots of August 1965, which began with an incident involving white law enforcement officers apprehending an African American motorist. The ensuing scuffle with concerned family members and the eventual participation of other nearby residents escalated into civil uproar. Three decades later, Korean Americans were also involved in highly publicized, racially motivated incidents.

Los Angeles has the highest concentration of Korean Americans in the nation. The outcome of the Rodney King police brutality trial led to greater destruction and civil unrest than had taken place in Watts, which took an estimated toll of $400 million in material damages and thirty-four deaths. In comparison, starting on April 29, over 4,500 businesses (about 2,500 immigrant-owned) were damaged or destroyed across Los Angeles County, accompanied by approximately $1 billion in total property losses. Fatality estimates range from fifty-three to sixty-three people, and there were thousands of injuries and more than 12,000 arrests. To Korean Americans, the civil disaster was known as *Sa-i-gu p'ok-dong*, or the "April 29 disturbance," with *Sa-i-gu* literally translating as "4-2-9" (Kim 1994, 71). A disproportionately high number of Korean-owned small businesses were targeted, vandalized, looted, burned, and destroyed. South Central Los Angeles and Koreatown became the riot's ground zero. The Los Angeles mayor's office estimated that 65 percent of all stores damaged or destroyed were Korean-owned and tens of thousands of Koreans lost their investments and hard-earned livelihoods during the chaos (Kim-Gibson 2004).

As attorney and filmmaker David D. Kim's documentary *Clash of Colors: LA Riots of 1992* (2012) illustrates, many Koreans felt they had been exploited by the nation's economic system, social structure, and media. Some Koreans felt that they were being treated poorly as the result of African Americans' anger toward what was viewed as a corrupt police force, denial about systematic racism, and an economic recession in the city. Many Korean Americans experienced immense stress over these racial tensions, which was especially difficult for a community that tends not to discuss mental health concerns openly. When non-Korean commentators displayed little to no sympathy for the working-class individuals whose businesses and livelihoods were destroyed in a matter of days, this perceived lack of compassion fueled feelings of bitterness, anger, and grief among many Koreans, described by a number of cultural critics as *han*. *Han* encompasses a history of colonial oppression in Asia (including the 1910–1945 occupation by Japan), devastating wars (including World War II and the Korean War, 1950–1953), and the ongoing yoke of U.S. and other imperialist influences that continues today in the divided, unstable peninsula. Many Koreans affected by the LA riots also felt isolated from and resentful toward other Asian Americans who acted ambivalent about supporting Korean Americans at the time.

Korean Culture in Los Angeles

Many Koreans immigrated to America seeking stability, freedom, and property ownership. A number of these immigrants moved to socioeconomically challenged areas of Los Angeles during the 1980s and 1990s due to the comparatively low rents in the area. Many chose small-scale entrepreneurship to support themselves because the freedom to be one's own boss relieved some of the disadvantages posed by language barriers and possible culture clashes with non-Asian employers. Rotating money pooling (or *kye* in Korean) among friends and community members could allow for large purchases such as a store. For many, the desire for self-sufficiency prevailed over other concerns, even though the investment could be highly stressful and very expensive. Many shopkeepers who were threatened, assaulted, or killed did not receive mainstream media coverage. Their own communities tended to downplay attacks to avoid making waves or provoking retaliation. As such, public displays of outrage and calls for accountability did not emanate far beyond the Korean community in Los Angeles.

At the time of the riots, approximately 200,000 Korean Americans lived in Los Angeles County (Kim-Gibson 1993). Small businesses like grocery stores, fruit stands, liquor stores, gas stations, dry cleaners, auto body and other repair shops, and convenience marts served as sites for social bonding among immigrants. However, internal divisions existed within the Korean American community, which became more apparent after the riots. Some of these divisions were based on feelings of competing for belonging and oppression based on social class, gender, age, linguistic abilities (such as English-language fluency), citizenship and immigration status, and degrees of affiliation with Korea (Kim 1994, 72). It was not obvious to many outside observers that Koreans who had recently arrived in the United States were not the same as those who had started settling in greater numbers decades earlier after the passing of the Immigration and Nationality Act of 1965. The influx of Korean immigrants to the city during Los Angeles's recession led to resentment from many long-time residents in South Central Los Angeles, especially given the newcomers' seeming lack of commonalities based on appearance, language, and ancestral histories.

The post-riot years were difficult for many Korean Americans in Los Angeles. They found themselves avidly dissected in media coverage by black, white, and a few (non-Korean) Asian American commentators. The glaring absence of direct testimonials by the worst-hit victims themselves did not go unnoticed; commentators like attorney Angela Oh infiltrated the cacophony of commentators. *East to America: Korean American Life Stories* (1997), edited by ethnic studies scholar Elaine Kim and sociologist Eui-Young Yu, helped share some of the experiences of Korean Americans and attempted to push back against the stereotype of "greedy Korean merchants."

Interracial Struggles

During the 1980s and into the 1990s, Korean American small-business owners sometimes found themselves depicted by other people of color as being arrogant, disrespectful, and un-American interlopers who infiltrated neighborhoods where they lacked historical presence. The black-focused newspaper the *Los Angeles Sentinel* published a number of articles that explored the unsavory nature of the group that was "taking over" the black community (Zia 2000, 173). Not everyone felt this way, but the accusations were hurtful to many. In 1988, the Asian and Pacific Islander Advisory Committee of the California Attorney General reported a worrying increase in anti-Asian hate crimes. In 1989, the Los Angeles County Human Relations Commission released the following statistics: while Asian Pacific Americans comprised 8.6 percent of the county's school population, they were victims of at least 14.5 percent of reported race-based hate crimes (Hata and Hata 2006, 96). Some local black activists spread rumors about special government programs that specifically benefitted Korean immigrants, as well as rumors that these immigrants were engaging in immoral business practices due to a sense of racial superiority (Oh 2010). Immigrant shopkeepers' limited English skills were sometimes held against them, and speaking English as a second language sometimes affected their opportunities for job growth and their ability to communicate their desires for social justice with native English speakers.

Korean shopkeepers were also sometimes singled out by non-Koreans for what was widely construed to be customer service lapses and deficiencies. They were criticized for defending themselves during robberies and were accused of watching customers with undue suspicion as a loss prevention measure. Other harmful stereotypes included perceptions that Koreans were not cheerful or welcoming and exhibited rudeness, such as not placing change directly into a customer's hand. Choosing not to comply with some conventional American service norms, or simply being ignorant of them, was perceived by many as rude behavior, instead of cultural differences.

Korean Americans lacked the same kind of unified activist community to engage in counter-picketing, boycotts, or other public demonstrations that well-known African American community groups like the Brotherhood Crusade engaged in when they felt disrespected. The 1991 death of fifteen-year-old Latasha Harlins, shot by Korean shopkeeper Soon Ja Du over an altercation relating to suspicion of theft, exponentially worsened relationships between the black and Korean communities. The strife likely harmed many of the positive inroads that religious and multicultural groups such as the Black-Korean Alliance (BKA) had made. This group was formed through the intervention of the Los Angeles Human Relations Commission after four Korean shopkeepers were killed by African Americans in a single month during 1986. According to scholar Edward T. Chang, a lot of the racial tension between Koreans and African Americans in Los Angeles during this era was fueled by rhetoric used in the media.

Violence was an undeniable reality of life in poor communities in South Central Los Angeles. Local Korean-language news outlets regularly ran stories of clashes between store owners and their customers of color, including threats by gangs and episodes of intoxicated individuals creating disruptions or committing various crimes on the premises (Oh 2010, 40). These interracial frictions were not isolated to Los Angeles. For example, an African American group boycotted the Korean-owned Family Red Apple Market in Brooklyn, New York, in 1990 as the result of a confrontation between a Haitian customer and a grocery store employee. During this era, many people and groups also acted as bridge builders and peace makers. The BKA and the African-Korean American Christian Alliance were two such groups. Despite peacemaking attempts, racial discourse continued to be heated after the riots took place. Filmmaker Dai Sil Kim-Gibson comments, "The mainstream media made it sound as if the 1992 LA riots were *caused* by black-Korean conflict. . . . Black-Korean conflict was one symptom, but it was certainly not the cause of that riot. The cause of that riot was black-white conflict that existed in this country from the establishment of this country" (Yamato 2017).

The Koreans and blacks who invested the time, patience, and open-mindedness for nonjudgmental dialogue and bonding often found ample grounds for commonality. However, this progress was hindered by the Harlins incident and resulting court ruling where Du did not serve jail time. Many felt that the media distorted the incident: for instance, the full video of Harlins's shooting was edited in a way that did not show the violence that led up to the shooting. Many felt that this edit portrayed Du as a heartless killer who was incensed about a container of orange juice, not someone who had been repeatedly struck (Kim-Gibson 2004). The Black-Korean Alliance, led by church and community leaders, tried for six years to create a useful interracial coalition before disbanding in 1991 due to mutual inflexibilities, including the reluctance of some black leaders to admit that racial prejudice does exist within black communities (Kim 1994; Kim and Yu 1997). Koreans like BKA co-chair Bong Hwan Kim who spoke out against the lenient sentencing of Du were criticized by some other Koreans as "race traitors" and felt invisible to the mainstream media. In October 1991, nine-year-old Juri Kang was shot at her parents' gas-mart by a black assailant whose identity was never discovered. After the shooting, some African Americans sought to quell tensions and seek cultural alliances, but these efforts were also not widely covered in the media. Despite the fact that Kang was even younger than Harlins, her name is virtually unknown, even to many Asian American activists. The Harlins case, in contrast, has spurred scholarly studies and extended civil rights commentary to underscore the failings of the American justice system. Some feel that even today, Harlins's name is brought up in criticism of Asian Americans, while Kang's incident and the racial tensions that may have led to it go undiscussed.

Issues of what many considered to be "media erasure" of Asian Americans' experience of the Los Angeles riots and surrounding events have been significant to those affected by it. The *Los Angeles Times*' white editor-in-chief justified the omission of Asian American voices from a post-riot survey of thousands of LA residents by arguing that these members of the community were statistically insignificant, even though their population approximated that of African Americans in the area (Zia 2000, 183). This series of events marked a turning point in cultural identity for Korean Americans. In the documentary film project *K-Town '92* (2017), which combines archival footage from 1992 with 2017 interviews, Annetta Wells, a political coordinator for the SEIU (Service Employees International Union), recalls a feeling of solidarity between blacks and Latinos that did not extend to Korean Americans in the 1990s (Lee 2017). In the words of lawyer Angela Oh, in the wake of the riots, "Korean America was born in April 1992" (2010, 43).

Toward Greater Leadership and Community Presence

The LA riots spurred the call for both renewed and new leadership among the Korean American community in the city, the county, the state, and the nation. A number of community organizers and activists, scholars, observers, and civic leaders in Los Angeles's Asian American communities likewise discerned the need for greater visibility and more pronounced political participation among the younger generations. Some of the major figures who mobilized in the Korean American community included Elaine H. Kim (literary and ethnic studies scholar from the University of California at Berkeley); Edward T. Chang (ethnic studies scholar from the University of California, Riverside and founding director of the Young Oak Kim Center for Korean American Studies); attorney Do Kim (who came to the United States at age three and eventually earned a Harvard degree specializing in African American studies and sociology); and Bong Hwan Kim (former co-chair of the Black-Korean Alliance before and after the riots, who was honored by the NAACP for his interracial coalition-building work).

The Korean American Coalition-Los Angeles (KAC-LA) is a nonprofit founded by Charles Kim, which has established branches in numerous U.S. cities. Founded in 1983, the organization seeks to better Korean American relations with non-Asian groups, support civic projects and civil rights initiatives, and work toward developing more pan-ethnic Asian American solidarity. The strategically named 4.29 Alternative Dispute Resolution Center, founded in 1997, uses mediation to solve legal problems and is also highly supportive of lower-income people who need community intervention. The KAC offers immigration counseling and citizenship advice, leadership development opportunities for college-age students and others, internships and other professionalization programs, voter registration assistance, and mentorship. KAC-LA was selected as the 2017 California Non-Profit of the Year and continues to fundraise, honor notable community members, and raise awareness of Korean American achievements and ongoing struggles (Korean American Coalition-Los Angeles 2018).

Post-Riot Healing and Reconciliation

The riots forced an abrupt, costly, and life-altering awakening for many Korean immigrants and their American-born descendants. Many of these immigrant entrepreneurs had invested over a decade of their lives and their hard-earned savings in building their businesses, only to see these structures, efforts, and dreams vanish. One year after the tragedy, only 28 percent of the destroyed Korean-owned businesses had reopened. Many of these were hindered in part by bureaucratic red tape and lack of government assistance in securing permits and filling out convoluted loan applications (Kim-Gibson 2004). Many felt the city failed to make satisfactory amends with the business owners. As a result, a number of Korean Americans engaged in dialogue about the importance of respecting other learning from and about other minorities and avoiding the urge to adopt racist, classist, and otherwise dehumanizing positions heard elsewhere. Korean Americans also expressed their right to live in safety and without fear, whether from direct physical attacks or verbal and psychological violence, including from the media. To many victims of *Sa-i-gu,* passivity and silence were no longer options, nor were they viable ways to combat harmful stereotypes. After the riots ended, many Korean Americans were no longer willing to contain their manifold frustrations. Some immigrant entrepreneurs whose businesses had been ruined returned to their homeland. Others held demonstrations demanding reparations and any approximation of collective justice. The sense that the city of Los Angeles did not adequately address Korean business owners' devastation remains an unresolved grievance for many even today. In 1992, the Peace March, an event convened to call attention to the victims' plight, was attended by more than 30,000 Korean Americans and was the largest convergence of Asian Americans up to that point in time (Chang 2014, 648). The Association of Korean American Victims of the L.A. Riot, led by Chung Lee (owner of the Watts Market and respected community figure who had made strides to quell black-Korean tensions as co-chair of the BKA), handled nearly $7 million in donations from South Korea, Southern California, and nationally. Unfortunately, financial mismanagement and conflict among Korean American leaders marred recovery efforts. There were fractious disagreements based on allegiances to particular South Korean politicians, and quarrels broke out about who should have jurisdiction over the distribution of funds. Others clashed on how best to avoid fraudulent claimants (McMillan 1992). Some first-generation Koreans butted heads with younger leaders. Having been hardest hit materially by the riots, the former did not feel that those Korean Americans who arrived in the United States at a young age (sometimes referred to as the 1.5 generation) and Korean Americans born in the United States to immigrant parents (referred to as second-generation immigrants) had the same interests or vision for recovery efforts.

There were some bright spots amid this internal dysfunction: individuals like Do Kim, a civil rights attorney and former member of the Black-Korean Alliance, focused on recovery efforts that were more inclusive. He fundraised with Harvard students to help black as well as Korean families and collaborated in the effort to create a Koreatown resource center where stricken shopkeepers could go to receive mental health counseling and legal advice, among other forms of community-based aid (Guidi 2012). Some Asian American groups stood up to provide nonpolitical forms of support, such as social services, fundraising, and legal assistance in pursuing and processing insurance claims. They also sought better representation of Korean Americans in the media. Overall, the political and economic dynamics of Koreatown have shifted from the low point of the early 1990s. Within Los Angeles, diversity has also increased to include people of many more racial, ethnic, and national backgrounds (Chang 2014).

Demographic shifts have witnessed the rise of Latino, Southeast Asian, and Arab American small businesses in South Central Los Angeles. The competition of these groups among one another and with Latino business owners especially, who make up the majority, has now taken center stage. The pre-riot emphasis on black-Korean tensions has largely become a thing of the past (Chang 2014, 649). K. W. Lee, founding president of the Korean American Journalists Association and creator of both the *Koreatown Weekly* and the *Korea Times* English edition, made an observation in 2012 about the factors that contributed to the 1992 disaster. He states that while white Americans have tended to have a "bird's-eye view" of urban areas, including their social problems, minorities have had a "worm's-eye view" in inner-city Los Angeles, which doesn't allow the same perspective that majority groups tend to enjoy (Kang 2012). What is required, as Lee sees it, is to help Los Angeles in the future through a diverse, revitalized police force that is connected to the neighborhoods they work in; communities that use contemporary media outlets as a vehicle for better communication across generations and cultures; and interaction between racial and ethnic groups through education, ethical leadership driven by young people, and respectful and open dialogues with those who are different.

Biographies of Notable Figures

Angela E. Oh (1955–)

Korean American educator, lawyer, writer, and public intellectual Angela E. Oh played an integral role during and after the riots as a de facto spokesperson for the Korean American community. Born in Los Angeles, Oh graduated from the University of California, Los Angeles with a Bachelor of Arts degree in 1977. She earned a master's in Public Health from her undergraduate alma mater in 1981 and subsequently attended UC Davis School of Law, where she graduated with a JD in 1986. Her legal expertise has concentrated upon trial advocacy in criminal practice, which proved to be instrumental in her rise to visibility. In 1992, Oh was appointed Special Counsel to the Assembly Special Committee on the Los Angeles Crisis.

Much of her prominence as a public presence stemmed from her seminal, if brief, appearance on a *Nightline* television interview after weeks of what many considered to be biased reporting on the riots by such mainstream outlets as ABC News and the *Los Angeles Times*. Oh inhabited the role of a sober, informed, and articulate English-language spokeswoman reflecting upon the events that transpired. She has been particularly adamant in her post-riot assessments about the lack of Korean American judicial and political presence in Los Angeles County and Southern California broadly and the need for such participation in the future (Oh 2010, 43). She represented a beacon of hope for many in the Korean American community, not only in the immediate Los Angeles area but also across the United States who felt unrepresented, under-represented, or caricatured. Her informed commentary refuted the media images and reports that portrayed Korean immigrant shopkeepers as potentially violent aliens who cared more about their property than people and who dismissed the needs or feelings of African Americans. Korean immigrant women, as scholar Elaine H. Kim explains in the documentary *Sa-I-Gu* (1993), were often portrayed as emotional and helpless, especially when it came to enunciating their feelings about the destruction of their property and livelihoods. Oh's demeanor helped to create a counter-discourse to these sensationalized portrayals.

Since 1992, her career trajectory has led to several noteworthy leadership positions in government, law, community outreach, and civil rights advocacy. She was recruited by the administration of President Bill Clinton to be part of the One America Initiative Advisory Board, offering perspectives on vital issues like racial cooperation and bridge building between vulnerable and minority communities. She served as president of the Korean American Bar Association of Southern California; commissioner to the City of Los Angeles Human Relations Commission; and executive director of the Western Justice Center Foundation, a nonprofit organization premised on peaceful conflict resolution and social justice advocacy. Oh has also participated in the Federal Judicial Nominations Committee for the Central District of California and consulted widely for state and federal criminal defense cases as well as state judicial appointments. Her more recent endeavors have involved lecturing, internationally as well as throughout the United States, primarily on diversity's intersection with activism, law, and civil rights history. Oh has served as a faculty member at a number of California universities, among them UCLA, UC-Irvine, and University of Southern California.

As a public intellectual, Oh has received her share of criticism from first-generation immigrant elders and a number of male community leaders. Some have even suggested that she was being an opportunist by benefitting from the devastation of the riots. Despite these detractors, she has continued her efforts. Oh was one of a number of Korean American perspectives comprising the interactive documentary *K-Town '92* (2017) directed by Grace Lee, a multimedia project that showcases silenced or under-represented voices who had a stake in the riots. Oh is adamant that policy change advocacy on behalf of Korean Americans and Korean immigrants remains vital to avoid the same kind of fallout experienced in 1992. Her collection of autobiographical reflections, *Open: One Woman's Journey* (2012), sheds light on her intellectual and spiritual coming to consciousness, as well as the tumultuous period of the riots and their aftermath. An ordained Zen priest, Oh uses contemplative spiritual practices to enhance her professional work as a mediator, activist, and community leader.

Edward "Eddie" Jae Song Lee (1973–1992)

Eddie Jae Song Lee was an eighteen-year-old Southern California teenager at the time of the riots. He was one of two children born to father Young Hi and mother Jung Hui, who immigrated to Los Angeles to pursue their American dream. He was the first Korean American casualty of the LA riots, dying of gunshot wounds on April 30, 1992, while standing alongside his friends and protecting a pizza shop from looters.

According to Dai Sil Kim-Gibson's documentary *Sa-I-Gu: From Korean Women's Perspectives* (1993), Lee grew up helping his working-class parents from an early age; he would accompany Jung Hui while she completed her nighttime cleaning job, even helping with the vacuuming and other labor. At the outset of the riots, Lee felt strongly about the need to fight back against the looting and destruction of the neighborhood businesses. He convinced his mother that complacency, inaction, and silence would result in only more oppression. Lee was picked up by his friends at his home that evening to join the makeshift brigades of shopkeepers, friends, and associates—largely immigrant Korean men of various generations—who were joining forces to protect their businesses. Their desire for self-defense stemmed from what they saw as a lack of reliable law enforcement presence or other municipal support in Koreatown, South Central Los Angeles, and other areas affected by the violence. A number of witnesses testified that LAPD officers were standing in the immediate area, even across the street, but were not stopping the riots. Instead, fires continued to burn, goods were stolen, and shopkeepers were left to fend for themselves.

Lee and three of his friends were shot by another Korean in a case of mistaken identity during a confused exchange of gunfire with looters. Bleeding profusely from the torso, Lee passed away on the sidewalk. *Los Angeles Times* photographer Hyungwon Kang captured an image of the teen's prone body on 3rd Street and Hobart Boulevard, with the three injured friends nearby being questioned by police officers. The image was published in the *Los Angeles Times* in color and the *Korea Times* in black and white. As *Sa-I-Gu* explains, Lee's mother held out hope that the deceased was not her son due to the fact that his shirt appeared to be a dark color in the *Korea Times*. She recalled that he had left the house that evening clad in a white top and blue jeans. She realized later that the dark hue had resulted from the white garment's saturation with blood, camouflaged by the black and white print of the newspaper.

Unlike Rodney King or Latasha Harlins, Lee's name does not evoke widespread recognition. Like Juri Kang, the nine-year-old Korean American victim who is thought to have died due to retaliatory racial violence, he is virtually unknown. As Kim-Gibson's follow-up documentary *Wet Sand: Voices from LA* (2004) implies, Lee stands as a tragic figure both for his family and the Korean American community broadly. His sister works as an elementary school teacher who instructs her pupils on the value of diversity, and his elderly parents regularly visit the Forest Lawn Cemetery in the Hollywood Hills to grieve and clean the gravestone (Kang 2012). Lee's death has led to conversations about conflict and harm created within communities, as well as failures of leadership by law enforcement and local politicians before, during, and after the riots.

DOCUMENT EXCERPTS

On March 3, 1991, four Los Angeles Police Department officers beat motorist Rodney King with batons after a high-speed chase in Los Angeles County. King suffered multiple fractures as a result. This violent "King incident" was filmed by a civilian nearby. The officers Stacey C. Koon, Laurence M. Powell, Theodore J. Briseno, and Timothy E. Wind were charged with assault with a deadly weapon and excessive use of force. On April 29, 1992, the jury acquitted the four officers of criminal misconduct against King. The People v. Stacey Koon et al. *decision surprised and angered many, especially African Americans in the Los Angeles area, and led to a series of riots, lootings, and civil disturbances. A federal jury convicted Koon and Powell, sentencing the men to thirty months in prison each for violating King's civil rights in April 1993. Briseno and Wind were acquitted.*

833 F. Supp. 769 (1993)
UNITED STATES of America, Plaintiff
v.
Stacey C. KOON, Laurence M. Powell, Timothy E. Wind, and Theodore J.
Briseno, Defendants.
No. CR 92 686 JGD.
United States District Court, C.D. California.
August 4, 1993.
(Excerpts)

*770 *771 *772 *773 Steven D. Clymer, Lawrence Middleton, Asst. U.S. Attys.,
Los Angeles, CA, Barry F. Kowalski, Deputy Chief, Civ. Rights Div., U.S. Dept.
of Justice, Washington, DC, for the U.S.
*774 Ira Salzman, Pasadena, CA, for Stacey C. Koon.
Harland W. Braun, Los Angeles, CA, for Theodore J. Briseno.
Michael P. Stone, Los Angeles, CA, for Laurence M. Powell.
Paul R. DePasquale, Los Angeles, CA, for Timothy E. Wind.

SENTENCING MEMORANDUM

DAVIES, District Judge.

INTRODUCTION

Four Los Angeles Police Officers, Stacey C. Koon, Laurence M. Powell, Timothy E.
Wind, and Theodore J. Briseno, were indicted by the United States in a Two-Count
Indictment filed August 4, 1992. The Indictment charges in Count One that defendants Laurence M. Powell, Timothy E. Wind, and Theodore J. Briseno violated Title
18, United States Code, Section 2, and Title 18, United States Code, Section 242,
and aided and abetted each other. The Government charges that while acting under
color of the laws of the state of California, said officers willfully struck with
batons, kicked, and stomped Rodney Glen King, resulting in bodily injury to him
and, thereby, willfully deprived him of the right preserved and protected by the
Constitution of the United States not to be deprived of liberty without due process
of law, including the right to be secure in his person and free from the intentional
use of unreasonable force by one making an arrest under color of law. The aiding
and abetting count was stated in Count One of the Indictment, but at trial was treated
as a separate count and was submitted to the jury as such.
Count Two of the Indictment alleges violation of Title 18, United States Code, Section 242, and is directed against Stacey C. Koon alone. He is charged with willfully

permitting the other officers in his presence, and under his supervision, to unlawfully strike with batons, kick, and stomp Rodney Glen King and with the willful failure to prevent the unlawful assault by said officers, all in violation of the right preserved and protected by the Constitution of the United States not to be deprived of liberty without due process of law, including the right to be kept free from harm while in official custody.

The case was tried to a jury commencing February 25, 1993. The jury reached its verdicts on April 16, 1993, and the verdicts were handed up on April 17, 1993.

By said verdicts the jury found that none of the defendants was guilty of aiding and abetting, that Officer Briseno was not guilty of the charges alleged in Count One and was acquitted, that Officer Wind was not guilty of the charges alleged in Count One and was acquitted, that Officer Powell was guilty of the charges other than aiding and abetting alleged in Count One, and that Sergeant Koon was guilty of the charges alleged in Count Two.

The matter is now before this Court for the sentencing of Laurence M. Powell and Stacey C. Koon. The Court has reviewed, read, and considered the presentence reports, the addenda thereto, the position papers and sentencing memoranda filed by the defendants and by the Government. The Court has reviewed and considered a multitude of letters relating to the trial of the case and sentencing, and letters written in support of the defendants. The Court has also considered the United States Sentencing Commission *Guidelines Manual,* effective November 1, 1992, and the arguments of counsel. Based thereon, the Court makes its findings as follows and sentences the defendants as follows.

FINDINGS OF FACT

The details of the arrest of Rodney Glen King in the early morning hours of March 3, 1991, on Osborne Street near Hanson Dam, Los Angeles, were disclosed at trial. Multiple motions were made before trial in an effort to resolve the many legal problems that emerged, and witnesses testified and evidence was taken between February 25, 1993, and April 6, 1993. The Government presented its case in great detail. It is hard to imagine that the Government overlooked any fact. However, because the verdicts *775 were general and no special findings were made by the jury, certain factual conclusions and findings remain undetermined. For the purposes of sentencing it falls to the Court to make those findings.

The essential facts proved at trial were as follows:

During the early evening hours of March 2, 1991, Rodney Glen King met with two friends and sat in his wife's Hyundai automobile in Altadena, a suburb of Los Angeles, drinking a malt beer beverage, Old English 800, packaged in 40-ounce bottles. Mr. King consumed at least two bottles. His friends also drank Old English 800.

Although it is not clear precisely how much they each consumed, it is certain that Mr. King consumed more than 80 ounces. Mr. King and his friends drank in the parked automobile for a number of hours. Late in the evening, they left Altadena in the Hyundai. Mr. King drove. Their intended destination is not clear. Mr. King testified that it was Hanson Dam, but his friend Bryant Allen testified that the three companions left Altadena to "look for women."

Mr. King was intoxicated. He drove the Hyundai from Altadena to the 210 Freeway, then west from Pasadena towards the city of San Fernando. While westbound, in the vicinity of La Tuna Canyon Road, CHP Officer Melanie Singer and Officer Tim Singer, her husband and training officer, observed the Hyundai speeding westbound on the freeway behind the CHP cruiser. Officer Melanie Singer was driving. The CHP vehicle exited and re-entered the freeway at Sunland Boulevard, and with red lights and siren activated followed the Hyundai, which was by then about one mile west of the CHP vehicle. Officer Melanie Singer estimated the speed of the Hyundai west of Wheatland Avenue as being in excess of 100 m.p.h.

Mr. King left the freeway at Paxton Avenue and commenced traveling on surface streets, followed by the Singers' CHP unit. Officer Melanie Singer called for backup. The CHP dispatcher alerted LAPD by radio call. The call was heard by patrol officers of the Los Angeles Unified School District in a unit nearby which joined the chase. In addition, Officers Powell and Wind in an LAPD unit responded to the call. During the pursuit, the CHP officers attempted to communicate with Mr. King as he drove on the surface streets, and ordered him to pull over. He failed to do so. Mr. King testified that he did not pull over because he was afraid of returning to prison.

Mr. King continued on the route chosen by him, at times stopping for red lights, at times proceeding through red lights. The CHP vehicle and the school district vehicle followed the Hyundai at varying speeds. They were joined by Officer Powell and Wind's vehicle. After the Hyundai left the freeway, the pursuit was always at moderate to slow speeds. The three police vehicles followed the Hyundai for a number of miles on surface streets to the point where it stopped at an entrance to the Hanson Dam recreation area on Osborne Street. In all, the CHP unit followed the Hyundai for approximately eight miles before the pursuit ended.

The CHP vehicle, the School District vehicle, and Officer Powell's vehicle came to rest in the immediate vicinity of the Hyundai. The occupants of the Hyundai were ordered out of the vehicle by Officer Singer. The two passengers exited the Hyundai and followed instructions of the police officers. Mr. King was slow to move from the driver's seat but ultimately did and was repeatedly ordered to lie on the ground. He emerged from the Hyundai smiling. This was the scene when Sergeant Koon arrived. Officers Briseno and Rolando Solano arrived in their unit moments after Sergeant Koon.

Mr. King did what appeared to be a dance step, and then waved at an LAPD helicopter overhead. Officer Melanie Singer ordered *776 Mr. King to move away from the Hyundai and to place his hands where she could see them, and then again ordered him to the ground. When she did so, he grabbed his buttocks. Officer Singer pointed her service revolver at him. Mr. King did not lie prone but moved around on his hands and knees.

Sergeant Koon took command and ordered Officer Melanie Singer to holster her service revolver. The LAPD officers then commenced the arrest process. Mr. King was a large muscular man and a felony suspect. Sergeant Koon testified that he thought Mr. King may have been recently imprisoned because Mr. King appeared to have engaged in the bodybuilding common among prison inmates. The officers ordered Mr. King to lie in the felony-prone position. He refused to do so. Officers Powell, Wind, Briseno, and Solano jointly attempted to place Mr. King in a felony-prone position. He resisted and became combative, forcing the officers to retreat. The subsequent events were captured by Mr. George Holliday on videotape, Exhibit 20 at trial. The tape does not capture the entire sequence. It records the events commencing with a view of Mr. King on the ground, surrounded by officers. The Holliday videotape became the focus of a good deal of testimony at trial and was analyzed in thorough detail by expert and other witnesses called by each side. The Court has reviewed the tape for the purpose of sentencing. Although the videotape creates a vivid impression of a violent encounter, careful analysis shows that it is sometimes an ambiguous record of the crucial events. A meaningful understanding of the events it depicts required the explanation of witnesses who are experts in law enforcement. At trial the Government and defendants agreed that much of the officers' conduct was justified and legal, yet vigorously disputed whether and when their behavior became illegal.

The principal question for sentencing not answered by the verdicts is, when did the offenses committed by Officer Powell and by Sergeant Koon occur? The answer to this question determines the extent to which these defendants are liable for Mr. King's injuries. Injury is an element of the offenses with which Officer Powell and Sergeant Koon were charged, and is relevant to the determination of their sentences under the Sentencing Guidelines.

Answering this question requires a two-tiered inquiry. The offenses the jury found to have been committed occurred when Officer Powell used excessive force and formed the intent to deprive Mr. King of his civil rights, and when Sergeant Koon intended to refrain from preventing the officers under his control from using excessive force which deprived Mr. King of his constitutional rights. Sergeant Koon's criminal liability is not derivative from Officer Powell's liability. *See United States v. Reese,* 2 F.3d 870, 889–90 (9th Cir. July 28, 1993). Sergeant Koon's conviction rests entirely upon the wrongfulness of his own conduct, that is, his willful refusal to prevent illegal use of force in his presence. *Id.* Thus, the Court must make separate determinations concerning Officer Powell's and Sergeant Koon's illegal behavior.

. . .

(3) Summary

Neither Officer Powell nor Sergeant Koon is liable for Mr. King's serious bodily injuries, namely, his facial injuries and leg fracture. Both officers are liable to differing degrees for Mr. King's bruises and abrasions sustained after 1:07:28. Because neither officer violated 18 U.S.C. § 242 prior to this moment, neither is liable for injuries sustained by Mr. King before the event recorded at 1:07.28 of the videotape, and the Court so finds.

. . .

IT IS SO ORDERED.

Source: *United States v. Koon*, 833 F. Supp. 769 (1993).

See also: The Delano Grape Strike and Boycott, 1965–1970; The First Asian American Studies Program Established at San Francisco State College, 1969; The Murder of Vincent Chin, 1982

Further Reading

Abelmann, Nancy and John Lie. 1995. *Blue Dreams: Korean Americans and the Los Angeles Riots*. Cambridge, MA: Harvard University Press.

Chang, Edward T. 2014. "Los Angeles Riots/Sa-I-Gu." In *Asian American Society: An Encyclopedia*, edited by Anthony Ocampo and Mary Yu Danico, 647–649. Thousand Oaks, CA: SAGE.

Chang, Edward T. and Eui-Young Yu, eds. 1995. *Multiethnic Coalition-Building in Los Angeles: A Two-Day Symposium, November 19–20, 1993*. Claremont, CA: Regina Books for the Institute for Asian American and Pacific Asian Studies, California State University, Los Angeles.

Guidi, Ruxandra. 2012. "Saigu, on April 29, Is a Landmark Date for Many of LA's Korean-Americans." *89.3 KPCC—The Voice of Southern California*, April 24. https://www.scpr.org/news/2012/04/24/32140/saigu-or-4-29-remembered-korean-americans/

Hata, Nadine and Donald Hata. 2006. "Into the Mainstream: Asians and Pacific Islanders in Post-1945 Los Angeles." In *City of Promise: Historical Changes in Los Angeles*, edited by Martin Schiesl and Mark Morrall Dodge, 87–108. Claremont, CA: Regina Books.

Itagaki, Lynn Mie. 2016. *Civil Racism: The 1992 Riots and the Crisis of Racial Burnout*. Minneapolis: University of Minnesota Press.

Johnson, Jr., John. 2011. "How Los Angeles Covered Up the Massacre of 17 Chinese." *LA Weekly*, March 10. http://www.laweekly.com/news/how-los-angeles-covered-up-the-massacre-of-17-chinese-2169478

Kang, Hyungwon. 2012. "Los Angeles: Home Sweet Home." *Reuters Photographers' Blog*, May 4. http://blogs.reuters.com/photographers-blog/2012/05/05/los-angeles-home-sweet-home/

Kim, Elaine H. 1993. "Home Is Where the *Han* Is: A Korean American Perspective on the Los Angeles Upheavals." *Social Justice* 20, no. 1–2: 1–21. http://www.jstor.org/stable/29766728

Kim, Elaine H. 1994. "Between Black and White: An Interview with Bong Hwan Kim." In *The State of Asian America: Activism and Resistance in the 1990s*, edited by Karin Aguilar-San Juan, 71–100. Boston: South End Press.

Kim, Elaine H. and Eui-Young Yu, eds. 1997. *East to America: Korean American Life Stories*. New York: New Press.

Kim, Kwang Chung, ed. 1999. *Koreans in the Hood: Conflict with African Americans*. Baltimore: Johns Hopkins University Press.

Kim-Gibson, Dai Sil, dir. 2004. *Wet Sand: Voices from L.A.* San Francisco: Center for Asian American Media.

Kim-Gibson, Dai Sil, and Cynthia Choy, dir. 1993. *Sa-I-Gu: From Korean Women's Perspectives*. San Francisco: Center for Asian American Media.

Korean American Coalition–Los Angeles. 2017. "Korean American Coalition–About." http://www.kacla.org/about.html

Lee, Grace, dir. 2017. *K-Town '92*. San Francisco: Center for Asian American Media and LeeLee Films. http://ktown92.com

McMillan, Penelope. 1992. "Fight Renewed over Funds to Help Korean Riot Victims." *Los Angeles Times*, August 18. http://articles.latimes.com/1992-08-18/local/me-5899_1_relief-fund

Oh, Angela E. 2002. *Open: One Woman's Journey*. Los Angeles: UCLA Asian American Studies Center Press.

Oh, Angela E. 2010. "An Issue of Time and Place: The Truth behind Korean Americans' Connection to the 1992 Los Angeles Riots." *Harvard Journal of Asian American Policy Review* 19: 39–48.

Smith, Anna Deavere. 1994. *Twilight: Los Angeles, 1992*. New York: Anchor Books.

Yamato, Jen. 2017. "'Look What Happens When We Don't Talk to Each Other': Korean American Filmmakers' L.A. Riots Stories." *Los Angeles Times*, April 28. http://www.latimes.com/entertainment/movies/la-et-mn-la-riots-korean-american-filmmakers-20170428-htmlstory.html

Yu, Eui-Young, ed. 1994. *Black-Korean Encounter: Toward Understanding and Alliance*. Claremont: Regina Books.

Yu, Eui-Young and Edward T. Chang, eds. 1995. *Multiethnic Coalition-Building in Los Angeles: A Two-Day Symposium, November 19–20, 1993*. Claremont, CA: Regina Books for the Institute for Asian American and Pacific Asian Studies, California State University, Los Angeles.

Zesch, Scott. 2012. *The Chinatown War: Chinese Los Angeles and the Massacre of 1871*. New York: Oxford University Press.

Zia, Helen. 2000. *Asian American Dreams: The Emergence of an American People*. New York: Farrar, Straus, and Giroux.

9/11 and Islamophobia, 2001–2018

Marie-Therese C. Sulit

Chronology

2001	9/11 begins with a series of four coordinated attacks by al-Qaeda, led by Osama bin Laden. Two planes fly into the twin towers of the World Trade Center in New York City; one plane aims for the Pentagon in Washington, D.C.; and another plane crashes in a field in Pennsylvania.
October 26, 2011	The USA Patriot Act is passed as a means to detect and prevent terrorism using surveillance tools that bridge the Federal Bureau of Investigation and the Central Intelligence Agency.
2002	The U.S. Department of Homeland Security is established.
2008	Barack Hussein Obama is elected the first African American president of the United States on November 8.
2012	Obama is re-elected on November 8.
2015	The USA Freedom Act is passed on June 2, delimiting the use of surveillance tools of investigation, including data collection and storage and intelligence gathering.
2016	Donald J. Trump is elected president of the United States on November 8.
2017	On January 27, Executive Order 13769 is signed, indefinitely halting the entry of refugees from Syria and banning entry for ninety days by citizens from Iraq, Syria, Iran, Libya, Somalia, Sudan, and Yemen.
January 28, 2017	Mass protests are held at multiple U.S. airports in opposition to the travel ban.
	Two federal judges in New York and Massachusetts block or place a temporary restraint on sections of Executive Order 13769.
January 29, 2017	Trump defends the order.

January 30, 2017	Obama criticizes the order.
	Attorney General Sally Yates, who declines to defend the travel ban, is fired.
January 31, 2017	John Kelly, the new secretary of the Department of Homeland Security, defends the order.
February 2, 2017	Trump eases travel ban restrictions.
February 3, 2017	James Robart, a district court judge, blocks the ban nationwide, halting key provisions of Executive Order 13769.
February 5, 2017	The U.S. government's request to resume the ban is denied by the Ninth Circuit Court of Appeals.
February 7, 2017	The arguments are presented by the Justice Department and the state of Washington in the Ninth Circuit Court of Appeals.
February 9, 2017	The travel ban remains blocked.
February 16, 2017	Trump promises a new immigration order.
March 6, 2017	Trump unveils a new travel ban excluding Iraq from the list of Muslim-majority countries whose citizens have been temporarily blocked. This new travel ban is set to take effect on March 16.
March 7, 2017	Hawaii files a lawsuit against the new travel ban.
March 15, 2017	U.S. District Court Judge Derrick Watson of Hawaii blocks the new travel ban.
March 16, 2017	U.S. District Court Judge Theodore Chuang of Maryland blocks the ninety-day travel ban.

Narrative

9/11 refers to a series of coordinated terrorist attacks in the United States by al-Qaeda, an Islamic group led by Osama bin Laden. These events took place on September 11, 2001, and caused close to 3,000 deaths, injured close to double that number, and amounted to at least $10 billion in property damage. Bin Laden is also held responsible for the bombing of the World Trade Center in 1993, the bombings of the U.S. embassies in Kenya and Tanzania in 1998, and the bombing of the USS

A Muslim American protester marched while holding up a sign calling for tolerance during an anti-war rally in New York City on April 9, 2011. Since 9/11 and the U.S. invasion of Iraq and Afghanistan, thousands of people have protested against Islamophobia and the wars. (Mario Tama/Getty Images)

Cole in Yemen in 2000. While the loss of life seemed on a much smaller scale than that caused by war, the ways in which 9/11 reflected, catalyzed, and galvanized age-old ideologies about race, religion, and the nation become quite evident in its striking aftermath, particularly through the long-standing Global War on Terrorism.

In U.S. history, the watershed moment of 9/11 crystallizes several notions that previously remained somewhat submerged in America's domestic, if not altogether global, consciousness. First, the advent of radical Islam with the fanatical Jihadist as its central trope in contemporary times harkens back to (if not predates) the Crusades throughout the early modern epoch across Europe. Second, the United States is seen as both a symbol of democracy and a target of capitalism, with the role of the military underscored. Third, "Muslim" ostensibly emerges as a racial category in the United States. Finally, in keeping with the aforementioned notions, Islamophobia develops as a form of racism in the United States.

People with Islamophobia believe the Muslim faithful are irrational, intolerant, and violent and that Islam's principles have become increasingly perceived as conflicting with American traditions. Prominent among those dispersing this specific narrative are elements within American far-right factions. Thus, the violence enacted against Americans by al-Qaeda on the fateful day of September 11, 2011, is refracted in hate crimes against those perceived to be Muslim, regardless of whether or not they are, in fact, Muslim.

Historical Background

Throughout the Middle Ages, the Crusades pitted Christians against non-Christians, typically referred to as Moors, Arabs, Muhammedans, Orientals, Turks, and Muslims. At the time, clear distinctions on the social level—not racial in today's terms—served to categorize these non-Christian peoples, whose origins spread across Southwest Asia and North Africa. The countries that comprise this immense geographic region, known as the Middle East, range from India and Pakistan to Algeria and Morocco, from North Africa through to Southwest and South Asia. These distinctions decisively separated these peoples from Europeans, typically those from Western Europe. The imperial expansionism of the Crusades thus subjected what we now consider the Middle East to the colonial oppression of European rule into modern times. Despite decolonization and independence effected in the twentieth century, Middle Eastern peoples still experience racism, dehumanization, and violence in the form of "American-led interventions." Rooted in the competing religious ideologies of Christianity and Islam, the dehumanization and racialization of the many peoples of the Middle East highlight the uneasy emergence of both the racial identification *and* the emergence of a stereotype of these peoples at times when heightened religious and racial violence are neither innocuous nor benign (Love 2017, 6, 37, 39–40).

Eric Hershberg and Kevin W. Moore have discussed the politics of war along religious and racial lines across the Middle East and pointed out the shortcomings of the political regimes throughout the Islamic world and the shortcomings of foreign policies by Western governments, implicating most strongly Great Britain and the United States. Hershberg and Moore note what they deem the "exclusionary and fundamentalist nature of the Saudi monarchy among other oil-exporting states in the Middle East," the arming of religious extremists by the United States (and its allies) in their historical campaign against the Soviet Union, and the ongoing conflict between Israel and Palestine (2002, 2). Abbas Amanat likewise identifies "a pattern of diplomatic, military and economic presence tying the fate of the Middle East and its resources to the West" (2001, 29) and implicates the more powerful Western influences in the political problems of the embattled region.

Despite disparate situations across the Middle East, scholars have suggested that the geographic boundaries of each nation-state outline the parameters of political structures and religious and/or secular affiliations, even as there may be conflicts and boundaries within each nation-state at times of ongoing crises. All of these are, to some degree, residual effects of imperial expansionism and colonialism throughout the region.

Mahmood Mamdani poses the seemingly rhetorical but no less authentic question: "Does it really make sense to write political histories of Islam that read like political histories of geographies like the Middle East, and the political histories of Middle Eastern states as these were no more than the political history of Islam in the Middle East?" (2002, 45). Mamdani further points out that the leaders of the United States (and its allies, such as Great Britain) have lapsed into generalizations by, for example, failing to differentiate between Iraq's government and its people and by continuing to support Israel in its conflict with Palestine. These are clearly two different situations that in no way implicate Islam. In short, Mamdani's questions are offered as caveats to the simplistic conflation of a country's government and its people when it is this simplification that elides the struggles—across politics, race and religion, and nation—within and throughout this region of the world.

All this said, Tariq Modood and Wang Gungwu note the debt that Western civilizations owe to what is now considered "a rival and inferior civilization," that is, Islam, arguably "one of the greatest religions of Asia," preserved by Arabs and translated by Muslims: scholarship, philosophy, scientific inquiry, medicine, architecture, and technology. This originary romantic narrative of the Middle East has since been supplanted and simplified by Osama bin Laden, who, according to Bergen, claims the United States leads a Western conspiracy to "destroy true Islam." According to bin Laden, U.S. foreign policy in the Muslim world led to the al-Qaeda attack on America (Bergen 2011, 26–27). Further, the Middle East, according to Amanat, is "still one of the least developed regions of the world" (2001, 31). This at least partially explains why there is a "staggering reorientation toward radical Islam"—characterized by Amanat as defiance, resentment, and violence—in light of the deeper crisis of identity in the Arab world" (2001, 28, 32). Despite what Gungwu refers to as "a revived discussion on the separation of religion and state" (2002, 229) across the three monotheistic faiths—Judaism, Christianity, and Islam—the events of 9/11 and their residue pit Islam against Christianity.

Orientalism, Islamophobia, and Racism

In his seminal work *Orientalism*, Edward Said notes that the same faulty, if not altogether stereotypical, characterizations of those from the vast regions that comprise the Middle East followed people originating in these regions from Western Europe to the United States. Those typically referred to as Moors, Arabs, Muhammedans, Orientals, Turks, and Muslims were arbitrarily assigned Asian qualities and characteristics—"orientalized"—and depicted as "backward, decadent, and untrustworthy" (Love 2017, 40). Such negative tropes found their basis in the late nineteenth and early twentieth centuries in modern American popular culture, from novels and advertising campaigns to the film industry, most notably in the popularity of the "Barbary captive" narratives of trans-Atlantic crossings wherein pirates of Middle Eastern descent captured those of English descent; in fact, the Barbary captive narratives established the major elements of the genre itself, and these elements have endured (Love 2017, 41). Further, American scholarship on the so-called Orient (i.e., the Far East) in the early twentieth century followed suit with its perpetuation of faulty tropes, developed by Europeans and disseminated by Americans. By the mid-twentieth century, American popular culture was well ensconced in colonial representations of so-called Orientals, thus partially explaining the conflation of those peoples from South Asia and Asia (i.e., part of the Middle East and the Far East, respectively). But these were also people of many faiths—Christians, Sikhs, Hindus, and Muslims (Love 2017, 4). Love contends that the nomenclature shift from "Saracen" to "Muslim" is similar to the shift from "Orientalism" to "Islamophobia" in that it reflects the emergence of "Middle Eastern" as a *racial* category in the United States. Thus, racial discrimination, social exclusion, and violence specifically target Arabs, Muslims, Sikhs, South Asians, and other brown-skinned peoples throughout the United States (Love 2017, 3, 42).

Proliferation of the term "Arab" in the United States took place from the 1950s through the 1970s by pro-Western leaders in Arab countries, including Iran (Love 2017, 43). Arguably, the strongest evidence of post–World War II Orientalism is the emergence of the "dangerous and uniquely violent Middle East" through the trope of the Arab in 1967, during the Six-Day War between the state of Israel and several Arab nations (Love 2017, 86). By the end of the 1990s, "Muslim" became a politically expedient term. It "spread direct influence (and military presence) to include non-Arab places in Central and South Asia, especially Afghanistan, Pakistan, and Turkey. Hence, 'Islamic terrorism' and 'Muslim extremists' came to dominate the political discourse, and conveniently 'Muslim' is today the most common term to mean 'person from the Middle East'" (Love 2017, 43). The shift of "Arab" to "Muslim" and/or its conflation with "Middle Eastern" is encapsulated historically by the acronym MENA, for Middle Eastern and North African. In 2010, two more collective terms emerged for this racial category: AMEMSA, for Arabs, Middle Easterners, Muslims, and South Asians; and SWANA, for Southwest Asians and North Africans. According to Love, these acronyms create the trope of a person of Middle Eastern descent, a racial image and a racial identity category for one who exists in American society and culture (2017, 8–10). Love also raises the problems of minority populations throughout the Middle East who trace their heritage to South Asia, Afghanistan, Bangladesh, Bhutan, India, Pakistan, Nepal, and Sri Lanka, and those minority populations who also comprise American communities: Bengali,

Kashmiri, Pashtun, and Punjabi. This convergence between geographical regions and majority-minority populations, such as the convergence of South Asian American and Asian American alongside North African and Southwest Asian American populations, forms a multi- and/or pan-ethnic and/or national-origin base (Love 2017, 54, 59, 61, 65).

The United States also has a history of attempting to block migrants from places outside of Western Europe throughout the 1800s and 1900s, including constituencies of the Middle East and South Asia as well as Asia itself. The Immigration Act of 1917 blocked peoples from India, Siam, Arabia, Indo-China, the Malay Peninsula, Afghanistan, New Guinea, Borneo, Java, Ceylon, Sumatra, Celebes, and parts of Turkestan and Siberia. Interestingly enough, through provisions in the Naturalization Act of 1790, there are case histories and legal appeals by Middle Eastern Americans to establish whiteness and gain citizenship. Historically, some groups were denied and some accepted, pending their nation-state of origin; for example, groups from present-day Syria, Lebanon, Jordan, Israel and Palestine, Iraq, and the Arabian Peninsula were denied. South Asians also faced challenges in "accessing the benefits of Whiteness" (Love 2017, 44, 45). The racial significance of this historical observation lies in the Asian exclusion acts of the late nineteenth century, in 1882 (The Chinese Exclusion Act) and 1892 (The Geary Act) and, definitively, with Executive Order 9066, former President Franklin Delano Roosevelt's call for Japanese internment on American soil during World War II. World War II also witnessed the Luce-Celler Act of 1946, which limited the migration of Indians and Filipinos to the United States. Love also underscores the massive immigration policies that were revised throughout the 1950s and 1960s, including the Immigration and Nationality Act of 1965 (also known as the Hart-Celler Act), which, to a limited degree, redressed the historical exclusion of Asians from the United States and brought in professionals of predominantly Southeast Asian descent (Love 2017, 49). However, whereas the U.S. Census, once upon a time, defined whiteness "as inclusive of many Middle Eastern Americans, including Iranian Americans," it also situates "Afghan, Indian, Pakistani, and other communities from the eastern edge of the Middle East region into the Asian American racial category" (Love 2017, 36). Thus, internal racial ambivalence, coupled with external racist logic, becomes manifest in the term "Middle Eastern" and the figure of the "Middle Easterner," both of which are heavily contested, particularly when coupled with the misapprehension and miscomprehension of the term "Muslim" as a racial category that includes Arabs, Muslims, Sikhs, and South Asians (Love 2017, 7).

Love enumerates the three central logics that shape and guide white supremacy: slavery/capitalism, genocide/colonialism, and Orientalism/war (Love 2017, 84). He further explains the "common ancestry in America's worst racial sins: the campaigns leading to the genocide of Native Americans, the brutal reign of chattel slavery, the *de jure* system of Jim Crow segregation, Japanese American internment camps, mass incarceration, deportation, and Islamophobia" (Love 2017, 85). By intrinsically connecting moments of racist violence with ongoing patterns of racist discrimination and exclusion, the ways in which racism informs Islamophobia cannot be denied as Islamophobia itself is a form of racism.

9/11 and Islamophobia

In the immediate aftermath of 9/11, more than 700 violent hate crimes occurred, including several murders of those who "looked Muslim," an increase of 1,600 percent. These ranged "from insults shouted at people walking by, to vandalism of private homes and places of workshop, to violent crimes like bullying in schools, assaults, and murder," as reported by the American-Arab Anti-Discrimination Committee (ADC) (Love 2017, 90). Employment discrimination claims filed with the U.S. Equal Employment Opportunity Commission (EEOC) by people of color continued to rise, accounting "for nearly 15% of all workplace discrimination charges filed in the United States between 2001 and 2006" (Love 2017, 91). The racial image of the "Middle Eastern American" and the racist stereotype of "terrorist" have become one and the same in the United States, figuratively and materially, Love asserts. There is a "lack of an accepted definition for 'Middle Eastern'" even as the racial image and the racist stereotype warn that such a person "contributes to terrorist impulses, that Middle Eastern Americans are prone to 'self-radicalize' into 'lone wolves', or to strike from shadowy 'sleeper cells'" (2017, 11). Love also contends that "to ignore diversity, to reject indigenous identity, and to promulgate its own version of history all at the same time" (2017, 6) are the costs of invoking the term "race." Given the history of racism against peoples of color in the United States, Love warns, "history might well repeat itself during the next era of racialized war hysteria" (2017, 49).

According to Love, the most effective perpetrator in developing and deploying the racial image and the racist stereotype of the Middle Easterner and the Muslim is the U.S. government, specifically in its "deeply flawed and often bigoted" counterterrorism programs, which are reductive of race, religion, ethnicity, and nation-state (2017, 10). While Love nuances the Federal Bureau of Investigation's (FBI) program of targeting Muslims as not racist per se, "the effect of this FBI program is racist, because of the way the program is justified, the methods by which it is sustained, and how the FBI presents its work to the public" (2017, 13). Love likewise emphasizes the decade-long multimillion-dollar campaign "that promoted using Islamophobia as a tactic throughout American politics"—a campaign that included research reports by so-called Islam experts, propaganda films utilizing the documentary form, and legislation law and policy regarding the banning of Islamic canonical law, also known as Sharia, in order "to stoke suspicion, to use Islamophobia as a wedge issue" in American politics (2017, 93). Thus, the FBI and the U.S. government contribute heavily and effectively to the racial image *and* the racist stereotype of the Middle Easterner and the Muslim, thus conflating the two into one particular figure.

Under former President George W. Bush and the newly established Department of Homeland Security, the USA Patriot Act that soon followed the terrorist attacks of 9/11 enacted a state of national emergency and a financial package into the multimillions, if not billions, of dollars for surveillance, border patrols, and financial interdiction. Most of the provisions of this act expired in 2015, but the new USA Freedom Act extended counterterrorism provisions to 2019 with the expansion of the so-called security state, including the Terrorism Information and Prevention System, or Operation TIPS, in 2001 and the curtailment of basic civil rights for Middle Eastern Americans. Stateside, the New York Police Department launched "a massive counterterrorism operation targeted directly at Middle Eastern Americans" that presented both the racial image and the racist stereotype, dating back to the Crusades (Love 2017, 104). The state of national emergency heightened racial profiling. For example, in 2012, FBI informants were allowed to enter mosques without specific cause, and even though new guidelines to curb racial profiling and racial discrimination on the basis of gender identity, sexual orientation, national origin, and religion were established, the loophole for "national security efforts" did very little to stop the racial profiling and discrimination (Love 2017, 108).

In her study *Terrorism TV: Popular Entertainment in Post-9/11 America*, Stacy Takacs illuminates the use of U.S. popular culture to generate affective investment on the War on Terrorism during the Bush administration, as she analyzes the discourse of national security and a development of a national consensus in the use of war to achieve peace:

> Though riddled with fantasy, the discourse on terrorism has generated very real material effects. It has reoriented social policy away from domestic needs and toward foreign affairs, sanctioned the conduct of wars with questionable merit, institutionalized surveillance and the suspension of civil liberties within the United States, and promoted an imperialistic expansion of U.S. power that many in the world find threatening (2012, 19–21).

Within the framework of trauma and fear, Takacs explores the emotional context of 9/11 that catalyzed Americans in such an effective way as to prime them, as a discourse community, for the counterterrorism programs set up by the Department of Homeland Security. Takacs also considers the role of the military in the production of war propaganda and various forms and genres, for example, satire and fantasy as well as drama, of U.S. popular culture in affirming and/or challenging the ideological war machine. Throughout her study, Takacs outlines the figure of the American, whether white American male or white American female, with the requisite "Good Muslim" figures in supporting roles. Through sanctioned methods of intelligence gathering, including torture, the U.S. public comes to view the FBI and/or the Central Intelligence Agency (CIA) as shifting from crime solving to intelligence gathering. She offers a striking example of the effectiveness of this ideological conditioning in regard to the 2004 elections, with Al Gore as the Democratic opponent voicing his objections to then incumbent president Bush. In spite of the voting controversy and the Electoral College, none of Gore's criticisms seemed to make an impact, and Bush was re-elected (Takacs 2012, 168). In so doing, Americans identified with what Takacs refers to as the virtual citizen-soldier, a "noble, self-sacrificing American" and, inevitably, an imperial grunt with an investment in a system of militarized discipline and the projection of power—all perpetuating the age-old myth of American exceptionalism (2012, 119, 145).

If the U.S. government and global history have created and manufactured the figure of the "Middle Easterner" as "terrorist," then U.S. popular culture has imbued the U.S. public with "a jingoistic climate that encouraged the popular withdrawal from public debate regarding issues of foreign policy" (Takacs 2012, 7) through tactics and strategies of public relations. Achin Vanaik asks a haunting question of the Global War on Terror: "Is this a terrorist war of revenge and imperial expansion, as many a longstanding critic of U.S. foreign policy would aver, or is it a just war?" (2002, 41). Vanaik continues, "In short, the United States has not only demanded that this war on Afghanistan be considered just, but also that it is declared a 'war on global terrorism'—the goals, forms, methods, targets, scale, and duration of which are all to be determined solely by the United States—be seen and endorsed as a just war" (2002, 43). Also in *Critical Views*, Amir Arjomand highlights two notions on which the reality of 9/11 can be constructed: the denial of the relevance of the Israeli-Palestinian conflict and the heightened significance of Islamic fundamentalism through the blurring of, if not altogether conflating with, "Islam as a whole" (2002, 165, 174). Thus, the U.S. public, through its manufactured consent, can be entrusted with the values of good citizenship and trust that its political leaders can handle the rest using the twin pillars in the politics of a liberal democracy: security and fear.

Advocacy Groups in America

As social constructions, race and ethnicity in regard to discrimination, exclusion, and violence have been foundational to American culture and society since its inception as a nation (Love 2017, 3). To reiterate, the ADC reported over 700 hate crimes, including murders, in the first nine weeks after 9/11 alone, and the EEOC reported a marked increase in employment discrimination claims by people of color. Such incidents were aimed at those perceived to be Muslim whether or not they were, in fact, Muslim, thus underscoring the need to see Islamophobia as a form of racism.

That said, even before 9/11, Muslim American advocacy organizations rose in response to global events that implicated America politically and affected Muslim Americans and those perceived to be Middle Eastern throughout the United States: the Palestinian Intifada, the Gulf War, and the Salman Rushdie affair, to name a few. These advocacy organizations appear to fall into two groups: community-based organizations and lobby groups within leadership organizations. They include Desis Rising Up and Moving (DRUM), Arab American Action Network (AAAN), Muslim Community Association (MCA), Arab Anti-Discrimination Committee (ADC), Arab American Institute (AAI), Council on American-Islamic Relations (CAIR), Muslim Public Affairs Council (MPAC), and South Asian Americans Leading Together (SAALT). Across these two types of organizations, two disparate advocacy strategies have been adopted—one race-neutral and the other race-conscious—to assuage "the sensibilities of an American public divided on race and concerned about terrorism" (Love 2017, 24). An obvious Catch-22 situation for the perceived Muslim or Middle Eastern American arises because a race-neutral strategy may ostensibly be more effective in establishing reforms, while a race-conscious strategy ignores or obscures ethnic, religious, or cultural diversity issues. The perceived Muslim or Middle Eastern American remains undifferentiated on the American landscape, where the construction of race has historically been writ large.

Coalition building for the Muslim American and the Middle Eastern American lies at the nexus of this historical moment but harkens back to the civil rights movement of the 1960s, with the establishment of the Civil Rights Act in 1964 and the leadership of American Muslims like Malcolm X and African Americans like Martin Luther King, Jr. The Asian American Movement also coalesced at that time and served as another platform for the Muslim American and the Middle Eastern American to build coalitions. "The question that remains," Love writes, "is whether Asian Americans were a unique case of racial rearticulation [*sic*] in the twentieth century, or if the work of Asian American advocates represents an option available to other civil rights advocates working in a similarly situated, racially marked community" (2017, 76). From that time, and in defining goals, there are thus two forms of coalitions: transactional and transformational. Transactional coalitions aim for short-term resolution, whereas transformational coalitions work for long-term resolution en route to social justice. In the wake of the Gulf War and atrocities committed by white American Christian terrorists (like the World Trade Center and Oklahoma City bombings), advocacy organizations aligned with transactional, but not transformational, coalitions. If Islamophobia is considered a form of racism, the need for coalition building towards social justice reforms can address both domestic violence and discrimination as well as immigration policy.

In October 2015, the International Center for Religion and Diplomacy in collaboration with Peace Catalyst International and the Dialogue Institute brought together thirty prominent U.S. evangelical leaders with selected representatives from the Muslim, Jewish, and non-evangelical Christian faiths to address the numerous aspects of Islamophobia, how they establish themselves, and what could be done to counter them. A number of scholars have written about different ways to combat Islamophobia, the policies of President Donald Trump and the controversy surrounding American Muslims and the alleged attempt at incorporation of Sharia law into American law and the U.S. Constitution, evangelical Protestant attitudes toward and writings about Muslims and their religious culture from colonial American times to the present day, and Islamophobia in schools of the United States and the bullying of Muslim students (Douglas Johnston 2016; Gourley 2017; David Johnston 2016; McCollum 2017).

The Travel Bans

In contrast to the U.S. Department of Defense, which is charged with military actions abroad, the U.S. Department of Homeland Security is charged with the protection of civilians in the United States. Established after 9/11, it remains the newest Cabinet of the United States, consolidating various agencies into one department and bridging the investigative and protective offices—both domestic and international—of the FBI and the CIA. The word "homeland" implies not only citizenship but also services across immigration, customs, and borders, all within the purview of protecting U.S. civilians.

Under the George W. Bush administration, the USA Patriot Act of 2001 morphed more than a decade later into the USA Freedom Act under the Barack Obama administration, when it was signed into law on June 2, 2015. While the Freedom Act restores many of the provisos under the Patriot Act, it also arguably improves the system of surveillance in accordance with protection of the privacy rights of U.S. citizens by dissolving flaws in the system regarding bulk data collection and storage. Further, under Obama, the oblique Global War on Terror (GWOT) was supplanted by Countering Violent Extremism (CVE) as citizens became part of the Shared Responsibility Committee (SRC), thus consolidating the role of the citizen in the ideological underpinnings of security and fear regarding those who look "Middle Eastern" and/or "Muslim" (Love 2017, 109, 112).

In a 2016 article for *The Washington Post*, Steven Heydemann specifically refers to Syria as "a case study in the globalization of violence." This descriptor aptly captures the troubling conflation of "Middle Eastern" and "Muslim" even as it implicates the United States' political stances regarding the different countries and populations that constitute the Middle East. For example, radical Islamist groups, such as al-Qaeda under Osama bin Laden and the Taliban, target Western countries in their calls for jihad, particularly the United States, for exploiting Muslims. Other radical Islamist groups—namely the Islamic State under Iraq and Syria (ISIS) and the Islamic State of Iraq and Levant (ISIL)—wish to establish an Islamic state across the Middle East. With the assassination of Osama bin Laden, the outbreak of civil war in Syria, and the rise of the Assad regime in 2011, ignorance about these disparate yet overlapping historical relationships during the Obama administration enabled this conflation of terms that, in 2015, culminated in restrictions on a visa admissions program that removed waiver benefits for foreign nationals who had visited certain countries—Iran, Iraq, Libya, Somalia, Sudan, Syria, and Yemen. These were deemed "countries of concern," or safe havens for so-called terrorists (Goodman 2017).

President Trump issued Executive Order 13769, commonly referred to as "the Muslim bans." These travel bans restrict the number of refugees allowed from Muslim-majority countries across the Middle East. The original order was redacted and rejected by Maryland and Hawaii state courts from January and March 2017. Its latest reiteration, Executive Order 13780, is commonly referred to as U.S. Travel Ban 3.0. This order amends a couple of "the countries of concern," that is, most citizens from Iran, Libya, Syria, Yemen, Somalia, and Chad, and adds North Korea along with perceived radicalized groups of people from Venezuela (Liptak 2017). As of this writing, the American Civil Liberties Union (ACLU) has vowed to dispute it.

According to David Sterman and Peter Bergen, there is no clear or direct correlation between the War on Terrorism and the imposition of these "Muslim" travel bans, even though Trump, with the aid and assistance of the senior White House policy advisor, insists upon this correlation. Sterman and Bergen argue that the terrorist attacks in the United States since 9/11 were carried out by American citizens or people who were in the country legally—that is, none were from the countries listed in the travel ban. Further, Judge Theodore D. Chuang of the Federal District Court in Maryland contends that "the new proclamation was tainted by religious animus and most likely violated the Constitution's prohibition of government establishment of religion," seemingly presenting an unprecedented "nationality-based travel ban against eight nations consisting of over 150 million people" (Sterman and Bergen 2017, 3–4). As of this writing, the third iteration of President Trump's ban on travel from several predominantly Muslim countries has been upheld by the Supreme Court.

Conclusions

The Democracy Index, produced by a company based in the United Kingdom, measures sixty indicators across five broad categories that measure the state of democracy in 167 countries worldwide, including the United States. These indicators include factors such as electoral process, pluralism, functioning of government, political participation, democratic political culture, and civil liberties. According to the index, the United States fell from a "Full" to a "Flawed" democracy as a result of the 2016 elections and continues its decline (as of January 2018). With the travel bans instituted by the Trump administration, a Republican-controlled Congress, and a rise in white supremacy organizations, time will tell if the rating of the United States will continue to fall on the Democracy Index.

The undifferentiated nature of the term "Middle Eastern" may prompt consideration of a sixth ethnoracial category, "Middle Eastern," for the 2020 census (Love 2017, 203). And in light of the hate crimes against those who are mistakenly perceived as either "Muslim" or "Middle Eastern," Islamophobia as a form of racism underscores two forms of profiling per state-sanctioned and state-governed counterterrorism programs: racial profiling and ethnic and religious profiling. It is clear that both perceived groups will undergo more discrimination, violence, legal hurdles, and limitations of civil rights protections, including reduction of burdens of proof and abandonment of the necessity of presenting public evidence before detention; criminal punishment without criminal statutes, judges, or juries; and avoidance of judicial, legislative, or voter participation in decisions regarding counterterrorism (Heymann 2003, 91–108).

Rethinking these broader categories are three choices affecting democratic freedoms and unity. The first is whether to concentrate investigative resources on nationals of Arab or Muslim states. The second is whether to spy on certain religious and political groups, and third is whether to diminish the privacy and anonymity of everyone. An additional three proposals remain unconsidered due to constitutional concerns: surveillance powers regarding visiting aliens, institution of an "incitement" offense, and membership crime legislation (Heyman 2003, 91–108).

While the constitutionality of the travel bans under the Trump administration has been disputed up to the Supreme Court with the assistance and advocacy of the ACLU, the Department of Homeland Security, created under the George W. Bush administration, continues to carry out policies regarding counterterrorism and border control as well as immigration and customs. However, in light of the political ramifications of 9/11 across three administrations, social, cultural, intellectual, and popular sites across the American landscape indicate a watershed moment that could witness the creation of additional Middle Eastern advocacy organizations and multiracial coalitions and the opportunity for fuller U.S. discourse on race relations informed by religion. Other possibilities include the rise and proliferation of artistic and literary works, shows, and performances, as well as nonfiction narratives by Middle Eastern and Muslim American artists.

In "Terror: A Speech after 9/11," Gayatri Chakravorty Spivak speaks of the role of youth, both male and female, in the Islamic Jihad Movement and notes the terror from within and throughout the United States. Spivak underscores the key role of the secular humanities in the development of a critical literacy for the moment in which we find ourselves. Her work subtly begs the question of the role of youth as leaders across the United States, youth who are now rising up and following others in this moment of terror. Currently, movements are occurring throughout the Trump administration across the various axes of cultural diversity. These include Black Lives Matter in response to police brutality, #MeToo and #NoMore in response to sexual assault and sexual awareness, the so-far-hypothetical wall between the United States and Mexico, Deferred Action for Childhood Arrivals (DACA) aka the Dreamers, and at least twenty school shootings amidst calls for stricter legislation regarding gun control. Together they seem to indicate that we are on the cusp of a new era of civil rights. As of the 2018 midterm elections, Rashida Tlaib and Ilhan Omar are the first Muslim women elected to Congress. Tlaib, born to Palestinian parents, won Michigan's 13th Congressional District, replacing long-time Rep. John Conyers. Omar, a former refugee, won in Minnesota's 5th Congressional District, replacing Rep. Keith Ellison. Omar is also the first Somali-American woman elected to Congress (Connley 2018).

DOCUMENT EXCERPTS

Executive Order 13769, titled "Protecting the Nation from Foreign Terrorist Entry into the United States" (also known as the Muslim Ban or the Travel Ban), is issued by President Donald J. Trump on January 27, 2017. It lowers the number of refugees to be admitted into the United States; suspends the U.S. Refugee Admissions Program; suspends the entry of Syrian refugees; and suspends entry of those from Iran, Iraq, Libya, Somalia, Sudan, Syria, and Yemen. This Travel Ban not only reflects the post-9/11 Islamophobia but also exemplifies how anti-immigration rhetoric and restrictive policies seem to be on the rise since the 2016 presidential election.

Executive Order: Protecting the Nation from Foreign Terrorist Entry
into the United States
(Excerpts)

By the authority vested in me as President by the Constitution and laws of the United States of America, including the Immigration and Nationality Act (INA), 8 U.S.C.

1101 *et seq.*, and section 301 of title 3, United States Code, and to protect the American people from terrorist attacks by foreign nationals admitted to the United States, it is hereby ordered as follows:

Section 1. Purpose. The visa-issuance process plays a crucial role in detecting individuals with terrorist ties and stopping them from entering the United States. Perhaps in no instance was that more apparent than the terrorist attacks of September 11, 2001, when State Department policy prevented consular officers from properly scrutinizing the visa applications of several of the 19 foreign nationals who went on to murder nearly 3,000 Americans. And while the visa-issuance process was reviewed and amended after the September 11 attacks to better detect would-be terrorists from receiving visas, these measures did not stop attacks by foreign nationals who were admitted to the United States.

Numerous foreign-born individuals have been convicted or implicated in terrorism-related crimes since September 11, 2001, including foreign nationals who entered the United States after receiving visitor, student, or employment visas, or who entered through the United States refugee resettlement program. Deteriorating conditions in certain countries due to war, strife, disaster, and civil unrest increase the likelihood that terrorists will use any means possible to enter the United States. The United States must be vigilant during the visa-issuance process to ensure that those approved for admission do not intend to harm Americans and that they have no ties to terrorism.

In order to protect Americans, the United States must ensure that those admitted to this country do not bear hostile attitudes toward it and its founding principles. The United States cannot, and should not, admit those who do not support the Constitution, or those who would place violent ideologies over American law. In addition, the United States should not admit those who engage in acts of bigotry or hatred (including "honor" killings, other forms of violence against women, or the persecution of those who practice religions different from their own) or those who would oppress Americans of any race, gender, or sexual orientation.

Section 2. Policy. It is the policy of the United States to protect its citizens from foreign nationals who intend to commit terrorist attacks in the United States; and to prevent the admission of foreign nationals who intend to exploit United States immigration laws for malevolent purposes.

Section 3. Suspension of Issuance of Visas and Other Immigration Benefits to Nationals of Countries of Particular Concern. (a) The Secretary of Homeland Security, in consultation with the Secretary of State and the Director of National Intelligence, shall immediately conduct a review to determine the information needed from any country to adjudicate any visa, admission, or other benefit under the INA (adjudications) in order to determine that the individual seeking the benefit is who the individual claims to be and is not a security or public-safety threat.

(b) The Secretary of Homeland Security, in consultation with the Secretary of State and the Director of National Intelligence, shall submit to the President a report on the results of the review described in subsection (a) of this section, including the Secretary of Homeland Security's determination of the information needed for adjudications and a list of countries that do not provide adequate information, within 30 days of the date of this order. The Secretary of Homeland Security shall provide a copy of the report to the Secretary of State and the Director of National Intelligence.

(c) To temporarily reduce investigative burdens on relevant agencies during the review period described in subsection (a) of this section, to ensure the proper review and maximum utilization of available resources for the screening of foreign nationals, and to ensure that adequate standards are established to prevent infiltration by foreign terrorists or criminals, pursuant to section 212(f) of the INA, 8 U.S.C. 1182(f), I hereby proclaim that the immigrant and nonimmigrant entry into the United States of aliens from countries referred to in section 217(a)(12) of the INA, 8 U.S.C. 1187(a)(12), would be detrimental to the interests of the United States, and I hereby suspend entry into the United States, as immigrants and nonimmigrants, of such persons for 90 days from the date of this order (excluding those foreign nationals traveling on diplomatic visas, North Atlantic Treaty Organization visas, C-2 visas for travel to the United Nations, and G-1, G-2, G-3, and G-4 visas).

(d) Immediately upon receipt of the report described in subsection (b) of this section regarding the information needed for adjudications, the Secretary of State shall request all foreign governments that do not supply such information to start providing such information regarding their nationals within 60 days of notification.

(e) After the 60-day period described in subsection (d) of this section expires, the Secretary of Homeland Security, in consultation with the Secretary of State, shall submit to the President a list of countries recommended for inclusion on a Presidential proclamation that would prohibit the entry of foreign nationals (excluding those foreign nationals traveling on diplomatic visas, North Atlantic Treaty Organization visas, C-2 visas for travel to the United Nations, and G-1, G-2, G-3, and G-4 visas) from countries that do not provide the information requested pursuant to subsection (d) of this section until compliance occurs.

(f) At any point after submitting the list described in subsection (e) of this section, the Secretary of State or the Secretary of Homeland Security may submit to the President the names of any additional countries recommended for similar treatment.

(g) Notwithstanding a suspension pursuant to subsection (c) of this section or pursuant to a Presidential proclamation described in subsection (e) of this section, the Secretaries of State and Homeland Security may, on a case-by-case basis, and when in the national interest, issue visas or other immigration benefits to nationals of countries for which visas and benefits are otherwise blocked.

(h) The Secretaries of State and Homeland Security shall submit to the President a joint report on the progress in implementing this order within 30 days of the date of this order, a second report within 60 days of the date of this order, a third report within 90 days of the date of this order, and a fourth report within 120 days of the date of this order.

Section 4. Implementing Uniform Screening Standards for All Immigration Programs. (a) The Secretary of State, the Secretary of Homeland Security, the Director of National Intelligence, and the Director of the Federal Bureau of Investigation shall implement a program, as part of the adjudication process for immigration benefits, to identify individuals seeking to enter the United States on a fraudulent basis with the intent to cause harm, or who are at risk of causing harm subsequent to their admission. This program will include the development of a uniform screening standard and procedure, such as in-person interviews; a database of identity documents proffered by applicants to ensure that duplicate documents are not used by multiple applicants; amended application forms that include questions aimed at identifying fraudulent answers and malicious intent; a mechanism to ensure that the applicant is who the applicant claims to be; a process to evaluate the applicant's likelihood of becoming a positively contributing member of society and the applicant's ability to make contributions to the national interest; and a mechanism to assess whether or not the applicant has the intent to commit criminal or terrorist acts after entering the United States.

(b) The Secretary of Homeland Security, in conjunction with the Secretary of State, the Director of National Intelligence, and the Director of the Federal Bureau of Investigation, shall submit to the President an initial report on the progress of this directive within 60 days of the date of this order, a second report within 100 days of the date of this order, and a third report within 200 days of the date of this order.

Section 5. Realignment of the U.S. Refugee Admissions Program for Fiscal Year 2017. (a) The Secretary of State shall suspend the U.S. Refugee Admissions Program (USRAP) for 120 days. During the 120-day period, the Secretary of State, in conjunction with the Secretary of Homeland Security and in consultation with the Director of National Intelligence, shall review the USRAP application and adjudication process to determine what additional procedures should be taken to ensure that those approved for refugee admission do not pose a threat to the security and welfare of the United States, and shall implement such additional procedures. Refugee applicants who are already in the USRAP process may be admitted upon the initiation and completion of these revised procedures. Upon the date that is 120 days after the date of this order, the Secretary of State shall resume USRAP admissions only for nationals of countries for which the Secretary of State, the Secretary of Homeland Security, and the Director of National Intelligence have jointly determined that such additional procedures are adequate to ensure the security and welfare of the United States.

(b) Upon the resumption of USRAP admissions, the Secretary of State, in consultation with the Secretary of Homeland Security, is further directed to make changes, to the extent permitted by law, to prioritize refugee claims made by individuals on the basis of religious-based persecution, provided that the religion of the individual is a minority religion in the individual's country of nationality. Where necessary and appropriate, the Secretaries of State and Homeland Security shall recommend legislation to the President that would assist with such prioritization.

(c) Pursuant to section 212(f) of the INA, 8 U.S.C. 1182(f), I hereby proclaim that the entry of nationals of Syria as refugees is detrimental to the interests of the United States and thus suspend any such entry until such time as I have determined that sufficient changes have been made to the USRAP to ensure that admission of Syrian refugees is consistent with the national interest.

(d) Pursuant to section 212(f) of the INA, 8 U.S.C. 1182(f), I hereby proclaim that the entry of more than 50,000 refugees in fiscal year 2017 would be detrimental to the interests of the United States, and thus suspend any such entry until such time as I determine that additional admissions would be in the national interest.

(e) Notwithstanding the temporary suspension imposed pursuant to subsection (a) of this section, the Secretaries of State and Homeland Security may jointly determine to admit individuals to the United States as refugees on a case-by-case basis, in their discretion, but only so long as they determine that the admission of such individuals as refugees is in the national interest—including when the person is a religious minority in his country of nationality facing religious persecution, when admitting the person would enable the United States to conform its conduct to a preexisting international agreement, or when the person is already in transit and denying admission would cause undue hardship—and it would not pose a risk to the security or welfare of the United States.

(f) The Secretary of State shall submit to the President an initial report on the progress of the directive in subsection (b) of this section regarding prioritization of claims made by individuals on the basis of religious-based persecution within 100 days of the date of this order and shall submit a second report within 200 days of the date of this order.

(g) It is the policy of the executive branch that, to the extent permitted by law and as practicable, State and local jurisdictions be granted a role in the process of determining the placement or settlement in their jurisdictions of aliens eligible to be admitted to the United States as refugees. To that end, the Secretary of Homeland Security shall examine existing law to determine the extent to which, consistent with applicable law, State and local jurisdictions may have greater involvement in the process of determining the placement or resettlement of refugees in their jurisdictions, and shall devise a proposal to lawfully promote such involvement.

Section 6. Rescission of Exercise of Authority Relating to the Terrorism Grounds of Inadmissibility. The Secretaries of State and Homeland Security shall, in consultation with the Attorney General, consider rescinding the exercises of authority in section 212 of the INA, 8 U.S.C. 1182, relating to the terrorism grounds of inadmissibility, as well as any related implementing memoranda.

Section 7. Expedited Completion of the Biometric Entry-Exit Tracking System. (a) The Secretary of Homeland Security shall expedite the completion and implementation of a biometric entry-exit tracking system for all travelers to the United States, as recommended by the National Commission on Terrorist Attacks upon the United States.

(b) The Secretary of Homeland Security shall submit to the President periodic reports on the progress of the directive contained in subsection (a) of this section. The initial report shall be submitted within 100 days of the date of this order, a second report shall be submitted within 200 days of the date of this order, and a third report shall be submitted within 365 days of the date of this order. Further, the Secretary shall submit a report every 180 days thereafter until the system is fully deployed and operational.

Section 8. Visa Interview Security. (a) The Secretary of State shall immediately suspend the Visa Interview Waiver Program and ensure compliance with section 222 of the INA, 8 U.S.C. 1222, which requires that all individuals seeking a nonimmigrant visa undergo an in-person interview, subject to specific statutory exceptions.

(b) To the extent permitted by law and subject to the availability of appropriations, the Secretary of State shall immediately expand the Consular Fellows Program, including by substantially increasing the number of Fellows, lengthening or making permanent the period of service, and making language training at the Foreign Service Institute available to Fellows for assignment to posts outside of their area of core linguistic ability, to ensure that non-immigrant visa-interview wait times are not unduly affected.

Section 9. Visa Validity Reciprocity. The Secretary of State shall review all nonimmigrant visa reciprocity agreements to ensure that they are, with respect to each visa classification, truly reciprocal insofar as practicable with respect to validity period and fees, as required by sections 221(c) and 281 of the INA, 8 U.S.C. 1201(c) and 1351, and other treatment. If a country does not treat United States nationals seeking nonimmigrant visas in a reciprocal manner, the Secretary of State shall adjust the visa validity period, fee schedule, or other treatment to match the treatment of United States nationals by the foreign country, to the extent practicable.

Section 10. Transparency and Data Collection. (a) To be more transparent with the American people, and to more effectively implement policies and practices that serve the national interest, the Secretary of Homeland Security, in consultation with the Attorney General, shall, consistent with applicable law and national security, collect and make publicly available within 180 days, and every 180 days thereafter:

. . .

(b) The Secretary of State shall, within one year of the date of this order, provide a report on the estimated long-term costs of the USRAP at the Federal, State, and local levels.

Section 11. General Provisions. (a) Nothing in this order shall be construed to impair or otherwise affect:

. . .

(b) This order shall be implemented consistent with applicable law and subject to the availability of appropriations.

(c) This order is not intended to, and does not, create any right or benefit, substantive or procedural, enforceable at law or in equity by any party against the United States, its departments, agencies, or entities, its officers, employees, or agents, or any other person.

Donald J. Trump

Source: "Executive Order: Protecting the Nation from Foreign Terrorist Entry into the United States." The White House, January 27, 2017.

See also: The First Sikh Gurdwara in the United States Established in Stockton, California, 1912; The Los Angeles Riots, 1992; The Murder of Vincent Chin, 1982

Further Reading

Alexander, Dean C. and Yonah Alexander. 2002. *Terrorism and Business: The Impact of September 11, 2001.* Ardsley, NY: Transnational.

Amanat, Abbas. 2001. "Empowered through Violence: The Reinventing of Islamic Extremism." In *The Age of Terror: America and the World after September 11*, edited by Strobe Talbott, Steve Almasy, and Darran Simon, 25–52. New York: Basic Books and the Yale Center for Globalization.

Arjomand, Said Amir. 2002. "Can Rational Analysis Break a Taboo? A Middle Eastern Perspective." In *Critical Views of September 11*, edited by Eric Hershberg and Kevin W. Moore, 162–176. New York: The New Press.

Berezin, Mabel. 2009. *Illiberal Politics in Neoliberal Times: Culture, Security and Populism in the New Europe.* New York: Cambridge University Press.

Bergen, Peter L. 2011. *The Longest War: The Enduring Conflict between America and Al-Qaeda.* New York: Free Press.

Connley, Courtney. 2018. "Meet Rashida Tlaib and Ilhan Omar, the First Muslim Women Elected to Congress." *CNBC*, November 7. https://www.cnbc.com/2018/11/07/rashida -tlaib-ilhan-omar-are-the-1st-muslim-women-elected-to-congress.html

Genoways, Ted. 2017. "The Only Good Muslim Is a Dead Muslim." *New Republic* 248, no. 5004: 30–41.

Goodman, Jack. 2017. "U.S. Travel Ban: Why These Seven Countries?" *BBC News*, January 30. http://www.bbc.com/news/world-us-canada-38798588

Gourley, Bruce. 2017. "Will the Real Theocrats Please Stand Up?" *Church & State* 70: 53–55.

Gungwu, Wang. 2002. "State and Faith: Secular Values in Asia and the West." In *Critical Views of September 11*, edited by Eric Hershberg and Kevin W. Moore, 224–242. New York: The New Press.

Hershberg, Eric and Kevin W. Moore, eds. *Critical Views on September 11*. New York: The New Press, 2002.

Heydemann, Steven. 2016. "Why the United States Hasn't Intervened in Syria," *The Washington Post,* March 14. https://www.washingtonpost.com/news/monkey-cage/wp/2016/03/14/why-the-united-states-hasnt-intervened-in-syria/?noredirect=on&utm_term=.d49415651a35

Heymann, Philip B. 2003. *Terrorism, Freedom, and Security: Winning without War.* Cambridge, MA, and London, England: The MIT Press.

Johnston, David L. 2016. "American Evangelical Islamophobia: A History of Continuity with a Hope for Change." *Journal of Ecumenical Studies* 51, no. 2: 224–235.

Johnston, Douglas M. 2016. "Combating Islamophobia." *Journal of Ecumenical Studies* 51, no. 2: 165–173.

Liptak, Adam. 2017. "Supreme Court Allows Trump Travel Ban to Take Effect," *The New York Times*, December 4. https://www.nytimes.com/2017/12/04/us/politics/trump-travel-ban-supreme-court.html

Love, Eric. 2017. *Islamophobia and Racism in America*. New York: New York University Press.

Mamdani, Mahmood. 2002. "Good Muslim, Bad Muslim: A Political Perspective on Culture and Terrorism." In *Critical Views of September 11*, edited by Eric Hershberg and Kevin W. Moore, 44–60. New York: The New Press.

McCollum, Sean. 2017. "Expelling Islamophobia," *Education Digest*. 82, no. 8: 14–18.

Modood, Tariq. 2002. "Muslims and the Politics of Multiculturalism in Britain." In *Critical Views of September 11*, edited by Eric Hershberg and Kevin W. Moore, 193–208. New York: The New Press.

Orsborn, Catherine. 2016. "Shoulder to Shoulder with American Muslims: What the Interreligious Community Is Doing to Combat Anti-Muslim Bigotry in America." *Journal of Ecumenical Studies* 51, no. 2: 257–263.

Scherer, Michael. 2016. "Why Did They Die?" *Time*, June 27.

Spivak, Gayatri Chakravorty. 2004. "Terror: A Speech after 9/11." *Boundary 2* 31, no. 2: 81–111.

Sterman, David and Peter Bergen. 2017. "Trump's New Travel Ban Still Doesn't Fly." *CNN*. https://www.cnn.com/2017/09/25/opinions/trump-travel-ban-still-doesnt-fly-opinion-bergen-sterman/index.html

Takacs, Stacy. 2012. *Terrorism TV: Popular Entertainment in Post-9/11 America*. Lawrence: University Press of Kansas.

Talbott, Strobe, Steve Almasy, and Darran Simon, eds. *The Age of Terror: America and the World after September 11*. New York: Basic Books and the Yale Center for Globalization, 2001.

Union Theological Seminary. 2017. "Statement by Union Theological Seminary in the City of New York Condemning the Trump Administration's Immigration Ban," *Network News*, February 18–21. http://www.pv4j.org/network-news/network-news-february-2017.pdf

U.S. Department of Justice. "The USA Patriot Act: Preserving Life and Liberty." https://www.justice.gov/archive/ll/highlights.htm

U.S. House of Representatives Judiciary Committee. "USA Freedom Act." https://judiciary.house.gov/issue/usa-freedom-act

Vanaik, Achin. 2002. "The Ethics and Efficacy of Political Terrorism." In *Critical Views of September 11*, edited by Eric Hershberg and Kevin W. Moore, 23–43. New York: The New Press.

Wright, Lawrence. 2006. *The Looming Tower: Al-Qaeda and the Road to 9/11*. New York: Alfred A. Knopf.

Bibliography of Recommended Resources

Abelmann, Nancy and John Lie. 1997. *Blue Dreams: Korean Americans and the Los Angeles Riots*. Cambridge, MA: Harvard University Press.

Aguilar-San Juan, Karin, ed. 1994. *The State of Asian America: Activism and Resistance in the 1990s*. Boston: South End Press.

Akhtar, Ayad. 2013. *Disgraced*. New York: Little, Brown and Company.

Alexander, Dean C. and Yonah Alexander. 2002. *Terrorism and Business: The Impact of September 11, 2001*. Ardsley, NY: Transnational Publishers.

Alexander, Saxton. 1975. *The Indispensable Enemy: Labor and the Anti-Chinese Movement in California*. Berkeley: University of California Press.

Anderson, Kay J. 1995. *Vancouver's Chinatown: Racial Discourse in Canada, 1875–1980*. Montreal and Kingston: McGill-Queen's University Press.

Bacon, Jean. 1996. *Life Lines: Community, Family, and Assimilation among Asian Indian Immigrants*. Oxford and New York: Oxford University Press.

Baldoz, Rick. 2011. *The Third Asiatic Invasion: Migration and Empire in Filipino America, 1898–1946*. New York: New York University Press.

Berezin, Mabel. 2009. *Illiberal Politics in Neoliberal Times: Culture, Security and Populism in the New Europe*. New York: Cambridge University Press.

Bosworth, Allan R. 1967. *America's Concentration Camps*. New York: W. W. Norton.

Cao, Lan and Himilce Novas. 1996. *Everything You Need to Know about Asian-American History*. New York: Plume.

Caplan, Nathan, John K. Whitmore, and Marcella H. Choy. 1989. *The Boat People and Achievement in America: A Study of Family Life, Hard Work, and Cultural Values*. Ann Arbor: University of Michigan Press.

Caplan, Nathan, John K. Whitmore, and Marcella H. Choy. 1991. *Children of the Boat People: A Study of Educational Success*. Ann Arbor: University of Michigan Press.

Chan, Kenyon S. 2000. "Rethinking of the Asian American Studies Project: Bridging the Divide between 'Campus' and 'Community.'" *Journal of Asian American Studies* 3, no. 1: 17–36.

Chan, Sucheng. 1986. *This Bittersweet Soil: Chinese in California Agriculture*. Berkeley: University of California Press.

Chan, Sucheng. 1991. *Asian Americans: An Interpretive History*. Woodbridge, CT: Twayne Publishing.

Chang, Edward T. and Jeannette Diaz-Veizades. 1999. *Ethnic Peace in the American City: Building Community in Los Angeles and Beyond*. New York: New York University Press.

Chang, Gordon H., Mark Johnson, and Paul Karlstrom, eds. 2008. *Asian American Art: A History*. Palo Alto, CA: Stanford University Press.

Chang, Grace. 2000. *Disposable Domestics: Immigrant Women Workers in the Global Economy*. Cambridge, MA: South End Press.

Chang, Kornel. 2012. *American Crossroads: Pacific Connections: The Making of the U.S.-Canadian Borderlands*. Berkeley: University of California Press.

Chang, Mitchell J. 1999. "Expansion and Its Discontents: The Formation of the Asian American Studies Programs in the 1990s." *Journal of Asian American Studies* 2, no. 2: 181–206.

Chang, Robert S. 1999. *Disoriented: Asian Americans, Law, and the Nation-State*. New York: New York University Press.

Choy, Bong-young. 1979. *Koreans in America*. Chicago: Nelson-Hall.

Choy, Philip P., Lorraine Dong, and Marlon K. Hom. 1994. *The Coming Man: 19th Century American Perceptions of the Chinese*. Seattle: University of Washington Press.

Collins, Donald E. 1985. *Native American Aliens: Disloyalty and the Renunciation of Citizenship by Japanese Americans during World War II*. Westport, CT: Greenwood.

Commission on Wartime Relocation and Internment of Civilians. 1982. *Personal Justice Denied*. Washington, D.C.: Government Printing Office.

Cooper, George and Gavan Daws. 1985. *Land and Power in Hawaii: The Democratic Years*. Honolulu: Benchmark Books.

Daniels, Roger. 1962. *The Politics of Prejudice: The Anti-Japanese Movement in California and the Struggle for Japanese Exclusion*. Berkeley: University of California Press.

Daniels, Roger. 2005. *Guarding the Golden Door: American Immigration Policy and Immigrants since 1882*. New York: Hill and Wang.

DeBonis, Steven. 1995. *Children of the Enemy: Oral Histories of Vietnamese Amerasians and Their Mothers*. Jefferson, NC: McFarland.

Devra, Weber. 1996. *Dark Sweat, White Gold: California Farm Workers, Cotton, and the New Deal*. Berkeley: University of California Press.

Dong, Lan, ed. 2016. *Asian American Culture: From Anime to Tiger Moms*. Santa Barbara, CA: ABC-CLIO/Greenwood.

Espiritu, Yen Le. 1992. *Asian American Panethnicity: Bridging Institutions and Identities*. Philadelphia: Temple University Press.

Espiritu, Yen Le. 1997. *Asian American Women and Men: Labor, Laws, and Love*. Thousand Oaks, CA: Sage.

Espiritu, Yen Le. 2003. *Home Bound: Filipino American Lives across Cultures, Communities, and Countries*. Berkeley: University of California Press.

Fadiman, Ann. 1997. *The Spirit Catches You and You Fall Down: A Hmong Child, Her American Doctors, and the Collision of Two Cultures*. New York: Farrar, Straus and Giroux.

Fawcett, James T. and Benjamin V. Carino. 1987. *Pacific Bridges: The New Immigration from Asia and the Pacific Islands*. Staten Island, NY: Center for Migration Studies.

Fenton, John Y. 1988. *Transplanting Religious Traditions: Asian Indians in America*. New York: Praeger.

Fong, Timothy P. 1998. *The Contemporary Asian American Experience: Beyond the Model Minority*. Upper Saddle River, NJ: Prentice-Hall.

Fong, Timothy P. and Larry H. Shinagawa, eds. 2000. *Asian Americans: Experiences and Perspectives*. Upper Saddle River, NJ: Prentice-Hall.

Freeman, James M. 1995. *Changing Identities: Vietnamese Americans, 1975–1995*. Boston: Allyn and Bacon.

Friday, Chris. 1994. *Organizing Asian American Labor: The Pacific Coast Canned-Salmon Industry, 1870–1942*. Philadelphia: Temple University Press.

Gibson, Margaret A. 1988. *Accommodation without Assimilation: Sikh Immigrants in an American High School*. Ithaca, NY: Cornell University Press.

Guyotte, Roland L. and Barbara M. Posadas. 2013. "Filipinos and Filipino Americans, 1870–1940." In *Immigrants in American History: Arrival, Adaptation, and Integration*, edited by Elliott Robert Barkan, 347–356. Santa Barbara, CA: ABC-CLIO.

Haines, David W. 1989. *Refugees as Immigrants: Cambodians, Laotians, and Vietnamese in America*. Totowa, NJ: Rowman and Littlefield.

Hawley, John Stratton and Gurinder Singh Mann, eds. 1993. *Studying the Sikhs: Issues for North America*. Albany: State University of New York Press.

Hayashi, Brian Masaru. 2008. *Democratizing the Enemy: The Japanese American Internment*. Princeton, NJ: Princeton University Press.

Hein, Jeremy. 1995. *From Vietnam, Cambodia, and Laos: A Refugee Experience in the United States*. Woodbridge, CT: Twayne Publishing.

Hing, Bill Ong. 1993. *Making and Remaking Asian America through Immigration Policy, 1850–1990*. Palo Alto, CA: Stanford University Press.

Hirabayashi, Lane Ryo, ed. 1998. *Teaching Asian America: Diversity and the Problem of Community*. Lanham, MD: Rowman and Littlefield.

Hsu, Madeline Y. 2000. *Dreaming of Gold, Dreaming of Home: Transnationalism and Migration between the United States and Southern China, 1882–1943*. Palo Alto, CA: Stanford University Press.

Hsu, Madeline Y. 2017. *Asian American History: A Very Short Introduction*. Oxford and New York: Oxford University Press.

Hune, Shirley. 1997. *Teaching Asian American Women's History*. Washington, D.C.: American Historical Association.

Hune, Shirley, Amy Ling, Stephen S. Fugita, and Hyung-chan Kim, eds. 1991. *Asian Americans: Comparative and Global Perspectives*. Pullman: Washington State University Press.

Hune, Shirley and Gail M. Nomura, eds. 2003. *Asian/Pacific Islander American Women: A Historical Anthology*. New York: New York University Press.

Ichioka, Yuji. 2006. *The Issei: The World of the First Generation Japanese Immigrants, 1885–1924*. New York: Free Press.

Jensen, Joan. 1988. *Passage from India: Asian Indian Immigrants in North America*. New Haven, CT: Yale University Press.

Kashima, Tetsuden. 1977. *Buddhism in America: The Social Organization of an Ethnic Religious Institution*. Westport, CT: Greenwood.

Kelly, Gail Paradise. 1977. *From Vietnam to America: A Chronicle of the Vietnamese Immigration to the United States*. Boulder, CO: Westview Press.

Kim, Hyung-chan, ed. 1977. *The Korean Diaspora: Historical and Sociological Studies of Korean Immigration and Assimilation in North America*. Santa Barbara, CA: ABC-CLIO.

Kim, Hyung-chan. 1996. *Asian Americans and Congress: A Documentary History*. Westport, CT: Greenwood.

Kitano, Harry and Roger Daniels. 1994. *Asian Americans: Emerging Minorities*. Upper Saddle River, NJ: Prentice Hall.

Kodama-Nishimoto, Michi, Cynthia A. Oshiro, and Warren S. Nishimoto. 1984. *Hanahana: An Oral History Anthology of Hawaii's Working People*. Honolulu: Ethnic Studies Oral History Project, University of Hawaii at Manoa.

Kondo, Dorinne. 1997. *About Face: Performing Race in Fashion and Theater*. New York and London: Routledge.

Kramer, Paul. 2006. *The Blood of Government: Race, Empire, the United States, and the Philippines*. Durham: University of North Carolina Press.

Kurashige, Lon and Alice Yang Murray, eds. 2003. *Major Problems in Asian American History*. Boston: Houghton Mifflin.

Kwong, Peter. 1997. *Forbidden Workers: Illegal Chinese Immigrants and American Labor*. New York: New Press.

Lai, Him Mark. 2004. *Becoming Chinese American: A History of Communities and Institutions*. Walnut Creek, CA: Alta Mira Press.

Lee, Erika G. 2003. *At America's Gates: Chinese Immigration during the Exclusion Era, 1882–1943*. Chapel Hill: University of North Carolina Press.

Lee, Erika G. 2015. *The Making of Asian America: A History*. New York: Simon and Schuster.

Lee, Joann Faung Jean. 1991. *Asian American Experiences in the United States: Oral Histories of First to Fourth Generation Americans from China, the Philippines, Japan, India, the Pacific Islands, Vietnam and Cambodia*. Jefferson, NC: McFarland.

Lee, Jonathan H. X. 2015. *History of Asian Americans: Exploring Diverse Roots*. Santa Barbara, CA: ABC-CLIO/Greenwood.

Lee, Jonathan H. X. and Christen T. Sasaki. 2016. *Asian American History: Primary Documents of the Asian American Experience*. San Diego, CA: Cognella Academic Publishing.

Lee, Robert G. 1999. *Orientals: Asians in Popular Culture*. Philadelphia: Temple University Press.

Lee, Sharon and Marilyn Fernandez. 1998. "Trends in Asian American Racial/Ethnic Intermarriage: A Comparison of 1980 and 1990 Census Data." *Sociological Perspectives* 41, no. 2: 323–342.

Lee, Shelley Sang-Hee. 2014. *A New History of Asian America*. New York: Routledge.

Lee, Shirley. 2013. *A New History of Asian America*. New York and London: Routledge.

Leonard, Karen Isaksen. 1997. *The South Asian Americans*. Westport, CT: Greenwood.

Leong, Russell, ed. 1996. *Asian American Sexualities: Dimensions of the Gay and Lesbian Experience*. New York and London: Routledge.

Lien, Pei-te. 2002. "Transforming Patterns of Contemporary Asian American Community Politics." *Asian American Policy Review* 10, no. 4: 59–73.

Lin, Jan. 1998. *Reconstructing Chinatown: Ethnic Enclave, Global Change*. Minneapolis: University of Minnesota Press.

Ling, Amy, ed. 1999. *Yellow Light: The Flowering of Asian American Arts*. Philadelphia: Temple University Press.

Ling, Huping and Allan Austin, eds. 2010. *Asian American History and Culture: An Encyclopedia*. Armonk, NY: M. E. Sharpe.

Lott, Juanita Tamayo. 2006. *Common Destiny: Filipino American Generations*. Lanham, MD: Rowman & Littlefield.

Mabalon, Dawn. 2013. *Little Manila Is in the Heart: The Making of the Filipina/o American Community in Stockton, California*. Durham, NC: Duke University Press.

Machida, Margo, Vishakha N. Desai, and John K. Tchen. 1994. *Asia/America: Identities in Contemporary Asian American Art*. New York: Asia Society Galleries and New Press.

McClain, Charles J. 1994. *In Search of Equality: The Chinese Struggle against Discrimination Nineteenth-Century America*. Berkeley: University of California Press.

McFerson, Hazel M., ed. 2002. *Mixed Blessing: The Impact of the American Colonial Experience on Politics and Society in the Philippines*. Westport, CT: Greenwood.

Melendy, H. Brett. 1977. *Asians in America: Filipinos, Koreans, and East Indians*. Boston: Twayne Publishers.

Miller, Stuart Creighton. 1969. *The Unwelcome Immigrant: The American Image of the Chinese, 1785–1882*. Berkeley: University of California Press.

Min, Pyong Gap and Rose Kim, eds. 1999. *Struggle for Ethnic Identity: Narratives by Asian American Professionals*. Walnut Creek, CA: Alta Mira.

Mokuau, Noreen, ed. 1991. *Handbook of Social Services for Asians and Pacific Islanders*. Westport, CT: Greenwood.

Ng, Franklin, ed. 1995. *The Asian American Encyclopedia*. New York: M. Cavendish.

Ng, Franklin, ed. 1998. *Asian American Issues Relating to Labor, Economics, and Socioeconomic Status*. New York: Garland.

Ngai, Mae. 2004. *Impossible Subjects: Illegal Aliens and the Making of Modern America*. Princeton, NJ: Princeton University Press.

O'Brien, David J. and Stephen S. Fugita. 1991. *The Japanese American Experience*. Bloomington: Indiana University Press.

Okamura, Jonathan Y. 1998. *Imagining the Filipino American Diaspora: Transnational Relations, Identities, and Communities*. New York: Garland.

Okihiro, Gary Y. 1994. *Margins and Mainstreams: Asians in American History and Culture*. Seattle: University of Washington Press.

Okihiro, Gary Y. 2001. *The Columbia Guide to Asian American History*. New York: Columbia University Press.

Omi, Michael and Howard Winant. 2015. *Racial Formation in the United States*. 3rd ed. New York and London: Routledge.

Ong, Aihwa. 2003. *Buddha Is Hiding: Refugees, Citizenship, The New America*. Berkeley: University of California Press.

Osajima, Keith. 1988. "Asian Americans as the Model Minority: An Analysis of the Popular Press Image in the 1960s and 1980s." In *Reflections on Shattered*

Windows: Promises and Prospects for Asian American Studies, edited by Gary Y. Okihiro, John M. Liu, Arthur A. Hansen, and Shirley Hune, 165–174. Pullman: Washington State University Press.

Park, Clara C. and Marilyn Mei-Ying Chi, eds. 1999. *Asian American Education: Prospects and Challenges*. Granby, MA: Bergin and Garvey.

Pascoe, Peggy. 2009. *What Comes Naturally: Miscegenation Law and the Making of Race in the United States*. Oxford and New York: Oxford University Press.

Patel, Eboo. 2007. *Acts of Faith: The Story of an American Muslim, the Struggle for the Soul of a Generation*. Boston: Beacon Press.

Patterson, Wayne. 1988. *The Korean Frontier in America: Immigration to Hawai'i, 1896–1910*. Honolulu: University of Hawaii Press.

Patterson, Wayne. 2000. *The Ilse: First Generation Korean Immigrants in Hawai'i, 1903–1973*. Honolulu: University of Hawaii Press.

Peterson, William. 1966. "Success Story, Japanese-American Style." *New York Times Magazine*, January 9.

Prashad, Vijay. 2000. *The Karma of Brown Folk*. Minneapolis: University of Minnesota Press.

Reimers, David. 2005. *Other Immigrants: The Global Origins of the American People*. New York: New York University Press.

Reinecke, John E. 1996. *The Filipino Piecemeal Sugar Strike of 1924–1925*. Honolulu: Social Science Research Institute, University of Hawaii.

Rhee, Helen Choi. 1995. *The Korean American Experience: A Detailed Analysis of How Well Korean Americans Adjust to Life in the United States*. New York: Vantage Press.

Robinson, Greg. 2010. *A Tragedy of Democracy: Japanese Confinement in North America*. New York: Columbia University Press.

Root, Maria P. P., ed. 1997. *Filipino Americans: Transformation and Identity*. Thousand Oaks, CA: Sage.

Rutledge, Paul James. 1992. *The Vietnamese Experience in America*. Bloomington: Indiana University Press.

Salyer, Lucy E. 1995. *Laws Harsh as Tigers: Chinese Immigrants and the Shaping of Modern Immigration Law*. Chapel Hill: University of North Carolina Press.

San Juan, E., Jr. 1998. *From Exile to Diaspora: Versions of the Filipino Experience in the United States*. Boulder, CO: Westview Press.

Shaffer, Robert. 2012. "J.J. Singh and the India League of America, 1945–1959: Pressing at the Margins of Cold War Consensus." *Journal of American Ethnic History* 31, no. 2: 68–103.

Shibusawa, Naoko. 2006. *America's Geisha Ally: Reimagining the Japanese Enemy*. Cambridge, MA: Harvard University Press.

Shinagawa, Larry Hajime and Gin Yong Pang. 1996. "Asian American Panethnicity and Intermarriage." *Amerasian Journal* 22, no. 2: 127–152.

Smith-Hefner, Nancy. 1999. *Khmer American: Identity and Moral Education in a Diasporic Community*. Berkeley: University of California Press.

Spickard, Paul R. 1996. *Japanese Americans: The Formation and Transformation of an Ethnic Group*. New York: Twayne.

Strand, Paul and Woodrow Jones, Jr. 1985. *Indochinese Refugees in America: Problems of Adaptation and Assimilation*. Durham, NC: Duke University Press.

Takaki, Ronald. 1983. *Pau Hana: Plantation Life and Labor in Hawai'i, 1835–1920*. Honolulu: University of Hawaii Press.

Takaki, Ronald. 1989. *Strangers from a Different Shore: A History of Asian Americans*. Boston: Little, Brown.

Takaki, Ronald. 1993. *A Different Mirror: A History of Multicultural America*. Boston: Little, Brown.

Takeda, Okiyoshi. 2001. "One Year after the Sit-In: Asian American Students' Identities and Their Support for Asian American Studies." *Journal of Asian American Studies* 4, no. 2: 147–164.

Tanaka, Chester. 1982. *Go for Broke: A Pictorial History of the Japanese American 100th Infantry Battalion and the 442nd Regimental Combat Team*. Richmond, CA: Go for Broke.

Tateishi, John. 1984. *And Justice for All: An Oral History of the Japanese American Detention Camps*. New York: Random House.

Taylor, Sandra C. 1993. *Jewel of the Desert: Japanese American Internment at Topaz*. Berkeley: University of California Press.

Tichenor, Daniel. 2002. *Dividing Lines: The Politics of Immigration Control in America*. Princeton, NJ: Princeton University Press.

Treuba, Henry T., Lila Jacobs, and Elizabeth Kirton. 1990. *Cultural Conflict and Adaptation: The Case of Hmong Children in American Society*. New York: Falmer Press.

Vang, Chia Youyee. 2010. *Hmong America: Reconstructing Community in Diaspora*. Urbana: University of Illinois Press.

Volpp, Leti. 2000. "American Mestizo: Filipinos and Antimiscegenation Laws in California." *U.C. Davis Law Review* 33, no. 4: 795–835.

Ward, Peter. 2002. *White Canada Forever: Popular Attitudes and Public Policy toward Orientals in British Columbia*. 3rd ed. Montreal and Kingston: McGill-Queen's University Press.

Welarantna, Usha. 1993. *Beyond the Killing Fields: Voices of Nine Cambodian Survivors in America*. Stanford, CA: Stanford University Press.

Whelchel, Toshio. 1999. *From Pearl Harbor to Saigon: Japanese American Soldiers and the Vietnam War*. London: Verso.

Wilkinson, Paul. 2000. *Terrorism versus Democracy: The Liberal State Response.* London and Portland, OR: Frank Cass Publishers.

Wong, K. Scott and Sucheng Chan, eds. 1998. *Claiming America: Constructing Chinese American Identities during the Exclusion Era.* Philadelphia: Temple University Press.

Woo, Deborah. 2000. *Glass Ceilings and Asian Americans: The New Fact of Workplace Barriers.* Walnut Creek, CA: Alta Mira.

Wright, Lawrence. 2006. *The Looming Tower: Al-Qaeda and the Road to 9/11.* New York: Alfred A. Knopf.

Xing, Jun. 1998. *Asian America through the Lens: History, Representations, and Identity.* Walnut Creek, CA: Alta Mira.

Yanagisako, Sylvia Junko. 1985. *Transforming the Past: Tradition and Kinship among Japanese Americans.* Stanford, CA: Stanford University Press.

Yoo, David, ed. 1999. *New Spiritual Homes: Religion and Asian Americans.* Honolulu: University of Hawaii Press.

Yoo, David and Eiichiro Azuma, eds. 2016. *The Oxford Handbook of Asian American History.* Oxford and New York: Oxford University Press.

Yung, Judy. 1995. *Unbound Feet: A Social History of Chinese Women in San Francisco.* Berkeley: University of California Press.

Yung, Judy. 1999. *Unbound Voices: A Documentary History of Chinese Women in San Francisco.* Berkeley: University of California Press.

Zhao, Xiaojian. *Asian American Chronology.* 2009. Santa Barbara, CA: ABC-CLIO/Greenwood.

Zhao, Xiaojian and Edward J. W. Park, eds. 2013. *Asian American: An Encyclopedia of Social, Cultural, Economic, and Political History.* Santa Barbara, CA: ABC-CLIO/Greenwood.

Zhou, Min and Carl L. Bankston III. 1998. *Growing Up American: How Vietnamese Children Adapt to Life in the United States.* New York: Russell Sage Foundation.

Zhou, Min and James V. Gatewood, eds. 2000. *Contemporary Asian America: A Multidisciplinary Reader.* New York: New York University Press.

Zia, Helen. *Asian American Dreams: The Emergence of an American People.* 2000. New York: Farrar, Straus and Giroux.

About the Editor and Contributors

Editor

Lan Dong is the Louise Hartman and Karl Schewe Professor in Liberal Arts and Sciences and an associate professor of English at the University of Illinois Springfield, where she teaches Asian American literature, world literature, and children's and young adult literature. She is the author of two books—*Mulan's Legend and Legacy in China and the United States* and *Reading Amy Tan*—and a number of journal articles and book chapters on Asian American literature, children's literature, and popular culture. She is the editor of three books: *Transnationalism and the Asian American Heroine*, *Teaching Comics and Graphic Narratives*, and *Asian American Culture: From Anime to Tiger Moms*.

Contributors

Maharaj "Raju" Desai is a scholar whose work crosses the disciplines of ethnic studies, education, and second language studies. His research explores participatory action research in educational spaces as ways to challenge colonially constructed narratives and identities. His writing has been published in *Red, Yellow, Black, and Brown: Decentering Whiteness in Mixed Race Studies*, *International Journal of Qualitative Studies in Education*, and *Educational Perspectives*, and is forthcoming in *Rethinking Ethnic Studies*. Prior to his doctoral studies, he was an educator in San Francisco Unified School District and City College of San Francisco. He is currently studying for his PhD in Curriculum and Instruction at the University of Hawaii at Mānoa.

Philip Deslippe is a doctoral candidate in the Department of Religious of Studies at the University of California, Santa Barbara. He has published articles in journals including *Amerasia*, *Contemporary Buddhism*, and *Sikh Formations*, and edited and introduced a definitive edition of the metaphysical classic *The Kybalion* (2011) for Tarcher/Penguin.

Rachel Endo recently became Founding Dean of the School of Education at the University of Washington, Tacoma. Her primary research and teaching areas include Asian American education, immigrant and refugee education, and the language and literacy practices of ethnically and racially diverse populations.

Karen Buenavista Hanna is Trinity College's Ann Plato Post-Doctoral Fellow in American Studies. Her research interests include social movements, transnational feminism, and disability justice. Her writing has been published in *Hyphen Magazine* and *Hypatia: A Journal of Feminist Philosophy*, and is forthcoming in *Frontiers: A Journal of Women Studies*, *CUNY Forum*, and *American Quarterly*. Prior to her doctoral studies, she was a New York City public school teacher, pre-GED instructor with the Brooklyn Public Library, and community organizer working alongside Filipina/o immigrant youth and domestic workers. She received her PhD in Feminist Studies from the University of California, Santa Barbara.

Tena L. Helton is an associate professor of English at the University of Illinois Springfield. Her primary expertise is in nineteenth-century American literature and culture. She has primarily published about African American, Native American, and Asian American history, literature, and film in various academic journals.

Teresa Hodges is a PhD student at the University of Hawaii at Mānoa. She received her MA in Asian American Studies at San Francisco State University and a BA in Ethnic Studies from the University of California, San Diego. She is currently a lecturer at California State University at San Marcos and is California State University Chancellor's Doctoral Incentive Program scholar. Her research interests include mixed race, especially mixed black and Filipina such as herself, intersectionality, Filipina/o/x American studies, black studies, and teaching and learning race.

Katelind Ikuma was born and raised in Honolulu, Hawaii, where she pursued her BA in Film at the University of Hawaii. She obtained her MFA in Film from San Francisco State University. She is currently living in Japan, increasing her skills in teaching and immersing herself in her native culture.

Hayley Johnson is the Head of Government Documents at Louisiana State University. She has worked with government documents for the past seven years and has been working to highlight the importance and relevance of government documents to both historical and present-day issues. She was previously at the Louisiana House of Representatives.

Nathan Jung, PhD, is an associate lecturer at the University of Wisconsin, Milwaukee. His research and teaching explore the relationship between migration, media, and democratic deliberation in contemporary American literature.

Nancy Kang is Canada Research Chair in Transnational Feminisms and Gender-Based Violence, Tier 2 at the University of Manitoba's Department of Women's and Gender Studies. Kang was a postdoctoral Faculty Fellow in the Humanities at Syracuse University (2007–2011) and was promoted to associate professor of Multicultural and Diaspora Literatures at the University of Baltimore (2012–2018). She is co-author, with Silvio Torres-Saillant, of *The Once and Future Muse: The Poetry and Poetics of Rhina P. Espaillat* (2018).

Rosie Kar is a second-generation South Asian American of Sindhi and Bengali descent. Born and raised in Southern California, she holds a PhD in Comparative Literature, with doctoral emphases on Feminist Studies and Asian American Studies, from the University of California, Santa Barbara. She teaches in the Department of Women's, Gender, and Sexuality Studies at California State University, Long Beach.

Martin Kich is a professor of English at Wright State University's Lake Campus. He is the author of *Western American Novelists* (1995) and co-editor of *Postcolonial Theory in the Global Age: Interdisciplinary Essays* (2013). His other publications include forty-three articles in professional journals, forty-nine book chapters and essays in collections, 326 entries for specialized reference books, 144 articles for general periodicals, ninety-seven book reviews, and 195 poems. In 2000, he received the Wright State's Trustees' Award, recognizing sustained excellence in teaching, scholarship, and service. He has received the Lake Campus awards for outstanding faculty member, research, and service. He has also received service awards from the American Association of University Professors and the Association for the University Regional Campuses of Ohio.

Andrea Kwon received her PhD in American History from the University of California at Berkeley. She teaches courses in U.S. history and Asian American studies.

Ying Ma is originally from China and obtained her BA and MA in Sociology from Nanjing University in China. She then decided to further her study in the United

States and received her PhD in Sociology from the University of Cincinnati. Her specialties are immigration, race and ethnicity, and gender and work. She is currently an associate professor in the Department of Sociology at Austin Peay State University in Clarksville, Tennessee.

Harveen Sachdeva Mann is an associate professor of English at Loyola University, Chicago. She has published and presented extensively on topics ranging from Third World feminism to postcolonial pedagogy, and from South Asian fiction to Bollywood films. Her current projects include an examination of cultural portrayals of the 1984 Punjab genocide and a study of Sikh diasporicity in the twenty-first century.

Ann Matsuuchi is an Instructional Technology Librarian and associate professor at LaGuardia Community College, CUNY. Her intersecting research and writing interests include science fiction (particularly the work of Samuel R. Delany), queer theory, comic books, technology, gender, and online cultures. She has worked with numerous college courses that utilize Wikipedia in educational projects.

Kimberly McKee is the director of the Kutsche Office of Local History and an assistant professor in the Liberal Studies Department at Grand Valley State University. Her monograph, *Disrupting Kinship: Transnational Politics of Korean Adoption in the United States*, is forthcoming.

Khoi Nguyen is a PhD student in American Studies at the University of Minnesota. They received an MA in Women's Studies with a concentration on queer Asian American literature from Southern Connecticut State University and a BA in English from Fairfield University. They previously taught in Asian American Studies at San Francisco State University and George Mason University. Their work examines the genealogy of queer refugees in the United States post-1975 to have a better understanding of the current global migration patterns. Their archival research traces the heteronuclear family structures within refugee narratives. Their project addresses the lack of engagement with issues of U.S. militarization and globalization in the current queer refugee scholarships.

William B. Noseworthy is an assistant professor of History at McNeese State University in Lake Charles, Louisiana. Among his diverse research interests, diaspora history and literature have been a significant focus of his work. He has published many essays on topics related to the history of migration, diaspora, and ethnoreligious minorities. Notable publications in the field include an essay on migration, culture, and trade in the history of the South China Sea (*Journal of Northeast Asian*

History, 2014), along with several contributions on topics related to Vietnamese American and Cambodian American culture in *Asian American Culture: From Anime to Tiger Moms* (2016). His most recent chapter for an ABC-CLIO project is "Caribbean Migration to New York City, 1870s–1920s" in *50 Events that Shaped Latino History* (2018).

Yuki Obayashi is a PhD candidate in Literature with a designated emphasis on Critical Race and Ethnic Studies at the University of California, Santa Cruz. She completed her MA in Asian American Studies at San Francisco State University. Her dissertation project examines the Japanese and U.S. imperialistic imaginary of the Pacific from the early twentieth century to today.

Laura Stanfield Prichard lectures regularly for the San Francisco and Chicago symphonies. Her twenty continuous years of college teaching have focused on interdisciplinary cultural analysis of music, dance, and art history. She is a specialist in African American, Latin American, and Pacific Rim culture. She teaches choral conducting in Boston and was the assistant conductor of the San Francisco Symphony Chorus (1995–2003).

Michael S. Rodriguez is an associate professor of Political Science at Stockton University and Coordinator of the institution's Washington Internship Program. He holds degrees in Political Science from Princeton University, the University of Texas at Austin, and Temple University. His research interests include race and identity, immigration, the pedagogy of critical thinking, and religion and politics. He is currently co-authoring a book on race and identity among Latinos in the United States.

Sarah Simms is the Undergraduate and Student Success Librarian at Louisiana State University. Before entering academic librarianship, she worked in the antiquarian book trade in New York City. Her interest in history, culture, and social justice advocacy has fueled her research on Japanese American internment during World War II.

Marie-Therese C. Sulit was born to immigrant Filipino parents and earned a doctoral degree with a specialization in Asian American Studies and Literature from the University of Minnesota, Twin Cities. As an associate professor at Mount Saint Mary College, she explores the historical and current directions of Filipino American studies and has contributed a number of book chapters on contemporary women writers of the Philippine diaspora. Her other research interest is the intersection between academic freedom and the axes of cultural diversity.

Kaori Mori Want received her PhD in English from the State University of New York, Buffalo. She is an associate professor of English at Konan Women's University in Japan. She is the author of several articles and book chapters on Asian Pacific Americans. She is the author of *Hapa America: The History and Culture of Multiracial Asian Pacific Americans* (2017).

Verna Wong is a high school teacher of English learners with the Anoka-Hennepin School District in Anoka, Minnesota. She supports teachers in incorporating language and literacy practices for linguistically diverse populations. Her research and advocacy pertain to mentoring and sustaining a diverse teaching force.

Philip Q. Yang received his PhD from the University of California, Los Angeles in 1993, and is a professor of Sociology and Director of the Sociology graduate program at Texas Woman's University. He is the author of three books, the editor of three books, the author of more than eighty articles in numerous referred journals and edited volumes, and a grantee of the National Science Foundation.

Index

Note: Page numbers in **bold** indicate the location of main events; *italics* indicate illustrations.